# MEETING THE DEMANDS OF REASON

Andrei Sakharov, 1987.

# Meeting the Demands of Reason

## THE LIFE AND THOUGHT OF ANDREI SAKHAROV

**Jay Bergman**

Cornell University Press  ITHACA AND LONDON

Frontispiece: MS Russ 79 (7263).
By permission of the Houghton Library, Harvard University.

First published 2009 by Cornell University Press

ISBN 978-0-8014-4731-0

Printed in the United States of America

Book Club Edition

To Julie and Aaron, with love

We must make good the demands of reason and create a life worthy of ourselves....

—Andrei Sakharov, Nobel Lecture, December 1975

He was a moment in the conscience of humanity.

—Anatole France on Emile Zola at Zola's funeral, 1902

# Contents

Illustrations follow page 196

# Preface and Acknowledgments

Andrei Sakharov (1921–1989) was one of the towering figures of the late twentieth century. He contributed much to our understanding of the origins of the universe, and his criticisms of the Soviet Union contributed in no small measure to its collapse. In this biography, I have focused on Sakharov's ideas, especially his political ideas: the influences that caused him to espouse them, how they changed or remained the same in the course of his life, and the effect they had on the larger Soviet society he inhabited. Even though the work he did in the early 1950s on thermonuclear weaponry is important in its own right, the emphasis is on Sakharov the dissident and on the movement of Soviet dissidence of which he was, with Alexander Solzhenitsyn, the most prominent member. The reader should know what Soviet dissidence was. By the term, one means a particular kind of opposition to the Soviet system that emerged in the late 1960s, continued through the 1970s, and ended in the mid-1980s when Mikhail Gorbachev's policies of perestroika (reconstruction) and glasnost (openness) incorporated aspects of this opposition and in the process rendered it largely moot. Substantively, Soviet dissidence was marked by the intensely moral character of its rejection of the political status quo; in this respect the dissidents resembled the intelligentsia under the tsars, which many of the dissidents, including Sakharov, recognized as their antecedent and intellectual inspiration. It was as a dissident that Sakharov came to the attention of the world outside the Soviet Union, and it was as a dissident that he will be most favorably and enduringly remembered. After December 1986, when Gorbachev allowed him to return to Moscow from internal exile, Sakharov's career as a dissident ended. But he remained active in a role that was new to him, that of participant in the politics of the state, and I have devoted considerable attention to his activities in this, the last stage of his life, because the ideas that informed these activities are traceable directly to his earlier dissidence.

Given the primacy of Sakharov's dissidence in his intellectual development, I have tried in the biography to explain three aspects of it: first, why he became a dissident; second, what his dissidence consisted of; and third, how it contributed to the collapse of the Soviet Union in 1991, two years after his death.

Sakharov's opposition to the regime—its origins, content, and consequences—reveals a great deal about the Soviet Union itself. In particular, it shows how a political leadership intent on perpetuating the paternalism it inherited from its tsarist predecessors felt compelled to grant its educated elite, to which Sakharov belonged as much by familial inheritance as by his training as a theoretical physicist, a vocational autonomy it strictly denied the remainder of the Soviet population. The government granted this autonomy because it recognized that scientists were indispensable to the modernization of the Soviet economy and society. Accordingly, it assigned Sakharov the task of designing thermonuclear weapons that would confirm the Soviet Union's status as a global power, deter the United States from practicing atomic diplomacy, and facilitate the expansion of Soviet influence. Because the regime considered these weapons and the scientists who built them essential to its survival, Sakharov and the physicists who worked with him were allowed privileges unimaginable to ordinary Soviet citizens, such as the freedom to discuss virtually anything, including anti-Soviet works like Orwell's novel *1984*. That Sakharov could discuss these works with impunity was the most astonishing piece of information uncovered in my research. But since these physicists, no less than the Soviet people from whom they were physically segregated (in an installation surrounded by barbed wire and police dogs), were also in the eyes of the regime little more than children, too immature and irrational to share in governance, the vocational autonomy they enjoyed would not, and could not, be accompanied by individual liberties or political freedom. There was an inherent contradiction between modernizing a backward society, which required that a segment of the population be treated in their jobs as adults, and maintaining a monopoly of political power, which required that the entire population be treated as children. Because it valued these two objectives equally, the Soviet leadership never resolved the contradiction its pursuit of them entailed. The result was dissidence such as Sakharov's.

Sakharov's campaign against the Soviet system was principally an ethical one, traceable intellectually to the intelligentsia, whose ethos of moral wholeness and consistency Sakharov inherited first from his father, Dmitrii Sakharov, and then from the renowned Soviet physicist Igor Tamm, Sakharov's mentor and role model while he was pursuing postgraduate training in physics in the late 1940s. The charge that the Soviet Union denied its people human rights was always paramount in Sakharov's indictment of it. To be sure, he also claimed the Soviet system was ineffectual in serving the material needs of its people, and the desiderata of human rights he elucidated included not only the intangible rights usually subsumed in the West under the rubric of civil liberties but also the provision of education, housing, and adequate medical care. That Sakharov considered the absence of these things primarily an ethical failing of the Soviet system was consistent with his belief that acting ethically was the paramount obligation of government.

When Sakharov determined what should replace the Soviet system, or how it could be reformed in ways that would make it more humane, he came up with a series of requirements that he claimed were based on universal principles of social justice, which he enshrined, just a few weeks before he died, in a constitution he drafted for a commission Gorbachev had established to write a successor to the so-called Brezhnev Constitution. The draft Sakharov produced includes nearly everything he stood for. But the guiding principles that informed it were based on a single and very simple proposition—namely, that a just and humane society was a society based on reason. To the emergence of this idea, Sakharov's training as a scientist was critical. The milieu he inhabited as a scientist was one where substantive disagreements and interpersonal conflicts were presumed to be amenable to reason. While Sakharov was never so naïve—a characteristic for which he was sometimes and wrongly criticized—as to deny the importance of feelings and emotions in human affairs, he never wavered in his conviction that social justice could be established only by people who were rational. The kind of society Sakharov considered most conducive to the emancipation of the individual personality—yet another moral imperative he inherited from the intelligentsia—was one governed by rational people and organized on the basis of rational principles. The exhortation in his Nobel Lecture in 1975 that "we must make good the demands of reason" encapsulates his political philosophy. By "we" Sakharov meant not only himself and other dissidents but humanity in general. Sakharov was a citizen of the world as well as of the Soviet Union, and the universalism he ascribed to his convictions makes his attempts to persuade the Soviet leadership to adopt them relevant to readers who know little or nothing about the Soviet Union and communism.

Writing a biography of Andrei Sakharov is not easy. To be done correctly, it requires a mastery, or at least a passing knowledge, of the disparate issues Sakharov dealt with in the course of his lifetime, from the cosmological issues he explored as a theoretical physicist to those of a more practical nature he confronted while designing thermonuclear weaponry. At the end of his life, while exhorting Gorbachev not to slacken in his effort to reform the Soviet system, Sakharov addressed several arcane questions of a political nature that one might think alien to someone trained as a scientist, such as whether the relationship between the central government and its constituent republics in a reformed union should be "federalist" or "confederalist" in nature. Moreover, since Sakharov was concerned with how the weapons he designed would be used, his biographer must be competent to discuss the paradoxical logic of nuclear deterrence in the Cold War, which in turn requires a familiarity with the various weapons systems to which this logic applied, such as ICBMs, IRBMs, the MX missile, and space-based missile defenses. Sakharov's awareness that the effects of science on nature and the environment were not always salubrious means that his biographer must also know something about radioactive fallout, the proper construction of nuclear power plants, and ecology.

Mine is not the first full-length biography of Sakharov. The most recent, by Richard Lourie, describes his personal life and political activities vividly. But it includes little analysis of Sakharov's ideas. For this reason I hope my book, with its emphasis on this aspect of Sakharov's life—not only the content of his ideas but how they evolved in response to changes both in his personal circumstances and in the larger political environment in which he lived—will satisfy prospective readers interested in Sakharov as a thinker and political actor who greatly influenced the history of the Soviet Union.

I have accumulated many debts in the course of writing this book. It is my great pleasure to acknowledge them now. Without the professionalism and exemplary assistance of Kimberly Farrington, Interlibrary Loan Librarian at Central Connecticut State University, and University Assistants Angie Staino-Zavatkay and Chris Tucker in acquiring books and other materials on Sakharov, most of them in Russian, I could not have done the research on which my book is based. To my great benefit, everyone at Cornell University Press who evaluated my manuscript—the director of the Press, John Ackerman, Senior Production Editor Karen Laun, and my superb copyeditor Jamie Fuller—improved it when I wrongly thought it was fine the way it was. I also thank David Coppen for sending me a copy of the bibliography of Sakharov's writings he compiled in partial fulfillment for a degree in Library and Information Science at the University of Illinois.

On my trips to the Andrei Sakharov Archives and Human Rights Center at Brandeis University (now at Harvard University), the archivist there, Alexander Gribanov, informed me of documents of which I was previously unaware and supplied essential information on aspects of Sakharov's life. Tatiana Yankelevich, the director of the archives and Sakharov's stepdaughter, patiently answered my seemingly endless questions on Sakharov, and to her enormous credit never tried to impose her own opinions on me. In Moscow Sakharov's widow, Elena Bonner, very kindly answered questions Tatiana transmitted to her, and in Israel Efrem Yankelevich clarified episodes in Sakharov's life of which he had personal knowledge. By reading the entire manuscript, excepting only the portions on physics and cosmology, Edward Kline, the president of the Andrei Sakharov Foundation in New York, saved me from many factual errors. He also offered excellent suggestions for improvement, and in our conversations provided insights into Sakharov's character accessible only to someone who knew the man personally, as Mr. Kline did.

On short notice Grant Mathews and Christopher Kolda, both physicists at the University of Notre Dame, agreed to read the sections of the manuscript that describe and evaluate Sakharov's contributions to physics and cosmology. They corrected errors of which only members of their profession would likely be aware, and for that I am enormously grateful.

I owe a special debt of gratitude to Kathleen Smith of Georgetown University, who read and evaluated my manuscript for Cornell University Press not once but twice. I believe that by incorporating into the manuscript her thoughtful and constructive suggestions I have improved it significantly. Whatever short-comings remain are of course my responsibility, and mine alone.

I am also grateful to Robert Crummey and Firuz Kazemzadeh, teachers of mine as a doctoral candidate at Yale University many years ago, who helped me acquire and hone the skills needed to write history. In Henry Turner, another of my teachers at Yale, I saw a historian scrupulous in using evidence, open-minded in testing hypotheses, and judicious in drawing conclusions that were as sensible and cogent as they were convincing. I learned a great deal from him, as I did even earlier in my life from Miriam Eisenstein's class on Problems of American Democracy at New Rochelle High School in New Rochelle, New York.

More recently, Geraldine Lenz provided much-needed moral support and gave me the confidence to believe that a press would judge my work favorably. Scott Seminer proved once again, as he has in the nearly half-century that I have known him, to be the best friend I could ever hope to have. Leonard Phillips spent countless hours reading my manuscript and correcting it the way a professional copyeditor would. I am certain that my book is better because of his efforts.

My colleague Katherine Hermes put her own scholarship on hold to read my manuscript and write a formal evaluation of it. That she did so with the intelligence, good cheer, and kindness I have come to value in her is an act of friendship I will always remember. My colleague Bolek Biskupski not only read my manuscript and commented on it in similar fashion; he also sustained me through the long hours of writing and revision with a wit that was as sharp as his friendship is enduring.

Marshall Shatz, who sparked my interest in Russian history as an undergraduate at Brandeis University and inspired me to become a Russian historian, read the manuscript with his unerring eye for the incorrect fact, the awkward phrase, and the unconvincing argument. Indeed, it is with Marshall's reaction in mind that I have written everything in the years I have known him variously as a teacher, mentor, role model, colleague, and friend. "What would Marshall think?" is the question I constantly asked myself when I was writing this biography, and the finest compliment I have received on it thus far is his good opinion of it.

My wife, Julie, and my son, Aaron, have enriched my life outside academia in so many ways that I could not possibly enumerate them all without exhausting the reader's patience. It is enough to say that their affection, love, and compassionate concern while I was writing I will always value. It is to them, with love, that this book is gratefully dedicated.

# Note on Transliteration

Transliteration of Russian words follows the Library of Congress system. The only exceptions are to render the "ks" in, for example, Aleksei, as "x"—hence, Alexei—and the names of persons and places well known in the West in the way they are spelled in the West—hence "Yeltsin" instead of "El'tsin," "Gorky" instead of "Gorkii," "Trotsky" instead of "Trotskii," "Yakovlev" instead of "Iakovlev" in the case of Alexander Yakovlev, and "Sharansky" instead of "Shcharanskii." The family name of Sakharov's stepdaughter is rendered in the same way, as "Yankelevich" instead of "Iankelevich."

# PART I

# Earliest Influences: 1921–1945

# 1 A Childhood of Culture and Ideas

The Soviet Union in which Andrei Sakharov was born and grew to maturity was radically different in many ways from the monarchy that preceded it. Mesmerized by the opportunity to remold human nature and create a communist society devoid of everything that had corrupted human existence prior to the Bolshevik Revolution in 1917, the original leaders of the Soviet Union were genuine zealots and ideologues. The orchestras without conductors and the communes whose members shared everything, including their underwear, that Soviet citizens created enthusiastically in the 1920s were just two expressions of the fanaticism implicit in the communism these leaders espoused, with its belief in the superiority of collective endeavor.[1] Indeed, the vast projects of social engineering the Soviet Union undertook in the late 1920s and early 1930s, most notably industrialization and the collectivization of agriculture, were intended to overcome the crippling backwardness that had afflicted Russia for generations and to provide the external conditions for the radical transformation not only of the Russian people but eventually of all people.

A regime with objectives such as these could not help but impinge on the private lives of its citizens, conscripting the most talented of them on behalf of its own agenda and objectives. This is what happened to Andrei Sakharov. In a country whose country roads were mostly unpaved and whose peasant villages were without modern plumbing, he was entrusted, along with others, with the task of constructing thermonuclear weapons. Russia in the early twentieth century was a country with a lot of catching up to do, and its Soviet leadership after 1917 believed this could be accomplished in a matter of decades. Many Soviet families, including Sakharov's, would be greatly and grievously harmed as a consequence of this.

Andrei Dmitrievch Sakharov was born in Moscow on May 21, 1921. He was the first child of Dmitrii Ivanovich Sakharov and Ekaterina Alexeevna Sakharova, whose family name before she married was Sofiano. Their second child, Georgii, whom they called Iura, was born four years later.[2] Both of Sakharov's parents came from families that were reasonably affluent. Many members were also well educated. Of course, education alone does not confer intelligence or provide critical insight; if it is sufficiently narrow, as it often was in Russia, it could easily limit, rather than liberate, a person intellectually. But the Sakharovs and Sofianos were fortunate. The education they received, combined with the sensibility to extract the larger lessons it contained, enabled them to pass on to their

1. Richard Stites, *Revolutionary Dreams: Utopian Vision and Experimental Life in the Russian Revolution* (New York, 1989), 135–40, 214.
2. Andrei Sakharov, *Memoirs*, trans. Richard Lourie (New York, 1990), 9–10.

descendants a penchant for examining intellectual issues critically that persons of lesser education, or of no education at all, would be less likely to have. In fact, while none of Sakharov's ancestors ever advocated the violent overthrow of tsarist autocracy, there runs through the history of the two families an awareness, fairly dim in early generations but more acute in later ones, that education was not only a prerequisite of vocational success but something to be valued for its own sake. For Sakharov and his ancestors, the capacity for rational analysis required by education was a uniquely human attribute that gave human beings their intrinsic and inviolable worth.

Sakharov's ancestors were not members of the intelligentsia, the term first used in Russia in the 1860s for those in the educated elite who in the nineteenth and early twentieth centuries expressed their alienation from the existing order by criticizing it in the name of moral and political principles they believed to be timeless, absolute, and universal. By this definition, members of the intelligentsia—the Russian word for them is *intelligenty*, the singular of which is *intelligent*—could be revolutionaries but did not have to be. Many intelligenty rejected revolution on ethical grounds or because they considered it impractical. What distinguished them from the educated elite from which they came was their belief in the dignity and worth of the individual not just as an end in itself but as the only possible basis on which a fair and just society could be constructed. While intelligenty were not oblivious to pragmatic arguments for the individualism they favored—for example, that only a society that recognized the sovereignty of the individual could satisfy the material needs of everyone—it was the intensely moral nature of their criticism of tsarist Russia, and the alienation of which their criticism was an undeniable expression, that distinguished this group from the much larger stratum of white-collar professionals who in the Soviet era were described, misleadingly, as the intelligentsia. The only persons in the Soviet Union to whom the original sense of the term applied were dissidents such as Sakharov.[3]

Boris Altshuler, a longtime friend and fellow physicist, writes that Sakharov came from "the lost world" of the intelligentsia.[4] Taken literally, his statement is not correct. Sakharov's ancestors, including his parents, were insufficiently alienated to be intelligenty. Nevertheless they tried to cultivate several of the qualities the intelligentsia possessed: an aversion to self-promotion and personal vanity, a respect for intellectual excellence, a firm belief in the primacy of ideas, and an ethos of "moral wholeness" requiring the application of moral principle

3. On the origins and attributes of the intelligentsia, see Marshall Shatz, *Soviet Dissent in Historical Perspective* (New York, 1980), 12–38, and Martin Malia, "What Is the Intelligentsia?" in *The Russian Intelligentsia*, ed. Richard Pipes (New York, 1961), 1–18. On the so-called intelligentsia in the Soviet Union, see Moshe Lewin, *The Gorbachev Phenomenon: Expanded Edition* (Berkeley, 1991), 46–50, 57–62, 124.

4. B. L. Altshuler, "A kogda upadesh'—eto nevazhno," in *Andrei Dmitrievich: Vospominaniia o Sakharove*, ed. Tatiana I. Ivanova (Moscow, 1990), 132. Raisa Orlova and Lev Kopelev, who knew Sakharov well, have written that "from childhood, Sakharov breathed the air of the Russian intelligentsia." Raisa Orlova and Lev Kopelev, "Istoki chuda," in *Sakharov: Takim on byl*, ed. A. O. Skonechnaia and F. L. Tsypkina (Zhitomir, 1991), 34.

to every aspect of life. As a consequence, Sakharov grew up in what he describes in a 1973 essay as "an atmosphere of decency, mutual help and tact, a liking for work, and respect for the mastery of one's chosen profession."[5]

As their name suggests, the Sofianos were Greek, and after settling in Russia in the late eighteenth century, they retained for a time a strong attachment to their ancestral homeland; one member even returned to Greece in the 1820s to fight in the war that won the Greeks their independence.[6] Once in Russia, several male members of the family, in what became a Sofiano tradition, served their adopted country as military officers, which did not preclude several of them from befriending figures prominent in Russian literature and politics— among them Pushkin, Griboyedov, and Tolstoy—and two of the so-called Decembrists who tried to overthrow the monarchy in 1825.[7] A half-sister of Sakharov's mother, Ekaterina, translated Chopin's letters into Russian.[8]

Sakharov's mother, Ekaterina (1893–1963), to whom Sakharov bore a physical resemblance, especially in the "Mongol cast" of his eyes, passed on to her son aspects of her personality—shyness, a certain obstinacy, and a sense of awkwardness in dealing with other people—that Sakharov says were impervious to all his childhood efforts to eliminate them and remained a source of irritation into his adulthood.[9] Ekaterina was from a small village in Belgorod District, and she was educated, as befitting a daughter of the nobility, at the Dvorianskii Institute. She married Dmitrii Sakharov in 1918. More religious than her husband, she was greatly perturbed by young Andrei's disenchantment with Russian Orthodoxy, which resulted in his announcement at the age of thirteen that, despite having been baptized into the Christian faith, he no longer believed in the existence of a deity.[10] Ekaterina's discomfiture over this declaration undoubtedly worsened when her son matured without ever reconciling himself to the Orthodox Church, an institution that, whatever Sakharov's musings as an adult on a "higher meaning" in nature and the universe, remained for him a force for ignorance and obscurantism; indeed, by compromising its independence in the Stalin era, the Church destroyed what little moral credibility it had for him.[11] In his memoirs, Sakharov mentions his mother less frequently

5. Andrei Sakharov, introduction to *Sakharov Speaks*, ed. Harrison E. Salisbury (New York, 1974), 30.

6. According to Sakharov's second wife, Elena Bonner, who after his death in 1989 endeavored to reconstruct his family history, the Sofianos before they emigrated were full-fledged members of the Greek aristocracy. She also notes that Sakharov did not know very much about his family history and that much of what he once knew he did not remember. For that reason her book's family trees for the Sakharovs and the Sofianos are invaluable in clarifying Sakharov's familial inheritance. Elena Bonner, *Vol'nye zametki k rodoslovnoi Andreia Sakharova* (Moscow, 1996), 3, 5–8, 42.

7. Ibid., 15.

8. Ibid., 20–22.

9. Sakharov, *Memoirs*, 3–4.

10. Ibid., 4; Bonner, *Vol'nye zametki*, 42–43.

11. Sakharov, *Memoirs*, 4–5; Iu. N. Smirnov, "Etot chelovek sdelal bol'she chem my vse...," in *On mezhdu nami zhil...vospominaniia o Sakharove*, ed. B. L. Altshuler, B. M. Bolotovskii, I. M. Dremin, L. V. Keldysh, and V. Ia. Fainberg (Moscow, 1996), 581. As an adult, Sakharov insisted he was not an atheist, and in keeping with his training as a physicist, he believed there was a higher

than he does his father, and his reticence in this respect may have been his way of shielding her from the criticism he would ordinarily level at people who reflected in their behavior and personality the specific qualities—inflexibility, narrow-mindedness, and a belief in the irrational and the supernatural—he often ascribed to the baleful influence of religion in general and of Russian Orthodoxy in particular. As it is, he describes his mother as "somewhat dogmatic" and "lacking in tolerance."[12]

Instead of producing military officers, as the Sofianos did, many of the Sakharovs gravitated to the priesthood. For several generations they lived and worked in a small village east of Moscow, sixty miles from Nizhnyi Novgorod and not far from the installation where, from 1950 to 1968, Sakharov worked in virtual isolation on various nuclear and thermonuclear weapons.[13] But Sakharov's grandfather, Ivan Nikolaevich Sakharov (1860–1918), broke family tradition: after studying law at the university in Nizhnyi Novgorod—which the Soviets would rename Gorky, after the writer Maxim Gorky, and where Sakharov would live in internal exile from 1980 to 1986—he moved to Moscow to pursue a career as a lawyer. Of his many achievements (in a trial in 1894 he delivered a plea of such eloquence and passion that it was included in a collection of attorneys' statements and summations published in the Soviet Union in the 1960s), the most impressive in his grandson's eyes was the collection of essays opposing capital punishment that Ivan edited when the original editor was arrested before the collection was completed. Indeed, Sakharov traced his own opposition to the death penalty to the essay on the subject Leo Tolstoy contributed to the collection, and in his memoirs he praises his grandfather's work on the collection as "an act of conscience and, to an extent, civic courage."[14] Ivan clearly was one of Sakharov's intellectual role models, even though Ivan, while obviously critical of certain aspects of Imperial Russia, was also a member of the Moscow legal establishment and never repudiated the tsarist system to the degree to which his grandson rejected the Soviet one.

---

power that invested the universe with a deeper meaning. In an interview in 1988 Sakharov proclaimed his belief in "some kind of internal essence" in the universe, albeit one that was entirely spiritual and immaterial. Andrei Sakharov, "O narodnom deputate A. D. Sakharove rasskazyvaet narodnyi deputat Galina Starovoitova," in Skonechnaia and Tsypkina, *Sakharov: Takim on byl*, 65; V. V. Borshchov, "Pravednik," in Ivanova, *Andrei Dmitrievich*, 94; Andrei Sakharov and Ales Adamovich, "Zhit' na zemle i zhit' dolgo," *Iskusstvo kino* 8 (1989): 169.

12. Sakharov, *Memoirs*, 3.

13. Bonner, *Vol'nye zametki*, 72–75. Bonner repeats the story, possibly apocryphal, that the name "Sakharov" came from one of the instructors at the seminary where Sakharov's great-great-grandfather, Ioann Iosifovich Sakharov (1789–1867), studied in the early nineteenth century. Favorably impressed by his young student—whose original name Bonner could not discover when she searched for it in the early 1990s—the instructor is supposed to have said to him: "As you are as pure and as white as sugar [*sakhar*], here you will be known as 'Sugarman.'" Ibid., 72. "Sakharov," loosely translated, means "of the sugar men."

14. Bonner, *Vol'nye zametki*, 114; Sakharov, *Memoirs*, 6; E. R. Gaginskaia and A. R. Gaginskaia, "Vospominaniia N. N. Raikovskoi (1865–1950)," in Ivanova, *Andrei Dmitrievich*, 241. Raikovskaia was a great aunt of Sakharov. Thus the Gaginskaias, who were her granddaughters, were his second cousins.

Ivan's wife, Maria Petrovna Sakharova (1859–1941), true to the ethos of the intelligentsia, rejected the paternalism in Russian culture that presumed women to be intellectually inferior and aspired to be the equal of her husband. To her credit, she very nearly succeeded. Educated at the Pavlovskii Institute in St. Petersburg, Maria Petrovna was able, at an early age, to think for herself, and as an adult she did not shrink from maintaining a friendship with a woman with ties to the terrorist organization Narodnaia volia, which in 1881 assassinated Tsar Alexander II. After marrying Ivan, who was her second husband, she joined the Union for the Equality of Women, an organization active in the 1905 Revolution. Remarkably, despite the demands of raising six children while simultaneously pursuing her outside interests, Maria Petrovna found time to read prodigiously, not just Pushkin and the Russian classics but foreign authors as well. She even learned English to appreciate the subtleties of British novels and American works such as *Uncle Tom's Cabin*.[15]

For her grandson, Maria Petrovna—or Babania, as her grandchildren called her—was not only a role model but also the object of genuine affection. In his memoirs Sakharov calls her "the guiding spirit of the Sakharov home" and lauds the personal qualities she possessed—"intelligence, goodness, and compassion, an appreciation of life's complexities, and a special talent for nurturing a family and raising educated, sensitive, self-reliant children able to cope with the demands of the turbulent times"—that helped to create a home environment as stimulating intellectually as it was protective and supportive psychologically.[16] Long after Babania died, Sakharov's second wife, Elena Bonner, once commented that her husband inherited from his grandmother her firmness and steadfastness of character and that he concealed these characteristics just as she did, beneath a soft and seemingly pliable exterior.[17] Moreover, it was Babania who more than anyone else introduced Sakharov to the pleasures of serious reading, which in due course included foreign authors such as Twain, Dickens, Hugo, Dumas, Verne, Swift, London, and Shakespeare, as well as the Russian classics. Andrei and his younger brother, Iura, came to know Pushkin's works so well that the two often played a game in which one of them would deliberately mumble one of the poet's verses, while the other would have to guess the work it came from.[18]

---

15. Bonner, *Vol'nye zametki*, 83, 89–90, 111; Sakharov, *Memoirs*, 11. Of Maria Petrovna's six children, only Ivan (1887–1944) voiced any doubts about the Soviet state. A skilled raconteur and conversationalist, Ivan was probably the most impulsive and spontaneous of the Sakharovs; on one occasion in the late 1920s or early 1930s he drew a caricature of Stalin, complete with fangs and a sinister smile, that in the wrong hands could easily have caused his imprisonment or worse. Of Babania's other children, Sakharov writes only about the eldest, his aunt Tatiana (1883–1977), who under the influence of Tolstoy became a vegetarian, taught English for many years, and married a great-grandson of the Decembrist I. D. Iakushkin. Sakharov, *Memoirs*, 10, 21; Gaginskaias, "Vospominaniia N. N. Raikovskoi," 241.

16. Sakharov, *Memoirs*, 6.

17. Bonner, *Vol'nye zametki*, 120.

18. Sakharov, *Memoirs*, 26–27; Andrei Sakharov, "Interv'iu Bolgarskoi zhurnalistke zhanne avisai. Moskva (July 1988)," *Zvezda* 5 (1991): 129; Altshuler, "A kogda upadesh'," 130.

Sakharov's father, Dmitrii (1889–1961), was by all accounts an outstanding intellect and pedagogue. Blessed with the rare ability to express complex ideas in simple, comprehensible language, Dmitrii made physics accessible to literally millions of Soviet students through the sixteen books and textbooks he wrote over the course of a distinguished career teaching physics at the Institute for Red Professors, Sverdlovsk University, and for twenty-five years at the Lenin Pedagogical Institute, from which his students went on to be teachers themselves.[19] An excellent classroom teacher who demanded as much from his students as he did of himself, Dmitrii refused to tolerate any frivolity and superficiality, which he took as evidence of a lack of commitment to science and to learning in general. However, he was also modest and self-effacing about his own achievements, and his patience with students having trouble with a particular problem was extraordinary, reflecting his belief that everyone who wanted to study science should be encouraged to do so regardless of aptitude.[20]

Not surprisingly, Dmitrii was his son's first physics teacher and in every sense an example of how someone who devotes his professional life to science should live. To his son, Dmitrii was as fine a human being as he was a teacher: "kind and gentle, a man of principle, wise and compassionate."[21] At the same time, Dmitrii was almost completely apolitical. When, in December 1934, Sergei Kirov, a leading Stalinist and the party chief in Leningrad, was assassinated, possibly on Stalin's orders, Dmitrii admitted that he did not know who Kirov was.[22] But in matters cultural and intellectual, Dmitrii's interests were as eclectic, his knowledge as broad, and his talents as diverse as those of anyone in the educated elite. In addition to his abilities as a science teacher, Dmitrii was a gifted pianist who in his youth had received a gold medal for his prowess from the music conservatory he attended.[23] His favorite composers were Bach, Chopin, Grieg, Mozart, Schumann, Borodin, Prokofiev, Rachmaninoff, Rimskii-Korsakov, Scriabin (whom he once met) and Beethoven (whose portrait hung over his mother's bed); the grand piano that dominated one of the two rooms of the communal apartment where the Sakharovs lived was perhaps his most cherished possession.[24] Music, for Dmitrii, was a way of expressing his belief that the finest and

19. N. E. Parfenteva and N. N. Malov, "Material bez kakikh iz"iatii perepechatan iz zhurnala 'Fizika v shkole,' no. 3 1989 god," in Ivanova, *Andrei Dmitrievich*, 262–65; Kevin Klose, *Russia and the Russians* (New York, 1984), 136. When Dmitrii Sakharov began working at the institute, it was called the Bubnov Pedagogical Institute, after the prominent Bolshevik and commissar of education Andrei Bubnov. Not long after Bubnov was arrested in 1937—he would be shot in 1940—the institute was renamed for Lenin. One of the textbooks Dmitrii wrote was still in print when he died in 1963; his son would edit the two subsequent editions. Sakharov, *Memoirs*, 12; Oleg Moroz, "Vozvrashchenie iz ssylki (Istoriia odnogo interviu)," in Ivanova, *Andrei Dmitrievich*, 344.
20. Parfenteva and Malov, "Material," 266.
21. Sakharov, *Memoirs*, 15.
22. Ibid., 31–32.
23. Parfenteva and Malov, "Material," 266; Sakharov, *Memoirs*, 7.
24. Andrei Sakharov, "Svoimi vospominaniami o Dmitrii Ivanoviche Sakharove delitsia ego syn, A. D. Sakharov (January 17, 1989)," in Ivanova, *Andrei Dmitrievich*, 267; Elena Bonner, "Do dnevnik: K izdaniiu Sobraniia sochinenii A. D. Sakharova," *Znamia* 11 (2005): 18 (unpublished copy received from Tatiana Yankelevich).

most uniquely human achievements can reside in the disembodied realm of ideas and artistic creation—from which his son would draw the conclusion that these achievements confer on human beings a dignity and worth that must be recognized, respected, and protected by the political leaders who rule them. In Dmitrii's music and his devotion to science and in the quiet moral goodness he exuded, his son would discern a humane and gentle wisdom that would remain the precious legacy of a father who loved him.

But this was not all that Dmitrii and Sakharov's other relatives provided. With few exceptions, the education the Sakharovs and the Sofianos received enabled them to enter professions that, for all the demands they imposed, left time for the pursuit of private interests and the cultivation of individual abilities. What this meant in practical terms was that those family members who used their leisure time in this fashion enjoyed a "zone of autonomy" from which the external world, no matter how oppressive or unpleasant, could be excluded. Indeed, as their childhoods evolved imperceptibly into adulthood, Sakharov's relatives imposed upon themselves a code of conduct they consciously followed, more or less consistently, for the rest of their lives. All that was missing from this, in terms of the intelligentsia, was the inclination to apply the ethical principles that informed their personal and professional lives to the existing political system and to formulate a coherent and morally superior alternative to it. This they left to their most illustrious descendant, who had to look no further than his own family to find the humane values he would champion as an adult in challenging the moral legitimacy of the second most powerful nation in the world.

## Early Childhood and Education

When Sakharov was eighteen months old, his parents moved from the basement apartment where he was born to a two-story building, also in Moscow, on a secluded side street, Granatnyi Lane, where, with other members of the family, they took over four of the six apartments the building contained. This was where Sakharov grew up. He, his parents, and eventually Iura occupied two rooms. One of these served as a bedroom, a dining room, and a nursery, while the other, which was really just an extended hallway, his father made into a study. Everyone who lived in the building, not just the Sakharovs, used the same bathroom and kitchen. While this might suggest that the Sakharovs were poor, such an arrangement, because of a chronic shortage of housing, was actually quite common in the Soviet Union in the 1920s. Fortunately for the Sakharovs, they could escape from their cramped quarters on Granatnyi Lane by renting rooms in a dacha outside Moscow for their vacations, which Sakharov says he found extremely enjoyable.[25]

Because of Sakharov's precocity—at the age of four he taught himself to read—his parents concluded that the Soviet school system would be inadequate, and they had him taught at home by private tutors. However, the instruction he

25. Sakharov, "Svoimi vospominaniami," 267; Sakharov, *Memoirs*, 9, 14; Sakharov, "Interv'iu Bolgarskoi zhurnalistke," 128.

received did nothing to further his social development. Sakharov states in his memoirs that his tutors not only failed to inculcate self-reliance and efficient work habits but increased his inability, which he wrongly considered innate and irreversible, to communicate his ideas effectively to others.[26]

In 1933, when Sakharov was twelve, his parents finally enrolled him in a public school, where his classmates included the children of high Soviet officials such as Karl Radek. But Sakharov's parents quickly soured on the idea. In early 1934 they withdrew him and resumed homeschooling, which this time proceeded smoothly enough so that the young boy could pass the examinations enabling him to reenter school—as it happened, a different one—the next fall one grade ahead of the students his age.[27]

This was when Sakharov first showed an interest in science. In all likelihood his interest was innate, but it was probably enhanced by the admiration preadolescent boys often have for their father's vocation. When his classes were not in session, Dmitrii Sakharov would bring his son to his laboratory at the Pedagogical Institute and perform experiments that the amazed young boy initially considered miraculous. However, Dmitrii would always supply a scientific explanation for what he did, and gradually his son understood that what he saw could be predicted on the basis of scientific laws and principles. This was an idée fixe for Sakharov as a physicist and later as a dissident, when he believed that political problems were just as amenable as scientific ones to rational analysis. Significantly, the young boy found his father's explanations of these experiments as impressive as the experiments themselves.[28] As a result, he learned early on that nature, despite its complexity, could be rendered comprehensible through the application of reason—an assumption that for every scientist is practically an article of faith.

Of course, young Sakharov, on the cusp of adolescence, could hardly know where his interest in science would lead. Years later, Sakharov described his indecision as follows: "Papa made me a physicist, but God knows where it will take me."[29] Still, Dmitrii's influence was enormous, and it even extended to how his son would write. As an adult, Sakharov praised his father for the lucidity and concision of his prose, and he states explicitly in his memoirs that Dmitrii's penchant for exactitude in this regard impressed him profoundly.[30] Indeed, Dmitrii impressed upon his son the larger lesson that the hypotheses scientists conjured had to be confirmed empirically or mathematically, that enthusiasm and curiosity were not enough, and that a good hypothesis required the most painstaking analysis of evidence and facts. What Dmitrii revealed to his son and young charge, in sum, was the tradition of rational inquiry that made possible the achievements of modern science. Dmitrii's motives in doing so included

26. Sakharov, *Memoirs*, 26–28. In fact, Sakharov's ability to communicate effectively improved with age. Correspondence with Edward Kline, September 18, 2007.

27. Ibid., 29–31.

28. Ibid., 12, 31; Sakharov, "Svoimi vospominaniami," 268.

29. Bonner, *Vol'nye zametki*, 153.

30. Sakharov, "Svoimi vospominaniami," 267; Sakharov, *Memoirs*, 13.

a personal and psychological element that Sakharov became aware of only as an adult: that as a mere teacher of physics, Dmitrii could satisfy his own aspirations for doing original and creative research only through his son.[31] Despite the eventual disparity in their accomplishments as scientists, Dmitrii's love and affection for his son never wavered, and the bond between them remained strong. In his late twenties and well on his way to becoming one of the most brilliant physicists in the Soviet Union, Sakharov spoke of his father only occasionally, but always lovingly and with the utmost respect.[32]

For the elementary physics and mathematics Dmitrii taught him, young Sakharov showed a natural inclination. Part of what made these disciplines exciting to him was the way the natural laws of physics could be given precise mathematical expression: "The whole gamut of natural phenomena [can be reduced] to the comparatively simple laws of interaction between atoms, as expressed by mathematical formulas. I did not yet fully understand all the subtleties of differential equations, but I sensed and delighted in their power. It may have been this more than anything else that kindled my desire to become a physicist."[33] For Sakharov there was something immensely satisfying and aesthetically pleasing about intellectual disciplines such as mathematics and theoretical physics that required the application of pure reason; the truths these disciplines revealed were marked by an elegance, a precision, and a permanence glaringly absent in the welter of emotions, feelings, impulses, and aspirations that so powerfully affect people in their everyday lives. Exercising pure intellect in the pursuit of scientific truth, Sakharov realized, was perhaps the highest calling to which a human being could aspire; and only the most pressing temporal concerns—human rights, social justice, and world peace—would finally divert Sakharov from his obligations as a scientist. Even then, he still considered himself primarily a physicist and only secondarily, and quite reluctantly, a dissident.[34] According to Bonner, there was never a day when her husband did not think about science, and several of Sakharov's scientific colleagues concurred in the opinion that, of all of Sakharov's activities, his work in physics was the most pleasurable.[35]

31. Sakharov, "Svoimi vospominaniami," 268; Sakharov, *Memoirs*, 16.

32. L. V. Pariiskaia, "On vsegda budet samim soboi," in Altshuler et al., *On mezhdu nami zhil*, 476.

33. Sakharov, *Memoirs*, 31.

34. Sakharov disliked the term "dissident." In his view it was not "politically meaningful." Sakharov, *Memoirs*, 361. At least to the mid-1970s, he preferred that he and other dissidents be called *volnomysliashchie* (freethinkers). Sakharov, *Memoirs*, 361. Sakharov may have avoided the term "dissident" because it implied that his beliefs were a deviation from a norm, in this case a communist one. But since "dissident" was the term most often used in English to describe Sakharov and the other members of the movement that fought for human rights in the Soviet Union from the late 1960s, I use it throughout. Sakharov, introduction to *Sakharov Speaks*, 36; Andrei Sakharov, "Why I Speak Out Alone," *Observer Review*, June 8, 1975, 19.

35. E. G. Bonner, "Chetyre daty," in Altshuler et al., *On mezhdu nami zhil*, 174; B. L. Altshuler et al., "Personalia," in Altshuler et al., *On mezhdu nami zhil*, 10. According to Bonner, Sakharov proclaimed once that what he loved most in life was "radio broadcast emanation"—present-day remnants of the creation of the universe. David Remnick, *Lenin's Tomb: The Last Days of the Soviet Empire* (New York 1994), 165.

Because the homework he was assigned in school did not challenge him, Sakharov could finish it very quickly, and in his spare time he read the science fiction and popular science he preferred. When the mood struck him, he also conducted scientific experiments. At first the young boy limited himself to those his father suggested. But as his knowledge and confidence increased, he devised and carried out his own. In keeping with the modesty and self-effacement that nearly everyone who knew him ranked among his most attractive and endearing personal qualities, Sakharov berates himself, in describing these early experiments in his memoirs, on his lack of manual dexterity, which he claims slowed his progress considerably. But he also acknowledges that he compensated for this shortcoming by his ability to improvise.[36]

Sakharov's education and intellectual development continued their upward trajectory in high school, from which he graduated with honors in the spring of 1938. That distinction enabled him to enroll the following fall in the physics department of Moscow State University (MGU) without having to take the entrance examinations required of other applicants.[37] During his first three years at MGU, which he completed just before the Nazi invasion of the Soviet Union in 1941, Sakharov devoted his efforts to his courses in physics and mathematics, and he was fortunate to make the acquaintance of teachers in these fields who were knowledgeable and stimulating enough to satisfy his intellectual curiosity. When Sakharov attended MGU, it was pervaded—as were other Soviet institutions of that time—by the spirit of Stakhanovism, an ethos of labor productivity named for a coal miner, Andrei Stakhanov, who, after mining an inordinately large amount of coal, was feted by Stalin himself in 1935 and extolled as a precursor of the New Soviet Man. At MGU Stakhanovism took the form of encouraging good students to take their final examinations before their courses ended; by graduating early, they could go to work for the Soviet state immediately. Sakharov made use of this particular expedient, even though he did not do so out of a sense of civic obligation. Rather, he simply wanted more time to read the scientific books that interested him.[38]

In the severe but factually accurate estimation of one of his classmates, Sakharov was a good student but, in spite of his estimable record, not a brilliant one.[39] In an independent research project he undertook in his second year on the weak nonlinearity of waves in water, a topic assigned to him by his adviser, Professor Mikhail Leontovich, Sakharov was unable to define clearly what he hoped to demonstrate, and the project, as a result, "got nowhere."[40] In addition, he did not do terribly well in the so-called social disciplines—history, sociology,

36. Sakharov, *Memoirs*, 33–34.

37. Ibid., 35.

38. I. L. Rozental, "Proshchaite, Andrei Dmitrievich," in Altshuler et al., *On mezhdu nami zhil*, 541–42. Rozental claims that the classes Sakharov took bored him. But this is contradicted by Sakharov himself, who in his memoirs praises—though not uncritically—the education he received at MGU. Ibid.; Sakharov, *Memoirs*, 35–37.

39. A. M. Iaglom, "Drug blizkii, drug dalekii," in Altshuler et al., *On mezhdu nami zhil*, 781.

40. Sakharov, *Memoirs*, 37.

economics, and political theory. In the Stalinist era in particular, these required a different kind of intellect from that which Dmitrii Sakharov had nurtured in his son. But according to another classmate, who would later distinguish himself as a physicist and mathematician, the grades Sakharov received were not commensurate with his natural abilities because his intelligence, especially his capacity for abstract logic, was superior to that of his teachers.[41] Indeed, several of the physicists who worked intimately with Sakharov as an adult would comment on his ability to think "outside the box," to solve problems that otherwise seemed immune to explanation by means of an intuitive and imaginative leap that lesser minds, more constrained by the reigning dogmas and intellectual assumptions of the time, could not conceive of, or even, in certain instances, understand.[42]

All things considered, Sakharov had a reasonably happy childhood. By Soviet standards it may even have been idyllic. This is reflected, albeit obliquely, in the memoirs he wrote as an adult, in which there is no indication of any psychological trauma or maladjustment severe enough to have affected his personal development adversely.[43] To be sure, Sakharov states in the preface to his memoirs that he did not intend them as a confession and that in writing them he tried to confine himself to describing the events he witnessed and to explaining their effects on him.[44] Questions of motivation, especially where they concerned his inner emotional state, he generally ignored: "I want these memoirs to focus less on me as a person and more on what I have seen and understood (or tried to understand) during my sixty-eight years of life."[45] One reason for Sakharov's reticence in this regard was his natural self-effacement. One senses that he wrote his memoirs reluctantly, as if his life was not really important enough for people

41. M. L. Levin, untitled remarks, in Ivanova, *Andrei Dmitrievich,* 46.
42. See, for example, V. B. Adamskii, "Stanovlenie grazhdanina," in Altshuler et al., *On mezhdu nami zhil,* 24, and L. V. Keldysh, "Slovo ob Andree Sakharove," in Altshuler et al., *On mezhdu nami zhil,* 317.
43. When Sakharov was ten, an older boy he knew was murdered by thieves to whom Sakharov, not knowing their intentions, had given the boy's address. In his memoirs Sakharov states that the death "weighed on me to this very day." But that is quite different from ascribing psychological impairment to the incident. Sakharov, *Memoirs,* 20.
44. Ibid., xx.
45. Ibid., 16. Sakharov's memoirs are divided into two volumes. All but the last chapter of the first volume, entitled *Memoirs* in English, he completed at the end of 1983, despite the KGB's having stolen parts of it in 1978 (the same year he started work on it), 1981, and 1982. In the absence of computer disks and copy machines, Sakharov had no choice but to rewrite the parts he lost from memory. B. L. Altshuler claims that Sakharov did not use carbon paper, as Bonner suggested, because he found writing over it difficult. The final chapter to the first volume, which was appended to the text at the very end of 1986 or the beginning of 1987, covers the period from the fall of 1983, when Sakharov was midway through the six years he would spend in internal exile in Gorky, to December 1986, when the Soviet government permitted him and Bonner to return to Moscow. A second, much shorter volume, entitled in English *Moscow and Beyond,* describes Sakharov's life from January 1987 to June 1989. Both volumes were first published in their original Russian in New York in 1990, the same year they appeared in English translation, and excerpts from them were published legally in the Soviet Union in the journal *Znamia* in 1990 and 1991. They appeared in book form in Russia in 1996. Ibid., xix; Altshuler, "A kogda upadesh'," in Ivanova, *Andrei Dmitrievich,* 128.

to spend their time reading about it. In fact, the reason Sakharov gives in his memoirs for writing them is a fairly limited one: that they would clear up misconceptions that had grown up about him—many of them fostered by the Soviet leadership to discredit him.[46] But there was perhaps a deeper and more substantive reason for Sakharov's refusal to speculate on his own psychology. He believed that the methods based on logic and evidence he used as a scientist to explain the natural world were the methods he should use to explain his own life. Much of what his life was concerned with outside science—politics, ethics, nuclear weapons and arms control, foreign policy and international affairs—was indeed amenable to such analysis. But there were other aspects of his life, such as his inner conflicts and unconscious motives, for which such analysis was useless. Thus the proper thing for him to do, as he saw it, was just to ignore these things and leave any psychologizing about their origins to others.

But Sakharov was too intelligent, too perceptive, and too honest in the way he described his intellectual development to ignore the role his emotions and feelings played in it. His memoirs are more introspective than he admits. In describing his formative years in particular, Sakharov pays attention to his internal psychological equilibrium and carefully calibrates the extent to which external events affected it. For that reason one can be fairly certain that if, as a youth, Sakharov suffered from some severe psychological malady that adversely affected him, he would have said so both in his memoirs and in other works that describe his maturation. But Sakharov does not do this, and the reason is that his childhood was neither tumultuous nor traumatic.

## The Intrusion of Politics

The Sakharov and Sofiano families were not oblivious to the harsh realities of Stalinism. Several members were victims of it. Sometime in the late 1920s—Sakharov's memoirs and other writings on his youth are not specific—Dmitrii's brother Ivan was arrested and imprisoned for two years after impulsively lending his passport to a friend of his who wanted to leave the country, which at the time and for many years afterward was a crime.[47]

After serving his sentence, Ivan was released on the condition that he give up his profession of law, and he found work as a draftsman instead. But in 1935 he was arrested again and this time sent to work on the Volga River as a buoy-keeper, after which he worked at a nearby hydrological plant. Sakharov is vague on what happened next. He writes that, not long after the Nazi invasion in 1941, Ivan was arrested yet again, and sent to the Krasnoiarsk prison, in the hospital of which he died of starvation in 1943.[48] Other relatives who lost their lives while

46. Sakharov, *Memoirs,* xx.
47. Ivan's wife, Evgeniia, had gone to school with Genrikh Iagoda, who was second in command of the secret police when Ivan was arrested. Concerned for Ivan's safety, she appealed to her former classmate for assistance. But Iagoda, for whom sentimentality was an alien emotion, refused to help her. Ibid., 21.
48. Ibid., 21; Klose, *Russia and the Russians,* 137; Sakharov, "Interv'iu Bolgarskoi zhurnalistke," 127–28. Bonner's account of these events diverges slightly from Sakharov's. She places Ivan's first

Sakharov was growing up included Ekaterina's brother Konstantin, who was arrested in 1937 and died a year later while being interrogated by the NKVD; Evgenii Sofiano, the son of Ekaterina's brother Vladimir, who drowned while rafting timber on a river in the labor camp to which he was confined; and the second husband of one of Ekaterina's cousins, who, having roused suspicion as a former officer in Admiral Kolchak's army, was arrested and shot.[49]

Young Sakharov seems to have endured these tragedies better than one might have expected. In his memoirs he describes them laconically, perhaps because he believed that their mere mention was sufficient to cause his readers to feel the same indignation he did: the depredations Stalin inflicted on his family were so similar to what millions of other Soviet citizens endured that detailed and lengthy descriptions were unnecessary. But the lack of emotion with which Sakharov approaches the whole issue of the Terror in his memoirs may be a reflection of something else, namely, a desire to describe it in a way that corresponded to his own emotional state when he was actually witnessing it. Caught up in the excitement of learning physics, engrossed in reading literature, enraptured by the classical music that was so much a part of his home, young Sakharov simply did not have time to concern himself with politics, which in any case was something people living in the Stalin era talked about only with their closest friends and most immediate family, and even then with a great deal of circumspection. Sakharov does write that by the early 1930s he had learned about "current events" from conversations he overheard and thus had some inkling of the horrors that the collectivization of Soviet agriculture entailed.[50] But of the Terror that followed it Sakharov writes even less, though he was older when the Terror began. It is significant that the failings of the Soviet system he cites while describing his childhood and adolescence were either those Ivan pointed out to him between his own serial arrests and imprisonment or those generic to the Soviet system throughout its existence: "the denial of civil liberties and of the rights of the individual, intolerance of other ideologies, and a dangerous pretension to absolute truth."[51] More to the point, these shortcomings were fully apparent to Sakharov only as an adult, and even then not until he became a dissident. In the sentence that follows this litany of the Soviet Union's deficiencies he writes the following: "I did not become conscious of these [deficiencies] until much later, and I don't know if my parents harbored any thoughts on these matters."[52] According to one of his classmates in high school and university, Sakharov showed

---

arrest in May 1930, his second in January 1934, and the year he died as 1944. She also states that when Ivan was arrested for the second time—eleven months before the assassination of Kirov—he was accused of conspiring with an émigré "Menshevik Center." Under questioning, Ivan admitted his preference for a less centralized regime that guaranteed economic and cultural autonomy. Bonner, *Vol'nye zametki*, 127–29, 146.

49. Sakharov, *Memoirs*, 21–22; Klose, *Russia and the Russians*, 137. Tatiana Yankelevich, Sakharov's stepdaughter, claims that the relative by marriage who was shot never actually fought with Kolchak in the civil war. Tatiana Yankelevich, conversation with author, January 13, 2004.

50. Sakharov, *Memoirs*, 20.

51. Ibid., 23.

52. Ibid.

no interest in politics in the years they were together—a perception Sakharov corroborates obliquely when he writes that he was "painfully introverted and totally immersed in my own affairs."[53] Not surprisingly, Sakharov never joined the Young Pioneers or the Komsomol.[54]

Clearly, family and science were a cocoon for the young Sakharov, protecting him not only from the larger world around him but also from any unsettling conclusions he might have drawn had his family encouraged him to think seriously about it. To be sure, Sakharov experienced at times in his childhood a certain "ferment" and "inner conflict" that he says made "moderation" very difficult to enjoy.[55] But this inner restlessness, whatever its origins, never found political expression. When as a schoolboy he encountered Marxism-Leninism—in the Soviet Union the ultimate source of political wisdom and a subject every student was expected to master—he objected to it on grounds having nothing to do with the political system based on it. Rather, what he disliked about Marxism-Leninism were its *intellectual* deficiencies—its verbosity, its materialism, and its crude determinism:

> The only subject that gave me trouble was Marxism-Leninism. It wasn't an ideological problem: at the time, it never entered my head to question Marxism as the ideology best suited to liberate mankind, and materialism too seemed a reasonable enough philosophy. What I didn't like was the attempt to carry over the outmoded concepts of natural philosophy into the twentieth century (the age of exact science) without amendment: for example, Engels with his Lamarckian theory of the role played by labor in turning apes into men (which conflicts with the modern theory of genetics) and the primitive, naïve use of formulas in *Das Kapital.* The very size of the book, so typical of nineteenth-century German pedantry, put me off. I have no patience with books so thick they can serve as doorstops. Lenin's *Materialism and Empirio-Criticism* seemed superficial, written on the level of journalistic polemic. But the absolute bane of my existence was the necessity of memorizing definitions: I was unable to absorb words devoid of meaning.[56]

In his understanding of the Soviet Union Sakharov—as a youth and indeed for many years as an adult—was like the proverbial blind man who is asked to describe an elephant by touch: he feels discrete parts of the elephant but is unable to gain any sense of the animal as a whole. In addition to what befell his uncles Ivan and Konstantin, he almost certainly knew children in the schools he attended whose parents disappeared in the Terror and who may have

53. Ibid., 32; Iaglom, "Drug blizkii," 779.
54. Ibid., 41; A. I. Ioirysh, *Uroki A. D. Sakharova: Gosudarstvenno-politicheskie vzgliady* (Moscow, 1996), 4.
55. Sakharov, *Memoirs,* 15.
56. Ibid., 36. Iurii Orlov, another scientist who became a dissident, like Sakharov comments in his memoirs on the antithesis he perceived between Marxism-Leninism and the intellectual rigor of genuine science. Yuri Orlov, *Dangerous Thoughts: Memoirs of a Russian Life* (New York, 1991), 115–16.

disappeared themselves. But young Sakharov could not know the magnitude of what was happening, that the suffering that intruded on his own life was the result not of isolated acts of brutality but rather of a systemic barbarism and inhumanity. If most Soviet adults in the 1930s lacked the knowledge and imagination to understand this, one can hardly expect someone as young and sheltered as Sakharov to have done so. What disturbed him about the Soviet Union was something else: that its ideology and the way its ideology was drummed into him seemed to deny his conviction, fostered by his father's teaching science to him, that he was old enough and rational enough to draw his own conclusions about things.

The only hint in Sakharov's childhood of the political views he would express later in his life was his reaction to the anti-Semitism he encountered because of his friendship with Grisha Umanskii, a Jewish boy of the same age who lived on the ground floor of the building the Sakharovs inhabited. With Grisha, young Sakharov shared his propensity for "daydreaming and fantasy."[57] At first Grisha's Judaism had no effect on their friendship. Having inherited his family's secularism and tradition of tolerance, Sakharov was inclined to consider his friend's religion irrelevant. But as time passed, Sakharov came to see in Grisha something distinctive, even unique: a capacity to create a vivid and satisfying inner life that in his memoirs he calls a "Jewish intelligence." Even poor Jews, he writes, are able to do this.[58]

Herein may lie the origin of the philo-Semitism Sakharov revealed as a dissident, when he considered the persecution of Soviet Jews emblematic of the inhumanity of the Soviet system as a whole. Obviously Sakharov knew none of this when he played with Grisha Umanskii in the late 1920s, any more than he did in 1942, in his last year at MGU, when he befriended another Jew, Iasha Tseitlin, whose "inner purity, contemplative nature, and melancholy empathy" Sakharov admired and ascribed to Tseitlin's Jewishness.[59] But these particular friendships, first with Umanskii, then with Tseitlin, provided the fertile soil in which Sakharov's subsequent perceptions of Soviet Jews took root. Like the intelligenty of the nineteenth century who saw in the plight of the Russian peasant a metaphor for what repulsed them about tsarist autocracy generally, Sakharov in the late 1960s and 1970s singled out Soviet Jews for what their persecution revealed about the Soviet Union and socialism.[60]

Still, it took many years for this perception to germinate, and neither Sakharov's friendships with Jews nor anything else he said or did in his childhood and adolescence can justify the conclusion that at this early stage in his life he was in any way alienated from the society in which he was living. He certainly did not reject the values his family instilled in him. By his own testimony, which one has no reason to disbelieve, Sakharov suffered no stigma, endured no external

57. Sakharov, *Memoirs*, 19.
58. Ibid.
59. Ibid., 47.
60. The analogy comes from Shatz, *Soviet Dissent*, 168–69.

oppression, or experienced any psychological or spiritual crisis in his youth that was severe enough to turn him against his own government, or even to create in his own mind the impression that there was something fundamentally wrong with it. Not even the physical destruction of several members of his family seemed to generate an antipathy for the Soviet regime. Because its members were so close to one another emotionally as well as physically, Sakharov's family could envelop the young boy and protect him from much of what was happening around him. And when Sakharov's family, depleted by arrests and imprisonment, could no longer do this, Sakharov's interest in science sufficed to perform the same function.

In the final analysis, Sakharov never focused the vague disquiet he felt on anything beyond his own personal milieu. While he retained from his early years an intellectual self-sufficiency that would enable him first to question, then to criticize, and finally to reject the moral and political bases of the Soviet Union, many experiences and observations would have to accumulate before Sakharov was ready to do this. In the meantime, his principal objective, as a student at MGU, was to pursue a career as a scientist, much the way his father had done. By the summer of 1941 this required only that he complete his last year of university education.

# 2  Expanding Horizons

The Nazi invasion of the Soviet Union on June 22, 1941, complicated Sakharov's life in ways he could not have previously imagined. Neither he nor anyone else in his course of study in mathematics and physics at MGU was conscripted because the Soviet government, despite the gravity of the situation, recognized how helpful to the war effort such persons would be once they graduated and could work for the government in their chosen profession. Sakharov chose not to volunteer for military service, believing that his chronic heart condition—from which he would suffer for the rest of his life—would disqualify him. As it was, he failed the physical examination all male students at MGU had to take for possible entry into the Air Force Academy. Sakharov also rationalized his failure to volunteer by convincing himself that the grief his parents would experience if he were killed in combat would be too painful for them to endure.[1] In his memoirs Sakharov implicitly acknowledges how self-serving his reasoning was when he asks rhetorically whether there was anyone of his age and gender in the Soviet Union in 1941 who could not truthfully have made the same claim. But he never explicitly apologized for his failure to serve and in his memoirs largely confines himself to

---

1. Sakharov, *Memoirs*, 41–42.

describing how he felt when the issue arose; in his words, he had "no desire to rush [his] fate, and preferred to let events take their course."[2]

Still, now that his country was under attack, Sakharov wanted to be socially useful, to contribute in some fashion to the war effort. Accordingly, he volunteered to repair radio equipment for the Red Army in a workshop in Moscow run by a professor he knew from MGU. When he realized that he lacked the necessary training for the task, he switched to another workshop, also directed by an MGU professor, where he devised a magnetic probe for detecting shrapnel in wounded horses. He also helped to extinguish incendiary bombs that were still burning after German air raids over the Soviet capital.[3]

Despite his aversion to military service, Sakharov believed the war was just. Stalin's Terror, as already mentioned, had not made a great impression on him, and the various actions Stalin took in foreign policy that were arguably immoral or in some way harmful to the national interest Sakharov barely mentions or ignores entirely in his memoirs. Of the secret protocol attached to the Nazi-Soviet Nonaggression Pact of 1939, which enabled Germany to attack Poland without the fear of Soviet intervention, Sakharov convincingly pleads ignorance. And about events he was surely aware of in the twenty-two months between the outbreak of World War II and the Nazi invasion—the partition of Poland, the war in Finland, and the absorption of the Baltic States and Bessarabia into the Soviet Union—Sakharov claims persuasively that they did not seem to him indicative of a larger systemic inadequacy or failure: "At the time very few of us understood all that was going on, and I was not among them."[4]

In the absence of any qualms about the political system the Soviet people were defending, Sakharov believed that a Soviet victory was both desirable and inevitable—if not a vindication of the Soviet regime, then at least a well-deserved reward for the bravery, fortitude, and perseverance the Soviet people showed in the face of a determined, relentless, and totally unsympathetic enemy. In addition, the war had the salutary consequence of "making us a nation once again."[5] When the war was over, Stalin abruptly ended the partial relaxation of repression he had permitted during the war that millions of Soviet citizens, including Sakharov, had hoped would be permanent. But while Sakharov was disappointed by this, he was not disillusioned by it.[6]

On October 23, 1941, with the Germans approaching Moscow, Sakharov left the city by train for Ashkhabad, the capital of the Turkmen Soviet Socialist Republic in central Asia, to which it had been determined that MGU students and faculty should be evacuated.[7] He did not arrive in Ashkhabad until December 6

---

2. Ibid., 42.
3. Ibid.
4. Ibid., 40.
5. Ibid., 40, 41.
6. Ibid., 41.
7. Coincidentally, on the same day Sakharov left Moscow a German bomb destroyed the family home on Granatnyi Lane. Fortunately, none of the relatives still living there were injured or killed. Ibid., 43.

because he had to change trains several times. Once there Sakharov completed what would turn out to be his last year of university education, which for several reasons he considered inferior to his previous years. Because of a shortage of trained instructors, the five-year course he was pursuing at MGU was shortened to four years, reducing the number of subjects he was able to study. In addition, the curriculum he had been following in Moscow was now altered to include courses with military applications—Sakharov chose to study magnetism and roentgen-structural analysis—for which, given his prior emphasis on theoretical subjects, he was poorly prepared. To make matters worse, the instruction he received, at least in his own estimation, was mediocre, so much so that Sakharov saw no reason to take notes.[8] To compensate for these inadequacies—his own and those of his instructors—Sakharov, along with another student, organized a group of students to study Einstein's General Theory of Relativity. But since food was scarce in Ashkhabad, the students quickly decided that finding it took precedence over physics, and the project never got off the ground.[9]

In Sakharov's estimation, the schooling he received in Ashkhabad was so poor that he was never able, as a theoretical physicist later on in his life, to overcome the gaps it left in his knowledge.[10] Making matters worse was the dysentery he contracted that briefly threatened his life. Lacking the material comforts he enjoyed in Moscow, Sakharov, like many others, had to scrounge for food, with the result that his diet lacked sufficient fat—a deficiency he corrected eventually by devising a method for frying potatoes in castor oil.[11]

Still, living in Ashkhabad was important in Sakharov's intellectual development. For the first time in his life, he actually experienced aspects of life in the Soviet Union that were unpleasant. Indeed, his train ride to the town was "my first real adventure beyond the confines of my family circle."[12] While Sakharov saw relatively little of the Turkmans themselves and thus had no idea of the enmity many of them harbored for Russians and the Russian political system, he did see enough workers to become aware of their living conditions and of the hostility many of them felt toward the educated elite. What is more, because his pronunciation of certain words caused some Turkmans to conclude that he was Jewish, Sakharov was himself the target of anti-Semitic slurs. All things considered, Sakharov's experiences and observations left "an indelible impression," even though he still drew no larger conclusions from them.[13] A friend and fellow student, I. M. Kapchinskii, reports that while he and Sakharov conversed freely

8. Ibid., 45–48; I. M. Kapchinskii, "Studencheskie kontakty. Ashkhabad," in Altshuler et al., *On mezhdu nami zhil*, 312.

9. Kapchinskii, "Studencheskie kontakty," 313; L. N. Bell, "Printsip nesootvetstviia," in Altshuler et al., *On mezhdu nami zhil*, 143.

10. Sakharov, *Memoirs*, 45.

11. S. M. Shapiro, "Vstrechi na Mokhovoi," in Altshuler et al., *On mezhdu nami zhil*, 772; E. L. Feinberg, "A Biographical Sketch," in *Sakharov Remembered: A Tribute by Friends and Colleagues*, ed. Sidney Drell and Sergei P. Kapitza (New York, 1991), 4; Kapchinskii, "Studencheskie kontakty," 312–13.

12. Sakharov, *Memoirs*, 45.

13. Ibid., 48, 49; Sakharov, "Interv'iu Bolgarskoi zhurnalistke," 130.

and frequently about physics in Ashkhabad, they never spoke about politics.[14] At the age of twenty-one, Sakharov was undoubtedly more intelligent, perceptive, cultured, and knowledgeable academically than most of his contemporaries. But his objective in studying physics was to join the Soviet establishment rather than to repudiate it.

Graduating from MGU in the summer of 1942 with a specialty in defense metallurgy, Sakharov turned down an offer from one of his professors to become an *aspirant* (the equivalent in the Soviet Union of a graduate student) in physics. As long as the war against the Nazis still raged, he was of the opinion that, despite his heart condition, he should contribute to it, even if only as a civilian. Graduate work in physics could wait. Accordingly, in July 1942 he welcomed the directive of the departmental committee that had overseen his studies at MGU that he leave Ashkhabad and work in a munitions factory in Kovrov, not far from the battle lines. But when Sakharov—in a reversal of his earlier attitude— told the general in charge of personnel at the factory that he had no objection to doing work that might expose him to military service, the general, probably fearful of losing an employee so soon after gaining one, resolved the matter by reassigning Sakharov to the Ministry of Armaments in Moscow. The ministry in turn directed him to a cartridge factory in Ulianovsk, 450 miles southeast of Moscow.[15] There the chief mechanic, realizing that his new charge lacked the practical knowledge to assist in the production of cartridges, sent him off to fell trees in the forest surrounding the town. In the course of his labors, Sakharov first heard someone openly criticize Stalin.[16] But whatever reaction this evoked in him he did not consider important enough to include in what he wrote about the episode many years later.

Just a few weeks after starting work, Sakharov injured his hand. It became infected, and as a result he was reassigned to a position indoors as a junior engineer in the "blanking" shop, where the cartridges were actually produced. In that capacity Sakharov was able to observe virtually every department in the factory and thus learned a great deal not only about cartridges but also about the generally wretched conditions of the workers who made them. What Sakharov saw astonished him. It was not just that the workers, female as well as male, worked long hours in unsafe conditions. He also observed that the food they ate was inedible and nutritionally inadequate and that female workers who left children behind in their villages could get permission to visit them only by becoming pregnant again, which made them, in the last months of their pregnancy, unemployable. What Sakharov found most objectionable about these arrangements was how destructive they were of the workers' dignity.[17]

14. Kapchinskii, "Studencheskie kontakty," 312.
15. Sakharov, *Memoirs*, 50–52. Ulianovsk, which was called Simbirsk when Lenin was born there in 1870, comes from Lenin's real family name, Ulianov.
16. Ibid., 51–52.
17. Ibid., 52–53.

In all likelihood this perception was heightened by the living conditions Sakharov himself endured: from September 1942 to July 1943 he lived in a barracks with anywhere from six to twelve people per room, sleeping on a three-tiered bunk bed with the only lavatory in an outside courtyard some seventy-five feet from the barracks door. And while Sakharov and his roommates could purchase food from women who brought it to them regularly, nothing could be done to rid the barracks of lice.[18] Of course conditions elsewhere in Russia during the war were just as bad, and in some cases worse. But for someone like Sakharov, who had been raised in relative comfort, living the way the vast majority of his countrymen lived could not help but broaden his horizons, sharpen his critical faculties, and generally make him cognizant of how much better his life had been before the war intervened to break down class distinctions and homogenize Soviet society.

One incident in particular seemed to heighten Sakharov's awareness that not everything was wonderful beyond the narrow milieu in which he had been raised. On a day when his superior, the senior engineer in the factory, happened to be absent, Sakharov took it upon himself to order the foreman to stop processing the metal caps that were a basic component of the cartridges the factory produced because on that day the caps were defective. The next morning a special meeting was convened at which the foreman upbraided Sakharov for abandoning his "battle station" without completing "a vital task."[19] No one at the meeting supported the foreman's charge or objected to it, and Sakharov himself said nothing. There the matter ended. But even in the absence of any punishment, the incident bothered him: in his memoirs he writes that it was "the last straw" for him (which suggested that perhaps there were other, similar incidents before this one) and that as a result of it he applied for a position elsewhere in the factory.[20] Evidently Sakharov did not think he had done anything wrong, believing that his actions were beneficial to the factory and perfectly consistent with the responsibilities his job entailed. But the initiative Sakharov took, along with the independent judgment he exercised in acting essentially as his superior's surrogate, was the kind of thing for which people in the Soviet Union were routinely shot, imprisoned, or exiled to labor camps. Because this was wartime and Sakharov was engaged in producing something essential to the war effort, he was treated leniently. But the insult to his sense of inner worth and the implication that, like a child, he needed constant supervision and direction undoubtedly hurt.

Still, Sakharov's patriotism and sense of civic obligation hardly wavered, and in November 1942 he was able to find a position in the factory laboratory more appropriate to his abilities as a scientist. His first assignment was to devise a better method of testing the hardness of armor-piercing bullet cores used by antitank guns. The method the factory used at the time was time-consuming and

18. Ibid., 53–54.
19. Ibid., 54.
20. Ibid.

crude: random samples of bullet cores would be removed from the box that contained them and smashed. If enough of the samples were defective, the entire box would be thrown away. Instead, Sakharov designed an apparatus in which cores would be dropped down a copper pipe, passing first a magnetic coil and then a demagnetizing coil before stopping just short of a magnet to which an indicator needle had been fastened. Because a soft core and a hard core would react to these coils differently, the cores could be tested for hardness quickly and with a minimum of waste. A hard core, after being magnetized by the first coil and then demagnetized by the second one, would have no effect on the magnet, and the magnet's needle would not move. A soft core, however, instead of being demagnetized by the second coil, would have its magnetic charge reversed, which would cause the magnet's needle to move. Remarkably, Sakharov was able to calibrate the indicators on the scale measuring the movement of the magnet's needle so precisely that he could determine exactly how much of the bullet core he was examining was soft or hard. As a reward for his achievement—the first of many he would receive from the Soviet government over the next fifteen years—Sakharov received a bonus of 3,000 rubles, 2,200 more than his monthly stipend, and in 1945 he secured a patent for his invention, which was used extensively in the Soviet Union for many years afterward.[21]

Additional evidence of Sakharov's ingenuity was a device he developed for testing the thickness of the brass coating on the jackets of special iron bullets fired by a particular automatic pistol. The device consisted simply of a steel rod that had been magnetized with a coil. On one side of the rod would be placed a bullet whose coating had already been determined to be of the required thickness. On the other side would be placed a bullet with a coating whose thickness was yet to be determined. When the bullets were pulled apart with the same degree of force, the steel rod, because it was magnetized, would adhere to, or bend in the direction of, the bullet with the thinner coating. Because the coatings were made of brass, which is nonmagnetic—unlike the bullets themselves, which were made of iron, which is magnetic—the magnetized steel rod would be attracted to the bullet whose nonmagnetic coating was thinner and thus less able to obstruct the attractive force between them. By measuring the degree of the attraction, one could determine the relative thickness of the coatings.[22]

Not everything Sakharov designed in the cartridge factory was built. In 1943, after his laboratory had acquired a spectroscope for determining the exact proportions of the steel and other metals mixed to form the various alloys used in the ammunition the factory produced, his superior at the laboratory asked him to explain how a spectroscope worked. To his regret, Sakharov was unable to do so. But he was not deterred by this failure. Recognizing how slowly the spectroscope worked, he decided to devise an instrument that would do what the spectroscope did but faster. But the higher-ups in the factory chose not to produce the instrument Sakharov designed, claiming that in testing the new device,

21. Ibid., 55–56.
22. Ibid., 61.

Sakharov had violated fire-safety rules. If his superiors were trying somehow to sabotage the entire project, they succeeded.[23]

Sakharov had better luck with an instrument he designed that could determine which cores in armor-piercing shells had cracks in them, making them more apt to explode in the bores of antitank guns before the guns could fire them. Incredibly, the method then used to detect defective cores was for inspectors to examine them visually after swabbing them down with kerosene, which was supposed to make the cracks more visible but did not always work. And when a core with a crack in it exploded during a test firing, all the cores in the batch that contained the defective one would be discarded because it would take too much time to reinspect them.[24]

To remedy the situation, Sakharov, working alone, developed an instrument that would measure the change a deformed core that had been magnetized would make on a magnetic field established around it. But the instrument worked only for cores with large cracks. To cores with small cracks the instrument reacted the way it did to cores with no cracks. But Sakharov persevered. He knew of the work a scientist from Leningrad was doing in the same area in a different laboratory in the cartridge factory, and he applied for permission to work with him. Permission was granted, and the two men, working together, designed and built a device in which a core was placed for no more than a second in an induction coil that, in Sakharov's words, "formed the arm of an induction bridge."[25] If the core was cracked, it enlarged the magnetized field around it, increasing induction and dissipative losses. These losses, in turn, threw the induction bridge out of balance, which tripped a relay the two scientists had connected to the apparatus, telling them the core was defective. Although in subsequent tests the device missed defective cores in roughly the same proportion as the inspectors did after swabbing the cores with kerosene, it examined cores far more rapidly than under the older method and with less expenditure of human labor. As a result, it was used during the rest of the war. When the device finally broke down, sometime in the summer or fall of 1945, it had to be discarded because both Sakharov and his colleague had left the factory and no one else knew how to repair it.[26]

The devices Sakharov developed demonstrate that he was a creative and resourceful engineer who could conjure solutions to problems with just the tools and equipment he possessed. This ability to apply the relevant theoretical principles to a particular problem of a practical nature, and in a way that confirmed these principles empirically, is quite unusual, particularly among theoretical physicists, who leave empirical verification to others or whose work requires such a high degree of abstraction that empirical verification is as yet impossible. This ability would serve Sakharov well in the years ahead. But in the early 1940s

23. Ibid., 64.
24. Ibid., 65–66.
25. Each batch contained approximately fifty thousand cores. Ibid., 66.
26. Ibid., 65–66.

he was more interested in the theoretical bases of the equipment he designed than in the equipment itself. Accordingly, he began in Ulianovsk what he later described as "an intensive study of theoretical physics." For this he was reprimanded, albeit mildly, by the head of the factory laboratory, who found him reading scientific works instead of Lenin and Stalin in the Party Education Center, to which Sakharov often repaired when he had time to himself.[27]

Undeterred by the reprimand, Sakharov continued his research. While in Ulianovsk, he even produced—without the benefit of a laboratory or any formal academic affiliation—four papers in physics. Perhaps because he was still unsure of his abilities, he did not try to publish them, even though one of them had a direct military application. In this particular paper, Sakharov argued that a chain reaction in which a quantity of uranium absorbs additional neutrons— and in that way becomes a heavier isotope of itself—could be triggered most easily if the uranium were not mixed with a moderator uniformly; instead, the uranium should be placed in the moderator in the shape of blocks. Given its content, Sakharov's paper almost certainly would have been classified as top secret if the government had known about it; when scientists the government commissioned came to the same conclusion Sakharov reached, the paper they produced was immediately treated in this fashion.[28] But regardless of the obscurity of its author, Sakharov's paper shows unmistakably how advanced and sophisticated his work in physics had become.

In Ulianovsk Sakharov did not concern himself exclusively with matters cerebral. In November 1942 he met the twenty-three-year-old Klavdia Alexeevna Vikhireva (known to her friends and family as Klava), who at the time was working as a laboratory assistant in the chemical department of the same factory where Sakharov worked. Klava's parents, with whom she lived in a workers' settlement not far from the factory, were minimally educated and thus very different from Sakharov's. In a matter of weeks, however, Sakharov and Klava became friends, their friendship deepened into love, and on July 10, 1943, they wed.[29] To reduce expenses, the couple moved in with Klava's parents in the workers' settlement, an arrangement Sakharov found congenial despite the obvious differences between his family and Klava's. In fact, Sakharov writes about Klava's parents in his memoirs in greater detail—and with greater affection—than he does about Klava herself, whose psychological problems, in particular her extreme lack of self-esteem, contributed to the eventual deterioration of their marriage. Paralyzed by self-doubt, Klava never worked outside her home after the war ended, and Sakharov plausibly suggests in his memoirs that his considerable professional achievements, which by the mid 1950s had been praised profusely and rewarded extensively by the Soviet government, only reminded her

27. Ibid., 63.
28. Altshuler et al., "Personalia," 10.
29. Sakharov, *Memoirs*, 56–57. Because Sakharov was afraid he would not express his intentions and his affection for Klava clearly enough, he proposed to her in writing. Ioirysh, *Uroki A. D. Sakharova*, 5.

of her own shortcomings. Not even the birth of their three children—Tatiana in 1945, Liuba in 1949, and Dmitrii in 1957—could bridge the emotional gap between them.[30] Evidently the emoluments and material comforts Klava enjoyed as Sakharov's wife never compensated for the loneliness and isolation she felt as her husband pursued his career; Sakharov admits in his memoirs that "the less I concerned myself with these seemingly insoluble personal problems, the more capable I was of leading an active and productive life outside the home."[31] The unequal relationship this reflected, in which the drudgery wives endured at home helped make possible the accomplishments their husbands attained outside it, was commonplace in the patriarchal Soviet society. But in Klava's case, this situation served to stimulate even further the internal demons that haunted her.

One wonders how much of this could have been predicted when the two of them married. Sakharov himself gives no indication. But he does make clear in his memoirs that, at least until the war was over, he and Klava were both reasonably contented. This in turn may have emboldened him, now that he was married and had reason to believe his personal life would be stable, to pursue his chosen career as a physicist. While still in Ulianovsk, Sakharov sent two of his scientific papers—he does not say which ones—to Igor Tamm (1895–1971), the director of the theoretical department of the Physics Institute of the Academy of Sciences (FIAN). Tamm, however, did not find them "interesting."[32] But Dmitrii Sakharov, whom Tamm knew and respected, asked Tamm to accept his son for graduate work at FIAN. In December 1944, possibly as a result of Tamm's intervention, Dmitrii brought his son to FIAN, presumably for an interview, whereupon Tamm tendered the younger Sakharov an invitation—which he eagerly accepted—to work under him there.[33] Leaving Klava, then pregnant with their

30. Sakharov, *Memoirs*, 57–58.
31. Ibid., 59.
32. Ibid., 63. Years later Tamm told Sakharov that, despite his misgivings about these papers, he recognized Sakharov's potential as a physicist. In his memoirs, Sakharov claims that in saying this, Tamm was merely being tactful, implying that the papers Tamm examined were mediocre or at least not up to Tamm's exacting standards. But Sakharov's modesty and penchant for self-deprecation—rather than the quality of the papers themselves—may account for Sakharov's implication. According to Iaglom, Tamm wanted Sakharov to come to FIAN so badly that he waived the requirement that Sakharov pass a qualifying examination. Sakharov, *Memoirs*, 63; Iaglom, "Drug blizkii, drug dalekii," 785.
33. Sakharov, *Memoirs*, 66–67. Others who have written about Sakharov's entry into FIAN provide different versions of it. V. A. Tsukerman, a fellow physicist who worked with Sakharov on the development of thermonuclear weapons in the 1950s, claims that Dmitrii Sakharov passed one of the four papers to a friend of his, A. M. Lopshits, who gave it to Tamm—implying that Tamm formed his opinion of the younger Sakharov at least partly on the basis of it and that Tamm's opinion of the paper was highly favorable. In an obituary of Sakharov they wrote in 1990, several scientists at FIAN identify the paper in question as the one on uranium—but contrary to Tsukerman, state that it was Andrei Sakharov, not Dmitrii Sakharov, who sent it. E. L. Feinberg reiterates this sequence of events but suggests that Sakharov sent Tamm all four papers. In fact it hardly matters which version is correct, since all agree on the result, which was that Sakharov came to FIAN under Tamm's sponsorship and tutelage. V. A. Tsukerman, "Ego nel'zia bycherknut' iz istorii," in Altshuler et al., *On mezhdu nami zhil*, 748; "A. D. Sakharov (obituary)," in Altshuler et al. *Andrei Sakharov: Facets of a Life* (Gif-sur-Yvette, France, 1991), 16; Feinberg, "Biographical Sketch," 5. *Andrei Sakharov: Facets*

first child, in Ulianovsk, Sakharov arrived in Moscow in January 1945, where he would remain for the next two years as an *aspirant* at FIAN.

## The Acquisition of Intellectual Independence and Autonomy

On the surface, there is little in Sakharov's youth and early adulthood to suggest that later in life he would oppose one of the most powerful and repressive political systems in the world. Rather, what is most obvious in Sakharov's early years is his undeniable aptitude for science and suitability for the life of a scientist. A life in science was also what his father, whom he greatly admired, wanted for him. Finally, the fate that members of his family suffered under the Terror probably only strengthened Sakharov's conviction, inherited from his parents, that the expression of political opinions should be avoided. All the evidence on his early years points inescapably to the conclusion that not only did he refrain in these years from ever questioning the moral and political legitimacy of the Soviet Union, but he was almost entirely oblivious to politics generally. The only experience beyond the realm of the purely personal that moved him to ponder what life was like for the Soviet people as a whole was World War II, which came to the Soviet Union when Sakharov was past his adolescence and entering adulthood. And because the patriotism it engendered was inclusive, the war was for many who experienced it the first external event in their lives that transcended politics.[34]

Still, it was largely in reaction to the war that Sakharov, almost in spite of himself, developed a social conscience, in the form of an inchoate, apolitical, but nonetheless deeply felt yearning to be useful to his country when its survival was at stake. Very slowly, under the impact of destruction and dislocation too obvious for someone of his intelligence to ignore, he was becoming aware of the existence of a larger world beyond the one he and his family inhabited that had protected him surprisingly well from the perils of Stalinism. He was also becoming aware, albeit very slowly and incrementally, that there were aspects of this larger world that were not particularly admirable or attractive.[35]

But the world Sakharov left behind when the war began—a world of family, science, high culture, and intellectual accomplishment—was not so insular and unique that the intellectual habits it fostered were of no use to him when he exchanged it for the larger, more complex, and more morally problematic world he encountered as an adult. In fact, the legacy of intellectual self-sufficiency Sakharov inherited from his family helped him immeasurably in developing the skills that enabled him later in his life to function more or less successfully

---

*of a Life* contains much, but not all, in English translation, of what is included in *On mezhdu nami zhil…: Vospominaniia o Sakharove.*

34.  Boris Pasternak makes this point in *Doctor Zhivago* (New York 1991), 507–8, where he writes that the horrors of the war "were a blessing compared with the inhuman reign of the lie" and that they "brought relief because they broke the spell of the dead letter."

35.  For a contrary view, see Susan Eisenhower and Roald Z. Sagdeev, "Sakharov in His Own Words," *Physics Today* 43, no. 8 (August 1990): 53, where it is argued—in my opinion incorrectly—that the war *delayed* Sakharov's political maturation.

as a dissident. In his youth he learned that thinking for himself was a good thing and that with the ideas he conjured he could create an "interior life" for himself, a life of the mind anchored in music, books, science, and culture that was in some sense more real to him than anything he encountered outside it. For this reason, from a fairly early age Sakharov was comfortable with abstractions and abstract reasoning—an attribute essential to a theoretical physicist studying phenomena such as the origins of the universe that are beyond the powers of human observation or subatomic particles whose behavior defies common sense and nearly everything that ordinary human experience leads one to expect.

To the extent that it facilitated Sakharov's development as a theoretical physicist, this ability to think in abstract terms had an immediate benefit. But it would prove useful as well when he trained his intellect on a brutal and dictatorial system that, in his adolescence and early adulthood, he was either oblivious to or disinclined, despite his vague disquiet, to reject. A belief in the reality and potency of ideas would prove exceedingly helpful to anyone who questioned the moral and political legitimacy of the Soviet Union. The fact that the Soviet system prohibited all political activity except that which it expressly prescribed meant that anyone who challenged the system, even for the purpose of reforming it, would have no chance to test his ideas empirically; these he would have to conceive and defend as pure abstractions, their attraction purely a function of their intellectual merit. For this reason Andrei Sakharov, with his training as a theoretical physicist, was just the person to challenge the system.

## PART II

# Designing Weapons for the Maintenance of Peace: 1945–1956

# 3 Tamm's Protégé at FIAN

"Never before or since have I been so close to the highest level of science—its cutting edge."[1] This is how Sakharov described in his memoirs the work he did at FIAN. Reading them one appreciates the enthusiasm Sakharov felt at the time for the academic discipline he had recently chosen as his profession. Sakharov probably had some inkling of what being Igor Tamm's protégé would be like even before arriving at FIAN in January 1945. One wonders, however, whether he was aware that the Soviet leadership viewed science as critical to the country's progress from capitalism to socialism and from socialism to communism. By joining the Soviet scientific establishment—which is what Sakharov did by becoming Tamm's student—he ensured a place for himself, however small it may have seemed at the time, in this enormous endeavor.

The original Bolsheviks espoused a Promethean ethos that considered science essential not only in mastering nature but in harnessing it for the larger endeavor of creating communism. Their ultimate objective was to create a New Soviet Man fully cognizant of the degree to which science had made possible the material comforts and prosperity communism provided. For this reason the Bolsheviks, once they took power, needed scientists even more than they needed writers and artists, however useful the latter might be in enforcing political and ideological conformity.[2] Stalin's famous description of Soviet writers as "engineers of the human soul" was mostly a conceit, for in the final analysis he believed it was science, far more than literature, that would remold human consciousness and transform human beings into the malleable automatons he wanted.[3]

For the Bolsheviks, science was a productive activity, not a creative one, and they viewed scientists essentially as instruments in the achievement of their transformationist objectives. As a result, the political reliability of scientists was as much a criterion for professional advancement as their competence. While scientific discoveries might be valuable for their own sake, for what they revealed about the natural world, the principal task of Soviet scientists was to strengthen the Soviet Union and facilitate the eventual emergence of communism.[4]

---

1. Sakharov, *Memoirs*, 85.
2. Several of the heroes in Soviet novels depicting communism were engineers and scientists. See, for example, *Red Star* and *Engineer Menni*, both by Alexander Bogdanov, who died in 1928 from a blood transfusion he performed on himself in an experiment he hoped would lead to the prolongation of human life. Kendall E. Bailes, "The Politics of Technology: Stalin and Technocratic Thinking among Soviet Engineers," *American Historical Review* 79, no. 2 (April 1974): 445–69.
3. Jay Bergman, "The Idea of Individual Liberation in Bolshevik Visions of the New Soviet Man," *European History Quarterly* 27, no. 1 (January 1997): 57–92, and Jay Bergman, "Valerii Chkalov: Soviet Pilot as New Soviet Man," *Journal of Contemporary History* 33, no. 1 (January 1998): 135–52.
4. Katerina Clark, "The Changing Image of Science and Technology in Soviet Literature," in *Science and the Soviet Social Order,* ed. Loren R. Graham (Cambridge, Mass., 1990), 263.

Science was critically important to the Soviet leaders. Without it, they could never achieve their objectives and the Soviet Union would lose its raison d'être. But the importance science held for the Soviets meant that scientists had to be watched extremely carefully so that they would not question the legitimacy of the system that had fostered them. Additionally, scientists were different from the bourgeoisie and all the other classes and social categories that existed under capitalism. Uniquely, they would survive capitalism's collapse and in fact play a critical role in the transformation of nature and the establishment of communism that would follow. Along with policemen, whose job was to enforce the regime's monopoly of power, scientists were the Soviet citizens the Soviet leadership needed most. If policemen—those who staffed the security forces that bore such acronyms as Cheka, GPU, NKVD, MVD, and KGB—were the ones ultimately responsible for keeping the Soviet regime in power, scientists were the ones whose accomplishments would give it moral legitimacy.

One might think that Soviet ideology—an amalgam of ideas and concepts drawn from Marx, Engels, Lenin, and Stalin that was known as Marxism-Leninism—would facilitate the pursuit of science. Marxism-Leninism, like the Marxism on which it was loosely based, claimed to be scientific, a rigorously objective set of philosophical propositions based on empirical evidence that proved the inevitability, as well as the desirability, of socialism. That Marxism-Leninism claimed for itself the mantle of science would therefore seem to ensure that any political leadership that espoused it would understand the requirements of science and do whatever it could to facilitate its pursuit.

The reality for Soviet scientists, however, was very different. Marxism-Leninism, like Marxism itself, purported to explain everything, with the result that once Stalin eliminated the limited freedom Soviet writers and scientists enjoyed in the 1920s, Marxism-Leninism was as much a hindrance to Soviet scientists as a help. By claiming to explain everything, Marxism-Leninism required the Soviet leadership to have a position on everything. This in turn made virtually inevitable the imposition of prescriptive as well as proscriptive censorship that not merely forbade what the government found objectionable but made obligatory what the government preferred. And with everything subject to government intervention, Soviet scientists found not just their politics but their scientific work as well subject to supervision and surveillance, a potential cause or excuse for their punishment, dismissal, or execution. Not surprisingly, scientists were disproportionately represented in the movement of Soviet dissidence that emerged in the mid-1960s.[5]

Reduced to its philosophical foundations, Marxism-Leninism stressed the materiality, the predictability, and under Stalin the plasticity and the malleability

---

5. Shatz, *Soviet Dissent,* 140, 144–48. Of the Soviet scientists who became dissidents, the most prominent were Valerii Chalidze, Zhores Medvedev, Iurii Orlov, Sergei Kovalev, Valentin Turchin, and Alexander Tverdokhlebov. All played a role in Sakharov's life. Also well represented in the dissident movement—and for many of the same reasons scientists were—were mathematicians, among them Alexander Esenin-Volpin, Revolt Pimenov, and Igor Shafarevich. It is often forgotten that Alexander Solzhenitsyn was trained originally as a mathematician.

of nature.[6] In doing so, it implied not only that communism was inevitable and inherent in the natural order of things but that committed communists in the Soviet Union could bring communism closer by transforming nature through gargantuan projects such as collectivization and rapid industrialization. Because Marxism-Leninism held that nature and the laws that governed it were comprehensible to man, nature was simply a resource man could utilize for his own undoubtedly enlightened and progressive purposes.

However much this Prometheanism emboldened the Soviets to believe they could build communism quickly even in a backward country such as Russia, it made them hostile to recent developments in science, such as Heisenberg's Uncertainty Principle, which denied the objective reality of nature, and Einstein's general theory of relativity, which argued that the laws that explain nature are not universally applicable. To the Bolsheviks, heretical ideas such as these seemed to limit their ability to harness nature for their own purposes—and scientists who espoused them had to be silenced, forced to confess their errors or be destroyed physically. It is telling that in the late 1940s several members of the Central Committee of the Communist Party informed a group of nuclear physicists who were briefing them on their progress in building nuclear weapons that relativity and quantum theory (which holds that the very act of observing subatomic phenomena changes their location and thus makes them quite literally unobservable) were "nonsense."[7] It is equally telling that one of the physicists at this meeting, P. A. Alexandrov, had to remind these Stalinist *apparatchiki* (careerists) that such "nonsensical" theories explained how nuclear weapons worked and that, unless the government permitted Soviet physicists to apply these theories, the Soviet Union would have to do without nuclear weapons entirely. In this instance, *raison d'état* took precedence over ideology, and the apparatchiki withdrew their objections.[8]

Sometimes Soviet science suffered when Soviet leaders thought they knew something about it. This was especially true for biology and plant genetics, about which both Stalin and Khrushchev claimed to speak knowledgeably because they were descended from peasants and had grown up among them.[9] But Soviet science also suffered, if not quite so dramatically, because Soviet leaders were often ignorant. Beria, after witnessing a nuclear chain reaction for the first time,

6. Robert C. Tucker, "Stalin and the Uses of Psychology," in *The Soviet Political Mind: Stalinism and Post-Stalin Change,* ed. Robert C. Tucker (New York, 1971), 143–72.

7. A. P. Alexandrov, "Kak delali bombu," *Izvestiia,* July 23, 1988, 3.

8. Ibid. In 1949, the Ministry of Higher Education planned to hold a conference at which "idealism" in Soviet physics would be condemned. When they learned of the conference, several nuclear physicists, understandably alarmed by the deleterious effect they believed the conference would have on their work, requested that Beria, who was in charge of the development of Soviet nuclear and thermonuclear weapons, persuade Stalin to cancel it. Their argument was the practical one that such a conference would delay the development of these weapons, perhaps permanently. Once again, the government had to back down. Paul R. Josephson, *Physics and Politics in Revolutionary Russia* (Berkeley, 1991), 322–23; Anatoly Sonin, "How the A-bomb Saved Soviet Physicists' Lives," *Moscow News,* April 1, 1990, 16.

9. Shatz, *Soviet Dissent,* 145.

was so unimpressed that he thought Igor Kurchatov, the scientist who arranged the demonstration, had tricked him: that what he saw was not a chain reaction at all and that Kurchatov's motive in tricking him was to conceal the failure of the physicists he supervised to develop nuclear weapons quickly enough.[10] Similarly, in the spring of 1949, when the nuclear physicists Kurchatov, Iulii Khariton, and Pavel Zernov met with Stalin in the Kremlin and showed him a plutonium core used in triggering an atomic bomb, Stalin expressed the opinion that the physicists were deceiving him: the core they brought with them, he said, was really made of iron. Only when Kurchatov informed Stalin that a plutonium core was hot, not cold as an iron one would be, and that by touching the core he could tell immediately which element it was made of did the Soviet dictator calm down.[11] It is hard to imagine presidents Roosevelt and Truman, who knew as little about physics as Stalin and Beria, summoning American scientists such as Robert Oppenheimer and Edward Teller to a meeting at which the latter would be required to demonstrate their competence as scientists.[12]

Nevertheless, because science was essential to both the survival of the Soviet Union and the establishment of communism, the Soviet government had no choice but to support it, even as it took measures to ensure that neither the privileges scientists enjoyed nor the intellectually liberating nature of the work they performed would cause them to oppose the government politically. Toward that end, the government created an enormous bureaucracy to direct scientific work and to ensure the ideological bona fides of Soviet scientists. In sociological terms Soviet science resembled a vertical hierarchy, at the very apex of which stood the Soviet Academy of Sciences. The academy stood in relation to the scientists who aspired to join it in much the way the Communist Party stood in relation to the Soviet people as a whole. Moreover, the individuals in charge of the academy were hardly figureheads, and membership—unlike membership in comparable organizations in the West, such as the American Academy of Sciences—was not just honorific. Real power and considerable privileges accrued from it.

Because its members were the elite of an elite, the very best the Soviet Union could produce, the Academy of Sciences enjoyed a degree of autonomy that not even its institutional counterparts in other spheres of Soviet society, such as literature and the visual arts, were permitted. Alone among the institutions of Soviet society below the Communist Party and the Soviet government, the academy elected new members by secret ballot and recorded split votes—as opposed to the bogus unanimous ones that other Soviet institutions reported—whenever

10. David Holloway, *Stalin and the Bomb: The Soviet Union and Atomic Energy, 1939–1956* (New Haven, 1994), 182.
11. Steven J. Zaloga, *Target America: The Soviet Union and the Strategic Arms Race, 1945–1964* (Novato, Calif., 1993) 58–59.
12. It is true that in 1944 the Danish physicist Niels Bohr met separately with Roosevelt and Churchill and that the meeting with Churchill went badly. But neither leader questioned Bohr's credentials or competence as a physicist, and their discussions with him concerned not the science of nuclear weapons but their military and political implications. Richard Rhodes, *The Making of the Atomic Bomb* (New York, 1986), 525–38.

they occurred.[13] In the autonomy it enjoyed, and in the relative freedom it exercised, the Academy of Sciences was very nearly sui generis in Soviet society.

Significantly for Sakharov, physicists were safer physically, and enjoyed considerably more autonomy, than their counterparts in other sciences. While physicists were hardly immune to persecution under Stalin, their work was less likely than that of other scientists to attract the government's opprobrium, and prior to the government's decision to build nuclear weapons, physicists were generally not conscripted to work on projects designed to advance political objectives. As a result, in Soviet physics no mini-Stalins prevailed the way Trofim Lysenko did in biology and plant genetics. What the Austrian physicist Alexander Weissberg-Cybulski wrote about the Ukrainian Physicotechnical Institute, where he worked before his arrest and imprisonment—that it was, up to 1935, "an oasis of freedom in the desert of Stalinist despotism"—applies almost as well to Soviet physics as a whole.[14]

There are several reasons why the government generally left Soviet physicists alone. For one thing, the research institutes that employed the majority of them provided a measure of security unattainable to Soviet scientists who taught at universities. Additionally, the profession of physics seems to have benefited from the caliber and international reputation of its leadership: Abram Ioffe in the 1920s and Lev Landau, Piotr Kapitsa, and Sakharov's mentor, Igor Tamm, in the 1930s and 1940s all seem to have recognized the extent to which scientific progress in the Soviet Union required that Soviet scientists go about their business unencumbered by the meddling of scientifically illiterate apparatchiki. None of these physicists ever challenged the moral and political legitimacy of the Soviet Union, and none of them, in contrast to Sakharov, became a dissident. But all of them were willing, in varying degrees, to oppose the regime on matters concerning their profession. For example, after his arrest in the mid 1930s, Landau escaped execution when Kapitsa intervened personally with Stalin and with his immense prestige forced the Soviet government to release him. In fact, for refusing Beria's "invitation" a decade later that he contribute his considerable expertise to the construction of nuclear weapons, Kapitsa endured as punishment only several years of house arrest, which in Stalinist terms was the equivalent of a slap on the wrist.[15]

13. Loren Graham, "Knowledge and Power," *Sciences* 8 (October 1980): 19; Loren R. Graham, *What Have We Learned about Science and Technology from the Russian Experience?* (Stanford, 1998), 83–84.

14. Alexander Weissberg-Cybulski, *The Accused* (New York, 1951), 158. In his memoirs Feinberg notes that in the late 1930s, when Stalin's Terror was at its worst, it was still possible for physicists "to be independent, to think creatively in their own area of expertise." E. L. Feinberg, *Epokha i lichnost'. Fiziki. Ocherki i vospominaniia* (Moscow, 1999), 69.

15. Zhores A. Medvedev, *Soviet Science* (New York, 1978), 37; Loren R. Graham, *Science in Russia and the Soviet Union: A Short History* (New York, 1994), 212. Kapitsa told Herbert York many years later that the reason for his refusal had nothing to do with politics or morality but rather reflected his concern that if he worked for Beria, he would no longer be able to conduct pure research. According to Loren Graham, Kapitsa had no objections to nuclear weapons but distrusted Beria and did not want to work for him. Herbert York, *The Advisors: Oppenheimer, Teller, and the Superbomb* (San Francisco, 1976), 38–39; Graham, *Science in Russia and the Soviet Union*, 169.

Finally, it bears mention that except for Soviet physicists who were conscripted like soldiers to work on the development of weapons, much of what they did was too arcane and esoteric to have the direct, practical, and immediate applications that piqued the interest, with its often murderous consequences, of the Soviet government. Compared with other sciences, such as botany and genetics, physics, and especially theoretical physics, was largely irrelevant to the regime's agenda.[16] Indeed, individuals such as Lysenko (who fraudulently claimed to be developing cold-resistant strains of wheat), Stakhanov (who mined unprecedented amounts of coal), Alexander Tupolev (who designed Soviet military aircraft), and Valerii Chkalov (who brought glory to the Soviet Union by flying an airplane across the North Pole to North America) were far more valuable to Stalin than the vast majority of Soviet physicists.

Of course Stalin's calculus would change when his perception of nuclear weapons and what they could do for him changed as well. But when that happened, in 1945–1946, physicists, or at least the physicists who worked on these weapons, would still be safer than other scientists in the Soviet Union not because they were irrelevant to the regime but for the opposite reason—because they were indispensable to it. Stalin's calculus was simple: if the majority of physicists—those who were not constructing nuclear weapons—were not important enough to be shot, the small minority of physicists who were constructing nuclear weapons were too important to be shot, however much he and Beria might have wanted at times to shoot them.[17]

Of course, conditions were hardly idyllic for Soviet physicists. The field itself, as Paul Josephson has pointed out, was riven by conflicts that were both substantive and ideological in nature.[18] In the 1930s physicists, like their counterparts in other sciences, were arrested, imprisoned, sent to labor camps, and shot. But the fact that these conflicts were allowed to continue unimpeded by any large-scale systematic purge, as occurred in other branches of Soviet science and in other spheres of Soviet life such as the military and the diplomatic corps, testifies to the relatively secure position physics enjoyed. And after World War II, when physicists were recruited to produce nuclear weapons for reasons of national security—and also for the enormous prestige these weapons would confer on the Soviet Union as only the second nuclear power in the world—physics would be the science whose achievements most dramatically reflected the validity of the whole Soviet experiment. What better proof of Soviet technological and scientific prowess could there be than the mushroom cloud produced by a nuclear bomb?

In sum, science was critically important to Stalin, and he could plausibly ascribe the successes Soviet scientists enjoyed to the superiority of socialism, which

16. Holloway, *Stalin and the Bomb*, 24. Gennady Gorelik with Antonina W. Bouis, *The World of Andrei Sakharov: A Russian Physicist's Path to Freedom* (New York, 2005), 123, 194–95, 200–201.

17. In December 1952, no fewer than eleven nuclear physicists, among them Sakharov, Landau, and Tamm, sent a strongly worded letter to Beria denouncing a recent attack in *Krasnyi flot* on relativity and quantum theory for the harm it did to Soviet physics. None of them was punished because of it. *The KGB File of Andrei Sakharov*, ed. Joshua Rubenstein and Alexander Gribanov (New Haven, 2005), 10.

18. Josephson, *Physics and Politics*, 247–75.

he claimed the Soviet Union had achieved in 1936. It was thus entirely appropriate for Stalin in 1945 to state: "If we [the Communist Party] help our scientists, they will be able to reach and surpass the achievements of science abroad."[19] And yet the professional autonomy, material privileges, and relative security Soviet scientists were granted in the furtherance of this objective meant that scientists would dissent more frequently and in greater numbers than would persons in any other class or category of the population; whatever their penchant for nonconformity, even writers and artists were not as cognizant of the disparity between professional autonomy and political freedom as Soviet scientists were. The result was a paradox: the very people the Soviet Union needed most—namely, its scientists—were the people most likely to oppose it politically. They would do so because their unique status in the Soviet Union, along with the nature of the work they performed, had the effect of imbuing them—or at least a certain percentage of them—with a sense of their own rationality and maturity, an awareness of their own identity as intellectually self-sufficient individuals who should be treated with the respect they deserved. From this perception it was only a small step—though for many scientists a very difficult and ultimately prohibitive one—to demand the civil and legal rights that were the formal desiderata of the dissident movement. In the case of Soviet scientists, dissidence was inherent in the Soviet system itself and thus would exist in varying degrees as long as the Soviet Union did. While dissidents like Andrei Sakharov would necessarily be few in number in the Soviet Union, they were also inevitable.

## Life and Work at FIAN

Given the unique role that science, and physics in particular, played in Soviet society, the community of physicists Sakharov joined in 1945 was, in David Holloway's apt description, "the closest thing to a civil society in the Stalinist regime."[20] By using the autonomy and independence he enjoyed to facilitate his development into a critically thinking individual with the intellectual and ethical wherewithal to challenge the Soviet regime directly, Sakharov benefited from this circumstance immeasurably.

For all the privileges Sakharov would come to enjoy, however, there were aspects of his tenure at FIAN that were unpleasant and reminded him that materially he was still only marginally better off than the rest of the population. Until January 1948, when FIAN secured a room for Sakharov and his family in a "hotel" run by the Academy of Sciences, the three Sakharovs lived in rooms in a succession of private residences, all of them inadequately heated, including one in the Moscow suburb of Pushkino where Sakharov had to wear a fur coat to stay warm. Making matters worse, young Tania Sakharova was often sick and once came down with a kidney infection. Because the allowance Sakharov received as an aspirant at FIAN was quite meager, the family had to make do with ration cards; when the ration card system was abolished, they paid for essential

---

19. Quoted in Medvedev, *Soviet Science*, 44.
20. Holloway, *Stalin and the Bomb*, 363.

commodities in rubles that, because of a currency "reform," had lost much of their purchasing power. At times, the family literally did not have enough to eat. When their various landlords inevitably evicted them—Sakharov implies that they did so for nonpayment of rent—as a last resort they moved in with Sakharov's parents. This, in turn, put Klava and her mother-in-law, Ekaterina Sakharova, in close quarters, which meant that their relationship, never especially harmonious to begin with, worsened.[21] At one point in this period, Klava, to her credit, refused an offer from the police that she spy on her husband in exchange for better living arrangements—an offer hardly unique to Klava and other Soviet women in similar circumstances.[22]

In addition, Sakharov spent time he would otherwise have used for research filling the gaps in his knowledge that his education at MGU had failed to fill. At Tamm's recommendation he read books and articles on relativity and quantum mechanics, fields in which his training had been especially poor.[23] In addition, the teaching he did that was required of all aspirants—he lectured for three semesters on nuclear physics, relativity, and electricity at the Moscow Energetics Institute and for one semester at the workers' night school of the Kurchatov Institute, also in Moscow—helped him make sense of the knowledge he was finally acquiring while having the collateral benefit of increasing his income. Sakharov enjoyed teaching and hoped he could continue it at both institutes, even though the caliber of the students at the Kurchatov Institute was not very high. But the head of the Energetics Institute, V. Fabrikant, who had given Sakharov useful pedagogical advice, was Jewish, and the government's suspicion that Fabrikant was guilty of "cosmopolitanism"—the common charge against Soviet Jews at the time—may have had something to do with Sakharov's own dismissal from the teaching staff there.[24] For Sakharov, this sequence of events, with its hint of a causal relationship, may have been a lesson in the perils of collegiality in a repressive and highly suspicious regime.

In spite of this, he found the working conditions at FIAN comfortable and the intellectual environment exhilarating. Short of membership in the Academy of Sciences, it is hard to imagine a more auspicious circumstance for a budding physicist like Sakharov than to be a protégé of Igor Tamm, who himself was flanked at FIAN by figures of nearly comparable stature and substance. Established by Sergei Vavilov—the brother of Nikolai Vavilov, the esteemed biologist who for opposing Lysenko was sent to prison and perished there—FIAN was the most prestigious and productive institute of physics in the entire country. Its department of theoretical physics, established by Tamm in 1934, was, if anything, even more exciting intellectually than the institute itself.[25] In many ways FIAN was for Sakharov a microcosm of the larger "Republic of Science" that would

21. Sakharov, *Memoirs*, 75–77; Altshuler et al., "Personalia," 11.
22. Sakharov, *Memoirs*, 76–77.
23. Ibid., 68–69, 75.
24. Ibid., 74.
25. V. L. Ginzburg, "O fenomene Sakharova," in Altshuler et al., *On mezhdu nami zhil*, 213.

remain for many years an idée fixe, a humane vision in which scientists would serve as a moral example for everyone because of their belief in the primacy of reason and their shared commitment to the pursuit of objective truth.

The individual most responsible for creating such a nurturing environment was Tamm himself, who more than anyone else in Sakharov's early adulthood served as a role model: "Perhaps the great fortune of my early years was to have had my character molded by the Sakharov family, whose members embodied the generic values of the Russian intelligentsia...and to have then come under the influence of Igor Tamm."[26] The qualities that made Tamm an excellent scientist were also those that made him admirable as a human being. By all accounts he combined a ferocious and unquenchable thirst for truth with a willingness to take almost any risk and endure almost any hardship in the course of pursuing it. Writing about Tamm in 1965, Sakharov and his coauthors, V. L. Ginzburg and E. L. Feinberg, physicists who worked intimately with Tamm and knew him nearly as well as Sakharov did, refer glowingly to Tamm's courageous struggle against "pseudo-science" (i.e., Lysenkoism) and "his passion for redressing wrongs whenever he perceived them."[27] Truly, Tamm followed Dmitrii Sakharov in exemplifying for the younger Sakharov what it meant to be a scientist in a political system in which scientists were valued more as machines than as human beings.

Earlier in his life, Tamm had professed Menshevik sympathies. Perhaps these were what caused him to eschew within his own bailiwick at FIAN the rigid hierarchies and the whole dysfunctional ethos of *mestnichestvo* (hierarchical ranking) endemic in Soviet science and Soviet society. The critical insight Tamm brought to FIAN from his earlier life was that scientific progress would be immeasurably more rapid if the artificial emoluments of rank, status, and title were not allowed to impede it. In keeping with this belief, Tamm gave Sakharov considerable leeway in the topics he chose for investigation; thus the latter's growth as a scientist came principally through "the scientific work I did on my own and brought to a publishable stage."[28] E. L. Feinberg comments on the "democratic atmosphere" Tamm fostered at FIAN, where academicians and junior researchers could discuss and debate essentially as equals, with truth the only criterion of critical judgment.[29] To the extent to which Tamm was able to influence it, the theoretical department of physics at FIAN was a model for Sakharov of how scientists should go about their jobs. For Sakharov and Tamm alike, science was as much a sacred calling as it was a profession; the truths it revealed were valued for much more than their practical application in the Promethean endeavor of transforming nature. Rather, these truths, in the rationalism that was required to discover them, were emblematic of the way in which scientists, as well as

26. Sakharov, *Memoirs*, 129.

27. V. L. Ginzburg, A. D. Sakharov, and E. L. Feinberg, "Igor' Evgen'evich Tamm (k sedesiateliiu so dnia rozhdeniia)," *Uspekhi fizicheskikh nauk* 86, no. 2 (June 1965): 353. See also A. Sakharov, "U chenyi i grazhdanin-akademiku I. E. Tammu—70 let," *Izvestiia*, July 8, 1965, 6.

28. Sakharov, *Memoirs*, 75.

29. E. L. Feinberg, "Dlia budushchego istorika," in Altshuler et al., *On mezhdu nami zhil*, 655.

persons in other professions, should live and work. United by this reverence for truth and emboldened to seek it out by a shared commitment to rational inquiry, the theoretical physicists at FIAN in the late 1940s were a true community of scientists—and for Sakharov striking confirmation that his original career choice was the right one.

From Tamm Sakharov also heard that science is international. Tamm always stressed to Sakharov that there was no Russian or Soviet science but only science—an endeavor that transcends, and thereby breaks down, the barriers that separate people by nationality. If one accepts this notion, as Sakharov did, then it follows logically that the community of scientists he inhabited was a model not only for how scientists should behave but for how everyone should behave; indeed, FIAN provided a model for how differences and disagreements should be settled everywhere—namely, through the application of reason. Applied to international relations, the result would be perpetual peace. For their part, scientists could help bring this about by internationalizing science, which in practical terms meant pressuring their own governments to eliminate restrictions on foreign travel, censorship of foreign journals, and the classification of information that had no possible relevance to national security. Should this be done, then everyone, not only scientists, would benefit.

Tamm's influence on Sakharov was immense. As a result of it Sakharov believed strongly in the social responsibility of scientists to profess humane values and try to apply these values in their lives as well as in their work. Also because of Tamm, Sakharov believed that, as a collection of like-minded and rational individuals, the community of scientists he inhabited could serve as a model for nonscientists, who by imitating scientists would enjoy the benefits of doing science without having to do it themselves. Finally, Tamm helped to nurture Sakharov's budding philo-Semitism, telling him in the early 1950s—when it was dangerous even to raise the topic of Soviet anti-Semitism—that there was "one foolproof way of telling if someone belongs to the Russian intelligentsia. A true Russian *intelligent* is never an anti-Semite. If he's infected with that virus, then he's something else, something terrible and dangerous."[30]

In his later years, Tamm, ironically, seemed to shrink from this ethos of social responsibility—an ethos that Sakharov, his protégé, fully embraced. For Tamm the responsibility of scientists was simply to be what they were; those in the larger society seeking a model for their own improvement and the improvement of society would extract the humane values science embodied and then apply these values to society themselves. Scientists, meanwhile, would go about their business, doing what they do best, namely, science. But in the late 1960s, Sakharov enlarged Tamm's vision to include the idea that scientists themselves had the moral authority—perhaps even a moral obligation—to try to influence society for the purpose of improving it. It was this view that led Sakharov to become a dissident. A regrettable consequence of his activism was that Tamm,

---

30. Sakharov, *Memoirs*, 123–24.

for the first time in the history of their relationship, expressed disapproval of Sakharov, mostly in the form of gentle reminders that by focusing on social and political questions he was neglecting his primary obligation, which was physics. In 1968 Tamm even withdrew his signature from a petition he had signed protesting the Soviet invasion of Czechoslovakia because he believed his action would harm FIAN specifically and Soviet physics and Soviet science more generally. Sakharov, who was sympathetic to the petition, was profoundly saddened by Tamm's reversal. That same year Tamm expressed disagreement with "convergence"—the idea that the western and communist systems were destined to merge into one that combined the best features of both of them—and some of the other ideas Sakharov was then developing.[31] But none of this, in the end, diminished Sakharov's admiration of Tamm or his gratitude to him. When Tamm died in 1971, Sakharov and three colleagues eulogized him simply and eloquently as "the epitome of decency in science and in public life."[32]

Sakharov's relationship with Iakov Zeldovich (1914–1987), another of the physicists with whom he worked closely at FIAN, was more complicated. A remarkably creative and resourceful physicist, Zeldovich nevertheless played the "operator" at times when standing on principle instead was the right thing to do, and, given Zeldovich's prestige and eminence in the field, a reasonably safe thing for him to do.[33] One example of this occurred in December 1975 when Zeldovich, well aware that Sakharov's private telephone in his apartment in Moscow was tapped, called Sakharov shortly after the latter won the Nobel Peace Prize to offer the opinion—which Zeldovich knew the government would approve of—that he should renounce it. Sakharov, not surprisingly, rejected such gratuitous and (since the police were listening in) wholly self-serving advice.[34] But he was also not one to hold a grudge, and the intimacy of his collaboration with Zeldovich in the early 1950s, when the two men occupied adjacent offices while working together on the development of thermonuclear weaponry, was apparently significant enough in Sakharov's evolution as a physicist so that when Zeldovich died in 1987, Sakharov not only attended the funeral but delivered a generous eulogy, with no mention of the occasional unpleasantness that marred their relationship. For his part, Zeldovich never questioned his colleague's extraordinary ability as a physicist and, like Tamm, disapproved only of Sakharov's involvement in politics; like Tamm, he thought it prevented Sakharov from achieving his full potential as a physicist.[35]

31. Ibid., 124.

32. V. L. Ginzburg et al., "Pamiati Igoria Evgen'evicha Tamma," *Uspekhi fizicheskikh nauk* 105, no. 1 (September 1971): 163.

33. Sakharov, *Memoirs*, 132.

34. Ibid., 137. Landau, who disliked Zeldovich for his outsized ego, often referred to him as a "bitch." Kip S. Thorne, *Black Holes and Time Warps: Einstein's Outrageous Legacy* (New York, 1995), 230.

35. Andrei Sakharov, "A Man of Unusual Interests," *Nature*, February 25, 1988, 671–72; Richard Wilson, "Priznanie pri zhizni," in Altshuler et al., *On mezhdu nami zhil,* 200. Zeldovich's pleasure when Sakharov returned to Moscow in December 1986 was genuine, and he called his former

All this, of course, was far in the future when Sakharov, with the gaps in his earlier education diminishing, set about earning the degree of doctoral candidate.[36] The topic on which he wanted to work—nonradiative nuclear transitions—was not original; Japanese physicists had investigated it many years earlier. But Tamm, who had more faith in Sakharov's abilities than Sakharov did at this stage in his life, thought the topic worth pursuing anyway and urged his charge not to abandon it.[37] In the thesis Sakharov produced, he explained why nonradiative transitions involving oxygen nuclei and a particular form of radium do not produce gamma rays; the reason for this, he concluded, was that the nuclear vibrations are spherically symmetrical when the "initial and final angular momenta" equal zero.[38]

After Sakharov received his candidate's degree and the title of junior researcher, he continued his work on these transitions, focusing on those that did not involve an electromagnetic field. Sakharov's conclusion, greatly simplified, was that these transitions were entirely independent of nonelectromagnetic effects. But when Tamm and Sakharov learned that an American physicist, Sidney Dancoff, had used calculations more complex than Sakharov's in an article on the same topic, Tamm advised Sakharov not to continue his work on the topic and to pursue others instead. In fact, Dancoff's calculations were wrong. But because Sakharov failed to check them and then to publish his findings, another physicist, Richard Feynman, would do so and receive credit for the "diagrams" he developed in doing correctly the calculations Dancoff had botched.[39]

Other research Sakharov pursued at FIAN proved more fruitful. Almost immediately after his arrival, he investigated the muffling effect oscillating bubbles in water have on sound. The matter was of practical as well as theoretical interest: submarines in turbulent water, in which there are many such bubbles, have more difficulty communicating by sonar than do submarines operating in more tranquil conditions. Sakharov postulated that sound traveling through water caused the bubbles created by turbulence to change their size and thereby experience large amplitude vibrations. The resulting oscillations changed the speed of sound in water and something called acoustic opaqueness, which hampers communication by sonar. In addition, Sakharov speculated that the heat generated along the boundary between the bubbles and the water when these bubbles expanded caused a dissipation of energy. This, he believed, was what caused sound in such circumstances to be muffled. Although the authorities at the Acoustics Institute of the Academy of Sciences to whom Sakharov spoke about his theory were not terribly impressed—they believed German scientists

---

colleague a "genius" when they met a short time later. B. V. Komberg, "Zastavil sebia slushat'," in Altshuler et al., *On mezhdu nami zhil,* 334.

36. The degree of doctoral candidate should not be confused with a doctorate itself, a higher degree that Sakharov received under unusual circumstances related to his election to the Academy of Sciences in 1953.

37. Sakharov, *Memoirs,* 81.

38. Ibid., 80.

39. Ibid., 82–83.

had already postulated much the same thing—Sakharov in this instance followed his instincts and pursued his research to completion.[40]

The same was true of his work on "mu meson catalysis." This was a term Sakharov invented to describe what he believed would happen if a vessel containing the hydrogen isotope deuterium—which contains a proton and a neutron, unlike ordinary hydrogen, which contains only a proton—were bombarded with mu mesons, a subatomic particle that behaves like a heavy electron and is found in nature only in cosmic rays; however, mu mesons are more massive than electrons and also highly unstable, decaying in two-millionths of a second. As the catalyst in Sakharov's scenario, the mu mesons themselves would not change as a result of their coming into contact with the deuterium. But this contact, according to Sakharov, would trigger nuclear fission, in which deuterium atoms that were hit by mu mesons would shed their neutrons—thus becoming hydrogen—and release considerable energy in the process. These neutrons in turn would smash into some of the deuterium the mu mesons had not hit directly, causing a similar emission of energy and neutrons. Neutrons from this second reaction would then collide with some of the deuterium that neither the mu mesons nor the neutrons released by the original fission reaction had been able to hit, more energy and neutrons would be released, and the chain reaction would continue until there was no longer any deuterium left to hit. Subsequent calculations by other physicists showed that the energy generated in this nuclear reaction would not exceed the energy that was required to produce mu mesons in the laboratory in the first place. For this reason mu meson catalysis was not a cost-effective method for generating nuclear energy. Still, the project served as the basis for Sakharov's first research paper, in which, on the basis of a model Tamm proposed to him, he estimated the "cross-section" for the production of mesons in cosmic rays.[41]

However gratifying these years were for Sakharov intellectually and personally, Sakharov could not escape the pernicious idiocies, not to mention the sheer odiousness and brutality, of late Stalinism, when the Communist Party claimed omniscience on everything, not merely politics and ideology, and anything less than total acceptance of party dominance was evidence of treason. At FIAN Sakharov had some exposure to this, even though his physical safety was never in doubt. In 1946 he wrote an article on the work he had been doing for several months on how mesons are produced. He then submitted the article to the *Journal of Experimental and Theoretical Physics,* one of the most prestigious and consequential journals of physics in the country. But the editors of the journal, after accepting the article, changed the title Sakharov proposed for it—"Meson Generation," which had the virtue of being both concise and descriptive of the article's contents—to the more obscure "Generation of the Hard Components

40. Ibid., 72–73.

41. Ibid., 86–88. A. D. Sakharov, "Generation of the Hard Component of Cosmic Rays," in Andrei Dmitrievich Sakharov, *Collected Scientific Works,* ed. D. ter Haar, D. V. Chudnovsky, and G. V. Chudnovsky (New York, 1982), 239–54.

of Cosmic Rays." Tamm explained to Sakharov that the reason for the change was that the editors, aware that bureaucrats in Glavlit (the official censorship) would think they knew what mesons were and thus consider themselves competent to rewrite the paper, thought they could prevent that by choosing a title less likely to tip off the censors to what the article was about. As it happened, Sakharov's article, with its title preemptively altered, appeared in print in 1947, its contents pretty much what Sakharov had written. In fact, by changing the title, the editors preserved not just the quality of the article but quite possibly Sakharov's political bona fides as well. In Glavlit, there were individuals eager to advance their careers by questioning the loyalty of those whose work they evaluated. The editors of this particular journal, to their credit, were aware of this and did what they could to protect one of their contributors from a repetition of it.[42]

A similar incident occurred in the summer of 1947. Because, in the course of his studies, Sakharov had read only a summary of N. G. Chernyshevskii's views on aesthetics, which Lenin admired, instead of the original works themselves, he received a grade on the examination in materialist and Marxist-Leninist philosophy lower than what he needed to be allowed to defend his dissertation in theoretical physics. Chastened by the experience, Sakharov read these works a few days later, retook the test, and received a passing grade. But in the interim the physicists who were to examine Sakharov on his dissertation had gone on vacation, and the defense could not be rescheduled until the fall. As a result, Sakharov did not receive for several months the larger stipend he would have been entitled to as the holder of a candidate degree. He does not mention in his memoirs what conclusions, if any, he drew from this particular instance of institutionalized stupidity, but it is safe to say that the delay could hardly have improved his opinion of the Soviet system that was ultimately responsible for it.[43]

The relevant point in all of this is not that Sakharov foolishly failed to prepare himself adequately for an examination he knew he would have to do well

42. Sakharov, *Memoirs*, 79–80.

43. Ibid., 81; Gorelik, "The Metamorphosis of Andrei Sakharov," *Scientific American* 280, no. 3 (March 1999): 94. The authors of "Personalia," in the biographical sketch in *On mezhdu nami zhil*, claim that the failing grade Sakharov received in Marxism-Leninism caused his defense to be delayed by nearly an entire year, a time span identical to that cited by M. S. Rabinovich in his reminiscences of experiences with Sakharov at FIAN. Rabinovich states that Sakharov was ready for his defense eighteen months after arriving at FIAN—which means his defense was originally scheduled for the summer of 1946. Altshuler et al., "Personalia," 11; M. S. Rabinovich, "Kak my nachinali," in Altshuler et al., *On mezhdu nami zhil*, 520. In his introduction to *Sakharov Speaks*, Sakharov claims that he defended his candidate's dissertation successfully in the spring of 1948. But in his memoirs, while not dating either the philosophy examination or the dissertation defense precisely, Sakharov intimates that these events occurred in 1947, within a few months, not a year, of one another, and that he took the philosophy examination in the summer of that year and defended his dissertation in the fall. E. L. Feinberg's chronology corroborates Sakharov's. Sakharov, introduction to *Sakharov Speaks*, 30; Sakharov, *Memoirs*, 81; Feinberg, "Biographical Sketch," 5.

on if he wished to receive his candidate doctor's degree. He immediately recognized his mistake and quickly rectified it. Sakharov did not do poorly on the examination deliberately, as a political protest, because he found Chernyshevskii in particular, or Marxist-Leninist philosophy in general, repugnant. At this time in his life, he was not hostile to Soviet ideology so much as indifferent to it. Rather, what is striking about the entire incident, and the aspect of it that was most likely to impress itself on Sakharov, was the requirement that he had to take and pass such an examination at all, an examination for which there was no equivalent in the accreditation of physicists in the West. Such a requirement, on the face of it, was absurd: what possible relevance could the views on aesthetics of a nineteenth-century philosopher and novelist have for theoretical physicists concerned with mu mesons and nuclear fission? Sakharov was too intelligent and perceptive and too clearheaded an observer of things not to have wondered about a political system that would impose such a requirement.

By this time in his life, Sakharov's penchant for thinking critically and independently had become an integral aspect of his personality. If this had not yet made him a dissident, it nevertheless enabled him, in late 1946, to reject an offer tendered by a General Zverov, probably on behalf of the police, "to work on state projects of the greatest importance" once he had finished his graduate study.[44] Sakharov knew immediately that Zverov's phraseology was code for working on nuclear weaponry, and perhaps because working on weapons earlier in his life had retarded his development as a scientist, he saw such work as a cul-de-sac from which he might never escape.[45] But the authorities apparently accepted his explanation to Zverov that he preferred continuing his collaboration with Tamm at FIAN after his dissertation was accepted and his candidate's degree conferred; the fact that Sakharov was not punished for his apostasy in refusing Zverov's offer is testament to the relative immunity he enjoyed as a theoretical physicist. In late June 1948, however, Tamm dramatically informed Sakharov that the Council of Ministers of the Soviet Union and the Central Committee of the Soviet Communist Party had created a special research group, that Tamm had been named to lead it, and that its purpose was to evaluate and, if necessary, to improve upon the work a group of physicists and chemists headed by Zeldovich was doing in the construction of thermonuclear weapons (commonly called hydrogen bombs). Possibly on his own initiative, Tamm recommended that Sakharov participate in this endeavor.[46] This time Sakharov accepted the assignment. For the time being, he would remain, together with Tamm, at FIAN. But with this assignment his life would change dramatically and in ways he could not have predicted.

44. Sakharov, *Memoirs*, 93.
45. Ibid.
46. Ibid., 94. Zh. S. Takibaev, "Operezhavshii vremia," in Altshuler et al., *On mezhdu nami zhil*, 621.

# 4 Arzamas-16—The Secret Installation

To facilitate the task of assessing the progress Zeldovich and his colleagues were making on the construction of a Soviet hydrogen bomb, Sakharov, Tamm, and two other physicists who were part of this project, Vitalii Ginsburg and Iurii Romanov, were moved to different offices and given new calculators. Because their task was by no means an easy one, Sakharov found himself working longer and harder than he ever had before, remaining in his laboratory late into the night.[1] Inevitably, Tamm's group began to do more than merely check on what Zeldovich's group had accomplished, and their suggestions for improvement eventually superseded, rather than merely complemented, the work the latter was doing.

While in their offices Tamm and his colleagues were guarded closely by security personnel.[2] Given their assignment, this is hardly surprising. By the late 1940s, building thermonuclear weapons was an objective of critical importance to Stalin and the rest of the Soviet leadership, no less so than the concurrent development of nuclear weapons (commonly referred to as atomic bombs). The most obvious reason for this was that both of these weapons, especially thermonuclear ones, are militarily effective. They kill far larger numbers of people and inflict more collateral damage than do conventional weapons, and because their use in war requires only a bomber crew or ground-based missile technicians, they are cheaper as well.

Sakharov played no role in the development of Soviet nuclear weapons. But both he and other Soviet scientists who were tasked with building thermonuclear weapons proposed that the energy that is released in the fission of atomic nuclei—which occurs when nuclear weapons are detonated—be used to trigger the fusion of atomic nuclei that occurs when thermonuclear weapons explode. For this reason the reader should know how nuclear weapons work.[3]

When detonated, nuclear weapons release enormous amounts of explosive energy, far more than is released by conventional weapons, which are based on chemical reactions. In the case of nuclear weapons, this is because the amount of energy released when an atomic nucleus is split (or fissioned) is directly proportional to the amount of energy required to overcome the nuclear force that binds the components of the nucleus—protons and neutrons—together. Because the nuclear force is many times stronger than the electromagnetic force that binds atoms that are altered in purely chemical reactions, greater amounts

---

1. Pariiskaia, "On vsegda budet samim soboi," 474.
2. Ibid.
3. An explanation of nuclear fission nonscientists can understand is Kip Thorne's in *Black Holes and Time Warps*, 221–22. For an explanation of nuclear fusion, see chap. 5.

of energy are required to trigger nuclear reactions than are needed to trigger chemical ones. But the greater investment of energy in initiating nuclear reactions results in the production of much more energy than that produced in chemical reactions.

Nuclear reactions begin when the nucleus of a heavy element such as uranium or plutonium is bombarded by a stream of neutrons that has been triggered externally. These neutrons hit the nucleus of the heavy element with sufficient force or energy to overcome the nuclear force (or "glue") holding it together. The nucleus splits, forming smaller and lighter elements, and in the process releases energy. The nuclei of a few heavy elements, such as uranium-238 (U-238), split naturally and spontaneously. But while U-238 is fairly plentiful, its fission does not trigger a chain reaction: its nuclei split, lighter elements are formed, and energy is released—but because a chain reaction is not triggered by this, not enough energy is released to be useful militarily. Uranium-235 is better. When its nucleus splits, it generates more neutrons than are produced by a U-238 nucleus fission, so there are additional, unattached neutrons even after light elements have formed. These additional neutrons smash into other U-235 nuclei, releasing additional energy as well as additional neutrons; these neutrons smash into yet other U-235 nuclei; and this chain reaction based on nuclear fission continues until the original nuclear fuel (the U-235) has fissioned entirely. But because U-235 is rare in nature, American scientists in the early 1940s transmuted U-238 into a new element, plutonium, with an atomic weight of 239, which could, like U-235, trigger a chain reaction when its nucleus was bombarded with neutrons.[4]

The key to using nuclear fission militarily, once sufficient quantities of U-235 or P-239 were procured, was to devise a container for these elements that was durable enough to be dropped from an airplane or placed on the tip of a rocket—but also large enough to enable the chain reaction inside it to proceed. Once the logistics of this were resolved, nuclear weapons could be developed that, in light of their power, made them greatly superior to any conventional explosives.

Nuclear weapons were not a high priority for Stalin until 1945. This is not to say he had no interest in them. A letter he received during World War II from the nuclear physicist G. N. Flerov pointed out that the sudden disappearance in American scientific journals of articles by prominent American nuclear physicists probably meant that these physicists were secretly making nuclear weapons. Stalin knew as well from notebooks found on killed or captured German officers that Nazi Germany, too, was in all likelihood trying to build an atomic bomb.[5] And he knew from spies such as Klaus Fuchs that the British were involved in the same thing. Accordingly, in 1943 Molotov, acting on Stalin's orders, appointed Igor Kurchatov, himself a nuclear physicist, to supervise atomic research in the Soviet Union for the purpose of developing nuclear weapons.[6]

4. Ibid.; Sakharov, *Memoirs*, 90–91; Rhodes, *Making of the Atomic Bomb*, 346–55.
5. Alexandrov, "Kak delali bombu," 3.
6. Holloway, *Stalin and the Bomb*, 86–90.

But Kurchatov's project remained small and underfunded during the war because Stalin continued to believe—as it turned out, correctly—that the Nazis could not build an atomic bomb quickly enough to prevent their defeat.[7] Still, Stalin's awareness of how destructive nuclear weapons were was fairly minimal, even after Hiroshima and Nagasaki. Up to his death in 1953, in fact, he largely accepted the view of Soviet military strategists that because its population was too dispersed to be destroyed completely by nuclear bombs, and because Soviet antiaircraft weapons and other air defenses were adequate to destroy most of the bombers an enemy might equip with nuclear weapons, the Soviet Union could survive a nuclear war. The advantages the Soviet Union possessed would even be sufficient to enable it to win a nuclear war with the United States. Given Stalin's assumptions, it was easy for him to conclude that the nuclear weapons the United States possessed after 1945 posed a threat only to capitalist countries rather than to the Soviet Union or to civilization as a whole.[8]

Other Soviet leaders were no less obtuse in their views on nuclear weapons and how the Soviet Union should respond to them. Beria was reluctant after Hiroshima and Nagasaki to put Soviet physicists to work on nuclear weapons because he feared the disappearance of their names from Soviet journals to which Western scientists had access would tip off Western governments to what the Soviet Union was doing.[9] As far as Beria was concerned, it was better that the Soviet Union not develop nuclear weapons than that it let Western governments know it was developing them—a paranoid logic in a political system that prized its ability to keep foreign governments, not to mention its own people, ignorant of its actions. In fact, Beria's limitations in understanding the science of nuclear weaponry and his frequent refusal to allow Soviet scientists to proceed with their work unimpeded by the police were positively harmful to the actual development of a Soviet atomic bomb. For example, until the Soviet Union finally exploded an atomic bomb in August 1949, Beria persisted in believing that the construction of the bomb was a purely technical matter, an exercise in practical engineering for which very little theoretical scientific knowledge was required.[10] One senses from the way he approached the whole issue of Soviet nuclear weapons that he was more concerned with ensuring his own control over the production of these weapons than with their political and military ramifications. Not until 1954, nine years after Hiroshima and Nagasaki, did a Soviet leader, Georgii Malenkov, finally state publicly that nuclear weapons were different from all previous weapons in that they could destroy civilization as well as capitalism, and that peace between countries that possessed nuclear weapons was therefore essential despite the differences in their economic systems.[11] It bears mention

    7. Ibid., 90.
    8. Ibid., 237–40, 332, 369; Jonathan Haslam, "Stalin's War or Peace: What If the Cold War Had Been Avoided," in *Virtual History: Alternatives and Counterfactuals*, ed. Niall Ferguson (New York, 1999), 348–67.
    9. Zaloga, *Target America*, 95.
    10. Alexandrov, "Kak delali bombu," 3.
    11. Holloway, *Stalin and the Bomb*, 336.

that by the time he made this statement, Malenkov had already lost his position as first party secretary and thus any chance of succeeding Stalin as the leader of the Soviet Union.

But once Stalin knew that the United States had nuclear weapons, he had no choice but to order Soviet scientists to build them. As David Holloway has pointed out, contrary to what many believe, Stalin sought nuclear weapons after Hiroshima and Nagasaki not because the United States posed an imminent threat to it but because it did not.[12] Stalin, in other words, wanted the Soviet Union to have its own bombs before the United States built more of them in order to neutralize, or at least to minimize, the latter's real but not yet decisive numerical advantage. And even then, the threat Stalin thought American nuclear weapons posed to the Soviet Union was primarily political. If, unlike the Americans and the British, he failed to recognize that these weapons were so destructive that their actual use was precluded if adversaries possessed a comparable retaliatory capability, he recognized something that the Americans and the British, for quite some time, did not: that nuclear weapons, by their very existence, intimidate and terrorize and for that reason are politically useful. As he observed, "[A]tomic bombs are designed to terrify those with weak nerves."[13] Unlike the United States, Stalin believed in the possibility of atomic diplomacy (or blackmail) and that if the Soviet Union ever enjoyed an atomic monopoly, he, unlike the Americans, would practice it.[14]

Thus in 1945–1946, Stalin made building nuclear weapons a priority. As in industrialization and collectivization in the 1930s, the emphasis was on speed, with the result that Soviet nuclear weapons and delivery systems were occasionally tested during the Cold War before it could be determined that they were reasonably safe. In 1960, for example, a Soviet ICBM (without a warhead attached to it) exploded before it was launched, causing the deaths of Soviet officials imprudent enough not to distance themselves sufficiently from the launch pad.[15]

Essential to the development of Soviet nuclear weapons was Soviet espionage, particularly in the United States and Great Britain, where nearly all the work in the West on nuclear weapons after World War II was conducted. The whole issue of espionage in the development of Soviet nuclear and thermonuclear weapons is a ticklish one for Soviet physicists like Sakharov who were involved in it. To ascribe the Soviets' success in developing these weapons to espionage is implicitly to minimize the contribution, and even the abilities, of the Soviet scientists who actually designed them. In fact, one need not have worked on nuclear and thermonuclear weapons in the Soviet Union to resent this implication. Anatolii Iatskov, who was a lieutenant colonel in the KGB, has argued, in the case of the atomic bomb, that while the intelligence gained through espionage was copious and very helpful during World War II, the flow of it stopped abruptly

12. Ibid., 153.
13. Quoted in Haslam, "Stalin's War or Peace," 354.
14. John Lewis Gaddis, *We Now Know: Rethinking Cold War History* (New York, 1998), 111.
15. Sakharov, *Memoirs,* 195–96.

in 1946, just when the Soviet nuclear weapons program was accelerating, and that after 1946 Soviet scientists were more or less on their own.[16] By contrast, V. I. Filatov contends that such intelligence was in fact absolutely essential to the creation of a Soviet atomic bomb.[17] In trying to assess these competing claims, one might cite Kurchatov's testimony that "50 percent" of the success Soviet scientists achieved was due to espionage, in particular the information transmitted by Klaus Fuchs and others in late 1945 that using high-explosive charges to compress plutonium was a more efficient way of triggering a nuclear chain reaction than fusing one piece of uranium into another (the so-called gun configuration American physicists had developed but then discarded when they realized the advantage of imploding a mass of plutonium).[18] Kurchatov's view that espionage played a significant role in the development of Soviet nuclear weapons is especially credible, since his own personal interest, as the director of the project to build an atomic bomb, would have been to acknowledge only a negligible role for espionage in the development of these weapons.

In light of what the Soviets have written about the role of espionage in the development of Soviet nuclear weaponry, the following seems more or less correct: that while they would have built atomic weapons even without the information espionage provided, they would not have done so as quickly (which might not have been a bad thing in that the quality of these weapons would have been better); where this information was helpful was in confirming what Soviet scientists already knew from their own work, which, in the absence of empirical corroboration, remained speculative and hypothetical.[19] Moreover, while the information gained through espionage did not tell Soviet scientists how to make nuclear weapons, it helped persuade Stalin of the necessity of making them. In fact, Soviet scientists, on Stalin's orders, began work on the development of thermonuclear weapons before American scientists did, which explains why in June 1948, fully fourteen months before the Soviet Union exploded its first atomic bomb, Andrei Sakharov, already one of the most able and imaginative theoretical physicists in the Soviet Union, was recruited to work on thermonuclear, rather than merely nuclear, weapons. In Stalin's mind, building hydrogen bombs was a way of nullifying the superiority the United States still enjoyed in atomic bombs.

To carry out this important objective, the government in 1946 ordered the creation of a special installation near the town of Sarov, approximately four hundred kilometers east of Moscow, for the construction of nuclear and thermonuclear weapons. When finished, it measured ninety square miles.[20] This

16. Anatoli Iatzkov, "Atom i razvelka," *Voprosy istorii estestvoznaniia i tekhniki* 3 (1992): 106. See also I. N. Golovin, "A. D. Sakharov—Osnovopolozhnik issledovanii upravliaemogo termoiadernogo sinteza v nashei strane," in Altshuler et al., *On mezhdu nami zhil*, 265–66.

17. Cited in Iatzkov, "Atom i razvelka," 106.

18. Zaloga, *Target America*, 25, 40–41.

19. The physicist P. A. Alexandrov generally agrees with Iatzkov's conclusion. Iatzkov, "Atom i razvelka," 106.

20. Richard Lourie, *Sakharov: A Biography* (Waltham, Mass. 2002), 113.

installation, which included living quarters for the scientists and support personnel who worked there, was called Arzamas-16, after the town of that name that was sixty kilometers north of it. The installation, of course, like the others in the country that were devoted to the development of nuclear weapons, was secret, and it was not until 1990 that the Soviet government publicly revealed its existence and its actual name.[21] Consistent with his promise never to divulge classified information, Sakharov, in all that he wrote, never used the terms "Arzamas" or "Arzamas-16" for this veritable city where he lived and worked for eighteen years.[22] Indeed, the descriptions in his memoirs of what he observed and did at Arzamas-16 (henceforth referred to simply as Arzamas) are far less detailed and comprehensive than those he supplies for earlier and later periods of his life.

In truth, the government selected this particular site because it was so isolated; the police guards who surrounded Arzamas and kept watch over the scientists and the other personnel who worked there did so not only to protect them but also to ensure they had no contact with ordinary people, who were denied the professional autonomy the scientists at Arzamas enjoyed. After 1954 Sakharov had his own personal bodyguards—as did Kurchatov, the director of the Atomic Energy Institute; Iulii Khariton, the research director of the installation; and, after 1956, Zeldovich. These personal bodyguards, armed always with pistols, lived in a cottage adjacent to Sakharov's and accompanied him on his periodic trips to Moscow and other places. Not until 1957, when Zeldovich's request that his bodyguards be removed was applied to Sakharov's as well, would Sakharov lose this protection.[23]

Sakharov finally received permission to visit Moscow in October 1950, and he returned to Arzamas a month later with Klava and their two daughters. The family was now together, but the reunion carried a price. Once they were there, the authorities had greater justification for preventing Sakharov from traveling elsewhere, and as a consequence he saw other family members, including his father, only occasionally. But the cottage the family lived in—which by coincidence had been previously occupied by the same Leningrad scientist Sakharov had worked with in Ulianovsk—was commodious enough, and Sakharov's monthly salary after March 1950 of twenty thousand rubles was more than sufficient to cover the cost of food and other expenses.[24] In a society in which poverty and material deprivation were still pervasive, Kaganovich's description of Arzamas and the

21. Holloway, *Stalin and the Bomb,* 196; Lourie, *Sakharov,* 113; L. V. Altshuler, "Riadom s Sakharovym," in Altshuler et al., *On mezhdu nami zhil,* 115.

22. Sakharov, *Memoirs,* 101. The English term most translators use for it is "the Installation."

23. Edward Kline, conversation with author, June 10, 2008. Anatoly Alexandrov, who was president of the Academy of Sciences when Sakharov was exiled to Gorky in 1980, tried later to minimize the hardships Sakharov endured by claiming that Gorky was no more isolated than Arzamas, and that since Sakharov had not suffered at Arzamas, there was no reason to think he suffered in Gorky. "Akademik Aleksandrov otvechaet...v 1990 godu," *Ogonëk* 35 (1990), reprinted in Skonechnaia and Tsypkina, *Sakharov: Takim on byl,* 62.

24. Edward Kline, conversation with author, June 10, 2008; Sakharov, *Memoirs,* 117–18; Bonner, *Vol'nye zametki,* 4.

other "atomic cities" the Soviet leadership created for its nuclear scientists as "health resorts" was only an exaggeration, not a total fabrication.[25]

To be sure, there were less pleasant aspects of life at Arzamas, to which Sakharov was hardly oblivious. On his arrival, he was told by Zeldovich that "there are secrets everywhere" and that "the less you know that doesn't concern you, the better off you'll be."[26] For someone like Sakharov, the secrecy the government imposed on the residents of Arzamas was sometimes stifling, especially when it affected him directly. While Sakharov acknowledged the need for secrecy on matters that concerned national security, such as the construction of thermonuclear weapons, he considered ridiculous the requirement that children traveling by airplane to Arzamas never divulge how long their flight took.[27] To be sure, he was aware of the government's obsession with secrecy even before he arrived at Arzamas: while still at FIAN he was required, when he was working on thermonuclear weapons, to place any notes he had written during the day in a special suitcase he would surrender to security personnel before he could leave the building and go home for the night.[28] But at Arzamas the secrecy imposed was more intrusive. Even the prizes Sakharov won for his work on the Soviet hydrogen bomb were awarded secretly, and for all his contributions to the Soviet state, his name hardly appeared in the Soviet press until his dissident days, when it became virtually a synonym for treason.[29]

Arzamas bore a resemblance to the *sharashkas,* actual laboratories in the Gulag Archipelago, where scientists carried out research for the very regime that had arrested and imprisoned them. Much of the menial labor that enabled Arzamas to function was performed by *zeks,* or labor camp inmates, who, because of the classified nature of what they observed or were proximate to, were rarely released; the government's reasoning was that if these prisoners were allowed to go home, they might write memoirs or tell others of their experiences.[30] Sakharov, of course, was aware of the *zeks* and the role they played at Arzamas, and their degradation and lack of freedom could not help but make an impression on him. Like the tsarist *intelligenty* he resembled, however, Sakharov did not merely observe the government's denial of freedom and human dignity at Arzamas. However briefly, he actually experienced it. One day, while walking on the grounds at Arzamas, he and several other scientists by mistake approached the barbed wire that separated, or more precisely isolated, the installation from the world beyond it. Guards armed with submachine guns saw them, thought they were prisoners trying to escape, and quickly apprehended them and put them in a truck, where they were told that if they tried to escape or even lifted their legs off the floor of the truck into a crouched position (presumably as a preliminary to jumping out), they would be shot.

25. "Delo Beriia," *Izvestiia TsKPSS,* February 1991, 168.
26. Sakharov, *Memoirs,* 108.
27. Ibid., 119.
28. Ibid., 103.
29. Robert G. Kaiser, *Russia: The Power and the People* (New York, 1976), 313.
30. Holloway, *Stalin and the Bomb,* 193.

Only after Sakharov and his colleagues were brought to police headquarters at Arzamas, where their bona fides were checked and confirmed, did their captors release them.[31]

Comparable secrecy, of course, prevailed at Los Alamos in the United States, where much of the work on the Manhattan Project was done. Like Arzamas, Los Alamos was surrounded by barbed-wire fences. General Leslie Groves, the operational director of the Manhattan Project, tried to maintain high security: after determining (without any evidence) that the venerable Hungarian émigré physicist Leo Szilard was a security risk, he had Szilard followed.[32] But there was far less compartmentalization at Los Alamos than at Arzamas, where even senior scientists were not told what kinds of weapons they were developing and where scientists from different departments could not exchange ideas or even interact socially, as their American counterparts at Los Alamos did.[33] More broadly, Los Alamos, with its guards, barbed wire, and lack of freedom, was not a microcosmic reflection of American society, as Arzamas was of the Soviet Union.

The scientists and other personnel who labored at Arzamas certainly believed their jobs, and possibly their lives, were in jeopardy if they did not perform to the government's satisfaction. Beria, their ultimate superior, had many of the qualities of a competent administrator. By all accounts, he was intelligent, energetic, hardworking, efficient, and even willing, on occasion, to ignore the ideological lapses of the scientists he supervised.[34] But according to Khariton, he placed informers everywhere at Arzamas and even had an entire cadre of "understudies" ready to replace the scientists he supervised if they failed to do their jobs satisfactorily.[35] Evidently Beria himself feared for his life before the initial test of a Soviet atomic bomb in 1949 proved successful.[36] But the experience hardly seemed to humanize him or temper the ruthlessness for which he was known. Kurchatov, who like Beria believed that the failure of the Soviet atomic bomb would cost him his life, found working under the Soviet police chief extremely stressful, and some of those who knew him thought that this was the principal cause of his premature death in 1960 at the age of fifty-eight.[37] Another administrator at Arzamas, P. M. Zernov, was so afraid of what Beria might do to him after an atomic bomb that was tested failed to explode that he suffered a heart attack.[38] Iulii Khariton, looking back on his experiences at Arzamas, summarized

31. Sakharov, *Memoirs*, 114, 119.

32. Rhodes, *Making of the Atomic Bomb*, 449–55, 506.

33. Zaloga, *Target America*, 54; Yuli Khariton and Yuri Smirnov, "The Khariton Version," *Bulletin of the Atomic Scientists* 49, no. 4 (May 1993): 21.

34. Khariton and Smirnov, "The Khariton Version," 26–27.

35. I. N. Golovin and Iu. N. Smirnov, *Eto nachinalos' v zamoskvorech'e* (Moscow, 1989), 9, quoted in Holloway, *Stalin and the Bomb*, 203.

36. Vladislav Zubok and Constantine Pleshakov, *Inside the Kremlin's Cold War: From Stalin to Khrushchev* (Cambridge, Mass., 1996), 151.

37. "Peter Kapitsa: The Scientist Who Talked Back to Stalin," *Bulletin of the Atomic Scientists* 46, no. 3 (April 1990): 31.

38. The heart attack was not fatal. Zaloga, *Target America*, 90.

his fears and those of his colleagues by commenting simply that "there were the times when a slip of the tongue could cost you your life."[39]

Despite these conditions, the physicists at Arzamas, as long as they did not challenge the regime publicly and maintained at least the appearance of ideological conformity, were reasonably safe, more so than they themselves were able to recognize. Indeed, the physicists were probably safer individually and collectively than the administrative personnel who oversaw them, including Beria, who behaved in Stalin's presence with a servility that reflected his awareness of how easy it would be for Stalin to have him shot. In reaction to this, Beria menaced his subordinates with commensurate cruelty and capriciousness. In his memoirs Sakharov describes a 1952 incident in which Beria gave a dressing down to an underling in the police who was responsible for the production of the materials required in the construction of the hydrogen bomb. In this particular instance, the unfortunate underling had made a wrong decision, with the result that the physicists lacked the materials they needed in the requisite amounts. Beria berated the terrified subordinate for "losing your Bolshevik edge" and after softening his onslaught by assuring him that he would not be punished, concluded by reminding him that "we have plenty of room [for people like you] in our prisons."[40] Referring to the physicists at Arzamas, Stalin is reputed to have told Beria that he should "leave them in peace [because] we can always shoot them later."[41]

But such threats, if not entirely empty, were more expressions of irritation and bewilderment, born out of a lack of comprehension of the scientific work the physicists were doing, than they were statements of actual intent. In the language of family relations so apropos in explaining Soviet politics, the physicists at Arzamas were like gifted children, so precocious in their intelligence and abilities that their parents (i.e., Stalin, Beria, and after 1953, Khrushchev) were unable to understand what they were doing, much less evaluate it. If, in the end, the bombs these children built did not explode or blew up before the missiles that would carry them were launched, then their parents would know something was wrong and punish them accordingly. But in the absence of such incontrovertible evidence of incompetence, the parents had no choice but to give their children a good deal of leeway—with the result that on matters of pure science, the children were able to prevail in most instances when they objected to what the government told them to do. This occurred, for example, in 1954, not long after Viacheslav Malyshev succeeded Beria, who was arrested in June 1953 and shot six months later, as overseer of the entire project. Sakharov and his colleagues had developed a different kind of bomb from the one the government had directed them to make. Malyshev, not surprisingly given his temperament and the fact that he was a typical product of a profoundly authoritarian and hierarchical system, considered what they had done insubordinate and believed

39. Ibid., 54.
40. Sakharov, *Memoirs*, 158–59.
41. I. Zorich, "Pis'mo," *Priroda* 9 (1990): 106, quoted in Holloway, *Stalin and the Bomb*, 211.

strongly that they all should be punished for it. But since Sakharov and his colleagues were producing bombs that exploded, Malyshev had no choice but to drop his objections.[42]

Compared with the rest of the Soviet Union, Arzamas was an oasis of professional and political autonomy, especially after Stalin and Beria died. Sakharov and his colleagues had access to the most prestigious foreign journals in their fields, such as the *Bulletin of Atomic Scientists,* established in the United States by Leo Szilard. In addition, according to Viktor Adamskii, they could discuss, and were not punished for discussing, anything and everything, including George Orwell's *1984,* as direct and relentless an attack on Soviet Communism as has ever been written.[43] According to Iurii Smirnov, another of Sakharov's colleagues at Arzamas, the physicists there, in moments of relaxation, discussed a wide variety of political issues, including "the tragedy of the 1930s."[44] It is a reflection of the amount of autonomy they enjoyed that a Communist Party functionary who worked at Arzamas relayed to the Central Committee the information that these physicists were "cranks" and what they believed politically was "baloney"—but they could not be prevented from expressing their opinions.[45]

Commenting on the free exchange of ideas at Arzamas, Adamskii acknowledges modestly that "we were neither dissidents nor heroes. It just happened."[46] As for Sakharov himself, Adamskii and others who observed him at Arzamas have written how uninterested he was in political issues until Stalin's death, focusing his time, energy, and formidable intellect on the scientific matters that concerned him. After Stalin's death, however, he began to examine political issues more closely, in the same methodical and dispassionate way he examined scientific ones; at the same time, he was, again according to Adamskii, the most outspoken of the theoretical physicists in expressing his opinions.[47] In his memoirs Sakharov does not contradict this general impression, stating at one point that before Tamm left Arzamas in 1953 he had long discussions with him on "the most sensitive questions: the repressions, the camps, anti-Semitism, collectivization, the ideal and real faces of communism."[48]

In their access to ideas the regime deemed ideologically dangerous, the theoretical physicists at Arzamas enjoyed a degree of intellectual freedom that was replicated nowhere else in the Soviet Union at any time prior to perestroika. Stalin's injunction to a subordinate that he "not bother our physicists with political seminars" captures the essence of the situation perfectly.[49] Stalin let physicists

42. Sakharov, *Memoirs,* 183–84.
43. Adamskii, "Stanovlenie grazhdanina," 30; Richard Rhodes, *Dark Sun: The Making of the Hydrogen Bomb* (New York, 1995), 513.
44. Smirnov, "Etot chelovek," 586.
45. Adamskii, "Stanovlenie grazhdanina," 34.
46. Ibid.
47. Ibid., 37.
48. Sakharov, *Memoirs,* 122.
49. Medvedev, *Soviet Science,* 46. Stalin probably said this in the late 1940s, when Soviet physicists were building an atomic bomb. But the comment applies as well to the physicists who in the early 1950s were developing a hydrogen bomb.

like Sakharov debate the merits of Soviet society because the work they were doing was indispensable; therefore, the physicists themselves were indispensable. In addition, the risks for the regime of their discussing political issues were practically nil: because the physicists were isolated so completely from the rest of the population, whatever unflattering conclusions they might reach about the Soviet system as a whole would remain literally in-house.

Paradoxically, the isolation to which Stalin consigned these physicists benefited them as much as it did the Soviet dictator. In short, it gave them leverage that some of them actually exercised when the regime, in a reflexive reversion to the way it treated everyone else in the Soviet Union, occasionally threatened them. An example occurred in 1950, when a commission arrived at Arzamas to confirm the political orthodoxy of the scientists who worked there. Responding to a member's question about Lysenko, Sakharov replied candidly that he disagreed with him and considered the Mendelian genetics Lysenko had repudiated scientifically correct. Because his intellectual brilliance rendered him untouchable, Sakharov was never punished or reprimanded for his impudence and ideological heresy.[50] But Sakharov's colleague, L. V. Altshuler (not to be confused with his son, B. L. Altshuler), was not so fortunate. Upon receiving from the elder Altshuler roughly the same answer Sakharov had given, the commission recommended his dismissal: by stating his opinion so blatantly and openly, Altshuler, who did not have the immunity Sakharov did, had violated the modus vivendi the regime and the physicists tacitly observed. His dismissal seemed a foregone conclusion. Sakharov, however, refused to let the matter rest. In much the way he would do as a dissident, when on countless occasions he tried to shield other dissidents from persecution, Sakharov, along with a colleague, Evgenii Zababakhin, interceded with the authorities on Altshuler's behalf and ensured his continuation at Arzamas.[51] A year later, however, Altshuler was summoned to Moscow and again threatened with serious punishment, this time for having expressed his views on various cultural issues more conspicuously than the authorities deemed acceptable. In his interrogation of Altshuler, Boris Vannikov, the head of the First Main Directorate of the Council of Ministers, the government agency with jurisdiction over Arzamas, explained why his conduct was intolerable: "You're working in an installation so secret even the party secretaries don't know about it and you're proposing your own party line in music, literature and biology. If we let just anyone say whatever he wants, we'd be crushed."[52] For a time, Altshuler feared he would be sent to a labor camp. But Khariton, who valued Altshuler's abilities as a scientist as much as Sakharov did, placed a telephone call to Beria, who was Vannikov's superior, and told him to leave Altshuler alone. Beria, instead of threatening Khariton and arresting him—as he might have done if Khariton had been in charge of

50. Sakharov, *Memoirs*, 135.
51. Ibid., 135–36; Zaloga, *Target America*, 97; L. V. Altshuler, "Tak my delali bombu," *Literaturnaia gazeta,* June 6, 1990, 13. Altshuler dates these events to 1951.
52. Quoted in Rhodes, *Dark Sun*, 515.

something less significant than the development of thermonuclear weapons—merely asked Khariton whether he needed Altshuler "very much." Khariton said yes, and Beria dropped the matter.[53]

Finally, the theoretical physicists at Arzamas had unprecedented access to the top Soviet leadership. Sakharov, Kurchatov, Khariton, and Zeldovich could all contact Presidium members directly, and after Beria's arrest in June 1953 Sakharov on at least one occasion briefed members of the Presidium on the nature of the weapons he and his colleagues were designing.[54] As a result, Sakharov could take his measure of the Soviet leaders and see for himself how cruel or mediocre, or both, many of them were. In his memoirs he offers this chilling rendition of how an encounter with Beria ended and his reaction to it immediately afterward: "Beria offered me his hand. It was plump, slightly moist, and deathly cold. Only then, I think, did I realize that I was face to face with a terrifying human being. It hadn't entered my mind before, and I had been completely free in my manner. At my parents' house that evening, I talked about my meeting with Beria, and their fear made me conscious—perhaps for the first time—of my own reaction."[55] Shortly after Beria was arrested, Sakharov, again because of his privileged position, was shown the letter of the Central Committee explaining Beria's arrest and detailing some of the atrocities he and his underlings had allegedly committed in Georgia—information of the kind ordinary Soviet citizens did not have access to until the late 1980s. Similarly, despite his not being a member of the Communist Party, Sakharov read Khrushchev's myth-shattering Secret Speech at the Twentieth Party Congress in February 1956 exposing and condemning some, though by no means all, of Stalin's crimes.[56] Observing Soviet leaders like Beria and having access to speeches and documents that served to confirm his personal observations of these figures were surely among the experiences that helped to shape the dissident ideas he articulated in the late 1960s. Sakharov's dissidence, in other words, did not emerge ex nihilo but was rather the culmination of experiences and observations germinating in his mind at Arzamas.

As the Altshuler imbroglio made clear, Sakharov was willing at Arzamas to use his own prestige and authority to help others more vulnerable to persecution and retribution. Another example of this occurred at the time of the infamous Doctors' Plot in January 1953, when nine Kremlin doctors, six of them Jewish, were accused of having murdered Soviet leaders and conspiring to murder Red Army generals. What prompted Sakharov's intervention was the removal of Mattes Agrest, who was Jewish, as head of the mathematics section at Arzamas. The authorities had recently discovered that Agrest had relatives in Israel, which

53. Khariton and Smirnov, "The Khariton Version," 27.

54. Adamskii, "Stanovlenie grazhdanina," 25; Sakharov, *Memoirs*, 180. Incredibly, when Beria was in power, one of his colleagues on the Politburo, Georgii Malenkov, and possibly others as well, were not informed of what Sakharov and his colleagues were doing. Sakharov, *Memoirs*, 169. At the Nineteenth Party Congress in 1952, the Politburo was renamed the Presidium.

55. Sakharov, *Memoirs*, 146.

56. Ibid., 167–68.

in their eyes was proof of dual loyalties and suggested he could not be trusted to keep state secrets. Equally abhorrent was the ritual circumcision of Agrest's newborn son, which was conducted openly at Arzamas. Sakharov could not in this instance cause the government to reverse itself. Rather, he invited his former colleague and his family to stay in the apartment in Moscow the Sakharovs had occupied before moving to Arzamas until they could find lodgings of their own.[57] Sakharov's action was not politically motivated. His offer was not a way of demonstrating his opposition to, or his dissatisfaction with, the Soviet state. Rather, it was simply an expression of compassion, something someone who is sensitive to the hardships of others does naturally and without regard for the consequences, and a manifestation of the philo-Semitism he had first shown in his childhood.

Notwithstanding its isolation, there was much about Arzamas Sakharov liked. Its collegial atmosphere, particularly in the department of theoretical physics, where Sakharov spent the bulk of his time, had the effect of minimizing the personal rivalries and recriminations he found unpleasant. But there was also a political dimension to this collegiality: it reflected an egalitarianism glaringly absent in the Soviet society that surrounded it. To the extent that Sakharov was aware of this disparity, it contributed to his political evolution.

That there was a formal hierarchy at Arzamas based on rank and professional accomplishment was undeniable. Kurchatov, based in Moscow but in charge of the nuclear weapons program at Arzamas, was at the top. He reported to Beria and then, after Beria's arrest, to Malyshev. Beneath Kurchatov was Khariton, who oversaw the heads of the various experimental and theoretical departments to which every scientist employed at the installation was assigned. Below Khariton were department heads, one of whom was Tamm, who directed the theoretical physicists and thus was Sakharov's superior. When Tamm returned to Moscow in 1953, Sakharov assumed his position. Two years later Sakharov and Zeldovich were named deputies to Khariton, which entitled them to serve with him as members of a scientific-technocratic council of the Ministry of Medium Machine Building, headed by Kurchatov until his death in 1960.[58] But while Kurchatov was mindful of the need to show the "civilian" authorities to which he was accountable that those below him at Arzamas showed their superiors the proper deference, he was also unafraid of intellectual excellence and was tolerant, even supportive, of scientists like Sakharov who spoke their minds.[59] Kurchatov was quite willing, in other words, to ignore the requirements of *mestnichestvo* (hierarchical ranking common in Muscovite as well as Soviet Russia) if a particular scientist had an idea he believed was worth pursuing. According to Smirnov, Sakharov himself, along with Zeldovich, helped to foster

57. Ibid., 112; According to L. V. Altshuler, Agrest lost his job because the authorities learned that as a teenager he had earned a diploma from a Jewish religious school. At the time of his arrest, Agrest was a rabbi. Lourie, *Sakharov*, 130; Altshuler, "Riadom s Sakharovym," 118.

58. Adamskii, "Stanovlenie grazhdanina," 25; Sakharov, *Memoirs*, 178.

59. Alexandrov, "Kak delali bombu," 3.

a "democratic" atmosphere within the theoretical department by not adhering to any hierarchy based on rank, prestige, or academic title. By welcoming into his office for discussions about scientific issues younger physicists like Smirnov who were understandably in awe of him, Sakharov set an example of accessibility that other senior physicists were inclined to follow.[60] In Viktor Adamskii's description, Sakharov always respected the opinions of others, even when he disagreed with them, and while chairing meetings at which scientific matters were discussed he always tried to give everyone present a chance to speak. While Sakharov would never change his mind solely for the sake of collegiality, he had the intellectual integrity to do so if someone else convinced him he was wrong.[61] In Adamskii's very laudatory estimation: "This respect for the opinions of others; this striving to maximize the democratic character of any discussion; this tendency to break free, wherever possible, from narrowly based decisions; or to say the same thing in more general terms, this unique intellectual-democratic style of behavior, no less than his scientific ability, created that lofty moral authority Sakharov wielded."[62]

By all accounts Sakharov was extraordinarily modest and self-effacing, always ready to credit the contributions of others; for example, in assessing his own role in designing the Soviet hydrogen bomb, he said it was "great but not exclusive."[63] He was also unflappable: slow to show anger, rarely irritated by the foibles of others, and almost never given to personal pique or professional jealousy. B. L. Altshuler, whose father worked with Sakharov, knew him well and wrote once that he never saw Sakharov irritated.[64] As a result, some of the younger physicists in the theoretical department asked Sakharov to arbitrate disputes and, more generally, to defuse conflicts created by the competitive impulses of highly motivated, intensely creative, and often personally idiosyncratic individuals working in close proximity on a project of enormous significance. When, in 1990, the elder Altshuler declared in an interview that Sakharov had worked on the hydrogen bomb in collaboration with others and that therefore it was inappropriate to call him the father of the Soviet H-bomb, he hastened to add that none of Sakharov's collaborators had ever objected to that title.[65]

60. Smirnov, "Etot chelovek," 577.

61. Adamskii, "Stanovlenie grazhdanina," 35–36; M. E. Perelman, "Vstrechi, besedy," in Altshuler et al., *On mezhdu nami zhil,* eds., 513.

62. Adamskii, "Stanovlenie grazhdanina," 36.

63. D. A. Kirzhnits, "Facets of a Talent," in Drell and Kapitza, *Sakharov Remembered,* 39; Sakharov quoted in Andrei Sakharov, "A Voice Out of Russia," *Observer,* December 3, 1972, 29.

64. B. L. Altshuler, "On ne bil naiven," in Ivanova, *Andrei Dmitrievich,* 225. See also P. I. Pimenov, "Kakim on byl," in Ivanova, *Andrei Dmitrievich,* 213.

65. L. V. Altshuler, "Tak my delali bombu," 13. Most of those who worked with Sakharov on the project would have disagreed with Altshuler's derogation. In 1953 Kurchatov told the Academy of Sciences that no one in the academy had done more than Sakharov to defend the Soviet Union. The same year, at a gathering of political and military leaders Kurchatov literally bowed to Sakharov and proclaimed him "the savior of Russia." V. A. Tsukerman and Z. M. Azarkh, "Liudi i vzryv," *Zvezda* 11 (1990): 121; Smirnov, "Etot chelovek," 596. Sakharov himself disliked such sobriquets, especially when they were applied to him. Ioirysh, *Uroki A. D. Sakharova,* 21.

For Sakharov, the community of physicists he inhabited was a prototype for something larger—a Republic of Science in which everyone, not just scientists, used reason to solve social and political problems as well as intellectual and scientific ones. To be sure, Sakharov never used the term himself, and one cannot emphasize enough that his principal focus at Arzamas was on science rather than on its moral and political implications. But it seems likely nevertheless that at Arzamas it occurred to him that the way scientists lived and worked was the way everyone should live and work, and that the kind of reasoning scientists used to comprehend the natural world should inform the way ordinary human beings conducted their lives, and how entire societies should be organized. From what Sakharov wrote about his experiences at Arzamas one gets a fairly clear idea of what he believed the relationship between scientists and everyone else should be in such societies: scientists would indicate to the political leaders the problems that had to be solved and offer solutions these leaders would be rational enough to accept, while the masses would be sufficiently rational to defer to the superior wisdom of scientists by removing democratically elected political leaders who for whatever reason failed to show these scientists the deference they deserved. Sakharov did not actually describe these elitist arrangements until the early 1970s.[66] But it was earlier in his life, mostly at Arzamas, that he first conceived the notion that the scientific method and the intellectual abilities science requires should be the arbiter of public policy and that scientists or persons possessing the attributes of scientists, especially rationality, should be accorded enormous influence in the formulation of public policy. Far from being the escape from society it was for Tamm, and perhaps for Dmitrii Sakharov as well, science, for Andrei Sakharov, was the model for it.

One should not, in assessing Sakharov's sensibilities and political maturity at Arzamas, make too much of this. Throughout the time he was there, he remained a loyal, if somewhat troubled, Soviet citizen, whose conviction that scientists should decide scientific issues themselves, without intervention by ignorant and overbearing government apparatchiki, never generated the broader conclusion that the Soviet system itself was corrupt, or even that it should be significantly reformed.[67] Sakharov's explanation for this in his memoirs deserves to be quoted in full. Commenting on the genuine grief he felt in 1953 when he learned that Stalin was dead, Sakharov wrote the following:

> I can't fully explain it—after all, I knew quite enough about the horrible crimes that had been committed—the arrests of innocent people, the torture, the deliberate starvation, and all the violence—to pass judgment on those responsible. But I hadn't put the whole picture together, and in any case, there was still a lot I didn't know....But above all, I felt myself committed to the goal which I assumed

---

66. For an analysis of Sakharov's political thought in the early 1970s that acknowledges its elitism, see Donald R. Kelley, *The Solzhenitsyn-Sakharov Dialogue: Politics, Society, and the Future* (Westport, Conn., 1982), especially 121, 125, 133–34.

67. This was roughly where Kapitsa's political evolution stopped.

was Stalin's as well: after a devastating war, to make the country strong enough to ensure peace. Precisely because I had invested so much of myself in that cause and accomplished so much, I needed, as anyone might in my circumstances, to create an illusory world, to justify myself.... The state, the nation, and the ideals of communism remained intact for me. It was years before I fully understood the degree to which deceit, exploitation, and outright fraud were involved in those notions, and how much they deviated from reality. In the face of all I had seen, I still believed that the Soviet state represented a breakthrough into the future, a prototype (though not as yet a fully realized one) for all other countries to imitate.[68]

At Arzamas Sakharov certainly objected to things. But up to 1957 he did so privately and on an ad hoc basis. For all his doubts and misgivings, he was not yet a dissident. At this stage in his life he lacked the ability to recognize what he saw and experienced as reflective of a larger social, political, and ideological malady that required intervention to cure.

# 5  The "Layer Cake" and Other Weapons

At Arzamas Sakharov was consumed by the task of constructing a hydrogen bomb. This was more difficult than constructing an atomic bomb, but the military benefits were commensurately greater. Even before the United States successfully tested nuclear weapons and dropped them on Japanese cities, Edward Teller and Enrico Fermi had dreamed of building what Teller called a superbomb (or "Super") based on the following process. Energy released in the fission of the nuclei of a heavy element such as uranium or plutonium raises the temperature of the atoms of a light element—Teller had in mind deuterium—to the point where their thermal motion overcomes their electrical repulsion and their nuclei fuse, creating a heavier element, in this case helium. In this nuclear fusion, enormous amounts of energy are released, far more than in nuclear fission, which is why hydrogen bombs are more powerful than atomic bombs. Because of the incredibly high temperatures fusion reactions require, the weapons based on them are called "thermonuclear."[1] In late 1945 the Soviet physicist Iakov Frankel suggested to Kurchatov the very sequence Teller and Fermi conjured and stressed its military implications.[2]

68. Sakharov, *Memoirs*, 164.

1. Thorne, *Black Holes and Time Warps*, 221; Holloway, *Stalin and the Bomb*, 294–95; Rhodes, *Dark Sun*, 247.
2. German Goncharov, "Beginnings of the Soviet H-bomb Program," *Physics Today* 49, no. 11 (November 1996): 50.

But the obstacles to building a bomb based on fusion were considerable. Nuclear fusion occurs spontaneously in nature, in the interior of stars, but temperatures of literally millions of degrees are required to trigger it. For this reason, while it is possible to predict from experiments in the laboratory how a fission bomb will perform, the enormous amount of heat required to detonate a fusion bomb makes comparable experiments impossible. This would be true even when the amount of nuclear fuel—the heavy element or elements whose nuclear fission would catalyze the fusion of light elements—was small.[3]

Confronted with this problem, Teller devised a solution. Since the temperature required to fuse deuterium nuclei was prohibitively high, in the hundreds of millions of degrees, he hypothesized that tritium—an isotope of hydrogen with two neutrons in its nucleus rather than one—should be used as well as deuterium (though not instead of it) because the temperature at which its nuclei fused was much lower. In other words, a mixture of tritium and deuterium would fuse at a lower temperature than would the same quantity of deuterium alone. But tritium, unlike deuterium, was rare in nature and hard to produce artificially. In addition, hydrogen and its isotopes, deuterium and tritium, were all gases, and in order for these isotopes to serve as a thermonuclear fuel, they would have to be either liquefied or combined with some other element to form a solid compound.[4]

Despite these difficulties, American and Soviet scientists persevered: the fact that the amount of energy a fusion bomb would generate was so much greater than what the largest practical fission bomb could produce made it too enticing a possibility for either superpower to ignore.[5] The foremost problem both sets of scientists faced was to direct energy, and therefore heat, from the fission reaction to the thermonuclear fuel so that it would reach the temperature at which it would ignite. Because the detonation of a thermonuclear weapon involved fission as well as fusion, there was a continuum in the relative amounts of nuclear and thermonuclear fuels that were needed. Teller's Super, for example, required far more thermonuclear fuel than nuclear fuel. For that reason, it would be so destructive—Teller conjectured that its explosive power would be ten megatons, the equivalent of ten million tons of TNT—that many believed it would be militarily useless. In fact, when Teller first conceived of the Super, he feared that the explosion it caused might literally incinerate the earth's atmosphere.[6] At the other end of this continuum were "boosted atomic weapons," in which a fission reaction involving a large amount of nuclear fuel would trigger a

---

    3. York, *Advisors*, 25, Rhodes, *Dark Sun*, 248.

    4. Holloway, *Stalin and the Bomb*, 295; Zaloga, *Target America*, 96; Yu. A. Romanov, "The Father of the Soviet Hydrogen Bomb," in Drell and Kapitza, *Sakharov Remembered*, 126.

    5. Because a thermonuclear reaction requires no critical mass except for the fissive materials that trigger it, theoretically there are no limits to its explosive power. Indeed, the very fact that fusion occurs in stars literally millions of times larger than the earth is proof of a sort that on earth there were no practical limits to the amount of energy a fusion reaction could generate. Rhodes, *Dark Sun*, 252–53, 400.

    6. Ibid., 254.

fusion reaction in a small amount of thermonuclear fuel; the neutrons released in the fusion reaction would complement the neutrons released in the original fission reaction to increase the efficiency of the fusion reaction and thus the cumulative explosive power of the bomb itself. In the so-called George tests in May 1951, the United States exploded such boosted atomic bombs.[7]

In the middle of this continuum were bombs that used more thermonuclear fuel than boosted atomic ones but less thermonuclear fuel than Teller's Super; in David Holloway's opinion, it is purely a matter of taste whether one calls these bombs hydrogen bombs.[8] A more accurate term for them might simply be "hybrids." But whatever one calls them, these bombs were preferable to the existing alternatives: boosted atomic weapons were hardly more powerful than ordinary atomic weapons, while Teller's Super required so much tritium that the laboratories where the isotope could be generated would have to cut back on producing the plutonium needed for atomic bombs. In addition, the American physicist Stanislaw Ulam determined in 1950 that the Super required even more tritium than Teller anticipated. For these reasons, Teller's Super was unworkable.[9]

As an alternative, Ulam proposed that the hydrogen bomb should physically be in the form of a cylinder, with the nuclear fuel for the fission reaction at one end and the thermonuclear fuel for the fusion reaction at the other. This was different from Teller's Super, in which the two fuels were basically packed together. There was a problem with Ulam's two-stage design, however: the shock waves the fission reaction generated could cause the casing in which the two fuels were enclosed to explode before the fusion reaction could occur. Ulam devised a solution: if the two fuels were separated somehow, the X-rays that were emitted in the fission reaction, because they traveled faster than the shock waves, would reach the thermonuclear fuel before the shock waves did and ignite the fuel before the waves could blow up the entire device.[10] In any case, when Ulam and another physicist, Cornelius Everett, informed Teller that his Super was unworkable, he was, understandably, furious. Ulam mollified him, however, and Teller gradually warmed to Ulam's idea; in the end, he even improved on it by suggesting that these X-rays could be used not only to heat the thermonuclear fuel but to compress it as well; by compressing the fuel, the X-rays would cause it to burn more quickly and thus more efficiently. In fact, by separating the two fuels, it would be possible to interpose a layer of plastic foam between them, which, when heated by the X-rays into a plasma (a hot, ionized gas), would itself serve to heat and compress the thermonuclear fuel considerably. Finally, when Teller and Ulam realized that even this arrangement would not generate from the fusion reaction the explosive force the bomb needed to be effective and thus to justify its being built in the first place, Teller had the idea that this

7. Holloway, *Stalin and the Bomb*, 299–300; York, *Advisors*, 76–77.
8. Holloway, *Stalin and the Bomb*, 308.
9. Rhodes, *Dark Sun*, 380, 455.
10. Rhodes, *Making of the Atomic Bomb*, 774.

plasma could trigger a second fission reaction, the heat from which would finally cause the bomb to explode.[11] Toward this end, he proposed encasing a layer of U-238 around both the plutonium that was fissioned and whichever isotopes of hydrogen were fused. To put it simply, Teller-Ulam posited the sequence fission-fusion-fission.[12]

With Teller-Ulam as their organizing principle, American physicists built a thermonuclear device and tested it on November 1, 1952. This was the test the Americans called "Mike." Eight hundred times more powerful than the Hiroshima bomb, it obliterated the island in the Eniwetok Atoll in the Pacific on which it was detonated. Because 75 percent of its explosive yield came from fission, Richard Rhodes calls it a "big, dirty fission bomb" instead of a real hydrogen bomb.[13] Whatever it was, the device was not deliverable in any militarily meaningful sense of the word. The liquid deuterium it burned required a temperature of $-250°$ centigrade to keep it from becoming a gas, and the device itself, which weighed fifty tons, was the size of a two-story house.[14] Two years later, on March 1, 1954, in a test code-named Bravo, the United States exploded another device with the Teller-Ulam configuration but with lithium deuteride—a chalky powder formed from the combination of deuterium and an isotope of lithium—instead of liquid deuterium as its thermonuclear fuel. Though deliverable by an airplane, this device, like the earlier one, was exploded on the ground.[15]

Sakharov and the other physicists at Arzamas who were designing thermonuclear weapons knew less about what their American counterparts were doing than did the Soviet scientists who were designing a nuclear weapon. After Sakharov began work on the hydrogen bomb in 1948, the two projects to build the bomb, the American and the Soviet, proceeded, as it were, on parallel tracks, with scientists in each country considering many of the same designs but deciding differently whether or not to build actual devices based on them. It will be recalled that Sakharov was recruited for the Soviet project originally to evaluate what a group headed by Zeldovich had already done. Barely two months after he began his assignment, however, Sakharov, in September 1948, conceived what he calls in his memoirs and in other writings the First Idea, a design for a thermonuclear bomb radically different from the one Zeldovich and his colleagues were pursuing. Because the bomb Zeldovich's group was designing was based partly on information received through espionage—most likely from Klaus Fuchs—in 1945,

11. Thorne, *Black Holes and Time Warps*, 243; Holloway, *Stalin and the Bomb*, 302–3; Rhodes, *Making of the Atomic Bomb*, 774.

12. Rhodes, *Making of the Atomic Bomb*, 776.

13. Rhodes, *Dark Sun*, 510. Kip Thorne, in contrast to Rhodes, calls the Mike device "a hydrogen bomb-type device." In terms of the continuum Holloway uses, it seems to me to have been a hybrid. Thorne, *Black Holes and Time Warps*, 231.

14. Khariton and Smirnov, "The Khariton Version," 29; York, *Advisors*, 82–83; German Goncharov, "The American Effort," *Physics Today* 49, no. 1 (November 1996): 47.

15. York, *Advisors*, 85; Rhodes, *Dark Sun*, 541.

it greatly resembled Teller's Super.[16] In contrast to this, Sakharov proposed a configuration that came to be known colloquially as *Sloika* (or Layer Cake). This consisted of alternate layers of light elements, deuterium and tritium, and a heavy element, U-238, surrounding an atomic bomb using plutonium as its nuclear fuel in the center. Sakharov's idea was that the fissioning of the plutonium would raise the temperature of both sets of elements to the point where they would be ionized, which in turn would equalize the pressure between them, making the fusion of the light elements, now greatly compressed, possible. The neutrons released in the fusion reaction would then cause the U-238 nuclei, now mixed with the light elements that were in the process of fusing, to fission, thereby increasing the explosive yield of the entire process. The layers of U-238 would serve the additional purpose of preventing the energy released in the fusion reaction from leaking out too quickly.[17] Because, by analogy, the heating and compression of the light elements in Sakharov's device resembled the carmelization of sugar, this particular phase in the detonation of the Layer Cake was called by the other scientists, in a playful acknowledgment of who conceived it, *sakharizatsiia*.[18]

When Sakharov broached his Layer Cake configuration to Tamm, the latter immediately recognized its superiority to what Zeldovich's group was pursuing, and Zeldovich himself also acknowledged it. In November 1948, two months after Sakharov proposed the Layer Cake, another physicist, Vitalii Ginzburg, improved on it (in just the way Bravo, in the United States, improved on Mike) by proposing what came to known as the Second Idea: that lithium deuteride, as a chalklike solid, was preferable as a thermonuclear fuel to deuterium or tritium.[19] Never one to reject a suggestion because he had not conceived of it, Sakharov incorporated Ginzburg's innovation into his initial proposal, which won the approval of Kurchatov as well. In February 1950 the Council of Ministers resolved that while the construction of a thermonuclear device similar to Teller's Super should continue along with Sakharov's Layer Cake, the latter should be given priority.[20]

To the extent that both devices, Sakharov's and Teller-Ulam, used considerable amounts of nuclear fuel and that this fuel produced a significant percentage of the energy each device would release, neither, strictly speaking, was a

16. Sakharov, *Memoirs*, 102–4; David Holloway, "Soviet Thermonuclear Development," *International Security* 4, no. 3 (1979/80): 193.

17. Rhodes, *Dark Sun*, 334; Holloway, *Stalin and the Bomb*, 298; Romanov, "Father of the Soviet Hydrogen Bomb," 127.

18. Goncharov, "Beginnings of the Soviet H-bomb Program," 53. The reader will recall that "Sakharov" means literally "of the Sugarmans."

19. Zaloga, *Target America*, 96–97; Sakharov, *Memoirs*, 102. Because Ginzburg's wife was imprisoned and exiled to a labor camp after the government accused her of conspiring to murder Stalin, Ginsburg was considered a security risk and remained in Moscow when Tamm and Sakharov went to Arzamas. It was from Moscow that he communicated to the latter his idea of using lithium deuteride. Thorne, *Black Holes and Time Warps*, 230.

20. Sakharov, *Memoirs*, 102; Holloway, *Stalin and the Bomb*, 299; Goncharov, "The Race Accelerates," *Physics Today* 49, no. 11 (November 1996): 56.

hydrogen bomb. But there the similarity ended. Sakharov's Layer Cake was basically a single-stage device in which the nuclear and thermonuclear fuels were physically proximate, so that the nuclear and thermonuclear reactions generated would be mutually reinforcing rather than sequential, as was the case in Teller-Ulam. And unlike Teller-Ulam, which theoretically could generate virtually unlimited amounts of energy, Sakharov's Layer Cake had built-in limits to its explosive power. This was because the thermonuclear fuel in the Layer Cake was not compressed nearly as much as it was in Teller-Ulam. As a result, the amount of thermonuclear fuel the Layer Cake could use was limited, which meant that its explosive power was limited as well. In addition, in the Layer Cake fusion was triggered by what were essentially explosions, rather than by radiation, as was the case in Teller-Ulam.[21]

Because only radiation made possible the high-megaton yields the Americans wanted, they basically skipped consideration of designs identical to, or comparable to, Sakharov's, and using Teller-Ulam proceeded directly from the boosted atomic bombs they had tested in 1951 to the hybrid they exploded successfully in the Mike test in 1952. For the Soviets, however, the Layer Cake for the time being was sufficient, despite the limits on megatonnage it entailed, to advance what was really their long-term objective—namely, a balance of terror in which Soviet superiority in hydrogen bombs nullified the American advantage in atomic ones. Sakharov's labors achieved fruition on August 12, 1953, when, at Semipalatinsk in Soviet Central Asia, the Soviet Union tested a bomb the Americans called Joe-4, in keeping with their practice of naming Soviet atomic tests, in numerical sequence, after Stalin.[22] Inasmuch as its thermonuclear fuel was the more manageable lithium deuteride, the bomb detonated in Joe-4 was an improvement over what the Americans had detonated the year before in Mike; in fact the Americans would not use lithium deuteride until Bravo in 1954.[23] In addition, the Soviet device exploded in Joe-4, unlike the American device in Mike, was potentially deliverable from an airplane. It was, however, not a genuine hydrogen bomb because not enough of its energy came from fusion.[24] Moreover, in keeping with the limits of its Layer Cake configuration, the Soviet device in Joe-4 was no more powerful than the largest fission device the United States had ever exploded and only 3–5 percent as powerful as the hybrid exploded in Mike. Its explosive yield was roughly four hundred kilotons, which made it approximately twenty times more powerful than the atomic bomb dropped on Hiroshima.[25]

As Patrick Glynn has pointed out, however, if Joe-4 was not a real hydrogen bomb, in its political effects it might as well have been, for it thoroughly surprised and frightened the American government, which spurred the physicists it

21. Rhodes, *Dark Sun,* 462–72, 524–25.

22. Ibid., 525; York, *Advisors,* 95; Holloway, *Stalin and the Bomb,* 308.

23. Thorne, *Black Holes and Time Warps,* 232; Goncharov, "Race Accelerates," 60.

24. Thorne, *Black Holes and Time Warps,* 231; Medvedev, *Soviet Science,* 52; David Holloway, "Soviet Scientists Speak Out," *Bulletin of the Atomic Scientists* 49, no. 4 (May 1993): 19.

25. York, *Advisors,* 10; Holloway, "Soviet Scientists," 19.

employed to develop thermonuclear weapons that would have even greater explosive power, relative to Joe-4, than Mike did.[26] Sakharov himself was rewarded handsomely by the Soviet government for his achievement. Even before the test at Semipalatinsk, he had applied for corresponding, or nonvoting, membership in the Soviet Academy of Sciences, for which he did not have to hold the degree of Doctor of Science. But because the government envisioned making him a voting member of the academy, an honor that required the degree, it deemed earlier works he had written the equivalent of a doctoral dissertation, and the degree of Doctor of Physical and Mathematical Sciences was conferred on Sakharov on June 8, 1953.[27] On October 23 of that year, Sakharov, at the unusually young age of thirty-two, was unanimously elected a full voting member of the academy. He was elected without having been a corresponding member, as Tamm was for twenty years before being elected a full member.[28]

With his election to the Academy of Sciences, Sakharov reached the pinnacle of the Soviet scientific establishment and of the entire Soviet educated elite. Full membership in the academy and the title of academician it conferred endowed him with even greater prestige than that enjoyed by persons in comparable positions in other professions.[29] The significance of Sakharov's accomplishment was not lost on the Soviet government or his colleagues. In recommending Sakharov for full membership in the academy, Kurchatov, Khariton, and Zeldovich described their colleague as follows:

> Andrei Dmitrievich Sakharov is unusually gifted as a theoretical physicist and at the same time an outstanding inventor....For six years A. D. Sakharov achieved the most significant results, putting him in first place in the Soviet Union and in the entire world in a critical area of physics....Beginning work in this area in 1948, A. D. Sakharov proposed entirely new ways of solving important problems. What he did required courage and a profundity of vision....In the years that followed, there was intensive work on realizing what Sakharov proposed, which led to brilliant success in 1953. Many academicians and corresponding members of the Academy of Sciences contributed to this. However, in this collective endeavor, Sakharov was always the leader, coordinating the various subgroups so that their work would be directed toward their common goal.[30]

In recognition of his accomplishment, the government awarded Sakharov the Stalin Prize, for which he received a half-million rubles; the title of Hero of

26. Patrick Glynn, *Closing Pandora's Box: Arms Races, Arms Control, and the History of the Cold War* (New York, 1992), 134.

27. Smirnov, "Etot chelovek," 598; Sakharov, *Memoirs*, 179; Perelman, "Vstrechi, besedy," 511–12.

28. Smirnov, "Etot chelovek," 597; Peter Dornan, "Andrei Sakharov: The Conscience of a Liberal Scientist," in *Dissent in the USSR: Politics, Ideology and People,* ed. Rudolf L. Tökés (Baltimore, 1975), 358. According to Smirnov, Tamm opposed Sakharov's skipping the stage of corresponding member because he believed Sakharov's election as a full member might preclude his returning to FIAN and realizing his full potential as a physicist. Smirnov, "Etot chelovek," 596.

29. Graham, *Science in Russia and the Soviet Union,* 183.

30. Quoted in Ioirysh, *Uroki A. D. Sakharova,* 22–23.

Socialist Labor; and a dacha in the elite Moscow suburb of Zhukova.[31] Malenkov, among others, singled him out for special praise, and at a meeting of the Presidium of the Supreme Soviet in February 1954, at which Sakharov formally received these various honoraria, Voroshilov, on behalf of the Presidium, praised Sakharov lavishly and then, in Russian fashion, kissed him.[32] Many years later, Nikita Khrushchev wrote simply that building the Soviet hydrogen bomb was "a great act of patriotism by Comrade Sakharov."[33]

Naturally the Soviet leadership hoped and expected that Sakharov would refine the Layer Cake so it could be incorporated into an actual warhead. In November 1953, on the basis of a report Sakharov had written describing how the Layer Cake device could be made deliverable, the Presidium ordered the Ministry of Medium Machine Building, which oversaw all the Soviet Union's nuclear and thermonuclear programs, to develop an intercontinental ballistic missile (the R-7 ICBM) that could carry this device once it was modified.[34] Over the next two months, however, Sakharov realized that his earlier expectation that he could increase the explosive yield of the Layer Cake was unrealistic, and he wanted the whole configuration abandoned in favor of something more powerful. Accordingly, in January 1954 Sakharov and Zeldovich proposed to Khariton what came to be known as the Third Idea: a two-stage device in which the nuclear and thermonuclear fuels were separated from each other and in which the radiation created in the initial fission reaction would trigger the subsequent fusion reaction.[35] What Sakharov and Zeldovich envisioned, in other words, was a Soviet Teller-Ulam but without the corrective the American physicists had conjured of some kind of damper that could minimize the destructive effect of the shock waves produced concurrently with radiation in the fission reaction.[36]

The paternity of the Third Idea is unclear. Apparently Sakharov and Zeldovich came to roughly the same conclusions simultaneously,[37] and neither Sakharov's memoirs nor any other account of the period indicates how much, or even whether, their work was enhanced by conversations they had with each other. But whatever its origins, Khariton and Kurchatov considered the Third Idea worth pursuing, and Kurchatov authorized the development of a device based on it. This, however, infuriated Malyshev, who considered what Sakharov,

---

31. Perhaps to prevent Sakharov from wanting to leave Arzamas permanently, the government did not inform him about the dacha for some time. Sakharov, *Memoirs*, 181.

32. Ibid., 174–75, 181. Even before the bomb Sakharov designed exploded to the Soviets' satisfaction, the government showed how valuable he was by insisting he be driven to Semipalatinsk, since at the time it was considered too dangerous to fly there. Ibid., 170.

33. Nikita Sergeevich Khrushchev, *Khrushchev Remembers: The Last Testament* (Boston, 1974), 68.

34. Sakharov, *Memoirs*, 180–81. Sakharov attended one of the meetings of the Presidium at which the matter was discussed, and only Molotov asked him questions. Still, what struck him most about the occasion was not only Molotov's unnaturally pallid complexion but the former foreign minister's extreme reluctance to say anything controversial. Kaganovich, he noted, said nothing at all. Ibid., 180.

35. Zaloga, *Target America*, 103; Goncharov, "Race Accelerates," 61.

36. Zaloga, *Target America*, 103.

37. Sakharov, *Memoirs*, 182.

Zeldovich, and Kurchatov had done rank insubordination, a violation of what the Presidium had ordered—namely, the further development of Sakharov's Layer Cake so that it could be mounted on the R-7 ICBM being developed concurrently. At a special meeting at Arzamas—for which Malyshev flew in from Moscow to ensure that the Presidium's orders were obeyed—Kurchatov and Khariton stood their ground, arguing that the new configuration Sakharov and Zeldovich were working on was worth pursuing. For his defiance, Kurchatov received a formal reprimand, which was rescinded a year later after the successful explosion of a bomb based on Sakharov's and Zeldovich's new idea.[38] In any other profession or in any other circumstance involving physicists, the Soviet authorities, confronted with comparable opposition, would have crushed it. But because these particular physicists and their administrative superiors were for all intents and purposes indispensable, their wishes, within the limits of their professional competence, had to be accommodated.

The standoff over the Third Idea ended in compromise. In early 1955, Avraamii Zaveniagin, who had replaced Malyshev after Malenkov, Malyshev's patron, was removed from power, ordered that the physicists at Arzamas continue perfecting the new configuration Sakharov and Zeldovich had proposed the year before, while an entirely new facility (code-named Cheliabinsk-70) would be built in Synezhinsk for the purpose of perfecting the Layer Cake device that had been tested in 1953. A refined version of the latter device was detonated at Semipalatinsk on November 6, 1955, in the form of a bomb that was dropped from an airplane—the first time a thermonuclear weapon had ever been detonated in this fashion.[39] The device Sakharov and his colleagues developed on the basis of the Third Idea was tested successfully sixteen days later, on November 22, 1955, also in the form of a bomb dropped from an airplane and also over the test site in Semipalatinsk. This device, unlike all those the Soviets and the Americans had tested previously, was a genuine hydrogen bomb and usable militarily as well. Based on the same general principles Teller and Ulam had first articulated in 1951, and using lithium deuteride as its thermonuclear fuel, its explosive power was approximately three hundred times that of the atomic bomb dropped over Hiroshima.[40] Ironically, Sakharov had been honored by the Soviet government for developing a Soviet hydrogen bomb two years before he actually developed one. Oblivious to the incongruity, in October 1956 the Council of Ministers honored the Soviet physicist for this, his second great success, by awarding him the Lenin Prize (the Stalin Prize renamed after de-Stalinization) and naming him a Hero of Socialist Labor once again.[41]

38. Ibid., 183; Zaloga, *Target America*, 104.

39. Zaloga, *Target America*, 104–5; Lourie, *Sakharov*, 173. The United States would not detonate a thermonuclear weapon by dropping it from an airplane until 1956. Goncharov, "Race Accelerates," 60.

40. Thorne, *Black Holes and Time Warps*, 232.

41. Sakharov, *Memoirs*, 195.

Some physicists have denigrated Sakharov's successes in 1953 and 1955, perhaps without meaning to, by arguing that without the information Sakharov gleaned from the radioactive fallout previous American thermonuclear tests had generated, the thermonuclear devices he developed might not have detonated successfully.[42] In his memoirs Sakharov admits that after the Mike test, he and one of the administrative heads at Arzamas collected snow and brought it back to analyze for any fallout it might contain. To Sakharov's great regret, however, the chemist who was supposed to analyze the snow absentmindedly discarded it—which still leaves open the possibility that the physicists at Arzamas got information about fallout from Mike in other ways, including espionage.[43] But Khariton, Smirnov, and A. I. Pavlovskii all maintain that in November 1952, when Mike was tested, Soviet scientists lacked sufficient knowledge of radiochemistry to glean useful information from any fallout they might have accumulated.[44] Indeed, Hans Bethe, after speculating in 1987 that Soviet scientists could have learned a great deal from analyzing radioactive fallout, three years later changed his mind and admitted that Sakharov "probably developed [the Third Idea] independently."[45]

Not everything Sakharov did at Arzamas resulted in thermonuclear weapons. Perhaps in response to charges in the 1970s that his work on thermonuclear weapons made him a warmonger, Sakharov made a point of mentioning, in his introduction to *Sakharov Speaks* in 1973, that his work had peaceful applications as well. Foremost among these was the "tokamak," a doughnut-shaped chamber with a magnetized wire wrapped around it that was a possible model for a thermonuclear reactor generating power for peaceful purposes.[46] It will be recalled that thermonuclear energy—energy released through the fusion of hydrogen or hydrogen isotopes—requires extraordinarily high temperatures, in the range of ten million to one hundred million degrees. Such temperatures exceed any reached naturally on earth, and they are easily high enough to vaporize any reactor in which thermonuclear fusion would occur.[47] In a hydrogen bomb, these temperatures are generated by nuclear fission; the thermonuclear fusion triggered by this fission destroys and is meant to destroy (though not too quickly) the casing in which these reactions occur. In a thermonuclear reactor, however, the plasma—the positively charged nuclei and negatively charged electrons of which the original thermonuclear fuel consisted before being heated—must somehow be confined or contained so that the walls of the reactor itself are not vaporized.[48] In 1950 Sakharov, working with Tamm, tried to devise a

42. See, for example, York, *Advisors*, 100.

43. Zaloga, *Target America*, 102; Sakharov, *Memoirs*, 158.

44. Rhodes, *Dark Sun*, 516; Holloway, "Soviet Scientists Speak Out," 19.

45. Hans Bethe in 1987 cited in Daniel Hirsch and William G. Mathews, "The H-Bomb: Who Really Gave Away the Secret?" *Bulletin of the Atomic Scientists* 46, no. 1 (January–February 1990): 28; Hans Bethe, "Sakharov's H-bomb," *Bulletin of the Atomic Scientists*, 46, no. 8 (October 1990): 9.

46. Gorelik, "Metamorphosis of Andrei Sakharov," 99; Sakharov, introduction to *Sakharov Speaks*, 30–31. "Tokamak" is the Russian acronym for "Toroidal Chamber with Magnetic Coil."

47. Michio Kaku, *Visions: How Science Will Revolutionize the 21st Century* (New York, 1998), 279.

48. Boris Altshuler, "Controlled Thermonuclear Reactions and Magnetoplosive Generators," in *On Sakharov*, ed. Alexander Babyonyshev (New York, 1982), 153–54.

structure that would do this. Serendipitously they learned of an idea a Soviet sailor had suggested in a letter to Beria, which was transmitted to Sakharov and Tamm: that the plasma might be confined electrostatically by creating electro-static "grids" (or fields) around it.[49] Sakharov and Tamm found the idea of confining the plasma attractive. They realized, however, that the positive charge of the nuclei in the plasma would be nullified by the negative charge of the electrons that had been stripped from them and that therefore any electric field that could be created around the plasma would fail to contain it. As an alternative, Sakharov and Tamm suggested that the plasma could be confined magnetically: because a magnetic field near the plasma would cause the motion of the plasma particles to curve, a magnetic field, if it were positioned properly, could prevent the plasma from touching and thus destroying the internal walls of the reactor.[50] Sakharov and Tamm then designed a structure in which this magnetic containment, as it was called, could occur. In 1952 other Soviet scientists confirmed their calculations, and fusion reactors based on the structure Sakharov and Tamm pioneered have been used subsequently around the world to generate thermonuclear power. Some of these are capable of generating significantly more power than the typical nuclear reactor can generate and in a much shorter time.[51]

## The Ethical Aspect

What role did building thermonuclear weapons play in Sakharov's intellectual development and in particular in his eventual emergence as a dissident? Did he become a dissident, as the KGB believed, to expiate the guilt that building such destructive weapons produced?[52]

In fact, Sakharov built thermonuclear weapons for several reasons, and he reaffirmed them in the years that followed. One reason he gave was that the physics thermonuclear weapons required for their construction was so engrossing that building the hydrogen bomb was an intellectual challenge. In 1988 he said that the work he completed was a way of proving, more to himself than to others, what he was capable of as a physicist.[53] The physics required to build these weapons was, in Fermi's phrase, "superb physics," a physics with the potential to reveal important truths about the lives of the sun and the stars and about the origins, sustenance, and ultimate future of life itself—in short a physics with which a young, imaginative, and energetic scientist like Sakharov could easily be infatuated.[54] In response to a question once posed to him about the applications of the bombs he helped develop, Sakharov said that at the time

49. Paul R. Josephson, *Red Atom: Russia's Nuclear Power Program from Stalin to Today* (New York, 1999), 167. The sailor's name was Oleg Lavrentiev. Sakharov, *Memoirs*, 139.

50. Josephson, *Red Atom*, 171–72; Altshuler, "Controlled Thermonuclear Reactions," 154; Roald Z. Sagdeev, *The Making of a Soviet Scientist* (New York, 1994), 35.

51. Sakharov, *Memoirs*, 139–44; Harold P. Furth, "Controlled Fusion Research," in A. D. Sakharov, *Collected Scientific Works* (New York, 1982), 53; Kaku, *Visions*, 279.

52. "Andropov to Brezhnev (January 18, 1971)," in Rubenstein and Gribanov, *KGB File*, 115.

53. Andrei Sakharov, "I Tried to Be on the Level of My Destiny," *Molodezh Estonii*, October 11, 1988, reprinted in *The Glasnost Reader*, ed. Jonathan Eisen (New York, 1990), 332.

54. Sakharov, *Memoirs*, 96.

he did not really think about that issue; all that concerned him was that "everything we had invented would in fact work."[55] Indeed, the genuine exhilaration he experienced at Arzamas seemed to neutralize temporarily—though not to eliminate permanently—the doubts about the Soviet system that were germinating in his mind.

Paradoxically, the very repression Sakharov saw in microcosm at Arzamas served to justify the larger enterprise of defending his country. Building thermonuclear weapons was not just an intellectual exercise but an act of patriotism far more consequential than his contributions to munitions in World War II. In his memoirs Sakharov states revealingly that "although I hadn't fought in [World War II], I regarded myself as a soldier in this new scientific war."[56] In the next paragraph, Sakharov includes the following explanation: "The monstrous destructive force, the scale of our enterprise and the price paid for it by our poor, hungry, war-torn country, the casualties resulting from the neglect of safety standards and the use of forced labor in our mining and manufacturing activities, all these things inflamed our sense of drama and inspired us to make a maximum effort so that the sacrifices—which we accepted as inevitable—would not be in vain. We were possessed by a true war psychology, which became still more overpowering after our transfer to the Installation."[57] For all his misgivings about the Soviet Union, Sakharov believed the Cold War, of which the arms race with the United States was a prime component, was worth fighting. For this reason it seems fair to conclude that working on peaceful uses of thermonuclear power like the tokamak was not a psychological necessity, an activity expiating the guilt induced by devising weapons that could kill large numbers of people. Rather, he worked on both of these applications of nuclear power because he considered both of them intrinsically useful, morally justified, and scientifically interesting.

Undoubtedly the most powerful argument Sakharov offered in defense of his building the Soviet hydrogen bomb was that by helping the Soviet Union achieve nuclear parity with the United States, he was making international peace and stability, and therefore the very survival of humanity, more likely. As he stated in a 1988 interview, "At the time we all were convinced that the creation from scratch of an atomic bomb (I did not participate in this) and then of a thermonuclear one was essential to the creation of a global equality in which our country could develop in peace and tranquility, without feeling itself under threat by the [nuclear] superiority of the other side [the USA]."[58] Throughout the time Sakharov worked on thermonuclear weapons, he believed that building them was the right thing to do because it was necessary, and on this particular point he never changed his mind.

---

55. Iaglom, "Drug blizkii," 789. In a 1990 interview Khariton confirmed Sakharov's recollection that his scientific work absorbed him totally at Arzamas and that he had no doubt it was morally justified. Reprinted as "Radi iadernogo pariteta," in Altshuler et al., *On mezhdu nami zhil*, 726.

56. Sakharov, *Memoirs*, 97.

57. Ibid. See also Sakharov's comments in November 1988, cited in Sidney D. Drell, "Andrei Sakharov and the Nuclear Danger," *Physics Today*, 53, no. 5 (May 2000): 41.

58. Sakharov and Adamovich, "Zhit' na zemle i zhit' dolgo," 168. See also Moroz, "Vozvrashchenie iz ssylki," 321.

From the earliest days at FIAN when he began working on thermonuclear weapons, Sakharov understood the paradoxical logic of deterrence. He recognized that all countries, not just the Soviet Union, benefited if both superpowers had nuclear and thermonuclear weapons. He knew that the nuclear monopoly the United States enjoyed until 1949 had failed to deter Stalin from acting provocatively in foreign policy, as he did by blockading West Berlin in 1948; what made the blockade dangerous was that, because American conventional forces in Europe after the end of World War II were no match for Soviet ones, it could conceivably have provoked an American response in the form of a nuclear strike. Thus, it would be in the interest both of the Soviet Union and of international peace and stability if the Soviet Union built nuclear and thermonuclear weapons in sufficient numbers to deter the United States from ever launching a nuclear or thermonuclear attack. As Sakharov recognized, deterrence is fundamentally a psychological construct requiring what John Lewis Gaddis calls "the deliberate cultivation of mutual vulnerability," an awareness that the nuclear retaliation a nuclear strike provokes renders nugatory whatever benefits such a strike might bring.[59] This in turn assumes that the political actors that are a party to it want to live: that they are rational enough to be concerned for their own survival. Furthermore, the threat to use nuclear weapons in response to a nuclear strike—what theorists of deterrence call a "second strike capability"—must be credible in terms of both intentions and capabilities: the parties to deterrence must possess nuclear weapons in numbers sufficient for some of them to survive a nuclear attack, and they must also make clear their intention of using these surviving weapons in the event of an actual attack. If these conditions obtain, deterrence is a guarantee, if not an absolute guarantee, of nuclear peace.

Once Sakharov had worked through the conceptual logic of this, he made the rational calculation that peace was more likely if the Soviet Union had nuclear and thermonuclear weapons than if it did not. As a result, there was no reason to feel guilty for helping his country acquire them. By the logic of deterrence, the only circumstance in which guilt would have been appropriate would have been if Sakharov had developed such weapons for the Soviet Union when the United States did not already have them. Stalin and Khrushchev, in possession of a nuclear monopoly, might well have launched a nuclear strike. Fortunately, they never had such a monopoly, and Sakharov could construct a hydrogen bomb with a clear conscience. He could view its successful detonation in 1955 as a personal triumph, as an affirmation of the prowess and the potentialities of science, and even as a vindication of the Soviet Union itself. As long as the weapons he developed were used to deter rather than to wage a nuclear war, he felt morally justified in building them. Sakharov explained his reasoning in 1988:

> I was recruited to do secret work in 1948, to work on the creation of a thermonuclear weapon.... This weapon was even more terrible than the one which was

59. Gaddis, *We Now Know*, 292.

used on Hiroshima and Nagasaki....So, we (and here I must speak not only in my behalf, for in such cases moral principles are formulated as though collectively-psychologically) believed that our work was absolutely necessary as a means of achieving a balance in the world. Lack of balance is very dangerous: The side which feels itself to be stronger could be encouraged to make the fastest possible use of its own temporary advantage, while the weaker side may be pushed into taking adventuristic, desperate steps to gain time while the advantage enjoyed by the opponent is not too great. I still think so. In the final account, the work which we did was justified, as was the work which was done by our colleagues on the opposite side.[60]

Unlike Robert Oppenheimer, who proclaimed after Hiroshima that he had "blood on his hands" and that the physicists who worked with him on the American atomic bomb "knew sin," Sakharov was not normally given to self-critical introspection once he made a decision he believed was grounded in reason.[61] As he insisted whenever anyone mentioned it, Sakharov never experienced an "Oppenheimer syndrome"; any doubts he experienced he quieted "by knowing that we lessened the chances of a war."[62] If, as Sakharov readily acknowledged, the construction of weapons of mass destruction was a tragedy, it was mostly a tragedy of circumstance for which no single individual was morally culpable—rather than one resulting from some human imperfection or failing for which the expiation of guilt was appropriate: "I and everyone else who worked with me [on thermonuclear weapons] were completely convinced of the vital necessity of our work, of its unique importance....What we did was actually a great tragedy, which reflected the tragic nature of the entire world situation, where in order to preserve the peace, it was necessary to make such terrible and horrible things."[63]

In the 1980s, however, Sakharov expressed the view that deterrence of the type that kept the peace through most of the Cold War had outlived its usefulness

60. Sakharov, "I Tried to Be on the Level of My Destiny," 330–31. Adamskii, Kurchatov, and Altshuler shared Sakharov's belief that deterrence justified the construction of these weapons. Adamskii, "Stanovlenie grazhdanina," 28; Holloway, *Stalin and the Bomb,* 206; Altshuler, "Kak my delali bombu," 13.

61. David Berlinski, "Where Physics and Politics Meet: The Extraordinary Life of Edward Teller," *Weekly Standard,* November 26, 2001, 36; Robert Oppenheimer, "Physics in the Contemporary World," *Bulletin of the Atomic Scientists* 4, no. 3 (March 1948): 66. Sakharov's career bears some resemblance to Oppenheimer's in that both men lost their security clearance and thus the opportunity to continue their work on nuclear weapons. But in personality Sakharov was very different from Oppenheimer—less tortured by doubts, less inclined to vacillate, more ready to live with decisions he made. Although they disagreed on a wide range of issues including radioactive fallout and space-based missile defense, Sakharov more closely resembled Oppenheimer's rival, Edward Teller, who like Sakharov had to endure the obloquy of fellow scientists who objected strongly to his views.

62. A. M. Adamovich, "Kliuchevoe slovo—Konvergentsiia," in Ivanova, *Andrei Dmitrievich,* 71; Sakharov and Adamovich, "Zhit' na zemle i zhit' dolgo," 168.

63. Quoted in Smirnov, "Etot chelovek," 593. Elena Bonner, it is true, once stated in an interview that Sakharov's conscience "began to torture him when he was involved in atomic bomb work." But Bonner went on in the same interview to say that Sakharov did not allow his conscience "to weigh him down" or "to threaten him." Klose, *Russia and the Russians,* 196.

because the assumptions on which it was based were no longer valid.[64] At some point—he never said precisely when—deterrence had become dysfunctional: nuclear weapons were more likely rather than less likely to cause wars. According to Sakharov, the very success of deterrence in keeping the peace was its ultimate undoing: political leaders who preside over enormous arsenals of nuclear weapons come to think, understandably, that these weapons, because of their deterrent effect, are the only kinds of weapons their countries need.[65] As a result, countries with nuclear weapons but inadequate conventional forces will have no choice but to use their nuclear weapons in wars against countries that have no nuclear weapons but superior conventional forces. Indeed, on the assumption implicit in deterrence that countries with nuclear weapons will never use them, countries without them might be emboldened to attack countries that possessed them because of the asymmetry in conventional forces that deterrence produced. Ironically, while deterrence prevented wars between nuclear powers, over the long run it increased the likelihood of wars between nuclear and non-nuclear powers.[66] The implication of this position is that while physicists like Sakharov were justified in building thermonuclear weapons in the early 1950s, they would not be justified in improving such weapons or developing new and even more powerful ones in the 1980s.

This is not to say that when Sakharov built thermonuclear weapons, he was not disturbed by them or that he was indifferent to the harm that could result even if they were used only to test how they worked. The necessity to test meant that even in peacetime radioactive fallout would increase. In the summer of 1953, prior to the Joe-4 test, Sakharov and some of his colleagues calculated the fallout the test would generate, and over Malyshev's and the military's objections, they succeeded in convincing the government to evacuate the villages they believed would be most intensely irradiated.[67] Still, Sakharov was appalled when the deputy to Defense Minister Zhukov to whom he had brought the estimates of radioactive fallout responded cavalierly that even ordinary army maneuvers often cause casualties, and that since the upcoming test was far more vital to national security, it hardly mattered that people would die as a result of it. It was encounters like this that caused Sakharov, in his own words, to become more aware of "the human and moral dimensions" of the scientific work he was doing.[68]

Two years later, after the successful test in November 1955, Sakharov experienced a similar unease, which was heightened when he learned that a soldier had died during the explosion when a trench that was protecting his platoon collapsed on him. He was even more distraught by the death of a two-year-old

64. See, for example, Moroz, "Vozvrashchenie iz ssylki," 328.
65. Sakharov might also have noted—though he did not—that nuclear weapons, compared with conventional ones, are inexpensive.
66. Sakharov and Adamovich, "Zhit' na zemle i zhit' dolgo," 168. See also "Stepen' svobody: Actual'noe interv'iu," *Ogonëk* 31, July 1989, 28.
67. Zaloga, *Target America*, 100.
68. Sakharov, *Memoirs*, 172, 179.

girl who had been left alone by her parents in a bomb shelter that collapsed from the shock waves produced in the explosion.[69] In his memoirs Sakharov is candid about the ambivalence these incidents created: "We were stirred up, but not just with the exhilaration that comes with a job well done. For my part, I experienced a range of contradictory sentiments, perhaps chief among them a fear that this newly released force could slip out of control and lead to unimaginable disasters. The accident reports, and especially the deaths of the little girl and the soldier, heightened my sense of foreboding. I did not hold myself personally responsible for their deaths, but I could not escape a feeling of complicity."[70]

Consistent with this attitude is the answer Sakharov gave in an interview in 1988 to a question about the psychological effect these two tests had on him:

> The impressions from the tests were of a dual nature. On the one hand, let me repeat, there was a sensation of the tremendous scope of the project. On the other, when you see all of this yourself, something in you changes. When you see the burned birds who are writhing on the scorched steppe, when you see how the shock wave blows away buildings like a house of cards, when you feel the reek of splintered bricks, when you sense melted glass, you immediately think of times of war.... All of this triggers an irrational and yet very strong emotional impact. How not to start thinking of one's responsibility at this point?[71]

Sakharov did not draw from either of these tests the conclusion that what he had done to make them possible was wrong. But the obvious fact that these tests were not cost-free, that they took the lives of people whose right to life was just as valid as anyone else's, touched him profoundly and helped to foster the idea he would champion as a dissident that the moral calculus one applies to intellectual and political abstractions must take into account the injury these abstractions may cause the individuals most directly affected by them. The harm human beings may suffer in the application of these abstractions cannot be written off as trivial.

Finally, Sakharov was deeply disturbed and shaken by the jocularity shown by Marshal Mitrofan Nedelin, the military director of the 1955 test, at the banquet he hosted that very same evening to celebrate its success. After Sakharov, at Nedelin's request, made the first toast, which he turned into a sober admonition that future tests be carried out far from inhabited areas, Nedelin expressed his contempt for this concern and for the solemnity Sakharov thought the occasion required by telling an off-color joke. Sakharov drew from the entire episode the following conclusion:

> We, the inventors, scientists, engineers, and craftsmen, had created a terrible weapon, the most terrible weapon in human history; but its use would lie entirely outside our control. The people at the top of the Party and military hierarchy

69. Ibid., 192.
70. Ibid., 193–94.
71. Sakharov, "I Tried to Be On the Level of My Destiny," 333.

would make the decisions. Of course, I knew this already—I wasn't *that* naïve. But understanding something in an abstract way is different from feeling it with your whole being, like the reality of life and death. The ideas and emotions kindled at that moment have not diminished to this day, and they completely altered my thinking.[72]

So shaken was Sakharov by what Nedelin said and how he behaved that he came to consider this incident "one of those shocks that made me a dissident."[73]

In sum, what Sakharov witnessed at Semipalatinsk in 1953 and 1955 forced him to acknowledge that the scientific work he was doing had relevance beyond the small and seemingly self-contained world of science he inhabited. In the course of recognizing the social consequences of science, Sakharov realized the importance of social and political issues in their own right. As he stated, "[W]hile working on nuclear weapons, in particular a thermonuclear one, I came to feel more responsible for broader societal problems, especially humanitarian ones."[74] In the next few years Sakharov came to understand the integral relationship between science and society. Consequently, he began trying to foster in other scientists the view that science should be a liberating force morally as well as technologically and that it should benefit not just the abstract interests of governments but the human beings these governments exist to serve.

In the course of Sakharov's exploration of this dynamic, which took up approximately the next ten years of his life, the range of his concerns widened, his intellectual self-confidence in matters outside physics increased, and his doubts about the Soviet Union deepened. Although he did not yet realize it, in 1955 he was already on the way to becoming a dissident.

72. Sakharov, *Memoirs*, 194–95.
73. Moroz, "Vozvrashchenie iz ssylki," 323. In 1960 Nedelin was among those burned to death because he was seated close to an ICBM that exploded prior to a launch he was observing. See chapter 4, note 15.
74. Andrei Sakharov, "V narode vsegda sokhraniaiutsia nravstvennye sily," *Knizhnoe obozrenie*, April 7, 1989, 7.

# PART III

# A Scientist with a Social Conscience: 1956–1968

# 6 Radioactive Fallout and Other Matters of Conscience

By the late 1950s Sakharov was sufficiently appalled by what he had seen of the Soviet ruling elite that on one occasion, in the winter of 1958, he described the top leaders of the Soviet Union, whom he had recently observed in meetings he attended in the Kremlin, as "monsters."[1] In time these same leaders would think similarly of Sakharov.

Obviously descriptions such as this reflected Sakharov's growing disillusionment not only with the personal qualities of the individuals who ruled the Soviet Union but with impersonal and institutional aspects of Soviet society and government as well. But it was by no means inevitable that Sakharov should have become a dissident as a result of it. He could easily have ignored his own observations of these things and instead of opposing the Soviet regime have spent the rest of his life as a pampered scion of the scientific establishment, basking in well-deserved acclaim for his achievements designing thermonuclear weaponry for his country. It would not have been dishonorable for him to do so. As a husband and father, Sakharov had responsibilities he could carry out most effectively by stifling his inclination to think independently, an attribute the Soviet leadership thought he should confine entirely to matters scientific. Sakharov, by all accounts, had great potential as a physicist, which Tamm in particular believed he had a responsibility to fulfill. But Sakharov's growing willingness to trust his moral intuition and use his training as a scientist in assessing rationally how he might rectify the wrongs he observed had the effect of propelling him in a different direction. He began examining carefully social and political issues that, in the end, would cause him to repudiate the very system on which he depended for his livelihood and professional identity. It is easy, with the benefit of hindsight, to see where Sakharov was headed. The dissidence he first espoused in the late 1960s was consistent with the moral sensitivity he displayed on several occasions earlier in his life. But as he concerned himself with issues that, like concentric circles, drew him farther and farther away from the familiar territory of physics, the transition from scientist to dissident could not have been easy. In the decade before he emerged as a dissident, Sakharov was still developing the critical intelligence needed to make sense of the larger political and social issues to which he was increasingly drawn. That he could not have known where his own insights were leading him makes the journey he began in the late 1950s truly an act of personal and intellectual courage.

Before 1956 the disobedience Sakharov occasionally displayed was limited to protecting people he knew personally. After that year, however, he was concerned

---

1. Adamskii, "Stanovlenie grazhdanina," 41.

increasingly with the fate of individuals unknown to him, people who were victims, in one form or another, of government policies he regarded as unwise, irrational, and morally suspect. At the same time, his protests had limits that he was unable or unwilling to exceed. Although Sakharov was confident enough in the late 1950s and early 1960s to voice objections to government policies related to scientific matters such as genetics and radioactive fallout, when he began expressing himself publicly on political issues in the mid-1960s, he did so mostly through letters of protest whose collective authorship afforded him a measure of protection. It was not until 1968 that he had the self-confidence to express himself individually on matters of broad public significance. Sakharov did not become a Soviet dissident overnight. This role was not the result of any spiritual epiphany or psychological crisis. Rather, it was the product of a slow accretion of intensely personal experiences and observations, which generated larger conclusions about Soviet society that he believed were grounded in both morality and reason. In this process Sakharov combined the moral stringency of the intelligentsia with the careful evaluation of evidence characteristic of the scientist. In retrospect, it is readily apparent in Sakharov's evolving ethic of social responsibility how very neatly each step in his political and intellectual evolution followed logically one from the other, and how they reflected a transformation in Sakharov's thinking in which the roles of scientist and *intelligent* were fused. In becoming a dissident, he harnessed the rational pursuit of truth to an ethical obligation to improve the world.

## Radioactive Fallout and Other Matters

The first issue Sakharov addressed in the mid-1950s with implications for social policy concerned the radioactive fallout from the nuclear tests at Semipalatinsk. This in turn caused him to question the kinds of nuclear weapons the Soviet government made and how it intended to use them. To be sure, Sakharov continued to believe that the government had the right to make these weapons and, given the circumstances of the Cold War, was acting rationally and reasonably in doing so. But he was troubled by the toll these weapons exacted in the diseases and genetic damage they caused when detonated atmospherically. Indeed, his concerns about radioactive fallout were the first that caused him to reevaluate the life he had imagined for himself years earlier under the influence of his father and Tamm and to consider the possibility that his life might be better spent combining science with the pursuit of social justice.

It is hardly surprising that Sakharov's concerns about radioactive fallout were prompted by his role in developing the weapons responsible for producing it. Some of the reading he did independently of his work on thermonuclear weaponry also alerted him to the genetic damage fallout causes. From an article by George Gamow in *Scientific American*—which Sakharov had access to at Arzamas—he learned of Watson and Crick's decoding of DNA and thus the role DNA plays in heredity.[2] He also read drafts of articles by Ovsei Leipunskii

2. Sakharov, *Memoirs*, 197–98.

specifying the radioactive isotopes of strontium, cesium, tritium, and carbon produced in the explosion of nuclear and thermonuclear weapons.[3] In addition, even though he does not mention it in his memoirs, Sakharov might have been aware of the Kyshtyn disaster in 1957, in which radioactive waste that had been stored carelessly at a nuclear weapons installation in the Urals heated up and exploded, spewing radioactive material into the atmosphere that wind carried to other parts of the Soviet Union, infecting untold numbers of people as it traveled.[4] Finally, his growing interest in the whole subject of radioactive fallout was given impetus and a degree of legitimacy by the fact that other Soviet scientists were concerned enough to establish radiological sections in existing scientific installations to examine its potential dangers and even to cause entire laboratories to be built in the Soviet Union to study the problem and alert the Soviet government of these dangers.[5]

But Sakharov did not merely decry the ill effects of radioactive fallout. He also calculated it. In an article he wrote in 1957 that, at Kurchatov's request and with Khrushchev's permission, appeared not only in the Soviet Union but in translations the Soviet government distributed from its embassies in other countries, he determined the amount of radiation all nuclear and thermonuclear tests had generated up to that time.[6] Evidently Kurchatov told Khrushchev to expect from Sakharov an article demonstrating that the "clean" hydrogen bomb the Soviets thought the United States was developing—a bomb containing no "dirty" fissionable material that would kill people only from the shock waves its detonation generated—was a fraud. The reason the Americans were supposedly developing such a bomb was partly political: by building clean bombs, they could excoriate the Soviets for building dirty ones, which harmed people not only from shock waves but from fallout as well. When he requested the article, Kurchatov presumed that Sakharov would expose and condemn what Kurchatov thought the United States was doing; the reputation for scientific excellence Sakharov would bring to this endeavor would surely enhance the credibility of his conclusions. But without actually advocating that the Soviet government do anything differently, Sakharov composed instead what was essentially a brief for not testing any nuclear weapons in the atmosphere at all. Instead they should be tested under ground, where radioactive leakage would be minimal. The closest he came to suggesting what the Soviet government should do was to mention in passing that a comprehensive test ban treaty would save lives. But he did not explicitly advocate such a treaty or call upon the Soviet Union to negotiate one with the other nuclear powers in the world.[7]

3. Josephson, *Red Atom*, 325.
4. Klose, *Russia and the Russians*, 147–50.
5. Valery Soifer, "Andrei Sakharov and the Fate of Biological Science in the USSR," in Babyonyshev, *On Sakharov*, 174.
6. Sakharov, *Memoirs*, 200–204. The English translation of Sakharov's article is "Radioactive Carbon in Nuclear Explosions and Nonthreshold Biological Effects" and can be found in *Soviet Scientists on the Danger of Nuclear Tests*, ed. A. V. Lebedinsky (Moscow: Foreign Languages Publishing House, 1960), 39–49.
7. Sakharov, "Radioactive Carbon," 49. This may be why Khrushchev did not rescind permission for publication.

In his article Sakharov stressed that there is really no such thing as a clean hydrogen bomb: all hydrogen bombs, even those in which nuclear fusion is not triggered by nuclear fission, emit neutrons, which are then captured by the nitrogen in the atmosphere in predictable and ascertainable amounts, resulting eventually in the formation of carbon-14, a radioactive isotope that is absorbed into human tissue. As it decays, it produces genetic damage, also in quantifiable and therefore predictable amounts. Strontium-90 and cesium-137 are among the other radioactive isotopes that are generated in the detonation of thermonuclear weapons in the atmosphere, and according to Sakharov, they have similarly lethal effects.[8] Sakharov knew from work others had done earlier on the epidemiology of illnesses caused by radiation—cancers and leukemias, immunological disorders, and various heritable diseases caused by the gene mutations radiation produces—that the probability of falling victim to these illnesses is a function purely of the degree, or dose, of radiation. Using data drawn from actuarial statistics on X-ray technicians and radiologists, he determined the rate per roentgen of the probability, and thus the incidence, of genetic damage caused by radioactive fallout from the decay of the aforementioned radioactive isotopes. Because he also knew how many roentgens of radiation are released per megaton in nuclear and thermonuclear explosions, Sakharov could calculate the damage caused by any atmospheric nuclear test: for every megaton of explosive power a nuclear or thermonuclear detonation generates, approximately ten thousand persons suffer damage of one sort or another as a result of it. Because in 1957, when Sakharov wrote the article, there had been exactly fifty such explosions of varying but ascertainable megatonnage, Sakharov was able to deduce that some five hundred thousand people in all parts of the world had been harmed by them.[9]

In the same article, Sakharov pointed out that because radioactive fallout affects future generations as well as the present one, a certain percentage of those who are harmed by fallout have not yet been born when the weapon that produces it is detonated.[10] For Sakharov, these were in some way the most innocent casualties of all; more than anyone else harmed by radioactive fallout, they bore no responsibility for the political system that caused it. One might plausibly speculate that the special empathy Sakharov later showed as a dissident for victims of Soviet repression who lacked the intellectual and material resources to defend themselves was an expression of the same concern he showed in the late 1950s for these particular victims, the most defenseless ones, of radioactive fallout.

When Sakharov wrote his article, he knew that while the probability of genetic damage from radiation is a function of the dose of radiation one receives, the

8. Ibid., 39–40.

9. Ibid., 41–48. Sakharov, *Memoirs*, 201–2. In 1990 Frank von Hippel, an American physicist who has written widely on nuclear nonproliferation and disarmament, evaluated Sakharov's estimate and affirmed its accuracy. Frank von Hippel, "Revisiting Sakharov's Assumptions," *Science and Global Security* 1, nos. 3–4 (1990): 185–86.

10. Sakharov, "Radioactive Carbon," 48.

severity of damage is not: even minimal exposure to radiation can have, albeit infrequently, extremely harmful effects. Indeed, there is no minimum dosage below which damage cannot occur.[11] This seemed to lend a special urgency to Sakharov's article, for there is something especially insidious about even the smallest dose of radiation causing life-threatening diseases such as cancer and leukemia, even if the incidence of persons who contract these diseases from such small doses is quite small. The fact that Sakharov was at the time unaware of the "self-healing" properties of living cells, which can undo the damage radiation causes and restore to these cells their original gene structure, only made the magnitude of the casualty figures he cited and the urgency of the problems he diagnosed more disturbing to him.[12]

Unlike his American counterpart, Edward Teller, Sakharov was not a nuclear evangelist. In his article, he took issue with several of the arguments Teller and other advocates of atmospheric nuclear testing advanced. To the notion that such testing should continue because the genetic damage it caused was less than that produced naturally by cosmic rays in the atmosphere, Sakharov countered that the fact that some dangers are unavoidable is hardly a reason for not protecting against other dangers that are avoidable.[13] Sakharov also responded to Teller's argument that since nuclear energy, like automobiles, is socially useful, the accidents and loss of life that are an inevitable concomitant of it must simply be tolerated. Sakharov disposed of this argument neatly and efficiently: "Automobiles improve people's lives; they only cause harm in case of an accident, and careless drivers can be held criminally responsible. In contrast, each and every nuclear test does damage. And this crime is committed with complete impunity, since it is impossible to prove that a particular death was caused by radiation."[14] To Sakharov, testing nuclear and thermonuclear weapons in the atmosphere was so pernicious in its effects on both present and future generations that over the long run it was only marginally less harmful than actually using such weapons in war.

In the late 1950s Sakharov still believed that science was fundamentally benevolent and, if properly used, could enhance human life immeasurably. Despite his concerns about its potential for misuse, Sakharov never considered science inherently evil. Even nuclear testing was reasonably safe if it was conducted under ground. Nevertheless, there is implicit in his concerns about atmospheric nuclear testing a questioning—though not an outright repudiation—of the Promethean ethos in Marxism and Soviet Communism that the transformation of nature by science is always beneficial.[15] What Sakharov is implying in his article

11. This is what is meant when scientists say that radioactive fallout has "nonthreshold effects." Sakharov, *Memoirs*, 197–98. See also V. I. Korogodin, "Assessing Radioactive Hazards," in Drell and Kapitza, *Sakharov Remembered*, 178.

12. Soifer, "Andrei Sakharov and the Fate of Biological Science," 176.

13. Sakharov, "Radioactive Carbon," 48.

14. Quoted in Sakharov, *Memoirs*, 202. This translation is superior to the one in "Radioactive Carbon," 48–49.

15. A classic statement of this Bolshevik Prometheanism is Leon Trotsky's 1924 extended essay, *Literature and Revolution* (Ann Arbor, 1960), especially 255–56. An example of this Prometheanism in the Stalin era is A. Morozov's prediction that through nuclear energy, people will melt snow,

is that in the wrong hands science can be harmful, even lethal, to humanity. For science to benefit humanity it must be tempered by an awareness of the catastrophes it can cause when the projects for which it is harnessed are not informed by a decent respect for human life. Had Sakharov been American or West European, his strictures would not merit special interest. In the West there is a long-standing tradition of protecting nature from the depredations of unbridled technology. But coming from someone who had grown up in a system that extolled science as a social good to be trusted unreservedly, these comments are truly remarkable.

The terrifying specter of damage done to innocent people by radioactive fallout caused Sakharov to modify his views on deterrence, though not to abandon them completely. He continued to believe that as long as one superpower possessed nuclear and thermonuclear weapons, it was incumbent on the other, both out of self-interest and in the interest of humanity, to stockpile such weapons in sufficient numbers to retain a second-strike capability. But Sakharov's calculations of the effects of radioactive fallout from nuclear testing sensitized him to its effects in an actual war. The result was an ambivalence that caused him to advocate deterrence and nuclear disarmament simultaneously, with the former a regrettable necessity that would keep the peace until the latter could be successfully negotiated. In the long run, disarmament was preferable to deterrence because while deterrence was a means of avoiding war, disarmament was a means of assuring peace.

One sees this ambivalence in the popular version of the article Sakharov wrote—the one that was displayed and distributed in Soviet embassies. In one passage he calls deterrence "a dangerous idea" that is "only one step away from preventive war."[16] In the very next paragraph, however, he seems to caution his readers against concluding from this that deterrence should be abandoned entirely. Explaining how deterrence began, he writes that "the Soviet state was compelled to develop nuclear weapons and conduct tests to provide for its security in the face of American and British nuclear weapons."[17] In his memoirs, while describing his anguish over radioactive fallout and atmospheric nuclear testing, Sakharov acknowledges that it was tempered somewhat by the conviction that building thermonuclear weapons was critical in maintaining the parity deterrence required.[18] During this phase of his life, when his views were in flux, Sakharov's concerns about deterrence seemed to parallel those he felt about Soviet Communism: however much he questioned each of these things, he was not yet prepared to abandon them, much less to repudiate them publicly.

Indeed, Sakharov's commitment to deterrence, however attenuated, served to anchor him to the Soviet system even as a multitude of other influences

transform deserts into gardens, and even create a "winter sun." A. Morozov, "Razrushiteli," *Smena* 9–10 (1946): 11–12.

16. Sakharov, *Memoirs*, 204.
17. Ibid.
18. Ibid., 221.

caused his allegiance to weaken. Even though, as he writes in his memoirs, he was "drifting further and further away from orthodox views," he continued to serve the Soviet Union loyally, "doing more than was required of me, taking initiatives, and generally doing the best I could."[19] Nowhere was this more apparent than in Sakharov's willingness in the early 1960s to design for the Soviet leadership an enormous torpedo that used an atomic-powered jet engine attached to it to travel hundreds of miles to enemy ports, which it would destroy with the nuclear or thermonuclear warheads it carried. In this design, the torpedo could be fitted with charges of up to one hundred megatons. In the end, the rear admiral Sakharov consulted on the project was properly horrified by what he was proposing, and Sakharov himself eventually recognized how morally abhorrent the whole concept was. Properly chastened, he never broached the matter again.[20]

The time lag in Sakharov's reaction is hardly surprising. His job, after all, was to conjure weapons of mass destruction, and it followed logically from the principle of deterrence that the more destructive these weapons, the more likely it was that nuclear war would be avoided. In fact, Sakharov's growing disquiet in the late 1950s seems to have resulted less from reevaluating his long-held ideas about deterrence and nuclear weapons than from examining social issues he had previously ignored. What drove him to do this was not a sense of guilt about the weapons he had developed but rather his opportunity as a weapons designer to witness and evaluate the Soviet system and the political leaders who administered it. Additionally, Sakharov displayed an innate ability, prominent among the original intelligentsia, to extrapolate from his own personal observations and experiences the larger moral and political lessons they contained. This was an incremental process. In the early 1960s Sakharov concerned himself with sciences other than physics; in the mid-1960s he focused on issues other than scientific ones; and finally, as his interests broadened even more, he turned his attention in the late 1960s to Soviet society as a whole and to issues of global significance.

There was one issue that Sakharov addressed in the late 1950s whose larger social implications he immediately grasped. In 1958, in an article he wrote with Zeldovich that was published in *Pravda*, he condemned the shortcomings he perceived in the scientific education Soviet students received and specified measures the government should take to rectify them.[21] Except for articles in scientific journals with limited readership, this was the first time Sakharov's name had appeared in the Soviet press. In their article the two physicists pointed out that because much of the best work in physics and mathematics was done by students who showed an aptitude for these disciplines while in their teens, the Soviet government should provide them with a curriculum weighted heavily in

19. Ibid.

20. Stalin thought of the same kind of weapon before Sakharov did. Gaddis, *We Now Know*, 237.

21. Ia. Zeldovich and A. Sakharov, "Nuzhny estestvenno-matematicheskie shkoly," *Pravda*, November 19, 1958, 3.

favor of these particular disciplines. In practical terms, this meant transferring these students from the existing school system into new boarding schools that the government would build and Soviet universities would sponsor. In these new schools, the social sciences and the humanities—what the Soviets called "humanitarian sciences"—would be deemphasized in favor of intensive study of physics, mathematics, and chemistry. Only as a result of intensive immersion in these disciplines, in an environment lacking the distractions to which they might succumb if they were still enrolled in traditional schools and living at home, could these students reach their full potential in the particular discipline for which they showed a predisposition. In this respect the boarding schools the physicists had in mind would be different only in degree—less intensive intellectually and not quite as isolated geographically—from scientific installations like Arzamas, for which these schools would presumably perform the role of feeders.

At these schools the subjects that were studied more intensively would be taught differently from the way they were in traditional schools. Sakharov and Zeldovich believed that recent developments in physics and mathematics in particular had rendered the existing curriculum passé. For example, they argued that in mathematics, analytical geometry, which was especially useful in physics, should be stressed instead of traditional Euclidean geometry; they also emphasized probability theory, calculus, and vector analysis. In physics, they underscored the centrality of quantum theory.

Possibly to preempt charges of elitism, Sakharov and Zeldovich included in their article the caveat that the curriculum they proposed should be taught, albeit in a simplified fashion, in the regular schools as well, so that traditional Communist constituencies—workers and peasants—would acquire at least a modicum of scientific and mathematical literacy. This, of course, was consistent with the Marxist and Soviet dogma that under communism the barriers between intellectual and physical labor would disappear and that people would be reasonably conversant in intellectual and cultural matters while retaining the practical skills they or their ancestors had learned under capitalism. Whether Sakharov and Zeldovich were paying anything more than lip service to this cliché when they acknowledged that all students, not just the gifted ones, would benefit from an updated curriculum must remain in the end a matter of speculation. Sakharov says nothing in his memoirs that would help to clarify his or Zeldovich's intentions. But it seems reasonable to suggest that while the two physicists truly intended that everyone should benefit from the curriculum changes they were proposing, they were more concerned about gifted students than about the far larger number of ordinary ones. Indeed, in the scenario they seemed to suggest, ordinary students would recognize their intellectual deficiencies and accept as part of the natural order of things that students superior to them would receive separate and special education.

Significantly, Sakharov and Zeldovich emphasized that while classes in the humanitarian sciences—which of course included instruction in Marxism-Leninism—might be reduced under the new regime they were proposing, political education per se would not be scanted. The implication was that students sent to the boarding schools would grow up to be just as loyal to the regime as the students who remained in traditional ones. The context in which Sakharov and Zeldovich were writing was significant. The article appeared just two years after Khrushchev's Secret Speech denouncing Stalin and Stalinism. That speech, when its content leaked out, served to stimulate criticism of the Soviet system and, to a certain extent, to legitimize it as well. But by ascribing Stalinism to Stalin rather than to the Soviet system that gave rise to it, the speech contained the implication that anyone emboldened by it to criticize the Soviet system should think twice before doing so. In addition, not long before the article appeared, Khrushchev had proposed publicly that students in the last year of high school spend approximately one-third of their time working in factories or on farms—an idea consistent with Khrushchev's belief, which reflected his origins as a *muzhik* (peasant), that physical labor was educational.[22] For this reason Sakharov and Zeldovich had to tread carefully. The elitism, apparent or real, in what they proposed might ruffle powerful feathers. Accordingly, they went out of their way in their article to stress the practical benefits of what they were proposing and with the proper ideological justification. Citing Lenin, the two physicists stated that "a distrust of science is profoundly alien to a socialist society."[23] And as if citing Lenin were not enough to demonstrate their political and ideological bona fides, they followed this with a rhetorical flourish: "[The Soviet people] are convinced that those who devote their youth to their studies are maturing into citizens who enjoy the complete and well-deserved trust of socialist society."[24] Undoubtedly such rhetoric was designed to obscure the unflattering implication in their article that the Soviet Union, despite its recent success in launching *sputniki,* was not producing the best scientists it was capable of producing. For that reason, the two physicists were probably not surprised that Khrushchev—who may not even have read the article or been apprised of its contents—never implemented their recommendations. Nor were they terribly surprised, one surmises, when the well-known author of children's books Evgenii Nosov penned a strident attack on the article in the journal *Krokodil.*[25]

This was the first time Sakharov was criticized in the Soviet press. The fact that the criticisms were as pointed as they were was proof that the article had touched a nerve in several people in the Soviet establishment. Still, one should not conclude from this that Sakharov henceforth was in disfavor with the government. He was still too valuable a resource to jettison entirely, and at this stage in his life the Soviet government had no reason to doubt his ultimate loyalty to the system; only a clairvoyant could see what the very specific and fairly muted criticisms he made of Soviet education would eventually lead to in the late 1960s.

22. George Bailey, *The Making of Andrei Sakharov* (New York, 1989), 238.
23. Zeldovich and Sakharov, "Nuzhny estestvenno-matematicheskie shkoly," 3.
24. Ibid.
25. Sakharov, *Memoirs,* 200.

In 1958, condemning the Soviet system as a whole was something Sakharov did not even consider. Still, the article and Nosov's attack on it were a harbinger of things of come.

The "small deeds" Sakharov performed for friends and colleagues in the early 1950s continued. In late 1957, Grigorii Barenblat, like Sakharov a physicist, asked him to intervene on behalf of his father, Isaak, an endocrinologist Sakharov had met some months earlier. The elder Barenblat had been arrested in the spring of 1957 for having joked about a supposed sexual relationship between Khrushchev and Ekaterina Furtseva, the first woman to serve on the Presidium. He was also accused of having obtained unlawfully some three hundred thousand rubles that were found when police searched his home. Finally, he had had the temerity to proclaim within earshot of others, shortly after Khrushchev delivered his Secret Speech, that the Soviet leader had no moral right to condemn Stalin unless he criticized himself for his own role in the crimes Stalin had committed.[26] Sakharov knew the Barenblats were Jewish, and the very real possibility that this was what caused the authorities to pursue them so vigorously surely heightened Sakharov's awareness of the special difficulties Soviet Jews encountered.

Sakharov responded to Grigorii Barenblat's plea for assistance by sending a letter directly to Khrushchev, who in turn passed the letter on to Suslov. In January 1958 Suslov summoned Sakharov to the Kremlin for a personal meeting, at which he told the Soviet leader that the "inadmissible things" Suslov claimed Barenblat had suggested about Khrushchev and Furtseva were, if true, just words, and hardly likely to hurt anyone.[27] Sakharov also pointed out that mere possession of a large sum of money was hardly proof it had been acquired nefariously: by saving most of what he earned as a physician, Barenblat over the years could easily have accumulated the large amount of money the government was now claiming he had stolen. Instead of responding, Suslov simply repeated his earlier accusations. But just when the conversation, in Sakharov's words, began to assume "a certain ominous quality," Suslov promised "to take another look at the case."[28] The Soviet leader then directed the conversation to other matters, including the unilateral halt in nuclear testing the Soviet government was about to announce—which Sakharov approved of.[29] Probably because of Sakharov's involvement, Suslov, after consulting with Khrushchev, ordered Barenblat's release; according to Barenblat's son, Suslov said at the time, "I must throw them a bone."[30] But rather than release Barenblat immediately, as Sakharov requested, the government detained him until May, probably to avoid any appearance of weakness.[31]

26. Ibid., 205; G. I. Barenblat, "Iz vospominanii," in Altshuler et al., *On mezhdu nami zhil*, 129–31.
27. Sakharov, *Memoirs*, 205.
28. Ibid., 206.
29. Ibid.
30. Barenblat, "Iz vospominanii," 133.
31. Ibid. Although Sakharov typically downplayed his own role in securing Isaac Barenblat's release, Grigorii Barenblat gives Sakharov full credit for it. Ibid., 207.

The effect of these events on Sakharov was immediate and, as it turned out, long-lasting. Viktor Adamskii reports that Sakharov reacted quite emotionally to the entire imbroglio, far more so than his fairly laconic recapitulation of the matter in his memoirs might suggest.[32] He expressed his disgust with Suslov repeatedly in the weeks following his Kremlin meeting and, in a conversation with Adamskii during this period, called the entire Soviet leadership monsters. In the same conversation Sakharov wondered how it was "that such monsters rule us" and then answered his own question by commenting pointedly that "anti-intellectualism with a dash of anti-semitism" was a prerequisite for serving in the highest echelons of the *nomenklatura*.[33]

At about the same time as the Barenblat affair, Sakharov, this time with Khariton at his side, met another high-ranking member of the government, Leonid Brezhnev, to whom the two physicists had gone to express their opposition to a draft resolution of the Central Committee allocating resources within the military sector of the economy. Brezhnev did not evoke in Sakharov the visceral dislike Suslov did, and while Brezhnev himself was noncommittal on the objections the two physicists raised, he promised to pass them along to his superiors. Perhaps because whoever ultimately received these objections found them meritorious, or simply because the Soviet government felt it had to mollify scientists who were especially prominent, the Council of Ministers did what Sakharov and Khariton wanted, rejecting the resolution the Central Committee bureau proposed. Sakharov had no hesitation in the late 1950s in exercising the influence he possessed, and because in personal encounters he was always civil and non-confrontational, his interventions, as in the Barenblat affair and in the matter Brezhnev addressed, were often successful.

The face of Soviet officialdom Sakharov saw most often in the late 1950s was Efim Slavskii's, and in this case his reaction was at least partially negative. Like Beria, Slavskii was intelligent and energetic, and a competent engineer as well. But he was also boorish, intolerant, and small-minded—in sum a Soviet careerist whose principal concern was his own advancement. In the summer of 1957, Slavskii was named minister of medium machine building after Mikhail Pervukhin, who had succeeded to the position after Zaveniagin died, was dismissed for his association with the "Anti-Party Group" of Malenkov, Molotov, and Kaganovich, which Khrushchev thwarted after it attempted to remove him from power.[34] In that capacity, Slavskii oversaw Sakharov's activities at Arzamas and was the first true apparatchik in the lengthy chain of command whose approval Sakharov needed for any proposals he made about the weapons he was charged with developing.

To a careerist, albeit a capable one like Slavskii, Sakharov was a potential threat, someone whose willingness to think for himself was just as incomprehensible

32. Adamskii, "Stanovlenie grazhdanina," 40.
33. Ibid., 41. *Nomenklatura* is a term from the Soviet era for those who held high positions in the government and Soviet society and enjoyed the privileges these positions conferred.
34. Sakharov, *Memoirs*, 212–13.

and bewildering as the theoretical physics Sakharov had made his profession. On one occasion, when he learned that Sakharov, on his own initiative, was working on a thermonuclear device the Soviet government had not yet approved, Slavskii criticized Sakharov for his actions publicly (though without naming him), telling him and the other physicists assembled at a formal staff meeting that he did not much care for "theorists who think up new devices while sitting on the toilet and propose them for testing before they've buttoned up their pants."[35] Sakharov must have recoiled viscerally at the crudeness of Slavskii's expostulation, which epitomized all that was arbitrary, banal, and irrational in the Soviet system. Slavskii's vulgarity, in other words, was just a microcosmic manifestation of the general lack of refinement and sensitivity in the Soviet political hierarchy that Sakharov had observed in the late 1950s and early 1960s. Twice before 1962 Sakharov and his family vacationed at the spa on the southern coast of the Crimea run by, and reserved for, the Council of Ministers.[36] There he rubbed elbows with Soviet leaders who, stripped of their sober public personae, appeared as the mediocrities they really were. The more Sakharov saw of the Soviet leadership, the less he respected it and the less inclined he was to accept its legitimacy.

# 7  Confronting Khrushchev

The substantive issue around which Sakharov's disaffection crystallized in the late 1950s was the testing of thermonuclear weapons in the atmosphere. He vehemently and unequivocally opposed it. Given his concerns about radioactive fallout, it was logical that he do so. Unlike nuclear tests conducted underground—which, by shifting massive amounts of subterranean material, had the effect, under certain circumstances, of preventing earthquakes or reducing their severity—atmospheric testing had no beneficial effects whatsoever.[1] To the latter Sakharov remained unalterably opposed, even though he was aware that any ban on atmospheric testing meant that the very weapons he and his colleagues designed could not be easily evaluated. Eventually, however, he came to believe and to argue forcefully that underground testing and forms of "modeling," often using computers, could serve as adequate substitutes.[2]

In September 1958 Sakharov included a plan for Soviet weapons testing that excluded detonations in the atmosphere among the proposals he asked Kurchatov

---

35. Ibid., 222.
36. Ibid., 215.

---

1. Vitalii I. Goldanskii, "Scientist, Thinker, Humanist," in Drell and Kapitza, *Sakharov Remembered,* 22–23.
2. Sakharov, *Memoirs,* 207–8.

to present to Khrushchev, then vacationing in the Crimea.[3] He requested that the Soviet Union, despite Khrushchev's threat to resume atmospheric tests after halting them unilaterally the previous March, wait an entire year, until the fall of 1959, before resuming them. By that time, Sakharov predicted, the United States and Great Britain would have completed the series of atmospheric tests they had already scheduled and thus be receptive to a comprehensive test ban treaty. Kurchatov agreed to present the idea to Khrushchev and flew to the Crimea. The Soviet leader, however, rejected the proposals and was so angry at Kurchatov for merely passing them on to him that, according to Sakharov, he never entirely trusted Kurchatov again.[4]

The first time Sakharov observed Khrushchev in person was in 1955, at a meeting of the Presidium to which Soviet physicists had been invited. Because his political position was still precarious, Khrushchev said little that was revealing, preferring, in Sakharov's phrase, to remain "in the shadows."[5] In 1959, with Khariton accompanying him, he saw Khrushchev again, this time to present the positions the physicists at Arzamas had formulated on a variety of military matters. In his memoirs Sakharov fails to specify what these matters were or what he and the other physicists thought about them. But he describes Khrushchev in considerable detail, calling him "brash," "susceptible to flattery," and "uncultivated"—qualities Khrushchev shared with Slavskii and many of the lesser Soviet bureaucrats Sakharov encountered in the course of his life.[6] But Khrushchev also impressed Sakharov as "intelligent" and "a leader of stature."[7] Sakharov apparently said nothing at the meeting to incur Khrushchev's wrath—which would not be the case in subsequent meetings at which the two men were present.

By 1959 Sakharov had calculated that every atmospheric nuclear test would cost, over thousands of years, no fewer than ten thousand lives.[8] Fortunately, the three nuclear powers had completed the atmospheric tests scheduled for 1958—the United States and Great Britain in the summer, the Soviet Union in the fall—and were now observing a de facto moratorium on nuclear testing. Zhores Medvedev speculates that the earlier, unilateral moratorium the Soviet Union had announced in March 1958 and maintained until the tests Khrushchev ordered for that fall was the result of the aforementioned nuclear accident in 1957 in the Urals, which forced the Soviet government to shut down temporarily the plant that produced the plutonium used in both fission and fusion devices.[9] But the moratorium that began in 1959 was a multilateral affair in which

3. Ibid., 208; Stephen Fortescue, *The Communist Party and Soviet Science* (London, 1987), 62.
4. Sakharov, *Memoirs,* 208.
5. Ibid., 211.
6. Ibid.
7. Ibid.
8. Ibid., 207.
9. Medvedev, *Soviet Science,* 96. In this explosion on September 29, 1957, involving some 70–80 tons of radioactive waste, 2.1 million curies of radioactivity were generated, in contrast to the 50 million curies released at Chernobyl in 1986. In all, some 270,000 people were contaminated. Zaloga, *Target America,* 219–24.

none of the countries that were a party to it wished to incur the opprobrium that would follow a decision by any one of them to violate it. Khrushchev was also aware that the "missile gap" alleged by John Kennedy in the 1960 American presidential campaign to disfavor the United States was actually bogus, and that it was really the Soviet Union whose thermonuclear capability was deficient both qualitatively and quantitatively. For this reason, Khrushchev hoped that the moratorium, by preventing the United States from testing new weapons and updating old ones, would prevent the real missile gap that disfavored the Soviet Union from increasing. In ordering this new moratorium, Khrushchev hoped to stabilize a situation that showed every indication of worsening for the Soviet Union, while the Soviet government could still reap the political benefits of the Sputniks, which seemed to prove the superiority of Soviet science and technology. At the same time, by refusing to test nuclear weapons, the Soviets, in the guise of furthering peace, could withhold technical assistance from their increasingly assertive and obstreperous ally, China, which did not trust the Soviet Union to defend it and thus wanted nuclear weapons of its own. For the foreseeable future, observing a moratorium on nuclear testing made sense for the Soviet Union.[10]

To be sure, by late 1959 neither Khrushchev nor President Eisenhower, albeit for different reasons, felt entirely comfortable with the moratorium each was tacitly following. Eisenhower preferred a formal treaty. But while he said that the United States was no longer bound by the moratorium, he still did not order the resumption of testing. In addition, he promised that he would do so only after giving prior notice to the Soviets. Khrushchev, in response, tried to lock Eisenhower into the position the American president had taken by declaring that the Soviet Union would resume testing only if the United States did.[11] Thus for the time being each superpower calculated that the political advantages of continuing the moratorium were greater than the military advantages of breaking it.

In the summer of 1961, however, Khrushchev made the critical strategic decision that the Soviet Union could compensate for its deficiencies in ICBMs by developing thermonuclear weapons of absurdly high megatonnage and then testing them in the atmosphere. Khrushchev did not want nuclear war. After consigning Malenkov to political oblivion, Khrushchev, in typical Soviet fashion, adopted Malenkov's position that nuclear war in any meaningful sense was unwinnable. Khrushchev also believed that the best way of avoiding a nuclear war was by acquiring and maintaining the means to fight one.[12] But the so-called Big Bombs Khrushchev envisioned, while militarily useless because most of their explosive power would be dissipated in the atmosphere, could still be useful politically.[13] In Khrushchev's scenario, these bombs and the tests that announced

10. In this I have followed mostly Gaddis, *We Now Know*, 221–59.
11. Herbert F. York, "Sakharov and the Nuclear Test Ban," in Babyonyshev, *On Sakharov*, 187.
12. Gaddis, *We Now Know*, 234–35.
13. Goldanskii, "Scientist, Thinker, Humanist," 22.

their existence would so frighten the Western, and especially American, public that their leaders would acquiesce in Khrushchev's updated version of atomic diplomacy and make concessions on issues, such as Berlin, in which the Soviet Union claimed a vital interest. For that reason, the moratorium on testing the Soviet Union had observed for nearly three years came to an end.

Khrushchev's decision made it harder for Sakharov to maintain the precarious strategy he had followed since the original thermonuclear test at Semipalatinsk in 1955 of designing thermonuclear weapons for the Soviet Union while trying to limit the damage that testing them caused. He states in his memoirs that at that time in his life he "had no idea [he] would become involved in public affairs."[14] But Khrushchev's decision made it necessary, as a matter of · principle, that he do so.

In July 1961, shortly before the Soviet Union resumed nuclear testing in the atmosphere, Khrushchev convened a meeting in the Kremlin to which Sakharov and other scientists were invited. Everyone who was present understood that the scientists were there simply to report on their work, not to make recommendations about policy. When it was Sakharov's turn to speak, he briefly cited the various projects on which he was working and then ventured to say in very general terms that resuming nuclear testing at that time was a bad idea. Describing the scene in his memoirs, Sakharov writes that "my remark registered, but evoked no immediate response."[15] Sakharov then did something he thought would be less confrontational and provocative: he wrote a note and had it passed to Khrushchev. In the note Sakharov specified his objections to atmospheric testing: it would favor the United States (which was a pragmatic argument to which Khrushchev might be susceptible), and it would jeopardize "test ban negotiations, the cause of disarmament, and world peace" (an argument that encapsulated Sakharov's own convictions on the subject). But the Soviet leader, furious that Sakharov had not only challenged the policy he had just reiterated but by expressing his own objections orally had changed the terms under which the meeting was being run, was not mollified by the note, and after glancing at Sakharov, simply pocketed it. At the lavish dinner that followed an hour later, Khrushchev, who had entered the banquet hall with the other Presidium members after the scientists who were assembled there had taken their seats, pointedly remained standing, presumably for the purpose of making a toast. Instead, the Soviet leader launched into a diatribe that lasted, according to Sakharov, for more than a half hour, with his face getting redder and his voice rising as he spoke.[16] What follows are excerpts as Sakharov recollected and recorded them in his memoirs:

Here's a note I received from Academician Sakharov. Sakharov writes that we don't need tests. But I've got a briefing paper which shows how many tests we've

14. Sakharov, *Memoirs*, 223.
15. Ibid., 215.
16. Ibid., 216.

conducted and how many more the Americans have conducted. Can Sakharov really prove that with fewer tests we've gained more valuable information than the Americans?...But Sakharov goes further. He's moved beyond science into politics. Here he's poking his nose where it doesn't belong. You can be a good scientist without understanding a thing about politics....Leave politics to us—we're the specialists. You make your bombs and test them, and we won't interfere with you; we'll help you. But remember, we have to conduct our policies from a position of strength. We don't advertise it, but that's how it is! There can't be any other policy. Our opponents don't understand any other language....Sakharov, don't try to tell us what to do or how to behave. We understand politics. I'd be a jellyfish and not Chairman of the Council of Ministers if I listened to people like Sakharov![17]

Everyone present remained perfectly still while Khrushchev was speaking, some looking nervously sideways, all of them maintaining the same blank expression. No one had the audacity to object to what Khrushchev was saying, and no one so much as looked in Sakharov's direction. Khrushchev's diatribe ended on a calmer note but not without sarcasm and condescension: "I can see Sakharov has got illusions. The next time I go for talks with the capitalists, I'll take him with me. Let him see them and the world with his own eyes, and then maybe he'll understand."[18]

Years later, Khrushchev expressed a quite different opinion of Sakharov. In his memoirs he wrote that he always considered Sakharov "a crystal of morality among scientists."[19] He also told his son Sergei that he regarded Sakharov "with a certain reverence," even though, in Sergei's recollection, he commented that people like Sakharov "live in their own world, far from the ups and downs of politics and interstate relations—where there's more dirt than there should be. Sakharov's views are naive, but they're interesting. They come from the heart, from his wish for everyone's happiness. We have to listen to him."[20] According to Sergei, his father came to regret his differences with Sakharov and regretted as well losing his temper at the 1961 meeting. In his son's interpretation, Khrushchev never got over his resentment of the luxury Sakharov enjoyed as a private citizen of being able to talk grandiloquently about moral principle, with no penalty for the appearance of political weakness that such a position might suggest.[21] But on at least one occasion he reminded his son that he had pushed through Sakharov's designation as a Hero of Socialist Labor for the third time in 1962 over the opposition of many in the Soviet bureaucracy.[22] In fact, at

17. Ibid., 215–16.
18. Sakharov, *Memoirs*, 216.
19. Khrushchev, *Khrushchev Remembers*, 69.
20. Sergei Khrushchev, *Khrushchev on Khrushchev: An Inside Account of the Man and His Era* (Boston, 1990), 342.
21. Sergei N. Khrushchev, *Nikita Khrushchev and the Creation of a Superpower* (University Park, Pa., 2000), 447.
22. Ibid., 527. Among the emoluments the designation conferred was having a seat reserved on special flights added to accommodate the Soviet elite when ordinary passenger flights were canceled. On at least one occasion, Sakharov availed himself of this privilege. Sakharov, *Memoirs*, 227.

the Kremlin banquet following the ceremony at which Sakharov received this honor, Khrushchev made only a casual reference to the unpleasantness of the year before and praised the physicist for his contributions to his country. In keeping with the occasion, Sakharov, in his response, avoided politics and said nothing controversial.[23]

But the damage had been done. What Khrushchev was actually saying to Sakharov on that fateful day in July 1961 was that, for all his achievements, abilities, knowledge, and unique contributions to his nation's security, he could have no say in governance or in the formulation of policy, not even in how the weapons he developed should be used. In common parlance, Khrushchev was telling Sakharov to mind his own business: that he could exercise his own judgment and express his own opinions as they pertained to his professional domain, but on matters beyond it he should keep his mouth shut. As far as Khrushchev was concerned, Sakharov's concept of Soviet citizenship, in which the Soviet people would loyally serve the Soviet government and in return be treated with dignity and respect, was plainly unacceptable. The importance of this in Sakharov's political maturation cannot be exaggerated. In an interview he gave in 1972, he pointedly described his protest against Khrushchev's resumption of atmospheric nuclear testing in 1961 as one of the principal turning points in his life.[24]

It was obvious to Sakharov that nothing he said or did could prevent the nuclear tests Khrushchev ordered. On August 31 the Soviet Union formally announced it would resume them. For Sakharov, this was a serious and significant defeat. But rather than respond with churlish indifference, he showed the pragmatism of which he was often capable: if he could not prevent atmospheric nuclear testing, he would try to minimize its deleterious consequences by constructing thermonuclear devices that contained a smaller fission component; in that way, less radioactive fallout would be released when they exploded.[25] This is precisely what Sakharov did, and in the middle of August, just after the Soviets and East Germans built the Berlin Wall, he and Khariton met with Khrushchev in the Kremlin to report on their progress. Khrushchev, however, would have none of it. He dismissed as factually inaccurate Sakharov's acknowledgment that the radioactive carbon these "cleaner" devices produced would still cause large numbers of casualties, and he made it clear to both men that the Big Bomb he

23. Sakharov, *Memoirs*, 224–25.

24. Andrei Sakharov, "A Voice Out of Russia," interview by Jay Axelbank, *Observer,* December 3, 1972, 29. Adamskii and Smirnov present a different view of Sakharov's attitude toward the Big Bombs Khrushchev wanted to detonate. They argue that Sakharov actually agreed with Khrushchev's decision because he hoped the bombs, once detonated, would demonstrate how awful and destructive thermonuclear weapons were. Victor Adamsky and Yurii Smirnov, "Moscow's Biggest Bomb: The 50-Megaton Test of October 1961," *Cold War International History Project* 4 (Fall 1994): 20. While this may have been Sakharov's fallback position, or one of several positions he adopted once he realized he could not change Khrushchev's mind on the subject, the argument fails to take into account what actually happened in the Kremlin in July 1961. Khrushchev's assorted references to the meeting in his memoirs do not in any way contradict or call into question Sakharov's own, more detailed, description of it.

25. Sakharov, *Memoirs*, 218.

desired would be tested in the atmosphere as soon as it was ready. Sakharov's response was simply to say that while he still held the same opinions, as an employee of the state he would do what he was told to do.[26]

In fact, Sakharov was successful in limiting the percentage of the bomb's explosive power that was produced by fission. When the bomb was tested, on October 30, 1961, roughly 97 percent of its megatonnage was the result of fusion.[27] Still, the bomb was truly frightening. Despite its military uselessness, it would prove to be the most powerful thermonuclear weapon either superpower detonated during the Cold War. According to Adamskii and Smirnov, if the bomb had been loaded with all the thermonuclear fuel it could hold, its explosive power would have increased from fifty-eight to approximately one hundred megatons. As it was, the bomb weighed more than twenty tons, and the T-95 bomber that dropped it over its target at Novaia Zemlia had to be specially modified; the blast it created was visible six hundred miles away.[28] In comparative terms, the bomb was four thousand times more powerful than the atomic bomb the United States dropped over Hiroshima, and it had ten times the explosive power of all the bombs, including the two atomic ones, that were dropped in World War II.[29]

The effect of the bomb's detonation on Sakharov was considerable. He concluded from it that limiting the harmful effects of atmospheric tests was insufficient and that even tests that contaminated the atmosphere only slightly should not be conducted. For this reason his concerns deepened in 1962—which he would characterize in his memoirs as "one of the more difficult years of my life"—when he realized that the test over Novaia Zemlia was just a forerunner of additional ones.[30] In the fall of that year, shortly after the United States and Great Britain resumed atmospheric testing, the Soviet government ordered what Sakharov calls the Duplicate Tests: the testing in the atmosphere of two thermonuclear devices, one of them designed at Arzamas, the other at Cheliabinsk-70, another secret installation established by the government in 1955. Sakharov believed that the first device—the one designed at Arzamas—was acceptable for testing because "it would be mass-produced and become a big element in our strategic armory."[31] But the second device—the one designed at Cheliabinsk—he was convinced should not be tested, much less deployed, because it was too much like the first device to diversify the Soviet nuclear arsenal; even worse, it could be enhanced to have far greater megatonnage than was militarily useful. Because Sakharov favored deterrence and a ban on atmospheric nuclear testing simultaneously, he could maintain that he was doing nothing unethical at Arzamas: he was developing weapons that by the logic of deterrence increased the likelihood of peace while at the same time doing everything

26. Ibid.
27. Adamsky and Smirnov, "Moscow's Biggest Bomb," 20.
28. Ibid., 3, 19–20.
29. Ibid., 19; Zaloga, *Target America*, 233.
30. Sakharov, *Memoirs*, 225.
31. Ibid., 226.

he could to prevent the atmospheric testing, and thus the eventual deployment, of weapons like the Big Bomb that by virtue of their redundancy and excessive megatonnage did not increase the likelihood of peace. As Sakharov saw them, such weapons were not only dirty but dangerous.

Accordingly, Sakharov, who may have contributed to the construction of the first device, did what he could in the fall of 1962 to stop the testing of the second. He first approached Khariton with a request for support. Khariton, however, believed that helping Sakharov would be misconstrued as an encroachment on the prerogatives of the other installation. He told Sakharov that regardless of what he might think personally of the second device and the decision to test it, he could not help him. But he also gave Sakharov the impression that he would not oppose Sakharov's enlisting others to pressure the government to cancel the test.[32] Encouraged by this, Sakharov went to see Slavskii in Moscow, where in conversation Slavskii agreed that if the first device were tested and shown to work, there was no need to test the other device. Sakharov then visited Zababakhin, his former colleague at Arzamas, who was now in charge of the other installation. Zababakhin told Sakharov that even if the first device were tested, he would still demand that the second one be tested. Unbeknownst to Sakharov, Zababakhin was already lobbying for the second device, in which he understandably had a proprietary interest, to be tested first. When Sakharov, back in Moscow, told Slavskii what Zababakhin had told him, Slavskii agreed with Sakharov's suggestion that both devices should be made ready but decided that only one device, Zababakhin's, should be tested. As an engineer, Slavskii knew, or should have known, that the device designed at Arzamas was technically superior to the one developed by Zababakhin's team.[33]

But Slavskii, after securing the approval of his superiors, broke his word to Sakharov and ordered a duplicate test with the caveat that the second device be tested seven days after the first device on September 19. Sakharov learned of this on September 25, only one day before the second test was to take place. Understandably furious, he telephoned Slavskii—there was not enough time to go to Moscow—and citing the thousands of casualties the duplicate test would potentially cause, implored him to cancel it. Sakharov then told Slavskii that testing a device that was both redundant and excessively powerful was pointless and criminal. When Slavskii still refused to cancel the test, Sakharov—either out of sheer exasperation or in an attempt to move him to do the right thing—told Slavskii he could no longer work with him. To this Slavskii responded that Sakharov could go to hell if he wanted to.[34]

At this point Sakharov, who was understandably angry, made one last attempt to stop the duplicate test. Audaciously, he decided to go over Slavskii's head and appeal directly to Khrushchev. He called Khrushchev, who happened, coincidentally, to be in Ashkhabad, where Sakharov had lived and worked during

---

32. Ibid.
33. The entire sequence of events is described in detail in Sakharov's memoirs, 226–27.
34. Ibid., 228.

World War II.[35] That Sakharov succeeded in getting through to Khrushchev was a measure of the prominence he enjoyed. Khrushchev, after listening to Sakharov's impassioned plea that the duplicate test be canceled, rebuffed him—which showed that there were limits to Sakharov's actual influence. Khrushchev told Sakharov the following: "My responsibilities in the post I hold do not allow me to cancel the tests....As the man responsible for the security of our country, I have no right to do what you're asking."[36] As had been the case at the Kremlin banquet in 1961, Khrushchev seemed annoyed as much by Sakharov's audacity in making such a recommendation as by the recommendation itself. By demanding that his views on nuclear weapons be taken seriously, Sakharov was implicitly questioning the Soviet leadership's presumed monopoly of wisdom. This, of course, was anathema to Khrushchev, to whom the larger meaning of what Sakharov was saying was clear.

Nevertheless, to mollify the Soviet physicist, or merely to end an unpleasant conversation without rupturing their personal relationship, Khrushchev told Sakharov he would tell Frol Kozlov, Khrushchev's colleague in the Presidium and then reputedly his heir apparent, to look into the matter of the duplicate test. Kozlov, in fact, called Sakharov the next day, a few hours before the test was to be carried out. He, too, was unyielding: the more the Soviet Union tested nuclear weapons, Kozlov insisted, the more amenable "the imperialists" would be to a treaty banning testing.[37] A frantic plea to yet another Soviet bureaucrat proved equally unproductive. One hour later, Sakharov learned that the test had been carried out and that, by the criteria with which the Soviet government measured such things, it was a resounding success.[38]

Sakharov was not merely disheartened by the duplicate test and his inability to stop it. He was genuinely crushed by it, in a way that had lasting effects on his subsequent actions. At the end of 1973 Sakharov stated that "the feeling of impotence and fright that seized me on that day has remained in my memory ever since, and it has worked much change in me as I moved toward my present attitude."[39] When he wrote his memoirs a few years later, he described his feelings before the duplicate test as follows: "It was the ultimate defeat for me. A terrible crime was about to be committed, and I could do nothing to prevent it. I was overcome by my impotence, unbearable bitterness, shame, and humiliation. I put my face down on my desk and wept."[40] In an interview with a Bulgarian journalist in 1988, Sakharov stated simply that he was "shaken" by the powerlessness he felt when he was unable to stop the test.[41]

35. Moroz, "Vozvrashchenie iz ssylki," 327.
36. Khrushchev, *Khrushchev Remembers*, 69, 70. Sakharov omits what Khrushchev told him from his own rendition of the conversation in his memoirs.
37. Sakharov, *Memoirs*, 229.
38. Ibid.
39. Andrei D. Sakharov, *Alarm and Hope* (New York, 1978), xiii.
40. Sakharov, *Memoirs*, 229.
41. Andrei Sakharov, "Interviu vtoroe, konets 1988 goda," *Zvezda* 5 (1991): 135.

By the steps he took to try to prevent the duplicate test, Sakharov virtually ensured that if the test were carried out, it would constitute a personal defeat. One
senses, in reading his account of the whole affair, that he truly believed he could
convince Khariton, and if not Khariton, Slavskii, and if not Slavskii, Khrushchev
himself that he was right and that the test would be stopped. No doubt this was a
reason for the anguish he experienced when the test took place. But more was at
stake in the matter than injured pride or even a recognition on Sakharov's part
that there were limits to his ability to influence events that pertained directly
to his professional expertise. The larger question was whether Sakharov's benign scenario of the humane scientist working within the system in ways that
were socially useful was actually feasible in the Soviet Union as it was presently
constructed. Sakharov's vision of the Republic of Science he first conjured in
the early 1950s was based on the assumption that scientists would have sufficient
access and influence to convince those with political power to use the fruits of
their expertise humanely. Sakharov was not like Saint-Simon, the nineteenth-
century French advocate of technocracy, or the Soviet engineer Palchinskii, who
believed that governments should be run by experts.[42] Neither in 1962 nor at
any other time in his life did he ever argue that scientists should actually wield
political power or coerce other people into doing what they wanted. Rather, in
Sakharov's scheme of things, scientists would exercise influence, and their influence would be a function of how well they could persuade both leaders and
laypersons alike that what they advocated was correct.

What Sakharov had failed to consider before the duplicate test—in spite of
everything he had seen on previous occasions—was that on issues where they
perceived their power and privileges to be at stake, the Soviet leaders were not
amenable to reason. It was this realization that made the test and the encounters
leading up to it so disturbing. When it became clear to him—probably on the
day the test was carried out—that Khrushchev would not come to his senses and
cancel it, it seemed to dawn on Sakharov that his faith in the system he was serving was, in some irreversible way, misplaced. While a few years would pass before
he would realize that to be a humane scientist in the Soviet Union one had to be
a social critic of the Soviet system, the duplicate test helped to move him toward
this awareness. The final outcome of the journey he had embarked upon many
years earlier was now, in 1962, a little clearer.

## The Test Ban Treaty

For the next four years little changed for Sakharov professionally. He remained
at Arzamas designing nuclear weapons (by one account, the Big Bomb that was
detonated over Novaia Zemlia was the last device "on which he worked intensely,
seriously, and without hesitation").[43] Sakharov's justification for continuing his

---

42. On Saint-Simon, see James H. Billington, *Fire in the Minds of Men: Origins of the Revolutionary
Facts* (New York, 1980), 210–18. On Palchinskii, see Loren R. Graham, *The Ghost of the Executed
Engineer: Technology and the Fall of the Soviet Union* (Cambridge, Mass., 1993).
43. Adamsky and Smirnov, "Moscow's Biggest Bomb," 20.

weapons work, as he recalled in his memoirs, was that he had decided to devote even more attention to ending nuclear tests that were biologically harmful and that the best and perhaps only chance of achieving this was by taking full advantage of the prerogatives and proximity to power that Arzamas, despite its geographical isolation, afforded him. In any case, the seeds of future dissidence that the duplicate test fertilized so effectively required time to germinate.

Among the events and experiences that assisted in this process was an incident in 1962 that Sakharov read about in *Nedelia,* the weekly supplement to *Izvestiia.* An old man, who was probably insane, had forged counterfeit coins to buy milk. After burying the coins in his garden, he made the mistake of dropping hints to friends and acquaintances about what he had done. When word of his actions reached the police, they searched his home, found the coins, and arrested him. In the trial that followed, he was required, in Stalinist fashion, not only to confess but to demand his own punishment. Coincidentally, the Soviet government had just enacted amendments to the Criminal Code of the Russian Soviet Federated Socialist Republic prescribing the death penalty for persons convicted of currency speculation, counterfeiting, and theft of state property on a massive scale. These amendments were enacted to silence two black marketeers who had previously been convicted and sentenced to fifteen years in prison and were now naming their accomplices, some of whom were highly placed in the government. Unfortunately for the counterfeiter, even though his transgressions were hardly comparable to those of the black marketeers, the government decided to treat him just as harshly. In the end, both the black marketeers and the counterfeiter were shot. To justify the extremity of the penalty, the government falsely claimed, in the case of the counterfeiter, that he had previously been convicted of armed assault.[44]

Because the article he read in *Nedelia* gave no indication that the counterfeiter's sentence had been carried out, Sakharov believed his intervention might still be useful. He sent a letter to the editor with a request that after reading it, the editor send it to the procurator's office; it is not clear whether Sakharov hoped the editor might print the letter or simply use whatever influence he had to stop the execution. In his letter Sakharov questioned whether what the old man had done was really a crime in light of his mental condition, and he argued that, regardless of how one viewed his actions, they hardly warranted the punishment the government had imposed. Although Sakharov does not quote from the letter in the section of his memoirs in which he describes it, it is clear from his comments about the case that, at the time it was adjudicated, he considered the counterfeiter's arrest—and particularly his punishment—a gross miscarriage of justice. Laws intended for persons whose malfeasance was immeasurably greater than the counterfeiter's had been applied in this instance mindlessly, unfairly, and arbitrarily.[45] This was the first criminal case Sakharov had investigated, and

44. Sakharov, *Memoirs,* 239–40.
45. Ibid., 240.

by his own testimony it left "a bitter taste" in his mouth.[46] Even if the incident, which occurred in the same year as the duplicate test, did not shatter Sakharov's faith in the Soviet system, it almost certainly weakened it.

Despite incidents like the one involving the counterfeiter, Sakharov was not diverted from his objective of reducing the harmful effects of nuclear testing in the atmosphere. In 1962 negotiations for a comprehensive test ban treaty still foundered on the problems of compliance and verification. Testing in the atmosphere is easy to monitor: wind inevitably carries the radioactive dust a nuclear test produces to other parts of the earth's atmosphere, enabling scientists in other countries to determine its origins. Tests conducted underwater or in space are only slightly less difficult to detect. But underground explosions, especially of weapons of relatively small megatonnage, are often indistinguishable from earthquakes or from lesser tremors of the earth's interior.[47] Given these facts and the skepticism with which the Western powers and the Soviet Union viewed each other's promises to abide by any agreements they negotiated, it was clear that a comprehensive test ban treaty would be meaningless unless the problem of verification could be resolved.

Sakharov proposed a solution to the stalemate. In the summer of 1962 Viktor Adamskii reminded him of a proposal floated by the Eisenhower administration four years earlier that any test ban the nuclear powers negotiated should explicitly exclude underground testing.[48] Sakharov immediately understood the advantage of this: while underground tests are harder to detect, they are also far less harmful biologically. In addition, Sakharov shared Khariton's conviction that testing in one form or another was necessary to ensure that nuclear weapons, which are complex and delicate mechanisms, remained operational. Without constant maintenance, including periodic testing, a nuclear arsenal would inevitably erode. To protect against defects in nuclear weapons that might arise later, periodic testing was critical in training the technicians who would actually have to operate these weapons in wartime.[49] Finally, Sakharov understood that even small changes in the composition and size of nuclear arsenals could change the perceptions about intentions and capabilities on which deterrence in a nuclear age ultimately depended. Circumstances might arise in which a comprehensive test ban treaty could in fact render deterrence obsolete and thus make nuclear war more likely. If, say, the United States' nuclear arsenal were older and therefore more prone to obsolescence and deterioration than the Soviet Union's, a comprehensive ban on testing would make it more difficult, despite modeling and computer simulations, for the United States to restore its arsenal to the point where it could once again deter the Soviet Union from launching a nuclear strike.

Sakharov recognized not only the substantive merits of the idea Adamskii passed on to him but its practicality as well: if a comprehensive test ban could

46. Ibid.
47. Ibid., 230.
48. Ibid.; Sakharov, "Interviu vtoroe," 135.
49. Sakharov, *Memoirs*, 207; Yu. B. Khariton, "For Nuclear Parity," in Altshuler et al., Andrei Sakharov, 413.

not be negotiated because the nuclear powers could not know when nuclear weapons were being tested underground in violation of it, then underground testing should be "decoupled" from testing in the atmosphere and elsewhere. Instead of a comprehensive ban on testing, the nuclear powers should negotiate a limited one that explicitly excluded underground testing. As it happened, Sakharov was aware that nuclear explosions had possible nonmilitary applications that were beneficial, and thus from his perspective such an exclusion was a positive virtue as well as a practical necessity. But Sakharov's ability to grasp the political wisdom of decoupling issues that were negotiable from those that were not suggested a pragmatism one might not ordinarily associate with a theoretical physicist whom admirers as well as detractors often criticized for his alleged naïveté.

Shortly after Sakharov saw the merit in this proposal, he asked Slavskii to recommend to his superiors that the Soviet government formally adopt it as a way of facilitating negotiations on a test ban treaty. Slavskii was sympathetic, or at least made an effort to appear sympathetic, telling Sakharov that he would pass on the suggestion—the American origins of which Sakharov commonsensically concealed—to Iakov Malik, the Deputy Minister of foreign affairs, who happened to be at the same spa where Slavskii was vacationing. Slavskii also cautioned Sakharov that on an issue of such gravity "the boss himself" (i.e., Khrushchev) would have to have the last word.[50]

Over the next few months, as the dispute over the duplicate test caused relations between the two men to worsen, Sakharov heard nothing further from his civilian superior. Suddenly, however, in late 1962 or at the very beginning of 1963, Slavskii called Sakharov to inform him that there was interest in his proposal at the highest levels of the Soviet government, which probably would be taking steps very shortly to implement it.[51] A few months later, on July 2, 1963, in a speech in East Berlin, Khrushchev proposed publicly what Sakharov had recommended privately, and on August 5, the Treaty Banning Nuclear Weapons in the Atmosphere, in Outer Space, and Under Water was signed in Moscow by representatives of the United States, the Soviet Union, and the United Kingdom. The treaty went into effect officially on October 10, 1963. Sakharov's statement, in his introduction to *Sakharov Speaks*, that "it is possible that my initiative was of help in this historic act," greatly underestimates his actual contribution.[52]

Even if the test ban treaty did not slow down the arms race, as Sakharov had hoped it would, it demonstrated that Soviet leaders could occasionally do the right thing, and it probably delayed his emergence as a dissident by several

50. Sakharov, *Memoirs*, 230–31.
51. Ibid., 231. In his memoirs Sakharov provides no specific dates for his conversations with Slavskii, so the chronology of this sequence of events is necessarily vague.
52. Sakharov, introduction to *Sakharov Speaks*, 34. In a letter sent to Gorbachev in October 1986 requesting permission to return to Moscow from internal exile in Gorky, Sakharov cited his contribution to the test ban treaty as evidence of his loyalty and past service to his country. A. D. Sakharov, "General'nomu sekretariu TsK KPSS M. S. Gorbachevu (October 22, 1986)," in Altshuler et al., *On mezhdu nami zhil*, 228.

years.[53] In addition, it showed Sakharov that, despite his earlier contretemps with Khrushchev, he could still influence government policy, which in turn confirmed the soundness of his earlier decision that he remain at Arzamas and work for changes within the Soviet system, while at the same time doing the "grand science" he enjoyed.[54] Even more important was that the test ban treaty, because it still allowed underground testing, would reduce the chances of nuclear war. For that reason Sakharov acknowledged in his memoirs that he was proud to have contributed to it.[55]

# 8  The Nuzhdin Affair

Sakharov scored another victory in 1964. In June of that year, he played a critical role in defeating the nomination of Nikolai Nuzhdin, an acolyte and accomplice of Trofim Lysenko—the longtime "Stalin" of Soviet biology, agronomy, and genetics—for full membership in the Academy of Sciences. By opposing Nuzhdin's nomination publicly—at the meeting of the general assembly of the academy at which the full members, in a secret ballot, formally rejected the nomination a few hours after Sakharov spoke—Sakharov was not merely criticizing specific policies obliquely and indirectly, as he and Zeldovich had done in their article in *Pravda* six years earlier concerning Soviet scientific education. Nor was he simply declaring that a particular individual the government favored was unworthy of the honor it wished to confer. By opposing Nuzhdin, Sakharov was frontally challenging the presumption of the Soviet government, central to its claims of moral legitimacy, that it alone had the right to determine Soviet ideology. Because this challenge was actually much broader than the specific issues it raised about the autonomy and integrity of Soviet science, the government, from its own perspective, would have been remiss had it not responded to it as forcefully and as vehemently as it did.

Nuzhdin, as David Joravsky has pointed out, was a more sophisticated fraud than Lysenko himself, even though Lysenko was Sakharov's real target when he determined to derail the Nuzhdin nomination.[1] There is a good deal about Lysenko's quackery that is misunderstood. In all the years he served as president of the V. I. Lenin All-Union Academy of Agricultural Sciences, Lysenko never claimed that his "discoveries" were applicable to humans or that they made the New Soviet Man easier to create.[2] As far as Lysenko was concerned, they would

53. Adamskii, "Stanovlenie grazhdanina," 39.
54. Sakharov, *Memoirs*, 231–32.
55. Ibid., 231.

1. David Joravsky, *The Lysenko Affair* (Chicago, 1970), 414.
2. Graham, *Science in Russia and the Soviet Union*, 123–24.

simply facilitate Soviet agriculture—no mean feat given its chronic deficiencies. These naturally concerned Soviet leaders like Stalin and Khrushchev who knew less about growing plants and raising crops than they thought they did, and who were therefore susceptible to Lysenko's seductive and thoroughly fraudulent claims that he could cure these deficiencies. Over his long career as a charlatan, Lysenko received seven Orders of Lenin, was awarded several Stalin Prizes, was named a Hero of Socialist Labor, and was accorded full membership in three separate scientific academies.[3] For all of this, he was never much concerned about the ideological implications of his chicanery, nor was his falsification of empirical data the most egregious aspect of his fraudulence. Rather, Lysenko was at heart a *praktik* (practical worker), whose explanations of what he falsely claimed his experiments demonstrated were at once illogical, refuted by reliable evidence, and so vague as to be literally incomprehensible—a kind of gibberish that probably not even Lysenko himself understood.[4] To the extent that they can be stated succinctly and coherently, Lysenko's views boiled down to the notion that heredity inheres in the entire organism and that there is nothing specific within the organism, like genes or chromosomes, that is concerned with it.[5] As Lysenko and his followers applied this bogus notion to the evolution of species, it suggested an extreme environmentalism: the example David Joravsky cites to demonstrate its absurdity is of dogs giving birth to foxes because they have been raised in a forest.[6]

All things considered, Lysenko was actually worse than a fraudulent scientist; in his disregard of the scientific method and his conviction that inquiries into the world of nature did not require rules about the accumulation, testing, and evaluation of evidence, he was not really a scientist at all. In fact, in his contempt for the canons of logic and evidence that inform all legitimate science, Lysenko revealed an anti-intellectualism and a disdain for the scientific elite he ruthlessly pilloried that was shared by Stalin and Khrushchev, his principal patrons and protectors in the Soviet government.

Ironically, the genetic damage caused by atmospheric nuclear testing seemed superficially to vindicate Lysenko's claim that environmental factors can directly alter an organism. When the first atmospheric tests were conducted, there was no way of knowing definitively that future generations would also be affected or that the damage they would suffer would be the result of mutations transmitted genetically in ways that contradicted Lysenko's theories. Sakharov may have opposed Nuzhdin, and by implication Lysenko as well, because unlike the vast majority of Soviet scientists, he was aware of this additional danger and had warned of it in his article on radioactive fallout. But Sakharov's concerns about Lysenko sprang from additional sources. He had always been interested in

3. Medvedev, *Soviet Science*, 102.
4. Joravsky, *Lysenko Affair* 187–201, 415.
5. Ibid., 213; Soifer, "Andrei Sakharov and the Fate of Biological Science," 173–74.
6. Joravsky, *Lysenko Affair*, 212. Lysenko himself once said that the plant world is "clay or plaster for the sculptor; we can easily sculpt from them the forms we need." Quoted in ibid., 313.

other sciences and, according to L. V. Altshuler, harbored the illusion for many years that by virtue of his access to Soviet leaders, he could persuade them to reform Soviet biology.[7] In January 1958, when Sakharov spoke to Suslov about Barenblat, he also criticized Lysenko, albeit without naming him, in the hope that the Soviet leader would take corrective action.[8] Indeed, as early as 1955, Sakharov and twenty-three other scientists, including Kapitsa, Landau, Tamm, and Georgii Flerov, wrote to the Central Committee decrying the state of affairs in Soviet biology; in response, Khrushchev called the letter scandalous.[9] A year later, Zeldovich took Sakharov to see Nikolai Dubinin, an opponent of Lysenko who had been disgraced for speaking out against him. Sakharov reports in his memoirs that he was impressed by "the range of [Dubinin's] intelligence" and "businesslike manner" when the biologist described in detail for the two physicists the harm Lysenko and his followers had caused.[10] Sakharov could not have been terribly surprised by what Dubinin told him because sometime before their meeting, he had received "briefings" on the situation from Tamm and other members of the Academy of Sciences.[11] Finally, the circle of physicists at Arzamas in the early 1950s felt a responsibility for all of the sciences, not just physics, and believed they had a special obligation to do whatever they could to help Soviet biology recover; conversely, many Soviet biologists believed their discipline could be salvaged only if Soviet physicists exercised their influence on behalf of it.[12] Toward that end, Kurchatov, who in 1956 had delivered to the government a letter signed by some three hundred geneticists repudiating Lysenko and calling for an end to his imperium, hoped to use funds he controlled as head of the Atomic Energy Institute in Moscow to make it a haven for legitimate but disgraced biologists, where they could pursue their research without intimidation or censorship.[13]

In light of all this, Adamskii's recollection that by the spring of 1964 Sakharov was perturbed enough by what Lysenko had done to take further action to stop him rings true. By that time Sakharov had read in samizdat Zhores Medvedev's manuscript enumerating Lysenko's offenses against Soviet biology.[14] This seemed to disabuse him of any hesitation he might have had in opposing Nuzhdin's nomination.[15] Nuzhdin, in Sakharov's estimation, was "an accomplice in Lysenko's

7. Altshuler, "Riadom s Sakharovym," 119; G. A. Askarian, "Vstrechi i rasmyshleniia," in Altshuler et al., *On mezhdu nami zhil,* 124.

8. Sakharov, *Memoirs,* 206–7.

9. Holloway, *Stalin and the Bomb,* 357–58. For some reason Sakharov does not mention this letter in his memoirs.

10. Sakharov, *Memoirs,* 199.

11. Ibid.

12. Adamskii, "Stanovlenie grazhdanina," 24.

13. Zhores Medvedev, "The Sakharov I Knew," *Observer,* July 7, 1974, 9.

14. Adamskii, "Stanovlenie grazhdanina," 41. This was how Sakharov learned of the Medvedev brothers, with whom he would have a complex and ambiguous relationship, marked by roughly equal amounts of mutual respect and suspicion. Zhores Medvedev's manuscript eventually reached the West and was published in English as *The Rise and Fall of T. D. Lysenko.* "Samizdat" was the term used for writings the dissidents self-produced and reproduced illegally.

15. Adamskii, "Stanovlenie grazhdanina," 24.

pseudo-scientific schemes and in his persecution of genuine scientists."[16] To be sure, if others in the scientific community took on Nuzhdin publicly, Sakharov would defer to them. But if it appeared that the nomination would be approved without debate or dissent, he would intervene.[17]

Elections for membership in the Academy of Sciences were routine. Negative votes were rare, and approval by a candidate's department was customary. According to the accepted procedure, within a specified time period the Council of Ministers would establish a quota for candidates for both full and corresponding membership, and then in a secret ballot each department (or scientific discipline) in the academy would vote on its particular slate of candidates. Candidates whose nominations the various departments approved would then be voted on again, also in a secret ballot, by the general assembly of the academy. This second vote was considered important enough that only the academy's president could excuse an academician's absence. Candidates who received favorable votes from at least two-thirds of the academicians who were present at the assembly became full or corresponding members of the academy, depending on their nomination.[18]

When the academy met on June 24, 1964, to consider a new set of nominations, the Lysenkoites did everything they could—even breaking the rules—to ensure that Nuzhdin's nomination would be approved by his fellow biologists; by a vote of 4–2, it was.[19] As a physicist, Sakharov could do nothing to prevent this. But when Nuzhdin's nomination reached the second stage of the process, at which the general assembly was required to consider it, Sakharov was ready. Unbeknownst to him, the highly regarded and world-renowned biochemist Vladimir Engelgardt had organized a group, which included Tamm and the physicist Mikhail Leontovich, for the purpose of defeating the nomination.[20] Sakharov declared in 1988 that, had he known this, he probably would have deferred to the group on the grounds that any statement he might make after such luminaries as Tamm had spoken would be redundant; presumably, he would then have voted silently against the Nuzhdin nomination.[21] But since Sakharov at the time knew nothing of this, he asked to be recognized when the general assembly convened and the president of the academy, the mathematician Mstislav Keldysh, opened the floor for discussion. With his customary eloquence,

16. Sakharov, *Memoirs*, 233.

17. Ibid., 233–34.

18. Ibid., 233.

19. "Stenogramma zasedaniia Obshchego sobraniia Akademii nauk SSSR, 22–26 iiunia 1964 goda," in Altshuler et al., *On mezhdu nami zhil*, 858. In his reminiscences of the affair, Valery Soifer refers to another biologist and Lysenkoite, G. V. Nikolskii, whose candidacy for full membership, he says, was proposed when Nuzhdin's was. Soifer, "Andrei Sakharov and the Fate of Biological Science," 178. But the stenographic record of the proceedings at which Nuzhdin's candidacy was debated and voted on fails to mention Nikolskii's—which probably was considered at some other time by the academy. Sakharov's memoirs make no mention of it either.

20. Sakharov, *Memoirs*, 234. Coincidentally, Leontovich had been one of Sakharov's teachers at Moscow State University.

21. "Kommentarii akademika A. D. Sakharova po povodu etoi stenogrammy, sdelannye im 8 iiulia 1988 g.," in Altshuler et al., *On mezhdu nami zhil*, 866.

Sakharov excoriated not only Nuzhdin but his mentor and protector, Lysenko, for all the harm they had inflicted on Soviet biology and genetics in particular and on Soviet science in general. Sakharov concluded his brief but powerful oration as follows:

> The academy's charter sets very high standards for its members with respect to both scientific merit and civic responsibility. Corresponding member Nikolai Nuzhdin, who has been nominated by the biology department for elevation to full member, does not satisfy the criteria. Together with Academician Lysenko, he is responsible for the shameful backwardness of Soviet biology and of genetics in particular, for the dissemination of pseudoscientific views, for adventurism, for the degradation of learning, and for the defamation, firing, arrest, even death, of many genuine scientists.[22]

Whoever prepared the stenographic record of Sakharov's remarks for publication pointedly altered what was perhaps his most passionate declaration—that "those who vote for Nuzhdin are those whose hands are dripping with the blood of Soviet biology"—to the more anodyne assertion that those who vote for Nuzhdin "caused the collapse of Soviet biology by the physical destruction of scientists."[23]

In Sakharov's view, Nuzhdin, while a despicable character in his own right, was mostly a surrogate for Lysenko and even more for all those in the Soviet government who encouraged Lysenko, protected him, or simply shut their eyes to the damage he did. Clearly, Sakharov was angered by what he perceived to be systemic failings that, in their magnitude and severity, could not be laid at the feet of any one individual, even one as powerful as Lysenko. He was angered by the perversion of Soviet science for nonscientific purposes and by the degradation of scientific scholarship and standards. He was angered not only by the fraudulence of Lysenko's claims but also by the arbitrariness with which the Soviet government, for purely political and ideological reasons, supported them and then, when expediency required it, rejected them. He was angered by the "exceptionalism" that Lysenko's sway over Soviet biology implied: that Soviet science should not be held to the same standards of evidence, logic, and proof by which the sciences in other countries and political systems were properly judged.[24] He was angry that Soviet science, degraded as it was by charlatans like Lysenko, should at the same time proclaim its superiority to Western science on the basis of ideological assumptions drawn from Marxism-Leninism that had little or nothing to do with science itself. And he was angry that Lysenko's rejection of Western science meant that the vision he had of science as an international endeavor, indeed as a supranational endeavor transcending

---

22. Quoted in Sakharov, *Memoirs*, 234.
23. Ioirysh, *Uroki A. D. Sakharova*, 73; B. M. Bolotovskii, "A Criminal Matter," in Drell and Kapitza, *Sakharov Remembered*, 53–54.
24. Loren Graham characterizes Lysenko's quackery as a form of "exceptionalism" in his *What Have We Learned?* 34–35.

the artificial and often restrictive barriers of nationality and nation-states, was that much further from being realized. For Sakharov, there could not be two sciences, a Marxist-Leninist one and a capitalist one.[25] There could be only one science, based on universally accepted canons of inquiry, experimentation, and verification. In sum, Nuzhdin's nomination evoked in Sakharov larger concerns about the profession he had chosen many years earlier under the salubrious influence of virtuous men, such as Tamm and his father, whom he deeply respected. Sakharov accordingly viewed the nomination almost as a personal affront, and the indignation that he says "boiled up" in him when he first learned of it was almost surely because of this.[26]

The initial response to Sakharov's denunciation was, as he puts it, "deafening silence." This was followed, eventually, by a mixture of applause and cries of "shame."[27] Lysenko, who, as an academician, was present for the occasion, proclaimed within earshot of Sakharov that he should be jailed and put on trial. Tamm, Engelgardt, and Leontovich presented their opinions next. Then Lysenko spoke, claiming that Sakharov had slandered Nuzhdin.[28] Among the other speakers was Zeldovich, who, like Sakharov, criticized Nuzhdin and eventually voted against him.[29] In an effort to calm the situation, Keldysh, from the podium, tried to be evenhanded: he admonished Sakharov for the substance of his criticisms and for what he called the "tactlessness" with which the physicist had delivered them.[30] But he also called on the assembled academicians to vote on Nuzhdin's nomination calmly and impartially and, addressing Lysenko directly, told him that Sakharov and every other member of the academy had the right to express their opinions when legitimate business was before them. Ironically, but perhaps appropriately in light of the critical role science played in the whole enterprise of achieving socialism and communism, the freedom of speech the academy enjoyed and the internal democracy it practiced were emphatically denied to the Soviet people, for whose benefit the academy purportedly existed.[31] In the voting that followed, Nuzhdin's nomination was defeated by a vote of 114–23.[32] A. I. Ioirysh's view that Sakharov's intervention was "decisive" was shared by many who were present at the meeting.[33] This was the first time since

25. Loren R. Graham, "The Impact of Science and Technology on Soviet Politics and Society," in Graham, *Science and the Soviet Social Order,* 2.

26. Sakharov, *Memoirs,* 233.

27. Ibid., 234.

28. Ibid., 234–35; Bolotovskii, "Criminal Matter," 54.

29. Bolotovskii, "Criminal Matter," 54.

30. "Stenogramma zasedaniia," 863; Sakharov, *Memoirs,* 235.

31. Sakharov, *Memoirs,* 235.

32. This is the tally in the official stenographic record of the proceedings. Several accounts of them offer different ones: 128–24, 126–24, and 126–22 or 126–24. Medvedev, "The Sakharov I Know," 9; Bailey, *Making of Andrei Sakharov,* 220; Dornan, "Andrei Sakharov," 363. Given that the stenographic record, which in other circumstances might be considered definitive, is not reliable, one has no way of knowing which of these tallies is correct. Sakharov does not provide one in his memoirs. The important point, of course, is that Nuzhdin's candidacy was defeated overwhelmingly and that Sakharov was more responsible for this than anyone else.

33. Bolotovskii, "Criminal Matter," 55; Ioirysh, *Uroki A. D. Sakharova,* 74.

the October Revolution that the academy had rejected a candidate for full or corresponding membership.

When he learned what had happened, Khrushchev, not surprisingly, was furious. According to Sakharov, the Soviet leader ordered the head of the KGB, Vladimir Semichastny, to gather "compromising material" on the Soviet physicist for having "poked his nose where it doesn't belong."[34] According to Adamskii, Khrushchev, before his anger subsided, even wanted to strip Sakharov of his title of academician and expel him from the academy.[35] Had it not been for Khrushchev's removal from power in October 1964, that might have happened. To Khrushchev, Sakharov's behavior was a personal betrayal. From his perspective, Sakharov was an unruly, ungracious, and insolent child who had responded with ingratitude to the perquisites and honors the Soviet government bestowed on him, in several instances by Khrushchev himself. But the Soviet leader was furious with the academy as well. At an official reception Khrushchev attended shortly after Nuzhdin's nomination had been defeated, he openly threatened to close the academy for having "meddled in politics."[36] With some cause, Khrushchev believed that the academy's action and the defeat it represented for the government had been made possible by the free and open debate that preceded it.

Not surprisingly, Sakharov was singled out for virulent criticism in the Soviet press. In August there appeared in the journal *Selskaia zhizn* an article by M. A. Olshanskii, the president of the Soviet Academy of Agricultural Sciences.[37] The title the editors chose for the article—in English translation, "Against Disinformation and Slander"—was apposite. In the article Olshanskii pointedly called Sakharov "an engineer by profession," which was a way of insinuating that Sakharov had no expertise in biology and thus did not know what he was talking about when he criticized Nuzhdin and Lysenko.[38] Olshanskii then went on to condemn Sakharov, whom he denigrated as "incompetent" and "naïve," for his "abusive, non-scientific attack against the Michurinist-scientists in the style of anonymous, slanderous letters."[39] Olshanskii also sent a letter to Khrushchev complaining that Sakharov had slandered Nuzhdin and that no one at the meeting had the good sense to stop him as he was doing so.[40] For good measure, he recommended that Medvedev be prosecuted criminally for sending Sakharov his manuscript on Lysenko.[41]

34. Sakharov, *Memoirs*, 236–37.
35. Adamskii, "Stanovlenie grazhdanina," 42.
36. Medvedev, "The Sakharov I Know," 9.
37. Sakharov, *Memoirs*, 236.
38. Quoted in Bolotovskii, "Criminal Matter," 58. One newspaper reporting the vote also called Sakharov an engineer. Goldanskii, "Scientist, Thinker, Humanist," 23.
39. Dornan, "Andrei Sakharov," 363; quoted in Bolotovskii, "Criminal Matter," 58. I. V. Michurin was a horticulturalist the Soviet regime esteemed highly in the 1920s and early 1930s and on whose ideas and methods Lysenko later claimed his own work was based. Joravsky, *Lysenko Affair*, 40–54.
40. Ioirysh, *Uroki A. D. Sakharova*, 75.
41. Joravsky, *Lysenko Affair*, 145, 395.

Olshanksii's article contained so many distortions and outright falsehoods both about Lysenkoism and Sakharov's reasons for condemning it that Sakharov felt compelled to respond. He sent a letter—which for some reason he fails to mention in his memoirs—to *Izvestiia* reiterating in greater detail the arguments he had mustered in the general assembly. He also stated that "for a scientist there is nothing more important than absolute scientific and professional objectivity.... I add my voice to the voices of those honest Soviet biological scientists who are struggling for the triumph of scientific truth in the interests of our native land."[42] In a letter he wrote concurrently to Khrushchev refuting Olshanskii's accusations, Sakharov expressed the same moral outrage, condemning Lysenko and his followers as "a group from which no scientific objectivity can be expected."[43] He also called—more than twenty years before Gorbachev did—for a kind of glasnost in which nothing would be off-limits to anyone wishing to investigate the history of Soviet biology. Stressing his pragmatic objections to Lysenko in light of his audience of one, Sakharov pointed out how much the Soviet Union could benefit from a frank and open discussion of how Lysenko had harmed not only Soviet biology but Soviet science and the Soviet Union itself.[44]

Following Khrushchev's ouster in 1964, the new leaders of the Soviet Union, Leonid Brezhnev in particular, sought to make amends. For the time being, they had no desire to antagonize Sakharov further, and in any event they still valued his abilities as a physicist. As Brezhnev told a regional party secretary in 1965 after Sakharov and Khariton had briefed the secretary on the projects they were working on at Arzamas, "Sakharov has some doubts and inner conflicts. We ought to try to understand and do all we can to help him."[45] But Sakharov, while not at all desirous of a formal break with the regime, was intent on preserving his autonomy and freedom of action. Once again he rejected an invitation—which in all likelihood originated with Brezhnev and was transmitted through Khariton—that he join the Communist Party.[46] In a sense, the invitation was a form of appeasement. Coming as it did on the heels of the contretemps in the Academy of Sciences, it was hardly likely to have its intended effect. In Sakharov's view, science was nothing less than "a keystone of civilization, and any unwarranted encroachment on its domain [was] impermissible."[47]

42. Quoted in Bolotovskii, "Criminal Matter," 55, 56.
43. Quoted in ibid., 58.
44. Ibid. Khrushchev's failure to show Sakharov's letter to the other members of the Presidium for two weeks after receiving it was one count in the "indictment" the plotters who later ousted him issued to justify their action. According to Suslov, who actually delivered the charges, Khrushchev's inaction reflected his long-standing inability to communicate with his colleagues effectively. Sakharov, *Memoirs*, 237. Regardless of whether this particular charge was accurate, the fact that Sakharov had sources in the government who informed him of this shortly after Khrushchev was ousted demonstrates how well placed he remained even after his repeated criticisms of government policy.
45. Sakharov, *Memoirs*, 232.
46. Ibid.
47. Ibid., 235.

For this reason the Nuzhdin affair was "another landmark...on my way to becoming active in civic affairs."[48]

## Finding Pleasure in Cosmology

By this time in his life, Sakharov was truly on his own. His father had passed away in December 1961, his mother in April 1963. In addition, Sakharov's estrangement from Klava had become deep and probably irremediable. Their marriage, long a troubled one, had become dysfunctional. Consistent with his sense of privacy and decorum, Sakharov writes about the deterioration of his marriage only fleetingly in his memoirs, in an early chapter that precedes his description of the other events in his life that were concurrent with it. This suggests that he may have felt compelled to establish some distance in his own mind between his deteriorating family life and the professional issues that were equally as important to him. Klava's very absence from the narrative, in other words, itself attests to her growing irrelevance. Not even the gastric hemorrhages she suffered in 1964 and 1965 could close the emotional gap between them.[49] The same can be said of Sakharov's three children. None of them rates any more than a perfunctory mention in his recollection of his life from 1954 to 1968.

From both his personal problems and the turmoil produced by issues like the Nuzhdin affair Sakharov found solace in exploring what he called "grand science."[50] By this he meant a kind of physics that sheds light on ultimate questions such as the origins and initial development of the universe. The theoretical physics he was able to pursue from 1963 to 1967, mostly at Arzamas but also in Moscow and on vacation in the Crimea, helped to make these years, in terms of scientific originality and productivity, the most fruitful of his entire life.[51] In Moscow in particular, where in the 1960s he frequently attended seminars at FIAN, he had the opportunity to exchange ideas with colleagues on topics of mutual interest.[52]

In 1965 Sakharov produced a paper in which he ascribed to quantum effects the existence in the universe of the "inhomogeneities" that are its galaxies, stars, and planets.[53] He assumed, as physicists in the 1960s were increasingly apt to do, that

48. Ibid.
49. Ibid., 295.
50. Ibid., 241.
51. Ibid.
52. B. L. Altshuler, introduction to Altshuler et al., *Andrei Sakharov,* 17–18.
53. Sakharov, *Memoirs,* 241–46; Feinberg, "Biographical Sketch," 6–7; A. D. Sakharov, "The Initial Stage of an Expanding Universe and the Appearance of a Nonuniform Distribution of Matter," in Sakharov, *Collected Scientific Works,* 65–83. The basic tenets of quantum physics were developed in the 1920s. At the risk of oversimplification, they can be boiled down to the mind-bending notion that in the subatomic world, where matter has the properties of both particles and waves, there are limits to what can be known about things when we are observing them; in fact, the very act of observing something—say, an electron—that we would consider objectively real has the effect of changing it. This implies an uncertainty about everything that is external to man. Einstein, for one, found this idea so troubling that he tried for many years, without success, to refute quantum theory. A concise and comprehensible explanation of it is John Gribbin's *In Search of Schrödinger's Cat: Quantum Physics and Reality* (New York, 1984).

the universe was expanding, and consequently it must have had a beginning, before which there was literally nothing. At the moment of its creation, the universe must have been infinitesimally small but at the same time unimaginably dense; for this reason its attributes could not possibly be simulated in a laboratory for the purpose of confirming them empirically. But this did not stop physicists and cosmologists from theorizing that at its beginning—in what has come to be known as the Big Bang and its immediate aftermath, measured in literally trillionths of seconds—the universe was more or less homogeneous, with matter and energy uniformly distributed, and that only the subsequent influence of gravity caused the "clumping" that explains the presence of discrete entities such as galaxies, stars, and planets. Cosmologists were convinced that once this clumping or clustering began, it was self-generating: the closer objects are to one another, the greater the gravity (that is, the attractive force) between them. But how did this clustering begin if, at the time the universe began, matter was uniformly distributed? As he acknowledged in his memoirs, Sakharov's answer was fundamentally flawed by his assumption that, at the moment of its creation, the universe was extremely cold. Since the time he wrote his paper, cosmologists have determined that the universe was in fact extremely hot. Sakharov's explanation, in other words, was wrong. But the fact that he had returned to studying such issues restored his confidence as a theoretical physicist—which had been shaken by devoting so much of his time over the years to the more practical task of designing thermonuclear weapons— and piqued his interest in other cosmological topics.[54]

Also in 1965 Sakharov collaborated with eight other authors on a paper describing how magnetic compression could be achieved by detonating a chemical explosion and transforming the thermal and mechanical energy it released into extraordinarily strong magnetic fields.[55] One year later, in another paper, Sakharov and Zeldovich produced a formula for the masses of subatomic particles, specifically protons and neutrons, on the basis of the arrangement of the quarks that comprise them.[56] In their paper Sakharov and Zeldovich also claimed, on the basis of what was known at the time about the kinds of quarks (called "flavors") that exist and about the different ways that quarks behave, that protons probably consisted of five quarks and in any case could not contain fewer than four. Subsequent research would prove their supposition wrong, but given what Sakharov and Zeldovich did not know, and could not have known, when they proposed it, their error hardly detracted from the intellectual brilliance of their speculation.[57]

54. Sakharov, *Memoirs,* 246.
55. Sidney Drell and Lev. B. Okun, "Physics, the Bomb, and Human Rights," in Drell and Kapitza, *Sakharov Remembered,* 112; A. D. Sakharov et al., "Magnetic Cumulation," in Sakharov, *Collected Scientific Works,* 23–27.
56. A. D. Sakharov and Ya. B. Zeldovich, "The Quark Structure and Masses of Strongly Interacting Particles," in Sakharov, *Collected Scientific Works,* 205–21; Harry J. Lipkin, "Elementary Particles," in ibid., 272–73. Physicists believe that quarks exist even though the force binding quarks together is so strong that they have never been seen individually.
57. Lipkin, "Elementary Particles," 273–74.

In 1967 Sakharov authored two papers on the nature of gravity. In his general theory of relativity, which he developed shortly before World War I, Einstein proposed that the universe, conceived as a four-dimensional space-time continuum, is curved, and that this curvature is a function of the gravitational force that all the mass exerts on the universe. Experiments conducted after the war confirmed this. But neither Einstein nor any other physicist knew precisely how the gravitational force worked. All they knew was that it existed. Einstein subsequently suggested that the force every body exerts on every other (to a degree that is a function of both mass and distance) was the result of the "deformation" gravity causes in the physical vacuum in which everything that is corporeal in the universe exists. Sakharov's contribution was explaining how this deformation can occur: because there are virtual particles that exist for an infinitesimal amount of time in this physical vacuum (which thus is not a vacuum at all). According to Sakharov, two bodies are attracted to each other because each somehow "recognizes" the deformation the other one has caused in this vacuum, which, because it contains these virtual particles, is not empty space; if there is no equivalent or countervailing force to prevent it, the two bodies will move closer together and eventually touch or collide.[58]

In this period Sakharov published other papers in cosmology.[59] Undoubtedly the most far-reaching, innovative, and original of these concerned "baryon asymmetry."[60] "Baryons" is the term physicists use to denote collectively not only protons and neutrons but also a variety of other, unstable particles that are created when protons and neutrons collide at extraordinarily high speeds. "Antibaryons" differ from baryons in that they carry the opposite electromagnetic charge. When baryons and antibaryons collide, they annihilate each another, producing in the process exotic, unstable particles, such as pi-mesons, which are lighter than baryons, as well as radiation in the form of "quanta" (or packets) of photons, which have no mass at all. The "background radiation" cosmologists discovered in the mid-1960s is really the remnant of the radiation that was produced in the annihilation of baryons and antibaryons that occurred when

58. D. A. Kirzhnits, "Sakharov-Physicist," in Altshuler et al., *Andrei Sakharov*, 424; A. D. Sakharov, "Vacuum Quantum Fluctuations in Curved Space and the Theory of Gravitation," in Sakharov, *Collected Scientific Works*, 167–69, 171–77.

59. A. D. Sakharov, "Magnetoimplosive Generators," in Sakharov, *Collected Scientific Works*, 29–41; A. D. Sakharov, "Maximum Temperature of Thermal Radiation," in *Collected Scientific Works*, 137–39.

60. A. D. Sakharov, "Violation of CP Invariance, C Asymmetry, and Baryon Asymmetry of the Universe," in Sakharov, *Collected Scientific Works*, 85–88; A. D. Sakharov, "Quark-Muonic Currents and Violation of CP Invariance," in Sakharov, *Collected Scientific Works*, 89–92; Andrei D. Sakharov, "The Symmetry of the Universe," in Drell and Kapitza, *Sakharov Remembered*, 217–23. In the exposition that follows, I have relied on Sakharov's memoirs, 247–59; Andrew M. Sessler and Yvonne Howell, "Sakharov's Contributions to Science," in *Andrei Sakharov and Peace*, ed. Edward D. Lozansky (New York, 1985), 184; and Martin Rees, *Before the Beginning: Our Universe and Others* (Reading, Mass., 1997), 155–58. On baryon asymmetry and Sakharov's insights into it, see also B. L. Altshuler, "Misunderstanding Sakharov," in Drell and Kapitza, *Sakharov Remembered*, 231–32; L. Susskind, "Matter-Antimatter Asymmetry," in Sakharov, *Collected Scientific Works*, 151–55; Gorelik, *The World of Andrei Sakharov*, 244–59; and V. A. Tsukerman, "Ego nel'zia vycherknut' iz istorii," in Altshuler et al., *On mezhdu nami zhil*, 750–51.

the universe was created or shortly afterward. Baryons and antibaryons, in other words, are one form of matter and antimatter, respectively; electrons, which have a negative electromagnetic charge, and their opposite, positrons, which have a positive charge, are another.

What Sakharov tried to explain was why baryon asymmetry exists: that is, how there came to be a surplus of baryons over antibaryons, without which there would be no matter at all. A universe without baryon asymmetry would thus be an empty universe, with nothing in it except this primordial radiation from when the universe was created. When Sakharov pondered the whole question, the consensus among cosmologists was that there had to be baryon symmetry when the universe began. But there was no consensus on how this symmetry broke down and asymmetry ensued.

Sakharov began by conjuring the conditions that existed shortly after baryon asymmetry appeared, before the overwhelming majority of baryons and anti-baryons were annihilated, leaving only the "small" surplus of baryons over anti-baryons (some $10^{80}$ of them protons) from which everything in the universe would subsequently be formed. He then argued that this asymmetry emerged out of an original state, less than $10^{-43}$ seconds after creation, in which there was baryon symmetry, and that this condition of symmetry could be followed by one that was asymmetrical.[61] According to Sakharov, for baryon asymmetry to occur, the universe at the quantum level had to know the future from the past—it had to have, in Christopher Korda's words, "an intrinsic arrow of time."[62] So important and original was Sakharov's hypothesis that physicists today refer to the sequence of events Sakharov described as "the Sakharov conditions."[63]

Sakharov's conclusion was that "baryon number"—the difference between baryons and antibaryons in the universe—was not constant, as most cosmologists before him believed. In fact, baryon number changes whenever a proton, having a baryon number of one, is transformed, say, into positrons and photons, which are not baryons at all and thus have a baryon number of zero. In this way, baryons, and in particular protons, can decay, and it was Sakharov's concept of proton decay and how it comes about that proved to be perhaps the most re-markable of all his contributions to cosmology. One of Sakharov's colleagues at FIAN, D. S. Chernavskii, went so far as to say that, by showing theoretically that the proton can disintegrate, he revealed "the basis of our universe."[64] Ironically,

61. Altshuler, "Misunderstanding Sakharov," 232. This baryon asymmetry or imbalance is extra-ordinarily slight when one considers the number of baryons and antibaryons that are annihilated. As the universe cooled, for every baryon that survived, there might be $10^9$ of them that did not. Rees, *Before the Beginning*, 157.

62. Communication with Christopher Korda, July 10, 2008.

63. Communication with Grant J. Mathews, July 10, 2008.

64. D. S. Chernavskii, "Osnova vselennoi mozhet raspadat'sia," in Ivanova, *Andrei Dmitrievich*, 68. Eisenhower and Sagdeev, among others, emphasize how unorthodox were Sakharov's views on baryon number conservation, while J. D. Bjorken, himself a theoretical physicist, claimed to see in both Sakharov's physics and his dissidence "a concern with fundamental issues, and an optimistic and often visionary viewpoint, but a viewpoint nevertheless tempered with pragmatic elements

Sakharov's ideas on the subject did not attract much attention for about a decade after he first expressed them. But the development of what were called gauge theories in the late 1970s sparked new interest in them, even though proton decay has yet to be confirmed experimentally.[65]

The intellectual world theoretical physicists inhabit is a world of pure reason. The subatomic particles they examine are too small, just as the outer reaches of the universe are too distant, to examine empirically, at least not with the same facility with which most other scientists are able to verify their theoretical hypotheses. Quantum theory even holds that the very act of observing something changes it, making precise measurements impossible. Sakharov seemed to flourish in this world where pure reason reigns supreme.

It hardly follows, however, that he functioned less well in other situations or that his cosmological interests and the intellectual habits he cultivated in pursuing them bore no relation to his life outside physics and science or were somehow harmful to it. Obviously, Sakharov did not become a dissident because he explored baryon asymmetry or tried to explain gravity. But his dissidence shared certain features with the way he explored cosmology and physics, most notably a willingness to challenge the conventional wisdom and to do so on matters that were of the utmost importance. In both roles he played, Sakharov showed irrefutably that he had the courage of his convictions. Moreover, while it is problematic to claim exact parallels between his dissidence and his physics, one sees in both areas a concern with fundamental issues—of morality and social justice in the case of the former, of existence itself in the case of the latter—and also an ability to integrate the microscopic and the universal in proposing a theory, or advancing an argument, that is itself comprehensive and complete.[66] As a dissident, Sakharov considered the universal human rights he advocated meaningless unless they were applicable to every individual. Similarly, he held that in order to understand how the universe works, a knowledge of the way subatomic particles react to one another is required. Relating the ridiculously large to the absurdly small in generating a thesis that applies to both of these realms seems to have been one of the skills Sakharov honed while pursuing his cosmological interests in the mid-1960s. He would have little difficulty applying this skill to the political realm.

---

as well." Eisenhower and Sagdeev, "Sakharov in His Own Words," 52; J. D. Bjorken, "Elementary Particle Physics," in Sakharov, *Collected Scientific Works*, 141.

65. Susskind, "Matter-Antimatter Asymmetry," 152; "Sidney D. Drell, "Tribute to Andrei Sakharov," in Drell and Kapitza, *Sakharov Remembered*, 86. Gauge theories hold that the interaction between elementary particles, rather than anything intrinsic to them, is what defines and determines their physical properties. Lee Smolin, *The Life of the Cosmos* (New York, 1997), 52–53, 62, 343.

66. D. S. Chernavskii states that Sakharov's genius as a physicist consisted in seeing the universe not as a collection of discrete and occasionally disparate elements but as a self-contained entity. Chernavskii, "Osnova vselennoi mozhet raspadat'sia," 68.

# 9 A Dissident at Last

Andrei Sakharov joined the dissident movement shortly after it became a recognizable phenomenon in the mid-1960s. A Soviet dissident could be generally described as someone who regarded the Soviet system as flawed, based his criticisms on moral principle, believed in the inherent dignity and worth of the individual, and whose efforts to change the Soviet system for the better prompted the leadership to try to silence him. To a remarkable degree, the trajectory of Soviet dissidence in the 1960s and 1970s—from isolated protests condemning specific actions of the government to a coordinated and organized movement for systemic reform—followed that of the prerevolutionary intelligentsia.

Before the mid-1960's, most critics of the Soviet Union couched their objections in terms strikingly similar to those Khrushchev had used in criticizing Stalin—they ascribed systemic problems to the moral failings of an individual or a small group.[1] These critics believed there was nothing wrong with the Soviet Union that the removal of individuals with defective character would not cure. The Soviet system was basically sound; Khrushchev's de-Stalinization showed that the system could reform itself, albeit within limits, and that the mistakes made and the crimes committed were primarily the result of a moral failure, the correction of which required the spiritual regeneration of individuals rather than the transformation of political institutions and society. Most of these critics were writers by profession who used literature to express their ideas not only because it was the genre for which they were specifically trained but because, as Marshall Shatz has pointed out, literature tends to transform political issues into moral ones. Thus, programmatic alternatives and specific recommendations of policy are largely absent in their work.[2] Since changing specific policies was not the intent of the critics anyway, literature was well suited for their purposes.

Examples abound of this kind of criticism in the Soviet Union from 1953, when Stalin died and de-Stalinization began, to the mid-1960s, when it gave way to outright dissidence. In 1953 Vladimir Pomerantsev's article "On Sincerity in Literature" called for an end to the strict limitations Stalin's doctrine of Socialist Realism had placed on Soviet writers in rendering accurate, three-dimensional portraits of the characters they created.[3] Three years later, Vladimir Dudinstev, in his novel *Not by Bread Alone*, decried what he considered the hypocrisy and narrow-mindedness of Soviet bureaucrats, whose collective foibles he neatly encapsulated in the figure of a thoroughly unappealing factory manager named Drozdov, who, after the novel appeared, became for many readers the prototype

1. For what follows, I found Shatz, *Soviet Dissent*, 100–12, very helpful.
2. Ibid., 115.
3. V. Pomerantsev, "Ob iskrennost' v literature," *Novyi mir* 12 (December 1953): 218–45.

of the unresponsive, self-interested Soviet apparatchik. Although Dudintsev located the problems he saw in Soviet society in an entire stratum rather than in a small number of individuals, he still believed that the regime, acting on its own, would resolve them. In the novel, a party official intervenes to save Drozdov's principal antagonist, who in the end is released from the labor camp to which he was exiled. In much the same way, Alexander Iashin's short story "Levers," which also appeared in 1956, describes how ordinary party members who were discussing matters that concerned them openly and honestly prior to a formal party meeting abruptly resort to the formulaic rhetoric of Marxism-Leninism when higher-ups arrive and the meeting begins.[4]

Mention should also be made of Pasternak's novel *Doctor Zhivago,* for which he won the Nobel Prize for Literature in 1958, which the Soviet government refused to allow him to accept. *Doctor Zhivago,* while rejecting the presumption of Bolshevism that objective reality is not only understandable but also predictable, nevertheless makes clear that the proper response to the fanaticism such certitude generates is not to confront it but to endure it (as the character, Iurii Zhivago, does) or to bear witness to it (as Pasternak did by writing the book). Alexander Solzhenitsyn's novella *One Day in the Life of Ivan Denisovich,* which Khrushchev in 1962 allowed to be serialized in *Novyi mir,* imparts a similar message: even though Stalinism ruined the lives of millions of people, most of them completely apolitical—Ivan Denisovich is the equivalent of the American John Doe—the most one could do to prevent its recurrence was to tell the truth about it. Under the circumstances, this was nothing to denigrate, and in Solzhenitsyn's opinion telling the truth about the Soviet Union was a necessary first step to reforming it. But the novella also leaves the reader with the impression (as does Solzhenitsyn's short story "Matryona's Place") that until the Soviet people experienced a moral and spiritual regeneration, changing the structure of Soviet society would be pointless. Indeed, in the absence of this ethical renaissance, which Solzhenitsyn thought should be based on Russian Orthodoxy, Stalinism could happen again.

The catalyst for the emergence of Soviet dissidence was the trial of the writers Andrei Siniavskii and Iulii Daniel in February 1966.[5] Although Soviet writers had been tried before, this was the first time they had been put on trial explicitly for the content of their work.[6] The reason for this is that although the government wanted to try Siniavskii and Daniel for sending their manuscripts abroad, where

---

4. Iashin's story can be found in English translation in *The Year of Protest, 1956: An Anthology of Soviet Literary Materials,* ed. Hugh McLean and Walter N. Vickery (New York, 1961), 193–210.

5. A transcript of the trial, with notes and commentary, is included in Max Hayward, ed., *On Trial* (New York, 1967). For analysis of the trial, see Shatz, *Soviet Dissent,* 117–21; Abraham Rothberg, *The Heirs of Stalin: Dissidence and the Soviet Regime, 1953–1970* (Ithaca, 1972), 151–67; and Ludmilla Alexeyeva, *Soviet Dissent: Contemporary Movements for National, Religious, and Human Rights* (Middletown, Conn., 1985), 274–79.

6. Rothberg, *Heirs of Stalin,* 152. The poet Iosef Brodskii, for example, was tried in 1964 on the charge of "parasitism." Because the literary work Brodskii did was intermittent, the government decided he was unemployed—which in the Soviet Union was a crime—and thus a "parasite." Ibid., 127–33.

they were published under pseudonyms, there was no law prohibiting foreign publication. So the government instead charged the two men with spreading "anti-Soviet agitation and propaganda," which under Article 70 of the Criminal Code of the Russian Soviet Federated Socialist Republic (RSFSR) was a crime punishable by a prison term or confinement in a labor camp.[7] As expected, both men were convicted and sent to labor camps—Siniavskii for seven years, Daniel for five. Although the proceedings, which took place in Moscow, were not show trials like those in the 1930s in which the defendants confessed to crimes they had not committed, the defendants in 1966 were allowed to mount a defense, even though the outcome was predetermined by the government. Sakharov himself was largely oblivious to the trial.[8] But the threat it posed to writers, who were now threatened with prosecution for what they wrote, was a serious one. And the denial of due process raised concerns among many in the educated elite that this might not be just an isolated occurrence but the beginning of a more general crackdown in which the limited criticisms Khrushchev allowed and even in some cases encouraged would no longer be tolerated.

If the Soviet leaders intended their punishment of Siniavskii and Daniel as an object lesson to others who might be contemplating following their example, their effort had the opposite effect. Through a "multiplier effect," the trial caused Soviet dissidence, over the next three years, to increase exponentially. Because it seemed to suggest so persuasively and ominously that no one was safe from the arbitrary exercise of judicial power, the trial prompted public protests against it. One of these, a demonstration in December 1965 in Pushkin Square in Moscow, occurred before the trial even began. The government in turn arrested the participants in these protests, and the trials that followed sparked additional protests. In this way, Soviet dissidence was self-perpetuating.

What caused this movement to emerge when it did was the nascent neo-Stalinism in the mid-1960s—the revival of some of the methods and objectives of Stalinism—of which the trial was just the most obvious expression. After Stalin's death in 1953 and throughout the Khrushchev era, the government's attitude toward the late dictator was a fairly accurate barometer of how repressive it was. The same was true of the mid-1960s. In those years, what the Soviet government said about Stalin and the actions it took that in some way concerned his reputation were an accurate indication not only that the reformist policies Khrushchev had stopped in 1963–1964 would not resume but that a new wave of repression in the form of increased police surveillance, greater restrictions on travel abroad, and more vigorous persecution of ethnic and religious minorities was about to begin. Among the actions the government took that suggested this were praising Stalin's wartime leadership as "beyond reproach" on the twentieth anniversary of V-E Day in 1965 and restoring the Stalin-era name "Politburo" to the Presidium in 1966. Even the rumor that the government was considering returning Stalin's body to the Lenin Mausoleum, from which it had been

---

7. Joshua Rubenstein, *Soviet Dissidents: Their Struggle for Human Rights* (Boston, 1980), 38–40.
8. Sakharov, *Memoirs*, 275.

unceremoniously removed in 1961, caused a small number of people, mostly Muscovites, to conclude that if this neo-Stalinism was to be thwarted and reform to resume, they would have to take action themselves. When they did so, they were acting, for all intents and purposes, as dissidents. Like their ancestors in the intelligentsia, they initially turned to petitioning their Soviet tsars for the redress of their grievances.

The mid-1960s were critical to Sakharov's intellectual and political development, the time in his life when, by concerning himself predominantly with social and political issues, he approached "a decisive break with the establishment."[9] In part this was because he was spending more time in Moscow, where he had an apartment. With Slavskii's permission, Sakharov attended seminars and worked on a part-time basis at FIAN (now renamed the Lebedev Institute). While in Moscow he met several dissidents, or people who were in the process of becoming dissidents, whose unorthodox ideas on the relative merits of socialism and capitalism he took back with him to Arzamas, where he and his scientific colleagues discussed them.[10] In particular, he learned much from Roi Medvedev, Zhores Medvedev's twin brother, who on his visits to Sakharov's apartment spoke to him at length about the exposé of Stalinism he was writing.[11] Roi Medvedev also trusted Sakharov sufficiently at this time to leave copies of his manuscript behind for safekeeping—thereby making Sakharov complicit in what the government could conceivably construe as a criminal conspiracy. From Roi Medvedev Sakharov also received samizdat copies of works such as *Journey into the Whirlwind*, a memoir by a Soviet schoolteacher, Evgeniia Ginzburg, of her travails as a victim of Stalin's Terror.[12] Although Sakharov would eventually reject Medvedev's view that Stalin alone was to blame for the Terror and other harmful distortions of Lenin's correct policies—in Sakharov's more commonsensical view Stalinism was traceable ultimately to Leninism—he nevertheless found Medvedev's work on Stalinism illuminating, especially on those aspects of it of which he was ignorant. In his memoirs he states that the information it contained "stimulated the evolution of my views at the crucial time in my life."[13]

Sakharov's initiation into the world of Soviet dissidence began in January 1966, when the enigmatic Soviet journalist Ernst Henri paid him a visit. Henri, a former Comintern agent whose real name was Semën Rostovskii, had ties to both the

9. Ibid., 267. Only once prior to becoming a dissident did Sakharov try to change government policy on an issue that did not concern Soviet science or thermonuclear weaponry. In 1954, in response to attacks in the Soviet press on a play, Leonid Zorin's *Gosti* ("The Guests"), that compared Soviet bureaucrats unfavorably with the honest Leninists in the population they purported to serve, Sakharov wrote a letter to Khrushchev defending the play. But he did so mostly at Zeldovich's urging and to no appreciable effect; all he received in response was boilerplate from a Central Committee underling. Ibid., 200.

10. Adamskii, "Stanovlenie grazhdanina," 42.

11. It was published in the West with the English title *Let History Judge: The Origins and Consequences of Stalinism.*

12. Sakharov, *Memoirs*, 271–72.

13. Ibid., 272.

Communist Party and the KGB.[14] In all likelihood he sought out Sakharov on behalf of people within these institutions who, while loyal to the regime, feared that the party congress scheduled to convene a month later would adopt a resolution rehabilitating Stalin. Henri showed Sakharov a letter he was circulating opposing such a resolution. Kapitsa, Tamm, and Leontovich had already signed the letter. Henry asked Sakharov to sign it as well, and he did so. Additional signers, of whom there would be twenty-five in all, included the writer Konstantin Paustovskii, the children's author Kornei Chukovskii, the dancer Maia Plisetskaia, the filmmaker Mikhail Romm, and the retired Soviet diplomat Ivan Maiskii.[15]

Addressed to Brezhnev, the letter was deferential, even obsequious, in tone. Describing the rumored rehabilitation of Stalin as "a cause for profound concern," the letter contained arguments that whoever actually composed the document thought might appeal, on purely pragmatic grounds, to the Soviet leader. Rehabilitating Stalin, it said, would only alienate Western Communist parties, the leaders of which would see renewed praise of Stalin as appeasement of the Chinese just when the Soviet Union needed these parties' support. In addition, the letter stated that Stalin "perverted the idea of communism so greatly" that, domestically, the Soviet people would find such praise incongruous, and there would be "great unrest" among Soviet intellectuals as a result of it.[16] Even worse, praising Stalin would "cause serious complications in the attitudes of young people."[17] Implicit in such formulations was reassurance that the signatories were all loyal Soviet citizens who wanted nothing but the best for the Soviet Union and that the criticism the letter contained was intended to be constructive.

Henri's gambit, if that is what it was, was only partly effective. While the party congress refrained from passing a resolution rehabilitating Stalin or ordering that his body be returned to the Lenin mausoleum, the increased repression the letter was intended to discourage continued apace.[18] For Sakharov the letter marked a milestone. Even though it was more the product of intraparty maneuvering than the handiwork of Soviet dissidents, it was nevertheless the first document Sakharov signed that circulated in samizdat and that protested government policy on a matter that was not limited to science. Indeed, Sakharov reports in his memoirs that the conversations he had with Henri and others about the letter had the effect of "greatly advancing" his understanding of a whole host of social issues.[19]

---

14. Henri was also a Soviet contact for the British spies Burgess, Maclean, Philby, and Blunt. In the late 1960s he reputedly wrote a samizdat essay critical of Stalin. Stephen F. Cohen, ed., *An End to Silence: Uncensored Opinion in the Soviet Union from Roy Medvedev's Underground Magazine "Political Diary"* (New York, 1982), 228–29.

15. L. A. Artsimovich et al., "Establishment Intellectuals Protest to Brezhnev," petition in ibid., 177–79.

16. Ibid., 178.

17. Ibid. Including Sakharov, seven academicians signed the letter. Sent to Brezhnev in February 1966, it appeared a month later in *Politicheskii dnevnik* (*Political Diary*), a samizdat compilation of documents and interpretive essays Roi Medvedev edited from 1964 to 1971.

18. Kevin Klose, "Andrei Dmitrievch Sakharov," in Lozansky, *Andrei Sakharov and Peace*, 81.

19. Sakharov, *Memoirs*, 269.

A few months later, Sakharov was active again. In September 1966, to facilitate the repression the Soviet leadership deemed necessary, the Supreme Soviet of the RSFSR secretly ordered the inclusion of two new articles in the Criminal Code of the RSFSR; comparable articles were added simultaneously to the codes of the other republics.[20] The article the government had previously used to legitimize the suppression of dissent—Article 70, which had been adopted in 1960—prohibited "agitation and propaganda" for the purpose of "weakening or subverting the Soviet regime."[21] The new articles, 190/1 and 190/3, said nothing about intent, which can be difficult to demonstrate even in a legal system like the Soviet, where legal definitions and terms were so elastic that they could be used to justify verdicts that defied both common sense and the plain meaning of ordinary language. The two articles simply declared unlawful, respectively, "the systematic dissemination by word of mouth of deliberately false statements derogatory to the Soviet state and social system" and "the organization of, or active participation in, group activities" that resulted in "a grave breach of public order, or clear disobedience to the legitimate demands of representatives of authority."[22] In addition, Article 190/3 effectively nullified Article 125 of the Soviet Constitution guaranteeing the right to assemble publicly and peacefully.[23] The penalties for violating these articles were actually less severe than those prescribed in Article 70, which they were intended, at least in practice, to supersede. But by absolving prosecutors of the necessity of proving intent, the new articles made the repression of dissent easier.

Many in the intellectual and cultural elite were alarmed by this. After the Siniavskii-Daniel Trial, the new articles seemed a harbinger of worse things to come. Sakharov shared this foreboding, and when he was asked to sign a petition to the Supreme Soviet protesting the new articles, he agreed immediately to do so.[24] The petition was signed by nine academicians, including Sakharov and Tamm, Romm, the writer Vladimir Voinovich, and the composer Dmitrii Shostakovich.[25] Like the letter on neo-Stalinism, it used an argument the Soviet leaders might find persuasive, or at least not terribly threatening—namely, that to the extent the two new articles facilitated "the subjective and arbitrary interpretation of any statement as deliberately false and derogatory to the Soviet state and social system," they were contrary to "Leninist principles of socialist democracy."[26] To indicate how strongly he felt about the articles, and perhaps also as an expression of his intellectual independence, Sakharov sent a telegram of his own, expressing the same concern, to the Chairman of the Supreme Soviet of the RSFSR.[27]

20. Dornan, "Andrei Sakharov," 364.
21. Pavel Litvinov, *The Demonstration in Pushkin Square* (Boston, 1969), 160.
22. Ibid., 13–14.
23. Rubenstein, *Soviet Dissidents,* 46. For some reason Sakharov omits any mention of 190/3 in his memoirs.
24. Sakharov, *Memoirs,* 270–71.
25. Litvinov, *Demonstration,* 15.
26. Ibid., 14.
27. Sakharov, *Memoirs,* 271.

In the end, the petition and Sakharov's protest were unavailing. Articles 190/1 and 190/3 remained part of Soviet law, as did their equivalents in the law codes of the outlying republics, and they would be used to repress dissidents and others who challenged the regime until the late 1980s, when they were purposely omitted from new law codes designed to facilitate perestroika and glasnost.[28] But this second venture into politics was still useful. By appealing to the Soviet government on its own terms, in the conviction that for all its willful misuse of power it was still receptive to rational arguments based on self-interest, Sakharov was honing a tactic he would use in the future: deliberately phrasing his appeals in ways that might strike a chord with the Soviet people even if the leadership was immune to them. Whether to change policy or to raise public consciousness, Sakharov continued this strategy adopted in 1966 even when faced with the more calculated and calibrated repression that followed in the 1970s. He justified this particular strategy in his memoirs: "Statements on public issues are a useful means of promoting discussion, proposing alternatives to official policy, and focusing attention on specific problems. They educate the public at large, and just might stimulate significant changes, however belated, in the policy and practice of top government officials."[29]

On the basis of these same tactical considerations, on December 5, 1966, which was Constitution Day in the Soviet Union, Sakharov attended a demonstration at Pushkin Square in Moscow in which the participants bore witness to their "respect for the Soviet Constitution," and to the guarantees of legal rights it contained, by observing a minute of silence on behalf of political prisoners incarcerated in violation of these rights. The KGB, which was filming the event, did not intervene, and Sakharov left the square unobtrusively once it was over.[30] Eventually he would have to resolve the tactical conundrum the protest suggested: if a regime enacts laws that contradict the principles its own constitution contains (as Article 190/3 of the RSFSR Law Code contradicted Article 125 of the Soviet Constitution), is there any reason for supporters of these principles to continue to support this constitution? Or should they instead demand an entirely new one? Or even propose a different version themselves? Only in the last months of his life, in the fall of 1989, did Sakharov resolve the issue by actually writing a draft for a new constitution for the Soviet Union.[31] In 1966 he may not have been aware of the incongruity inherent in what he and the other demonstrators in Pushkin Square were demanding. But his presence at the demonstration, the first one he attended, was an indication of his deepening political conviction.

28. Martin McCauley, *Gorbachev* (New York, 1998), 102.
29. Sakharov, *Memoirs,* 271.
30. Ibid., 273.
31. Ioirysh, *Uroki A. D. Sakharova,* 54–61; Andrei Sakharov, "Draft Constitution," *New Times* 52 (1989): 26–27. The constitution Sakharov produced in the fall of 1989 conspicuously omitted any clause proclaiming the Communist Party the guiding force in Soviet society. It was on the basis of this assertion, enshrined in Article 6 of the Soviet Constitution, that the government enacted laws in violation of the constitution and applied them arbitrarily and inconsistently.

Given Sakharov's concerns and his willingness to express them publicly, it was perhaps inevitable that he should eventually suffer personally for them. Early in 1967 Sakharov learned of the arrests of Alexander Ginzburg, Iurii Galanskov, Alexei Dobrovolskii, and Vera Lashkova, who would be tried together and convicted of various offenses in 1968. Their trial would be the first since the 1930s to be publicized nationally.[32] Galanskov, Dobrovolskii, and Lashkova had been arrested for helping Ginzburg compile a White Book of documents and other materials on the Siniavskii-Daniel Trial. Ginzburg himself was arrested a week later for organizing a demonstration in Moscow on their behalf.[33] He had previously edited a collection of verse called *Sintaksis;* it and Galanskov's collections *Feniks-61* and *Feniks-66* were early samizdat journals.[34]

Sakharov's response to these arrests was to write to Brezhnev and request that everyone charged be released: the government's action was a violation of its own legal norms and procedures. Probably because he believed his protest would be more effective if it remained private, Sakharov did not try to publish his letter or circulate it clandestinely. In this respect, he was reverting to the tactics he had used on behalf of Barenblat and the counterfeiter and when he sought through moral suasion to convince Khrushchev not to test thermonuclear weapons in the atmosphere. But despite his best efforts to be discreet, the Soviet government, for the first time in Sakharov's life, exacted a penalty for something he did: Slavskii reportedly told the participants in a party conference that, while Sakharov was a fine scientist who had contributed much to his country, "as a politician he's muddleheaded, and we'll be taking measures."[35] Shortly afterward, Sakharov was removed from the directorship of his department at Arzamas and saw his salary slashed nearly in half.[36] Now he was not just protesting injustices but experiencing injustice himself.

Viewed as a whole, Sakharov's emerging dissidence was not just a reaction to the neo-Stalinism he feared and increasingly deplored. It was also a consequence of his belief that science must be used in the interests of humanity and that when it was not, scientists had an obligation to speak out. In Sakharov's view, which had been germinating in his mind since the early 1950s, scientists had to have a social conscience. They had to be cognizant of the larger social implications of their work and to be aware at all times that science was not inherently benevolent, that it had the potential to destroy as well as to create,

---

32. Nicolai N. Petro, *The Rebirth of Russian Democracy: An Interpretation of Political Culture* (Cambridge, Mass., 1995), 127. Vladimir Bukovskii, Vadim Delaunay, and Evgenii Kushev would in turn be tried in August–September 1967 for protesting these arrests in a demonstration in Pushkin Square. Pavel Litvinov, who compiled materials on this later trial, would himself be arrested for protesting the Soviet invasion of Czechoslovakia in 1968 in a demonstration in Red Square. When the Ginzburg-Galanskov trial in 1968 predictably sparked protests against it, Mstislav Keldysh, the president of the Academy of Sciences, threatened reprisals against scientists who participated in them. Rothberg, *Heirs of Stalin,* 208–17, 246–49.

33. Litvinov, *Demonstration,* 2–3.

34. Petro, *Rebirth of Russian Democracy,* 127; Rubenstein, *Soviet Dissidents,* 18, 58.

35. Sakharov, *Memoirs,* 275.

36. Ibid.

and that it was only as virtuous as the human beings who practiced it. In the wrong hands, science could seriously damage the earth and in a nuclear age could destroy the earth and everything on it. Throughout his life, Sakharov tried to make his actions conform to his convictions, and much of what he did in the mid-1960s was consistent with this vision he held of the humane and socially conscious scientist. At Arzamas, he worked increasingly—and apparently to some extent by choice—on nonmilitary applications of nuclear power, such as the use of carefully calibrated nuclear charges to release underground oil reserves.[37] At the same time, he read even more intensively than he had in the late 1950s on radioactive fallout and missile technology and in the process became familiar with the arcana he would have to master to write knowledgeably about the issue of arms control. In the case of the latter, his reading only strengthened his conviction, arrived at earlier in his life, that nuclear disarmament, properly negotiated, was the only permanent solution to the nuclear arms race.[38]

Sakharov's recognition—so contrary to the Prometheanism in Marxism and Soviet Communism—that science was not inherently beneficial, and even potentially destructive, also caused him in 1967 to become involved in an effort to save Lake Baikal in Siberia from pollution. The deepest lake in the world and a natural resource of incomparable beauty, Lake Baikal at that time had not yet come to symbolize the struggle between those who saw nature as something to be exploited for human purposes and those who believed that preserving nature took precedence over every other consideration.[39] Instead, the fight over the lake and its environs was conducted mostly within the confines of the Communist Party. Sakharov's involvement was triggered by an invitation from a member of the Komsomol's Committee to Save Baikal to attend a meeting at which committee members discussed various strategies for publicizing the damage to the lake and its attendant wildlife that toxic wastes, air pollution, and deforestation had caused.[40] Sakharov not only attended the meeting but also did research on a factory producing rayon cord for airplane tires that had been built on the lake because its fresh water facilitated the process by which the rayon fibers in the cord were strengthened. The factory was situated over a seismic fault and had been rocked by one earthquake already. What was worse, the aircraft designers on whose behalf the factory was built had determined shortly after construction began that metallic cord was preferable to rayon cord in the construction of airplane tires. This change meant that the entire rationale for building the factory on a freshwater lake like Baikal was outmoded. But in typical Soviet fashion the factory was built anyway. To protect the lake from further depredations, Sakharov and the members of the committee proposed that no new industries be built near the lake or on its shores and that industries that were already there be relocated elsewhere. Presumably, the factory

37. Sakharov, *Memoirs*, 267.
38. Ibid., 268.
39. Medvedev, *Soviet Science*, 91.
40. Sakharov, *Memoirs*, 277–80.

producing rayon cord either would be shut down or would produce something else if it were moved.

The committee was a duly constituted entity of an institution, the Komsomol, that was an integral part of the Soviet system. However critical it was of the government's actions (or really inaction) in this particular instance, the committee's report was not, strictly speaking, a dissident document. Sakharov and the other members of the committee who signed the report secured the approval of the Komsomol Central Committee before they sent it to the Central Committee of the Communist Party, along with a sampling of letters on the subject received by two newspapers, *Literaturnaia gazeta* and *Komsomolskaia pravda*. Sakharov himself telephoned Brezhnev—the last time he would speak directly to the Soviet leader—in the hope that he would take action and rectify the situation, which, as general secretary of the Communist Party, he had the power to do. That Sakharov in this instance petitioned a Soviet leader for redress of his grievances shows that he still believed the Soviet system could respond favorably to requests and appeals that were rational, respectful, and couched in terms of patriotism and national self-interest. One can imagine Sakharov's dismay, and the effect it would have on his confidence in the Soviet Union's ability to reform itself, when Brezhnev simply deflected Sakharov's request by suggesting he contact Alexei Kosygin, the head of the Soviet government and thus a step lower in the Soviet hierarchy. Sakharov did not know Kosygin personally and partly for that reason ignored Brezhnev's suggestion. This in itself is quite revealing: for all his growing estrangement from the Soviet system, Sakharov still placed great stock in personal communication with the Soviet leadership and at some level still believed the contacts he had developed over the years were useful. In the end, he never placed the call, and an investigation commissioned by the Academy of Sciences concluded, in the face of overwhelming evidence to the contrary, that the existing safeguards protecting Lake Baikal were adequate and that therefore the lake was not polluted.[41]

In spite of this setback, or possibly because of it, Sakharov continued to speak out on issues of social significance. In 1967 he agreed to be interviewed by Ernst Henri on "the present-day role and responsibility of the intelligentsia."[42] After the interview was conducted, Henri submitted it in the form of an article to *Literaturnaia gazeta*, which, at Henri's request, had previously agreed in principle to publish it. But the editors of the journal deemed its contents too controversial and discreetly told Henri he would need permission from "higher-ups" before it could appear. Henri asked Sakharov to send the article to Suslov with a letter of explanation, which Sakharov did. Suslov never responded personally to the letter, and the article never appeared in *Literaturnaia gazeta*.[43] Instead, it

41. Ibid., 279. Sakharov was not invited to the meeting at which the Council of Ministers received and ratified the bogus conclusions its investigation had reached. Babyonyshev, *On Sakharov*, xxi.

42. This is how Sakharov describes the article in his memoirs. Sakharov, *Memoirs*, 276.

43. In fact, Suslov's secretary sent Sakharov a letter stating that Suslov found the manuscript interesting but unsuitable for publication. Edward Kline, conversation with author, June 10, 2008.

made its way, without Sakharov's knowledge or permission, to Roi Medvedev, who included it in an issue of *Politicheskii dnevnik.*[44]

The interview began with Sakharov proclaiming that "progressive scientists and intellectuals" had an obligation to discuss issues of public importance "openly and without prejudice."[45] Science, he said, was ideally an international endeavor. If they worked together, Western and Soviet scientists would not only advance the cause of science but could even help the cause of international peace.[46] For Sakharov, there was nothing more important. Contrary to what Soviet military theorists believed, Clausewitz's famous dictum that war was a continuation of politics did not, according to Sakharov, apply to nuclear war, which, by its very destructiveness, could never achieve political ends. Because it was qualitatively different from conventional war, a war fought with nuclear weapons could only lead to the end of politics—indeed, to the end of civilization.

At this point in the interview Sakharov turned to a topic he clearly wished to discuss—namely, the negotiations then being conducted by the two superpowers on a treaty to prohibit the research, development, and deployment of antiballistic missile (ABM) systems. At about the same time as the interview with Henri, Sakharov sent a memorandum to the Central Committee of the Communist Party arguing that the moratorium on such systems proposed by the United States would also benefit the Soviet Union.[47] He enclosed with his memorandum a request—which the government rejected—that an article he had written explaining his reasoning in terms understandable to the Soviet people be published in the Soviet press.[48] The interview with Henri gave Sakharov the opportunity—or so it seemed at the time—to speak directly to the Soviet people, or at least to those who read *Literaturnaia gazeta,* on an issue of great political significance.

An ABM system, Sakharov argued, was not, under present circumstances, technologically feasible. Far from reducing the chances of nuclear war, it would make nuclear war more likely and at the same time more destructive. He enumerated three reasons for this. First, the technology of offensive nuclear weapons was presently more advanced than that of defensive weaponry, and thus any country whose offensive capability was impaired by the introduction of a defensive system in response to it could easily regain its original advantage. Second, offensive weapons were cheaper to produce. Third, in nearly all military confrontations, including nuclear ones, the offensive power would always retain

44. Ibid.,; Roy Medvedev, "How *Political Diary* was Created," in Cohen, *End to Silence,* 20; Gennadii Gorelik, "Andrei Sakharov: Ot teoreticheskoi fiziki k prakticheskomu gumanizmu," in *Razmyshleniia o progresse, mirnom sosushchestvovanii i intellektual'noi svobode: Materialy konferentsii k 30-letiiu raboty A. D. Sakharova* (Moscow, 1998), 125. For the text of the article, see Andrei Sakharov and Ernst Henry, "Scientists and the Danger of Nuclear War," in Cohen, *End to Silence,* 229–34.

45. Sakharov and Henry, "Scientists and the Danger of Nuclear War," 229.

46. Ibid.

47. Elena Bonner, "Letter to the Editor," *New York Times,* October 27, 1999, A26.

48. Sakharov also hoped that American scientists opposed to ABM systems would read the article and use its arguments in debates with other scientists who favored these systems. Gorelik, "Metamorphosis of Andrei Sakharov," 101.

a tactical advantage in that it could target its missiles and decoys on a limited number of targets, thereby "exhausting" the capabilities of all but the most expensive antiballistic missile systems to repulse them. An ABM system, in other words, simply would not achieve its intended purpose.[49] Both in the late 1960s and in the early 1980s, when he joined the debate on space-based missile defenses, Sakharov believed in the inherent superiority of the power that strikes first: the only deterrent, short of disarmament, to such a strike would be the ability of the intended target to deliver a retaliatory strike powerful enough to deter the aggressive power from launching its own missiles in the first place.[50] As Sakharov saw it, the existing state of weapons technology, which enabled nuclear powers to protect offensive missiles in hardened silos or to launch them from virtually undetectable nuclear-powered submarines made an antiballistic missile system not worth the time, money, and effort required to build it.

The main problem with an ABM system, as Sakharov shrewdly realized, was not just that it would not defend against a nuclear strike but that it would not deter a nuclear strike. If, say, the United States should construct an ABM system that "worked" (i.e., that enabled the United States to shoot down every nuclear missile the Soviet Union could launch), all the Soviet Union would have to do to make the system obsolete would be to build more offensive missiles. At the same time, by giving the nuclear power that built an ABM system the illusion that it was invulnerable, such a system would make it more likely that that power would launch a first strike of its own.[51] Paradoxically, an ABM system would make both nuclear powers more likely to take action leading to an even more destructive nuclear exchange. In sum, an ABM system would yield neither victory nor peace. Only at the tactical level—say, on a battlefield, where predominantly conventional forces were deployed—did Sakharov think that missiles with nuclear warheads would have their intended effect of destroying other missiles.[52]

For all these reasons, Sakharov supported the ABM treaty the United States and the Soviet Union negotiated and signed in Moscow in 1972.[53] Indeed, this treaty, like the nuclear test ban treaty, was cause for personal satisfaction: the arguments Sakharov and other scientists at Arzamas marshaled against the ABMs helped make the Soviet government more amenable to a treaty prohibiting them. In the late 1960s Sakharov still believed that, short of total disarmament,

49. Sakharov and Henry, "Scientists and the Danger of Nuclear War," 232–33.

50. See, for example, Christopher Walker, "Sakharov Casts Doubt on Feasibility of SDI," *Times* (London), December 29, 1986, 8; "A Conversation with Andrei Sakharov and Elena Bonner," *SIPIscope* 15, no. 2 (June–July 1987): 8; Interview with Zora Safir, December 4, 1988, 8–9, Sakharov Archives, Brandeis University, Waltham, Mass.

51. Sakharov and Henry, "Scientists and the Danger of Nuclear War," 230.

52. Ibid., 233.

53. According to the terms of the treaty, the United States and the Soviet Union were allowed to construct two ABM sites, one near the national capital, the other anywhere else, with up to one hundred launchers and interceptors per site. The Soviet Union built a site near Moscow; the United States did so at Grand Forks, North Dakota, near an ICBM launch area. In 1974, the superpowers by mutual agreement reduced the number of permissible sites from two to one; two years later the United States deactivated its site in North Dakota. William J. Durch, *The ABM Treaty and Western Security* (Cambridge, Mass., 1988), 9–10.

deterrence, rather than antiballistic missile systems, was the only way of keeping the nuclear peace. His later opposition to the American Strategic Defense Initiative (SDI), in which missiles launched from space would intercept ballistic missiles launched from earth, was consistent with his belief that antiballistic missiles would neither defend nor deter, regardless of their launching point. One wonders whether he would have had the same opinion today, when the principal threat to peace comes not from nuclear powers whose leaders are rational enough to accept the paradoxical logic of deterrence but from fanatical dictators or terrorists who might launch nuclear missiles against a nuclear power no matter how much death and destruction such a strike and the inevitable retaliation would cause. Sakharov's animadversions on ABM systems required a presumption of rationality on the part of political leaders that in the twenty-first century may be unwarranted.

It was no coincidence that Sakharov's concerns about the environment and nuclear weapons evolved in the late 1960s into full-fledged dissidence. The change from Sakharov the scientist to Sakharov the dissident, while hardly inevitable or preordained by what had transpired previously in his life, was entirely logical. If the Soviet government would not grant him satisfaction on the issues relating to science that concerned him, then there was something seriously wrong with the Soviet government and perhaps even with the Soviet system as a whole. This was the conclusion Sakharov came to in the late 1960s—a conclusion that Tamm and Kapitsa, for whatever reason, were either unable or unwilling to reach. There is an underlying logic to Sakharov's assuming the role and responsibilities of a dissident that is evident even in the way he describes this transformation retrospectively in his memoirs:

> By the beginning of 1968, I felt a growing compulsion to speak out on the fundamental issues of our age. I was influenced by my life experience and a feeling of personal responsibility, reinforced by the part I'd played in the development of the hydrogen bomb, the special knowledge I'd gained about thermonuclear warfare, my bitter struggle to ban nuclear testing, and my familiarity with the Soviet system. My readings and my discussions with Tamm (and others) had acquainted me with the notions of an open society, convergence, and world government....
> I shared the hopes of Einstein, Bohr, Russell, Szilard, and other Western intellectuals that these notions, which had gained currency after World War II, might ease the tragic crisis of our age.[54]

One must recall that Sakharov's acquaintance with the Soviet system was originally and for a long time in an area—the design and development of thermonuclear weapons—in which the cost to the Soviet Union from error and miscalculation was immense. For this reason, he seemed to be more aware than persons working in a different niche within the system of just how harmful the capriciousness, petty brutality, and mediocrity of Soviet officials could be. A bad

---

54. Sakharov, *Memoirs*, 281.

decision made out of personal pique would have far more serious consequences if it concerned thermonuclear weaponry than if it involved Soviet pipe casting (the industry Dudintsev used in *Not by Bread Alone* to make the point that Soviet bureaucrats were often narrow-minded and incompetent). The consequences of Drozdov's personal foibles were serious; those of Slavskii were potentially catastrophic. For this reason, when Sakharov encountered representatives of Soviet officialdom outside the insular world of nuclear weaponry—as he did in the Barenblat affair, in the case of the counterfeiter, and in the effort to save Lake Baikal from further despoliation—he was already aware of how much damage such individuals, by their personal failings, could cause. The work he did on thermonuclear weapons lent a seriousness, even an urgency, to his concerns about other issues. As he came to enumerate them in the mid-1960s, the failings of the Soviet Union were a seamless web; the failure to provide human rights or to protect the environment suggested a lack of sufficient concern for the preservation of the earth and the avoidance of nuclear war. For this reason, the importance Sakharov placed on his own dissidence and that of others over the next two decades would be very high: on its success would depend not only the moral health and material welfare of the Soviet people but possibly even the survival of humanity itself.

It was Sakharov's fears and forebodings about a revival of Stalinism—however benign it might be in comparison with Stalinism itself—that catalyzed his decision to speak out on what he calls "the fundamental issues." This was where he was in his intellectual and political evolution when 1968 began. By then he had already done most of the things dissidents did: he had signed petitions, participated in demonstrations, written letters, and consented to interviews in which he opined that the Soviet Union's policies violated fundamental moral principles, in particular the ethical imperative that every individual was entitled to social justice.

There was just one weapon the dissidents used that Sakharov, as 1968 began, had not employed: he had not yet articulated a positive vision of what life would be like in the Soviet Union and of how the Soviet state should be governed if its leaders were rational and ethical enough to accept his admonition that the only proper political system was a just one. In short, he had not produced a programmatic alternative to the status quo. But in a matter of months, he would produce such an alternative and in doing so achieve international fame. It took the form of a statement of First Principles. The title Sakharov gave to the essay was *Razmyshleniia o progresse, mirnom sosushchestvovanii i intellektual'noi svobode* (*Reflections on Progress, Coexistence and Intellectual Freedom*).

# PART IV

# Challenging the Soviet Goliath: 1968–1973

# 10 Reflections on Progress, Coexistence, and Intellectual Freedom

*Reflections* made Sakharov famous. Incredibly, some 18 million copies were sold or distributed globally in the first year of its publication.[1] An American edition, with an introduction, notes, and commentary by the American journalist Harrison Salisbury, was published in 1968 and remained in print in the United States for many years.[2] From 1968 to 1992, no fewer than sixty-five editions of the essay, in seventeen languages, appeared around the world.[3] Andrei Grachev, who in the late 1980s served as one of Gorbachev's secretaries and advisers, claims in his reminiscences of those years that he never had to ask the KGB for the copies of the essay it kept, closely guarded, in its vaults because he had already received a copy from someone who had purchased it abroad.[4] *Reflections* circulated widely in Eastern Europe and the Soviet Union.[5] As early as the summer of 1968 Czech intellectuals were familiar with it, as were students at Sakharov's alma mater, Moscow State University, where, after reading the essay, some of them deliberately left their copies on their desks for others to read.[6] At the end of August, a copy was discovered in the suitcase of a student arrested after demonstrating in Red Square against the invasion of Czechoslovakia. Three months later, the government sent the dissident Soviet general Piotr Grigorenko to a psychiatric hospital after the KGB found a review Grigorenko had written of the essay while searching his apartment for incriminating materials.[7]

1. Sakharov, *Memoirs*, 288.
2. Andrei D. Sakharov, *Progress, Coexistence and Intellectual Freedom*, ed. with introduction, afterword, and notes by Harrison E. Salisbury (New York, 1968). In the original Russian, the title begins with the phrase "Reflections on." For that reason, although all references in the notes are to Salisbury's edition, which omits this phrase, I refer to the essay in the text as *Reflections*.
3. Bela Koval and Ekaterina Shikhanovich, "'Razmyshleniia': Variant i izdanie," in *Razmyshleniia o progresse, mirnom sosushchestvovanii i intellektual'noi svobode*, 36.
4. A. S. Grachev, *Kremlevskaia khronika* (Moscow, 1994), 97.
5. The authorities had better luck apprehending readers who sent the essay to others by regular mail than they did with persons who circulated it in samizdat. Persecution for mailing the essay, involving a student in Dushanbe in Tajikistan, is noted in *Khronika tekushchikh sobytii*, May 20, 1972, 4, in *Sobranie dokumentov samizdata* vol. 10b (Munich, 1972), no. AS1130.
6. Walter C. Clemens Jr., "Sakharov: A Man for Our Times," *Bulletin of Atomic Scientists* 27, no. 10 (December 1971): 6; Rubenstein, *Soviet Dissidents*, 86.
7. V. D. Poremskii, "Diskussia po memorandumu akademika A. D. Sakharova v inostrannom mire," in *Memorandum Akademika A. Sakharova. Tekst, otkliki, diskussiia* (Frankfurt, 1970), 84. The KGB did not find the essay itself because Grigorenko had returned it to Sakharov with suggestions for improvement that, according to Grigorenko, the author adopted. Petro G. Grigorenko, *Memoirs* (New York, 1982), 336–37.

Ironically, Sakharov was not entirely satisfied with *Reflections* when he finished it in April 1968. In his opinion it lacked "literary taste."[8] Nonetheless, he gave a copy to Roi Medvedev, who, with Sakharov's permission, circulated it in samizdat. By the third week in May, a copy (with the first five pages missing) had reached the KGB, which passed it on to Brezhnev.[9] For his part, Sakharov showed the Soviet leader the courtesy—which was consistent with his purpose in writing the piece—of sending him a copy directly.[10] According to both Solzhenitsyn and Zhores Medvedev, Sakharov tried to keep *Reflections* secret, in the sense of limiting its circulation beyond the government to samizdat.[11] In Medvedev's account of how the essay was written, Sakharov had different typists type different parts of it so that none of them would understand the work in its entirety. The reason for their doing so, supposedly, was that any report a typist provided the police would necessarily be fragmentary, leaving the latter ignorant of the larger themes the essay advanced.[12] But Sakharov insists in his memoirs that only one typist at Arzamas ever saw the essay, and he acknowledges that no matter how few were the number of persons assisting him, he knew that word of the essay would eventually reach the authorities. Thus it made sense for him to send Brezhnev a copy preemptively. In that way, the Soviet leader would see it without any of the errors or omissions samizdat copies might contain. In fact, Brezhnev received two versions of the essay, the first one in May from the KGB, the second one in June from Sakharov directly.[13]

Also in June, the Soviet dissident Andrei Amalrik gave a copy of the essay to Karel van het Reve, the Moscow correspondent for the Dutch newspaper *Het Parool;* van het Reve then showed it to Raymond Anderson, the Moscow correspondent for the *New York Times.*[14] Anderson gave the copy to another foreign correspondent who was about to leave the Soviet Union for New York. On his arrival, the correspondent brought the copy to the *Times,* which printed it in full on July 22, sixteen days after it appeared in Holland.[15] A month later, it appeared as well in the émigré newspapers *Russkaia mysl,* published in Paris, and *Posev,* produced in Frankfurt by the anticommunist émigré organization, NTS (short in Russian for the Popular Labor Alliance).[16] According to Zhores Medvedev, it was the essay's appearance in these émigré publications that prompted the Soviet government, in August 1968, to rescind Sakharov's security clearance,

8. Sakharov, *Memoirs,* 284. Sakharov revised the essay several times in the months that followed, and eventually thirteen separate versions circulated in the Soviet Union and abroad. Koval and Shikhanovich, "'Razmyshleniia,'" 24.

9. "Andropov to the Central Committee (May 22, 1968)," in Rubenstein and Gribanov, *KGB File,* 86–87.

10. Sakharov, *Memoirs,* 285.

11. Ibid.

12. Medvedev, "The Sakharov I Knew," 9.

13. Sakharov, *Memoirs,* 284. Koval and Shikhanovich, "'Razmyshleniia,'" 25.

14. Koval and Shikhanovich, "'Razmyshleniia,'" 27; Sakharov, *Memoirs,* 286.

15. Raimond Anderson, "Vystupleniia," in *Razmyshleniia o progresse, mirnom sosushchestvovanii i intellektual'noi svobode,* 93–95; Poremskii, "Diskussia po memorandumu," 73.

16. Bailey, *Making of Andrei Sakharov,* 240.

thereby making his continued work at Arzamas impossible.[17] Still, Sakharov was not expelled from the Academy of Sciences. And in addition to retaining the dacha at Zhukova the government had given him in 1956, he continued to have access to the special health care facilities he and his family had used for many years.[18] But the order rescinding Sakharov's security clearance came from none other than Suslov, the éminence grise of the regime, which suggests that despite his best efforts to be conciliatory, especially in sending the essay to Brezhnev, its contents and the enormous publicity it subsequently received had seriously antagonized the Soviet leadership.[19] After *Reflections*, Soviet scientific journals—almost surely on orders from higher-ups—either minimized Sakharov's prior scientific accomplishments by ascribing them to Tamm and unspecified "others" or ignored them entirely.[20]

Still, the Soviet government, given Sakharov's newfound prominence, could not easily have arrested him or otherwise harmed him in a way that would have jeopardized the improvement in Soviet-American relations it desired; paradoxically, *Reflections* antagonized the government but also provided Sakharov some protection from it. As a result, he found new employment fairly easily. In May 1969, Slavskii asked Sakharov to return to the Lebedev Institute, where fortuitously there was a vacancy in the department of theoretical physics. Although the department was still headed by Tamm, by this time Sakharov's old mentor was too sick from the cancer that would take his life two years later to direct the department, or even to appear at the institute on a regular basis.[21] Nevertheless, Sakharov accepted Slavskii's offer with alacrity. In August 1969 he cleaned out his office and vacated the residential cottage he had occupied at Arzamas for nearly two decades. On his arrival at the institute, Sakharov, who did not want to ruffle any feathers unnecessarily, told the director, Dmitrii Skobeltsyn—who was dubious about Sakharov's appointment and may have actively opposed it—that he would refrain from speaking out on political issues if there were no "serious reasons" to do so. This last caveat fairly absolved Sakharov of disingenuousness in the event he spoke out on matters of public importance in the future.[22]

Despite its providential outcome, Sakharov's dismissal from Arzamas was a sobering experience, which caused him to question even more the beneficence of the Soviet system. By writing *Reflections* and losing his job as a result, he was now a victim of his own dissidence as well as an advocate of it. Indeed, as a way of demonstrating their displeasure, the authorities made sure Sakharov was hired at the institute at the lowest rank possible for a member of the Academy

17. Medvedev, "The Sakharov I Knew," 9.

18. Ibid.; Sakharov, *Memoirs*, 358; Klose, *Russia and the Russians*, 160; Barenblat, "Iz vospominanii," 137.

19. B. M. Bolotovskii, "Kak Ia vospityval A. D.," in Ivanova, *Andrei Dmitrievich*, 152.

20. Smirnov, "Etot chelovek," 601.

21. Sakharov, *Memoirs*, 298–99. Since Sakharov was last at FIAN, it had moved from a small building on a side street in central Moscow to a larger and more impressive one on Lenin Boulevard on the outskirts of the city. Lourie, *Sakharov*, 216.

22. Sakharov, *Memoirs*, 299; Note in *Khronika tekushchikh sobytii*, April 30, 1969, 26, reprinted in *Sobranie* vol. 10a, no. AS196; Medvedev, "The Sakharov I Knew," 9.

of Sciences.[23] Along with the monthly stipend of 400 rubles Sakharov received as an academician, he earned a yearly salary of 4,200 rubles; by comparison his *monthly* salary at Arzamas was 2,000 rubles.[24] Since the regime could not punish Sakharov to the extent it wanted to—say, by arresting him or forbidding him from doing physics entirely, it took pleasure in exacting vengeance in the form of deprivations, like the gratuitously diminished rank, that were no less hurtful for being mostly symbolic.

At the same time that the government was hounding dissidents like Grigorenko for reading Sakharov's essay, commenting on it, or distributing it, it provided copies to individuals it considered sufficiently reliable not to be swayed by the criticisms it contained. Among this select group were the members of the presidium of the Academy of Sciences.[25] Evidently the government thought the scientific elite should know what Sakharov had actually written so that his conclusions could be refuted effectively.[26] In this endeavor it succeeded admirably, probably more than it actually intended. As early as 1969, the American physicist Bernard Feld stated that, on his most recent trips to the Soviet Union, every Soviet scientist he met had either read *Reflections* or was familiar with it.[27] But if the authorities thought that the Soviet scientists to which they showed Sakharov's essay would be immune to its arguments, in a remarkably large number of instances they were wrong. Several scientists both at the institute and in the academy openly expressed support for Sakharov after his involuntary separation from Arzamas.[28] Even Kapitsa, perhaps the Soviet scientist with the greatest prestige among scientists abroad, expressed the opinion at a press conference he gave while in the United States in 1969 that at least some of what Sakharov had written was right.[29] Among the scientists in the West who read *Reflections,* its admirers were legion. Jerome Wiesner of MIT said he would be proud to have written the essay himself, and even Edward Teller, as critical as he was of the essay's arguments for socialism, said that he liked what the Soviet physicist had written about freedom.[30] In light of this, it seems fair to speculate that Sakharov was named a foreign member of the American Academy of Sciences in 1969 as much for writing *Reflections* as for his scientific accomplishments.[31]

23. Kelley, *Solzhenitsyn-Sakharov Dialogue,* 103.

24. Sakharov, *Memoirs,* 299.

25. Goldanskii, "Scientist, Thinker, Humanist," 24.

26. Mstislav Keldysh thought that for this reason the essay should be published officially and made available to the general population. Filipp Bobkov, *KGB i vlast* (Moscow, 1995), 202.

27. Bernard T. Feld, "Sakharov Chooses Survival," *Tech Engineering News,* April 1969, 5.

28. Tsukerman and Azarkh, "Liudi i vzryvy," 123.

29. "Ot izdatel'stva," in *Memorandum Akademika A. Sakharova,* vi. On February 28 of that year, in a speech to the presidium of the Academy of Sciences, Kapitsa, without endorsing Sakharov's proposals, argued that the issues they raised should be discussed in the academy and by Soviet "ideologists" as well. P. L. Kapitsa, "Vystuplenie na zasedanii Prezidiuma AN SSSR 28 fevral 1969 g.," *Voprosy filosofii* 5 (1969): 148, reprinted in P. L. Kapitsa, *Nauka i sovremennoe obshchestvo* (Moscow, 1998), 347.

30. Louise Campbell, "Sakharov: Soviet Physicist Appeals for Bold Initiatives," *Science,* August 8, 1968, 557.

31. Herman Feshbach, "Razmyshleniia i vospominaniia," in Altshuler et al., *On mezhdu nami zhil,* 716.

## Reflections: Origins and Content

*Reflections* was not conceived in a vacuum. The ideas it expressed had been germinating in Sakharov's mind for many years, some of them since his earliest years at Arzamas, when his views on thermonuclear weaponry were being formed. But the impetus for putting these ideas to paper came not from Sakharov himself but from Iurii Zhivliuk, a Ukrainian physicist with ties to Ukrainian dissidents who previously had brought the cases of Ginzburg and Galanskov to his attention. In January 1968 Zhivliuk suggested to Sakharov that he write a reflective piece on the role of the intelligentsia in Soviet society.[32] Sakharov, who had addressed the issue briefly in his conversation with Henri the year before, welcomed the opportunity to express his views at greater length; over the next few months, working mostly in the evenings, he completed a first draft.

The timing of Zhivliuk's suggestion was fortuitous. When Sakharov was writing *Reflections,* he was also listening avidly to the BBC and Voice of America for information about the Prague Spring, the program of democratic socialism reformers in Czechoslovakia were then trying to implement. In this endeavor, the reformers took pains to avoid antagonizing the Soviets, whose intervention, they knew, would be as disastrous for their own cause as it had been for the Hungarians, whose objectives were far more radical, twelve years earlier.[33] By their moderation, the Czech reformers were trying to demonstrate not only that the socialism they advocated could be humane and pluralistic but that the Soviet Union could be persuaded to accept it or at least to tolerate it. For that reason they deliberately refrained from calling either for the privatization of property or for the withdrawal of their country from the Warsaw Pact, both of which the Hungarians, perhaps imprudently, had advocated. As it was, the Prague Spring stood for many of the things Sakharov would advocate in *Reflections:* freedom of speech, the abolition of censorship, the truthful telling of history, reform of the economic system, and a sharp reduction in the coercive power of the police. Both Sakharov and the Czechs deliberately excluded from their respective programs the dismantling of the collective farms and the denationalization of heavy industry. Obviously the Prague Spring was emotionally exhilarating for Sakharov: the peaceful changes it was producing seemed to augur a similar transformation of the Soviet Union. But intellectually the Prague Spring confirmed Sakharov's beliefs without actually contributing to them. He could have written *Reflections* even if the whole movement of reform in Czechoslovakia had never occurred. It is true that in 1978 Sakharov would write that the Prague Spring "considerably shaped my own personal destiny [and] my own inner development."[34] But most

32. Sakharov, *Memoirs*, 282. In his memoirs, Sakharov speculates that Zhivliuk may have had a "relationship" with the KGB—which may explain Sakharov's allowing the friendship to deteriorate and eventually to end. Ibid., 274.

33. Ibid., 281.

34. Andrei Sakharov, "Human Rights Struggle Will Continue," *Guardian Weekly,* August 27, 1978. Sakharov told the Czech physicist František Janouch that, because he knew little about the Prague Spring, it hardly influenced the ideas he expressed in *Reflections*. František Janouch, "My 'Meetings' and Encounters with Andrei Dmitrievich Sakharov," in Altshuler et al., *Andrei Sakharov,* 386.

of what he said in *Reflections* was implicit in the ideas he had expressed in the letters he signed, the protests he attended, and the interviews he gave—not to mention the discussions he had with other physicists at Arzamas—well before the Prague Spring began.[35]

Indeed, *Reflections* reveals a familiarity not only with the ideas of individuals cited in the essay—such as Norbert Wiener, who in the 1950s helped to develop the new discipline of cybernetics, with which Sakharov was profoundly impressed—but with unacknowledged sources as well. Among the most significant of these were theorists such as Milovan Djilas, to whose writings on "the new class" in communist countries Sakharov may have had access at Arzamas.[36] In contrast to what ordinary Soviet citizens were allowed to read, his essay is distinguished by an eclecticism of sources that reflects the eclecticism of its ideas.

What, then, is *Reflections* about? Sakharov begins the essay with a general statement of the problems the world faces. In it he barely mentions the Soviet Union and then only at the very end. What this suggests is that the principles that will follow in the text are timeless, absolute, and universal. Sakharov is writing the essay not only, or not primarily, for the Soviet people but for all people. The problems he deems worthy of attention are global problems, transcending national boundaries and requiring international solutions. Only if peoples and governments in all parts of the world act together on the basis of universal principles they all accept can these problems be solved, social justice be provided, and the material security to which everyone is entitled be guaranteed.

Sakharov states at the very outset of his meditation—which is what *Reflections* truly is—that his views developed "in the milieu of the scientific and scientific-technological intelligentsia." He further asserts that the scientific method that drives all legitimate scientific study—"a method based on deep analysis of facts, theories and views, presupposing unprejudiced, unfearing open discussion and conclusions"—must be applied to social problems as well.[37] One sees in this the convergence of Sakharov the scientist and Sakharov the *intelligent:* through the application of reason, people will voluntarily come to uphold the universal moral principles that exist eternally in nature.[38] Running like a thread though the essay is the conviction, which Sakharov seems to think is self-evident, that there are universal truths that are knowable to people once they exercise their innate capacity for reason. Indeed, humanity is capable of progressing from ignorance to knowledge, from barbarism to civilization, and from poverty to material affluence through the purposeful application of science. As long as those who decide how the benefits of science are to be distributed inform their decisions with a commitment to social justice, the undeniable ability of science

35. Viktor Adamskii writes that the ideas Sakharov expressed in *Reflections* originated in these discussions at Arzamas. Adamskii, "Stanovlenie grazhdanina," 40, 43.

36. Alexander Gribanov, "Ob izuchenii istochnikov pervoi 'gumanitarnoi' raboty Sakharova," in *Razmyshleniia o progresse, mirnom sosushchestvovanii i intellektual'noi svobode* (Moscow, 1998), 17–18.

37. Sakharov, *Progress*, 25.

38. Bernard Feld is the only commentator on *Reflections* I am aware of who explicitly made the same point. Feld, "Sakharov Chooses Survival," 5.

to destroy life as well as enhance it can be controlled. Sakharov's essay, as he saw it, was an effort to accelerate this natural progress of humanity.

As he states in an introductory paragraph, Sakharov intended *Reflections* merely as a basis for discussion.[39] Given his hope that the Soviet leadership, to whom he sent the essay, would respond favorably, it made sense for him to present his proposals not as demands but as suggestions. By not calling into question, even obliquely and indirectly, the monopoly of wisdom Brezhnev and his colleagues claimed to possess, he hoped to avoid antagonizing them. But the calm and deferential tone he adopted, at least in the second version of the essay he produced, was more than just a tactical ploy. It also reflected the way he thought and how he presented his ideas to others. Sakharov's essay is truly a clarion call to moderation, reason, and evolutionary change. And it was directed not only to the Soviet government but to the Soviet people as well, who in his view were nearly as rational and amenable to reason as the scientists at Arzamas had been many years earlier when they discussed not only science but some of the social issues Sakharov explored further in *Reflections*. When he wrote the essay, Sakharov was not so foolish as to think that, under the circumstances existing in 1968, large numbers of Soviet citizens would actually read it. But by rejecting "all extremes [and] the intransigence shared by revolutionaries and reactionaries alike," he could convince the readers he did reach of the value and utility of what he was proposing.[40]

Stylistically the essay leaves much to be desired. Sakharov himself acknowledged its deficiencies in this regard, and there is reason to think he tried to correct them in the revisions he made in the spring and early summer of 1968. In 1973 he admitted that the essay in a number of places was "pretentious" and that even in later editions it remained "imperfect in terms of form."[41] To a Western reader, Sakharov's use of Marxist-Leninist phraseology—his references to "dogmatism," "ruling classes," "monopolist capital" in Nazi Germany and "militarist circles" in the United States—are jarring and seriously detract from the strength of his arguments.[42] He also came to regret his criticism of the director of the Central Committee Department of Science, Sergei Trapeznikov, as ad hominem and therefore inconsistent with the dispassionate tone of the rest of the essay.[43] But *Reflections* is still an impressive achievement. Nearly everything in it could have been written by a non-Russian, and Sakharov's ability to transcend the political culture in which he was raised and address issues from a truly global perspective—the first Soviet dissident to do so—is absolutely breathtaking. Perhaps only a scientist accustomed to dealing with cosmological questions could have achieved this.

In *Reflections* Sakharov describes humanity as an indissoluble entity, with common interests, a common destiny, and, ideally, common values.[44] He strongly

39. Sakharov, *Progress*, 25; Sakharov, *Memoirs*, 282.
40. Sakharov, *Memoirs*, 283; Poremskii, "Diskussia po memorandumu," 88.
41. Sakharov, introduction to *Sakharov Speaks*, 37.
42. Sakharov, *Progress*, 29, 37, 51.
43. Sakharov, *Memoirs*, 284.
44. Sakharov, *Progress*, 47.

implies, moreover, that these shared values have in common a quality—something like the Platonic idea of the Good—for which all countries, in their foreign and domestic policies, should strive. According to Sakharov, in the relations between states there should be a genuine identity of national and international interests, so that advancing the national interest advances the interests of humanity. Foremost among these global interests was peace. By this Sakharov did not mean the complete cessation of hostilities everywhere. He was never a pacifist. Rather, "peace" for him meant the avoidance of thermonuclear war. He repeats in *Reflections* the ideas he advanced earlier in the Henri interview about thermonuclear war rendering Clausewitzian concepts of war as a political instrument untenable; in the essay he also reiterates his qualified endorsement of deterrence and his unqualified rejection of antiballistic missile defense.[45] The only issue he treats without the calm and understated tone he maintains throughout the rest of the essay is thermonuclear war. Sakharov's description of what such a conflagration would lead to is chilling in its graphic detail: "A complete destruction of cities, industry, transport, and systems of education, a poisoning of fields, water, and air by radioactivity, a physical destruction of the larger part of mankind, poverty, barbarism, a return to savagery, and a genetic degeneracy of the survivors under the impact of radiation, a destruction of the material and information basis of civilization—this is a measure of the peril that threatens the world as a result of the estrangement of the world's two superpowers."[46]

Because the consequences of a nuclear exchange between the United States and the Soviet Union would be so dire, Sakharov insisted that the two superpowers redefine their relationship on the basis of "unified and general principles" that are universally accepted.[47] Especially in a nuclear age, national interest must be sensitive to the interest of all people and it must be based on moral principles, of which the most important was the pursuit and preservation of peace. One suspects that Sakharov's rather striking hostility toward, and trepidation about, Chinese Communism (referred to in the essay as "Maoism," which was how the official Soviet press always described it) stemmed not just from the atrocities the Chinese committed during the recent Cultural Revolution but from his fear of their using nuclear weapons against Taiwan or some other enemy.[48] Despite his visceral antipathy to violence, Sakharov comes very close in *Reflections* to sanctioning the use of force not just by the Chinese people but by other countries as well if that became necessary to liberate China from its odious and aggressively expansionist regime. But this principle of justifiable outside intervention was not confined to China. In later writings, he would argue that the interests of nations and those of humanity are synonymous, and for that reason the domestic policies countries adopt are the legitimate concern of all other countries, especially when these policies violate human rights.

45. Ibid., 35–36.
46. Ibid., 37.
47. Ibid., 41.
48. Ibid., 57.

Several other aspects of Sakharov's views on international affairs, as he expressed them in *Reflections,* deserve mention. Well before it became fashionable, Sakharov saw the world in terms not only of East and West but also of North and South. While the differences between East and West, between communism and capitalism, were potentially very dangerous because the superpowers that dominated the two blocs possessed nuclear and thermonuclear weapons, the differences between North and South were even more deserving of amelioration because of the huge disparities in living conditions. Accordingly, Sakharov devoted considerable attention in *Reflections* to world hunger and the deficiencies in agriculture that he believed were responsible for it. For example, he writes in some detail about increasing food production in underdeveloped countries by using better fertilizers, improved irrigation, and synthetic fuels.[49] Implicit in this is a benevolent Prometheanism in which the industrialized countries of the world, out of rational self-interest as well as altruism, extend to these countries the benefits of science and technology both communist and capitalist countries have enjoyed. Sakharov's innate sympathy for the less fortunate, which manifested itself in his everyday affairs as well as in his dissidence, makes his compassion for Third World people understandable. He held that the poverty these peoples endured was not of their own making. Rather, it was the result of a natural imbalance in which the developed countries for whatever reason had harnessed man's innate capacity for rational thought in the conquest and transformation of nature more efficaciously than underdeveloped countries had been able to do.

Fortunately this imbalance could be redressed fairly easily. According to Sakharov, there should commence a transfer of technology and scientific knowledge to the Third World so that people there would be assured the same material comfort and security that the peoples of the First World (the capitalist countries) and the Second World (the Soviet Union and the Soviet bloc countries in Eastern Europe) took for granted. What Sakharov writes in *Reflections* about the dire need to transfer scientific and technological expertise to underdeveloped countries should dispel the notion—which his concerns the year before about Lake Baikal might plausibly suggest—that when he wrote *Reflections,* he no longer considered science and technology benevolent. In the essay, and in everything else he wrote subsequently on ecology and the preservation of the environment, one sees an awareness on his part of the degree to which, and the ease with which, science can be misused and abused for inhumane purposes. But one also sees in *Reflections* Sakharov's conviction, in which he never wavered at any time in his life, that science, as a form of intellectual inquiry, as a means of understanding nature and the universe, and as a way of improving the material and spiritual lives of human beings, was a worthwhile and even noble endeavor.

Sakharov argued passionately in *Reflections* that the affluent and the educated had a moral obligation to help the impoverished and that the transfer of knowledge he called for should be accompanied by a transfer of wealth, specifically

49. Ibid., 44–45.

20 percent of the "national income" of all developing countries.[50] On what basis such a sum should be calculated—as a percentage of tax revenues or of gross national product (GNP)—Sakharov gave no indication. Nor did he take into account the likelihood, or perhaps the near certainty, that countries like the Soviet Union would not agree to what he was proposing unless it advanced their own interests: not long before Sakharov wrote *Reflections,* the Soviet Union refused to relinquish to the UN Commission on Trade and Development even the 1 percent of its GNP the commission requested from advanced industrialized countries to assist underdeveloped ones.[51] Additionally, Sakharov failed to consider that Third World countries simply could not absorb the enormously large amounts of foreign aid, whether in money or material assistance, that he envisioned.[52] He did not take into account when he made his proposal that throwing money at problems often makes them worse, not better. In this instance his natural compassion for the underprivileged clouded his judgment.[53]

On Soviet-American relations, to which he devoted considerable attention in the essay, Sakharov posited a rough moral equivalence: while the United States had behaved badly in Vietnam, so, too, had the Soviet Union in the Middle East, where it had shamefully egged on the Arab states in their ongoing effort since 1948 to destroy Israel, whose existence, but not all of whose policies, Sakharov strongly supported.[54] He pointed out that while the Middle East was obviously an arena in which Soviet-American rivalry was displayed, this rivalry aggravated the existing tensions in the region but was not responsible for creating them.

The moral equivalence Sakharov affirms in *Reflections* would be hardly worthy of note if he had been a Westerner. During the Cold War many in the West accepted and even celebrated this implicit equation of capitalism and socialism. It is the fact that Sakharov was Russian and thus hectored practically from birth into believing that Soviet policies were inherently virtuous and incomparably superior to those of any Western government that makes his moral equation of Soviet and American foreign policy so extraordinary. Indeed, from Sakharov's suggestion that in material terms capitalism and socialism had "played to a tie," the reader could easily infer that the superpowers themselves, not just their foreign policies, were morally equivalent.[55] What Sakharov was suggesting, in other words, was that not everything about the United States was bad and not everything about the Soviet Union was good. Soviet propaganda notwithstanding, in terms of labor productivity, living standards, and what Sakharov vaguely called "the development of productive forces," the two countries and their respective

50. Ibid., 46–47.

51. "Aid to Underdeveloped Nations: Interview of Professor Max Millikan," *Tech Engineering News,* April 1969, 25.

52. Clemens, "Sakharov," 55.

53. Robert Conquest, *Tyrants and Typewriters: Communiqués from the Struggle for Truth* (Lexington, Mass., 1989), 29.

54. Sakharov, *Progress,* 38–39.

55. Ibid., 71.

economic systems were nearly identical. This is another equivalence that Sakharov explained by pointing to the social category, which he called "managerial," of the persons who in each country oversee the distribution of goods and services.[56] In doing so, Sakharov was indicating that at least in the attitudes and social composition of those who distributed goods and services in the two countries, the United States and the Soviet Union were the same. One cannot emphasize enough how audacious a claim this was. Although Sakharov in *Reflections* did not go so far as to claim that these managers exercised political power as well as economic power or that they constituted within each country a new class (as Milovan Djilas did), the very fact that Sakharov used the term "managerial," which the Soviets loathed, to describe the Soviet system was remarkable.[57]

But for all of Sakharov's misgivings about socialism and the Soviet Union, he still considered the Soviet Union socialist and remained, by conviction as well as convenience, a socialist himself. At one point in *Reflections* he describes his views not only as socialist but as "profoundly socialist," and in another he writes about socialism that "there is only one justifiable conclusion and it can be formulated cautiously as follows: We have demonstrated the vitality of the socialist course, which has done a great deal for the people materially, culturally, and socially and, like no other system, has glorified the moral significance of labor."[58] While Sakharov acknowledges in *Reflections* that capitalism has not led in every instance to the "absolute impoverishment" of the working class, he implies that the "economic progress" that has occurred under capitalism is the result of its incorporating "the social principles of socialism," by which he means socialism's emphasis on the inherent dignity of honest labor.[59] For all his criticisms of the Soviet Union, Sakharov does not call anywhere in *Reflections* for the dismantling of the Soviet economy or of the "Sovietized" economies of Eastern Europe. It is important to bear in mind that his socialism was as much an ethical imperative as an organizing principle of society. For that reason it did not really matter to him whether agriculture was entirely or only partially collectivized or whether local and regional institutions rather than the central government in Moscow actually ran the factories the government continued to own. The important point was that socialism ensured a more equitable distribution than capitalism did of the goods and services each system produced because in socialism the ethos of self-enrichment inherent in capitalism was absent.

According to Sakharov, what accounted for the Soviet Union's current predicament—the censorship and lack of freedom, the persecution of dissidents and ethnic minorities, the proliferation of drug abuse and substandard education—was not socialism but Stalinism. In *Reflections,* Sakharov is less interested in analyzing and categorizing Stalinism than in denouncing it. As he

56. Ibid., 76.
57. Milovan Djilas, *The New Class: An Analysis of the Communist System* (New York, 1957).
58. Sakharov, *Progress,* 54, 73.
59. Ibid., 73–74.

describes it, the system of prophylactic terror Stalin established was far worse than the betrayal of Leninism Roi Medvedev denounced in *Let History Judge*.[60] Stalinism, in Sakharov's view, was a species of absolute evil so monstrous that speaking the truth about it was a moral imperative of the highest order. In *Reflections* he devotes several pages to a litany of Stalin's crimes, from the murder of millions in the Terror to the incarceration in labor camps of Soviet POWs the Red Army "liberated" in World War II in the course of advancing westward to Berlin.[61] But for the Soviet reader, perhaps the most audacious aspect of Sakharov's indictment was his equation of Stalinism with German fascism. In commenting on the coercive power of secret police forces in Europe, he lumps together in a single sentence none other than Eichmann, Himmler, Beria, and Ezhov, thereby suggesting that not only were these notorious police chiefs equally repugnant, but so were the systems and the dictators they served. At another point in the essay Sakharov draws the same moral equivalence more clearly by stating flatly that "the torture chambers of the NKVD...were in fact the prototypes of the fascist death camps" and that most of those who died in them were Jews.[62] Such assertions, unremarkable for a Westerner, were extraordinary coming from someone raised in the Soviet Union, where nearly everything written about the Nazis included a statement that their principal victims, in some cases their only victims, were Russians.

In explaining what might prevent a full-scale reemergence of Stalinism in the Soviet Union, Sakharov is content in *Reflections* to offer general principles rather than specific prescriptions. De-Stalinization under Khrushchev, he says, was a good start but did not go far enough. One thing Khrushchev should have done but did not or could not do was to expel Stalin posthumously from the Communist Party.[63] At one point in the essay Sakharov counsels the Soviet government to tell the truth about itself. This was really a polite way of telling the regime to tell the truth about Stalinism. For Sakharov, the complete exposure of the enormity of Stalin's crimes was absolutely essential to the moral health of the Soviet people and the Soviet system. In emphasizing this, Sakharov and Alexander Solzhenitsyn were at one, though their respective notions of the kind of freedom this truth telling required varied greatly. For Sakharov, intellectual freedom—rather than the spiritual freedom Solzhenitsyn favored—was the only true guarantor or measure of a country's willingness to reform itself; it was not for nothing that he used the term in the title of his essay.[64] As a scientist, he was obviously also an intellectual, and it was only natural that he would consider intellectual freedom—by which he meant freedom of opinion and the right to open and unfettered intellectual inquiry—uniquely conducive to what he termed "the progressive restructuring" of government. The only other

60. Roy Medvedev, *Let History Judge: The Origins and Consequences of Stalinism* (New York, 1989), 872.

61. Sakharov, *Progress,* 52–54.

62. Ibid., 51–52.

63. Ibid., 55.

64. Ibid., 29.

corrective to Stalinism Sakharov mentions is the rule of law, by which he means a legal system in which what people are allowed to do is clearly distinguished from what is forbidden.[65] Applied to Russia in 1968, the intellectual freedom Sakharov espoused might have produced glasnost some twenty years before Gorbachev permitted it.

Sakharov said very little in *Reflections* about democracy. His comments on it were mostly limited to the prediction that the Soviet Union and other socialist countries would have a multiparty system when the ruling authorities, by refusing to practice democracy, finally forced the people to demand it.[66] A multiparty system, he cautioned, was neither a "panacea for all ills" nor "an essential stage in the development of the socialist system."[67] In the terminology Sakharov and many other dissidents employed, democracy and democratization were different things, with the latter meaning not elections and multiple parties but rather the participation of people in the culture and intellectual life of their country. While favoring democratization, many dissidents, including Sakharov, were quite equivocal about democracy. For them, it was not the unqualified virtue democratization was: where democratization would produce material prosperity and intellectual freedom, democracy could conceivably lead to chaos and anarchy, which might be followed by tyranny. Neither inevitable nor, in many circumstances, desirable, democracy for Sakharov in 1968 was at best irrelevant to, and at worst destructive of, the humanistic socialism and liberalism he espoused. Indeed, in his explicit rejection in *Reflections* of Lenin's dictum that every cook in a socialist society should know how to govern; in his condemnation of what he called "the opium of mass culture"; in his contention that societies now were too complex and specialized for the masses to participate actively in the formulation of public policy; and in his implication that the technocratic elite should render advice to government leaders that these leaders would willingly accept, Sakharov was actually advocating a kind of humane elitism he would not modify significantly until the mid-1980s.[68]

Sakharov could espouse, or strongly suggest, such elitism with equanimity because he believed its benefits would facilitate the progress of humanity to a higher state of being, in which conflicts and social antagonisms no longer escalated into war, and people lived with one another in perpetual peace. Indeed, with their material needs satisfied, the freedom they enjoyed could assist them in realizing their full potential as human beings. In this vision of history as fundamentally progressive, one sees a fascinating mixture of the rational and the romantic, of the analytical and the prophetic, that is traceable ultimately to Sakharov's intellectual roots in the world of science, with its emphasis on dispassionate inquiry, and the intelligentsia, with its belief in the perfectibility of humanity. In fact, although Sakharov's religious beliefs were unconventional and his ties

65. Ibid., 67.
66. Ibid., 82.
67. Ibid.
68. Ibid., 29, 61.

to Russian Orthodoxy tenuous at best, there is something profoundly religious about his vision of how history ends in a utopia of moral rectitude and material satisfaction. In the last pages of the essay, Sakharov supplies a time line to indicate the stages leading to this goal and precisely when they will be reached. At the same time, he describes, albeit sketchily, the astonishing feats of science and technology of which people will be capable in the not-too-distant future: the colonization of outer space and "the effective control and direction of all life processes...from fertility and aging to psychic processes and heredity."[69] The only caveat diminishing his optimism is his fear that those who govern this technologically superior society might not always demonstrate the necessary "care and concern for human values of a moral, ethical and personal character."[70] But as long as the political elites absorb from scientists the humane values with which they practice their profession, the process of moral improvement Sakharov predicts will continue. According to Sakharov, writing in 1968, this utopia in which science and moral virtue have been harnessed in the pursuit of human happiness and self-fulfillment will prevail globally as early as 1980 and no later than 2000. This in itself testifies to his optimism.

The process by which this secular utopia would emerge Sakharov always called "convergence." Although in *Reflections* he used the word only twice, he would use it freely and frequently in subsequent writings, and it would be the closest thing to an idée fixe in the years that followed. By convergence Sakharov meant specifically the process, already under way when he wrote *Reflections,* by which the capitalist and socialist systems would incorporate all that was best in each of them and then merge into one indivisible entity. In this scenario peace would prevail, and the intellectual and artistic aspirations of people, no less than their material needs, would be fully and permanently satisfied. And because conflicts between peoples would be eliminated, nation-states could be dispensed with as well, thus making deterrence, arms control, and international organizations like the United Nations (all of which presupposed the existence of nation-states) unnecessary. From the perspective of this utopia, the above would be seen as little more than temporary and imperfect expedients humanity adopted for preventing thermonuclear war before convergence was completed, thereby guaranteeing mankind's survival.

By convergence Sakharov meant not just a rapprochement of the United States and the Soviet Union and the melding of their political systems into one. Nor did he mean merely the prominence of a managerial class or stratum that distributed goods and services efficiently and equitably.[71] Convergence meant also a mutual

---

69. Ibid., 84.
70. Ibid.
71. Ibid., 76. Again, one sees here the influence of Djilas and possibly also of James Burnham and Pitirim Sorokin, with whose writings in the 1940s on the emergence of a managerial elite Sakharov might have been familiar, though his views differed from theirs. Although Burnham described convergence in terms similar to Sakharov's, he thought the system it produced would be a bad thing: more efficient than socialism but also more exploitative than capitalism. He also thought the managers running this global system would be bellicose and that frequent wars would

acceptance by the two superpowers, and eventually by all the peoples of the world, of the moral and philosophical principles that Sakharov, as an *intelligent,* believed to be timeless, absolute, and universal. The irresistible implication in everything Sakharov wrote about convergence is that there is one good way to live, which is worth adopting everywhere and at all times and is informed by ethical principles that, like convergence itself, are embedded in nature and discoverable through reason. In his belief in the inevitability and desirability of secular progress and in his conviction that such progress would lead ultimately to a state of perfection in which every individual would achieve his full potential as a human being, Sakharov was proclaiming himself in 1968 a product not only of the intelligentsia but also of the Enlightenment from which the intelligentsia emerged. Where Sakharov differed from the Marxists, who themselves could trace their intellectual lineage to the Enlightenment, was in thinking that progress was the result not of the irreconcilability of capitalism and socialism but rather of the fact that they are destined to merge. In comparing Sakharov's vision with Marx's, it is also worth pointing out that the utopia that follows convergence in Sakharov's scenario is no less inevitable, and no less desirable, than that which follows the violent overthrow of capitalism in Marx's. When he wrote *Reflections,* Sakharov still shared the historical determinism of Marxism-Leninism. But by substituting convergence for the Marxist dialectic, he conjured a vision of how history would end that Marxists and Marxist-Leninists would have to reject.

## *Reflections:* Criticism from Friends and Enemies

While several of the scientists who had access to *Reflections* found it cogent and convincing, the Soviet government, predictably, was appalled by it, angered as much by Sakharov's impudence in challenging its prerogative of making policy autocratically as it was by his specific criticisms. For all its mediocrity, the Soviet leadership recognized the challenge Sakharov's essay posed to it.[72] The Soviet Union's claim of legitimacy rested partly on the presumption that its leaders possessed a monopoly of wisdom as well as power. To question the policies the

likely result. For this reason there could be no world government, no matter how similarly individual societies and economies were organized. In contrast to Burnham, Sorokin thought that the Grand Alliance in World War II, as well as the existence in the Soviet Union of a "national dictatorship" that under Stalin had jettisoned many of the more egregious elements of Marxist-Leninism, would cause the hostility between the United States and the Soviet Union to diminish and lead eventually to the two countries' adopting a "managed economy." Sakharov, by contrast, realized that the Grand Alliance had collapsed and that no such synthesis had occurred after World War II; moreover, he considered Stalinism and the forces in the Soviet Union seeking to revive it totally inimical to convergence. Yet another intellectual who wrote about convergence was John Kenneth Galbraith. Like Sakharov he thought it was already occurring, but unlike Sakharov, he believed that the Soviet people enjoyed the same rights Americans did and that that was a concomitant rather than a consequence of convergence. In *Reflections* Sakharov allowed for the persistence of market mechanisms after convergence, but Galbraith believed these would eventually disappear. James Burnham, *The Managerial Revolution: What Is Happening in the World* (New York, 1941), 127–34, 169–74; Pitirim Sorokin, *Russia and the United States* (New York, 1944), 96, 208; John Kenneth Galbraith, *The New Industrial State* (Boston, 1967), 343.

72. This was true particularly of Andropov, who described the essay in some detail in his report to the Politburo on May 22, 1968. Rubenstein and Gribanov, *KGB File,* 86–88.

government had already promulgated was thus to question the legitimacy of the system itself. Sakharov did precisely that in his essay, and for that reason the Soviet government had to respond by pointing out to him and to anyone else who might conceivably be persuaded by the essay how wrongheaded and destructive to Soviet socialism it actually was. Of course the arguments the authorities mustered were illegitimate by most standards of reasoned debate: instead of responding to what Sakharov had written, they attacked Sakharov the man—his character, objectives, and motives—and they did this either through the press or through people they knew would transmit their disapproval to others.

Iulii Khariton, who himself disagreed with *Reflections* and opposed its circulation, was called in by Iurii Andropov, the head of the KGB, in May. After expressing his own objections to the essay, the Soviet police chief implored Khariton to convince Sakharov to withdraw it. Not surprisingly, when Khariton transmitted Andropov's plea to Sakharov, he summarily rejected it. In July, after the essay had circulated widely both in samizdat and in newspapers abroad, Slavskii summoned Sakharov and asked him to renounce the essay. Once again, Sakharov refused. Three days later, Slavskii tried to argue with him, indicating point by point why nearly everything he had written was wrong.[73] Nor surprisingly, Slavskii found convergence especially abhorrent: by acknowledging that capitalism was changeable and could therefore form the basis, along with socialism, of a good society, Sakharov was implying that it was potentially benign—a notion that to an apparatchik like Slavskii was inconceivable. What angered Slavskii most, however, were not the particular criticisms Sakharov made of the Soviet Union but rather the hypocrisy he saw in the fact that someone in Sakharov's position could make them. "You criticize the leaders' privileges [yet] you've enjoyed the same privileges yourself" was how Slavskii summarized his indictment.[74]

At the beginning of August, without mentioning either the essay or its author by name but with sufficient specificity that anyone familiar with the essay would know it was Sakharov's, an article in *Izvestiia* took strong exception to the essay's tacit equation of communism and capitalism, claiming flatly that "only communism can resolve fundamental social problems."[75] The article also expressed the view prevalent among the elite that Sakharov, quite apart from being wrong in his views, had no business expressing them.[76] Finally, in October 1969 there appeared in *Pravda* an article that, without identifying Sakharov or *Reflections* by name, went on at some length about how convergence was a convenient cover for seeking in the Soviet Union the full restoration of capitalism, and a theoretical justification for anticommunism, which in the Soviet scheme of things was practically the most egregious form of human depravity imaginable.[77]

73. Sakharov, *Memoirs*, 285–88.
74. Ibid., 287.
75. V. Cherpakov, "Problemy poslednei treti veka," *Izvestiia*, August 8, 1968, cited in *Razmyshleniia o progresse, mirnom sosushchestvovanii i intellektual'noi svobode*, 40.
76. Ibid.
77. A. Rumiantsev, M. Mutin, and V. Mshvenieradze, "Aktual'nye voprosy bor'by protiv antikommunizma," *Pravda*, October 13, 1969, 4–5.

Soviet apparatchiki were not the only ones who criticized the essay. Several dissidents and others who had access to it did so as well. Andrei Amalrik, who was quite familiar with *Reflections,* claimed that Sakharov's notion of convergence was naïve, that quite apart from whatever happened to capitalism, socialism could not be humanized or liberalized in any meaningful way. In somewhat the same vein, Leonid Pliushch—who, like Amalrik, greatly admired Sakharov—noted that convergence could conceivably result in the survival of all that was bad, rather than all that was good, in capitalism and socialism, and that what would exist once the two systems merged would be no better, and possibly worse, than what existed now.[78] Other readers of *Reflections* thought that convergence, while desirable, was impractical and hardly likely to come about, while others considered it simply a capitulation to capitalism.[79] Some believed that as an ideal and a prediction, it ignored the virtues and the persistence of national culture, especially the Russian one.[80]

Another common criticism of *Reflections* was more philosophical: that by stressing intellectual freedom, Sakharov had minimized the importance of what several Estonian intellectuals called "the internal, the spiritual, the political, and the organic."[81] By this they meant that Sakharov had erred in placing too much emphasis on Stalin and not enough on socialism as the source of Soviet society's ills. More profoundly, he had failed to emphasize, or even to recognize, the centrality of inner moral and spiritual regeneration in rescuing the Soviet people from their own repression, the responsibility for which they shared with the Soviet government. The satisfaction of material needs mentioned in the essay, while hardly objectionable, was just a prerequisite for moral improvement, not a substitute for it, as Sakharov, in the opinion of the Estonians, seemed to suggest.[82] While lauding Sakharov as "the foremost intellect in our society," the Estonians, somewhat incongruously, called for a multiparty system within the context of political as well as intellectual freedom—a scenario conspicuously absent in *Reflections* for the simple reason that when Sakharov wrote the essay, he was a liberal but not a democrat.[83]

78. Andrei Amalrik, *Will the Soviet Union Survive Until 1984?* (New York, 1981), 27–28; Michael Scammell, *Solzhenitsyn: A Biography* (London, 1985), 697; Leonid Plyushch, *History's Carnival: A Dissident's Autobiography* (New York, 1979), 142.

79. Marina Panova and Efim Pivovar, "Diskussiia o 'Razmyshlenniiakh...' v samizdate (1968–1974 gg.)," in *Razmyshleniia o progresse, mirnom sosushchestvovanii i intellektual'noi svobode,* 48. This was in contrast to the concerns a number of Western readers expressed that convergence would not destroy socialism sufficiently to bring about societies that were just, and that Sakharov did not acknowledge this because he valued socialism too highly. This was the view of the German physicist Max Born, who admired Sakharov greatly and agreed with most of his conclusions. Sakharov, *Memoirs,* 289.

80. Alexander Solzhenitsyn, "As Breathing and Consciousness Return," in Alexander Solzhenitsyn et al., *From Under the Rubble* (Boston, 1976), 13. The essay was a revised and expanded version of the impressions of *Reflections* Solzhenitsyn had communicated to Sakharov in 1968.

81. "Nadeiat'sia ili deistvovat'?: O broshiure akademika A. D. Sakharova 'Razmyshleniia ob intellektual'noi svobode,'" in *Memorandum Akademika A. Sakharova,* 65.

82. Ibid., 70.

83. Ibid., 67, 70.

The most important critique of Sakharov's essay was Alexander Solzhenitsyn's, which sparked the debate between the two men who in the 1970s personified two of the three principal strains of Soviet dissidence: the liberal and secular one embodied by Sakharov and the theological and at times authoritarian one advocated by Solzhenitsyn.[84] These two towering figures in the history of Soviet dissidence had first met after the invasion of Czechoslovakia in August 1968, when Solzhenitsyn asked Sakharov to sign a statement condemning the action. In this instance, Solzhenitsyn, uncharacteristically, was reluctant to act alone and wanted allies.[85] In the months that followed, even though Solzhenitsyn saw in Sakharov a potential rival, he came to respect him for his courage in opposing the Soviet regime. After reading *Reflections*, Solzhenitsyn proclaimed it "a fearless public statement" and praised its author for having broken out of "the deep, untroubled cozy torpor in which Soviet scientists too often conducted their scientific work," oblivious to the regime of lies they tacitly supported.[86] He also noted "the honesty of its judgments" and called its publication "an important event in modern Russian history."[87] But he also claimed that many of the ideas in *Reflections* were insufficiently "thought out," and those that were were "unsound."[88] More broadly, Solzhenitsyn, like the Estonians, insisted that socialism, not Stalinism, was at the core of the Soviet Union's moral degeneracy and that this degeneracy was all that socialism would ever produce. As for Sakharov's vision of convergence, Solzhenitsyn condemned it unequivocally for denying "the vitality of the national spirit"; thus convergence was not only a myth but a dangerous myth.[89] According to Solzhenitsyn, nations had an internal essence that was unchangeable no matter how they might be organized and governed at any particular time; for this reason convergence was not only a bad idea but contrary to the natural order of things.

Finally, Solzhenitsyn claimed that the intellectual freedom Sakharov championed was only "external freedom," incapable of ever yielding the social justice he desired as much as Sakharov. The only freedom that really mattered was spiritual freedom, the freedom that resulted not when people were emancipated from external things like repressive laws but when the moral vacuum in which they were living was replaced by moral principles grounded in humble deference to God—a point that Sergei Zheludkov, an Orthodox priest and another critic of Sakharov, also stressed.[90]

In the early 1970s, Sakharov and Solzhenitsyn debated larger and more fundamental issues, most portentously the kind of system Russia should have instead of the Soviet one and the philosophical and ethical principles on which this new system should be based. These substantive disagreements, as well as

84. The third was the Marxist dissidence of the Medvedev brothers and several others.
85. Scammell, *Solzhenitsyn,* 640.
86. Solzhenitsyn, "As Breathing and Consciousness Return," 3.
87. Ibid.
88. Ibid., 6.
89. Ibid., 13–14.
90. Sergei Zheludkov, "K 'Razmyshleniiam ob intellektual'noi svobode.' Otvet akad. Sakharovu," *Khronika tekushchikh sobytii,* April 30, 1969, in *Sobranie* vol. 10a, no. AS196: 22–23.

a series of incidents in which Solzhenitsyn behaved badly, severely strained their personal relationship, which in any case ended when Solzhenitsyn was expelled from the Soviet Union in 1974. But in 1968 the two men, feeling vulnerable, quickly recognized how much they needed each other and how much they might help each other. The proximity of Sakharov's dacha at Zhukova to that of Mstislav Rostropovich, a close friend of Solzhenitsyn, enabled the two men to meet easily when they had matters to discuss.[91] As a result, despite radically different personalities and points of view, their relations remained amicable in the immediate aftermath of Reflections and Solzhenitsyn's response to it.


# 11  An Equal Partner in Politics and Life


Largely because of *Reflections* and the publicity it received around the world, by 1969 the Soviet government considered Sakharov its principal domestic opponent.[1] In his memoirs, Sakharov describes his newfound notoriety matter-of-factly, perhaps because his life was changing even more dramatically in other ways, for reasons having nothing to do with politics. In 1968 Klava's health deteriorated rapidly, the result of stomach cancer that metastasized because her doctors had been unable, even with X-rays, to detect it; Sakharov may have considered their incompetence, which verged on malpractice, symbolic of the larger failings in Soviet society he deplored.[2] By the new year there was nothing even the finest doctors could do, and on March 8, 1969, she died. The only real cause for joy in the last months was the birth in October 1968 of her first grandchild. Despite the deterioration in their relationship, Sakharov was profoundly troubled by Klava's illness and distraught by her death. When she was admitted to a sanitarium five months before she died, Sakharov, who also entered the sanitarium for a lengthy examination, was discovered to be suffering from a "cardiovascular disorder" that would plague him periodically for the rest of his life. It is a measure of Sakharov's distress over Klava's terminal illness that, despite the professional skepticism with which he normally viewed perversions of science, he investigated all sorts of bogus miracle cures in the futile hope that her life might be saved. In 1969 he donated a portion of the 139,000 rubles he had saved in his years at Arzamas to the building fund of a cancer hospital, donating the rest of it to the Soviet Red Cross and a children's fund at Arzamas.[3]

---

91. Scammell, *Solzhenitsyn*, 798.

1. Iu. I. Krivonosov, "Landau i Sakharov v 'razrabotkakh' KGB," *Voprosy istorii estestvoznaniia i tekhniki* 3 (1993): 125.
2. Sakharov, *Memoirs*, 295–96.
3. Ibid., 298–99; "Stepen' svobody," 26. On Klava's illness and death I have relied on Sakharov's memoirs, 295–98.

Eventually Sakharov regretted this donation. He came to believe that dissidents in special difficulty with the authorities and persons who needed material assistance were actually more deserving of his largesse.[4] He also realized that by giving most of his life savings to the building fund, the children's fund, and the cancer hospital, all of which were owned and run by the Soviet government, he was indirectly helping the very entity that was now the object of his political animus. In his memoirs Sakharov explains his mistake as the result of his belief that he was still "part of the [Soviet] establishment."[5]

For months after Klava's death, Sakharov remained "in a daze," so immobilized by grief that he could do neither scientific work nor anything political.[6] Because her death occurred just two months before his removal from Arzamas and because he did not begin work at the Lebedev Institute immediately afterward, he happened to have a great deal of time on his hands, which made his depression worse. But gradually his melancholy lifted, and in the fall of 1969 he produced an article on a "multisheet cosmological model," which he took as confirmation that he was once again a functioning scientist.[7] By the spring of 1970 he had resumed his political activities.

That fall, while visiting the home of the dissident Valerii Chalidze (who was also a physicist), Sakharov saw Elena Bonner, an attractive woman two years his junior who impressed him immediately by her "serious, energetic, and businesslike manner."[8] Over the next year their affection for each other deepened into love, and on January 7, 1972, in a ceremony at a civil registry office in Moscow, they wed.[9] Theirs was not just a marriage. It was also a political partnership, forged in adversity and strengthened by mutual respect. Sakharov and Bonner together were a more powerful political force than they would have been if they had remained alone, leading separate lives without the sustenance and strength each drew from the other. Sakharov's second marriage was very different from his first, and infinitely more satisfying. If his marriage to Klava was an aspect of his life that was distinct from everything else in his life, his marriage to "Lusia" (a childhood name Sakharov always used for Bonner) was so integral a part of his life that it is hard to imagine what his years as a dissident would have been like without her.

Elena Bonner's childhood, adolescence, and early adulthood were very different from Sakharov's. Her family was more political than Sakharov's and suffered

4. Sakharov, introduction to *Sakharov Speaks*, 38.

5. Sakharov, *Memoirs*, 299.

6. Ibid., 298.

7. Ibid., 300; A. D. Sakharov, "A Multisheet Cosmological Model," in *Collected Scientific Works*, 105–14.

8. Sakharov, *Memoirs*, 315. Sakharov does not specify in his memoirs or anywhere else the exact date on which he first saw Bonner. But in his memoirs, it is in the context of describing preparations for the Pimenov-Vail trial, which occurred in September–October 1970, that he mentions meeting her. In "Kakim on byl" Pimenov gives 1969 as the date of the marriage.

9. Sakharov, *Memoirs*, 353, 359. Almost certainly because of his estrangement from his own children, Sakharov did not inform them of his intentions, and they learned of his wedding only after the ceremony was performed. Ibid., 359.

considerably in the Stalin era because of their views. Her mother, Ruf Bonner, was from a Jewish family in Siberia, far removed from the Pale of Settlement in European Russia to which most Russian Jews were confined after Catherine the Great acquired the territory in the partitions of Poland in the late eighteenth century.[10] This may explain the family's distance from a traditional, religious Judaism that might have frowned upon the iconoclasm and intellectual independence both Ruf and her daughter displayed. Bonner grew up with her Armenian stepfather, Gevork Alikhanian, to whom she was closer than she was to her biological father, who also was Armenian. A committed communist, Alikhanian—who, to pass as ethnically Russian, called himself Alikhanov—worked with Anastas Mikoian before the October Revolution and afterwards helped him establish the Armenian Communist Party. When Alikhanov became head of the personnel department of the Comintern, the institution Lenin founded in 1919 to foment world revolution and advance international communism, he, Ruf, their son Igor, and Elena lived in a Moscow hotel reserved for Comintern officials. There young Elena played parlor games with Tito, Togliatti, and other foreign communists visiting Moscow as "Comintern Reps" to report on their activities and receive instructions for future operations.[11]

Until the mid-1930s, Bonner's childhood was uneventful. But in 1937 Alikhanov was arrested and sent to a labor camp. He was executed six months later. Ruf was arrested as well for the "crime" of being his wife. She spent eight years in a labor camp in Kazakhstan, several more in exile elsewhere, and was finally rehabilitated in 1955, when she was allowed to rejoin the Communist Party and return to Moscow. There she lived on Chkalov Street in an apartment the government provided her. Sakharov and Bonner lived in this apartment after they married.[12]

Elena used the name Bonner because after her parents disappeared, she was raised by Ruf's mother, Tatiana. Although as a child she belonged to the Komsomol, after her parents were condemned as traitors, Bonner refused for many years to join the Communist Party. Conversely, the party would not have wanted her as a member. Only after Ruf was rehabilitated did Bonner join, becoming a candidate member in 1964 and a full member in 1965.[13] In October 1941, while serving as a nurse's aide in World War II, she suffered a concussion when a bomb exploded near her. Sakharov speculates that this was the original cause of the cataracts and other ophthalmological problems Bonner suffered from later in life.[14]

As an injured war veteran Bonner had access, after the war was over, to the special stores only members of the Soviet elite could enter.[15] To the extent that

10. Ibid., 347.
11. Ibid., 347–49; Elena Bonner, *Alone Together*, trans. Alexander Cook (New York, 1986), 32–33; Klose, *Russia and the Russians*, 171.
12. Sakharov, *Memoirs*, 348.
13. Elena Bonner, *Alone Together*, 35.
14. Sakharov, *Memoirs*, 349–50.
15. Bailey, *Making of Andrei Sakharov*, 243.

she came to privilege through adversity, however, she was never really part of this elite in the manner Sakharov was. Indeed, she revealed an independent streak much earlier in her life than Sakharov did. While studying to be a pediatrician at the Leningrad Medical Institute in the early 1950s, she refused to imitate her fellow students in advocating the death penalty for one of the accused in the Doctors' Plot. For this she was expelled from the institute. Her expulsion, however, was only temporary, for after Stalin's death, she was reinstated. While studying at the institute Bonner met her first husband, Ivan Semënov, with whom she would have two children, Tatiana, born in 1950 (and named for Bonner's grandmother), and a son, Alexei, born in 1956. She and Semënov divorced in 1965.[16]

While teaching pediatrics in a Moscow medical school in the 1960s, Bonner became disenchanted with communism. In 1966 she made a trip to Armenia, where she examined KGB and party archives in preparation for an article on the Armenian Communist Party she had been asked to write for the fiftieth anniversary of the Bolshevik Revolution. There she learned how cruel and repressive the Soviet government had been in the Lenin era. Trips to Poland and France in the late 1960s showed her that the Soviet system in the years since Lenin and Stalin had not improved.[17] The Prague Spring, it seems, marked a turning point for her. When it was crushed in August 1968, Bonner realized that joining the Communist Party had been a mistake, and in November 1972 she formally renounced her membership.[18]

Bonner became a dissident before Sakharov did, and her dissidence in the early 1970s was more radical than his. By 1972 Bonner, unlike her husband, no longer cared whether the Soviet Union obeyed its own laws or adhered to its own principles.[19] And because she was more skeptical than her husband that the authorities would respond positively to his appeals to reason, she was also more willing to challenge them directly. Bonner obviously influenced Sakharov, who always valued her opinions and suggestions, and it was through her that he met literary figures and other dissidents such as Bulat Okudzhava, Alexander Galich, and Vladimir Maximov.[20] But he was never her puppet or tool, as many of his enemies insinuated.

Sakharov and Bonner, whatever their political agreements and mutual needs, were separate individuals with personalities that were in many ways diametrically opposite. Sakharov was shy, self-effacing, and slow to anger; Bonner was outgoing, comfortable with other people, occasionally acerbic, and quick to take umbrage when she thought she or anyone close to her, especially her husband, had not been treated fairly. These differences, which for others might

16. Sakharov, *Memoirs*, 347, 350.
17. Ibid., 351–52.
18. Bonner, *Alone Together*, 35. At a meeting of the Moscow party committee to which she had been summoned to explain her decision, she was asked why she was so hostile to the Soviet system after it had "given [her] everything." Sakharov, *Memoirs*, 376.
19. Sakharov, *Memoirs*, 377.
20. Ibid., 354–55.

have prohibited a harmonious relationship, drew Sakharov and Bonner closer together and made their union stronger both personally and politically.[21] What one partner lacked, the other supplied. Together, they instilled genuine fear in the leaders of the second most powerful country in the world.

# 12  Moral Anchor of a Dissident Movement

In the early 1970s Sakharov became a central figure among the dissidents. For this reason he could not remain aloof from the effort to create permanent organizations as a vehicle for pursuing the goals they shared. Through these organizations Soviet dissidence became an actual movement, as opposed to sporadic, ad hoc, and generally amateurish expressions of opposition whenever a particular instance of repression or mistreatment presented itself. Unlike Solzhenitsyn, for whom intellectual independence was an end in itself, Sakharov could see the practical benefit of collective action, and in the years that followed participated in organizations of a political nature without compromising his principles. Political disagreements, he knew, were inevitable, but his ability to keep them from becoming personal grudges helped to maintain an unusual degree of amity in the organizations and informal groups to which he belonged. Under the circumstances, personal feuds and recriminations were very likely. It is easy to forget how harried, defenseless, and insignificant in terms of numbers the dissidents were. But Sakharov provided ballast to the fragile ship the dissidents launched in those years, and it navigated the turbulent waters it was meant to sail with a minimum of self-induced leaks. What is surprising about the dissident organizations is not that they eventually collapsed but that they lasted as long as they did.

Also, from 1970 to 1973 Sakharov selected several issues he had tentatively raised in *Reflections* for special emphasis and elucidation; under the press of current events, he explored their implications for the Soviet system as a whole. In these years Sakharov grew as a dissident to the point where he offered specific proposals for reforming the Soviet Union based on the abstract moral and philosophical principles he professed. Intellectually, he was operating on two distinct levels of thought, the practical and the philosophical, and his ability to explicate complex problems from both perspectives made him a compelling and persuasive social critic. The plight of Soviet Jews who wished to leave the country, the desire of the Crimean Tatars and the ethnic Germans to return to their ancestral homes inside the Soviet Union, the question of amnesty for political prisoners, the use of psychiatry as an instrument of political repression,

21.  Sakharov and Adamovich, "Zhit' na zemle i zhit' dolgo," 172.

and the suppression of religion and the persecution of ethnic nationalism—
these were all issues Sakharov emphasized from 1970 to 1973. Because his time
and energy were limited, he had to be selective in the individuals and the causes
he championed. But since his natural tendency was to defend everyone who had
been victimized, in the early 1970s Sakharov seemed to be everywhere: appearing in every courtroom, participating in every demonstration, giving interviews
to every journalist who requested one, affixing his name on every petition he
was asked to sign.

At this stage in his development, he was still getting to know his fellow dissidents. One of these was another physicist, Valentin Turchin. While visiting
his home for seminars on contemporary and historical issues that Turchin and
his wife hosted periodically, Sakharov met other dissidents, the most impressive of whom, in Sakharov's estimation, was Grigorii Pomerants, a philosopher
who like Sakharov found Solzhenitsyn's ideas deficient in a number of ways.[1]
At one such seminar Turchin suggested to Sakharov that they write a letter to
the Soviet government showing how democratization was a prerequisite of scientific progress. Sakharov drafted the letter, and Turchin and Roi Medvedev
added their names to it after Sakharov reluctantly agreed to changes they suggested. When others they approached—including Kapitsa, Romm, and Lev
Artsimovich—refused to sign the letter, the three men sent it directly to the
Supreme Soviet of the USSR and released it publicly on March 19, 1970. The
fact that Sakharov not only drafted the letter but actively sought public support
for it was an indication of how prominent a role in the burgeoning movement
of Soviet dissidence he was willing to play.[2]

The letter was essentially a brief for democratization, by which the authors
meant not democracy but rather a kind of glasnost in which "freedom of information, the open airing of views, and the free clash of ideas" would be allowed
or even encouraged. Quite deliberately, the letter did not characterize democratization as a basic human right to which people everywhere were entitled.
Instead, it was extolled for its utility: democratization was essential to technological, scientific, and political progress; without it the Soviet Union would become
a "second-rate, provincial power."[3] There is no doubt that the authors believed
this. But it is also true that advocating democratization in purely utilitarian
terms was politically shrewd. Only a pragmatic justification of democratization,
one based on *raison d'état*, would have any chance of persuading the Soviet leadership to support it. The letter was meant to persuade, not to alienate. Just as in
*Reflections,* Sakharov, this time with two other dissidents, was seeking a dialogue
with the Soviet government out of which would emerge a program of reform as

1. Philip Boobbyer, *Conscience, Dissent and Reform in Soviet Russia* (London, 2005), 125. It was
for these seminars that Sakharov read *Vekhi,* a collection of essays published in 1909 that warned
against the fanaticism the contributors believed was endemic in the intelligentsia and the product
of its moral and philosophical absolutism. Sakharov, *Memoirs,* 305.

2. Ibid., 300–305.

3. Andrei Sakharov, Roy Medvedev, and Valentin Turchin, "A Reformist Program for Democratization," in Cohen, *End to Silence,* 318, 327.

beneficial to the Soviet people as it was supportive of the Soviet state. In 1970 Sakharov, unlike Bonner, still believed that a reformed Soviet Union was worth preserving and that if and when the country reformed itself, it would again be worthy of his loyalty. For this reason, Sakharov and his coauthors assured the recipients of their letter that it had been written with the aim of finding "a positive and constructive approach that will be acceptable to the Party and government leadership of the country."[4] Furthermore, the democratization they advocated must promote "the maintenance and consolidation of the Soviet socialist system" and be carried out "under the leadership of the Soviet Communist Party in collaboration with all strata of society."[5]

One sees in this a variant of the liberal elitism Sakharov espoused: in the beginning of democratization, the Soviet government would do well to limit the amount of information it released and thereby circumscribe the debate that would follow. This position assumed that the Soviet people were still irrational. In the lexicon of the letter, there were too many potential "demagogues" and "supporters of a 'strong state'" in Soviet society for there to be a completely free marketplace of ideas.[6] Sakharov and his coauthors truly seemed to believe that Brezhnev, Kosygin, and Podgorny would agree. Indeed, the three dissidents hoped that, by demonstrating their moderation to the Soviet leadership, they could more easily persuade it to approve the other reforms they requested, such as multicandidate (not multiparty) elections. Proclaiming that the threat China posed to the Soviet Union was an exceedingly serious one was yet another point on which its authors thought the leadership would agree.[7]

As deferential as it was, the letter proved to be too radical for the Soviet leadership.[8] As was the case with *Reflections*, its very existence posed a challenge to the government's presumed monopolies of wisdom and initiative. Soviet citizens, even a thrice-named Hero of Socialist Labor who had constructed the first Soviet thermonuclear bomb, could not be allowed to participate as equals with the Soviet leadership in the formulation of policy. Although the letter appeared in the émigré press, in the journal *Posev,* in the same year it was written, it did not appear in the Soviet press until 1990.[9]

Two months after the letter was sent, Sakharov felt compelled to protest for the first time the abuse of psychiatry as a means of repression. In May 1970 Valerii Chalidze, after introducing himself to Sakharov and requesting a meeting with him, asked the physicist to sign a complaint protesting the confinement of Piotr Grigorenko in a psychiatric hospital. Before being demoted for publicly

---

4. Ibid., 318.
5. Ibid.
6. Ibid., 323.
7. Ibid., 325, 327.
8. On April 20, slightly more than a month after the letter was sent, the KGB requested permission from the Central Committee to place listening devices in Sakharov's apartment. "Andropov to the Central Committee (April 20, 1970)," in Rubenstein and Gribanov, *KGB File,* 99.
9. A. D. Sakharov, V. F. Turchin, and R. A. Medvedev, "Neobkhodima postepenniia demokratizatsiia," *Posev* 7 (1970): 36–42; Archie Brown, *The Gorbachev Factor* (New York, 1996), 7–8. The letter appeared in *Izvestiia TsK KPSS* 11 (1990): 150–59.

criticizing Khrushchev, Grigorenko had been a major general in the Red Army. Grigorenko's confinement, for supporting the Crimean Tatars in their struggle to return from central Asia to their ancestral homeland, was actually his second one. In 1964 he had been confined for distributing leaflets demanding that the Soviet government return to the principles of Leninism. Sakharov not only signed the complaint, which implored the procurator general to investigate irregularities in the way Grigorenko's investigation and trial had been conducted, but also agreed to deliver it.[10]

Two weeks later, Roi Medvedev asked Sakharov to assist in the campaign to secure the release of his brother, Zhores, from a psychiatric hospital where he was confined, ostensibly for treatment for "psychological psychopathy" but in fact as punishment for his manuscript exposing Lysenko.[11] Again, Sakharov agreed to participate. The next day, at an international seminar in Moscow on genetics and biochemistry, he dramatically walked to the blackboard before the seminar began and wrote that he was seeking assistance in the effort to release Medvedev. Over the next two weeks Sakharov worked feverishly on Medvedev's behalf. At one meeting in Chalidze's residence, he met Tatiana Velikanova, Grigorii Podiapolskii, and Sergei Kovalev, the last of whom would be a close confidant and ally for the rest of his life.[12] Finally, on June 17, after a meeting at the Ministry of Health, to which Sakharov, Kapitsa, and other supporters of Medvedev had been invited (and at which the future president of the Academy of Sciences, Anatoly Alexandrov, told Sakharov that he was insane for assisting Medvedev), Medvedev was released. This was undeniably a genuine victory for Sakharov and his fellow dissidents. It showed that even if the Soviet system was not reformable, protests such as theirs could at least reduce its malevolence; under pressure, the regime might make similar exceptions in the future, albeit arbitrarily and on an ad hoc basis, to its repressive policies. But Medvedev himself was released only provisionally, on the condition that he refrain from anti-Soviet political activity in the future, and Sakharov, for his involvement in the matter, lost access to the special hospitals, health clinics, pharmacies, and sanitariums he and his family had previously frequented.[13]

Over the next three years Sakharov protested other instances in which dissidents had been arrested and then sent without trial to psychiatric hospitals where, under the guise of treatment, they endured what amounted to physical torture. In some cases, doctors acting on orders of the KGB dispensed narcoleptic and other powerful drugs that caused the recipients, depending on the

10. Sakharov, *Memoirs*, 309–10.

11. Ibid., 310; Rothberg, *Heirs of Stalin*, 300.

12. Sakharov, *Memoirs*, 311. Sakharov's stepson-in-law, Efrem Yankelevich, in a conversation on February 18, 2004, confirmed my estimation of Kovalev's closeness to Sakharov. A biologist by profession, Kovalev became a dissident because he found the Soviet system incompatible with the intellectual freedom science requires. But this transformation occurred more quickly and earlier in life in Kovalev's case—when he was a student at MGU—than it did in Sakharov's. Emma Gilligan, *Defending Human Rights in Russia: Sergei Kovalyov, Dissident and Human Rights Commissioner, 1969–2003* (New York, 2004), 2, 26.

13. Sakharov, *Memoirs*, 297, 311; Rothberg, *Heirs of Stalin*, 300, 337.

medication, to suffer uncontrollable tremors or to degenerate into a vegetative state. Among the many reasons Sakharov opposed this form of repression was that it turned the whole idea of treatment on its head. Under the pretense of making patients better, Soviet psychiatrists were deliberately trying to make them worse.[14]

There are several reasons the Soviet government adopted this particular tactic. Clearly, the emergence of dissidence in the late 1960s had thrown the Soviet leadership off balance. It flew in the face of everything the Soviet leaders believed about the passivity and immaturity of the Soviet people. Flustered, the regime experimented with various means of repression; calling the dissidents crazy was just one of them. Exiling them or stripping them of their Soviet citizenship while they were abroad (which is what was eventually done to Solzhenitsyn and Zhores Medvedev, respectively) was another. A further ploy was promising dissidents leniency if they denounced the Chinese. But declaring them insane and incarcerating them in hospitals had certain advantages over these other means of repression. Certainly it was a quieter and more expeditious way of silencing people. Public trials required preparation: indictments had to be prepared, witnesses rounded up and coached, and evidence discovered or, if necessary, manufactured. All of this took time. Public trials were also risky in that they could easily trigger protests by foreign governments and organizations or by Soviet citizens themselves. It was, after all, a trial, that of Siniavskii and Daniel, that had triggered the emergence of public dissidence in the first place. Finally, psychiatric concepts and categories, especially definitions of normalcy, were often so vague and elastic that political disagreement could be construed as evidence of psychological dysfunction.[15] Because no actual evidence of dissidence was required to declare an individual insane, psychiatry could be applied prophylactically to Soviet citizens who might merely be contemplating disobedience, or retroactively to actual dissidents for whom the government lacked sufficient evidence to try them in court. In short, psychiatric repression impressed upon the Soviet people the sobering realization that they could be punished, and punished severely, even if they never did anything wrong.

In the early 1970s it seemed that whenever the government sent a dissident to a mental hospital, Sakharov responded by denouncing the action. Among the other dissidents, in addition to Grigorenko and Medvedev, whose incarceration and subsequent mistreatment Sakharov denounced and whose release he insistently demanded, were Viktor Fainberg, who was declared insane for participating in the Red Square demonstration against the invasion of Czechoslovakia;[16] Vladimir Borisov, with whom Fainberg staged a hunger strike while incarcerated

---

14. Sakharov's brother Georgii suffered for much of his life from schizophrenia. Sakharov does not mention his brother's illness in his memoirs or in any of his other writings. However, Elena Bonner states that Georgii's illness did not affect Sakharov's views on psychiatry and was not what made him sensitive to its abuse. Edward Kline, *Moskovskii Komitet prav cheloveka* (Moscow, 2004), 47; Tatiana Yankelevich, conversation with author, February 9, 2009.

15. Alexeeva makes this point in *Soviet Dissent*, 310.

16. Sakharov, *Memoirs*, 327.

and who kept notes of his experiences that, along with Fainberg's, helped give Sakharov a greater sense of their predicament;[17] and the Ukrainian mathematician Leonid Pliushch, who was also psychiatrically hospitalized and on whose behalf and Borisov's Sakharov and Podiapolskii in 1973 requested the assistance of the United Nations.[18]

In the same year Sakharov, Podiapolskii, and Igor Shafarevich sent a pointed letter to the International Congress of Psychotherapists in Oslo, Norway, denouncing it for failing to issue a statement condemning abuses of psychiatry in both the Soviet Union and Eastern Europe.[19] When the Soviet psychiatrist Semën Gluzman was arrested in 1972 for disseminating an article (which never existed) on the Prague Spring that the government claimed had been written by Sakharov, the Soviet physicist, after pointing out the absurdity of arresting someone for distributing something that did not exist, reaffirmed Gluzman's integrity as a psychiatrist and called on psychiatrists everywhere to demand that the Soviet Union produce all relevant facts about the abuses of psychiatry for which it was responsible. Sakharov believed that the real reason the government had arrested Gluzman was that he had written a report attesting to Grigorenko's sanity, albeit without ever having examined the Soviet general.[20]

Sakharov's criticisms of the abuses of psychiatry evolved. In 1970, in a letter he sent to Brezhnev shortly after Zhores Medvedev was incarcerated, he noted, inter alia, that confinement of a scientist like Medvedev was inimical to Soviet science and a threat to its integrity. He also stressed the illegality of what the government had done, expressing incredulity that "such lamentable lawlessness [could be] sanctioned by the highest authorities."[21] In an open letter Sakharov sent in March 1971 to the Ministry of Internal Affairs he decried the continued confinement of Fainberg and Borisov, once again stressing the illegality of their punishment and their original arrest. As he had in his protest on behalf of Medvedev, Sakharov added to these objections the pragmatic argument that by treating dissidents like Fainberg and Borisov so cruelly—the two men were compelled by the barbaric treatment they received to stage a hunger strike for nearly three months—the government was seriously damaging its reputation abroad.[22]

17. Ibid., 328; Hilary Sternberg, "Sakharov and Solzhenitsyn: Champions of Freedom," *Index* 2, no. 4 (1973): 7.

18. Andrei Sakharov and Grigory Podyapolsky, "To the Secretary-General of the UN, Mr. Kurt Waldheim (June 25, 1973)," in *Sakharov Speaks*, 241–43.

19. Grigory Podyapolsky, Andrei Sakharov, and Igor Shafarevich, "Announcement of the Committee for Human Rights (July 9, 1973)," *Samizdat Bulletin*, no. 5 (September 1973).

20. Sakharov, *Memoirs*, 310; A. D. Sakharov, "Otkrytoe obrashchenie k psikhiatram vsego mira s prizyvom vystupit' v zashchitu Semena Gluzmana (November 15, 1972)," in *Sobranie* 24 (Munich, 1977), AS1221: 1; "Andrei Sakharov Demands International Investigation: An Open Appeal," *Samizdat Bulletin*, no. 3 (July 1973).

21. A. D. Sakharov, "Otkrytoe pis'mo L. I. Brezhnevu v sviazi s nasil'stvennym pomeshcheniem Zh. A. Medvedeva v psikhiatricheskuiu bol'nitsu (June 6, 1970)," in *Sobranie* 7 (Munich, 1972), AS471: 2.

22. Sternberg, "Sakharov and Solzhenitsyn," 7; A. D. Sakharov, "Otkrytoe pis'mo Ministru vnutrennikh del N. A. Shchelokovu v podderzhku V. Fainberga i V. Borisova, a takzhe drugikh

In that same year Sakharov called for an amnesty for everyone confined illegally in psychiatric hospitals and for the passage of new laws to prevent the repetition of what Fainberg, Borisov, and others had had to endure. He wrote that every Soviet citizen should be presumed sane until shown conclusively to be otherwise and that persons in psychiatric institutions did not lose their legal rights when they entered them. He also noted the vagueness of the whole concept of mental health and stressed the need for safeguards to prevent a faulty diagnosis. The most reliable would be a special board or agency to review every diagnosis of mental illness that was made; if it determined that the diagnosis was unfounded, it could prevent the individual in question from being committed to a psychiatric hospital. Furthermore, the individual had to have the option of contesting his own diagnosis legally, with the burden of proof in cases of confinement resting on those who claimed the person was mentally ill rather than on the person himself. Finally, psychiatric treatment could be compulsory only if the individual receiving it posed a real danger of physical harm to himself or others.[23]

As the cases of psychiatric abuse multiplied, however, Sakharov increasingly stressed the immorality, rather than the illegality, of incarceration. Gradually he came to recognize that its purpose and effect were "to demoralize, discredit, and humiliate" and rob its victims of their dignity as human beings.[24] Psychiatric incarceration was an especially repugnant form of repression. When normal, functional human beings were turned into "vegetables" because of unwarranted and harmful medication, when they were subjected to repeated beatings or wrapped tightly in wet canvas that shrank when dry, they experienced not only physical pain but dehumanization. To Sakharov, declaring normal people insane was not merely punishment but a way of stigmatizing them as well.

In most of the protests Sakharov lodged in the early 1970s he collaborated with others. No doubt this was partly because in those years the number of dissidents willing to make common cause with him, and with whose views he was mostly in agreement, was large. In many cases he worked with others on an ad hoc basis, writing a letter with one dissident, attending a demonstration with another, and so on. But he also belonged to an organization, the Human Rights Committee (HRC), with which he coordinated many of his activities until the organization faded away in 1974, decimated by deaths and departures from the Soviet Union among its membership.[25]

The impetus for the creation of the HRC came from Chalidze, who in the fall of 1970 proposed that he, Sakharov, and Tverdokhlebov form an organization that would do more than issue appeals on behalf of persons who were persecuted

lits, podvergshikhsia repressiiam v marte 1971 g. (March 30, 1971)," in *Sobranie* 8 (Munich, 1972), AS609: 2.

23. A. D. Sakharov, A. N. Tverdokhlebov, V. N. Chalidze, and I. P. Shafarevich, "Mnenie Komiteta prav Cheloveka po probleme lits, priznannykh psykhicheski bol'nymi (July 3, 1971)," in *Sobranie* 24 (Munich, 1977), AS1268: 2–4.

24. Sakharov, *Memoirs*, 330.

25. Ibid., 381. Edward Kline, conversation with author, June 10, 2008.

or make proposals for specific changes in Soviet policies and Soviet law. Instead, the organization's principal purpose would be informational: by providing the Soviet people with knowledge and understanding of human rights, it would raise their political consciousness to the point where the monopoly of wisdom the Soviet government claimed for itself would be broken.[26] If all went well, the government, even if it never agreed to elections or to the establishment of a genuine legislature, would have to deal with the Soviet people as the coequals Chalidze and the other dissidents believed they were. But since it would take time for this consciousness raising to succeed, for the immediate future the HRC would serve as the Soviet people's mentor and surrogate, in much the way the technocrats Sakharov referred to in *Reflections* would recommend policies that everyone would agree to once convergence had occurred. Of course the HRC, by trying to communicate with the Soviet people directly—indeed, by its mere existence as an entity independent of the government—posed a threat to it. But Chalidze believed that if the HRC espoused nonviolence and proclaimed that it wanted the government merely to uphold its own laws—in Chalidze's scheme of things, that was tantamount to saying that human rights and Marxist-Leninism were compatible—the government would allow the HRC to function, oblivious to its ultimate objective of helping the Soviet people create a public life for themselves outside the Soviet system.[27]

Sakharov joined the HRC with reservations. For one thing, he feared that such an organization, as Chalidze explained it to him, would raise false hopes. For another, he was troubled by its legalistic approach. In addition, he may have been reluctant to join any organization, especially one with strict rules and elaborate hierarchies of membership, that reminded him of the centralism he detested in the Communist Party.[28] But Sakharov also realized that isolated tracts like *Reflections* and the ad hoc protests he participated in after the essay appeared had not achieved the desired result of convincing the Soviet leaders to reform the country. He now understood that this objective could be achieved only if it was pursued collectively by organizations in which the dissidents worked together toward shared goals. The public criticism in 1970 that the Central Committee had directed at Soviet scientists for the insufficiency of their ideological vigilance against Western ideas only heightened Sakharov's sense that Soviet dissidence had to be organized if it was to have a chance of succeeding.[29]

Despite his misgivings, Sakharov therefore signed on to Chalidze's endeavor. On November 11, 1970, the two men, joined by Tverdokhlebov, held a press conference at which they distributed to the foreign correspondents daring enough

26. Ibid., 318–19; Alexeyeva, *Soviet Dissent*, 293.
27. On Chalidze's and the HRC's commitment to the rule of law, see Shatz, *Soviet Dissent*, 133–36, and Michael Scammell, "The Prophet and the Wilderness," *New Republic*, February 25, 1991, 30.
28. Sakharov, *Memoirs*, 319; Alexeyeva, *Soviet Dissent*, 291.
29. The Central Committee's rebuke appeared in *Partiinaia zhizn'*, October 25, 1970, and is referred to in "Soviet Physicists Rebuked by Party," *New York Times*, October 26, 1970, 10.

to attend it a detailed statement of the organization's founding principles.[30] To be sure, the HRC was not the first organization Soviet dissidents had created. In May 1969 Piotr Iakir and Viktor Krasin had established an Initiative Group for Human Rights, which lasted until 1973, when Iakir was arrested. While it existed, the group was little more than a name that gave people who signed petitions the illusion that they were part of a larger movement of political protest.[31] Chalidze's organization, by contrast, had a genuine structure (however grandiloquently he chose to describe it) and what might even be called a corporate identity. Indeed, the HRC was intended to be nothing less than a microcosm of a reformed Soviet society, its members joined to one another and to the organization itself by enlightened self-interest.

Still, the group was strictly, almost rigidly, hierarchical. Below the three founding members was a stratum of "experts" consisting of Alexander Esenin-Volpin and Boris Tsukerman; below them were "corresponding members" who included Galich and, at Chalidze's suggestion, Solzhenitsyn.[32] The problem with these arrangements, however, was not that they were too restrictive but that they were not restrictive enough. In the months that followed the committee's creation, Sakharov would become increasingly irritated by Chalidze's penchant, which he shared with Volpin and Tverdokhlebov, for raising theoretical issues of no practical relevance. What was worse, the three men, like Soviet apparatchiki, used the committee's bylaws to ensure that it devoted large amounts of time to such trivialities.[33] Still, Sakharov maintained his membership. He believed that the committee, whatever its flaws, was worth preserving, and that the chances the regime would disband it were minimized by the proviso in its original declaration of principles that only persons who were not members of any political party could join it. This, to Sakharov, was proof of a sort that the HRC was nonpolitical and thus could not be accused by the Soviet leadership of trying to supplant the Communist Party.[34]

The declaration of principles the committee released reads like a legal brief. In fact, the legalese in which it was written was cause for criticism, and some hilarity, among dissidents; in English translation the first sentence alone is 179 words long.[35] Substantively, the declaration stressed the group's commitment to act "in accordance with the laws of the state" in the furtherance of its objectives. These included assisting "state agencies in creating and applying safeguards for human rights, [helping] persons occupied with constructive investigations of the theoretical aspects of human rights, [and furthering]

30. Sakharov, *Memoirs*, 319–20.

31. Rubenstein, *Soviet Dissidents*, 122–24; Edward Kline, conversation with author, June 10, 2008.

32. Ludmilla Alexeyeva and Paul Goldberg, *The Thaw Generation: Coming of Age in the Post-Stalin Era* (Pittsburgh, 1993), 255; Scammell, *Solzhenitsyn*, 795.

33. Sakharov, *Memoirs*, 327.

34. Alexeyeva, *Soviet Dissent*, 294.

35. Plyushch, *History's Carnival*, 293; Alexeyeva and Goldberg, *Thaw Generation*, 254. The translation I used is in Roy A. Medvedev, *On Socialist Democracy* (New York, 1977), 355–56.

legal education and, in particular, the dissemination of documents of international and Soviet law concerning human rights."[36] This last objective was especially noteworthy. The HRC was the first organization in the history of the Soviet Union to affiliate itself with international organizations of human rights.[37] It claimed in its founding declaration that it was guided by the Universal Declaration of Human Rights, the nonbinding declaration of principles adopted by the UN General Assembly in December 1948 despite the Soviet Union's abstention in the vote to approve it.[38] In 1971 the committee was also accepted as an affiliate of the International League for the Rights of Man, which had consultative status at the United Nations. And in that same year it joined the International Institute of Law, headed by René Cassin, the author of the Universal Declaration.[39] Because the HRC saw human rights as indivisible, applicable everywhere and at all times regardless of the circumstances, it often issued appeals to these and other human rights organizations on behalf of Soviet citizens whose rights had been violated. These appeals, which Sakharov readily signed and wholeheartedly supported, were precedents for the literally hundreds of similar appeals he would issue on his own or with others long after the HRC had disappeared.

Another aspect of the HRC of which Sakharov approved was the fastidiousness with which it adhered to the procedures it had established for itself. Chalidze in particular believed that the Soviet people could learn as much from how the committee functioned as they could from what it said and did. He considered it a model of how a reformed Soviet Union would function. For that reason it was essential that, in its deliberations, the committee follow parliamentary procedure, no matter how ridiculous that might be given the small number of people who belonged to it.[40] By establishing its own rules and scrupulously adhering to them, the committee gained for its criticisms of the Soviet authorities a certain credibility that contrasted sharply with the latter's practice of disobeying their own laws.[41] Many, if not most, of the protests the HRC issued concerned the abuse of Soviet law by the Soviet government. Chalidze's insistence that he and the other members of the Committee practice in their own affairs what they advocated as a matter of principle was consistent with the concern for "moral wholeness" so pervasive among the Russian intelligentsia—the belief that the moral principles a person espouses must be

36. Medvedev, *On Socialist Democracy*, 355–56; "Human Rights Committee Statement of Purposes," in *Samizdat: Voices of the Soviet Opposition*, ed. George Saunders (New York, 1974), 414.

37. Alexeyeva and Goldberg, *Thaw Generation*, 257.

38. "Principles of the Human Rights Committee," in *Sobranie* 30 (Munich, 1977) AS657-b: 2; Mary Ann Glendon, *A World Made New: Eleanor Roosevelt and the Universal Declaration of Human Rights* (New York, 2001), xv, xviii, 218.

39. Alexeyeva and Goldberg, *Thaw Generation*, 257; Alexeyeva, *Soviet Dissent*, 294; Edward Kline, conversation with author, June 10, 2008.

40. Alexeyeva, *Soviet Dissent*, 293–94.

41. See, for example, A. Sakharov, A. N. Tverdokhlebov, V. N. Chalidze, and I. P. Shafarevich, "Mnenie Komiteta po povodu doklada A. N. Tverdokhlebova o bor'be sovetskogo zakonodatel'stva s paraziticheskim obrazom zhizni (June 29, 1972)," in *Sobranie* 24 (Munich, 1977) AS1256: 1–3.

applied to every aspect of his life.[42] In this respect, Sakharov's sensibility and Chalidze's coincided.

Eventually, however, Sakharov became disenchanted with the HRC and Chalidze. Though he never regretted joining the organization, he disliked the high-handed manner in which Chalidze, on occasion, tried to run it. Equally irritating from a purely tactical point of view was Chalidze's insistence on taking minutes when the committee met, which left a paper trail the government could easily follow should it seek to arrest or intimidate the membership.[43] By 1973 Sakharov was so disillusioned by the committee's ineffectiveness that he called it the "Pickwick Committee"—after the character in Dickens's novel—for issuing lengthy papers no one read.[44] After the fall of 1972, when Tverdokhlebov and Chalidze resigned from the committee, the organization was largely directionless; shortly afterward Chalidze left the Soviet Union. While its remaining members, bolstered by the inclusion of Shafarevich, continued to write reports and protest the violation of legal norms in trials the government staged of dissidents it was seeking to silence, the committee lost its original justification. Eventually it simply faded away.[45]

Sakharov's experience with Chalidze and the HRC was sufficiently unpleasant and disquieting that in 1976 he refused to join the Moscow Helsinki Group. He explained this decision in his memoirs: "It had been a relief to escape the constraints imposed by the Human Rights Committee, and I had no wish to find myself again saddled with such obligations."[46] But Sakharov's affiliation with the HRC was not without its benefits. The committee provided him with an "address" from which his views could be expressed, ensuring him a larger audience than he would have had if he, like Solzhenitsyn, had remained on his own. He also benefited from the opportunity to meet weekly with other dissidents, such as Alexander Esenin-Volpin, and to exchange ideas with them.[47] Finally, while

42. Isaiah Berlin has written eloquently on this in "The Birth of the Intelligentsia," in *Russian Thinkers*, ed. Henry Hardy and Aileen Kelly (New York 1979), 128–31.

43. Sakharov, *Memoirs*, 320; Alexeyeva and Goldberg, *Thaw Generation*, 255.

44. Hedrick Smith, "The Intolerable Andrei Sakharov," *New York Times Magazine*, November 4, 1973, 43.

45. Sakharov, *Memoirs*, 380–81; Alexeyeva, *Soviet Dissent*, 316–17. Sakharov believed that Chalidze left the Soviet Union by mutual consent: the government wanted Chalidze gone, and Chalidze, for reasons Sakharov implies were less than honorable, wanted to leave or at least was willing to leave. According to Solzhenitsyn, Chalidze manipulated Sakharov and used him for his own purposes—which was why Sakharov's work on the committee took up so much time. But Sakharov, whatever his feelings about Chalidze, was never anyone's puppet, and thus the decision to spend so much time on the committee was his alone. Sakharov, *Memoirs*, 380; Aleksandr I. Solzhenitsyn, *The Oak and the Calf: Sketches of Literary Life in the Soviet Union* (New York, 1980), 372–73.

46. Sakharov, *Memoirs*, 456. To be sure, Sakharov goes on to say that he had no objection to endorsing appeals of the Helsinki group when he agreed with them. Sakharov's experience with the HRC was not the reason, or not the main reason, he, unlike Bonner, did not join the chapter of Amnesty International Turchin and Tverdokhlebov established in 1973. As he indicates in his memoirs, Sakharov stayed away from that particular human rights organization because he considered impractical under Soviet conditions the rule the London headquarters imposed on its foreign chapters that, to ensure impartiality, they refrain from protesting the treatment of political prisoners in their own country. Ibid., 448–49.

47. Ibid., 320.

Sakharov's criticisms of the committee, as well as those of other dissidents, were well founded, the limits on what it could reasonably hope to accomplish were real. In the early 1970s the Soviet authorities saw no pressing reason to reform the system. Since most of the dissidents, as products of the educated elite, were as far removed temperamentally and sociologically from the Soviet people as the Soviet government was, the committee had no choice but to adopt a strategy geared to the long run. Thus its emphasis on pedagogy, on raising the political consciousness of the Soviet people, made sense. In pursuing its objectives, the HRC seemed to follow a two-stage strategy: its short-term goal of reducing the regime's malevolence would improve conditions temporarily until its long-term objective of educating the Soviet people would bear fruit. Under the circumstances, it is hard to imagine what else the committee could have done. Forming an underground party for the purpose of confronting the regime directly, as Grigorenko and some other dissidents tried unsuccessfully to do, was something for which neither Sakharov nor Chalidze was suited temperamentally and surely would have caused the government to arrest them.[48] For tactical reasons and as a matter of moral principle, Sakharov always rejected tactics like those the Bolsheviks had adopted prior to the October Revolution.

Sakharov's affiliation with the HRC was critically important in the evolution of his dissidence because it gave him a vehicle for expressing his belief in the rule of law. This belief was not incidental to his dissidence. Rather, it was at the core of it: a just society was one ruled by law, a society in which the supremacy of law was recognized by everyone, regardless of whether political power was exercised democratically. To be sure, Sakharov was not averse to breaking laws he considered unjust. But the permanent opposition and harsher methods some Russian émigrés recommended he emphatically rejected not only because he was temperamentally unsuited to these kinds of tactics but also because their illegality would undermine the very concept of the supremacy of law.[49] Sakharov was intent on creating a culture of law in the Soviet Union and for that reason eschewed tactics inimical to it. His objective in the early 1970s was to convince the Soviet authorities to obey those of its laws that were just and to change or rescind those that were not.

For the immediate future Sakharov thought he could foster this culture of law by bearing witness to, and thereby calling attention to, specific instances in which the Soviet government acted unlawfully. For this reason he tried, as much as his physical stamina and the demands of other commitments permitted, to attend the trials of people, many but not all of them dissidents, who were unjustly prosecuted. In the beginning, Sakharov seems to have believed that by attending these trials, he could increase the chances that the defendants in them would be treated fairly. This was certainly true of the first trial he attended, that of Revolt Pimenov and Boris Vail in Kaluga in October 1970. The two men had been arrested and charged with circulating materials in samizdat, including several

---

48. Edward Kline, conversation with author, June 10, 2008.
49. V. Tretiakov, "Strategiia i taktika," *Posev* 3 (March 1971): 2.

copies of *Reflections*.[50] Possibly because of Keldysh's intervention, Sakharov was allowed into the courtroom. During a break in the proceedings, in response to an informal question from the prosecutor, Sakharov informed him that Vail had not done what he was charged with—circulating "subversive" materials, among them Milovan Djilas's *The New Class*—and that the trial was therefore a farce. Tellingly, when Zeldovich advised Sakharov just before the trial began that by going to it, he would be putting himself "on the other side of the fence," Sakharov told him that he was *already* on the other side of the fence.[51] In the end, Pimenov and Vail got off fairly easily. Although they were convicted, they were sentenced to only five years in a labor camp, which Sakharov ascribed partly to his own presence in the courtroom.[52]

What was remarkable about how the Soviet government treated its dissidents in the early 1970s was not that they were treated cruelly but that the cruelty was sometimes leavened by leniency. It was not unheard of in this period for the government to release dissidents charged with serious crimes before being tried; among those released in this fashion were I. Kaplun and V. Bakhmin.[53] The reason was not that the authorities on occasion experienced pangs of conscience or that they had some inkling of the inhumanity of their own legal system. Rather, as Sakharov gradually realized, they were lenient because the Soviet system allowed the authorities to apply Soviet laws arbitrarily and capriciously, because the authorities had come to consider the law an instrument for the satisfaction of their personal whim. The Western concept of law as something external to those who applied it was entirely alien to the Soviet leadership. Sakharov, like many other dissidents, became aware of this. By attending political trials like Pimenov and Vail's in which the laws were ignored or misrepresented to ensure the convictions the government demanded, he became, in his own words, "more familiar with the problems of defending human rights."[54] If, for Solzhenitsyn, the network of labor camps he called the Gulag Archipelago was a metaphor for the Soviet Union as a whole, for Sakharov the emblematic expression of the Soviet Union was the legal (or rather, illegal) proceedings in which the Soviet government arbitrarily punished those who challenged it.

The legal abuses Sakharov protested were both substantive and procedural. Substantive abuses included the arrest, trial, and punishment of persons who had not committed the crimes with which they were charged or whose actions did not, or should not, constitute crimes. Pimenov and Vail were in this category. Andrei Amalrik was another. His arrest, under an article of the law code

50. Sakharov, *Memoirs*, 315; Rothberg, *Heirs of Stalin*, 338.

51. Sakharov, *Memoirs*, 316–17.

52. Ibid., 317. Others, including Vail himself, shared Sakharov's self-assessment. Bailey, *Making of Andrei Sakharov*, 281; V. S. Imshennik, "Epizod pravozashchitnoi deiatel'nosti," in Altshuler et al., *On mezhdu nami zhil*, 305.

53. V. N. Chalidze, A. D. Sakharov, A. S. Volpin, and P. I. Iakir, "Prezidiumu Verkhovnogo Soveta SSSR," *Posev* 11 (1970): 62.

54. Sakharov, introduction to *Sakharov Speaks*, 40.

of the RSFSR making unemployment a crime, Sakharov considered "a legal monstrosity."[55] Although Sakharov was unable, because of prior commitments, to attend Amalrik's trial in Sverdlovsk in November 1970 and thus to point out its flaws, the absurdity of the charges showed that the problem with Soviet jurisprudence was not merely that the Soviet government ignored its own laws but that the laws themselves were often deliberately and maliciously vague. As a result, practically anyone the government wanted to silence could be silenced simply by invoking one or several of them. Among the other trials Sakharov protested because he considered the arrests unlawful was Vladimir Bukovskii's in 1972, in which Bukovskii was convicted for having sent abroad various materials documenting the Soviets' abuse of psychiatry. That Bukovskii himself had been incarcerated in a psychiatric hospital once before (in the 1960s for possessing a copy of *The New Class*) lent credibility to Sakharov's criticisms of this particular punishment.[56] Perhaps in recognition of Bukovskii's fortitude in surviving it and of his willingness to endure a repetition by exposing its brutality to foreigners, Sakharov asked the celebrated airplane designer and former political prisoner Andrei Tupolev to join him in protesting Bukovskii's trial. Perhaps with two celebrities attending the trial in silent protest, the judge would be more inclined to acquit the defendant or at least to reduce his punishment. Tupolev, however, refused Sakharov's invitation on the grounds that Bukovskii was an "idler," and for good measure he told the Hero of Socialist Labor that he needed a psychiatrist himself.[57]

The procedural violations Sakharov sought to publicize were those that occurred once a dissident had been arrested and charged. These could include the refusal by the presiding judge at the trial to permit exculpatory witnesses to testify, as happened at the trial of Valerii Kukui. In Kukui's case, Sakharov determined that this was so egregious a denial of due process that Kukui's conviction was itself unlawful, and with Chalidze he petitioned the Soviet Supreme Court, without success, to reverse it.[58] Similarly, in the fall of 1972 Sakharov informed Hedrick Smith, the Moscow correspondent of the *New York Times*, of the government's refusal for six months even to consider the offer of "surety" he and Bonner had extended on behalf of the dissident mathematician Iurii Shikhanovich shortly after his arrest. According to Soviet legal procedure, if two persons offered surety, or assurance, that the arrested individual would appear in court when his trial began, the individual could be released. What Sakharov objected to was not only that Shikhanovich was not released—in Soviet law the receipt of two offers of surety did not require the government to honor them—but that the authorities refused his and Bonner's requests for an explanation of why their offers had been rejected.[59] In fact, just prior to Sakharov's

55. Sakharov, *Memoirs*, 321.
56. Ibid., 334.
57. Ibid., 356–57.
58. A. Sakharov and V. Chalidze, "O strannom protsesse v Sverdlovske (July 16, 1971)," *Khronika tekushchikh sobytii*, September 11, 1971, in *Sobranie* 10b (Munich, 1972) AS1000: 8.
59. Sakharov, *Memoirs*, 372–73.

contacting Smith, the government summoned him to KGB headquarters, where Shikhanovich's investigator, after pointedly excluding Bonner from the conversation, informed Sakharov that because he was not "trustworthy," his offer of surety could not be accepted. In his memoirs Sakharov notes laconically that this was his first official encounter with the KGB.[60]

By this time, Sakharov had been barred from courtrooms where dissidents were tried. The first trial from which he was excluded was evidently Bukovskii's, in January 1972.[61] At some point prior to the trial the authorities concluded that Sakharov's protests would be less credible if they were based on hearsay rather than on what he had personally observed—which only strengthened Sakharov's conviction that the government had a great deal to hide. Indeed, to ensure that his presence was a matter of public record, he now bore witness to official lawlessness in Soviet judicial proceedings by standing in silent protest outside courtrooms, sometimes outdoors. At the trial of Kronid Lubarskii, who had been arrested for distributing the *Chronicle of Current Events*—the principal samizdat compendium of dissident activities and Soviet violations of human rights—when Sakharov and a few others who tried to enter the courtroom were pushed back forcibly by KGB agents, they simply stood vigil outside in the cold for nine hours.[62] Not surprisingly, Sakharov considered public access to trials part of the due process he believed everyone charged with a crime was entitled to.[63]

Sakharov's abhorrence of the violation of legal norms in the Soviet Union crystallized in 1972 in his calls for a blanket amnesty for political prisoners. These calls followed logically from the legal abuses he decried: if dissidents were denied due process in their arrest, interrogation, trial, and conviction, then the punishments they consequently endured were unlawful as well and should be ended by granting amnesty. The same reasoning applied, a fortiori, to dissidents unlawfully incarcerated in psychiatric hospitals. In calling for such an amnesty when he did, just prior to the official celebration in December 1972 of the fiftieth anniversary of the establishment of the Soviet Union, Sakharov may also have calculated that the Soviet government, given the circumstances, would be receptive to it. As it happened, the amnesty the government granted on December 28, 1972, fell short of what Sakharov wanted. Conspicuously, it excluded political prisoners and persons confined against their will in psychiatric hospitals. A few weeks later, Sakharov, Shafarevich, and Podiapolskii, in the name of the HRC, expressed their opposition to these exclusions to the Cassation Committee of

60. Ibid., 372. Shikhanovich, in fact, was not tried but declared insane and sent to a psychiatric hospital. Sakharov, Bonner, and Podiapolskii strongly protested this. E. Bonner, G. Podiapolskii, and A. Sakharov, "Otkrytoe obrashchenie v sviazi s priznaniem Iu. Shikhanovicha dushevnobol'nym (July 5, 1973)," in *Sobranie* 25 (1977) AS1445: 1–2.

61. Sakharov, *Memoirs*, 359; Bailey, *Making of Andrei Sakharov*, 295; A. P. Lavut, "Na zakrytykh 'otkrytykh' sudakh," in Ivanova, *Andrei Dmitrievich*, 163.

62. Sakharov, *Memoirs*, 375–76; Sakharov, "Voice Out of Russia," 29. The *Chronicle of Current Events* was a samizdat journal that mostly presented just the facts of the Soviet Union's denial of human rights because its editors believed that editorializing about them was unnecessary.

63. See, for example, Andrei Sakharov, "Memorandum (March 5, 1971)," in *Memoirs*, 642.

the International League for the Rights of Man.[64] But even before this selective amnesty was granted, Sakharov waged a veritable campaign for an inclusive one, circulating a petition he had written with the assistance of Tatiana Litvinova, Chalidze's mother in-law and also the daughter of the Soviet foreign minister in the Stalin era, Maxim Litvinov. Rebuffed by Solzhenitsyn and Kapitsa, Sakharov persevered in this endeavor, even after he and Bonner were tailed by KGB agents while soliciting signatures in Komarov outside Leningrad. For much the same reason that he advocated a general amnesty, Sakharov also agitated in 1972 for the abolition of the death penalty in the Soviet Union, which, like his grandfather Ivan, he opposed not only in principle but because in the Soviet Union it was applied frequently to people who had never committed the crime for which they were executed. Accordingly, he and Litvinova circulated an appeal proclaiming that the death penalty was morally wrong, which they sent to the Presidium of the Supreme Soviet.[65] It is not clear from the text of the appeal whether the other signatories, mostly dissidents and other figures from the Soviet elite, shared Sakharov's rationale for abolition.[66]

## Defending Ethnic and Religious Dissidents

Of course Soviet dissidents were not the only ones whose persecution Sakharov deplored. In the early 1970s he learned in greater detail and from a variety of sources—in his memoirs he cites Shafarevich, Mikhail Agurskii, the *Chronicle of Current Events,* and conversations he had with Catholics, Baptists, Uniates, Pentecostals, and Seventh Day Adventists—of the government's denial of religious liberty and its efforts to silence those who protested it.[67] In much the same way, he also became aware of movements of various ethnic minorities in the Soviet Union that wished to reclaim their cultural heritage and assert their ethnic identity. What linked the abstract moral and philosophical principles Sakharov espoused with the particular individuals he defended was his belief that his principles were meaningful only if he protested their violation in as many instances as possible. By the very diversity of the people he defended, he demonstrated that the rights he championed were truly universal rights and that every individual was entitled to them precisely because they were inherent in the very concept of humanity. Sakharov felt obliged to defend Baptists, Ukrainians, and Latvians not only because these were ethnic groups that were collectively persecuted but because the individuals who comprised these groups were human beings.

64. A. Sakharov, I. Shafarevich, and G. Podiapolskii, "Otvety na voprosy, kasaiushcheesia Komiteta prav Cheloveka (January 1973)," in *Sobranie* 24 (1977), AS1246: 1–3.
65. Both alone and with Bonner, Sakharov circulated the petitions for amnesty and the abolition of the death penalty. In the end, the petitions, which Sakharov released in November 1972, contained an impressive list of fifty signatories, including Leontovich, Chukovskaia, Rostropovich, Maximov, Roi Medvedev, and Viktor Nekrasov. Sakharov, *Memoirs,* 364–66; "51 in Soviet Ask Amnesty for Political Prisoners," *New York Times,* November 19, 1972, 2.
66. The texts of both petitions are in Sakharov, introduction to *Sakharov Speaks,* 239–40.
67. Ibid., 337.

Dmitrii Sakharov (Andrei Sakharov's father), ca. 1910–1919. MS Russ 79 (6922). By permission of the Houghton Library, Harvard University.

Ekaterina Sofiano (Andrei Sakharov's mother), ca. 1910–1919. MS Russ (6923). By permission of the Houghton Library, Harvard University.

Andrei Sakharov, 1945. MS Russ (6954). By permission of the Houghton Library, Harvard University.

Sakharov with Igor Kurchatov on the grounds of the Institute for Atomic Energy, Moscow, 1957. AIP Emilio Segre Visual Archives. Physics Today Collection.

Sakharov, first wife Klavdia Vikhireva, and children, ca. early 1960s. AIP Emilio Segre Visual Archives. Physics Today Collection.

Sakharov and his second wife, Elena Bonner, 1973. MS Russ (6995). By permission of the Houghton Library, Harvard University.

Sakharov, Gorky, 1975. In the apartment of Yurii Tuvim on the day Nobel Peace Prize was awarded. MS Russ (7034). By permission of the Houghton Library, Harvard University.

"We want the Olympics to be a sporting event—not an opportunity for the Western news media to lionize dissidents and to play politics." *Washington Post*, 25 January 1980. Cartoon by Edmund S. Valtman. Prints and Photographs Division, LOC, LC-DIG-ppmsc-07973.

Sakharov and Elena Bonner, ca. 1980s.
MS Russ (7133). By permission of the
Houghton Library, Harvard University.

Sakharov at the Institute for Atomic
Energy, Moscow, 1988. AIP Emilio
Segre Visual Archives, Physics Today
Collection.

Sakharov with Vice President George W. Bush and unidentified man, Washington, D.C., 1988. MS Russ (7275). By permission of the Houghton Library, Harvard University.

Sakharov in the House of Scientists beneath a bust of Lenin, Moscow, 1989. AIP Emilio Segre Visual Archives, Physics Today Collection.

Sakharov at the Congress of People's Deputies, Mikhail Gorbachev in background, Moscow, 1989. MS Russ. (7303). By permission of the Houghton Library, Harvard University.

Sakharov and Elena Bonner at the Nobel Institute, Oslo, 1989. MS. Russ. (7307). By permission of the Houghton Library, Harvard University.

Elena Bonner beside Sakharov's coffin, Moscow, December 1989. MS Russ (7313) By permission of the Houghton Library, Harvard University.

For example, in May 1971 Sakharov attended the trial of Anatolii Krasnov-Levitin, a devoutly Orthodox believer who wrote books on the history of the Orthodox Church while simultaneously protesting the persecution of his coreligionists. Arrested for anti-Soviet slander in 1969, only to be released for no apparent reason almost a year later, Krasnov-Levitin was taken into custody again for protesting the arrest of an elderly woman who had forged some of the names on a petition she was circulating calling for the reopening of an Orthodox Church that had been converted into a warehouse.[68] When he learned of the matter, Sakharov understood immediately that the forgery charge was just a pretext for the woman's arrest, as well as for Krasnov-Levitin's, and that the real issue their cases raised was religious liberty. He sent an appeal to the Soviet president, Nikolai Podgorny, and when it became clear that Podgorny would not respond, he helped write a second appeal that the HRC sent a few months later to the Supreme Soviet. In both of these Sakharov stressed that Krasnov-Levitin was being persecuted for his religious beliefs and that practicing one's religion was not a crime.[69] From what he observed of the case—a KGB agent, in a reversal of what by then had become the standard procedure, ushered him into the courtroom so he would be unable to address the protesters gathered outside it—Sakharov concluded that "religious liberty is an important part of the human rights struggle in a totalitarian state."[70] Similarly, in 1972, Sakharov and Bonner traveled to Kiev to protest the trial of the Ukrainian poet Anatolii Lupynos, who had been arrested both for distributing Sakharov's writings and for publicly reading a poem he had written condemning the desecration of the Ukrainian national flag; as a Ukrainian he considered it a sacrilege that in the Soviet Union it was used as a rag. The government therefore deemed his poem "anti-Soviet," and his trial, which was postponed with no explanation and then rescheduled with no prior announcement, was a farce: the crime of which Lupynos was convicted was considered evidence of insanity, and he soon found himself in a psychiatric hospital.[71] In large part because of travesties like the Lupynos case, Sakharov in that same year called for amnesty for everyone who had been punished for practicing religion.[72]

Some ethnic activists did not take kindly to Sakharov's interventions. In 1970 several Ukrainians objected strongly to his call for the elimination of any indication of nationality on the internal passport every Soviet citizen was required to carry. They believed that this was an affirmation of ethnic identity and that regardless of the government's reason for requiring it, an indication of nationality was something of which every Ukrainian should be proud.[73] These Ukrainian

68. Ibid., 336.

69. A. D. Sakharov, "Pis'mo N. V. Podgornomu v zashchitu A. Ye. Levitina-Krasnova (May 23, 1972)," in *Sobranie* 9 (Munich, 1972), AS685: 1.

70. Sakharov, *Memoirs*, 337.

71. Ibid., 358; Note in *Khronika tekushchikh sobytii*, November 10, 1971), 19, reprinted in *Sobranie* 10b (Munich, 1972), AS1038: 16–17.

72. Sakharov, "Memorandum," 642.

73. Dornan, "Andrei Sakharov," 370.

nationalists were championing a self-limiting and particularist agenda, in which the rights they demanded for their own nationality they refrained from demanding for others. Sakharov's conception of rights was radically different. By his own definition they were universal, and one senses that his misgivings about Ukrainian nationalism, and about nationalism generally, stemmed largely from its inherent exclusiveness, which he believed was reinforced by the way Soviet citizens were identified on their passports.

Still, the right to proclaim one's ethnic identity and to find its satisfaction in the creation of an independent state was a human right like any other in Sakharov's scheme of things, and his defense of it never wavered even when it threatened the very survival of the Soviet Union in the late 1980s. In fact, there were several ethnic minorities in the Soviet Union whose cause Sakharov always advocated with special zeal. Among these were the Crimean Tatars and the ethnic Germans. During World War II Stalin considered both groups disloyal; accordingly, they were removed from their homes and resettled in dreadful camps in Soviet Central Asia and Siberia. Unlike other minorities, such as the Kalmyks, Chechens, Karachai, Ingush, and Balkars, that were exiled under similar circumstances, the Crimean Tatars were not permitted after Stalin's death to return to their homes.[74] In 1956 the government allowed them to live outside the special settlements to which they were confined. And in 1967 the Presidium of the Supreme Soviet formally exonerated them of the charge of treason. But without the residence permits they needed to live there, the Tatars were still excluded from the Crimea.[75]

In the spring of 1971, a Tatar couple sought Sakharov's assistance in acquiring these permits. He agreed to help and shortly afterward wrote to the minister of internal affairs on their behalf. In response, two subordinates of the minister informed Sakharov while he was visiting the ministry that because Khrushchev had "given" the Crimea to the Ukraine as a "gift" in 1954, their hands were tied and thus he would have to take the matter up with the proper authorities in the Ukraine.[76] Undaunted, Sakharov, in the months that followed, issued appeals on behalf of the Crimean Tatars generally, including one supporting the Meskhi Turks as well as the Tatars in their desire to return to their respective national homelands (which, it must be remembered, were inside the Soviet Union).[77] What Sakharov objected to in the government's recalcitrance was not merely its denial of the right to choose one's place of residence. Equally repugnant to him was the collective guilt imputed to the Tatars as the basis for the government's denial. The Crimean Tatars, Sakharov pointed out, had not collaborated with the Nazis during World War II more than other ethnic minorities and therefore should not be singled out for special punishment. He also noted that, whatever the extent of collaboration, individual Tatars should not be penalized for

74. Alexeyeva, *Soviet Dissent*, 7.
75. Ibid., 138–39, 144–45; Sakharov, *Memoirs*, 331.
76. Sakharov, *Memoirs*, 332.
77. A. D. Sakharov et al., "Komitet prav Cheloveka, Obrashchenie v Presidium VS/SSSR o vosstanovlenii prav nasil'stvenno pereselennykh narodov (April 21, 1972)," in *Sobranie* 24 (Munich, 1977), AS1254: 1.

the actions of other Tatars. Sakharov abhorred the concept of group guilt because it so obviously denied the notion of individual moral responsibility. While the Crimean Tatars as a group had suffered persecution incommensurate with that which other ethnic groups endured, it was almost always in the context of defending individual Tatars that Sakharov raised with the government its persecution of the Tatars collectively. For Sakharov, human rights belonged to individuals, not groups.

Ethnic Germans were in a similar situation. Exiled to Siberia in 1941–1942 because Stalin feared they would collaborate with the advancing Germans armies, and then confined to special settlements in 1948, the ethnic Germans were allowed to leave these settlements in 1955 and were absolved of treason in 1964.[78] But they still could not return to their ancestral homes, mostly along the Volga River. Because of their comparatively small numbers in and around Moscow, most foreign diplomats and correspondents ignored them.[79] Sakharov, aware of this, realized that if he did not take up their cause, no one would. In addition, some of the ethnic Germans wanted to leave the country entirely. This, too, according to Sakharov, was a human right to which every Soviet citizen was entitled. And so, when Frederick Ruppel, an ethnic German who had been stymied in his efforts to secure an exit visa, solicited Sakharov's assistance in November 1970, the Soviet physicist, despite his limited stamina and resources, agreed to help him. Ruppel's predicament was complicated, which severely hampered Sakharov's efforts to help him. In addition to his request to secure an exit visa, Ruppel was trying to secure his mother's posthumous rehabilitation; in the Stalin era, she had been charged with anti-Soviet agitation and shot.[80] But Sakharov labored indefatigably on Ruppel's behalf, and finally in 1974 Ruppel was allowed to emigrate to West Germany. In his memoirs Sakharov describes approvingly what motivated Germans like Ruppel to want to leave the Soviet Union: "German emigration stems from a natural human desire to return to the land of their forefathers, to share in its culture and language, to enjoy its economic and social achievements. It is understandable that Germans should want to leave a country where they have been victims of appalling injustice—in effect genocide—and where they have been discriminated against in education and employment."[81] The fact that Ruppel's case ended satisfactorily, particularly in light of the issues it raised, pleased Sakharov immensely. Once again his actions demonstrated that while the dissidents might not be successful in changing Soviet policy, they could on occasion force the government to make exceptions to it.

## Soviet Jews and Emigration

For Sakharov, the right to emigrate was always an individual right even though collective entities like an ethnic minority could be denied it. Ultimately, his view

78. Alexeyeva, *Soviet Dissent,* 168–69.
79. Sakharov, *Memoirs,* 341.
80. Ibid., 338–39.
81. Ibid., 340.

reflected a liberal nationalism neither exclusionary nor chauvinistic. Peoples like the ethnic Germans and the Crimean Tatars may have had particular grievances other groups lacked, but the rights they were denied they were entitled to as individuals and as human beings. In the innumerable statements Sakharov issued over his long career as a dissident in defense of the right to emigrate (which was a subset, as it were, of the right to choose one's place of residence), he was always careful to describe this right as one to which everyone was entitled regardless of ethnicity, nationality, or religion. In fact, in October 1971, in an appeal to the Supreme Soviet requesting that it guarantee this right in the form of actual legislation, he underscored his belief in its universality by including it among the corpus of rights he claimed were "universally acknowledged"—a clear reference to the Universal Declaration of Human Rights, which specifically includes a right of emigration.[82] The fact that the Soviet Union abstained on the motion in the United Nations to adopt the declaration was for Sakharov irrelevant: the Soviet Union, whether it liked it or not, as a member of the UN had a moral, if not a legal, obligation to follow the declaration and allow its citizens to emigrate.

Of all the human rights Sakharov extolled, the right to emigrate was the one he championed most persistently. There were several reasons, both circumstantial and philosophical, for this. For one thing, it took up the preponderance of his time. In the 1970s, by Sakharov's own reckoning, of the literally hundreds, if not thousands, of people who sought his assistance, more than half wished to emigrate.[83] For another, unrestricted emigration, from the perspective of the regime, suggested unmistakably that its achievements were hollow, its promises illusory, and its legitimacy doubtful. Given all the good the Soviet Union had done since its creation—so the Soviet authorities reasoned—there was no reason, other than wanting to be reunited with a relative abroad (which was the only grounds for issuing an exit visa), for anyone to want to leave it. Whereas for Western democracies the personal freedom emigration implied was a source of strength, for the Soviet Union it was a tacit acknowledgment not only of weakness but of failure—that the grand experiment in building socialism and creating a New Soviet Man had gone terribly wrong. In light of what the Soviet government risked by permitting emigration, what is remarkable about the struggle Sakharov and other Soviet dissidents waged to secure exit visas is not how many Soviet citizens were denied them but that any actually received them. Obviously foreign pressure played a role in this. But dissidents like Sakharov were the ones who alerted foreign governments and organizations to the problem and pushed them to do something about it.

In articulating a right to emigrate and claiming that the Soviet government was obliged to honor it, Sakharov was playing for high stakes. At issue was not only a philosophical and ethical principle but the moral legitimacy of the Soviet Union

---

82. "Universal Declaration of Human Rights," in Glendon, *World Made New*, 312; Andrei Sakharov, "Let Soviet Citizens Emigrate (October 7, 1971)," in *Sakharov Speaks*, 162.
83. Sakharov, *Memoirs*, 344.

itself. Sakharov seemed quietly cognizant of this, as did the Soviet government. Partly for this reason, he was especially sensitive to Solzhenitsyn's charge, repeated in *The Oak and the Calf,* that he was concerned about emigration only because Bonner was interested in the subject (presumably because she was Jewish).[84] In his memoirs, Sakharov notes with satisfaction that he had mentioned the issue of emigration in *Reflections,* long before he knew her.[85]

In the 1970s, the majority of those who sought Sakharov's assistance in leaving the Soviet Union were Jews. Jews wishing to do this—those who applied for exit visas were called "refuseniks"—had no interest in changing the Soviet Union, which of course is what the dissidents wanted to do. Still, despite the differences in their respective objectives, relations between dissidents and refuseniks were generally harmonious. In Sakharov's case, it is not hard to understand his concern for Soviet Jews. His marriage to Bonner clearly strengthened the philo-Semitism he had harbored since childhood. So, too, did his contacts with Jewish dissidents such as Shikhanovich, Boris Tsukerman, and Alexander Galich; several others Sakharov met were half-Jewish, such as Esenin-Volpin.[86] Most of these were dissidents first and Jews second. They believed that the oppression of Jews in the Soviet Union was a concomitant of the oppression experienced by everyone in the country and that therefore Soviet Jews would not receive a measure of justice until everyone did. Indeed, many Jewish dissidents believed that Soviet Jews should fight not for Jewish rights but for human rights. While most of them did not deny their Jewish identity, they were neither particularly observant in their private lives nor especially vocal in calling for the revival of Judaism inside the Soviet Union.

Soviet dissidents like Sakharov also recognized that the situation for Soviet Jews was more complicated, and in some ways more precarious, than it was for the other ethnic and religious minorities in the Soviet Union. The pervasiveness of Soviet anti-Semitism and the virulence with which it was expressed by the government and ordinary citizens alike, especially after the Six-Day War in 1967, were not lost on the dissidents, for whom Soviet Jews became what the peasants were for the intelligentsia—the most obvious and identifiable victims of a political system that was unjust. For this reason, they responded sympathetically to pleas for help from this group, even though agitation for exit visas probably increased the hostility toward the vast majority of Soviet Jews who still wished to remain in the Soviet Union.[87]

---

84. Solzhenitsyn, *Oak and the Calf,* 375.
85. Ibid., 345.
86. Leonard Schroeter, *The Last Exodus* (Seattle, 1979), 385–86.
87. In this respect, Solzhenitsyn was an exception. While not anti-Semitic, he considered Soviet Jews, despite the unrivaled virulence of the anti-Semitism they endured, just one minority among many, undeserving of any special recognition or consideration. Because Russia, beneath its communist exterior, was always his homeland, he was especially unsympathetic to Jews—or to anyone else, for that matter—who wished to leave the Soviet Union for another country, whether it be Israel or the United States. Solzhenitsyn's second wife, Natalia, even criticized Sakharov to his face for helping Jewish refuseniks when *kolkhozniki* in her opinion were worse off. D. M. Thomas, *Alexander Solzhenitsyn: A Century in his Life* (New York, 1998), 342.

The first issue Sakharov addressed concerning Soviet Jews was the Leningrad hijacking affair in 1970. In June of that year seven Soviet citizens, five of them Jewish, were arrested before they could hijack a Soviet commercial airliner for which they had purchased all the tickets. Their plan, as conceived by their leader, Eduard Kuznetsov, was to commandeer the plane after flying from Leningrad to Priozersk, where they would pick up four confederates and release the crew members they had previously overpowered. From Priozersk one of the hijackers, Mark Dymshits, who was a pilot, would then fly the plane to Sweden, from which they would eventually make their way to Israel. Upon their arrest, the would-be hijackers disclaimed any animus toward the Soviet Union. Theirs was not a political protest, they said; all they wanted was to go to Israel.[88]

At no time in the course of his protests over the government's treatment of the hijackers did Sakharov ever consider their arrest illegal or a violation of human rights. He readily acknowledged that hijacking an airplane was morally wrong and a crime. But he and Bonner were appalled when they learned that the hijackers had been charged with treason, for which the penalty, though it did not have to be imposed, was death. This led Bonner, with Sakharov's concurrence, to claim falsely that she was Kuznetsov's aunt and should thus have the right to secure defense counsel for him and the other defendants; her justification was that Kuznetsov's mother was ill and could not do this herself.[89] Though perhaps understandable, what Bonner did was wrong, one of the few times she and Sakharov were duplicitous in pursuing their objectives. When the trial ended in December with Kuznetsov and Dymshits sentenced to death, Bonner and Sakharov reverted to a tactic they had used before: Sakharov wrote to Brezhnev requesting commutation of the sentence on the grounds that the hijackers had not committed the crime of air piracy for which they were charged.[90] He also sent letters to Podgorny and President Nixon requesting clemency for the hijackers and for the American communist Angela Davis, respectively; rightly or wrongly, Sakharov's pairing of the two cases suggested their moral equivalence and, more subtly, the moral equivalence of the Soviet and American legal systems.[91] Sakharov also tried to call Brezhnev about the matter, but the latter's secretary rebuffed him. Because of this, Sakharov and Bonner were pleasantly surprised when, on December 31, following weeks of protests by foreign organizations (not all of them Jewish), the government announced it was commuting the death sentences to fifteen years' confinement in labor camps.[92]

---

88. Sakharov, *Memoirs*, 321; Alexeyeva, *Soviet Dissent*, 182. How ill prepared the hijackers were for the difficult feat they were attempting is clear from the fact that the pistol they intended to brandish to keep the crew from resisting did not work. Alexeyeva, *Soviet Dissent*, 182.

89. Sakharov, *Memoirs*, 322–23. The notes Bonner took while attending the trial were included in an appendix to the manuscript Kuznetsov wrote, called *Prison Diaries*, that Bonner helped smuggle out of the Soviet Union three years later. Ibid., 322, 390.

90. Sakharov and Adamovich, "Zhit' na zemle i zhit' dolgo," 174.

91. Sakharov, *Memoirs*, 323; A. D. Sakharov, "Otkrytoe obrashchenie k Prezidentu SShA R. Niksonu i Predsedateliu Prezidiuma Verkhovnogo Soveta SSSR N. V. Podgornomu, 28 dekabria 1970," in *Sobranie* 7 (Munich, 1972) AS512: 1–2. Davis had been indicted for her involvement in an attempt to free the Black Panther George Jackson from a California prison.

92. Sakharov, *Memoirs*, 324–25.

In 1971 Sakharov focused even more intently on the issue of emigration. At first, he took up mostly cases of Soviet Jews who sought to emigrate for the purpose of "repatriation," which was the euphemism both the government and the Jews used for Zionism.[93] Gradually, however, Sakharov grew less concerned with the reason the Jews he was helping wanted to leave and more inclined to support emigration under virtually all circumstances for the sake of the principle itself. For example, in the appeal he sent to the Supreme Soviet in October 1971, he proclaimed that "the freedom to emigrate…is an essential condition of spiritual freedom. A free country cannot resemble a cage, even if it is gilded and supplied with material things."[94] Consistent with this, Sakharov listed in his appeal Lithuanians, Armenians, Estonians, Ukrainians, ethnic Germans, and Meskhi Turks, as well as Jews.[95] This practice continued in 1972 and 1973. In fact, he interceded in these years not only on behalf of Soviet Jews who sought to emigrate but on behalf of relatives of theirs the government took to harassing in an effort to persuade them to stay. This was what prompted Sakharov's calls for an international campaign on behalf of Evgenii Levich, who had been seized and forced into military service after his father, the prominent physicist Veniamin Levich, had applied for exit visas for himself and his family.[96]

Not surprisingly, Sakharov's philo-Semitism ripened into visceral, but by no means uncritical, support for the state of Israel. He had long admired the Jewish state for the courage and vigor with which it defended itself. This was particularly the case after the Six-Day War in 1967, when Israel acted preemptively against Arab states that were planning to attack it. But in the early 1970s, he increasingly identified Israel as the weaker party and the one more frequently and unfairly criticized in its relations with its larger Arab neighbors.[97] This was certainly true in September 1972, when, after the Palestinians' massacre of Israeli athletes at the Munich Olympics, Sakharov and Bonner's children and son-in-law (Bonner herself was ill at the time) joined a silent vigil in Moscow to protest that atrocity. Shortly after Sakharov and his stepchildren arrived at the vigil, the KGB briefly detained them. This was the first time this had happened.[98] Given the threats to its survival from the stronger countries that surrounded it, Israel, for Sakharov, was analogous to Soviet Jewry, which was obviously weaker than the Soviet government and whose predicament he considered emblematic of the Soviet people's.

## The Memorandum and Postscript

However much the cause of unrestricted emigration occupied pride of place in Sakharov's dissidence, he always viewed it within the larger context of the

---

93. Schroeter, *Last Exodus*, 386.

94. Sakharov, "Let Soviet Citizens Emigrate," in *Sakharov Speaks*, 162.

95. Ibid., 160.

96. Andrei Sakharov, "Otkrytoe pis'mo rektoru tel'avivskogo universiteta prof. Iuvalu Neemanu v zashchitu Evgeniia Levicha (May 30, 1973)," in *Za i protiv: 1973 god, dokumenty, fakty, sobytiia* (Moscow, 1991), 46.

97. When asked once why he did not criticize the Israelis as much as he did the Palestinians, Sakharov replied that "there will always be enough critics of Israel without me." N. A. Dmitriev, "Politicheskii opponent," in Altshuler et al., *On mezhdu nami zhil*, 278.

98. Sakharov, *Memoirs*, 374; Dornan, "Andrei Sakharov," 392.

struggle for human rights. It is noteworthy that the aide-mémoire he hoped to use in persuading Brezhnev to commute the Leningrad hijackers' death sentences turned out to be a prescription for comprehensive reform.[99] This was the so-called Memorandum, which Sakharov sent to Brezhnev on March 5, 1971. To avoid antagonizing the Soviet authorities unnecessarily, he deliberately did not release it to foreign correspondents or circulate it in samizdat.[100] In his memoirs Sakharov states that he sent the Memorandum without expecting the government to accept immediately any of the specific reforms it suggested. Its purpose was actually more ambitious: to put before the Soviet government "a comprehensive, internally consistent alternative to the official Party program."[101] Sakharov may have viewed this as an existential act of protest, something that was worthwhile for its own sake even though its chances of producing tangible changes in the immediate future were nil. By this time, Sakharov was much less optimistic about the dissidents' prospects for influencing the Soviet government than he had been when he wrote *Reflections* or when he joined the HRC. Whatever his expectations, he received no response for what must have been a period of several months. (Sakharov nowhere indicates in his writings the exact duration.) Finally, however, he heard from Brezhnev's chief assistant that a reply would follow shortly. But none ever did.[102]

Still, the Memorandum was important for what it revealed about the evolution of Sakharov's thought. Bonner commented once that in the Memorandum Sakharov broadened the concept of intellectual freedom into a comprehensive exposition and defense of human rights.[103] According to Oleg Moroz, the Memorandum prefigured much of what perestroika and glasnost would usher in under Gorbachev's leadership fifteen years later.[104] In many ways the document served as a way station, an intermediate point for Sakharov between the optimism that informed *Reflections* in 1968 and the pessimism that pervades *My Country and the World,* an essay he wrote in 1975.

As a compendium of policy recommendations—far more elaborate and detailed than those Sakharov included in *Reflections*—the Memorandum grounded its claim to moral legitimacy in the larger philosophical and political principles alongside which these policy recommendations were presented. The majority of these Sakharov put forth, as he had in *Reflections,* in the form of "discussion points." His reason, again, was primarily tactical. However unlikely it was that Brezhnev would adopt his ideas, Sakharov did not want to alienate him unduly by claiming they were nonnegotiable (even though philosophically and morally they were).[105] Once he made his intentions plain in this respect, Sakharov

99. Sakharov, *Memoirs*, 324, 326.
100. Ibid., 326–27.
101. Ibid., 326.
102. Ibid.
103. Elena Bonner, "Stupitel'noe slovo," in *Razmyshleniia o progresse, mirnom sosushchestvovanii i intellektual'noi svobode,* 11.
104. Moroz, "Vozvrashchenie iz ssylki," 311.
105. Sakharov, "Memorandum," 643.

presented his central point: "The basic aim of the state is the protection and safeguarding of the basic rights of its citizens. The defense of human rights is the loftiest of all aims."[106] Human rights are not only the foremost objective of all states; their preservation is the very reason states exist. Ideally, all the laws states enact are consistent with human rights and "observance of the law is obligatory for all citizens, agencies, and organizations."[107] Sakharov then goes on to claim that in a society that values human rights, laws exist to liberate the individual more than to limit him: "The happiness of the people is safeguarded, in particular, by their freedom of work, freedom of consumption, freedom in their private lives and in their education, their cultural and their social activities, freedom of opinion and of conscience, and freedom of exchange of information, and of movement."[108]

With these general principles as justification, Sakharov then proposes a whole laundry list of reforms, from the abolition of the internal passport and the jamming of foreign radio broadcasts to measures against noise, air, and water pollution, the death penalty, alcoholism, and cruelty to animals. To the desiderata of legal rights and guarantees he deems essential, he adds an entire paragraph on the explosive issue of self-determination for the national and ethnic minorities of the Soviet Union. Consistent with the tenor of the document, he adopts what under the circumstances is a moderate position: on the one hand, he calls for the Soviet government to reiterate explicitly the right of secession guaranteed in the Soviet Constitution, while on the other, he assures Brezhnev (and anyone else in the government who might happen to come upon the document and read it) that few, if any, minorities would actually avail themselves of this right, and those that did would almost certainly retain close ties with Moscow.

On the Soviet economy as well, Sakharov tries to be reasonable. He advocates a fairly small private sector enjoying limited autonomy within the context of a socialist economy. Individual enterprises should have greater autonomy in how they organize themselves and in how they operate on a daily basis, and management personnel should be chosen democratically in multicandidate elections. But conspicuously absent are the denationalization of property and the privatization of industry and the collective farms.[109] In 1971, there were still some things, like the creation of a market economy and a multiparty system, that Sakharov was not ready to suggest or even consider seriously. He still believed that adherence to legal norms would make the transformation of political institutions unnecessary. Only at the very end of his life would he call explicitly for an end to the monopolies of power and initiative the Soviet Constitution reserved exclusively for the Communist Party.[110] On foreign policy, which Sakharov mentions

106. Ibid., 644.
107. Ibid.
108. Ibid.
109. Ibid., 646–48.
110. See, for example, A. D. Sakharov, V. A. Tikhonov, G. Kh. Popov, A. N. Murashev, and Yu. N. Afanasyev, "The Appeal of a Group of People's Deputies of the USSR (December 1, 1989)," in Altshuler et al., *Andrei Sakharov,* 717–18.

only briefly in the Memorandum, he also seeks common ground with the Soviet authorities, warning ominously, albeit obliquely, of a possible Chinese attack on the Soviet Union, which he implies would have to be repulsed militarily.[111] Also, in much the way he recommended in *Reflections* that technical experts advise the Soviet government, he calls for the creation of an international body of experts, possibly under United Nations auspices, that would make nonbinding recommendations to individual governments.[112]

In June 1972, having received no reply to his Memorandum from Brezhnev or anyone else in the Soviet government, Sakharov decided to distribute it in samizdat and give copies to foreign correspondents. Parts of it quickly appeared in Western newspapers, including the *New York Times*.[113] Shortly before releasing the Memorandum, Sakharov added a Postscript that differed in tone from the original document and touched on several points it omitted.[114] While in the Memorandum he had said nothing about convergence, in the Postscript he reiterated what he had written earlier about it in *Reflections,* though with greater urgency. "Only through the convergence of capitalism and the socialist regimes," he wrote, "will it be possible to overcome the tragic conflicts and dangers of our time."[115] For the first time, Sakharov evoked convergence not just as a means of achieving peace and harmony but as the only means of preventing war. Just as he had in *Reflections,* he suggested a moral equivalence between capitalism and socialism. Both systems, he wrote, were characterized by a pervasive militarism that degraded politics under capitalism just as much as it harmed the economy under socialism.[116] In addition, capitalism was no less deficient in protecting the rights of workers than socialism was in fostering "a Party-state bureaucratic monopoly" in ideology, the economy, and culture.[117] Notably absent from Sakharov's comparisons is the conclusion he might logically have drawn from them: that there was no longer any reason for him to remain a socialist or, in the alternative, no reason to believe that the Soviet Union was still socialist. Although Sakharov was clearly evolving toward both of these positions, he may have deliberately refrained from embracing them for fear that doing so in a document intended specifically for the Soviet authorities would be gratuitously provocative and antagonistic. Clearly, Brezhnev would be more receptive to calls for the Soviet Union's reform if they came from someone who proclaimed himself a socialist, or at least refrained from stating that he was not.

---

111. Sakharov, "Memorandum," 645. In 1973 Sakharov expressed regret over what the Memorandum said about the Chinese, acknowledging that tough talk about China, even from dissidents, would only encourage the Soviet leaders to militarize the Soviet Union, making democratic reforms impossible. Sakharov, introduction to *Sakharov Speaks,* 47.

112. Sakharov, *Memoirs,* 645.

113. Ibid., 649; David Peter Coppen, "The Public Life of Andrei Sakharov, 1966–1989: A Bibliographical Chronicle" (master's thesis, University of Illinois at Urbana-Champaign, 1998), 34.

114. Sakharov, *Memoirs,* 326, 366.

115. Andrei Sakharov, "Postscript to Memorandum (June 1972)," ibid., 649.

116. Ibid.

117. Ibid.

In the document there is nevertheless a pessimism, or at least a sense of chastened optimism, that one does not find in Sakharov's previous writings. In the Postscript he does not merely single out for special criticism those aspects of Soviet society, specifically medical care and education, of which the Soviet leadership was most proud and with which Sakharov, as a former member of the Soviet elite, was intimately familiar. Nor does he merely bemoan the harsh treatment to which dissidents such as Bukovskii, Grigorenko, Fainberg, Borisov, and Vladimir Gershuni had been subjected.[118] What most clearly distinguishes the Postscript from the Memorandum is his concern for the spiritual and moral health of the Soviet Union and the Soviet people—a concern he had first raised fleetingly a few months earlier in an appeal he wrote on Bukovskii's behalf immediately after the latter's trial and conviction.[119] In Sakharov's diagnosis, the Soviet Union—by which he means its people and its government in roughly equal measure—is "infected by apathy, hypocrisy, petit-bourgeois egoism, and hidden cruelty."[120] What is more, the alcoholism he deplored in the Memorandum is so pervasive that it has assumed "the dimensions of a national calamity" leading to "the moral degradation" of Soviet society as a whole.[121] Given the magnitude of this degradation, reversing it will require "the spiritual regeneration" of the entire country, which in Sakharov's teleology will be possible only when the social conditions producing "feelings of impotence, discontent, and disillusionment" have been ameliorated.[122] And the only way this can happen, he insists, is as a consequence of the government's providing "opportunities for advancement in work, education, and cultural growth."[123]

Not surprisingly, the spiritual regeneration Sakharov called for in the Postscript caught Solzhenitsyn's eye and pleased him greatly. Despite his contention that Sakharov had failed to publicize the Postscript sufficiently because he was still too involved in other, less important, matters, Solzhenitsyn was sufficiently enamored of what Sakharov had written—which seemed surprisingly similar to what he himself believed—that he invited the Soviet physicist to contribute to *From Under the Rubble,* a compendium of essays he was creating that stressed the necessity of moral self-improvement and to which he would contribute three essays of his own.[124] But Solzhenitsyn's belief that Sakharov had now adopted his position was unwarranted. Although Solzhenitsyn may not have realized it at the time, he and Sakharov actually viewed the causal relationship between individual moral regeneration and social justice very differently. For Solzhenitsyn the former was a prerequisite of the latter. For Sakharov it was exactly the reverse. According to Sakharov, it was precisely the lack of social justice, the rule of law,

118. Ibid., 650–51.

119. Andrei Sakharov, "Appeal to the General Secretary of the Central Committee and the USSR Prosecutor General (January 18, 1972)," in *Sakharov Speaks,* 236.

120. Sakharov, "Postscript," 650.

121. Ibid.

122. Ibid.

123. Ibid.

124. Solzhenitsyn, *Oak and the Calf,* 373; Scammell, *Solzhenitsyn,* 798.

personal freedom, and material prosperity that had caused the spiritual and moral degeneration he bemoaned in the Postscript. Sakharov seemed to recognize the differences between their two positions more clearly than Solzhenitsyn did and politely but firmly turned down his invitation.[125]

After releasing the Postscript in June 1972, Sakharov issued appeals that encompassed the full range of his dissidence. Fainberg's and Borisov's continued incarceration in a psychiatric hospital,[126] the denial of due process in legal proceedings involving Lubarskii and Piotr Iakir,[127] and the inability of the Jewish mathematician Vladimir Gershovich to secure an exit visa[128] were just a few of the injustices he deplored. In November, in an interview he gave to Jay Axelbank of *Newsweek*, Sakharov returned to the larger themes of the Postscript. He first answered questions about his personal life: the authorities harassed Bonner's children because they were afraid to go after his own children; he had no hobbies but liked skiing; he earned 750 rubles monthly; and he lived plainly and unostentatiously. But in responding to Axelbank's subsequent, more substantive questions, Sakharov took the opportunity of revising some of the ideas he had expressed in earlier writings, especially *Reflections*.[129]

Sakharov told Axelbank that in *Reflections* he had seriously underestimated the responsibility the Soviet Union, China, and North Vietnam should bear for the turmoil and instability that existed in the world. He explained that he had written the essay "from what you call a position of abstraction" and that much of what he had subsequently learned convinced him that his original commitment to socialism was unwarranted.[130] Intellectual honesty required him to acknowledge this. In simple, declarative sentences, Sakharov described his disavowal of socialism in much the way a scientist might reject a hypothesis he was testing experimentally because the empirical evidence for the hypothesis was lacking: "When I wrote this book [*Reflections*] I was a little idealistic. Remember that Czechoslovakia had not yet been invaded.... Now I know many more things and am a much more disappointed man. I called myself a socialist then, but now I have modified my beliefs. What I stand for now is contained in the postscript to the Memorandum, which became known this summer. I would no longer label myself a socialist. I am not a Marxist Leninist, a Communist. I would call myself a 'liberal.'"[131] Sakharov went on to say that he was compelled by his experiences in the Soviet Union and by what he knew about how socialism had fared in other countries to admit that socialism could only be considered "a grave disappointment"; whatever benefits it provided, other ideologies provided just as

125. Scammell, *Solzhenitsyn*, 799.
126. "Soviet Physicist Pleads for Dissenters," *New York Times*, August 3, 1972, 3.
127. A. Sakharov et al., "Telegram to Rudenko on Admission to Trial of Lubarsky (October 27, 1972), cited in *Chronicle of Current Events*, December 31, 1972, 21.
128. Coppen, "Public Life of Andrei Sakharov," 47; "Notes on People," *New York Times*, July 22, 1972, 17.
129. Sakharov, "Voice Out of Russia," 29. References are to the interview as reprinted in the London newspaper the *Observer*, December 3, 1972) 29.
130. Ibid.
131. Ibid.

well. In fact, it was precisely because capitalism was no less effective than social-ism in ameliorating the problems capitalist and socialist societies shared that he favored convergence.[132]

Just as he had in the Postscript, Sakharov acknowledged to Axelbank the moral and spiritual dimensions of the problems facing the Soviet Union. Shrewdly, he recognized that the arrangement the government had tacitly fashioned with the Soviet people was effective: by regurgitating Marxist-Leninist shibboleths publicly, the Soviet people were permitted to mock the system and pursue their material interests privately, leading in the latter case to a pervasive black market the government tolerated because it defused popular anger and resentment. In the Soviets' calculation, beating the system was easier than overthrowing it, and the number of actual dissidents would thus be few. But the result of this cyni-cal arrangement was a generation of "Moscow taxi drivers"—Sakharov's meta-phor for the Soviet people—who were in equal measure apathetic and cynical, recognizing that the system was corrupt but doing nothing to reform it.[133]

Sakharov's deduction is quite sobering. "Our struggle," he said to Axelbank, "is really useless and senseless. . . . We stand outside courthouses and we write pro-test letters. But who listens?"[134] While acknowledging that a half-century from now things might be better, Sakharov predicted ruefully that in ten years nearly nothing would have changed, even though what the dissidents had been asking of the regime—namely, that it adhere to its own laws and protect the liberties its constitution guaranteed—was hardly extreme. In response to Axelbank's ques-tion why he continued the struggle for human rights in the Soviet Union if it was futile, Sakharov gave a justification very different from the one that had driven him to write *Reflections*, when he thought his chances of changing the system were better. He said he was still fighting for human rights "because for us it is not a political struggle, and I must emphasize I really know nothing about politics or political theory. It is a moral struggle for all of us. We have to be true to ourselves."[135] In explaining his position, Sakharov rejected Axelbank's implication that he was now "a pessimist." On the contrary, he said, he was actu-ally an optimist, and his views were simply the result of analyzing the situation objectively.[136] At first glance, Sakharov's position is inexplicable. How can he be optimistic about changing a situation he freely admits is unchangeable, at least for the foreseeable future? The answer lies in his notion of optimism, which had a moral component lacking in most other people's understanding of the term. For him, optimism was warranted not only when existing circumstances were objectively auspicious for the outcome or result one desired. It was justified also when moral principles were involved because these principles were valid every-where and at all times, even when there was no one ethical enough to put them

132. Ibid.
133. Ibid.
134. Ibid.
135. Ibid.
136. Ibid.

into practice. As a result, though the Soviets could eliminate the dissidents, they could never eliminate the principles the dissidents espoused.

Obviously Sakharov's repudiation of socialism did not emerge ex nihilo. Changes in his own life and in the Soviet Union precipitated it. The severity with which the government persecuted the dissidents in 1972 seemed to belie Sakharov's belief, which he held from 1968 through 1971, that whatever their shortcomings, the Soviet leaders were amenable to reason. Therefore, in any discussions they might conduct with the dissidents the possibility of finding common ground was real. But the capriciousness and brutality the authorities displayed in 1972—in punishing Bukovskii yet again and in arresting Piotr Iakir, the son of the executed Soviet general Iona Iakir, for protesting what he feared was a revival of Stalinism—convinced Sakharov that his hopes were sadly misplaced. By requesting a dialogue with the government, as he did successively in *Reflections,* the Memorandum, and the Postscript, Sakharov may have thought he was being conciliatory and in that way demonstrating his bona fides as a partner in reforming the Soviet Union. But the Soviet authorities viewed Sakharov's attempts at conciliation as a challenge. Allowing a private citizen a role in the formulation of policy—especially one as open-minded and reasonable as Sakharov—was simply inconceivable to a regime that claimed a monopoly of wisdom in the formulation and execution of policy. Dissidents were not supposed to exist in such a regime—hence the brutality, born of frustration, irritation, and bewilderment, with which they were treated.

It is clear that the decline of the HRC, which Chalidze's departure from the Soviet Union in 1972 greatly accelerated, also played a role in convincing Sakharov that changing the country was more difficult than he had previously imagined. So too, one suspects, was Bonner's decision in 1972 to discard her party card, an action that formalized her earlier break with the Soviet Union and socialism in 1968 when she had left the party in all but name. In her view, the Soviet Union was incapable of reforming itself because its ideology was untenable as an organizing principle of society. The problem, which Sakharov acknowledged four years later than Bonner, was therefore not just with the Soviet Union but with socialism itself. From this he drew the logical conclusion, which became clear in his interview with Axelbank, that he had no reason to remain a socialist himself.

By the time Sakharov repudiated socialism, dissidence had become a way of life, obliterating the small barrier that still existed between his politics and his personal life. His interventions by this time were devoted, in varying proportions depending on the circumstances, to dissidents he knew who were harassed, Soviet citizens he did not know who were harassed, and members of Bonner's family who were harassed. As noted earlier, Bonner's children had participated with Sakharov in the September vigil protesting the Munich massacre of Israeli athletes. This was probably the reason Bonner's older child, Tatiana (or Tania, as everyone called her) was expelled from the Moscow night school she attended.[137]

---

137. Sakharov, *Memoirs,* 374; Bonner, "Do dnevnik," 40–41. After Tania's expulsion, the Massachusetts Institute of Technology in the United States tendered her an invitation to study there.

By now Bonner's children (far more than Sakharov's, who were more or less estranged from him) had become, in effect, hostages to Sakharov's and Bonner's dissidence, their fates inextricably linked to those of their mother and stepfather. Emigration was not a real option. The Soviet government might not agree to it, and if it did, Sakharov and Bonner, who almost certainly would be allowed to leave the country, would never see them again. The only option Sakharov and Bonner had was to continue their dissidence. By protesting Soviet policies, the couple provoked the authorities to mistreat them in ways that were harmful to the Soviet Union's reputation abroad. For that reason the government would not want the additional adverse publicity an assault on Bonner's family would undoubtedly generate. This, at any rate, appeared to be the couple's calculation, and at the time and for several years afterward, it worked. Bonner's children, while harassed, were not actively persecuted; neither Tania nor Alexei was arrested, exiled internally or abroad, or sent to a psychiatric hospital.

The interview with Axelbank, as well as other statements, prompted the Soviet government to criticize Sakharov publicly and severely. On February 14, 1973, there appeared in *Literaturnaia gazeta* a review by its editor in chief, Alexander Chakovskii, of a recent book by Harrison Salisbury, who Chakovskii knew had edited the American edition of *Reflections*.[138] Midway through the review Chakovskii abruptly attacked Sakharov's essay and, by implication, Sakharov himself. That Chakovskii's assault came five years after *Reflections* was written shows that its purpose was to discredit the author rather than the essay itself; by 1973, it was largely unknown or forgotten outside dissident circles. In its sheer vituperation, Chakovskii's diatribe deserves to be cited at length:

> Some time ago I read this concoction [i.e. *Reflections*] that was published in the Western press. I found it to be a naïve conglomeration of wishful thinking and passages taken from the Gospel, *The Social Contract* of Rousseau, and the Soviet and American Constitutions.... The way in which Sakharov hopes to achieve universal peace is by creating a world government that would reconcile the interests of Soviet workers and *kolkhozniki* [collective farmers] with those of Texas oil barons, Pentagon generals, "heroic patriots" in South Vietnam, Black Panthers, racists from the John Birch Society, and neocolonialists and present-day participants in national liberation movements in Rhodesia and Angola.[139]

Chakovskii then goes on to write confusingly that Sakharov's naïveté comes not from some misguided virtue but rather from what Chakovskii calls "an evident coquettishness" that causes the Soviet physicist to "posture majestically over conflicts" while simultaneously seeking to aggravate them as an unwitting tool of

---

But the authorities refused to grant her an exit visa. Sakharov, *Memoirs*, 381. In the end, it took two years of protests by Sakharov before Tania was reinstated. She finally graduated from the school in 1975. Bonner, *Alone Together*, 35.

138. A. Chakovskii, "Chto dal'she: Razmyshleniia po prochtenii novoi knigi Garrisona Salsberi," *Literaturnaia gazeta*, February 14, 1973, 14.

139. Ibid. This was the first time *Reflections* had been cited by name in the Soviet press. Sakharov, Introduction to *Sakharov Speaks*, 50.

Western capitalists and imperialists.[140] A naïf like Sakharov, he implies, should stick to what he knows best (in Sakharov's case, presumably physics) and leave politics to those who are better informed.

Here again one sees the Soviet leadership, through its spokesman, arrogating to itself the individual's right to his own convictions and the collateral right to act responsibly on the basis of them to influence the government's policies. These were rights that Sakharov now believed belonged not just to him but to everyone. Of course his belief challenged what was perhaps the principal justification of the Soviet system—that the Soviet people were insufficiently rational to share in its governance. Indeed, the lengths to which Chakovskii went to discredit Sakharov were an indication that the Soviet leadership recognized how direct a threat he posed to its legitimacy. For this reason, Sakharov's moral probity had to be denied, his political intelligence derided, and his patriotism questioned.

But as harsh and potentially threatening as Chakovskii's criticisms were, worse would follow soon.

# 13  The Regime Reacts

Five weeks after Chakovskii's piece appeared, Sakharov was summoned to answer questions from the KGB. This was the first time the Soviet police had demanded this of him. At the meeting, which the KGB termed an interview but which quickly became a unilateral denunciation, the KGB informed Sakharov that he was not "morally sound."[1] In addition, he was told that his membership in the HRC was in itself "slanderous" of the Soviet Union, that his attempts to attend trials of dissidents were improper, and that foreign correspondents like Axelbank who interviewed him did so for the purpose of weakening the Soviet Union.[2] Although the police did not explicitly order him to cease his activities, they made it clear that by continuing them he could find himself in serious jeopardy. If Sakharov, in the estimation of the police, was not a traitor, he was perilously close to becoming one.[3]

But Sakharov was not easily intimidated. No amount of harassment, whether of him personally or of the dissidents generally, seemed to faze him. In the pursuit of his own objectives he remained indefatigable. In the spring of 1973, however,

---

140. Ibid.

1. Dornan, "Andrei Sakharov," 394.
2. Ibid., 394–95.
3. Ibid., 395. A rumor that Sakharov was mentally ill was circulating in Moscow—possibly with the connivance of the KGB—when the KGB summoned him. Sternberg, "Sakharov and Solzhenitsyn," 7.

the government had some success in disrupting the dissidents, though not to the point of eliminating the movement entirely. Piotr Iakir, after renouncing his dissidence in exchange for leniency, sent Sakharov a letter criticizing the Soviet physicist for acting in ways that, in Iakir's newfound estimation, were harmful to the Soviet Union. Sakharov's principal transgression, according to Iakir, was that he allowed himself to be used by émigré organizations like NTS that sought the Soviet Union's destruction. Obviously, Sakharov could not have been pleased by Iakir's defection, accompanied as it was by an ad hominem denunciation that was obviously orchestrated by the government. Equally distressing was the fate of the *Chronicle of Current Events,* which, along with *Veche* (a samizdat journal espousing the virtues of Russian Orthodoxy), had to cease publication, albeit temporarily, after a prohibitively large number of people involved in producing it were arrested. This was also when Zhores Medvedev was stripped of his citizenship while abroad in England, and Andrei Amalrik was sentenced yet again to confinement in a labor camp.[4] In spite of these setbacks, or possibly because of them, Sakharov persisted, protesting instances of injustice even though the chances of preventing further ones were rapidly diminishing. Leaving the Soviet Union voluntarily was not an option for him. Because of his prominence, his defection would be a public-relations disaster for the Soviet government. Accordingly, his acceptance in the spring of 1973 of an invitation to lecture at Princeton University in the United States was purely pro forma.[5] The only real alternative to his current situation was to renounce his dissidence entirely. And that was something Sakharov, unlike Iakir, was unwilling to do.

In fact, the dissidents were stronger in some ways than they thought they were. The sudden upsurge in repression in 1972–1973 was a reflection of the threat they posed. As Peter Reddaway has pointed out, with the exception of the Human Rights Committee, the relative openness and fluid membership of the groups the dissidents established made them less vulnerable to surveillance than they might have been had they created organizations with elaborate rules and regulations requiring frequent and predictable communication.[6] Moreover, by the spring of 1973, the dissidents had succeeded in informing foreign governments, newspaper correspondents, and organizations of their existence. To that extent they ensured that should the Soviet government try to do away with them or subject them to punishments more severe than those it was already inflicting, it would pay a considerable price in public opprobrium, which was something the Soviet leadership, increasingly intent on securing foreign investments and economic assistance, could not afford. Brezhnev and company could not simply shoot the dissidents, which is surely what Stalin would have done.

---

4. Sternberg, "Sakharov and Solzhenitsyn," 7–8.

5. Sakharov, *Memoirs,* 381–82. The grounds on which the Soviet government would deny a request for an exit visa would almost surely be that, while abroad, Sakharov might divulge state secrets learned while developing thermonuclear weapons in the 1950s. In fact, by the 1970s, much, though not all, of the secret information to which Sakharov had been privy was obsolete.

6. Peter Reddaway, "Dissent in the Soviet Union," *Problems of Communism* 32, no. 6 (November–December 1983): 1.

If, by 1973, Sakharov and his fellow dissidents had ample reason to fear the Soviet government, the government, despite the vast machinery of repression it commanded, had good reason to fear the dissidents. However small their numbers, however limited their resources, the dissidents questioned the moral legitimacy of the Soviet system itself, and they did so in ways that enabled people in other countries to assist them in their endeavor. For that reason, they posed a challenge the Soviet leadership could not ignore. Indeed, in 1973, the leadership made a conscious decision to ratchet up its harassment incrementally. Because it now needed more than ever before economic expertise and investment from foreign governments and individuals abroad who would strongly disapprove of its eliminating the dissidents entirely, the Soviet government realized, no doubt reluctantly, that it would have to tolerate the dissidents for the immediate future, carefully calibrating both the quality and quantity of the repressive measures it took on the basis of what it thought world opinion would tolerate. Because of his prominence both at home and abroad, Sakharov was a particular beneficiary of this calculus of repression. There were things he could do that other dissidents could not, and there were things the government could do, and did do, to other dissidents that it could not do to him. Indeed, Sakharov's prominence occasionally conferred unusual boldness on persons who were associated with him. For example, the government wanted the head of the theoretical department at the Lebedev Institute, E. S. Fradkin, to circulate among the scientists who worked under him a petition denouncing Sakharov. When Fradkin refused, quoting Suslov's earlier admonition that Sakharov was not the government's responsibility, the Soviet government backed down, and no such petition was circulated.[7]

The epic struggle between Sakharov and the Soviet authorities continued into the summer of 1973, with the protagonists exploring the practical limits of how far they could go in opposing each other. Sakharov, while always true to his ideals, was not oblivious to the leverage his prominence provided him in his relationship with the Soviet government. One senses that in the spring and summer of 1973 he tried to ascertain precisely how much he could say and do without provoking the government to silence him completely. By this time, Sakharov had concluded that reasoning with the Soviet government was pointless, that the chances were nil of the Soviet Union's reforming itself as a result of pressure from the dissidents alone, and that the only hope the dissidents had of achieving their objectives was persuading governments and private organizations in the West to pressure the Soviet government.[8]

This was evident in an interview Sakharov gave, probably on July 1, to the Swedish journalist Olle Stenholm.[9] On July 2 a shortened version of it aired on Swedish radio and television; on July 4 the text appeared in the Swedish newspaper *Dagens Nyheter;* and in the weeks that followed, it appeared in *Der Spiegel,*

---

7. Bolotovskii, "Kak Ia vospityval A. D.," 152.
8. Efrem Yankelevich, conversation with author, February 18, 2004.
9. The interview is reprinted in Sakharov, *Memoirs,* 623–30.

the *Washington Post,* and other Western newspapers.[10] For merely conducting the interview, Stenholm, in December, would lose his visa and be forced to leave the Soviet Union.[11] Many who have written about Sakharov claim that the Stenholm interview, more than anything else, was what triggered the sustained campaign in the press against both Sakharov and Solzhenitsyn in the late summer and early fall of 1973.[12] In the interview, Sakharov acknowledged that when he wrote *Reflections* in 1968, he was still "materially privileged and isolated from the people" and not fully cognizant of what socialism was.[13] But the years since then had shown him its fundamental fraudulence: that beneath misleading rhetoric about its superiority to capitalism in distributing goods and services equitably, socialism in practice was nothing more than a form of state capitalism in which the state monopolized the economy and exploited people more egregiously than pure capitalism could ever do through private enterprise and a market economy. Responding to a question from Stenholm about the genesis and evolution of his views, Sakharov explained his apostasy from communist orthodoxy as follows:

> I began by thinking that I understood [socialism] and that it was good. Then gradually I ceased to understand a great deal—I didn't even understand its economic basis; I couldn't make out whether there was anything to it but mere words and propaganda for internal and international consumption. Actually what hits you in the eye is the state's extreme concentration—economic, political, and ideological—that is, its extreme monopolization of these fields. One may say, exactly as Lenin did at the beginning of our revolution, that it is simple state capitalism, that the state has simply assumed a monopoly role over the economy. But in that case this socialism contains nothing new.[14]

The problem with the Soviet Union was not that it had betrayed socialism but that the socialism it practiced was really a variant of monopoly capitalism in which the state, rather than big business, owned the vast majority of property and misused the enormous power it retained. In Sakharov's words, "[socialism] is only an extreme form of that capitalist path of development found in the United States and other Western countries but in an extremely monopolized form."[15]

Sakharov's point in the interview was that by living in a system that was an amalgam of socialism and capitalism, the Soviet people suffered all the disadvantages of living in a society in which the government owned the means of production while enjoying none of the advantages of living in a system based on private property and a market economy. They had neither economic freedom (which is what pure capitalism provides) nor economic prosperity and security (which is what socialism purportedly provides); the hybrid that would

10. Bailey, *Making of Andrei Sakharov,* 298; Coppen, "Public Life of Andrei Sakharov," 55–56.
11. "Jews Tell of KGB Threat," *Times* (London), December 28, 1973, 5.
12. Moroz, "Vozvrashchenie iz ssylki," 329.
13. Interview with Olle Stenholm, in Sakharov, *Memoirs,* 623.
14. Ibid., 623–24.
15. Ibid., 624.

exist after convergence would be better because all that was best in both socialism and capitalism had been preserved. In the hybrid the Soviet leadership governed the reverse was true. In the Soviet Union, socialism was just a euphemism
for a kind of authoritarianism that in its malevolence was worse than any system
based on private enterprise. Because those in the Soviet Union who owned the
means of production did not have to account to anyone for their actions, they
could act as selfishly and rapaciously as the worst robber barons under capitalism. And because they had monopolized the material resources of the country
to a much greater extent than even the most affluent private individuals under
capitalism, the inequalities they enjoyed had been formalized in a strict hierarchy of privilege that was based more on access to limited goods and services
than on income or inheritance and was extremely destructive to the spiritual
and moral health of the Soviet people. In Sakharov's own words:

> I am skeptical about socialism in general. I don't see that socialism offers some
> kind of new theoretical plan, so to speak, for the better organization of society.
> Therefore it seems to me that while we may find some positive elements in our
> life, on the whole our state has displayed more destructive features than con-
> structive ones. Our society has witnessed such fierce political struggles, such de-
> struction, such bitterness, that now we are reaping the sad fruits of all this in a
> kind of tiredness, apathy, [and] cynicism, from which we find it most difficult to
> recover, if recovery is possible at all.[16]

In response to another question, Sakharov described life in the Soviet Union
as "boring" and "dreary" and far more demoralizing, in the literal sense of the
word, than it would be if the *nomenklatura*'s dominance of the economy were not
as stifling of individual initiative as it was.[17]

Pointedly, Sakharov did not exempt the intelligentsia from the spiritual mal-
aise and degradation he detected among the Soviet people as a whole.[18] Instead
of providing moral leadership, as an intelligentsia was supposed to do, it had
retreated on the one hand to a narrow professionalism in which no thought
whatever was given to moral and political issues, and on the other hand to a
dual intellectual life, sometimes called "radish communism," in which the truth
was spoken only rarely and within the confines of family or friends.[19] In every
milieu the intelligentsia inhabited in Soviet society, its members corrupted
themselves by cynically repeating the shibboleths of communist orthodoxy the
regime required as its price for tolerating the black market and the ethos of
self-enrichment the black market fostered.[20] As he had in the Postscript, in the

16. Ibid., 627.
17. Ibid., 629.
18. In the interview Sakharov used the term "intelligentsia" in the Soviet sense of signifying
everyone who made his or her living through intellectual labor.
19. Radish communists were Soviet citizens who conformed to the orthodoxies of communism publicly while mocking them privately. Like radishes they were red (i.e., communist) on the
outside but white (i.e., noncommunist or anticommunist) on the inside.
20. Interview with Olle Stenholm, 629–30.

Stenholm interview Sakharov, like Solzhenitsyn, stressed the moral and spiritual costs of socialism and communism. But unlike Solzhenitsyn, Sakharov thought that a socialism grounded in ethical principles was preferable to one that was not. If, in Solzhenitsyn's view, socialists were incapable of ever acting ethically because their ideology was the product of a rationalist tradition that was soulless and amoral, in Sakharov's opinion, the problem was that by concentrating enormous power in the state, socialism corrupted those who ran the state to act unethically regardless of their original intentions. But for Sakharov all was not lost. The ethical aspects of socialism could be salvaged in convergence and combine with the technological prowess and economic productivity of capitalism to form a world government that would act humanely.

Nevertheless, by 1973 Sakharov had realized that convergence would be a lengthy and protracted process and that its benefits were not apt to be apparent any time soon. Referring mainly to dissidents, he confessed to Stenholm that for the immediate future "[w]e really have no hopes, and unfortunately, experience shows we are right. Our actions don't lead to positive results."[21] Even Western protests, he admitted ruefully, were practically useless: the Soviet Union was largely immune to them, and the only possible benefit in the dissidents' apprising foreigners of what went on in the country was in preventing them from making the same mistakes the Soviets had made. As Sakharov put it, "the history of our country should serve as a warning."[22]

Given prospects so bleak, one could easily forgive Sakharov if he eschewed dissidence entirely and returned on a full-time basis to physics. As it was, he spoke in the Stenholm interview, as he had in the Axelbank interview, of the need to speak out on moral issues even though the chances of achieving positive results immediately were nil. To Sakharov, speaking out on moral issues was one of the obligations that informed his very concept of humanity. The cynicism of radish communism was not for him. He would continue to protest violations of human rights. But notwithstanding his comments to Axelbank and Stenholm, Sakharov was also too much the optimist, the activist, and the *intelligent* in his vision of a positive future to protest the Soviet regime for the sake of protest itself. In the same interview in which he confessed that none of the demands he had made had been met, he reiterated several of them anyway as if to suggest that things were not nearly as bad as he said they were. For example, in response to another question from Stenholm, Sakharov repeated his call for the Soviet government to grant exit visas to Soviet citizens: "[A] country from which it is not possible to leave freely," he said, "is a country that is unsound, a closed system where all processes develop differently from those of an open system."[23] Indeed, in response to a question about what he thought might benefit the Soviet Union in addition to unrestricted emigration, he reiterated his previous demand for glasnost and then, albeit elliptically and cautiously, called

21. Ibid., 627.
22. Ibid.
23. Ibid., 628.

for a multiparty system in the Soviet Union, the first time he had ever done so publicly: "A single-party system is excessively rigid. Even under the conditions of a socialist economic system a multiparty system is possible. Actually, on some levels of the people's democracies, the one-party system is not needed. And in some of the people's democracies some elements of a multiparty system exist, although they are a travesty of the real thing."[24]

Reaction to the interview from the Soviet government was quick, harsh, and ad hominem. On July 12 the Soviet press agency TASS carried an article, entitled in English translation "A Purveyor of Libel," by the journalist-apparatchik Iurii Kornilov. Six days later, the article appeared in *Literaturnaia gazeta*.[25] As Kornilov described him, Sakharov was hardly the political innocent previous critics in the Soviet press considered him. Rather, the Soviet physicist was malevolent, an enemy of socialism who, while posing as a "knight" in the noble struggle for human rights, "deliberately blackens the Soviet Union and the Soviet way of life.[26] Although Kornilov refrained from saying so, he surely knew that under Soviet law slandering the Soviet Union was a criminal offense.[27] The problem with Sakharov, as Kornilov described it, was not that he allowed evil imperialists and capitalists seeking the Soviet Union's destruction to use him for their nefarious ends. Rather, it was that Sakharov knew all too well that what he was saying about the Soviet Union was false. Instead of acknowledging the regime's achievements honestly, he maliciously distorted them "as if in a funhouse mirror."[28] This was particularly true of Sakharov's criticisms of Soviet education and health care, institutions that Kornilov, not surprisingly, said were irreproachable. And to Sakharov's contention that Soviet society was closed, Kornilov retorted that because the number of tourists to the Soviet Union was large and showed every indication of increasing, Soviet society was actually open. Only someone seeking to harm the Soviet Union, as Sakharov was, would state otherwise. In his eagerness "to slander his own country," Sakharov had sold his soul to "reactionary circles in the West" that were only too happy to quote the words of a decorated hero of the Soviet Union against the very system that had rewarded him so lavishly for his services.[29] Once again Sakharov was guilty of ingratitude. To Soviet critics like Chukovskii and Kornilov, Sakharov's contributions to the Soviet Union, far from bolstering his credibility as a critic of the country, in reality destroyed it. Because he was not sufficiently grateful for the emoluments he had received in recognition of these contributions, they actually demonstrated his unreliability and lack of character. Reading Kornilov's article, it is easy to infer that its author (and by extension, the Soviet authorities) considered Sakharov a traitor. Articles

24. Ibid., 629.
25. Dornan, "Andrei Sakharov," 400; Iurii Kornilov, "Postavshchik klevety," *Literaturnaia gazeta*, July 18, 1973, 9.
26. Kornilov, "Postavshchik klevety," 9.
27. Scammell, *Solzhenitsyn*, 804.
28. Kornilov, "Postavshchik klevety," 9.
29. Ibid.

that appeared concurrently with Kornilov's reached practically the same conclusion, and they were just as vitriolic in their ad hominem attacks.[30]

Clearly, the proverbial noose around Sakharov's neck was tightening. At the beginning of August, he learned that Bonner's son Alexei had been rejected for admission to Moscow State University, despite his having earned excellent grades at the school of mathematics he attended. His ties to Sakharov and his refusal to join the Komsomol, however, had caused the authorities at the university, on orders from higher-ups, to fail him on the entrance examinations he had taken and passed. As a result, Alexei had to enroll instead in the mathematics department at the Lenin Pedagogical Institute in Moscow, where the caliber of instruction was not as good as at MGU.[31] Although Alexei would do very well at the institute, he would eventually be expelled in his last year there for failing to finish his military training.[32]

A few days later, a more direct and sinister threat to Sakharov emerged. On August 15, he received a summons from the deputy procurator general, Mikhail Maliarov. In the conversation in Maliarov's office that followed, the deputy procurator warned Sakharov that anti-Soviet statements he had made recently might be grounds for legal action.[33] With Maliarov's threat, the government's persecution of Sakharov escalated from discrete attacks, issued usually in response to particular statements or actions of his, into a veritable campaign in the Soviet press in which his personal character and integrity were repeatedly and unrelentingly impugned. Qualitatively as well as quantitatively, the rhetoric with which he was attacked in this new press campaign was more sarcastic, bitter, and vituperative than any criticism the government had ever directed against him. In the lexicon of Stalin's Terror, Sakharov was vilified essentially as an enemy of the people. Had he been living in Stalin's time, he undoubtedly would have been shot or sent to a sharashka in a labor camp.

Sakharov was more alone in the late summer of 1973 than he had ever been since becoming a dissident in the mid-1960s. Even with Bonner at his side and the small but dedicated cadres of Soviet dissidents behind him, he seemed practically defenseless, a lonely David confronting the Soviet Goliath. But the Soviet physicist was not without resources in the struggle he would wage in the months ahead. By the summer of 1973 foreign governments and organizations were aware of Sakharov's precarious situation, and the Soviet leaders were sufficiently concerned about their country's reputation to take into account the reaction of foreigners in determining how harshly it could treat the physicist it previously lauded but now condemned. Even if foreign protests could not prevent the government from persecuting Sakharov, they could limit the severity and duration of his punishment.

30. Sakharov, *Memoirs*, 383.
31. Ibid., 384; Bonner, *Alone Together*, 35. Ironically, this was the same institute where Dmitrii Sakharov had taught physics many years earlier.
32. Bonner, *Alone Together*, 35.
33. Sakharov, *Memoirs*, 385.

Equally important in this regard was that by 1973 Sakharov had effectively defined the intellectual contours of his dissidence and articulated with considerable clarity the relationship between the particular individuals he championed and the larger philosophical and ethical principles that caused him to intervene on their behalf. He knew very well what he was fighting for, and this knowledge gave him the self-assurance he needed intellectually and psychologically to survive the storm that was brewing around him. From the political neophyte of *Reflections* who intended its suggestions as a basis for collegial discussion—as if the Soviet Union were just a genial debating society—Sakharov had become considerably more astute politically and self-sufficient intellectually. Hardened by many defeats and strengthened by his few victories, he was now capable of defending himself against any additional assaults the Soviet authorities might direct against him. No longer a socialist or a Marxist-Leninist but rather a dissident with a positive vision of what his country should look like once the system that oppressed the Soviet people was transformed, Sakharov entered the fray with a fairly clear idea of what had to be done so that the human rights he favored would become a practical reality.

PART V

# "Domestic Enemy Number One": 1973–1980

# 14  Orchestrated Vituperation

"Sakharov, that traitor." This is how Sakharov characterized the slander he heard several Soviet citizens utter in September 1973, not long after the press campaign began, when they spotted him on a beach in Batumi on the shore of the Black Sea. He and Bonner had hoped to find a brief respite there from the incessant attacks.[1] Sakharov does not reveal in his memoirs what his reaction was to the charge, but one can be fairly certain he was not pleased by it. Not only was it completely false but it also showed that the government's rhetorical onslaught was having an effect on a population that habitually ignored or ridiculed government directives prescribing what it should think about a particular issue or individual. From the reaction of the bathers on the beach, it seemed that the press campaign was serving its purpose.

But the public vilification Sakharov endured following his interview with Maliarov in August 1973 was no ordinary exercise of the traditional prerogative Soviet leaders adopted to discredit people they considered hostile to the Soviet system. Sakharov's case was different. Exceeding anything any Soviet citizen had experienced since Stalin's death, the campaign against him was even more vituperative and shrill and of a longer duration than that directed at Pasternak in 1958 after he won the Nobel Prize for literature but was prevented from going to Sweden to accept it. The campaign was also better coordinated than previous attacks on other dissidents.[2] In Soviet history the only analogue to what Sakharov was now enduring were the attacks in the Soviet press on some of Stalin's victims, such as Zinoviev and Kamenev, in which their reputations were blackened and their achievements either ignored or maligned. It is true that Solzhenitsyn was attacked concurrently with Sakharov. But the transgressions for which Solzhenitsyn was excoriated were different from those attributed to Sakharov. Because Sakharov, unlike Solzhenitsyn, had worked for the Soviet government and had been rewarded handsomely for his services, there was a bitterness, born out of a sense of betrayal, in the criticisms the government directed against him. Partly for that reason, Sakharov and Solzhenitsyn did not coordinate their responses in defending themselves.[3]

The press conference Sakharov called on August 21—the fifth anniversary of the Warsaw Pact invasion of Czechoslovakia—triggered the press campaign against him. From the Soviets' perspective, the very act of calling a press conference was a provocation, a way of showing both the Soviet government and the rest of the world that nothing the Soviet leadership could say about him would

1. Sakharov, *Memoirs*, 387.
2. Dornan, "Andrei Sakharov," 403.
3. Solzhenitsyn, *Oak and the Calf*, 359.

frighten him and that he would continue to speak out whenever he had something newsworthy to say. Maliarov's reason, or excuse, for his warning five days earlier of serious, if unspecified, consequences if Sakharov were to grant any more interviews was that the Soviet physicist might reveal secret information from his days at Arzamas. Holding the press conference was therefore a way of showing Maliarov and everyone else in the Soviet leadership that their concerns were groundless and that the discretion he would exercise was actually proof of his patriotism. Finally, the press conference, which took place in Sakharov's apartment, rankled the Soviets because it called into question the government's claim, on which a good deal of its political legitimacy depended, that the Soviet people were children, too immature to answer rationally and in a way that was supportive of the Soviet Union the probing questions of hostile reporters, all of them foreigners.

Sakharov began the press conference by reading a prepared statement in which he described his meeting with Maliarov.[4] In responding to questions, he reiterated his support for human rights, expressed in general terms his reservations about détente, and declared again that he and the other dissidents were acting on the basis of moral principle rather than out of political expediency. What the dissidents were doing, he said, was "normal human activity," the kind of thing ordinary people with a minimal degree of decency would do.[5] The implication of Sakharov's comments, which he hoped the reporters would comprehend, was that by trying to silence him, the Soviet leaders were not only morally wrong but were engaged in an enterprise that was irrational, unnatural, and abnormal. At the very least, they, not Sakharov, should be the ones called to account for their behavior.

In as public a forum as any to which he had access, Sakharov boldly threw down the gauntlet to the Soviet regime, calling its actions and even its legitimacy into question. The Soviet government had no choice but to respond, and it did so in a way that was designed to intimidate Sakharov and to impress upon the Soviet people the magnitude and malevolence of his transgressions. For three weeks the government mobilized the Soviet press, which it controlled completely, to show that Sakharov was not only a bad person whose character and integrity were suspect but also an enemy of the Soviet Union and socialism. Though the invective the Soviet press discharged never included an actual accusation of treason, the implication that the Soviet physicist was disloyal was too obvious for even the most inattentive and unsophisticated reader to miss.

The first shot in the campaign was fired, undoubtedly in response to a directive from the highest levels of the Soviet government, by Sakharov's colleagues in the Academy of Sciences. On August 29 in *Pravda* and in various

4. The full text of the press conference, which was the first one Sakharov held by himself, can be found in *Sakharov Speaks*, 194–207. At about this same time Sakharov produced a transcript, reconstructed from memory, of his talk with Maliarov, which he made available to foreign reporters and, through samizdat, to other dissidents. Sakharov, *Memoirs*, 385.

5. Press conference, *Sakharov Speaks*, 202.

other newspapers around the country there appeared a letter signed by forty academicians (out of a total membership, excluding candidate members, of two hundred).[6] Mstislav Keldysh, who with commendable impartiality had presided over the academy's deliberations in the Nuzhdin affair, this time took the lead in defaming the physicist, not only signing the letter but circulating it among his colleagues as well. The fact that Keldysh respected Sakharov and felt sympathy for his predicament only made his actions more reprehensible.[7] Another signatory from whom Sakharov expected better was Iulii Khariton. But Keldysh and Khariton were not the only colleagues of his in the academy who refused to defend him. Though he refused to sign the letter or to assist in any way in its circulation, Piotr Kapitsa remained silent as well.[8] Although the academy shrank from the ultimate punishment of expelling Sakharov and rescinding his membership—a course of action for which there were probably not enough votes—he would be ostracized for years by most of his fellow academicians and by a somewhat smaller percentage of his colleagues at the Lebedev Institute. As Turchin shrewdly recognized at the time, those in the Soviet elite who sympathized with Sakharov but chose nonetheless to attack him or to remain silent could assuage whatever guilt they felt by simply accepting as true all the bad things the Soviet press was saying about him.[9] In the political system Soviet scientists inhabited, people of residual integrity like the ones Turchin described were as likely to comply with the regime as were people with no integrity at all.

In their letter, the academicians referred their readers to Sakharov's interview with Stenholm—of which the Soviet people, with the exception of the dissidents, had previously been ignorant. They asserted that the content of the interview provided clear evidence of Sakharov's perfidy and moral degradation: in spite of the awards he had won and the privileges he enjoyed, the Soviet physicist really cared little about "the interests of progressive people"; whatever his original intentions, his current criticisms of the Soviet Union were unfounded and constituted "a rude rebuke of Soviet achievements."[10] Moreover, by aligning himself with "the most reactionary and imperialist circles," Sakharov was acting objectively as "a mouthpiece for hostile propaganda against the Soviet Union and the other socialist countries."[11] For that reason he must be subjected to the most stringent criticism and condemnation, particularly by those in the scientific establishment who knew him best and who considered particularly abhorrent his discrediting "the honor and the accomplishments of Soviet science."[12]

6. "Pis'mo chlenov Akademii nauk SSSR," *Pravda*, August 29, 1973, 3.

7. Iu. B. Khariton, "Radi iadernogo pariteta (interv'iu Olegu Morozu)," in Altshuler et al., *On mezhdu nami zhil*, 733; V. S. Imshchennik, "Epizod pravozashchitnoi deiatel'nosti," in Altshuler et al., *On mezhdu nami zhil*, 307.

8. Sakharov, *Memoirs*, 386, 632–33.

9. Scammell, *Solzhenitsyn*, 808.

10. "Pis'mo chlenov," 3.

11. Ibid.

12. Ibid.

By the time the letter appeared, Sakharov, Bonner, and Alexei had left Moscow for a vacation in Armenia and Azerbaijan.[13] Returning to Moscow on September 5, Sakharov began organizing his defense. He called foreign reporters to his apartment the same day and twice in the next four days, each time refuting as best he could the seemingly endless derogations of his character. These came from nearly every institution and social stratum in the country. Among those denouncing the Soviet physicist after August 21 were war veterans; steelworkers; scientists; writers such as Sholokhov, Simonov, and Fedin; and musicians and composers including Oistrakh, Khachaturian, and Shostakovich. Most signed group letters purporting to represent the prevailing opinion in their respective profession or place of work. The Academy of Agriculture, the Writers' Union, the I. A. Likhachev automobile factory, the Academy of Pedagogical Sciences, the Medical Academy, and the Bauman Technical Academy were just a few of the institutions contributing to the cacophony of vitriol.[14] Some of Sakharov's critics sent letters individually, while others sent letters that, while not denouncing Sakharov, expressed approval of those that did.[15] The obvious purpose of these letters was to demonstrate that by his words and deeds Sakharov had not merely betrayed the Soviet government but, in the inimitable phraseology of Stalinism, had rendered himself an Enemy of the People. In case the Soviet people missed the point, *Pravda* on September 8 carried a particularly unpleasant piece of character assassination entitled "To Be a Scientist Means to Be a Patriot."[16]

For the most part such reminders were unnecessary. The animus toward Sakharov, as the incident on the beach at Batumi revealed, was real, and the fact that most of the dissidents, including Sakharov, came from the educated elite and that a number of them had once enjoyed the same privileges as the Soviet leadership, meant that they were viewed with a certain suspicion irrespective of the efforts of the Soviet government to reinforce it. Because the government enjoyed a virtual monopoly of information, it was exceedingly difficult for the dissidents to refute the lies and misinformation the government spread about them. A measure of how strongly the Soviet leaders despised Sakharov by this time and wanted to ruin him both personally and politically is that what they said about him privately was no less scathing and ad hominem than what their sycophants in the press were told to say about him publicly. Iurii Andropov privately informed his colleagues in the Politburo (to which he had recently been elevated) in the fall of 1973 that Sakharov was both insane and actively collaborating with Western intelligence agencies, especially Zionist ones.[17]

---

13. Sakharov, *Memoirs*, 386. The incident on the beach at Batumi occurred during this vacation.
14. Scammell, *Solzhenitsyn*, 807. A representative sample of the denunciations is reprinted in Sakharov, *Memoirs*, 633–40.
15. For example, E. Borzenkov, "Nedostoinye deistviia," *Pravda*, September 5, 1973, 3.
16. Reprinted in Sakharov, *Memoirs*, 639.
17. "Iz rabochei zapisi zasedaniia Politiuro TsK KPSS (August 30, 1973)," in *Kremlevskii samosud*, ed. A. V. Korotkov, S. A. Melchin, and A. S. Stepanov (Moscow, 1994), 245. Christopher

Though they came from all directions, the attacks on Sakharov boiled down to a surprisingly small number of accusations and insinuations. The most frequent charge was that he was opposed to peace because he criticized the Soviet Union, which favored peace. Sometimes his attackers made this point indirectly, claiming that, by aligning himself with "reactionary circles" opposed to peace, Sakharov, regardless of what he might personally have wished for, was "objectively" an enemy of peace.[18] However absurd, unfair, and unsubstantiated by empirical evidence this line of reasoning was, its attribution of bellicosity to the foreign entities Sakharov supposedly supported helped to justify the Soviet Union's ongoing effort to improve its military capabilities to the point of parity with the United States.[19]

Should this particular line of reasoning prove too abstruse or subtle for Soviet readers to follow, Sakharov's attackers could always claim that Sakharov, by betraying his country, was demonstrating his ingratitude toward it—a form of character assassination used effectively against him in the past. This, in fact, is what they did. As members of the Academy of Pedagogical Sciences wrote in the letter they signed that appeared in *Izvestiia* on September 4, Sakharov "has lost his sense of responsibility toward his people, who educated him and gave him every opportunity for scientific creativity."[20] The problem, in the words of the twenty-eight Soviet filmmakers whose denunciation appeared in *Pravda* on September 5, was not merely that Sakharov, in his words and deeds, was "defaming the reputation of his own country and his own people."[21] What made Sakharov the most despicable of the dissidents was that he was criticizing a government that had treated him well—a government that had recognized his abilities as a scientist, provided him with the wherewithal to hone these abilities to the point where his contributions to the state were rewarded handsomely, and generally satisfied his every need. However unfair this argument was—Sakharov surely gave to the system as much as he received from it—there was sufficient plausibility to what Sakharov's critics were alleging for the charge of ingratitude to resonate in a way nothing else did except perhaps the charge of disloyalty. Ingratitude is a human frailty more easily understood and resented than many others, and however much the campaign against Sakharov was manufactured by the Soviet government, the fervor with which Sakharov's critics berated him was probably genuine. One senses this in the following denunciation by E. Borzenkov, whose status as a Hero of Socialist Labor, coupled with his working as a forger in a Magnitogorsk metallurgical combine, gave him a credibility in attacking Sakharov that few others in the Soviet Union could match: "It is

---

Andrew and Vasili Mitrokhin, *The Sword and the Shield: The Mitrokhin Archive and the Secret History of the KGB* (New York, 1999), 317.

18. Sakharov, *Memoirs*, 387; "Pis'mo chlenov," 3.

19. Martin Malia calls the attainment of military parity in the late 1970s the foremost achievement of the Soviet Union. Martin Malia, *The Soviet Tragedy, A History of Socialism in Russia, 1917–1991* (New York, 1994), 372–73.

20. Reprinted in Sakharov, *Memoirs*, 638.

21. G. Alexandrov et al., "Pozitsii, chuzhdaia narodu," *Pravda*, September 5, 1973, 3.

incomprehensible how someone who grew up under Soviet rule, who received an education and scientific titles, and who worked alongside Soviet workers, can slander our way of life so unconscionably."[22] According to N. Erugin, who got the chance to denounce Sakharov in the Soviet press before Borzenkov did, the Soviet dissident was not only a puppet of "malicious imperialist forces"; what was even worse, he was living well while condemning the very system that had done so much for him personally as well as professionally.[23]

Along with anger and resentment, the attacks on Sakharov exuded an underlying frustration, an inability to comprehend just what it was that drove him to such extremes of behavior. To most Soviet people, Sakharov's dissidence was inexplicable. Many of Sakharov's critics, perhaps most of them, were genuinely perplexed and even mystified by him. This is certainly the impression one gets from the criticisms that appeared in an unsigned article in *Kommunist* in September 1973, shortly after Sakharov, with Galich and Maximov, sent an appeal to the recently empowered General Pinochet in Chile decrying the house arrest of the left-wing writer Pablo Neruda, who at the time was quite ill.[24] Implicit in this particular article—as well as in many others that appeared in the late summer and early fall of 1973—was the notion that no one living in the Soviet Union who was sane would repudiate such a virtuous system and that the only possible explanation for Sakharov's doing so was that he was deranged or a traitor. Not surprisingly, some of the diatribes managed to combine the two attributes, insanity and treason, in explaining Sakharov's motivation. It is telling that while the press campaign was under way and for some time afterward, the KGB circulated rumors that Sakharov was mentally disturbed, that he had suffered a breakdown,[25] even that his mind had been altered physiologically by the radioactive materials he handled while designing thermonuclear weapons. Even more preposterous was the rumor that Sakharov was actually dead and that the "Sakharov" who was criticizing the Soviet Union was an impostor.[26]

Given the pride Sakharov took in his intellectual independence, charging him with being a tool of the Soviet Union's enemies was bound to be especially hurtful to him. Perhaps for this reason, the Soviet government stressed in its attacks—not only in the fall of 1973 but for the remainder of Sakharov's career as a dissident—that he was more misguided and weak than malevolent and strong. Thus he was easily used by more sophisticated and sinister persons who recognized that his reputation for moral probity made him a perfect instrument for their nefarious designs. Describing Sakharov in this fashion was clearly intended to diminish him, and in keeping with this, the Soviet government never

22. Borzenkov, "Nedostoinye deistviia," 3.

23. N. Erugin, "Otpoved' klevetniku," *Pravda*, August 31, 1973, 3.

24. "Mezhdunarodnye otnosheniia i ideologicheskaia bor'ba," *Kommunist* 14 (September 1973): 221–22. See also Theodore Shabad, "Soviet Portrays Sakharov as Backer of Chile's Junta," *New York Times*, September 26, 1973, 3. The original appeal Sakharov coauthored is reprinted in *Sakharov Speaks*, 243–44.

25. Dornan, "Andrei Sakharov," 401.

26. Kaiser, *Russia*, 462.

enlarged him into a devil figure the way Stalin had done with Trotsky.[27] Were the government to do so, it would be ascribing to Sakharov not only real political power but the very independence and intellectual autonomy on which he prided himself. For purely tactical reasons, it was better for the Soviets to call Sakharov a dupe. At the end of September 1973, when they finally called off the press campaign, they largely redirected their rhetorical fusillades against Bonner, who would henceforth be depicted in the Soviet press as Sakharov's master, from whom he deferentially and unquestioningly took orders. With Iurii Andropov's ascension to the Politburo, the Soviet government included at its highest levels someone of cunning and sinister intelligence who knew very well the weaknesses and vulnerabilities of the dissidents. It was Andropov who, at Politburo meetings, reiterated the opinion most forcefully that by silencing Bonner, the government would be silencing Sakharov as well.[28]

Many Soviet dissidents realized that the attacks against Sakharov were attacks against all of them: if Sakharov, with his celebrity, was not safe, then no one was safe. Shafarevich, Litvinov, Boris Shragin, and Lidiia Chukovskaia all defended Sakharov, in Chukovskaia's case with such flowery language that Sakharov was acutely embarrassed by it.[29] Solzhenitsyn, who had won the Nobel Prize for Literature in 1970, on September 11 nominated Sakharov for the Nobel Prize for Peace; on September 14 Siniavskii "seconded" the nomination in a letter to *Le Monde*.[30] Because its rules prescribed that Nobel Prize winners could nominate candidates only in the category in which they themselves had won, the Nobel Committee had to reject Solzhenitsyn's nomination.[31] But Sakharov and Bonner, who were desperate for support, were undeterred by the rejection, and

27. At a Politburo meeting on September 17, 1973, Brezhnev compared Sakharov to Trotsky. But the general secretary failed to explain exactly how the two men were similar, and I am unaware that Brezhnev or any other Soviet leader made the same comparison publicly. At the same meeting Brezhnev raised the possibility, without making a formal motion or recommendation, of exiling Sakharov to Siberia and permitting him membership in the Siberian section of the Academy of Sciences. Eleven days later, Roman Rudenko, the procurator general of the Soviet Union, and Viktor Chebrikov of the KGB formally proposed exiling Sakharov internally but only after a trial in which he would be convicted of violating Soviet law. That the two men also contemplated stripping him of his honors and expelling him from the Academy of Sciences shows the difficulty the Soviets had in deciding on a strategy for dealing with Sakharov before finally exiling him, without a trial, to Gorky in 1980. The option of exiling Sakharov internally was first discussed in the Politburo in March 1972. "Iz rabochei zapisi zasedaniia Politbiuro TsK KPSS (September 17, 1973)," in Korotkov, Melchin, and Stepanov, *Kremlevskii samosud*, 329–30; "Chebrikov and Rudenko to Kosygin (September 28, 1973)," in Rubenstein and Gribanov, *KGB File*, 161–64; "Iz rabochei zapisi zasedaniia Politbiuro TsK KPSS (March 30, 1972)," in Korotkov, Melchin, and Stepanov, *Kremlevskii samosud*, 208, 212, 215–16.

28. Rubenstein and Gribanov, *KGB File*, eds. Rubenstein and Gribanov, passim.

29. Lydia Chukovskaia, "Otkrytoe pis'mo 'Gnev naroda' o travle A. D. Sakharova [September 7, 1973]," *Sobranie* 25 (Munich, 1977), AS1480: 1–11. Despite Chukovskaia's penchant for overblown rhetoric, Sakharov valued her enormously for her integrity and courage and included her among his closest friends. Sakharov, *Memoirs*, 388–89.

30. Sakharov, *Memoirs*, 389; Scammell, *Solzhenitsyn*, 810; Andrei Siniavskii, "Pis'mo v parizhskuiu gazetu 'Mond,' September 14, 1973," reprinted in *A. Sakharov v bor'be za mir*, ed. Ia. Trushnovich (Frankfurt/Main, 1973), 231–32.

31. *Guardian*, September 11, 1973, reprinted in Trushnovich, *A. Sakharov v bor'be za mir*, 257–58.

they were buoyed by the alacrity with which the dissidents closed ranks behind them. Although there were several dissidents who failed to defend Sakharov, the only ones who criticized him in the fall of 1973 were Zhores and Roi Medvedev; for doing so, they earned Sakharov's quiet but enduring contempt and Bonner's as well.[32] The matters on which the brothers took issue—détente and disarmament—were substantive and significant. But to Sakharov, their criticisms were ill timed, gratuitous, and, in Zhores Medvedev's case, possibly prompted by requests from the KGB, to whose blandishments many dissidents believed he was susceptible.[33] In addition, several of Sakharov's supporters thought that, in light of all that Sakharov had done for Zhores Medvedev in 1970 when the government confined him to a psychiatric hospital, the least the brothers could have done now that Sakharov was the one being persecuted was to remain silent until the pressures on the Soviet physicist eased. Both Maximov and Mikhail Agurskii wrote scathing denunciations of the Medvedevs that circulated in samizdat, and Maximov additionally dictated his by telephone to a correspondent of the *Daily Telegraph* in London, which published it.[34]

Several dissidents who defended Sakharov suffered as a result. Turchin and Iurii Orlov lost their jobs, while Chukovskaia was expelled from the Writers' Union, which made it more difficult for her to find work of any kind; because unemployment in the Soviet Union was a crime, she was now subject to arrest.[35] But in relative terms, the protests of dissidents probably did not bother the government as much as the refusal of the 160 academicians to sign the letter the academy issued denouncing Sakharov. Whether they did so out of sympathy for Sakharov or from fear that Western scientists in response would sever contacts they considered essential to their work is not clear.[36] From the perspective of the government, their motives for refusing to join in the campaign against Sakharov hardly mattered. In the perfervid atmosphere the government had created, even a discreet silence from Soviet scientists was a tacit protest, an implicit rejection of the participatory dictatorship Soviet leaders from Lenin onward had fostered in which character assassination of one person by others, especially professional colleagues, was commonplace.

32. Bonner has recently condemned the Medvedevs' book, *Solzhenitsyn i Sakharov. Dva proroka*, published in 2004, for the lies she claims it contains about her late husband. Bonner, "Do dnevnik," 54.

33. Dornan,"Andrei Sakharov," 409; Sakharov, *Memoirs,* 430.

34. Vladimir Maximov, "Otkrytoe pis'mo brat'iam Medvedevym—V sviazi s ikh vyskazyvaniami o Sakharove i Solzhenitsyne," *Sobranie* 26 (Munich, 1978) AS1507: 1–2; M. S. Agurskii, "V chem pravy i nepravy brat'ia Medvedevy (November 17, 1973)," *Sobranie* 26 (Munich, 1978) AS1508: 1–2.

35. Sakharov, *Memoirs,* 388–89; Turchin's eloquent defense of Sakharov, "Otkrytoe pis'mo v zashchitu akademika A. D. Sakharova," which he wrote on September 1, is reprinted in *Sobranie* 25 (Munich, 1977) AS1464: 1.

36. Kevin Klose has argued that Soviet scientists were particularly afraid that the severance of contacts would preclude trips to the West to see colleagues (and also, one suspects, to enjoy the material comforts absent in the Soviet Union). Klose, *Russia and the Russians,* 131.

However much the silence of these scientists must have annoyed the Soviet government, the protests that surely unnerved it were those from Western governments and Western scientists. In the case of the latter, because their protests were usually issued by the professional organizations to which they belonged, the Soviets had to take them very seriously. Both in its intensity and in the fact that much of it came from the political left, the support Sakharov received from abroad was impressive. The Austrian chancellor Bruno Kreisky, the Swedish foreign minister Krister Wickman, the Italian Social Democratic Party, and the left-wing German writer Gunter Grass all made known their displeasure with the press campaign, as did the prime minister of Denmark, 100 British psychologists, 300 French physicians, 188 Canadian intellectuals, Norwegian and Swiss writers, and the Consultative Assembly of the European Community.[37] In the American House of Representatives several congressmen, as a symbolic gesture of support, proposed a resolution making Sakharov and Solzhenitsyn honorary citizens of the United States.[38] What attracted the Soviets' attention most effectively, however, was the threat Philip Handler, the president of the National Academy of Sciences in America, included in a telegram to Keldysh, his counterpart in the Soviet Academy of Sciences, on September 9, occasioned by Chalidze's letter in the *New York Times* of September 7 that Sakharov was under attack.[39] "Harassment or detention of Sakharov," Handler wrote, "will have severe effects upon relationships between the scientific communities of the U.S.A. and U.S.S.R. and could vitiate our recent efforts toward increasing interchange and cooperation."[40] In his reply, which did not appear in the Soviet press until October 18, Keldysh disingenuously assured Handler that, despite what he might have thought or been told, Sakharov, in fact, had never been harassed.[41]

Handler did not indicate in his letter exactly what retributive measures the American academy had in mind. But the mere possibility that scientific contacts might end or be severely limited caused the Soviet government to recalculate the benefits of silencing Sakharov. Not only did it need the expertise that Western, and especially American, scientists could offer, but the scientific exchanges that were now in jeopardy were also an excellent vehicle for espionage. Moreover, the campaign against Sakharov had increased Western doubts about the Soviets' commitment to détente. On September 10, Congressman Wilbur Mills, who as chairman of the Ways and Means Committee had considerable influence over whether the Jackson-Vanik Amendment to the trade bill providing Most Favorable Nation status to countries permitting emigration would be approved by the Congress, proposed expanding the amendment to

37. Sakharov, *Memoirs*, 389; Hedrick Smith, *The Russians* (New York, 1976), 603; Solzhenitsyn, *Oak and the Calf*, 355.
38. Scammell, *Solzhenitsyn*, 811.
39. Edward Kline, conversation with author, June 10, 2008.
40. Quoted in Smith, *Russians*, 603.
41. Sakharov, *Memoirs*, 390.

require that the Soviet Union cease its persecution of Sakharov and Solzhen-itsyn.[42] Mills's proposal was probably unnecessary: on the day he made it, Brezhnev, who had previously been on vacation, convinced his colleagues in the Kremlin that the press campaign should stop.[43] Although the campaign would resume a week later, it would proceed with somewhat less ferocity. Encouraged by this turn of events, Sakharov kept up the pressure, sending a letter to the Congress on September 14 supporting the Jackson-Vanik Amendment whole-heartedly.[44] Sakharov's letter proved persuasive: politicians issued statements praising him, and newspaper editorials extolled both his personal virtues and the ideas he espoused. But not everyone thought Sakharov and his supporters in the Congress, most prominently Senator Jackson and Congressman Vanik, were proceeding wisely. The secretary of state, Henry Kissinger, believed that only private diplomacy would yield changes in Soviet emigration policy and that the public pressure Jackson-Vanik exerted would backfire, harming the dissidents and Soviet citizens seeking to emigrate. Kissinger was clearly irritated by what Sakharov had done, and his irritation would continue long after the events that precipitated it. In the context of explaining his opposition to Jackson-Vanik in his memoirs, Kissinger comments acidly that "men on the firing line" (by whom he meant dissidents like Sakharov) should not be deciding American foreign policy.[45] Of course Sakharov would not have described what he was doing so pejoratively. He emphatically rejected the realpolitik Kissinger's position entailed, not because he believed the United States should deal with the Soviet Union on the basis of moral principle per se but because he believed it was in America's national interest to do so. In Sakharov's opinion, the only pressure to which the Soviets responded was public pressure, and using private diplomacy exclusively, as Kissinger preferred, would be viewed by the Soviets as a sign of weakness.[46] For this reason, Sakharov was pleased when the

42. The amendment, which eventually was approved by Congress, modified the annual trade bill to make the granting of MFN status to the Soviet Union—which meant that tariffs on Soviet goods would equal the lowest tariff the United States imposed on any other country's imports—conditional upon the Soviet Union's increasing the number of exit visas it granted Soviet citizens (not just Soviet Jews) who applied for them. For slightly more than a year, the Soviets refused to agree to this. In October 1974, however, they agreed to terms transmitted privately by Kissinger that were nearly identical to those the amendment prescribed; prior to transmitting these terms, Kissinger had secured Senator Jackson's approval of them. But when Jackson publicized the agreement, the Soviets angrily repudiated it. In the end, the Soviet Union did not receive MFN status. Nevertheless, the number of exit visas the Soviets issued for the rest of the decade did not diminish. Walter Isaacson, *Kissinger: A Biography* (New York, 1992), 611–21; Joseph Albright, "The Pact of Two Henrys," *New York Times Magazine*, January 5, 1975, 16–34; Petrus Buwalda, *They Did Not Dwell Alone: Jewish Emigration from the Soviet Union 1967–1990* (Baltimore, 1997), 221.
43. Boris Altshuler, "Evoliutsiia vzgliadov Sakharova na global'nye ugrozy sovetskogo VPK: Ot 'Razmyshlenii...(1968 g.) do knigi 'O strane i mir' (1975 g.)," *Razmyshleniia o progresse, mirnom sosushchestvovanii i intellektual'noi svobode,* 166.
44. Andrei Sakharov, "A Letter to the Congress of the United States (September 14, 1973)," in *Sakharov Speaks,* 212–15.
45. Henry A. Kissinger, *Years of Upheaval* (Boston, 1982), 989.
46. Sakharov included this argument in "Letter to the Congress," 214.

*Washington Post* published his letter to the Congress.[47] Even though he was not an American citizen, Sakharov believed he had the right, even the obligation, to address the American people through its elected representatives on an issue involving a universal human right, in this case the right of people to choose their place of residence.[48]

The respite Sakharov enjoyed as a result of the pressure that was brought to bear on the Soviet government benefited other dissidents as well. Grigorenko, who was still in a psychiatric hospital when Sakharov mounted his counterattack, to his surprise found himself transferred to a regular one. For the first time since 1945, the Soviet government, on September 13, stopped jamming foreign radio broadcasts. On September 21 it signed the universal copyright convention.[49] These concessions were not lost on Sakharov. When the press campaign resumed, more carefully calibrated now so as not to provoke a new round of threats from foreign governments and organizations whose assistance the Soviet Union needed, he seemed to regain some of the leverage he had lost when the campaign began; one senses that Maliarov's summons had thrown him momentarily off balance. As the struggle between Sakharov and the authorities continued into the fall of 1973 and the winter of 1973–1974, it became increasingly a war of attrition not unlike the nuclear stalemate that existed simultaneously between the superpowers, a prolonged struggle in which the protagonists tested the limits of what they could do without provoking a response from the other that could lead to total defeat. In the Soviets' case, that meant avoiding threats like Handler's that would force them to reduce their attacks on Sakharov further or to stop them entirely. In Sakharov's case, it meant avoiding needlessly provocative actions or statements that would force the government to arrest him, or worse.

With their options severely circumscribed, the Soviet leaders resolved to wear Sakharov down to the point at which he would conclude that opposing the government was not worth the psychological and physical toll it was exacting. Sometimes their harassment took the form of ad hominem attacks in the press, as in the article the Soviet propagandist Nikolai Iakovlev penned for *Golos rodiny* (*Voice of the Motherland*) in February 1974, in which he derogated *Reflections* as "drivel" and castigated its author as a latter-day Kadet who "wallowed in anti-Sovietism" in his role as a lackey of the capitalists.[50] Some of the other actions the government took or instigated were more menacing. In October 1973, after Sakharov in an interview had called for Arab recognition of Israel as a condition for a negotiated settlement of the Yom Kippur War that was still raging,

---

47. Michael Scammell believes Sakharov's letter was decisive in persuading the Congress to pass the amendment over the strenuous opposition of the Nixon administration. Scammell, *Solzhenitsyn*, 809.

48. Sakharov, *Memoirs*, 394.

49. Scammell, *Solzhenitsyn*, 811.

50. Nikolai Yakovlev repeats these charges verbatim in *CIA Target—The USSR* (Moscow, 1982), 227. The Kadets were the liberal party in Russia prior to the Bolshevik Revolution. "Kadet" in Russian is the acronym of Constitutional Democrat.

two men, whom Sakharov judged to be Arabs, appeared at his apartment door. When, against his better judgment, he let them in, they announced that they were members of the Palestinian terrorist organization Black September and threatened to kill Bonner, her children, and grandchild unless Sakharov disavowed what he had said in the interview and publicly declared his ignorance of the entire Middle East.[51] At that point the doorbell rang, whereupon the Arabs, suddenly unnerved, ran away but not before promising that the next time Black September paid Sakharov a visit, it would be to carry out their threat. Understandably, Sakharov, Bonner, and Alexei were unnerved by the whole experience. But Sakharov quickly recovered his composure and once the terrorists were gone, informed foreign correspondents of what had happened and asked the police to investigate, which they made only a feeble pretense of doing.[52] Upon reflection, Sakharov realized that the incident, which he was sure the KGB had staged using either its own agents or Arabs it had recruited, was designed to intimidate not only him but Bonner and her children as well.

In this deadly serious game of move and countermove, Sakharov, in November, raised the stakes by taking the first step toward acquiring the visa he would need to lecture at Princeton University, which had extended an invitation the previous spring. In accordance with the requirements for obtaining a visa, Sakharov requested a letter from his employer, the Lebedev Institute, attesting to his loyalty.[53] When it became clear that, on orders from higher-ups, no one at the institute would write such a letter, Sakharov issued a statement to foreign correspondents promising inter alia that, if he went abroad, he would neither defect nor reveal secret information.[54] In response, the government, which had acquired a copy of the statement, broadcast its contents on state radio but without the parts containing these assurances.[55] The emotional strain caused by the entire sequence of events took its toll on Sakharov and Bonner. In December 1973 they were both hospitalized—Bonner for treatment of a chronic thyroid condition, which now required the gland's removal, and Sakharov to have his heart condition reevaluated. On her release, Bonner, who was dissatisfied with her treatment, consulted other doctors and not long afterward found a surgeon at another hospital who agreed to perform the thyroidectomy she needed. But as the day for the operation drew near, the surgeon decided he would have nothing more to do with her, almost surely because of her relationship to Sakharov. In the end, it was not until February 1974 that the operation was finally performed.[56]

51. Sakharov, *Memoirs*, 392; P. I. Pimenov, "Kakim on byl," 213.
52. Sakharov, *Memoirs*, 393–94.
53. Andrei Sakharov, "My Place Is in My Homeland (November 30, 1973)," *Samizdat Bulletin*, no. 10 (1974).
54. Sakharov, *Memoirs*, 396.
55. Ibid., 396.
56. Ibid., 396–97, 405.

# 15 Debating Solzhenitsyn

Sakharov's revelation in early September of the Princeton invitation caused his relations with Solzhenitsyn to worsen. The two men met for the last time on December 1, 1973. At the meeting, Solzhenitsyn argued strenuously against Sakharov's leaving the country. When Sakharov assured Solzhenitsyn he had no intention of defecting in the unlikely event he received a visa, Solzhenitsyn, who knew that both Chalidze and Zhores Medvedev had been stripped of their Soviet citizenship while abroad after receiving official permission to leave, told Sakharov that the same fate might befall him as well. To this Sakharov replied unrealistically and with a touch of bravado that if he went abroad and the government refused to let him return, he would camp out at the Soviet border until it relented.[1] The whole issue of visas and emigration touched a raw nerve in Solzhenitsyn, who considered leaving the Soviet Union even temporarily a betrayal of one's country and, in the case of the dissidents, of their cause. Even more harmful to their relationship was that the two men differed in their view of what should replace the Soviet system they both deplored. This, along with their personal differences, would be the catalyst, in the fall and winter of 1973–1974, for a near severance of their personal relations.

The more Sakharov and Solzhenitsyn saw each other, the less they liked each other. Inevitably, this colored their appraisal of the political and philosophical issues that divided them. Sakharov disliked especially the Soviet writer's theatricality, his view of the world as a stage and the history of the Soviet Union as a morality play in which Solzhenitsyn simultaneously performed the roles of actor and onstage commentator. Although Sakharov, in his own words, "bowed deeply" before Solzhenitsyn for telling the sordid truth about the Soviet Union, he quickly realized to his dismay that Solzhenitsyn did not always report the particulars of their conversations accurately. Sakharov also rejected Solzhenitsyn's claim that he, Sakharov, had become a dissident because he felt guilty about developing thermonuclear weapons and living in conditions while doing so that Solzhenitsyn, who spent years in a Soviet labor camp, persisted in describing as luxurious.[2] In addition, Sakharov was angered by Solzhenitsyn's accusations of naïveté, by which Solzhenitsyn meant that Sakharov failed to apportion his energy and attention sensibly. Among the causes to which he believed Sakharov devoted too much of his time was emigration.[3] Most infuriating, however, were Solzhenitsyn's insinuations, which mirrored those of the Soviet government,

1. Scammell, *Solzhenitsyn*, 823.
2. Sakharov, *Memoirs*, 399; Smith, *Russians*, 595; Solzhenitsyn, *Oak and the Calf*, 367–68.
3. Solzhenitsyn, *Oak and the Calf*, 375.

that Bonner was a neurotic busybody and that after marrying Sakharov, she made him her puppet.[4] Even Solzhenitsyn's calling Sakharov "a miracle" struck the Soviet physicist as the kind of grandiloquent claim only someone oblivious to the primacy of rational explanations of human behavior would make. In contrast, Sakharov explained his dissidence in his memoirs as simply "the natural consequence of what life has made me."[5] It is significant that *The Oak and the Calf,* in which Solzhenitsyn expresses his reservations about Sakharov most candidly, is the only book from which Sakharov quotes frequently and extensively in his memoirs. Solzhenitsyn's criticisms obviously struck a nerve. Conversely, Solzhenitsyn seemed always to hold Sakharov's service to the Soviet Union, and especially the emoluments he received as a result of it, against him. For that reason he thought Sakharov's dissidence was always tainted by the events in his life that had preceded it. In light of all this, it was probably beneficial to what remained of their relationship that the two men saw each other only once from the spring of 1973 to February 1974, when Solzhenitsyn was exiled from the Soviet Union.[6]

The political and philosophical differences between the two men became clearer after Solzhenitsyn, in the fall of 1973, wrote his celebrated *Letter to the Soviet Leaders,* which is as much a meditation on what it means to be Russian as it is an elucidation of the problems then afflicting the Soviet Union and the Soviet people.[7] In the *Letter,* which he knew Brezhnev and his cronies would ignore, Solzhenitsyn made explicit his long-standing belief that Russia's destiny and the West's were profoundly different. He stated that once the Russians threw off the Soviets' tyranny, they should retreat from the West philosophically, culturally, and even geographically to a preindustrial, agrarian order in the pristine wilds of Siberia informed by the moral and theocratic principles of Russian Orthodoxy. In doing so, Russia would be turning her back on the whole tradition of secular progress in Western civilization, which in Solzhenitsyn's view bore the onus of having created democratic capitalism and Soviet Communism—the two dominant twentieth-century political and economic systems that confronted each other oblivious to their common origins in the Enlightenment. It is hard to imagine prescriptions for Russia more antithetical to Sakharov's.

When he read the *Letter,* which circulated in samizdat, Sakharov realized immediately how profoundly he disagreed with it. This did not mean he rejected everything Solzhenitsyn believed or that he considered his other works devoid of merit. In an interview in January 1974, Sakharov made a point of praising

4. About the Princeton invitation, for example, Solzhenitsyn implied that in accepting it, Sakharov was deferring "to those close to him [who had] ideas not his own." Ibid.

5. Solzhenitsyn, *Oak and the Calf,* 367; Sakharov, *Memoirs,* 399.

6. Solzhenitsyn, *Oak and the Calf,* 398; Scammell, *Solzehnitsyn,* 799. As head of the KGB, Andropov was aware of the personal differences between the two men and seemed to enjoy repeating for the benefit of his colleagues the invective Solzhenitsyn occasionally directed at Sakharov, such as the charge that the latter was "irresponsible" and "insane." "Informatziia Komiteta Gosudarstvennoi Bezopasnosti pri Sovete Ministrov SSSR (July 24, 1974)," in Korotkov, Melchin, and Stepanov, *Kremlevskii samosud,* 501.

7. Aleksandr I. Solzhenitsyn, *Letter to the Soviet Leaders* (New York, 1974).

Solzhenitsyn's magnum opus, *The Gulag Archipelago,* as "a stone that will at long last destroy the barriers dividing humanity."[8] In the same interview he acknowledged that the roots of the repression both he and Solzhenitsyn were experiencing predated Stalin and Stalinism—which meant that Solzhenitsyn was right in claiming that Stalinism was the result of Leninism rather than a betrayal of it.[9] Also in January 1974, as the Soviet leadership was finalizing plans to deport Solzhenitsyn and making his daily existence in Russia as unpleasant as possible, Sakharov wrote an appeal, for which he solicited additional signatories, to permit the publication in the Soviet Union of Solzhenitsyn's works, which, with the exception of *One Day in the Life of Ivan Denisovich,* were forbidden.[10] A week later, in an interview with the *Sunday Times* of London, Sakharov expressed agreement with Solzhenitsyn's point that only by preserving the Soviet people's collective memory of the Soviet past could "the force, devastation, and fanatical dogmatism" of the Soviet system be brought to an end.[11] For the rest of his life Sakharov generously acknowledged all that Solzhenitsyn had done to raise awareness abroad and in the Soviet Union of the evils Soviet leaders from Lenin to Brezhnev had committed, and in 1988 he could say about *The Gulag Archipelago* that it "reflected the greatest tragedy of our people more than any other work published in the USSR."[12]

After receiving and reading Solzhenitsyn's letter, Sakharov thought it best to contemplate its full meaning before responding to it. Finally, in April 1974, he did, in a fifteen-page pamphlet that circulated in samizdat and was published abroad, in Russian by the Kontinent Press in Paris and in English in the *Sunday Times* of London.[13] Sakharov's disagreements with Solzhenitsyn were profound. In expressing them as emphatically as he did, he seemed to be drawing a line in the sand, indicating to everyone concerned that his views and Solzhenitsyn's were irreconcilable. To Solzhenitsyn's view that peace would come when Russia withdrew from the world, Sakharov insisted it would come when the Soviet Union finally accommodated itself to the world. For Sakharov convergence was the alternative not only to the communism Marxist-Leninists predicted but also to the isolationism Solzhenitsyn espoused. To Solzhenitsyn's contention that Russia, in its history and culture, was sui generis, Sakharov argued that,

8. Andrei Sakharov, "Interv'iu, dannoe korrrespondentu gazety 'Tribiun de Zhenev' o knige 'Arkhipelag GULag' i o svobode slova i material'nom polozhenii v SSSR (January 20, 1974)," in *Sobranie* 28 (Munich, 1978) AS1579: 2.

9. Ibid., 1.

10. Andrei Sakharov, Alexander Galich, Vladimir Maximov, Vladimir Voinovich, and Igor Shafarevich, "Declaration on Solzhenitsyn (January 5, 1974)," in *Sakharov Speaks,* 232–33.

11. A. D. Sakharov, "Interv'iu, dannoe korrespondentu ezhenedel'nika 'Sandi Taims,' o vysylke A. Solzhenitsyna iz SSSR i o 'Moskovskom obrashchenii' (February 20, 1974)," in *Sobranie* 28 (Munich, 1978), AS1593: 3.

12. Interview with Zora Safir, 11.

13. Coppen, "Public Life of Andrei Sakharov," 86. The original title of Sakharov's rejoinder was *O pis'me Aleksandra Solzhenitsyna "Vozhdiam Sovetskogo Soiuza."* An English translation, entitled "On Aleksandr Solzhenitsyn's *Letter to the Soviet Leaders,*" can be found in *The Political, Social and Religious Thought of Russian 'Samizdat': An Anthology,* ed. Michael Meerson-Aksenov and Boris Shragin (Belmont, Mass., 1977), 291–301.

notwithstanding certain cultural and historical idiosyncrasies, none of which was determinative, Russia was participating in a universal process of modernization based on science and technological advancement in which Russia differed from the West only in lagging behind it. While Solzhenitsyn believed that the moral values the Russian people should reclaim had emerged organically in Russian culture before the communists corrupted it, for Sakharov those values were the natural emanations of a rational and technologically modern order that transcended the artificial boundaries imposed by religion and national culture. And to Solzhenitsyn's insistence that science was incompatible with morality and ecology, Sakharov responded by arguing that science was not inherently destructive of either morality or the environment and that as long as it was used by rational individuals for appropriate purposes, it could not help but improve people's lives spiritually as well as materially and be a force for progress in the ongoing evolution of humanity.[14] Sakharov's disagreement with Solzhenitsyn over the very concept of progress caused him to reiterate his long-standing optimism about the future. As he explained this disagreement in his memoirs:

> I do not share Solzhenitsyn's antipathy toward progress. In my opinion, the ecological and social dangers entailed are more than offset by the better life for everyone that progress brings. It can temper social, racial, and regional conflicts. It can minimize basic inequities and bring relief to millions who suffer from hunger, poverty, and disease. And if mankind is the healthy organism I believe it to be, then progress, science, and the constructive application of intelligence will enable us to cope with the dangers facing us. Having set out on the path of progress several millennia ago, mankind cannot halt now—nor should it.[15]

The political differences the two men expressed were just as stark and incapable of resolution as their philosophical ones. For Sakharov, the very pluralism and freedom Solzhenitsyn condemned as evidence of weakness and irresolution in a society were actually a source of strength, proof that those exercising political power believed their policies and opinions were defensible by reason. Sakharov criticized Solzhenitsyn severely for opposing democracy in his *Letter*. This in itself was quite remarkable. Prior to 1973, Sakharov's support for democracy—as distinguished from democratization—was tepid at best, hedged by qualifications about its necessity, desirability, and appropriateness for people like the Soviet who had no practical experience with it nor any memory of it from any previous political system. Until the late 1980s, Sakharov's advocacy of democracy would always be qualified by the presumption that everyone who exercised it should be rational; whether evidence of irrationality (short of insanity) would be disqualifying was something he never clarified. But Solzhenitsyn's categorical rejection of democracy on utilitarian, philosophical, and ethical grounds seemed to cause Sakharov, in response, to think better of it. In his reply

14. Sakharov, "On Aleksandr Solzhenitsyn's *Letter*," 295, 299.
15. Sakharov, *Memoirs*, 409.

to Solzhenitsyn, Sakharov's endorsement of democracy could not have been more emphatic: "I consider the path of democratic development to be the only favorable one for any country. I consider the slavish, servile spirit which existed in Russia for centuries and which was combined with contempt for anything foreign, alien, or heterodox to be the greatest misfortune, not an indication of national well-being. Only under democratic conditions can a national character be elaborated and be capable of a reasonable existence in a world growing ever more complex."[16] In order to show that precedents for democracy existed in Russian history, in the very same paragraph Sakharov even described the reforms of Tsar Alexander II in the 1860s and 1870s, which were conceived and imposed on Russian society autocratically, as "democratic."[17]

The philosophical assumption on which Sakharov's response to Solzhenitsyn ultimately rested was that there were universal standards for judging not just moral behavior but literally everything. Sakharov came close to stating this principle in the course of arguing, in contrast to Solzhenitsyn, that the Russian people were not the only ones to suffer under communism: other nationalities and ethnic groups were persecuted just as much as the Russians and in some cases more.[18] From this he concluded that the principles germane in reforming the Soviet Union were applicable everywhere, to all peoples regardless of the degree to which national culture and history made them different. Sakharov's vision of the future was supranational. In contrast to Solzhenitsyn, he believed that there was no uniquely Russian path to salvation, happiness, material prosperity, or spiritual contentment. However different and diverse nations and cultures might be, they would all share eventually in a common destiny—by which Sakharov of course meant convergence—in which human rights would be acceptable to, and accepted by, everyone. But convergence, once it occurred, would not bring any uniformity of thought or impose any stifling intellectual orthodoxies. Freedom to think differently would be protected, and it would generate genuine diversity—not in the manner in which societies would be organized (because convergence implied that socialism and communism would fuse and form a hybrid that was universally accepted) but in the ideas, beliefs, aspirations, and attitudes people would hold. In this Sakharovian vision, universal moral principles would justify an astonishing degree of individuality in people's preferences, talents, inclinations, and abilities. Although the moral principles that would exist under convergence would be universally the same, everything in life that was ideational and emotional would be marked by the full flowering of the individual personality.

Philosophically, Sakharov was a monist who, like Isaiah Berlin's celebrated hedgehogs, believed in a small number of universal principles—Sakharov called

---

16. Sakharov, "On Aleksandr Solzhenitsyn's *Letter*," 297–98.

17. Regarding his emancipation of the serfs in 1861, the tsar declared, "The autocracy established serfdom and it is up to the autocracy to abolish it." *The Politics of Autocracy: Letters of Alexander II to Prince A. I. Bariatinskii, 1857–1864*, ed. Alfred J. Rieber (Paris, 1966), 54.

18. Sakharov, "On Aleksandr Solzhenitsyn's *Letter*," 292.

them "human rights"—the validity of which had nothing to do with whoever happened to espouse them.[19] In contrast to Solzhenitsyn's "particularist" vision of Russia's destiny, in which there were Russian ideas to be adopted and Western ideas to be avoided, in Sakharov's there were only ideas, and they were evaluated by universal canons of evidence, logic, and moral reasoning that scientists, in particular, were trained to uphold. After rejecting Solzhenitsyn's view that Marxism, because it was a Western ideology, diverted the Russian people from the natural evolution for which their history and culture had prepared them, Sakharov argued for the universality of ideas and of the criteria by which their correctness and applicability were determined: "In general I cannot comprehend this very separation of ideas into Western and Russian. In my opinion the only division of ideas and concepts in a scientific, rational approach to social and natural phenomena can be in categories of right and wrong."[20] By idealizing Russian history while at the same time consigning the Russian people to a permanent, albeit benevolent, authoritarianism, Solzhenitsyn was denying them the common destiny they shared with everyone else.

There was yet another disagreement that Solzhenitsyn's *Letter,* and Sakharov's response to it, clarified. To Solzhenitsyn's argument that the Soviet people would recover their moral goodness through a process of spiritual purification informed by the moral principles of Russian Orthodoxy, Sakharov replied that regardless of how moral virtue was acquired (or, in Solzhenitsyn's scheme of things, recovered), its existence would always remain precarious unless societies were based on the rule of law and upheld human rights. For Sakharov it was not enough for human beings to reform themselves morally and spiritually. Quite apart from his conviction that Russian Orthodoxy was hardly the proper instrument for this, he was always skeptical that individual moral regeneration, by itself, would yield a society that was just. In addition to the spiritual regeneration of the individual, a transformation was required of the social and political institutions that mediated the relationships individuals forged with others in the larger society. After all, it was the laws, institutions, unwritten traditions, customs, and accepted practices of societies that, once created, inevitably molded people and, in Russia's case, unfortunately robbed them of their moral discernment. This lack of moral sensibility in the Soviet people troubled Sakharov profoundly and prompted him to describe them in an unflattering light in the Postscript to his 1971 Memorandum. Ironically, this view also caused Solzhenitsyn to believe erroneously, but only temporarily, that he and Sakharov basically shared the same opinions. But on the necessity of law and other external constraints on human behavior and on the universality of the moral principles that informed these constraints Sakharov could not have been more emphatic and more at

19. In the terminology Berlin borrowed from the Greek poet Archilochus to classify Russian and European thinkers, the antithesis of hedgehogs, who "know one big thing," are foxes, who "know many things" and thus are less likely to ascribe universal validity to their beliefs. Among the former he includes Dante, Plato, Hegel, and Ibsen. Isaiah Berlin, "The Hedgehog and the Fox: An Essay on Tolstoy's View of History," in *Russian Thinkers,* 22–23.

20. Sakharov, "On Aleksandr Solzhenitsyn's *Letter,*" 294.

odds with Solzhenitsyn. His differences with Solzhenitsyn boiled down to three fundamental postulates: first, the Russians were really no different from other people; second, like all people they required laws and other external restraints to ensure a just society; and third, the moral principles that undergirded this just society were absolute, timeless, and universal.

In understanding Sakharov, one must bear in mind that the universal moral principles he called human rights were not deduced merely through an exercise in pure reason. They were also the result of personal experience and observation. That in itself is unremarkable. But what makes the observations from which Sakharov inferred or induced abstract moral principles unusual is that they were always of people or institutions that were themselves devoid of moral principles. What concerned Sakharov most of all about Soviet society was its amorality, which manifested itself in a pervasive cynicism holding that what was right was nothing more than what one could safely get away with. In place of this could be substituted any number of ethical systems, Solzhenitsyn's just as easily as Sakharov's. But there was a significant difference. Solzhenitsyn's alternative to the Soviet Union drew much of its moral and political content from an older Russia that had existed before the communists came and that, despite the communists, continued, albeit tacitly and unobtrusively, to exist. In contrast to Solzhenitsyn, Sakharov found nothing in Russia's past that could serve as a realistic alternative to its Soviet present. As a result, he had to conjure an alternative and the moral principles that informed it ex nihilo—a remarkable intellectual achievement and one for which he has been praised insufficiently, even by his admirers.

Sakharov demonstrated this ability on several occasions throughout the 1970s, when his dissidence most severely tested the limits of the Soviet government's tolerance. One such occasion was in December 1977, when Sakharov, Bonner, and Alexei visited the Mordovian labor camp to which Eduard Kuznetsov had been exiled. This was the first time Sakharov had spent any length of time in a camp (albeit as a visitor) or even examined one closely; what he saw in the early 1950s of the camp adjacent to Arzamas was fairly minimal.[21] The experience confirmed for him the validity of the argument, implicit in Solzhenitsyn's *Gulag Archipelago*, that the system of labor camps was a microcosm of the Soviet Union itself. He returned from the visit more convinced than ever of the Soviet system's malevolence. However, he drew from this experience, and from the metaphor it suggested, a conclusion different from Solzhenitsyn's. For Solzhenitsyn the horrors of the Gulag underscored the need to tell the truth about the Soviet Union. Sakharov's observations of the camp in Mordovia underscored the need for the Soviet people to have human rights. Foremost among these was the right to human dignity, and the very pettiness with which this dignity was denied the inmates in the camp seemed, paradoxically, to magnify rather than reduce its importance to Sakharov. The lack of adequate ventilation for prisoners varnishing furniture, the absence of protective goggles for those cutting glass

21. Sakharov, *Memoirs,* 478–81.

(both of which Sakharov cites in his reminiscences of the trip in his memoirs), and the absence of safety precautions seemed to Sakharov to constitute a denial of human dignity not only to the inmates of the camp but, by analogy, to the Soviet people as a whole.[22] And for Sakharov, the only way human dignity could be preserved when people were not virtuous themselves was by restraining their behavior through the application of law. Ironically, it was Sakharov the secularist and quasi-atheist rather than Solzhenitsyn the Christian theocrat who had a keener sense of the intractability of human imperfection, evidence in Christianity of man's inherent sinfulness. For Sakharov this imperfection was mostly impervious to amelioration through religious education. If (or rather when) these efforts failed, then the rule of law would be required for ethical behavior to prevail. Indeed, over the long run the rule of law would create a culture of law, which would generate moral virtue more effectively than religion could. This was Sakharov's corrective to what he thought was lacking in Solzhenitsyn's scenario of the Russian people's salvation.

The debate the two men engaged in touched on matters educated Russians had considered for centuries, such as the attitude Russia should adopt toward Western rationalism, science, and technology. Not surprisingly, other dissidents felt compelled to contribute to it. In April 1974, for example, Vladimir Osipov, the founder and original editor of *Veche (The Assembly)*, criticized Sakharov strenuously and called on him to accept unequivocally Solzhenitsyn's prescriptions for Russia and the Russian people.[23] Sakharov, in Osipov's opinion, was insufficiently attentive to the suffering of the Russian people—a charge the Soviet physicist rejected.[24] From his exile in Vermont, Solzhenitsyn escalated his criticisms of Sakharov, condemning him harshly for making emigration, as a human right, of paramount importance.[25] In 1976 Solzhenitsyn wrote for *Kontinent,* the émigré journal Vladimir Maximov edited in Paris, a wide-ranging rebuttal of Sakharov's criticisms in which the Soviet writer proclaimed the virtue of "national consciousness" while condemning as "vehement" and "rash" the Soviet intelligentsia of which Sakharov, despite his dissidence, was still a member. In Solzhenitsyn's jaundiced view, the present-day intelligentsia "cannot without anger hear the words 'Russian national rebirth.'"[26]

By the time Solzhenitsyn's critique appeared, Sakharov had moved on to other things. But the polemics he exchanged with Solzhenitsyn were critical to his intellectual and political maturation. In a way that no one else could have done, Solzhenitsyn forced Sakharov to clarify the moral and philosophical

22. Ibid., 479.

23. Vladimir Osipov, "Piat' vozrazhenii Sakharovu (1974)," in *Tri otnosheniia k rodine* (Frankfurt/Main, 1978), 173–80.

24. Ibid., 179. That Osipov strongly disagreed with Sakharov did not deter the latter from defending Osipov when he was arrested in November 1974. Alexeyeva, *Soviet Dissent,* 441.

25. "O budushchem Rossii: Press-konferentsiia A. I. Solzhenitsyna (November 16, 1974)," *Posev* 12 (December 1974): 6.

26. Alexander Solzhenitsyn, "Sakharov and the Criticisms of 'A Letter to the Soviet Leaders,'" in *Kontinent* (Garden City, New York, 1976), 20, 23.

principles that would inform the good society he hoped would succeed the Soviet one once convergence was a global reality. As it happened, an opportunity to describe this society in detail presented itself just when Sakharov was formulating his response to Solzhenitsyn's *Letter*. In the winter of 1974 he was asked to participate in a symposium sponsored by the American magazine *Saturday Review* on what the world would look like fifty years in the future.[27] For his contribution, Sakharov received five hundred American dollars, the first hard currency he had received.[28]

In his contribution, Sakharov assumed that by 2024 convergence as a process would be complete. Nations would have demilitarized entirely and conventional weapons as well as nuclear and thermonuclear ones would be a thing of the past. Human rights, individual freedom, and the culture of law he hoped to cultivate in the Soviet Union would exist everywhere and be respected by everyone. While Sakharov did not state explicitly that nation-states would have disappeared, the melding of socialism and capitalism would presumably have eliminated their very reason for being. But even if nation-states did exist in 2024, their sovereignty would be severely limited: in his essay Sakharov referred to the United Nations as a prototype for a "world government" committed to protecting "global human rights."[29] In terms of the world economy, convergence would have rendered it a hybrid, a mixture of socialist and capitalist elements yielding "maximum flexibility, freedom, social mobility, and opportunities for worldwide regulation."[30] Unfortunately, Sakharov failed to explain how this system would be flexible if it were also regulated, presumably by the world government that oversaw it.

What interested Sakharov more than these macropolitical and economic arrangements was the question of how ordinary people would live. In the article he seemed especially intent on describing the ways in which science and technology would make daily life easier. In many respects, the future society Sakharov described—a society he considered inevitable as well as desirable—was the ultimate expression of the humane Prometheanism he had always advocated under which rational human beings used science and technology to harness nature for their own purposes. In this model society of the future, Sakharov envisioned something called the Work Territory, where people would either produce food on farms using the most advanced techniques of animal husbandry or produce consumer goods in enormous automated or semiautomated factories. But people would also live in the Work Territory, either in "super cities" with multistoried apartment buildings in which the lighting and temperature would be carefully controlled or in suburbs marked by "silent and comfortable public transportation, clean air, arts and crafts, and a free and varied cultural life."[31]

27. Andrei D. Sakharov, "Tomorrow: The View from Red Square," *Saturday Review*, August 24, 1974, 12–14, 108, 110.
28. Sakharov, *Memoirs*, 410.
29. Sakharov, "Tomorrow," 13.
30. Ibid.
31. Ibid., 14.

All that was worthwhile and rewarding about life in the Work Territory, and in the entire society of which it was an integral element, was attributable ultimately to what Sakharov called "the rational solution of social and international problems" by those who had laid the groundwork for the society as a whole.[32]

Adjacent to the Work Territory would be the Preserve Territory. Here people would go not only for recreation—which Sakharov considered essential to the maximum performance of labor—but "to work with their hands and their heads, read, and think."[33] Living in tents ("the way their ancestors did") for the long periods of time they spent there, presumably on weekends or vacations, people would "listen to the noise of a mountain stream or simply relish the silence, the wild beauty of the outdoors, the forests, the sky, and the clouds. Their basic work [would] be to preserve nature and themselves."[34] In Sakharov's description, the Preserve Territory would enable people to merge with nature rather than to dominate it, as they did in the Work Territory. In this way, the Prometheanism that prevailed in the Work Territory would be tempered somewhat so that the vast projects of social engineering it inspired would benefit humanity without at the same time destroying nature. Among the most imaginative and technologically advanced of these projects were space exploration and the search for extraterrestrial life; the development of battery-powered cars, atomic-powered dirigibles, and high-speed trains running both underground and aboveground on monorails; and a universal information system not unlike the World Wide Web that came into existence shortly before Sakharov died in 1989.[35] The kind of modernization the Soviet Union engaged in under Stalin, in which the environment was considered just a resource to be exploited in serving the purely selfish interests of a self-contained elite, had no role to play in this Sakharovian future in which the benefits of progress would be enjoyed by everyone.

In 1974, when Sakharov indulged in this imaginative exercise in futurology, progress was not just a matter of science and technology. It also required a healthy respect for nature and a commitment to preserving it. Toward this end, Sakharov predicted that by 2040 any productive activity that could pollute or otherwise damage the earth's atmosphere would be carried out in "flying cities" (really satellites circling the earth), where pollutants could be dispensed with safely. Meanwhile, back on earth, nuclear and solar power would have become the fuels of choice: to the extent that coal was used, the pollution it produced would be harmless. Finite natural resources would be carefully recycled, and the battery-powered vehicles that predominated would have mechanical legs sufficiently soft that asphalt roads would not be necessary. Instead, these vehicles would be driven over grass, which would not even be crushed in the process. In agriculture, not only would the Green Revolution by 2024 have produced artificial soil that was "superfertile" in comparison with the best soils of 1974, but because extraterrestrial travel would be commonplace, food would be extracted

32. Ibid.
33. Ibid.
34. Ibid.
35. Ibid., 108.

from whatever was edible on other planets of the solar system as well as from bacteria and algae on earth. (By 2024 all of these planets would have been explored.) Thus man's supply of food, once thought to be finite, would be practically inexhaustible.[36]

In sum, Sakharov's vision of life in 2024 was a very modern one, limited only by his awareness that scientific progress, to be truly lasting and beneficial, cannot be rushed. Sakharov's was not a vision in which his imagination ran rampant in defiance of what was scientifically and technologically possible. Despite his excitement at writing the article, he did not lose his sense of reality. At the same time, he included very little in the article about how this future society would be governed politically. The reader thus has to infer this from the descriptions Sakharov provided of how people would live on a daily basis and of the values they would have to hold. But Sakharov's future society cannot be understood without understanding the political arrangements it seems to necessitate—arrangements that reflect the rational elitism one finds in earlier writings of his, such as *Reflections*.

Politically, Sakharov's ideal society was not unlike Plato's Republic, in which knowledge of the good was a prerequisite of power. To function effectively, Sakharov's society, like Plato's, would be divided politically into three basic constituencies: first, a stratum of governors, all of them rational, who would be democratically elected; second, a scientific-technological elite, also rational, that would advise the governors on the policies they should adopt; and third, the masses, who would accept the policies the governors adopted because they reflected the superior wisdom of the scientific-technological elite that recommended them. The entire society, while practicing democracy, would be hierarchical, as Plato's Republic was; to the extent that everyone accepted his place in it, it would be conservative as well. In the end, the rationality each of these constituencies possessed would be the social glue holding society together. The technocratic elite would be rational enough to recommend policies beneficial to everyone; the governors would be rational enough to defer to the technocrats' superior wisdom in accepting them; and the masses would be rational enough both to elect governors who were rational and to accept the policies the governors adopted. Unlike the technocracies Saint-Simon conjured in the nineteenth century and H.G. Wells imagined in the twentieth century, in which scientists and technocrats wielded power, Sakharov's society was one in which such people would have influence rather than power.[37] But because these scientists and technocrats would identify problems and contemplate solutions that those wielding power accepted, they would be just as essential to Sakharov's model society as they were to Saint-Simon's and Wells's. As David Kelley has pointed out, Sakharov

36. Ibid. 108, 110.
37. Wells expressed his preference for societies run by scientists and technocrats in one of his novels, *The Shape of Things to Come* (New York, 1933). In the novel, scientists who have previously developed a superior civilization far removed from the rest of the world suddenly emerge to bring order and peace to people reduced to a Paleolithic existence in which warfare is rampant.

considered decision making in a democracy a matter not of compromise but of planning and problem solving.[38] Because Sakharov had been raised in a country whose history and political culture were traditionally paternalistic and authoritarian, he had no exposure until the late 1980s to what democracy in practice entailed—in particular the compromises, mutual accommodations, and inevitable disparities between what was best and what was possible and practical. For this reason his notion of what a model democracy would look like was so idealized as to be completely unattainable.

The elitism Sakharov's model society entailed had a long pedigree in Sakharov's political thought. In *Reflections* he described the intelligentsia as society's tutor, instructing the masses in the correctness of the policies it recommended.[39] In the letter to the Soviet leaders he coauthored with Turchin and Roi Medvedev in 1970, he endorsed the view that political reform "must be supplemented by a plan for economic and social measures worked out by specialists."[40] And in his critique of Solzhenitsyn's *Letter*, he called, oxymoronically, for "a world-wide scientific and democratic regulation of the economy and society."[41] What was implicit in all of this was that the rationality the scientific elite possessed was somehow superior to everyone else's. In Sakharov's scheme of things, the rationality of the masses and that of the governors were grounded in deference, a kind of wisdom that boiled down to an awareness of one's own intellectual limitations. Because the masses and the governors understood their limitations, they wisely deferred to those who knew more than they did—namely, the intellectual elite—and they did so willingly because they understood their own intellectual inferiority.

Despite the elitism this opinion implies, Sakharov was not a snob. In his relations with those intellectually inferior to him (a category that encompassed nearly everyone he met), he was always a model of egalitarianism, treating people with enduring decency. But as an integral aspect of his political thought, the elitism he expressed sporadically in his various writings and that is implicit in his futurological essay in 1974 was nonetheless very real, and any biographer of Sakharov must acknowledge it and recognize it for what it reveals about him. The grounds on which one can criticize Sakharov's elitism are several. For one thing, human beings, even the most rational ones like Sakharov himself, are subject to emotions and feelings that often cause them to act in ways that are irrational and also contrary to the best interests of their society. In terms of the society Sakharov believed would exist after convergence, this might cause either the masses or the governors, or both, to reject the pride of place the intellectual elite was meant to enjoy. The result, if that were to occur, would be conflict and perhaps even violence. Second, the kind of technical and scientific knowledge

38. Kelley, *Solzhenitsyn-Sakharov Dialogue*, 137.

39. Sakharov, *Reflections*, 25, 84–85.

40. They went on to say that "we emphasize that democratization alone in no way solves economic problems, but will create the prerequisites for their solution." Sakharov, Medvedev, and Turchin, "A Reformist Program for Democratization," 325.

41. Sakharov, "On Aleksandr Solzhenitsyn's *Letter*," 295.

this elite possessed was hardly a sufficient basis on which to make policy. Translating abstract recommendations into policies people would accept and uphold required political skills that the governors in Sakharov's good society, accustomed as they were to deferring to the technocrats and scientists, might not possess. Indeed, it was entirely possible that despite their superior knowledge and rationality, the technocrats and scientists might simply be wrong. But since the governors were conditioned to defer to them and the masses conditioned to defer to the governors, there might be no one in the society able to recognize this. Finally, it must be said that Sakharov's elitism bore some resemblance to the long-standing paternalism in Russian culture—a paternalism that in many other aspects of his life he emphatically and unequivocally rejected. In both cases, an elite class presumed to know more than the masses, and this disparity in wisdom was reflected in a comparable disparity in influence in Sakharov's case (where the intellectual elite advised) and in power in the case of Russia (where only rarely had the people and the educated elite been allowed to share in governance). But there was a significant difference between Sakharov's elitism and the paternalism so prevalent in Russian history and culture: while for Sakharov the masses were adults and thus sufficiently rational to recognize their own shortcomings, for both the tsars and the Soviet leaders they were essentially children and thus not even capable of that. Unlike paternalism, the hierarchies Sakharov preferred were not inherently incompatible with democracy because they were based on knowledge and rationality.

Understandably, Sakharov took pleasure in the futurological exercise he was asked by *Saturday Review* to perform. As one who had believed throughout his life in secular progress, it was only natural that he should relish describing the society to which this progress would lead. Convergence, of course, was Sakharov's preferred term for what would exist when no more progress was necessary; it was the closest equivalent in his teleology to the religious concept of the end of history or the kingdom of heaven on earth. For all his pessimism about the prospects for short-term improvements in the Soviet Union in the mid-1970s, his faith in convergence was still sufficient for him to write confidently in 1974 about the kind of future society he believed humanity was capable of creating. Although Sakharov, as a scientist, found religion too dogmatic for his tastes, his faith in convergence was always precisely that, an article of faith.

# **16**  Détente and Human Rights

However much futurology attracted him, Sakharov devoted most of his attention in the 1970s to issues of immediate concern both to him and to the Soviet Union. The most pressing and prominent of these was détente. Sakharov himself never defined the term, but he used it repeatedly to describe a relationship between

states that was less bellicose than that in a cold war but without the shared interests implicit in ententes and alliances. What most clearly distinguished détente
from a cold war, as these terms were used in the West in the 1970s, was that,
while the former suggested a striving for peace, the latter suggested an ideological struggle using all methods short of nuclear war.

One of the problems in discussing détente, as it pertained to the United States
and the Soviet Union in the 1970s, was that the two superpowers defined it differently, had different reasons for adhering to it (or for pretending to adhere to
it), and had different expectations of what would result from it. For the United
States, as the Nixon, Ford, and Carter administrations pursued it with varying
degrees of enthusiasm, détente was basically a substitute for the Cold War and
as such was an end in itself. The principal architect of détente, Henry Kissinger,
who served as secretary of state under presidents Nixon and Ford, saw it as a
necessity or a virtue or both, depending on the circumstances. The opposition
to the Vietnam War in the United States when Nixon was elected president in
1968 had become by the early 1970s so intense and widespread that Kissinger
believed containment was no longer sustainable politically as the basis for American policy toward the Soviet Union. As a result, a different policy was required,
one that took into account not only the realities of American domestic politics
but also the fact that the Soviets' worsening relations with China seemed to require an improvement in relations with the United States. If the Soviets could
not see that improving relations with the United States was in their own interest, a carefully calibrated mixture of inducements and threats from the United
States would convince them of this. The result would be a new international
equilibrium—one that would, in Kissinger's phrase, usher in "a new generation
of peace" because the relationship between the two superpowers and between
each of the superpowers and China would now be based not on ideology but
on a rational calculation of national interest. In popular parlance, this new calculus, as it applied to Soviet-American relations, would be called détente. Not
surprisingly, both Kissinger and Nixon took very seriously the defining document of détente, the statement of Basic Principles of Soviet-American relations
signed in Moscow by Nixon and Brezhnev on May 29, 1972. In it both countries
agreed to avoid military confrontations, exercise restraint in their bilateral relations, and reduce tensions in their relations with other countries.[1]

Kissinger did not believe that détente required the Soviets to modify their
domestic policy: how the Soviets treated their dissidents should not influence
American policy toward the Soviet Union. There were some in the West, such
as Senator Henry Jackson, who opposed détente precisely because they feared
it excluded the Soviet dissidents from its jurisdiction. And there were others
in the West, such as John Kenneth Galbraith and Willy Brandt, who favored
détente because they thought it would cause the liberalization of the Soviet
system and perhaps its eventual disintegration. But that was not the reason the
Nixon administration chose to pursue it. The purpose of détente, rather, was

---

1. Theodore Draper, "Appeasement and Détente," *Commentary* 61, no. 2 (February 1976): 30.

to improve Soviet-American relations and reduce the chance of nuclear war—objectives that did not require on the Soviets' part any alteration in the way they ruled the Soviet people.

The Soviet leadership had a very different view of détente. In fact, Soviet leaders rarely used the term, preferring instead the phrase "relaxation of tensions." For them, détente (in Martin Malia's formulation) was not a way of transcending the Cold War, as it was for the Americans, but a way of winning it.[2] Regardless of détente, the inexorable laws of historical development leading ultimately to the triumph of communism still pertained, and for that reason *Izvestiia* pointed out in December 1975 that "the process of détente does not mean and [has] never meant the freezing of the social-political status quo in the world."[3] As Brezhnev informed the Twenty-fifth Party Congress in February 1976, "détente does not in the slightest abolish, and cannot abolish or alter the laws of class struggle."[4] Nuclear war, to be sure, was to be avoided. But what prevented it was not détente but Soviet military strength—as well as the peaceful intentions of the Soviet Union and its allies around the world. In fact, throughout the Cold War and détente, many Soviet military leaders believed that nuclear war would not be the unimaginable catastrophe for communism that it would be for capitalism; only the latter, they believed, would be destroyed by it. Were nuclear war to occur, it would not supersede or render nugatory the Marxist dialectic or any of the other principles of Marxism-Leninism. To say that no one could win a nuclear war was to play into the hands of the imperialists, and the Soviet Union should thus be able to fight a nuclear war and win it. Détente or no détente, the Soviet Union should still seek nuclear parity with the United States, which would bring with it significant political, psychological, and military advantages. Paraphrasing Clausewitz, nuclear war, no less than conventional war, was an extension of politics.[5]

This, at any rate, is what Soviet military strategists believed. In practical terms it hardly mattered whether they were correct or not. For them nuclear war was just a more destructive form of conventional war, and for that reason détente, as a means of reducing the chances of nuclear war, was hardly a necessity. To be sure, the Soviet civilian leaders wanted détente but only so long as they were the ones who defined it. For them, détente was principally a way of ameliorating the deficiencies of Soviet society without correcting them.[6] As Georgii Arbatov explained the rationale for détente in his memoirs:

> Why bother developing your science and technology when you can order entire plants from abroad? Who needs to find radical solutions to the food problem when it's so easy to buy tens of millions of tons of grain, and no small amounts of

---

2. Malia, *The Soviet Tragedy*, 378.

3. Quoted in Draper, "Appeasement and Détente," 31.

4. Quoted in Holloway, *The Soviet Union and the Arms Race* (New Haven, 1984), 91.

5. A. I. Bulanov and I. A. Krylova, "Sootnoshenie politiki i iadernoi voiny: Analiticheskii obzor literatury: 1955–1987," *Voprosy filosofii* 5 (1988): 113–14. See also Richard Pipes, "Why the Soviet Union Thinks It Could Fight and Win a Nuclear War," *Commentary*, 64, no. 1 (July 1977): 21–34.

6. Wolfgang Leonhard, "The Domestic Politics of the New Soviet Foreign Policy," *Foreign Affairs* 52, no. 1 (October 1973): 70.

meat, butter, and other produce from America, Canada, and West Europe? Who needs to salvage the dreadfully backward construction industry when there are Finnish, Yugoslav, or Swedish construction companies to build or renovate the most important sites, when you can import the materials in shortest supply—the plumbing and the fixtures from West Germany, the wallpaper and the furniture from other Western countries?[7]

It is conceivable that if the Soviet leaders had taken better advantage of détente and refrained from invading Afghanistan in 1979, which effectively ended it, the Soviet Union might have survived longer than it did. As it was, détente significantly benefited the Soviet Union by blinding the West to the Soviets' objectives, which never changed as a result of it. Soviet foreign policy was no less aggressive in the 1970s, when détente existed, than it was in the 1960s, when it did not. From the Soviets' perspective, détente made a great deal of sense, not only because of the economic benefits it generated for the Soviet Union but also because of the illusion it fostered in the West that the Soviets had finally forsaken an aggressive foreign policy.

Paradoxically, détente worked also to the advantage of the dissidents. However skillfully the Soviets used détente to achieve their principal objective (which from the end of World War II to perestroika remained the expansion of Soviet power and influence), they had to be concerned throughout this period that if they treated the dissidents too harshly, the West might withdraw the economic assistance the Soviets desperately needed. This consideration especially affected how the Soviets treated Sakharov himself. In 1975 the leadership considered exiling him to Sverdlovsk (where his path and Yeltsin's, then the Communist Party boss in the city, might have crossed) but in the end chose not to, fearing the adverse effect such an action would have on Soviet-American relations.[8] Of course there were other reasons why Sakharov generally escaped harsher treatment. Certainly his celebrity had the effect of protecting him to some extent, as did the fact that by virtue of his earlier work on thermonuclear weapons, he remained, even as a dissident, tangible evidence that the Soviet system could produce scientists equal to those in the West. For all his dissidence, Sakharov embodied all that was best in the Soviet Union and socialism. To kill him, to exile him abroad, or even just to exile him internally would be

---

7. Georgii Arbatov, *The System: An Insider's Life in Soviet Politics* (New York, 1992), 215.

8. "Andropov, Ustinov, and Rudenko to the Central Committee (November 16, 1975)," in Rubenstein and Gribanov, *KGB File*, 201; Walter Laqueur, "Andrei Sakharov," in *Fin de Siècle and Other Essays on America and Europe* (New Brunswick, N.J., 1997), 210. Laqueur argues that it was not détente but the need to justify the whole machinery of coercion and control in the Soviet Union that prevented Brezhnev from ordering the KGB to suppress the dissident movement entirely. The Soviet leadership, in other words, had a vested interest in the continued existence of the dissidents so long as they were weak and did not try to overthrow the regime. But Laqueur's argument ignores the fact that once détente ended in 1980, the Soviets *did* try to eliminate the dissident movement and largely succeeded. According to one of Gorbachev's chief advisers, Alexander Yakovlev, the government did not put Sakharov on trial in the 1970s, before détente ended, because of the "political costs" a trial would exact. Alexander Yakovlev, *A Century of Violence in Soviet Russia* (New Haven, 2002), 149.

a tacit admission of failure, an acknowledgment that the Soviet system was profoundly flawed.[9]

By the time détente was proclaimed in the early 1970s, Sakharov was sufficiently skeptical of the good intentions of the Soviet Union to warn repeatedly of the harm détente could cause if the West allowed the Soviet Union to take advantage of it. He always made a distinction between genuine détente, one that served the interests of peace, and a fraudulent détente that merely advanced Soviet interests. For Sakharov, a fraudulent détente was one in which the West would confer on the Soviets all the economic benefits they desired—credits, technical expertise, and investment—while ignoring violations of human rights and efforts to seek political and military advantage abroad. In foreign affairs the Soviets would continue the Cold War as if détente had never existed. On détente Sakharov was like a Cassandra, warning the West of the dire consequences of misunderstanding what the Soviets meant by it and what they hoped to gain from it. In October 1973, in response to a letter in *Le Monde* by Samuel Pisar criticizing him for making the democratization of the Soviet Union a prerequisite of Western economic assistance, Sakharov stated that while such assistance should continue as long as the Soviet Union observed the terms of détente, it would not by itself lead to the liberalization of the Soviet system and that Western liberals like Samuel Pisar who thought it would were naïve. According to Sakharov, the only way the Soviet system would reform itself was if Western governments insisted on it. As a first step in this endeavor, Sakharov suggested that the West demand, as a condition of détente, that the Soviets proclaim a general amnesty for political prisoners and issue exit visas to all those who were demanding them: only after the Soviet government had done these things would there exist in the Soviet Union "a new atmosphere, more favorable for the process of détente as well as for the solution of internal social problems which affect all layers of our society."[10] Détente, as Sakharov defined it, required reciprocity. Without it, the Soviets would be emboldened by what they rightly considered Western weakness to use the economic assistance they received from the West to advance their own interests, which would be detrimental to international peace and stability. Should Western governments not hold the Soviets to the promises they made when détente was originally proclaimed in 1972, the Soviets would construe détente as carte blanche to smash the dissidents and to make the Soviet system even more repressive than it already was. In an interview Sakharov gave in August 1973, he spoke eloquently and at length on what a fraudulent and one-sided détente would entail:

Détente without democratization [in the Soviet Union], détente in which the West in effect accepts the Soviet rules of the game, would be dangerous, it would

9. Alexander Gribanov, archivist, conversation with author, June 7, 2001, Sakharov Archives, Brandeis University, Waltham, Mass.

10. Samuel Pisar, "Otkrytoe pis'mo 'Voprosy k akademikiu Sakharovu,' opublikovannoe vo frantsuzskoi gazete 'Le Mond' (September 16, 1973)," reprinted in *Sobranie* 25 (Munich, 1977), AS1483-a: 4–8; "Text of the Sakharov Reply to Lawyer," *New York Times*, October 8, 1973, 4.

not really solve any of the world's problems and would simply mean capitulating in the face of real or exaggerated Soviet power. It would mean trading with the Soviet Union, buying its gas and oil, while ignoring other aspects. I think such a development would be dangerous because it would contaminate the whole world with the anti-democratic peculiarities of Soviet society, it would enable the Soviet Union to bypass problems it cannot resolve on its own and to concentrate on accumulating still further strength. As a result, the world would become helpless before this uncontrollable bureaucratic machine. I think that if détente were to proceed totally without qualifications, on Soviet terms, it would pose a serious threat to the world as a whole. It would mean cultivating a closed country where anything that happens may be shielded from outside eyes, a country wearing a mask that hides its true face.[11]

For détente to be real, the Soviets would have to stop viewing it as an opportunity to advance their own interests and consider it instead an end in itself.

In the 1970s Sakharov tried to define the policies Western governments should pursue to ensure that the Soviet Union complied with the agreements on which the continued existence of détente ultimately depended, principally the 1972 agreement on Soviet-American relations and, in 1975, the Helsinki Accords, which ratified the de facto division of Europe since 1945 into Soviet and Western spheres of influence. Sakharov thought the West was right to pressure the Soviets to comply with these documents, but he did not consider all forms of pressure acceptable. Some he rejected on ethical grounds; others he advised against because he believed they were counterproductive. In an interview he gave to *Newsweek* in February 1977, Sakharov indicated that "a partial boycott of scientific and cultural contacts" and "a partial cutback in the supply of certain types of technology" were not only acceptable but essential should the Soviets continue to violate the agreements they had signed.[12] However, he ruled out as morally unacceptable a refusal to sell grain to the Soviet Union and, more generally, using humanitarian aid as a form of political leverage. In addition, Sakharov argued that a complete cessation of Western assistance might cause the Soviets to conclude that détente was no longer worth pursuing—with the result that the leverage the West possessed as a result of détente would disappear. Sakharov recognized that the West had to consider carefully how far it could push the Soviets. Too little pressure would embolden them to ignore the constraints détente imposed, but too much pressure might cause them to repudiate détente entirely. Moreover, there were limits on the methods the West could use in this endeavor. Sakharov was certainly mindful of the Soviets' vulnerabilities, of how much they needed Western scientific and technological expertise, and of the degree to which they would be willing to behave differently if the West were to threaten seriously to withhold this expertise. He also believed, pace Kissinger, that sometimes public pressure could yield better results than private diplomacy. But he emphatically ruled out public threats and ultimatums on

---

11. Quoted in Smith, *Russians,* 594.
12. Andrei Sakharov, Interview, *Newsweek,* February 24, 1977, reprinted in Andrei D. Sakharov, *Alarm and Hope* (New York, 1978), 25.

the grounds that such tactics would force the Soviets into a corner, where they would have no choice, because their honor was at stake, but to repudiate concessions to which they might otherwise agree.[13]

Sakharov shrewdly recognized that the leverage détente conferred on the West carried with it dangers as well as possibilities. Properly exercised, this leverage was potentially advantageous. He could even imagine its leading eventually to the democratization and liberalization of the Soviet Union. Where he disagreed with Pisar and other advocates of what he considered a one-sided détente was in insisting that economic aid and technological assistance be accompanied by demands that the Soviets respect human rights; unless this happened, the Soviet Union would never liberalize or democratize. These processes, which Sakharov previously had considered inevitable and inherent in history, he now realized were not automatic. Someone had to advocate them and insist on them if they were to occur. And since the dissidents were neither numerous enough nor influential enough to do this, others—principally individuals, organizations, and governments in the West—would have to do it for them. But these surrogates for the dissidents would have to be careful that the pressure they exerted on the Soviets was not so great as to cause them to conclude that détente was not in their interest and therefore reject it entirely. Then the Soviet Union would become economically autarchic, its people suffering from shortages far greater than those that presently existed. Without the rewards for good behavior that détente implied, Soviet foreign policy would become even more bellicose. For these reasons, Sakharov often cautioned that any suspension of scientific contacts the West might impose on the Soviets for their bad behavior should always be temporary. In an interview he gave to the *Guardian Weekly* in August 1978, for example, he argued that while "temporary and partial suspension" of contacts was an effective way of showing the Soviets that "détente [was] inseparable from respect for human rights," making this suspension permanent would reduce "the contacts between people, including scientists from different countries" that contributed to the mutual confidence among nations on which international peace ultimately depended.[14]

Sakharov believed that, despite its requirements for good behavior, détente was in the Soviet Union's best interests and that the Soviet leaders, despite their moral degradation, were still rational enough to recognize this. It was precisely for this reason that he believed Western pressure on the Soviet leaders to treat the Soviet dissidents and the Soviet people more humanely would be effective and was justified morally. While Sakharov believed that foreign governments and individuals had no right to intervene in the purely economic affairs of other countries, he believed they had the right, even the obligation, to do so when human rights were violated.[15] That is why he supported Jackson-Vanik in 1973–1974 and why, in his September 1973 letter to the Congress expressing

---

13. Andrei Sakharov, "The Human Rights Movement in the USSR and Eastern Europe: Its Goals, Significance, and Difficulties (November 8, 1978)," in Babyonyshev, *On Sakharov*, 257–58.

14. Andrei Sakharov, "Human Rights Struggle Will Continue," 15.

15. Sakharov, *Memoirs*, 431.

his support of it, he described the amendment as a model of the correct response to the Soviet Union when it violated the human rights of its citizens.[16]
But Sakharov justified this pressure not simply as a matter of principle. It was
also essential because under the circumstances imposed by détente—or more
precisely by the Soviets' economic deficiencies and their interest in rectifying
them—it was likely to be effective. As a result of it, the moral health of the Soviet
Union might be appreciably improved and the general sum of happiness in the
country increased.

For Sakharov, détente entailed a genuine, if mostly tacit, alliance between the
dissidents and Western governments. Working together, they were likely to have
more effect on the Soviets than if Western governments were to absolve themselves of all responsibility for human rights and leave the dissidents to confront
the Soviets alone, as they had done before détente existed. So crucial was this
alliance, in Sakharov's scheme of things, to the survival of Soviet dissidence and
the reform of the Soviet Union that in 1975 he practically equated détente with
Western governments' adopting the dissidents' agenda: "To some extent it is
being decided right now whether détente is to be a comprehensive, in-depth
process of historic significance involving the democratization of Soviet society
and making it more open, or whether it is to be a cynical political game serving some persons' local and temporary political and economic interests, while
in reality constituting a plot behind the backs of peoples, and capitulation to
Soviet pressure and blackmail."[17] Because by 1975 Sakharov no longer believed
the dissidents by themselves could reform the Soviet Union, he had no choice
but to believe that Western pressure, added to whatever pressure the dissidents
could still muster, would yield the desired result. If it was true that only the dissidents could tell the West what the Soviet Union was really like, it was also true
that only the West could extricate the dissidents from the oblivion to which the
Soviet authorities were seeking to consign them. Sakharov desperately wanted
help from Western governments and elites, and never dismissed them, as Solzhenitsyn did, as unconscionable hypocrites.[18]

For Sakharov, what was at stake was more than merely the dissidents' survival
and safety or even the introduction and preservation of human rights in the
Soviet Union. The success of détente was a prerequisite for convergence itself.
In a message to the AFL-CIO convention in Los Angeles in November 1977, Sakharov described starkly how critical the success of détente was to the eventual
merger of capitalist and socialist societies:

> Détente is not only the attempt, through establishing contacts, trade, and tech-
> nological and cultural ties, to weaken the threat of universal destruction. It is
> also the complex, many-sided antagonism of two systems against each other, at
> the basis of which lies the contradiction between totalitarianism and democracy,

16. Andrei Sakharov, "A Letter to the Congress of the United States (September 14, 1973)," 213.
17. Andrei D. Sakharov, *My Country and the World* (New York, 1975), 56.
18. Sakharov, introduction to *Sakharov Speaks,* 52–53.

between violations of human rights and their observance, between the striving to close society and the striving to open it. On the outcome of this struggle depends the convergence of our societies—which is the alternative to the collapse of civilization and to general destruction.[19]

This was not a conclusion Sakharov came to in 1977. Four years earlier, in December 1973, he had written no less emphatically, and more succinctly, that convergence was "the only way to the salvation of mankind."[20]

Because so much depended on it, détente obliged the West, and indeed all of humanity, to take up the cause of human rights the dissidents championed. This was the corollary of Sakharov's linking détente and convergence. But his pleas for human rights in the mid-1970s were qualitatively different from those he had issued earlier in the decade. In these later ones there was an urgency and, at times, a despondency entirely missing in *Reflections* and in the other programmatic statements he had issued when he was still confident the Soviet leadership would listen to him. The following was Sakharov's view in January 1974 on the relationship between a fraudulent détente, in which Western pressure on the Soviets was absent, and the persecution of dissidents that détente facilitated: "We do not see any inclination toward liberalization and great openness in our society, toward less power for the KGB and the ideological party leaders.... True détente is not compatible with the persecution of those who, in their attempts to be truthful, try bravely and honestly to justify their convictions in the struggle for social justice, human rights, and genuine world peace."[21] Six months later, in June 1974, in announcing the hunger strike he was initiating to protest the treatment of political prisoners in the Soviet Union, Sakharov juxtaposed the benefits of true détente against the harmful consequences of a fraudulent détente more starkly than he ever had before: "I am for détente, but détente by collusion; détente by capitulation would be a catastrophe, a betrayal of people throughout the world. Genuine détente and a genuine guarantee of security means not just talks between statesmen, but in the first instance contacts, mutual trust and mutual understanding between ordinary citizens."[22]

19. Andrei D. Sakharov, "Speech to the AFL-CIO Convention in Los Angeles (November 28, 1977)," in *Alarm and Hope*, 166.
20. Sakharov, introduction to *Sakharov Speaks*, 54.
21. "Sakharov: Hardliners Gaining Power in Kremlin," *Washington Post*, January 21, 1974, A14.
22. Andrei Sakharov, "Declaration of a Hunger Strike (June 28, 1974)," *Chronicle of Current Events*, no. 32 (July 17, 1974): 96. Sakharov deliberately timed his hunger strike—the first of four he undertook in his lifetime—to coincide with the arrival of President Nixon in the Soviet Union. Nixon arrived on June 27, 1974, and Sakharov began his hunger strike at midnight on June 28–29. Because additional Western media would be in Moscow when Nixon was, Sakharov calculated that his protest would be more widely publicized. In fact, he was interviewed by a television crew trailing Nixon, but the Soviets succeeded in blocking transmission of the interview. Among the political prisoners whose confinement and mistreatment Sakharov hoped his hunger strike would call attention to were Bukovskii, Pliushch, Valentin Moroz, and Igor Ogurtsov. In addition, Bonner was a patient in the Moscow Eye Hospital when Sakharov began his strike, and the refusal of the doctors there to perform the surgery she needed for her glaucoma was an additional reason for Sakharov to resort to a tactic that, while obviously jeopardizing his health, was dramatic enough to interest foreign reporters. But Sakharov states in his memoirs that Bonner's condition was not the

A year and a half later, in December 1975, Sakharov described succinctly what he thought the West, through détente, should seek to accomplish: "Détente is more than ripping the mask off communism. It involves real changes. There must be a very deep liberalization of Soviet society and a breakdown of East-West barriers to create a basis for trust."[23] Finally, in February 1977, Sakharov reiterated the absolute necessity of détente as a means of exerting pressure on the Soviet leadership. It should not be forgotten, he said, "that only détente created the possibility of exerting even minimal influence on both the domestic and foreign policies of the Socialist countries. In the name of détente, they are required to accommodate their actions to universal humanitarian standards. It would be a great misfortune to return to the past."[24]

From Sakharov's strictures on the requirements of détente one can construct the sequence by which he linked humanity's future salvation in convergence to the current treatment of Soviet dissidents. Convergence required trust between nations and the free exchange of ideas and information; trust and the free exchange of ideas and information required that the Soviet Union liberalize and democratize itself; the liberalization and democratization of the Soviet Union required that its leaders observe the human rights of its citizens; and the Soviet Union's observing the human rights of its citizens would begin with restoring the human rights of its dissidents. Still, there were no guarantees this would actually happen. By the mid-1970s Sakharov's faith in the inevitability of convergence, though not in convergence itself, had been gravely shaken. He was now ready to concede, in sharp contrast to what he had previously believed, that history was not inherently progressive. Things could get worse as well as better. Whether life on earth would improve or deteriorate depended not on impersonal laws of nature but on the choices of fallible human beings whose actions determined how, or even whether, humanity would continue to evolve. Should any of the stages leading to convergence fail to emerge for any reason, convergence would remain, whatever its abstract virtues, a mirage, as much a chimera in the history of humanity as the pure communism the Bolsheviks erroneously believed was inevitable.

Like René Cassin, the author of the Universal Declaration of Human Rights, Sakharov saw human rights transcending the relations between states; for this reason he probably shared Cassin's conviction that the declaration was one of *universal* rather than *international* moral principles.[25] For Sakharov, nations as well as individuals were indivisible moral entities and should be treated as such: just as unethical individuals tended to act unethically in nearly every

---

reason for his action. Whatever the truth of the matter, Sakharov ended his hunger strike six days later, on July 4, both because his health had worsened and because he believed it had achieved its objective. Sakharov, *Memoirs*, 411; Coppen, "Public Life of Andrei Sakharov," 91–92.

23. Quoted in James Hoge, "Sakharov Urges West: Keep Pushing Detente," *Los Angeles Times*, December 2, 1975, 7.

24. Sakharov, Interview, *Newsweek*, 25–26.

25. Jeremy Rabkin, "The Legacy of Eleanor Roosevelt: The Promise and Problems of a Universal Declaration of Human Rights," *Weekly Standard*, May 28, 2001, 32.

aspect of their lives, so countries that acted aggressively (which is to say unethically) in their foreign policies tended to violate the human rights of their own people. And since the human rights that countries violated domestically were just as essential to the survival of humanity as the covenants countries violated in their foreign policies, everyone, not just the Soviet dissidents, had an obligation to ensure that these rights were restored in every instance. Not only convergence but the peace of the entire world depended on it. For this reason, the requirement that human beings observe human rights transcended national boundaries, and the plight of the Soviet dissidents should be the concern of everyone. In return, the Soviet dissidents should support human rights, to the extent it was feasible for them to do so, everywhere such rights were in jeopardy.

Sakharov's dissidence transcended the Soviet Union. By the mid-1970s he was truly a citizen of the world, protesting violations of human rights wherever they occurred, certainly wherever his intervention was requested. No political prisoner was too insignificant, no violation of human rights too inconsequential, no denial of human dignity too distant for him to ignore. Everyone, not just the Soviet people, was entitled to human rights, and Sakharov acted as a global defense attorney, with all of humanity his potential clientele. As he stated succinctly in December 1973, the struggle for human rights in the Soviet Union was just a forerunner of "a worldwide movement for the salvation of all mankind."[26] For this reason Sakharov protested violations of human rights in the Soviet Union even more faithfully and persistently than he had before, and the causes he pursued in the early 1970s he supported for the rest of the decade as well: the right of Soviet citizens, whether they be ethnic Germans,[27] Crimean Tatars,[28] or Soviet Jews,[29] to emigrate and to choose their place of residence; the right of religious minorities, such as the Baptists[30] and the Pentecostals,[31] to practice their religion freely; a general amnesty for political prisoners and the abolition of the death penalty;[32] the incarceration and mistreatment of dissidents and

26. Sakharov, introduction to *Sakharov Speaks*, 44.

27. "The Case of the German Residents in Estonia," *Chronicle of Human Rights*, no. 10 (July–August 1974): 11–12.

28. A. D. Sakharov et al., "Obrashchenie k General'nomu Sekretariu OON K. Val'dkhaimu s pros'boi posodeistvovat' vozvrashcheniiu krymskikh tatar na rodinu (January 1974)," in *Sobranie* 12 (Munich, 1974), AS1725: 1–2.

29. Andrei Sakharov et al., "Appeal for Davidovich (1976)," *Chronicle of Current Events*, no. 39 (1978): 198; A. Sakharov, E. Bonner, and V. Maksimov, "Obrashchenie v Mezhdunarodnyi PEN-klub i Evropeiskoe soobshchestvo pisatelei v sviazi s otkazom v razreshenii na vyezd v SShA Aleksandru Galichu (January 16, 1974)," in *Sobranie* 28 (Munich, 1978), AS1546.

30. A. Sakharov et al., "Defense of the Khailo Family," *Chronicle of Current Events*, no. 48 (March 14, 1978): 127.

31. A. Sakharov, "Request on Behalf of Pyotr Vins' Family (January 3, 1978)," *Chronicle of Current Events*, no. 48 (March 15, 1978): 22.

32. Andrei Sakharov, "Message to the 1979 Sakharov Hearings (September 5, 1979)," *Samizdat Bulletin*, no. 78 (October 1979); A. Sakharov, "Otkrytoe obrashchenie (October 24, 1979)," *Khronika tekushchikh sobytii* 54 (November 15, 1979): 137.

others in psychiatric hospitals;[33] the mistreatment of political prisoners in labor camps;[34] and the denial of due process to these prisoners in the course of their being arrested, detained, interrogated, tried, convicted, and sentenced.[35] As he had in the early 1970s, Sakharov still considered the right to emigrate critically important. In 1975, in an interview with a reporter for the *Los Angeles Times*, he expressed his reason for doing so as follows: "All other human rights are predicated upon the basic right of free movement. Only by ensuring this basic right can we correct all the injustices committed against those accused in the Soviet Union."[36] By this time, however, Sakharov had come to recognize that Soviet violations of human rights harmed not just the Soviet people but everyone and thus constituted "a direct threat to international trust and to peaceful relations among states."[37] Since their violation in one part of the world made more likely their violation in other parts of the world, human rights were a seamless web.

As a result, the causes and individuals Sakharov supported in the 1970s comprised a United Nations of the persecuted and the oppressed. Political prisoners in Indonesia;[38] the Kurds in Iraq;[39] victims of the Khmer Rouge in Cambodia;[40] blacks segregated by apartheid in South Africa;[41] dissidents in Yugoslavia,[42] Poland,[43] and Czechoslovakia;[44] and people everywhere who were tortured in plain violation of their human rights[45] were all proper objects of his moral passion. As if to emphasize that human rights were universal rights, Sakharov, in October 1975, called for amnesty for political prisoners not just in the Soviet Union but everywhere.[46] In addition, he often expressed his high regard for organizations, such as Amnesty International, that protested human rights violations in all parts of the world, and he once called on the United Nations to

33. Andrei Sakharov, "In Defense of Leonid Plyushch (October 23, 1975)," *Chronicle of Human Rights*, nos. 17–18 (October–December 1975): 18.

34. Andrei Sakharov et al., "Political Prisoner's Day," *Chronicle of Human Rights*, nos. 17–18 (October–December 1975): 24–25.

35. Andrei Sakharov et al., "V zashchitu Andreia Tverdokhlebova," in *Delo Tverdokhlebova*, ed. Valerii Chalidze (New York, 1976), 97.

36. Quoted in Erno Easterhas, "The Tragic State of Soviet Workers," *Los Angeles Times*, March 19, 1975, 7.

37. "Andrei Sakharov on Emigration (April 22, 1975)," *Chronicle of Human Rights*, no. 15 (May–June 1975): 10.

38. A. Sakharov, "Appeal to General Suharto (April 4, 1974)," *Chronicle of Current Events*, no. 32 (July 17, 1974): 101.

39. Sakharov, *Memoirs*, 414.

40. A. Sakharov, "Predsedateliu PVS SSSR L. I. Brezhnevu," *Khronika tekushchikh sobyti* 54 (November 15, 1979): 137–38.

41. Sakharov, *My Country*, 83.

42. Ibid., v.

43. Sakharov, *Memoirs*, 496–97.

44. Andrei Sakharov et al., "Czechoslovak Trials and Moscow Support," *Chronicle of Human Rights*, no. 36 (October–December 1979): 19; Andrei Sakharov et al., "In Support of Charter 77 (February 12, 1977)," *Chronicle of Human Rights*, no. 25 (January–March 1977): 67.

45. A. D. Sakharov et al., "Obrashchenie k Predsedateliu GA OON s prizyvom zapretit' pytki," *Materialy samizdata*, no. 1/76 (January 16, 1976), AS2451-a: 3.

46. Andrei Sakharov, "Nobel Acceptance Speech (December 11, 1975)," in *Alarm and Hope*, 16–17.

judge severely member states that violated the human rights of their people.[47] For his efforts, Sakharov in 1976 was elected vice president of the International League of Human Rights, an entirely honorific position but one that nonetheless was consistent with the supranational breadth of his concerns.[48] In the late 1970s, Sakharov did what he could to help Westerners sympathetic to the Soviet dissidents hold hearings designed to publicize their plight. From 1975 to 1979 Sakharov Hearings (as they were called) were held in Copenhagen, Rome, and Washington.[49] It was in the address that was read on his behalf at the hearings in Rome in November 1977 that Sakharov made the point that "by defending human rights wherever they are being violated, we protect all humanity and ensure our common future."[50]

In the terminology au courant throughout the Cold War, Sakharov believed strongly in "linkage": that how a country behaved in its domestic affairs was a good indication of how it acted in foreign affairs and that other countries should consider the former as well as the latter in determining their relations with it. In the case of the Soviet Union, linkage meant that other countries, particularly Western ones, should base their relations with it at least partly on how well or how badly the Soviet government protected the human rights of its citizens. In practical terms this meant that other countries should support all those in the Soviet Union who supported human rights—namely, the dissidents.

But Sakharov made an exception, a very significant one, to the linkage he advocated—namely, arms control and the negotiations conducted through most of the 1970s to achieve it. Sakharov's position was a subtle one, and to understand it one must bear in mind the distinction he maintained between arms control negotiations on both nuclear and conventional weapons on the one hand and nuclear disarmament on the other. Nuclear disarmament, he insisted repeatedly, was impossible without the democratization and liberalization of the Soviet system.[51] However, arms control, on which the maintenance of international peace depended until convergence occurred, was of such paramount importance that negotiations to achieve it—that is, to regulate the

---

47. Andrei Sakharov, "Obrashchenie v 'Mezhdunarodnuiu Amnestiiu,' Gen. sekr. Martinu Ennalsu i mezhdunarodnoi obshchestvennosti v zashchitu Andreia Tverdokhlebova i Mikoly Rudenko (April 18, 1975)," *Materialy samizdata*, no. 18/75 (May 2, 1975) AS2129: 1; Sakharov et al., "V zashchitu Zosimova (October 26, 1976)," *Khronika tekushchykh sobytii* 43 (December 31, 1976): 86–87.

48. Babyonyshev, *On Sakharov*, xxvi. Until that year, the organization was called the International League for the Rights of Man.

49. Three days before the Sakharov hearings in Copenhagen began, a delegation of Soviet apparatchiki arrived in the Danish capital to hold hearings of their own to counter the publicity the hearings would generate. Leading the delegation was none other than Alexander Chakovskii, author of the scurrilous attack on Sakharov in *Literaturnaia gazeta* two years earlier. To Chakovskii's acute embarrassment, another member of the delegation, a psychiatrist who sent dissidents to mental hospitals, found himself at the delegation's press conference face-to-face with one of these dissidents, who promptly denounced him. Bailey, *Making of Andrei Sakharov*, 333–34.

50. Andrei Sakharov, "Address to the Second Sakharov Hearing (October 30, 1977)," in *Alarm and Hope*, 132.

51. In 1975 Sakharov declared nuclear disarmament "impossible without changes in the nature of the Soviet system." Sakharov, "Why I Speak Out Alone," 19.

increase in nuclear arsenals or to stabilize them without necessarily reducing
them—should continue regardless of how the Soviet Union behaved toward its
own people or toward other nations.[52] At first glance, Sakharov's position on
arms control appears untenable: if the Soviet Union behaved badly toward its
own people, how could it be trusted to abide by arms control agreements—any
more than it could be trusted, for example, to exercise restraint in its political
relations with the United States? What good, after all, were arms control agreements if the Soviet Union was likely to violate them?

Sakharov's response, which can gleaned from what he wrote about arms
control in the 1970s, was threefold. First, Soviet leaders were rational enough
to understand that arms control was in their own interest and in the interest
of the Soviet Union. Second, if for some reason they did not recognize this,
then the economic and other pressures real détente would exert would force
them to negotiate arms control agreements anyway. Third, the democratization
produced by real détente would cause them to negotiate even if neither of the
other two factors did. In any case, nuclear disarmament would be a concomitant
of convergence, and if arms control for some reason had not occurred before
convergence, the need for it once convergence occurred would be moot. The
problem with Sakharov's scenario, of course, was that while arms control might
in fact have been in the interests of the Soviet Union in the 1970s, the Soviet
leadership did not share that assessment and sought nuclear parity with the
United States instead. Additionally, since Sakharov no longer believed in the
inevitability of convergence, it was entirely possible, given his linkage of convergence and disarmament, that while arms control agreements (which did not
require convergence as a precondition) might be signed, disarmament itself
might never occur.

This, at any rate, was how Sakharov viewed the complex relationship between human rights in the Soviet Union, arms control, disarmament, and convergence. Because each of these elements was linked in some fashion to every
other one, Soviet violations of human rights effectively precluded international
peace in either the present or the future. To no one's surprise, the Soviet government emphatically rejected the teleology Sakharov predicted and rarely lost
an opportunity to denigrate him personally for it. In September 1973, an article
in *Kommunist* that criticized him for his attacks on the Soviet Union condemned
convergence as an alien concept no different from that of "bourgeois ideologues
in the West such as Walt Rostow and Raymond Aron." The article also expressed
dismay that someone who had constructed thermonuclear weapons should now
advocate policies detrimental to the "relaxation of tensions" to which the Soviet
Union was committed.[53] In 1975, Igor Kon, in *Filosofskaia entsiklopediia*, without
naming Sakharov explicitly, included convergence among the "antiscientific
corruptions permeated with the spirit of anticommunism."[54] And in 1976 Iurii

---

52. Andrei Sakharov, "Alarm and Hope (1977)," in *Alarm and Hope,* 109. In the essay, Sakharov
states that arms control negotiations should have "absolute priority." Ibid.
53. "Mezhdunarodnye otnosheniia i ideologicheskaia bor'ba," 215–16.
54. Igor Kon, "Sotsiologiia," *Filosofskaia entsiklopediia,* vol. 5 (Moscow, 1970), 92.

Andropov bluntly called the Soviet physicist "domestic enemy number one."[55] More serious and substantive criticisms came from Roi Medvedev. In his 1975 treatise, *On Socialist Democracy,* Medvedev argued that democratization in the Soviet Union would come about not from Western pressure and certainly not from anything the dissidents did but from the modernization Russia would undergo in accordance with universal and irreversible laws of historical development. According to Medvedev, not détente, not human rights, not convergence, but rather modernization would cure the Soviet Union of its ills.[56]

## My Country and the World

The changes that occurred in Sakharov's views in the 1970s can be seen most clearly in the lengthy essay he wrote in the first six months of 1975, despite cardiac problems that made writing very difficult for him.[57] The essay is titled in English *My Country and the World.* Although it originated in conversations he had in late 1974 with Senator James Buckley and a group of American scientists led by Wolfgang Panovsky, it addressed topics Sakharov and his interlocutors had not discussed.[58] *My Country* (as the essay will henceforth be referred to) made clear the changes in Sakharov's thinking since *Reflections,* of which it was in many ways a corrective. In comparison with the earlier work, *My Country* is more realistic in its estimation of the changes the Soviet system required and far more pessimistic about the chances that the Soviet leadership would make these changes in the absence of external pressure from the West. *My Country* bluntly describes the Soviet Union as a real and immediate threat to global peace and stability, and the urgency with which Sakharov calls for this threat to be recognized and countered makes the essay as much a plaintive plea for help as a piece of political analysis. In *My Country* Sakharov emphatically rejects the "optimistic futurology" he admits marred *Reflections;* moreover, while he reiterates his idée fixe that convergence is the only permanent solution to everything that ails humanity, he acknowledges that those who desire convergence cannot count on its appearing automatically. If convergence is to occur, hard work, dedication, and a hard-nosed acknowledgment of human frailty are required. Far more than in *Reflections,* Sakharov is interested in *My Country* in exposing "the illusions" about the Soviet Union and socialism to which people both in the Soviet Union and in the West are still prone.[59] Indeed, the various arguments Sakharov advances in the essay seem to suggest that the optimism in Western liberalism and in the rationalist tradition in Western Civilization of which this liberalism is a prominent expression may be unwarranted.

What is perhaps most striking about Sakharov's critique of the Soviet Union in *My Country* is his calling it "totalitarian."[60] He does not explain in the essay

---

55. Oleg Kalugin, *The First Directorate: My 32 Years in Intelligence and Espionage against the West* (New York, 1994), 261–62.
56. Medvedev, *On Socialist Democracy.*
57. Sakharov, *Memoirs,* 424.
58. Ibid., 424, Bonner, "Chetyre daty," 176.
59. Sakharov, *My Country,* 5.
60. Ibid., vi, 64, 90, 92, 103, 108.

how totalitarian regimes like the Nazi and the Soviet differ from traditional authoritarian ones. Nor does he explain, more fundamentally, what totalitarianism actually is. In *My Country,* he uses the term primarily as a pejorative, even as an epithet, to express his disgust with the Soviet Union; for Sakharov, calling the Soviet Union totalitarian is a way of signaling his realization that Soviet Communism is far worse than he ever imagined. In *My Country* there is none of the moral equivalence he posited in *Reflections* between the United States and the Soviet Union. In the later work, the Soviet Union is clearly evil, and one senses that one of the reasons Sakharov wrote the essay was to impress this central fact on all those in the Soviet Union and the West who still refused to accept it. But at the same time that Sakharov denounces the Soviet Union for its totalitarianism, he reiterates his commitment to peaceful and nonviolent change—without considering that totalitarian regimes by definition can change only through violence and only if the violence is applied by other, even more powerful ones.[61]

In *My Country* Sakharov reiterates the same desiderata of domestic reforms he had been advocating for nearly a decade—amnesty, democratization, due process, freedom of speech, and unfettered emigration. He also repeats his call for committees of experts under the aegis of the United Nations to issue reports on various social, legal, and political issues.[62] As he did in the Stenholm interview, he calls flatly and unequivocally for a multiparty system on the grounds that the monopoly of power the Communist Party enjoys makes people "hypocrites, timeservers, mediocre, and stupidly self-deceiving."[63] The bogus elections in which party hacks receive 99 percent of the votes are "an insult to common sense and human dignity."[64] But Sakharov says nothing about the parties that would participate in such a system, leaving the reader with the distinct impression that they would resemble the fairly monolithic interest groups with limited objectives characteristic of Soviet society rather than the sprawling and often amorphous conglomeration of competing constituencies that define political parties in the West.[65] The only admonition Sakharov offers in other writings of his about how the parties in a multiparty system should be organized is a negative one: they should not be organized territorially (because the problems the Soviet Union faces are systemic) or on the basis of ethnicity (because ethnic tensions in the country are so combustible).[66] But on how these parties should be organized he is silent.

To be sure, Sakharov addressed issues in *My Country* on which he had not previously taken a position. For example, he affirmed the right of the constituent republics of the Soviet Union to secede; and while he believed at the time that secession was neither practical nor necessary, the Soviet authorities, not surprisingly, claimed that by sanctioning secession, he was effectively advocating

61. Ibid., 102.
62. Ibid., 101, 104, 106–7.
63. Ibid., 30.
64. Ibid.
65. Kelley, *Solzhenitsyn-Sakharov Dialogue,* 140.
66. Ibid.

the dissolution of the Soviet Union.[67] Obviously, because under socialism ethnic tensions were supposed to have disappeared, the whole issue of secession, which implied that these tensions still existed, was a sensitive one for the Soviets, and Sakharov's addressing secession, regardless of how tentatively he did so, was bound to infuriate them.

In *My Country* Sakharov advocated for the first time the partial denationalization of the Soviet economy. By this he meant something similar to the New Economic Policy (NEP) Lenin adopted in 1921 to repair the damage World War I, the civil war, and the Bolsheviks themselves with their policy of war communism had caused to Russia's economy. Heavy industry and the principal agencies of transportation and communication were the only aspects of the economy Sakharov excluded from the denationalization he advocated (in much the way that Lenin excluded the same sectors of the Soviet economy a half-century earlier). Even these, he acknowledged, might be placed eventually under private ownership. In agriculture, Sakharov called for "partial decollectivization"—without indicating what he meant by that—and for "government encouragement of the private sector as the most productive and the one best able to help restore social and psychological health to the rural areas, now under the threat of a complete lapse into drunkenness and torpor."[68] As he had been when he wrote the Postscript and spoke to Stenholm, Sakharov in *My Country* was sensitive to the toll Soviet Communism had taken on the spiritual sensibilities and material condition of the Russian people.

In what he advocated for the Soviet economy, Sakharov anticipated an outcome that was the exact opposite of Lenin's after announcing the NEP: whereas Lenin believed that the socialist sector of the Soviet economy would outperform and eventually absorb the capitalist sector the NEP permitted, Sakharov was fairly sure the reverse would occur. In his view, the newly permitted capitalist sector would outperform the socialist sector and possibly even absorb it; for Sakharov this was part and parcel of convergence. For this reason Bonner was right when she commented in 1998 that in *My Country* Sakharov disavowed not merely socialism but also Socialism with a Human Face—the slogan coined during the Prague Spring in 1968, which suggested that a humane socialism, as distinguished from Soviet socialism, was both desirable and attainable.[69] As Sakharov acknowledged explicitly in the essay, the political power socialism concentrated in the state made even a humane socialism, one that would reward individual initiative and protect human rights, extraordinarily difficult if not impossible to create and sustain.[70]

As its title suggests, Sakharov's essay was addressed as much to Western governments and public opinion as it was to the Soviet government and people.

67. Sakharov, *My Country*, 102; Sakharov, *Memoirs*, 431.

68. Sakharov, *My Country*, 100.

69. Elena Bonner, "Pochta Sakharova v sviazi s 'Razmyshleniiami…'," *Razmyshleniia o progresse, mirnom sosushchestvovanii i intellektual'noi svobode: Materialy konferentsii*, 79.

70. Sakharov, *My Country*, 91–92.

There is no mention in *My Country,* as there was in *Reflections,* of pursuing a constructive dialogue with the Soviet leadership. Instead, Sakharov stressed the role the West could play in the Soviet Union's reform—provided that Western elites no longer excused, denied, or minimized Soviet malevolence at home and abroad. Just when Soviet surrogates in Indochina (the North Vietnamese), the Middle East (Arab dictatorships), and Latin America (the Castro regime in Cuba) were repressing their own people and acting aggressively abroad, Western intellectuals—whether out of ignorance, lack of imagination, communist propaganda, or simply a penchant for simple and easy solutions—were professing themselves either agnostic on Soviet Communism or explicitly in favor of it, despite the fact that Soviet totalitarianism, like all forms of totalitarianism, was inherently expansionist.[71] To remain in power, Sakharov insisted, Soviet leaders had to invent or exaggerate a foreign threat, which they cited to justify their own aggression and expansionism. And it was precisely this expansionism that Western intellectuals, in their moral obtuseness and willful ignorance, had chosen to ignore. Sakharov's charge in *My Country* that Western intellectuals had sacrificed truth and moral principle on the altar of their ideological predilections was reminiscent of the 1909 critique of the Russian intelligentsia in *Vekhi,* a collection of essays by seven prominent intellectuals. Though previously sympathetic to the intelligentsia, they subjected it to withering criticism based in some cases on Russian Orthodoxy and in others on secular ideologies such as neo-Kantianism.[72] There is, however, a significant difference between the two critiques: whereas *Vekhi* condemned the intelligentsia for its excessive rationality and corresponding lack of spirituality, Sakharov ascribed all that was wrong with Western intellectuals to an insufficiency, rather than an excess, of reason. Far from being the cause of their moral and intellectual degeneration, reason, as a means of ascertaining moral principles, was precisely what these Western intellectuals needed.[73] Unlike the *Vekhi* group (and Solzhenitsyn as well), Sakharov believed that reason and moral improvement were mutually reinforcing.

Once Western intellectuals recovered the rationality they had lost, they would recognize the truthfulness of what Sakharov and the dissidents were saying about the Soviet Union and then pressure it to respect the human rights of its citizens. This, at any rate, was Sakharov's expectation, and he clearly hoped that *My Country,* in its own small way, would assist in this global renaissance of Western rationalism he desired. More than in *Reflections,* Sakharov expressed in *My Country* his moral universalism, his belief that in the final analysis human rights must be defended everywhere to exist anywhere, and that violations of human rights in one country threatened those rights in all countries.[74]

---

71. Ibid., 75–98.

72. *Vekhi: Landmarks,* ed. Marshall S. Shatz and Judith E. Zimmerman (Armonk, N.Y., 1994).

73. The irrationality Sakharov bemoaned in Western intellectuals manifested itself most clearly, in his opinion, in their inability "to evaluate critically" what they knew about the Soviet Union. Sakharov, *My Country,* 87.

74. Ibid., iv.

*My Country* was not just a theoretical exegesis of moral first principles. It also contained practical recommendations Sakharov thought the West should follow. For example, it called upon the West to be proactive in deterring human rights abuses in the Soviet Union by making clear the price the Soviets would pay for committing them; in that way, the number of abuses the Soviets committed would most likely be fewer and perhaps also less serious. At the same time, he made clear that he considered actions in Soviet foreign policy just as violative of human rights—in particular the right of every person to live in a peaceful world—as anything the Soviet Union did to its own people. Once again, Sakharov, unlike Henry Kissinger and other practitioners of realpolitik, made no distinction between Soviet domestic policy and Soviet foreign policy. Both were morally deficient because both were destructive of human rights. As for the latter, its victims numbered literally in the millions. But Sakharov was not so consumed by sentimentality to the point where he absolved all the victims of injustice in the world of responsibility for improving their own situation. In contrast to *Reflections,* in which the people of the Third World were described as the beneficiaries, rather than the agents, of their own liberation and material advancement, in *My Country* Sakharov stated that while the United States and the West should assist Third World people materially, these people could no longer blame all their problems on the two superpowers and expect them to solve them. To improve their own lives Third World peoples would have to take action themselves.[75]

On arms control and disarmament, Sakharov reiterated in *My Country* the distinction he drew in earlier writings between arms control negotiations (which should proceed regardless of Soviet misbehavior either domestically or abroad) and nuclear and thermonuclear disarmament (which required the democratization of the Soviet Union and thus was best served by Western governments and Western elites vigorously protesting Soviet violations of human rights). In short, Sakharov rejected linkage in arms control but embraced it wholeheartedly in disarmament. In fact, by 1975 the arms race had developed such momentum that the weapons the two superpowers possessed conferred hardly more than a temporary advantage, which when dissipated required that even more destructive weapons be built. For this reason it was critical that the arms race be slowed and possibly reversed. As he had in earlier writings, Sakharov rejected ABM systems as destabilizing and very possibly the worst way to try to slow down the arms race. In *My Country,* however, he also proclaimed his opposition to placing Multiple Independently Targetable Reentry Vehicles (MIRVs) on a single missile, which had the effect of dramatically increasing the damage a single missile could do.[76] Sakharov severely criticized the recently concluded agreement in Vladivostok signed by the two nuclear superpowers not only because he believed the ceiling it placed on delivery systems (particularly missiles) was too high but also because the agreement failed to cap their payload, in terms of both megatonnage and the number of warheads they could carry. Vladivostok, in sum, failed to reduce

75. Ibid., 108.
76. Ibid., 108.

the "strategic instability" created by the MIRVing of missiles because the Soviets could MIRV so many of their missiles that they might seriously consider a nuclear first strike. He was much less concerned about the Americans in this regard because he acknowledged their basically peaceful intentions and their recognition that nuclear war was unwinnable. Finally, Vladivostok was deficient because it failed to include adequate means of verification: although surface and underground launchers could be detected by satellites, underwater and mobile launch platforms could not.[77] Although he did not say so explicitly in *My Country,* he probably believed that, for a country like the Soviet Union, only on-site inspections by American or UN observers could ensure compliance with the terms of any arms control agreement the Soviets signed.

The concerns Sakharov expressed about arms control negotiations in *My Country* show that he was now far less sanguine about the Soviet Union than he had been when he wrote *Reflections;* the concerns he mentioned also reflect a realism in his view of international relations that was far less evident, and in certain respects altogether absent, in earlier writings. While convergence remained in Sakharov's scheme of things the deus ex machina that would make everything right in the world, in *My Country* he placed its emergence sufficiently far into the future that it no longer obscured his judgment about what he and the other dissidents could hope to accomplish in the Soviet Union in the weeks and months to come.

# 17 Nobel Laureate

Sakharov did not confront the Soviet goliath in a vacuum. His ideas and objectives and his sense of what was politically possible were all colored in varying degrees by the circumstances of his personal life. In 1974 and 1975 these were dominated by Bonner's medical problems. In the spring of 1974 her glaucoma worsened, the result, in Sakharov's view, of the thyroidectomy she had undergone in February of that year. Untreated, her affliction would leave her blind. In June Bonner entered the Moscow Eye Hospital for surgery, fully expecting it to be performed once the preoperative procedures were completed. But her doctors procrastinated for an entire month, perhaps on orders from the KGB. In exasperation Bonner finally checked herself out of the hospital, at which point she and Sakharov determined that she should seek treatment abroad.[1]

In August 1974, with her eyesight deteriorating rapidly, Bonner applied for an exit visa. In the Soviet Union this was an extraordinarily laborious process,

---

77. Ibid., 68–71.

1. Sakharov, *Memoirs,* 405, 411.

just as difficult as joining the Communist Party and requiring many of the same testimonials to the applicant's personal probity. Still, Bonner managed to amass the requisite documentation. But after months in which she heard nothing from the visa registration office, she finally learned in April 1975 that her application had been rejected. The reason given was that medical treatment for her particular condition was available in the Soviet Union. Sakharov sought assistance from higher-ups he knew personally, including Keldysh, but they refused to help.[2] In May, after Sakharov and Bonner threatened to go on hunger strikes simultaneously, the authorities suggested a compromise: Bonner could be treated by foreign doctors but only if they came to the Soviet Union. Sakharov and Bonner considered this a ploy to buy time and were convinced that if she agreed to it, she would never receive the treatment she needed. In the next few weeks, foreign protests the couple solicited generated worldwide awareness of Bonner's predicament. Willy Brandt, the West German chancellor, and Queen Juliana of the Netherlands were just a few of the dignitaries who expressed support. Finally, in July 1975, Bonner received the visa she had requested eleven months earlier. Elated, she made plans to leave for Italy, where arrangements had been made for the surgery. Her departure date was August 9.[3]

On that very day, however, the Yankelevichs' son Matvei, now two years old, almost died from convulsions. Bonner and Sakharov surmised that the little boy had been fed poison by a KGB agent who had appeared two days earlier when the little boy was playing in the hallway outside the dacha Sakharov still retained. In his memoirs, Sakharov cites circumstantial evidence—principally a phone call to the hospital where Matvei was taken from someone identifying himself as a doctor and inquiring how "the Yankelevich child" was doing—that suggested foul play.[4] Bonner postponed her departure a week, but just before she was to leave, she received in the mail what she considered yet another form of KGB intimidation: an envelope with a Norwegian postmark containing gruesome photographs of eyes being gouged out of their sockets, slit by knives, or depicted with the image of a skull reflected on them. This time, however, Bonner kept to her schedule, and on September 4, in Siena, Italy, she finally underwent the operation; while not improving Bonner's vision, it prevented for two years further deterioration of it. Predictably, the KGB got word to Sakharov that the operation had failed before he could hear from his wife or her doctors that it had succeeded. For several years afterward at Christmastime, the KGB sent Bonner and Sakharov photographs of automobile accidents, brain surgery, and monkeys whose brains had electrodes planted in them.[5]

2. Ibid., 422–23; Andrei Sakharov, Pis'mo Prezidentu AN SSSR akademiku Keldysh M. V., March 25, 1975, Sakharov Archives, Brandeis University, Waltham, Mass.
3. Sakharov, *Memoirs*, 423, 426. Lourie speculates that the government granted Bonner a visa so that she would be outside the country when the Helsinki Accords were signed on August 1, an occasion she and Sakharov were sure to capitalize on in publicizing the plight of the dissidents. Lourie, *Sakharov*, 268.
4. Sakharov, *Memoirs*, 427–28.
5. Ibid., 428; Tatiana Yankelevich, conversation with author, January 13, 2004.

This kind of harassment, compared with the punishments of which the KGB (not to mention the NKVD in the 1930s) was capable, was fairly petty. But its objective was a serious one: to break Sakharov's will incrementally to the point where he would stop protesting. In fact, its inanity only emboldened him. As a result, the government also went after Bonner, her family (which by now was as much his as hers), and on occasion friends and acquaintances who were not even dissidents. Among these last was the Associated Press correspondent in Moscow, George Krimsky, one of the few Western reporters to become a friend of the couple. For this, the tires of his car were slashed, among other indignities he endured before being expelled from the Soviet Union in early 1977.[6] In the 1970s the KGB engaged in a disinformation campaign against Bonner, planting stories in Western newspapers that she habitually seduced men; in one of these, it was even claimed that she had advised one of her conquests to murder his wife.[7] In addition, in late 1974 Bonner's son, Alexei, was lured to an obscure location in Moscow and beaten by a gang of youths who were either from the KGB or paid off by it.[8]

Other dissidents experienced the same kind of harassment. One of the tactics the KGB used to prevent them from organizing their protests effectively was to schedule political trials to coincide; dissidents like Sakharov could not be in two places simultaneously. An example of this was the trials of Andrei Tverdokhlebov in Moscow and of Mustafa Dzhemilev in Omsk.[9] Both were scheduled to begin on the same day, April 6, 1976. Tverdokhlebov had been a founding member of the HRC, and Sakharov valued him highly as a friend and a colleague, which made the illegality of his arrest a personal affront.[10] But perhaps because Dzhemilev was a Crimean Tatar and on a hunger strike in the labor camp where he was confined when new charges were filed against him, Sakharov opted for Omsk.[11] When, accompanied by Bonner, he arrived in the city, he learned that the KGB had postponed the trial, no doubt deliberately, and Sakharov and Bonner returned to Moscow. To the KGB's astonishment, however, he reappeared with Bonner a week later when the trial finally began—only to be arrested and briefly detained when, along with other protesters, he shoved KGB agents who had shoved him first. According to one account, Sakharov hit a KGB agent in the face after the agent started to drag Bonner away.[12] Virtually the same thing happened in May 1978 at Iurii Orlov's trial in Moscow (which was deliberately timed to coincide with that of the Georgian dissident Zviad

6. Sakharov, *Memoirs*, 459.

7. Andrew and Mitrokhin, *Sword and the Shield*, 326.

8. Sakharov, *Memoirs*, 418.

9. Ibid., 449–50; "Mustapha Dzhemilev Continues His Hunger Strike," *Chronicle of Current Events*, no. 38 (1978): 123–26.

10. Sakharov, "Obrashchenie v 'Mezhdunarodnuiu Amnestiiu,'" 1.

11. "Mustapha Dzhemilev Continues His Hunger Strike," 125.

12. A. P. Lavut, "Na zakrytykh 'otkrytykh' sudakh," in Ivanova, *Andrei Dmitrievich*, 166; Andrei Sakharov, "A Statement (April 17, 1976)," *Chronicle of Human Rights*, no. 20–21 (April–June 1976): 15. In the end, Dzhemilev was convicted and sentenced to two and a half more years of exile in a labor camp. At Sakharov's urging, he ended his hunger strike. Sakharov, *Memoirs*, 451.

Gamsakhurdia in Tiflis), where, in a melee outside the courthouse, Sakharov in the heat of the moment hit a KGB agent. He and Bonner were arrested, fined for "hooliganism," and released.[13] He was not charged with assault, a more serious offense, largely because of his celebrity. But the harassment of Bonner and her children was real, and it frightened them greatly.

Increasingly, Sakharov had to defend Bonner's family the way he defended prisoners and others who were persecuted for their beliefs. Largely because of this, he began to emphasize the suffering the Soviet regime was causing for the relatives of political prisoners as well as for the prisoners themselves.[14] Of course, punishing the families of people it persecuted was nothing new for the Soviet regime. In the case of the Tukhachevskiis, for example, Stalin punished a whole family for the supposed treason of one member of it.[15] Still, when Sakharov saw firsthand how the regime avenged his own dissidence by harassing his family, in the tradition of the intelligentsia he extrapolated from this a concern for all those who were similarly harassed. In June 1974 he even donated the fifty thousand francs he had received for winning the Cino del Duco Prize, given annually in France for humanitarian activities, to establish a fund in Paris for the children of political prisoners.[16]

Estranged from his own children, Sakharov took special pleasure in the birth of Tania's second child, a girl she and her husband, Efrem Yankelevich, named Anya, in September 1975. He experienced the same parental pride when Alexei and Olga Levshina, who had married in November 1974, had a girl, whom they named Katya, in October 1975.[17] But Sakharov was also aware of the troubles his dissidence caused Bonner's children and in-laws—though not so troubled by it that he would cease his activities entirely. It must be said in Sakharov's defense that had he done this, the government, in all likelihood, still would have persecuted him. In fact, had he no longer been a public figure about whose personal safety Western governments and organizations were concerned, the government might have persecuted him and his family anyway, and more severely than it actually did. From Stalin onward, Soviet leaders were known for their long memories and penchant for settling scores with long-standing antagonists.

---

13. Sakharov, *Memoirs*, 482–84; Andrei Sakharov, "Statement (July 20, 1978)," *Chronicle of Human Rights*, no. 31 (July–September 1978): 30. Just before his trial, Gamsakhurdia recanted his dissidence. Remarkably, thirteen years later, just before the collapse of the Soviet Union, he was elected president of the Georgian Republic and retained the office until 1992, when he was driven from power and from Georgia itself in a coup d'état.

14. Sakharov, *Newsweek* interview, in *Alarm and Hope*, 136.

15. Robert Conquest, *The Great Terror: A Reassessment* (New York, 1990), 204–5.

16. Coppen, "Public Life of Andrei Sakharov," 99; A. D. Sakharov, "Statement on Receiving 'Cino del Duca' Prize (September 24, 1974)," *Chronicle of Current Events*, no. 33 (December 10, 1974): 173. The fund should not be confused with the one Solzhenitsyn established, the Russian activities of which were managed by Alexander Ginzburg.

17. Sakharov's younger daughter, Liuba, gave birth to a boy in the spring of 1978. To Sakharov's genuine regret, he would see his new grandson only rarely. Perhaps a measure of his estrangement from his children is that he barely mentions them in his memoirs, and when he does so it is out of sequence chronologically in the narrative. In the case of Liuba he mentions her marriage, which occurred in 1973, in a chapter entitled "1978." Sakharov, *Memoirs*, 482.

One can easily imagine, therefore, how much the announcement on October 9, 1975, that Sakharov had won the Nobel Prize for Peace cheered and invigorated him and reaffirmed his belief that the cause of human rights to which he had given so much of himself was worth pursuing. The prize did not come as a complete surprise to him. After Solzhenitsyn's nomination of Sakharov two years earlier was rejected on a technicality, British and Danish members of parliament had nominated him, and their nominations were accepted and considered by the Nobel Committee.[18] Still, the news was electrifying. Sakharov very quickly proclaimed that his winning was not just a personal triumph but a tribute to the dissident movement generally. In impromptu remarks he made to foreign correspondents shortly after learning of the award, he said that he shared it with "prisoners of conscience in the Soviet Union [who] have sacrificed their most precious possession, their liberty, defending others by open and nonviolent means."[19] Sakharov also told the correspondents that the first words he uttered on hearing the news were "This will help our political prisoners."[20] With some of the $140,000 he received for the award, he established a fund, which Bonner oversaw, to help the children of political prisoners.[21]

Sakharov knew he would not be allowed to go to Oslo to receive the prize. He applied for a visa not because he expected to receive one but because its denial would preclude any uncertainty on the part of the Nobel Committee about his absence at the actual ceremony, then scheduled, as was customary, for December 10.[22] It seemed logical that Bonner, who was in Italy when the prize was announced, should go to Norway and accept it on Sakharov's behalf. Sakharov and Bonner's mother, Ruf, however, were fearful that the Soviet government would revoke Bonner's citizenship if she went to Norway and thought that Alexander Galich, who was also already abroad, should go in her stead. In the end, Sakharov's stepson-in-law, Efrem Yankelevich, convinced him that only Bonner could properly represent him, and she traveled without incident to Oslo on December 8. On December 11 she delivered the Nobel Lecture Sakharov had written.[23]

On that day Sakharov was in Vilnius, attending the trial of Sergei Kovalev, who had been arrested a year earlier and charged with coediting the *Chronicle of Current Events*, which the government now condemned as "libelous"—the first time it had ever done so explicitly.[24] Given Sakharov's belief that he had won the award on behalf of the dissidents, his presence at the trial was appropriate. The only deviation Sakharov permitted himself from his customary procedure of standing vigil outside the courthouse was to break away for a few hours to listen to a radio broadcast of the Nobel ceremony at the home of the Lithuanian dissident Viktoras Petkus.[25] Neither TASS nor Soviet state radio reported Sakharov's award, and

18. Solzhenitsyn, *Oak and the Calf*, 355; Trushnovich, *A. Sakharov*, 257–58.
19. Sakharov, *Memoirs*, 429.
20. "What the Nobel Prize Means, by Sakharov," *Sunday Times* (London), October 12, 1975, 10.
21. Edward Kline, conversation with author, June 10, 2008.
22. Sakharov, *Memoirs*, 431–32.
23. Ibid., 432–33, 438.
24. Rubenstein, *Soviet Dissidents*, 149–50.
25. Sakharov, *Memoirs*, 435.

thus the broadcast Sakharov heard was likely transmitted from Western Europe, from either Oslo or Munich, where Radio Liberty was located.[26]

In his Nobel Lecture, which recipients of the peace prize traditionally delivered after receiving the prize, Sakharov reiterated many of the themes he had stressed in *My Country,* especially the notion that countries that behaved aggressively abroad were bound to violate human rights domestically as well; for that reason, he said, "the defense of human rights [is] the only sure basis for genuine and lasting international cooperation."[27] But Sakharov also made the point that human rights were a prerequisite for secular progress: "Freedom of conscience, together with other civic rights, provides both the basis for scientific progress and a guarantee against its misuse to harm mankind, as well as the basis for economic and social progress, which in turn is a political guarantee making the effective defense of social rights possible."[28] "Peace, progress, and human rights," he claimed, were "indissolubly linked."[29] Achieving any one of these was impossible without achieving the others. Thus for progress to occur, countries had to behave ethically both in their foreign policy (which in practice meant striving for peace) and in their domestic policies (which more than anything else entailed protecting the human rights of their citizens).

Sakharov also stressed in his lecture the personal qualities political leaders needed in order to strive for peace and preserve human rights. Foremost among these was rationality, by which he meant the quality not just of being reasonable, of thinking logically and analytically, but also of recognizing the role reason plays in the advancement of civilization. Reason was the prerequisite of nearly everything in life worth preserving, and progress was possible only if it were "subject to the control of reason."[30] By the time he received the Nobel Prize, Sakharov no longer took man's rationality for granted. At the same time, he had not become so cynical as to consider it nothing more than a convenient fiction people contrived to flatter themselves. At the very least, human beings could use the rational component of their minds to contain the less generous and less altruistic impulses they all possessed. At their best, they could meet successfully what Sakharov succinctly called "the demands of reason."[31]

News of the Nobel Prize rejuvenated not only Sakharov but the dissident movement as a whole. For the dissidents, the prize was a vindication of their struggle for human rights, proof that their efforts, while not forcing changes in the Soviet Union, were at least being recognized and lauded in the West.[32]

26. James O. Jackson, "Russian Dissident Wins Nobel Peace Prize," *Chicago Tribune,* October 10, 1975, 15. The Soviets may have tried Kovalev in Vilnius rather than Moscow to get Sakharov, who they knew would attend the trial, away from the Soviet capital and thus out of reach of Western correspondents there when he won the Nobel Prize. Efrem Yankelevich, "Vspominaia podrobnosti" (unpublished manuscript), 19.

27. Andrei Sakharov, "Nobel Acceptance Speech," 5.

28. Ibid.

29. Ibid., 4.

30. Ibid., 9.

31. Ibid., 18.

32. For example, Andrei Amalrik et al., "Goriacho pozdravliaem Andreia Dmitrievicha Sakharova," *Posev* 11 (November 1975): 5. Although Sakharov was congratulated warmly on the award

Conversely, the Soviet leaders were appalled by what had transpired in Oslo. For them, the Nobel Prize was a public relations disaster, and for Brezhnev, who thought he deserved the award for signing the Helsinki Accords, it was a personal rebuff.[33] The fact that Sakharov was the first Russian to win the peace prize only aggravated the insult. In response, the government began another campaign maligning Sakharov's character, this time by passing statements to Western newspapers depicting the award as the work of those opposed to détente and international peace and by filling the Soviet press with ad hominem denunciations. Like those that appeared in 1973, diatribes signed by luminaries from the literary and scientific elites (but actually written for them by government functionaries) defamed the Soviet physicist in terms that were as venomous as they were ridiculous. To their credit, Kapitsa, Khariton, and Zeldovich all refused to sign one especially egregious piece of invective to which seventy-three members of the Academy of Science had appended their signatures.[34] This time, however, the campaign had undeniable anti-Semitic overtones. Writers acting on the direct orders of the government compared Sakharov's prize money to the thirty pieces of silver Judas had received for betraying Jesus to the Romans.[35] Because Bonner was Jewish and because a disproportionate number of dissidents were Jewish as well, such analogies were innately appealing to the large number of Soviet citizens who considered Jews somehow responsible for all that was wrong in their country. Given the invective that was directed at Bonner's family in this period, Sakharov and Bonner were probably not surprised when Tania's husband, Efrem, lost his job. But they were profoundly shaken a few weeks after the announcement of the prize in October, when a legal consultant from Leningrad, after visiting Sakharov at his dacha, fell to his death from the train on which he was traveling, probably as a result of being pushed, presumably by an agent of the KGB. At least that was how Sakharov and Bonner interpreted the event.[36]

## The Personal Dimension—How Sakharov Lived

To the discomfiture of the authorities, who wanted nothing more than to cause a rift between Sakharov and Bonner, these events in Sakharov's life only solidified their relationship. The circumstances in which the family lived contributed to this as well. In the mid-1970s, Sakharov and Bonner, like most

---

by Roi Medvedev, he heard nothing from Zhores Medvedev, whose comment in 1974 that Sakharov's work on thermonuclear weapons disqualified him for the award clearly rankled Sakharov, as the reference to it in his memoirs makes clear. The Medvedevs—Zhores especially—harbored an intense dislike of Bonner, which they expressed in letters that found their way to her and Sakharov. Sakharov, *Memoirs*, 430; Tatiana Yankelevich, conversation with author, January 13, 2004.

33. Klose, "Andrei Dmitrievich Sakharov," 49; Sagdeev, *Making of a Soviet Scientist*, 254–55.

34. Andrew and Mitrokhin, *Sword and the Shield*, 323; Sagdeev, *Making of a Soviet Scientist*, 246. The petition the three scientists refused to sign appeared in *Izvestiia* on October 25, 1975, and is cited in the *Chronicle of Current Events*, no. 35 (December 31, 1975): 72.

35. Andrew and Mitrokhin, *Sword and the Shield*, 323; Sakharov, *Memoirs*, 431.

36. Sakharov, *Memoirs*, 439–41.

married Russians, lived with extended family. Their two-bedroom apartment at 48B Chkalov Street in Moscow was also home for Ruf Bonner (its original inhabitant), Tania, Efrem, and their children.[37] With only 375 square feet of space, the apartment was barely adequate for two people; for seven it was, by Western standards, unlivable.[38] In February 1977, hoping that Tania and Efrem and their children, who lived elsewhere in Moscow, could join them in a larger apartment, Sakharov formally applied for one. But his request was rejected.[39] The family had no choice, then, but to make the best of it on Chkalov Street. Every morning, the beds were turned into couches, but the plethora of papers and documents Sakharov's activities generated caused the entire apartment to retain the appearance of an office much too small for all the business it attracted.[40] To make matters worse, the apartment was in perpetual need of repairs: a pan was positioned permanently under the single radiator to catch the water that perpetually dripped from it. Skis and ice skates were stored in the tiny bathroom, while in the kitchen, to which Sakharov, in Russian fashion, usually repaired with any guests that arrived, there was an enamel-topped table on which dishes were invariably piled.[41]

Notwithstanding the chauffeured limousine and dacha to which Sakharov, as an academician, still had access, finances were tight. In addition to their living expenses, Sakharov supported his son, Dmitrii, on a regular basis, and his daughters occasionally. He and Bonner supported Alexei and Olga as well.[42] Sakharov's monthly income consisted of the 400 rubles he received as an academician and the 300 rubles he received from the Lebedev Institute. He and Bonner could add to this the 120 rubles Bonner received as an injured war veteran and Ruf's monthly pension of 85 rubles as the wife of a purge victim who had been rehabilitated. Fortunately, Sakharov had no desire to live extravagantly. It was enough for him that the refrigerator was full and that Elena, who was an excellent cook, had on hand the beets he ate for breakfast and the tea with chunks of apples in it that he favored at meals and while conversing with guests.[43] Because he did not like the taste of it, Sakharov drank very little alcohol.[44]

In many ways Sakharov was an eccentric genius, as absentminded and unconcerned about his physical appearance as Einstein had been. Indoors he often wore just a running suit, occasionally with tennis shoes or slippers on his feet, more

37. Ibid., 467; Klose, *Russia and the Russians,* 165–66; Andrei Sakharov, Interview, *France-Soir, February 23, 1977,* reprinted in *Alarm and Hope,* 94–95.

38. Sakharov, *Memoirs,* 467.

39. Ibid., 468.

40. Klose, *Russia and the Russians,* 165–66.

41. Smith, *Russians,* 590.

42. Sakharov, Interview, February 23, 1977," 94–95; Bonner, "Do dnevnik," 33; Tatiana Yankelevich, conversation with author, January 13, 2004.

43. M. A. Vasiliev, "Tri poezdki v Gor'kii," in Altshuler et al., *On mezhdu nami zhil,* 192; Smith, "Intolerable Andrei Sakharov," 43. The apartment Sakharov vacated when he moved into Bonner's mother's apartment in 1971 he left to his daughter Liuba and his son, Dmitrii. Edward Kline, conversation with author, June 10, 2008.

44. Moroz, "Vozvrashchenie iz ssylki," 309.

often with only his socks on.[45] When he wore pants, which were usually baggy, they were held up with suspenders; when he had to put on a tie, it was almost always a clip-on.[46] As in so many other aspects of his life, Bonner was indispensable in minimizing Sakharov's absentmindedness, or at least the effects of it, as much as was humanly possible; she was also successful in persuading her husband to pull a handkerchief, rather than a towel, from his pocket when he needed to wipe something or to blow his nose.[47] But Sakharov's reputation for being sui generis in his personal habits persisted, sustained in part by his remarkable ability—which many who admired him took special pleasure in mentioning—to write equally well with both hands.[48] He was even capable of writing with one hand the mirror image of what he was writing simultaneously with the other hand.[49] In the realm of sports and recreation, Sakharov, the brilliant physicist who designed the Soviet H-bomb and unraveled the mysteries of baryon asymmetry, much preferred checkers to chess because the latter, as he freely acknowledged, was too difficult for him. Uncoordinated physically, he never learned to swim.[50]

Given his political commitments, Sakharov had little time for frivolities or even for the reflection he would have used productively had he remained exclusively or even primarily a physicist. As large numbers of people, not all of them mentally competent, requested his assistance, the telephone in the apartment rang incessantly.[51] In the end he had no choice but to find an assistant, and he was fortunate that Sofia Kalistratova, a lawyer "for whom the fate of the individual was always the most important thing," agreed to help him.[52] Together they determined which of the requests he received deserved his immediate attention: those from political prisoners or their families generally took precedence over those from people who were convicted of ordinary crimes, who could not make ends meet, or who complained that their apartments were too small. Sakharov's limited energy, depleted as it was by his persistent cardiac insufficiency and by the strain of defending himself and his family, forced him to make difficult choices. But wherever possible, he took the cases of people whose problems most insistently tugged at his conscience:

> The vast majority of the letters I received were sent by prisoners or their families.
> It was terrible to read in their letters or to hear directly from visitors tales of

45. Smith, *Russians,* 590; Fred Coleman, *The Decline and Fall of the Soviet Empire: Forty Years That Shook the World from Stalin to Yeltsin* (New York, 1966), 107.

46. Smith, *Russians,* 590. Even the KGB noted Sakharov's dishevelment: "His dress is unusually untidy, he wears old clothes, and his general appearance is one of neglect." "Andropov to Brezhnev (January 18, 1971)," in Rubenstein and Gribanov, *KGB* File, 115.

47. Perelman, "Vstrechi, besedy," 502.

48. Pariiskaia, "On vsegda budet samim soboi," 469; Smirnov, "Etot chelovek," 583; V. F. Diachenko, "Vse bylo vperedi...," in Altshuler et al., *On mezhdu nami zhil,* 293.

49. Gorelik, *World of Andrei Sakharov,* 247. But Tatiana Yankelevich, in a conversation on August 21, 2001, denied Revolt Pimenov's claim that Sakharov could write different things with each hand simultaneously.

50. Smirnov, "Etot chelovek," 580; Takibaev, "Operezhavshii vremia," 623.

51. Peter Osnos, "Too Many Protests," *Washington Post,* January 13, 1975, A9.

52. Sakharov, *Memoirs,* 502.

judicial errors caused by debased legal standard, of bias in trials and investigations, especially towards ex-convicts, of beatings and torture during investigations, of arbitrary brutality in places of detention, of the judiciary's subservience to local party officials and the bureaucracy, and of the futility of appeals to the Procurator's Office or appellate courts, which barricaded themselves behind an endless series of form letters.[53]

Somehow, despite the chaos of his daily life, Sakharov continued his scientific work. As a theoretical physicist, he needed only pen and paper, access to scientific journals, and contact with colleagues—all of which he had—to be productive. Although he had no formal duties at the academy or the institute, not even the government's excision of references to his work in the scientific journals it published dampened his commitment to remaining a productive member of his profession.[54] Under the circumstances, Sakharov's productivity as a physicist was astonishing, and the quality of his work, in the estimation of physicists competent to evaluate it, was consistently outstanding.[55] Among the most provocative and imaginative of his ideas in the 1970s concerned the reversibility of time: the mind-boggling possibility that either at the point of the maximum expansion of the universe or at the point just beyond a black hole called the singularity, at which the laws of physics cease to apply, time, in the ordinary sense of the word, runs backward. At some point in the 1970s, Sakharov even considered the possibility that there are regions in the universe that, in the words of the Soviet physicist A. D. Linde, "differ from each other by the direction of time, by the compactification of spacetime, and by the number of time coordinates."[56] In plain English, Sakharov was speculating that time might not run in the same direction everywhere in the universe.[57]

Sakharov's principal political commitment, of course, remained the preservation and advancement of human rights. Nothing, not even science, and certainly not the harassment he endured from a regime that sought to ruin him morally and politically, could deter him from this. The very chaos of his personal life that Bonner was only partially successful in reducing lends to his struggle a poignancy that in some fashion heightens its moral legitimacy. In David Remnick's pithy phrase, 48B Chkalov Street seemed "the moral center of an immoral empire."[58]

53. Ibid., 504.
54. Hoge, "Sakharov Urges West" 7.
55. The texts of the articles he produced can be found in Sakharov, *Collected Scientific Works*.
56. A. D. Linde, "Inappropriate Questions: Courage or Insanity?" in Drell and Kapitza, *Sakharov Remembered*, 215. Although the article in which Sakharov suggested this appeared in 1980, one can reasonably infer that the work he did on it occurred in the late 1970s. Andrei Sakharov, "Cosmological Models of the Universe with Reversal of Time's Arrow," *JETP* 52 (1980): 349–51, reprinted in Sakharov, *Collected Scientific Works*, 131–36.
57. As Sakharov points out in his memoirs, this did not mean that in a universe with time's arrow reversed, physical processes would run backward as well. Water spilled from a cup, for example, would not return to it. Sakharov, *Memoirs*, 544.
58. David Remnick, "The Missing Man," *New Yorker*, May 21, 2001, 38.

## The Helsinki Accords

Sakharov's Nobel Prize was not the only thing that invigorated the dissidents and gave their cause greater legitimacy. So, too, did the Final Act of the Conference on Security and Cooperation in Europe (referred to informally as the Helsinki Accords), signed by thirty-four countries and the Vatican on August 1, 1975. Politically, the Helsinki Accords were the result of a quid pro quo in which the West formally recognized all of the post-World War II frontiers—thus legitimizing the division of Europe into Western and Soviet spheres of influence—in exchange for the Soviet Union's promising to respect human rights and fundamental freedoms. Because the accords were not a treaty per se and thus not legally binding on their signatories, they lacked any enforcement mechanism; instead they prescribed periodic conferences to report on compliance. Nevertheless, they were considered one of the crowning achievements of détente.[59]

The Helsinki Accords were the first international agreement in which human rights and security issues were addressed in the same document. Among the rights the signatories promised to respect were freedom of speech, religion, and conscience. They also committed themselves to protecting the right of people "to enter or leave their territory temporarily, and on a regular basis if desired, in order to visit members of their families"; toward that end, "the preparation and issue of [travel documents] and visas will be effected within reasonable time limits, [and] cases of urgent necessity—such as serious illness or death—will be given priority treatment."[60] Finally, the accords guaranteed ethnic minorities legal equality and committed their signatories to act in conformity with the Universal Declaration of Human Rights and, for those nations that had ratified them, with the International Covenants on Human Rights.[61] As a result, by signing the Helsinki Accords, the Soviet Union finally committed itself to upholding the Universal Declaration, twenty-seven years after abstaining on the original vote in the United Nations to ratify it.[62]

In what turned out to be a serious miscalculation, the Soviets agreed to these human rights provisos. They did so because they thought they could safely ignore them, believing that Western governments had cynically insisted on them only to placate public opinion in their own countries. In fact, by signing the accords and promising publicly to abide by them, the Soviets thought they would demonstrate their benign intentions to the West and thereby gain a political advantage.[63] But even if the Soviets' expectations were mistaken, de jure recognition of Soviet frontiers and those of its East European satellites, because this implied acceptance of Soviet domination of Eastern Europe, was itself

59. Glendon, *World Made New*, 218.

60. "The Final Act of the Conference on Security and Cooperation in Europe, Aug. 1, 1975, 14 I.L.M. 1292 (Helsinki Declaration)," http://www1.umn.edu/humanrts/osce/basics/finact75.htm.

61. Ibid.

62. Glendon, *World Made New*, 228. As Glendon points out, the Helsinki Accords were the first document on human rights the Soviet Union ever signed.

63. Alexeyeva, *Soviet Dissent*, 335–36. Glendon, *World Made New*, 218.

a significant victory. For this reason the Soviet leadership had the full text of the accords published in *Pravda* and *Izvestiia*.[64]

The Soviets failed to consider the effect the accords would have on the Soviet dissidents, who began to cite them as a way of legitimizing their demand for human rights. By signing the accords, the Soviet Union had obliged itself to uphold its provisos, including those on human rights. As a result, when it violated human rights, both the dissidents and their supporters in the West could claim that the Soviet Union was violating not only its own constitution and laws but an agreement that had the imprimatur of international law. The Helsinki Accords, in other words, legitimized foreign involvement in Soviet domestic affairs; in the area of human rights they eradicated the distinction between foreign affairs and domestic affairs entirely. For the dissidents, the practical benefits of this were enormous. Charging the Soviet Union with violating an international agreement was a far more effective rhetorical device than charging it with violating its own laws. Moreover, by signing the accords the Soviet government had acquiesced in the dissidents' preference for evaluating the Soviet Union on ethical grounds rather than on grounds of economic productivity or material security. But the Helsinki Accords were helpful to the dissidents in yet another and in some respects even more fundamental way. Because they were an international agreement, they implicitly legitimized the dissidents' contention that human rights, because they were universal rights essentially limitless in time and in space, should be applied and protected everywhere. The universalism the accords conferred meant that people everywhere in the world should consider human rights, and also the courageous individuals in the Soviet Union who advocated them, very seriously. Thus the Helsinki Accords underscored the moral seriousness of the whole dissident movement.

The dissidents did what they could to take advantage of the opportunity the Helsinki Accords provided. In May 1976 Iurii Orlov founded the eleven-member Moscow Helsinki Group to monitor Soviet compliance with the accords. In November similar groups were established in Ukraine and Lithuania. Georgians and Armenians formed their own organizations in 1977, Seventh-Day Adventists in 1978, and Pentecostals in 1980.[65] The accords and the campaign to monitor compliance strengthened the often tenuous ties between the dissidents and the religious and ethnic minorities, whose advocates in most cases were concerned only with their own people's interests and rights and no one else's. As a result, the geographical base of the dissidents expanded beyond the cities of Moscow and Leningrad, where to a large degree it had previously been confined.[66] In addition, although Israel discouraged would-be Jewish emigrants (known as refuseniks) from participating in dissident activities, believing these would complicate and possibly even terminate the issuance of exit visas to Israel, the establishment

64. Rubenstein, *Soviet Dissidents*, 221.
65. Sakharov, *Memoirs*, 456; Alexeyeva, *Soviet Dissent*, 17.
66. Alexeyeva, *Soviet Dissent*, 345–46; Daniel C. Thomas, *The Helsinki Effect: International Norms, Human Rights, and the Demise of Communism* (Princeton, 2001), 160–66.

of the Moscow Group in particular facilitated a partial merger of the dissidents and the refuseniks. For the few years it lasted, until arrests in the late 1970s made it impossible to continue, this melding of the two groups, their working in tandem on issues of mutual interest, was beneficial to both. The Moscow Group included not only dissidents such as Grigorenko, Ginzburg, Alexeeva, Malva Landa, and Orlov himself but also refuseniks such as Vitaly Rubin, Iosif Begin, Vladimir Slepak, and Anatolii Sharansky, who served as Sakharov's translator at many of the press conferences the Soviet physicist called in the mid-1970s and whose arrest, trial, and conviction for treason in 1977–1978 became a cause célèbre for both the dissidents and their supporters in the West.[67]

This alliance was not without its tensions and disagreements. The dissidents and the refuseniks had different, even opposite, objectives: whereas the dissidents wanted to reform the Soviet Union, the refuseniks, by definition, wanted to leave it. But the dissidents wholeheartedly supported the right of the refuseniks to do this, and the refuseniks' ability to educate Western opinion about their predicament was undoubtedly strengthened by the working relationship the two groups had established. Although the Moscow Group did not attempt to report all injustices that occurred in the Soviet Union, it did produce copious reports of human rights violations in that country, including violations of the right to emigrate, that it sent to foreign organizations like Amnesty International and to the conferences that convened to monitor compliance with the Helsinki Accords.[68]

As has already been noted, Sakharov did not join the Moscow Helsinki Group. But he and Bonner hosted the press conference at which Orlov announced the group's creation, and they allowed it to meet at their apartment because of the relative security their presence afforded against arrest.[69] More important, Sakharov never considered his not joining the group an impediment to his using the accords as a petard with which to hoist the Soviet leadership. Repeatedly Sakharov called its mistreatment of political prisoners and denial of human rights blatant violations of the Helsinki Accords.[70] In March 1978, for example, after calling the charge of espionage against Sharansky itself a violation of the Helsinki Accords, he condemned the Soviets for acting in the entire matter not only brutally and unethically but also hypocritically.[71] On another occasion, while acknowledging the value of the Belgrade Conference—the first

67. Rubenstein, *Soviet Dissidents*, 218; Alexeyeva, *Soviet Dissent*, 187–88; Sharansky, *Fear No Evil* (New York, 1988), xxi.

68. Rubenstein, *Soviet Dissidents*, 218, 228.

69. Sakharov, *Memoirs*, 456–57. L. B. Litinskii, "Ob A. D. Sakharove i vokrug," in Altshuler et al., *On mezhdu nami zhil*, 406. Bonner, however, was a founding member, and as time passed and members were arrested, she assumed a leadership role. Edward Kline, conversation with author, June 10, 2008.

70. A. Sakharov, M. Landa, E. Bonner, and T. Khodorovich, "100-dnevnaia golodovka politzakliuchennykh mordovskikh lagerei-trebovanie statusa politzakliuchennogo (April 21, 1977)," *Khronika tekushchikh sobytii*, no. 45 (May 25, 1977): 47.

71. A. Sakharov, "Statement in Defense of A. Sharansky (March 8, 1978)," *Chronicle of Current Events*, no. 48 (March 14, 1978): 14.

of several conferences in the late 1970s and 1980s to monitor compliance with the accords—as a means of raising public consciousness in the West about the plight of Soviet dissidents, he also criticized the conference for not citing many instances of noncompliance of which the Soviets were guilty.[72] Indeed, Sakharov vigorously condemned as a violation of the accords the Soviets' suppression of the various Helsinki Watch Groups (as they were often referred to) that were created in the Soviet Union to monitor Soviet compliance with the accords.[73]

For his efforts, the KGB exacted its revenge. In September 1977, even before the Belgrade Conference convened, Sakharov's car was vandalized, its radiator punctured, and its locks immobilized by glue that was poured over them, almost certainly by KGB agents.[74] By this time, Sakharov and Bonner had determined that Bonner's children and their spouses were in danger of reprisals far more injurious than punctured radiators and sticky car locks and that they should therefore leave the Soviet Union as quickly as possible. Tania and Efrem, they believed, might even be prosecuted criminally. To their surprise, Tania and Efrem received exit visas shortly after requesting them; evidently the KGB had reassessed its tactics and concluded that the two of them were less useful to Sakharov safely abroad than they would be as martyrs to his struggle inside the country. Because Bonner needed more surgery, this time on her right eye, and had received an exit visa herself, she, Tania, Efrem, and the couple's two children all left the following month for Italy, where Bonner's operation was performed, while the Yankeleviches continued on to the United States, establishing residence in Newton, Massachusetts, near Boston.[75] Their emigration, however, left Alexei dangerously exposed. In the fall of 1977 he was expelled from the Teachers' Institute in which he was enrolled and was thus liable for induction into the military, where, invisible to Western reporters, he could be mistreated, perhaps egregiously. In light of this, Sakharov and Bonner thought it best that Alexei, too, go abroad. The plan was for Alexei, Olga, and their daughter to leave together for Israel after Sakharov secured from the Israeli government an invitation to establish residence there. But in December 1977 the couple separated. In March 1978, Alexei therefore left the Soviet Union alone, leaving behind not only Olga, whom he promised he would wait a full year before divorcing, but also a classmate of his at the institute, Liza Alexeeva, with whom he had fallen in love. Her request for the visa she needed to join Alexei in Israel the KGB, with its customary cruelty and petty sadism, refused to grant. Alexei then enrolled as a graduate student in mathematics at Brandeis University in Waltham, Massachusetts, near Tania.[76] Sakharov would do what he could over the next several years to help Liza receive a visa, and his efforts on her behalf would exact an enormous toll on his time, energy, and physical health.

72. A. Sakharov, "About the Belgrade Conference (March 9, 1978)," ibid., 174–75.
73. Sakharov, "Statement in Defense of A. Sharansky," 14.
74. Sakharov, *Memoirs*, 474–75.
75. Ibid., 472–74.
76. Ibid., 477–78, 482.

## Sakharov and Carter

The other development, in addition to the Nobel Prize and the Helsinki Accords, that encouraged Sakharov and raised his spirits, if only temporarily, in the mid-1970's was the so-called Human Rights Campaign President Carter pursued after his inauguration in January 1977. Carter's campaign came at a particularly inauspicious time for dissidents. On January 8, an explosion in a Moscow subway car had killed seven people and left forty-four others injured.[77] Normally the Soviet government did not publicize such breaches of public security. This time, however, the government carried news of the explosion in the Soviet press, albeit minimizing the number of casualties. In addition, there appeared on January 10 in the *Evening News* of London an article by Viktor Louis, a Soviet journalist with KGB connections, citing unnamed Soviet sources blaming Soviet dissidents for the explosion, which Louis claimed was the result of a bomb.[78] Sakharov, who immediately thought the KGB might have set the explosion as a provocation, considered Louis's article, when he got wind of it, a way of justifying yet another wave of repression of Soviet dissidents. The searches the police conducted concurrently of members of the Moscow Helsinki Group strengthened his suspicion.[79]

Prior to the explosion, Sakharov had sent to Carter an appeal on behalf of a Soviet citizen, Piotr Ruban, who had made a wooden book cover commemorating the American Bicentennial and depicting the Statue of Liberty. For this he was tried and convicted of stealing state property and private enterprise.[80] The previous October, before Carter was elected, Sakharov had appealed to him and President Ford, his opponent in the election, to uphold human rights globally.[81] Possibly in response to this, Carter sent a telegram to the refusenik Vladimir Slepak expressing support for his right to leave the Soviet Union.[82] Still, Sakharov must have been pleasantly surprised when, in his inaugural address on January 20, the new president proclaimed his commitment to human rights and

77. Alexeyeva, *Soviet Dissent*, 128–30.

78. Andrei Sakharov, "Statement on Moscow Bomb (January 12, 1977)," in *Alarm and Hope*, 59. Who actually caused the explosion has never been determined conclusively. Three Armenian nationalists—Stepan Zatikian, Akop Stepanion, and Zaven Bagdasarian—were arrested shortly after the incident and, in January 1979, tried, convicted of the crime, and sentenced to death. Sakharov and others protested the convictions as well as the sentences, which were carried out shortly after the verdict. Although Sakharov believed the explosion was a KGB provocation, he had no proof of this, and in his memoirs he acknowledges that only in an impartial court of law could the matter be resolved. But he was convinced the three Armenians were innocent of any wrongdoing, and in his memoirs notes that the evidence the government cited as proof of Zatikian's involvement was particularly dubious. Some dissidents, however, thought the three men, given their nationalism, could easily have set the explosion, while others were inclined to give credence to a rumor circulating in Moscow shortly afterward that it was the work of Russian workers protesting food shortages. Sakharov, *Memoirs*, 490–92; Alexeyeva, *Soviet Dissent*, 129.

79. Sakharov, *Memoirs*, 463.

80. Ibid., 462; Andrei Sakharov, "Appeal on Behalf of Pyotr Ruban (January 3, 1977)," in *Alarm and Hope*, 42.

81. Andrei Sakharov, "Message to Ford and Carter (October 11, 1976)," in *Alarm and Hope*, 44.

82. Cited in Andrei Sakharov, CBS interview, February 10, 1977, in *Alarm and Hope*, 49.

stated that his commitment was "absolute." The language Carter used made it clear that it was not nearly enough to support human rights rhetorically. Such support, he said, had to be translated into policy and practical action: "[O]ur moral sense [requires that we prefer] those societies which share with us an abiding respect for individual human rights."[83]

To Sakharov, Carter seemed to be expressing explicitly and unequivocally the same commitment to human rights that animated his own endeavors. Although Carter's commitment to human rights sprang from impulses and experiences very different from those that galvanized Sakharov, this seemed at the time no impediment to what the latter evidently thought would be a collaborative effort in which the American president and the Soviet dissidents would advance a common agenda on behalf of principles they both considered universally applicable. At the very least, Carter's inaugural address emboldened Sakharov and greatly encouraged him. On January 21, he gave an American lawyer in Moscow a letter intended for Carter listing the names of political prisoners on whose behalf he thought the president should intervene with the Soviet government. The lawyer, Martin Garbus, had asked for ten names; Sakharov provided him with sixteen.[84] Garbus made the letter public when he returned to the United States, and it appeared on January 29 in both the *New York Times* and the *Los Angeles Times*. In the letter Sakharov mentioned the Moscow subway explosion, comparing it to the Reichstag Fire in 1933 and the Kirov assassination in 1934, both of which he described as government provocations. The implication that the explosion was also a provocation was unmistakable. Describing the situation of the dissidents as almost unbearable, the letter had a desperation about it generally absent in the other missives Sakharov intended for foreign leaders, in almost all of which he avoided flowery rhetoric and tried to appeal to these leaders on the basis of reason.[85]

On January 24, three days after Sakharov met with Garbus, he was summoned to the procurator's office, where the deputy procurator warned him that the statement he had released shortly after the explosion expressing his suspicion that it was the work of the government was itself legitimate grounds for criminal prosecution.[86] On January 26, the warning appeared in the Soviet press in short notices in *Izvestiia* and *Vechernaia Moskva*, along with an excerpt from Article 190–1 of the Criminal Code of the RSFSR.[87] In response, on January 27 the U.S. State Department, in a written statement, warned the Soviet Union that "any attempt... to intimidate Mr. Sakharov will not silence legitimate criticism in the Soviet Union and will conflict with accepted standards of human rights."[88] On January 30, however, in impromptu remarks to reporters, Carter seemed to disavow the statement, or at least to distance himself from it, by observing that anything the United States

83. Sakharov, *Memoirs*, 464.
84. Ibid.; Sakharov, *Alarm and Hope*, 45.
85. Andrei Sakharov, "Letter to Carter (January 29, 1977)," in Sakharov, *Alarm and Hope*, 46–48.
86. Ibid., 62; Sakharov, *Memoirs*, 465.
87. Sakharov, *Alarm and Hope*, 73.
88. Quoted in Sakharov, *Memoirs*, 465.

government had to say officially about Sakharov would come from him or the secretary of state, Cyrus Vance.[89] Vance, in fact, had expressed his own reservations about the statement on January 28, shortly after the Soviet ambassador to the United States, Anatoly Dobrynin, had called to complain about it.[90] Over the next several months, Carter tried to convince Dobrynin that his statements supporting Sakharov and human rights in the Soviet Union were not intended to harm Soviet-American relations and that in the future he would limit the number of public statements he made on these subjects.[91]

Still, on February 5 Carter replied to Sakharov in a letter the Soviet government allowed him to read at the American embassy.[92] Although Sakharov had undoubtedly irritated the Soviets by praising Carter's support for human rights, they realized that harassing Sakharov now that the president of the United States had expressed his personal concern for him would be a colossal mistake—hence the privilege accorded Sakharov of entering a foreign embassy and being allowed to return from it.[93] In his letter to Sakharov (whom Brezhnev described as "a renegade" and "an enemy of the Soviet state" in a letter of his own to the American president), Carter reiterated his previously stated commitment to human rights: "The American people and our government will continue... to promote human rights not only in our own country but also abroad [and] to seek the release of prisoners of conscience."[94] In his reply of February 17, after thanking Carter for his letter, Sakharov expressed his own commitment to human rights and brought to the president's attention the names of members of various Helsinki Groups who had recently been arrested. He also implored the president to do what he could to help Sergei Kovalev, who was then in a labor camp and suffering from a tumor that required surgery.[95]

It is impossible to know whether a campaign for human rights by the Carter administration would have helped the Soviet dissidents because the campaign petered out shortly after Carter's exchange of letters with Sakharov. After the breakdown of Strategic Arms Limitation Talks (SALT) II negotiations in March—which many in the West ascribed to Soviet umbrage at the intervention in Soviet domestic affairs that Carter's statement supporting Sakharov seemed to entail—the administration continued to speak out publicly on violations of human rights in the Soviet Union. In September 1977, Carter broached Sharansky's fate with Soviet foreign minister Andrei Gromyko; in May 1978 Health, Education, and Welfare Secretary Joseph Califano canceled a trip to the Soviet Union following Orlov's arrest; and in June 1979, at the summit conference with Brezhnev in Vienna, Carter told the Soviet leader that the Helsinki Accords made human

89. Ibid.

90. Sakharov, *Alarm and Hope*, 58.

91. Anatoly Dobrynin, *In Confidence: Moscow's Ambassador to America's Six Cold War Presidents (1962–1986)* (New York, 1995), 385–86.

92. Coleman, *Decline and Fall of the Soviet Empire*, 108.

93. Sakharov, CBS interview, 48.

94. Sakharov, *Memoirs*, 466. Brezhnev's characterization of Sakharov is in Zbigniew Brzezinski, *Power and Principle: Memoirs of the National Security Advisor, 1977–1981* (New York, 1983), 155.

95. Sakharov, *Memoirs*, 466. On March 1 Kovalev was in fact transferred to a hospital in Leningrad. Ibid.

rights a relevant issue in Soviet-American relations.[96] He also received Bukovskii at the White House and pressured the Soviets to release Alexander Ginzburg, which they did. But that was the extent of the campaign. The Carter administration seemed increasingly receptive to the self-serving argument of many in the West that better relations with the Soviets should take precedence over human rights and that statements by Western governments supporting the dissidents forced the Soviets to treat them more harshly; Sharansky's arrest in March on charges of espionage was often cited as evidence of this.

Sakharov rejected this argument on empirical grounds and as a matter of principle. On the snag in arms control negotiations, he believed it was caused not by any American rhetoric about the dissidents or human rights but rather by the American proposal Vance presented to Gromyko shortly before negotiations broke down that required the Soviets to relinquish the advantage in "throw weight" (i.e., the megatonnage their ballistic missiles could deliver) ratified by the Vladivostok Agreement just fifteen months earlier.[97] In addition, as it became evident that Carter's human rights campaign was petering out, Sakharov reiterated that Western protests of Soviet human rights violations actually furthered the cause of arms control and disarmament and that the protection of human rights in the Soviet Union was a prerequisite of peace and genuine détente.[98]

To Sakharov, Carter's response to Soviet criticisms of his support for human rights should be to continue it, even to intensify it. He believed the Soviets would negotiate arms control for reasons of national interest; in addition, pressuring the Soviets to uphold human rights was simply the right thing to do, and ideally it should be accompanied by protests over violations of human rights in other countries as well. In Sakharov's opinion, any campaign a government conducted for human rights should protest the violations committed by its allies just as forthrightly and unambiguously as it did those of its enemies. In an interview in 1981, Sakharov argued that Carter's human rights campaign had failed not for a lack of good intentions but because he and his administration had not pursued it forcefully and consistently.[99] By this Sakharov meant that Carter should have condemned human rights violations wherever they occurred and that his rhetoric should have been accompanied by actions or the threat of actions. These, in Sakharov's opinion, would have prevented additional violations: a human rights campaign, if conducted properly, would, like nuclear weapons, have a deterrent effect.

Although Carter's commitment to human rights was genuine, there were several reasons it ended so quickly. Originally, Carter saw human rights as good politics domestically: after Watergate and the Vietnam War, with their imputations

96. Gaddis Smith, *Morality, Reason and Power: American Diplomacy in the Carter Years* (New York, 1986), 68.

97. Andrei Sakharov, Interview on Swedish/Norwegian Radio and Television, April 4, 1977, in *Alarm and Hope*, 118.

98. Sakharov, CBS interview, 115–16; Andrei Sakharov, ABC interview, March 25, 1977, in *Alarm and Hope*, 117.

99. Andrei Sakharov, Interview by Kevin Klose, June 1, 1981, *Chronicle of Human Rights*, no. 43 (July–September 1981): 20.

of American immorality, an emphasis on moral principle in foreign policy might play well politically.[100] But when it became clear that the American people considered other issues, such as the state of the economy, more important, the campaign for human rights became, if not a liability, at least extraneous to the political fortunes of the administration. In addition, the Carter administration wanted arms control negotiations more than the Soviets did and thus had no qualms about downplaying human rights violations if that would enhance the chances that these negotiations would result in a meaningful agreement.[101] For such considerations Sakharov had little sympathy. The political and intellectual gulf between the two men was immense, and to the whole issue of human rights in particular they brought very different perspectives. Sakharov was a private citizen and had no power. Living in the Soviet Union, he was also unfamiliar (at least until perestroika) with the constraints under which democratically elected leaders like Carter had to operate. For this reason he failed to realize that the American president had to factor into his decisions constituencies and considerations that often limited his options. In the case of human rights, there were elements in the American government and the public who viewed Carter's human rights campaign as a frivolity no superpower could afford to undertake in a nuclear age, when a miscalculation or a hasty and ill-conceived response to an adversary's criticism could lead to the destruction of humanity. Secretary Vance, in particular, considered arms control and human rights campaigns, under the particular circumstances that pertained in the late 1970s, incompatible.[102]

Although they generally agreed on what constituted human rights—namely, those that protected the individual's freedom from the state as well as those that provided a minimum level of material security, such as unemployment compensation and adequate health care—Sakharov and Carter championed human rights for different reasons, which in turn reflected their different views of human nature, self-improvement, and redemption. Whereas for Sakharov, human rights were inherent in nature and thus ascertainable through the application of reason, for Carter they were inseparable from Christianity. Indeed, it was a spirit of Christian charity that moved him to deplore the racial discrimination he had first observed as a youth in the American South.[103] For Sakharov, human rights were eternal, and it was political ideologies like Stalinism and Marxism-Leninism, not human beings themselves, that were evil. For Carter, evil was inherent in the human condition, and therefore upholding human rights was not a natural part of being human; only a belief in Christ would move people to live righteously. From this it followed logically that neither the Soviet Union nor communism was uniquely evil—as Sakharov, after 1975, was increasingly

---

100. Smith, *Morality, Reason and Power,* 28, 50.

101. Jody Powell, the president's press secretary and adviser, naïvely believed the Soviets would understand that domestic politics was a reason for the president's criticisms and would continue negotiations. Burton I. Kaufman, *The Presidency of James Earl Carter, Jr.* (Lawrence, Kans., 1993), 39.

102. Smith, *Morality, Reason, and Power,* 68.

103. Jimmy Carter, *Keeping Faith: Memoirs of a President* (New York, 1982), 143.

inclined to believe. Because he saw the Soviet Union as the single greatest force for evil in the world, Sakharov would never have criticized Americans, as Carter famously did in 1977, for their "inordinate fear of Communism."[104] By the time Carter announced his human rights campaign, Sakharov already believed the worst about the Soviet Union. And unlike Carter, he was unwilling to reject containment for détente, or deterrence for arms control, as the Carter administration seemed willing to do. Finally, although Sakharov saw convergence almost in religious terms, as a deus ex machina that would rid the world of the Soviet Union prior to ushering in a secular paradise that would last forever, he believed that before this happened, battling the Soviet Union was a better way of reducing evil in the world than engaging in the spiritual introspection persons more religiously inclined than he, such as Solzhenitsyn and Carter, were apt to advocate.

## Sakharov on Totalitarianism

An expression of Sakharov's pessimism in the mid-1970s was his calling the Soviet Union, with increasing frequency and desperation, totalitarian. In 1977, in a short essay entitled in English "Alarm and Hope," Sakharov wrote more extensively on totalitarianism than he had two years earlier in *My Country and the World*. In the later essay, he explicitly and repeatedly condemned the Soviet Union for its totalitarianism, by which he meant a form of rule uniquely repressive not just in the power rulers amassed and exercised but in the way they used their power to exclude foreign influences that might otherwise generate internal resistance against them.[105] The stability and security of totalitarian systems, Sakharov argued, were traceable ultimately to the absence of any foreign models against which these systems could be evaluated and judged adversely. Totalitarian regimes, he insisted, were particularly derelict in providing social equality and material security. Moreover, without any basis of comparison, the people they ruled had no way of knowing how dismal their living conditions were. Nor would they know, if they were living in socialist totalitarian regimes, that Western capitalism, under the humanizing influence of Christianity and the Enlightenment, had lost much of its original rapaciousness and was therefore preferable to socialist systems on moral grounds as well as on purely utilitarian ones.[106]

In "Alarm and Hope" Sakharov made the important point that the powerlessness of the Soviet people prevented them from thwarting the expansionism of the Soviet state that he believed was inherent in totalitarianism. According to Sakharov, totalitarian regimes sought total power not only over their own people but over all people. They were expansionist, he insisted, because it was simply in their nature to be so, because there was an irrational, almost primal, impulse in the collective mentality of these regimes that caused them to expand regardless

---

104. Quoted in Smith, *Morality, Reason and Power,* 66.
105. Andrei Sakharov, *Alarm and Hope,* 99–111. Sakharov wrote the essay for an anthology the Nobel Committee published of the writings of Nobel Prize winners.
106. Ibid., 102–3.

of whether expansion served their self-interest or not. And because people living under totalitarianism were unable to thwart this expansion, people in countries without the constraints totalitarianism imposed had a special obligation to thwart this expansion on their behalf; in Sakharov's view, nothing less than the survival of humanity was at stake. Totalitarianism was as much a threat to those who were not yet living under it as it was a horrible reality to those who were. In the essay, Sakharov duly castigated those in the West who were inclined to give the Soviets the benefit of the doubt in evaluating Soviet foreign policy precisely because they were oblivious to the totalitarianism that motivated it.[107]

Because Sakharov now considered the Soviet Union totalitarian, he had to revise somewhat the rate at which, and the way in which, he expected convergence to come about. His conclusion was that, for convergence to occur everywhere in the world, the Soviet Union would have to change more than the West would. And because the Soviet Union was totalitarian, changing it was far more difficult than changing the West now that the latter almost everywhere guaranteed its people the human rights Sakharov extolled. In fact, Sakharov even expressed in "Alarm and Hope" uncertainty that the Soviet Union, because it was totalitarian, would ever merge with the humane and efficient capitalism he saw developing in the West. Convergence, in other words, might be something that only a portion of humanity, rather than all of humanity, would enjoy. Even worse, it might even be a mirage, something that, however desirable in the abstract, could never be attained. In the essay Sakharov described in some detail how Soviet totalitarianism over the next decade might distort the historical process so severely that the global emancipation he envisioned as the ultimate result of convergence was no longer inevitable. This is how he expressed this idea:

> Today's capitalist society, with a few reservations, can be called "capitalism with a human face." The great achievements of science and engineering, which I view as the root of this material progress, have created a profusion of consumer goods which, in itself, has alleviated the problem of the distribution of material wealth. But the *ideas* of social justice, human rights, and democracy which have permeated social consciousness...play a no less significant role in capitalist society....Socialist ideas, in their pluralistic, anti-totalitarian form, will continue to play a definite role in Western social development. This will in fact be the movement of the West toward convergence with the socialist world. I feel less certain of a reciprocal evolution of totalitarian socialism toward pluralism. That will depend on many internal and external conditions, the most important of which is to overcome the "closed" aspect of totalitarian-socialist society.[108]

Sakharov's characterization of the Soviet Union as totalitarian could be questioned on a variety of grounds. One could argue that the Soviet Union under Brezhnev was not totalitarian at all, that it lacked the total power totalitarian regimes by definition possess or at least come close to possessing. Indeed, given

107. Ibid., 104.
108. Ibid., 103.

that its policy objectives did not entail massive projects of social engineering like the collectivization of agriculture, the Soviet Union in the Brezhnev era had no particular need for total power: the regime's tolerance of a black market that provided much of what the Soviet people needed made the violent overthrow of the system unnecessary; thus the total power to prevent it was unnecessary as well. Finally, some of the obligations imposed by détente limited the power the Soviets possessed. However much they tried to avoid implementing these obligations, such as the human rights provisos of the Helsinki Accords, these undoubtedly limited the amount of coercion they could use against the dissidents and anyone else in the Soviet Union inclined to challenge them, such as the ethnic and religious minorities. Ironically, Sakharov had to look no further than his own situation to find proof of this: the very fact that the Soviets refrained from shooting him—which one must reiterate is surely is what Stalin would have done—shows that the Soviet Union no longer fit Sakharov's description of it as totalitarian. At most, the Soviet Union by the 1970s had evolved into a "post-totalitarian" regime—one that did not use terror against its own population in the systematic manner and massive scale previously employed. In the 1970s the mere threat of terror and the still vivid memory of it kept the population as quiescent as its actual application had done in the 1930s.

The frequency and alacrity with which Sakharov called the Soviet Union totalitarian in the mid- and late 1970s suggests that for him the term was as much an epithet for condemning the Soviet system as it was an analytical tool that helped him explain it. He could have explained the Soviet Union without ever invoking the term, and there were occasions in the late 1970s when he did so. In an interview with an Italian journalist in 1979, Sakharov noted that the Soviet Union presently was different from what it had been in the Stalin era only in "the scale of political repressions... [But] the basic structures of society which were created in the Stalin era are still preserved."[109] The enormous apparatus of control and coercion that enabled the Soviet system to endure—what he often called the "party-state monopoly" over "politics, culture and ideology"—originated, for the most part, under Stalin.[110] Despite the reforms Khrushchev had instituted, the Soviet system Brezhnev inherited in 1964 was a Stalinist one; and trying to rid the Soviet Union of all that was morally reprehensible in it would require that its Stalinist foundations be uprooted and destroyed. The fact that this foundation had persisted largely untouched in the quarter century since Stalin's death made this task, according to Sakharov, extraordinarily difficult.

As a purely intellectual matter, Sakharov would have been better off avoiding the totalitarian analogy entirely. By subsuming dictatorships like the Soviet one under a generic category from which the peculiarities and uniqueness of national culture were necessarily excluded, the concept of totalitarianism obscured more than it clarified. What is more, Sakharov could explain the Soviet system

---

109. A. Sakharov, "Answers to Questions from the Italian Journalist Laccua (December 21, 1979)," *Chronicle of Current Events*, no. 55 (December 31, 1979): 66.
110. Ibid.

coherently—as he did in the interview with the Italian journalist—without using the term, by stressing the origins of the Soviet system not in totalitarianism but in Leninism and Stalinism. Nevertheless, Sakharov's use of the term is understandable. With his family harassed to the point where it had to disperse, with détente fostering hopes about the Soviet Union that Sakharov believed were illusory, and with an American human rights campaign that gradually weakened after the fanfare with which it had begun, he understandably latched onto a rhetorical device that, whatever its analytical shortcomings, assisted him in making the case for human rights despite the unlikelihood that it would persuade the Soviet leadership to behave differently. Under the circumstances, expressing his deep animus toward the Soviet leaders by implicitly equating the Soviet Union with Nazi Germany, which he knew they would find outrageous and insulting, probably provided Sakharov with a great sense of satisfaction.

# 18  The Noose Tightens

From 1977 to 1980 the government's persecution of both the dissidents and the refuseniks increased. Paradoxically, the more the government harassed these groups, the more it seemed to fear them. In March 1979 Andropov told a conference of KGB officials assigned to the Fifth Directorate (which had the task of combating ideological subversion) that "every act" a dissident carried out against the Soviet Union "represent[ed] a danger."[1] Because the dissidents chose to challenge nothing less than the moral legitimacy of the Soviet system, the paucity of their popular support and the smallness of their numbers were irrelevant. Moreover, by seeking support from the West, the dissidents were linking themselves with self-professed enemies of the Soviet Union—countries, organizations, and individuals that genuinely sought to harm it and in some cases destroy it. In this sense, Western support for the dissidents was a double-edged sword: while on the one hand it alleviated their political and psychological isolation, on the other it made plausible the damaging charge that they were traitors consorting openly with their country's enemies.[2]

What was true for the dissidents was doubly so for the mostly Jewish refuseniks, whose efforts to leave the Soviet Union were an even more obvious and overt rejection of the Soviet system than were the dissidents' efforts to reform it. In light of this, the Soviet government acted accordingly. In 1978 alone, Ginzburg, Slepak, Begin, and Ida Nudel were all arrested, and Sharansky, who had been arrested the year before, was tried and convicted of treason, a crime for

---

1. Andrew and Mitrokhin, *Sword and the Shield*, 330.
2. Petro, *Rebirth of Russian Democracy*, 132.

which no dissident or refusenik had previously been charged.[3] In the same year, Grigorenko and the cellist Rostropovich, who, while not a dissident himself, never tried to conceal his friendship with Solzhenitsyn, had their citizenship revoked while they were outside the country.[4] Among the dissidents arrested in 1979 were Tatiana Velikanova, who was a founding member of the Initiative Group for Human Rights in 1969 and helped revive the *Chronicle of Current Events* in 1974, and Viktor Nekipelov, who was an active member of the Moscow Helsinki Group.[5]

Through all of this, Sakharov and Bonner tried as best they could to keep the dissident movement alive, cognizant that their international fame had saved them from a comparable fate. But the petty harassments they had endured earlier in the decade continued and in some ways caused them serious harm. The KGB, which had previously interrupted their mail, now tampered with and even fabricated it. On one occasion it sent Sakharov a letter ostensibly from Sweden inviting him and other Soviet scientists to a conference there; in the letter the police enclosed clippings from Swedish journals with drawings pasted on them of arrows piercing a person's eyes—undoubtedly a morbid reference to Bonner's ophthalmological ailments.[6] Because these letters would serve their purpose only if Sakharov knew who was sending them, the KGB made little effort to conceal its authorship. To be sure, there were times when the government tried to appear conciliatory. But its benevolence was always the consequence of hard-nosed political calculation, designed in most instances to keep the couple off balance. In January 1979, for example, the government gave Bonner the exit visa she needed to go to Italy to consult doctors there about yet another operation on her eyes. But it did so only after Sakharov and Bonner threatened to go on a hunger strike if the visa she requested was not granted.[7] The previous November, in fact, the KGB had picked the lock of their apartment and ransacked it, making off with the manuscript of Sakharov's memoirs (the first of several versions he would have to write as a result of similar KGB operations in the future). In April 1979, while he was at the airport meeting Bonner on her return from the trip abroad she had begun in January, KGB agents punctured the tires of his car.[8]

3. Rubenstein, *Soviet Dissidents*, 242–43. Under Soviet law, treason was a crime punishable by death. Sharansky, however, was sentenced to three years in prison and ten years in a labor camp, largely because of the outcry his conviction had generated abroad. President Carter stated publicly that Sharansky had no ties to American intelligence agencies. Sakharov, *Memoirs*, 484–85.

4. Rubenstein, *Soviet Dissidents*, 241.

5. Because Sakharov had enormous respect for Velikanova and Nekipelov and valued their services to the dissident movement, he considered their arrest an especially egregious loss to it. Sakharov, *Memoirs*, 499.

6. T. M. Velikanova, "Khodoki," in Ivanova, *Andrei Dmitrievich*, 105.

7. The doctors Bonner saw in Italy advised against the operation and recommended she wear glasses instead. From Italy Bonner traveled to the United States, where the doctors who treated her supported what those in Italy had advised. On her visit, Bonner took the opportunity to spend time with her children and grandchildren in Massachusetts, which explains why she did not return to the Soviet Union until April. Sakharov, *Memoirs*, 488.

8. Ibid., 486, 495–96.

Undaunted by this, Sakharov continued his activities, protesting, among other injustices, a resolution of the Council of Ministers in August 1978 giving the minister of the interior the authority to deport Crimean Tatars from the Crimea. Shortly thereafter, deportations began. With the same alacrity he had shown in previous years in protesting instances of repression he considered especially egregious and reprehensible, Sakharov protested the resolution, and the actions that followed it, before any Tatars asked him to do so.[9] By the end of the decade the government's violations of human rights were so frequent that Sakharov could no longer devote large amounts of time to any particular case. His tendency to protest human rights violations whenever they occurred seemed now unchecked by any recognition of his own limitations; as a result, his physical and psychological resources were stretched to their breaking point. From an offhand comment in Sakharov's memoirs one learns that in 1979 he was calling press agencies regularly, often more than once a week, to notify them of the human rights violations the Soviet government was committing with increasing frequency.[10]

Occasionally Sakharov professed optimism. For example, in an interview with the BBC in 1978, he expressed confidence that "a handful of honest, brave, and gifted people like the dissidents can in fact change the psychological attitude of the whole society."[11] More often, however, he expressed a pessimism that verged on genuine despondency. Because the Soviet Union still lacked "the ecology of freedom" every society required to ensure the protection of human rights and because human rights had to be guaranteed everywhere for convergence to occur, in a 1979 review written for the *Washington Post* of Freeman Dyson's semifuturological book *Disturbing the Universe,* Sakharov extended even further into the future the emergence of the world government he thought convergence would entail.[12] In the review, Sakharov reiterated the support he had expressed for space exploration in his article for *Saturday Review* in 1974.[13] This time, however, he supported space exploration as a necessary prerequisite to transporting humanity to another planet or to some other celestial body should either a natural disaster (such as a comet heading for earth) or a man-made disaster (such as a nuclear war) seem imminent.[14] Whereas in 1974 Sakharov had endorsed space exploration as a way of enhancing human life, in 1979 he did so as a way of preserving it.

In the five years between the 1974 article and the 1979 book review, what really changed in Sakharov's mind was the role of science itself. While in 1979

---

9. Ibid., 489.
10. Ibid., 490.
11. John Simpson, "Interview with Andrei Sakharov," BBC (July 3, 1978): 15.
12. Andrei Sakharov, review of *Disturbing the Universe,* by Freeman Dyson, *Washington Post Book World,* September 23, 1979, 1, 8. The phrase "ecology of freedom" is Mary Ann Glendon's, but it encapsulates Sakharov's belief that human rights, to be preserved and respected in perpetuity, had to become part of the larger culture of a society. Glendon, *World Made New,* 240.
13. Sakharov, "Tomorrow," 110.
14. Sakharov, review of *Disturbing the Universe,* 8.

science for Sakharov was just as essential to human existence as it was for him in 1974, it was essential in a very different, almost opposite way, its role now that of protecting man from his own worst impulses instead of assisting him in acting on his most laudable ones. What this meant for scientists, who for Sakharov served always as the ultimate repository of a society's moral and intellectual resources, was that they had an even greater responsibility. In 1974 Sakharov believed scientists should be concerned with making human life better; in 1979 he implored them to find ways to prevent man from destroying himself. Ironically, the less convinced Sakharov was that people generally acted rationally or understood the importance of reason, the more he valued rationality and the commitment to reason scientists embodied. In a message he sent in December 1979 to the New York Academy of Sciences, which the president of the academy read on his behalf to the audience assembled for its annual meeting, the Soviet physicist wrote with great eloquence on the responsibility scientists bore as avatars of reason at a time when many were questioning the utility and value of science itself:

> Sometimes one reads or hears about a crisis of rational thought—that rational thought is impotent when confronted by the complexity and irrationality of human life. I am convinced that such doubts are unfounded. Historically, it has been the representatives of science—that is, of rational thought—who have recognized and tried to solve the problems of economic and social regulation, environmental protection, pollution control, the management of irreplaceable resources, population planning, the maintenance of an open society with the free exchange of information, and disarmament including the control of nuclear weapons.
>
> I am convinced that humanity's survival depends upon open and tolerant societies, and their ability to progress guided by scientific principles. This method does not promise paradise on earth, but then, does the essence of human existence reside in utopias? Our future depends on persistent and unselfish effort, on our sense of responsibility, and on our wisdom.[15]

Consistent with this view was Sakharov's renewed interest, in the late 1970s, in the peaceful applications of nuclear energy. In October 1977, at the suggestion of the Czech physicist František Janouch, Sakharov wrote an article for the *Bulletin of the Atomic Scientists* arguing that nuclear power could be used for peaceful purposes. He pointed out that nuclear power is cleaner than coal and cheaper than oil. Moreover, because the natural resources needed to generate it are ubiquitous, nuclear power could make countries "energy independent," which would make the preservation of political independence easier.[16] In July 1979, in correspondence with the German writer Heinrich Böll, Sakharov disagreed

15. "Andrei Sakharov on Science and Society (December 6, 1979)," *Chronicle of Human Rights* 36 (October–December 1979): 25.

16. Sakharov, *Memoirs*, 475; Andrei Sakharov, "Nuclear Energy and the Freedom of the West," *Bulletin of the Atomic Scientists*, July 1978, reprinted in *Alarm and Hope*, 124–28.

strongly with the latter's contention, popular among the so-called Greens in Germany and among ecologically conscious organizations elsewhere in Western Europe and in America, that nuclear power was dangerous given the technology required in the construction and maintenance of nuclear reactors.[17] In reply, Sakharov wrote that the danger of nuclear accidents was greatly exaggerated and that nuclear power, properly harnessed, was neither carcinogenic nor productive of harmful gases the way other fuels were. In fact, nuclear power was presently the only viable substitute for the dirty fuels then existing: while in the distant future solar energy, hydroelectric power, and even floodwaters might be suitable substitutes for nuclear power, because the existing technology for using these things was still primitive, they were all inadequate to meet the current global demand for energy.[18]

As his calls for energy independence suggest, Sakharov did not advocate nuclear power for ecological reasons alone. There were also sound political reasons for nations to use it. In this sense, his support of nuclear power was integral to his politics: by using nuclear power instead of the oil and natural gas it imported from the Soviet Union, the West could achieve a freedom of action in dealing with the Soviets it currently lacked. Conceivably, the energy independence nuclear power could provide would make it easier for Western governments to criticize Soviet human rights violations, and it might even advance the larger goal of convergence. But how could Sakharov be sure governments would have the good sense to use nuclear power in the first place? He did not answer this question explicitly either in his article or in his correspondence with Böll, but the confident tone with which he writes about the benefits of nuclear power suggests that he believed Western governments would use it because they were democracies. In other words, Western governments would switch to nuclear power because the people to whom these governments were accountable would demand that they do so. And in Sakharov's scenario they would make this demand because both the people in the West and the rulers they elected were fundamentally rational.

In this respect one discerns in Sakharov's thought in the late 1970s a strict dichotomy between people in the West, whom he considered rational enough to do the right thing politically (which in practice meant voting for political leaders who supported human rights), and the Soviet people, whom he denigrated for perpetuating the attitudes that helped make Soviet totalitarianism possible. One might even infer that Sakharov believed the Soviet people, because they were not sufficiently rational, could not be trusted to use nuclear power safely in the unlikely event that anyone other than party and government officials would make the decisions involved in this. Certainly his comments earlier in the decade disparaging the Soviet people for their ethical degeneration under communism makes such an inference plausible.

17. "Perepiska s Genrikhom Bëllem," reprinted in Andrei Sakharov, *Vospominaniia*, vol. 2 (Moscow, 1996), 476–79. In his memoirs, Sakharov misdates the correspondence to 1978. Sakharov, *Memoirs*, 475.
18. Ibid., 479–81.

Yet another issue Sakharov addressed toward the end of the decade, when it seemed that the causes he believed in were not advancing, was arms control. To his great credit, Sakharov recognized at the time what many in the West denied or chose to ignore: that the Soviet Union in the 1970s sought nuclear parity with the United States and, once that was achieved, perhaps even nuclear superiority in the form of a first strike capability.[19] By 1971 the number of Soviet ICBMs exceeded the number of American ones that were fully operational. Moreover, many of the ICBMs the Soviets built and deployed legally under the terms of the SALT agreement of 1972 were designed to destroy the Minuteman missile, on which America's ICBM retaliatory capability was based.[20] In the 1970s the Soviets also MIRVed their ICBMs; they produced large numbers of Backfire bombers (which, like the American B-52, had intercontinental range and could carry nuclear and thermonuclear weapons); and they experimented with new technologies intended to make their own missiles less vulnerable, such as "cold launches," which greatly reduced the time it took to fire a missile once a decision to launch had been made. Throughout the decade, the Soviets in a variety of ways also violated the ABM treaty they had signed in 1969.[21]

The SALT II agreement in 1979 (which the United States Senate never ratified but which American presidents chose to observe nonetheless) worked to the Soviets' advantage in much the way the SALT I agreement did. For example, SALT II contained no acknowledgment that the American MX missile—which, to decrease its vulnerability to an incoming missile, would be placed on mobile launchers that could be moved quickly from one launch site to another on tracks in underground tunnels in Utah and Nevada—was permitted. In addition, the limit on new ICBMs the agreement imposed still allowed older ones to be modernized, which worked to the advantage of the country with less money to spend on defense (in this case the Soviet Union) because modernizing old missiles was cheaper than designing and producing new ones. What is more, the number of intermediate-range cruise missiles the United States could deploy under the terms of the agreement to neutralize the threat the Soviet SS-20 posed to Western Europe was strictly limited, while the development of air defenses against these missiles (which only the Soviets, of course, would ever have to deploy) was not. Finally, the agreement failed to limit the deployment of the SS-20 itself.[22] Although the Reagan administration in the 1980s would shelve the MX missile as impractical, the Carter administration, in December 1979 in the wake of the Soviet invasion of Afghanistan, ordered deployment of

---

19. Bulanov and Krylova, "Sootnoshenie politiki i iadernoi voiny," 113–14; Glynn, *Closing Pandora's Box*, 216, 245.

20. Glynn, *Closing Pandora's Box*, 216, 236.

21. Ibid., 260.

22. Ibid., 303. The designation "SS" in "SS-20" was short for "surface-to-surface," thereby designating a missile that is fired from the earth's surface toward a target somewhere else on the surface. The nomenclature, which included "SA" for "surface-to-air" and AA "for air-to-air," was exclusively American.

464 cruise missiles and 108 Pershing II IRBMs in Western Europe in response to the Soviets' development and deployment of the SS-20 in the Soviet Union.[23] But by this time, the Soviets had concluded that for the Americans, arms control was an end in itself rather than a means of advancing their national interests, which is how the Soviets viewed it. As a result, in any arms control negotiations only the Soviets would use the threat to break off negotiations as a bargaining chip if the negotiations were not proceeding in ways that were consistent with their interests. While breaking off negotiations was not really an option for the Americans, given what they believed about arms control, this tactic could conceivably advance the Soviets' objective of achieving nuclear parity.[24] It was hardly a coincidence that, as American defense spending in the 1970s declined as a percentage of gross national product, Soviet defense spending, both absolutely and as a percentage of GNP, increased. As Harold Brown, Carter's secretary of defense, commented sardonically, "[W]hen we build weapons, they build; when we stop, they nevertheless continue to build."[25]

Although Sakharov did not know all of the arcana of arms control, he understood very well the larger issues involved. Most important, he understood the Soviets' basic objectives and for that reason never succumbed to the tendency among some in the Carter administration (including the chief American arms control negotiator, Paul Warneke, Cyrus Vance, and Carter himself) to consider arms control an end in itself. To be sure, Sakharov always considered arms control unique among the issues in the Cold War in its taking precedence over Soviet human rights violations: no matter how egregiously the Soviets violated the human rights of their citizens, arms control negotiations should continue. But this did not mean that arms control was inherently beneficial or that the United States should sign any and all arms control agreements. There might be some agreements from which the United States, both to protect its own interests and to advance the cause of international peace, should walk away. At the very least, it should negotiate toughly and always enter into negotiations from a position of strength. For this reason, Sakharov favored the MX as a way of restoring parity in ICBMs, and he thought the United States was wrong not to insist on a condition in SALT II explicitly permitting its deployment. For the same reason, he favored deployment of the cruise and Pershing missiles as a bargaining chip, to be removed in exchange for the Soviets' removal of their SS-20s.[26] The conditional nature of Sakharov's support for arms control negotiations is evident in what he

23. Ibid., 313, 325. Only twice—in 1959 in East Germany and in 1962 in Cuba—did the Soviet Union deploy nuclear weapons outside its borders during the Cold War, despite the reduction. Matthias Uhl and Vladimir Ivkin, "'Operation Atom'—The Soviet Union's Stationing of Nuclear Missiles in the German Democratic Republic, 1959," *Cold War International History Project Bulletin*, no. 12/13 (Fall/Winter 2001/2002): 299.

24. In the 1980s the Reagan administration showed that it viewed arms control differently than previous administrations had done. While it never broke off arms control negotiations (as opposed to rejecting particular Soviet proposals), it simply waited out the Soviets after they stopped negotiating a treaty on intermediate range ballistic missles in November 1983—which did not prevent a treaty from being signed four years later. Ibid., 334.

25. Quoted ibid., 304.

26. Sakharov, review of *Disturbing the Universe*, 8; Sakharov, *Memoirs*, 578.

wrote about SALT II in an article that appeared in 1979 in *Trialogue*, the publication of the Trilateral Commission. Before signing such a treaty, he insisted, the United States "must ask whether it will lessen the danger and destructive power of a nuclear war, strengthen international stability, or prevent a one-sided advantage for the U.S.S.R. or a consolidation of its already existing advantages."[27] The implication of Sakharov's article was that SALT II might not do these things and should not be signed by the United States if it did not.

As Bonner pointed out in one of several reminiscences she wrote about her husband after his death, Sakharov grasped the essential truth about arms control in a nuclear age—namely, that in order to reduce or eliminate nuclear and thermonuclear weapons, countries sometimes have to produce more of them (and also, although Bonner did not mention this, a greater variety of them).[28] Drawing on his years of experience dealing with Soviet leaders personally, Sakharov recognized that strength was something they desired for themselves and respected in others. Therefore, an aura of strength, whether warranted by the objective facts or not, was precisely the quality the Soviets' adversaries should cultivate if they wanted the Soviets to take them seriously. American strength, not American weakness, made deterrence, and thus the absence of nuclear war, possible throughout the Cold War.

To ensure that the American nuclear deterrent remained credible to the Soviets, Sakharov called on the United States to eliminate "the weak points" in its nuclear arsenal and not become "complacent" about its conventional forces so that "the parity of forces in all basic types of weapons" could be maintained.[29] He recognized the linkage, in a nuclear age, of conventional and nuclear forces. He understood that the casualties American conventional forces in Western Europe would suffer following a Soviet invasion with conventional forces would trigger an American nuclear strike. Thus the Soviets' fear of such a strike would deter them from launching an invasion in the first place. This scenario presumably made increasing American conventional forces in Europe unnecessary. But Sakharov also saw these forces, in sufficient numbers, as a symbol of American resolve—of its commitment to do whatever was necessary to ensure that the Soviet Union did not achieve such a preponderance in purely nuclear and thermonuclear weaponry (to complement the superiority in conventional weapons it had enjoyed since the early 1950s) that it would consider launching a first strike against the United States directly. American conventional forces in Western Europe, in other words, deterred not only a Soviet invasion of Western Europe but also a Soviet nuclear strike on America.

## The Soviets Come to a Decision

For Sakharov, the Soviet invasion of Afghanistan in December 1979 was the logical outcome of all that was wrong with détente and irrefutable proof that

27. Sakharov, "The Human Rights Movement in the USSR and Eastern Europe," 257.
28. Elena Bonner, "U nego byl kharakter pobeditelia," *Kuranty*, May 21, 1991, 5.
29. Sakharov, review of *Disturbing the Universe*, 8. Sakharov also warned in very general terms against "dangerous complacency in regard to conventional weapons." Ibid.

the Cold War had never ended. It was also the equivalent in foreign policy of the persecution of Jews in domestic affairs, the embodiment of everything he considered abhorrent in the Soviet Union. Specifically, the Afghan operation seemed to confirm his diagnosis of the Soviet Union as totalitarian: only a society as closed as the Soviet Union would acquiesce in the aggression the government was committing. The obvious corollary to Sakharov's contention was that if the Soviet people had more information about the invasion and if they could somehow use that information in forging a public consensus against the war, the government would have no choice but to reverse its policy and withdraw its troops from Afghanistan. To be sure, Brezhnev and company sent troops into Afghanistan in 1979 not to establish a Soviet client state but to preserve the one they had established in April 1978, when they installed Nur Mohammed Taraki as their puppet. But Taraki proved inadequate to the role and was replaced a short time later by Hafizullah Amin. Amin, however, no more met Soviet expectations than Taraki had done and by the fall of 1979 had become a liability. Shortly after Soviet forces captured Kabul, the Afghan capital, in the opening hours of the operation, KGB agents murdered Amin, along with all witnesses. It is not clear what, if anything, the Soviets intended to do once the country had been pacified and their new surrogate, Babrak Karmal, installed. After their initial success, Soviet troops encountered greater resistance than they had anticipated, and Afghanistan in the early 1980s became the Soviet Union's Vietnam—a constant drain on its resources without any apparent solution, short of unilateral withdrawal. Sakharov, however, believing as he did that expansion was an integral aspect of totalitarianism, was convinced the Soviets intended Afghanistan as a base for further expansion. Indeed, it was partly for this reason that he condemned it so loudly.[30]

Sakharov deplored the invasion for other reasons as well. The brutality Soviet forces displayed—bombing villages; using napalm, land mines, chemical weapons, and booby traps; the occasional atrocity of Soviet helicopter crews firing on Soviet troops that were about to surrender—all repulsed him.[31] More than most critics of the war, Sakharov recognized how the entire operation made the soldiers involved in it complicit in war crimes. This, along with a Soviet public oblivious to the horrible things Soviet soldiers were doing in Afghanistan, Sakharov ascribed to the dehumanization caused by totalitarianism.[32] In his memoirs he calls the invasion "a major blunder [that] cast doubt on the Soviet Union's respect for international obligations and undermined confidence in its policies and its sincerity in preaching peace and security."[33] In addition, it was something for which the Soviet Union should be punished. Prior to the invasion Sakharov had opposed foreign countries' boycotting the Olympic Games sched-

---

30. Sakharov, *Memoirs*, 507.
31. Ibid., 508. Sakharov also condemned the atrocities of the Afghan resistance, such as shooting Soviet soldiers after capturing them. Ibid.
32. Ibid., 509. On the same page, Sakharov calls Soviet soldiers in Afghanistan "murderers and oppressors."
33. Ibid., 508–9.

uled for the following summer in Moscow on the pragmatic grounds that any boycott was likely to fail, reflecting badly on the countries that called for it, and also because he thought the Olympics, by drawing foreign spectators to Moscow, would facilitate genuine détente. After the invasion began, he changed his mind. On or around January 1, 1980, he told a correspondent for the German newspaper *Die Welt* that because the Soviet Union was at war, the games should be canceled, and that if the Soviet government refused to cancel them, other countries should boycott them. In his remarks, Sakharov referred to the cancellation of the games during World Wars I and II because so many of the athletes were from combatant countries. In the case of Afghanistan, however, Sakharov made clear that the games should be canceled on ethical grounds because Soviet actions in Afghanistan were in violation of universal standards of morality.[34]

In the first three weeks of January 1980, Sakharov condemned the invasion of Afghanistan in a variety of venues. In an interview on January 2 with Anthony Austin, the Moscow correspondent of the *New York Times,* he expressed concern that the war could escalate into a great-power confrontation, possibly leading to the ultimate catastrophe of nuclear war.[35] In response, the Soviet government, on January 8, stripped Sakharov of his awards and titles, though he would not learn of this for another two weeks.[36] On January 17, he told Charles Bierbauer of ABC News that the United States and other Western countries should suspend trade and scientific exchanges with the Soviet Union absent a complete and unconditional withdrawal of Soviet troops from Afghanistan, which he believed should be demanded by the UN General Assembly.[37] On January 21 Sakharov and Bonner hosted in their apartment the Soviet writer Georgi Vladimov and his wife, with whom they spent the evening discussing a statement of the Moscow Helsinki Group they had agreed to sign condemning the invasion unambiguously as reflective of a political system that systematically violated human rights.[38] Vladimov and his wife stayed until ten o'clock. At one o'clock in the morning, Bonner took a call from Vladimov (now in his own apartment), who told her that he had just heard from someone who had been present at a recent meeting of "political propagandists" that the government had decided to arrest Sakharov and exile him someplace far from Moscow; where exactly he would go Vladimov did not know.[39] When Bonner relayed this information to Sakharov, he replied simply, "A month ago, I wouldn't have taken it seriously, but now, with Afghanistan, anything's possible."[40] Nevertheless, one doubts that

34. Ibid., 496, 509.

35. Anthony Austin, "Sakharov Proposes Soviet Withdrawal," *New York Times,* January 3, 1980, A13.

36. Sakharov, *Memoirs*, 509.

37. Sakharov, Andrei, "Otvety na voprosy korrespondenta Bi-Bi-Si Ch. E. Birbaura 17/I-1980g," Sakharov Archives, Brandeis University, Waltham, Mass.

38. Coppen, "Public Life of Andrei Sakharov." 205.

39. Sakharov, *Memoirs*, 510.

40. Ibid.

Sakharov's sleep that night was restful. The following day, the Soviet government arrested him and a few hours later exiled him to Gorky, a closed city five hundred miles east of Moscow, where he would remain for almost seven years. However well Sakharov might have prepared himself psychologically for such an eventuality, neither he nor anyone else could know just how radically his life would be altered by it.

The Soviet invasion, of course, had lasting consequences for Soviet-American relations and the subsequent course of the Cold War. Shortly after the Afghan operation began, the Carter administration asked American athletes to boycott the Moscow Olympics (as Sakharov had suggested) and took several other steps to punish the Soviet Union for what President Carter called its naked aggression. The invasion also heightened doubts about the SALT II treaty, which the Senate refused to ratify. The invasion effectively ended détente, and Carter's pursuit of it contributed significantly to his crushing defeat in the 1980 presidential election. As for Sakharov, the end of détente gave the Soviets the option of dealing harshly with him, which they had refrained from doing before 1980.

In January 1980 Sakharov faced a supreme test of his character and his convictions, an ordeal more difficult and dangerous than any he had encountered earlier in his life. But the preponderance of power and initiative the government enjoyed now that détente had ended was not the only factor affecting the outcome of the struggle that would soon be waged on different terms and, quite literally for one of the two parties to it, on different terrain. Sakharov had advantages his adversaries lacked. For one thing, he knew what he was fighting for far better than the Soviets did. By 1980, the Marxism-Leninism they still claimed to believe in had become less a means of inspiring the Soviet people to create a glorious communist future than a concatenation of empty slogans legitimizing an increasingly dysfunctional status quo. For another, nearly everything he had done as a dissident—even the mistakes he had made and the ideas he had once held but then rejected—prepared him fairly well for what he would face after January 22, 1980. By this time, Sakharov had mostly shed the illusions he had previously entertained about the Soviet Union—that it was immediately reformable, that its leaders were reasonable, and that these same leaders were mostly receptive to constructive dialogue with their critics. Even more significant, by 1980 he no longer saw the Soviet people as inherently sympathetic to the liberal and humane agenda he and the other dissidents had advanced. In the years immediately preceding his exile to Gorky, Sakharov in fact had erred in the opposite direction, arguing wrongly that the Soviet Union was a totalitarian regime, with all that that implied about the permanence of the regime and its inability ever to reform itself. As it happened, the Soviet Union would begin to reform itself radically less than a decade after Sakharov was sent to Gorky, and it would collapse just a few years after that.

Of course Sakharov could not have known any of this as he awaited somberly, on the evening of January 21, the internal exile he had good reason to believe would begin the next day. What he did know was that his immediate prospects were grim. Western support, while personally gratifying, would not help him very much now that the leverage the West possessed during détente had disappeared. Nor were the dissidents, their ranks depleted by arrests and persistent harassment, in a position to provide meaningful support, much less force the Soviet government to reverse its decision to exile him. Although the dissidents, or whoever might follow them, might succeed eventually in securing human rights for the Soviet people, many years, perhaps decades, would have to pass before this happened. On the evening of January 21, 1980, as he contemplated how his life would change in the weeks and months ahead, Sakharov may have acknowledged yet again what he had come to recognize, however reluctantly, in the late 1970s—namely, that the hopes the Nobel Prize and the Helsinki Accords had raised were illusory. Nevertheless, by shedding these illusions, Sakharov had readied himself fairly well for whatever calumnies and deprivations the Soviet government might inflict on him in addition to those he had already endured. The intellectual journey from political naïf to political realist that began with *Reflections* in 1968 and continued with *My Country* in 1975 was by no means over when Sakharov was exiled to Gorky in 1980. But by 1980 he had journeyed far enough to have become a formidable adversary of the Soviets— physically weakened by years of harassment and character assassination but also capable of drawing on deep reserves of moral courage and political conviction that the government, because it lacked these same things, persistently underestimated. By 1980 the Soviet leadership had come to fear Sakharov. But it never understood why Sakharov did not fear it in return.

# PART VI

# In Exile, Unrepentant: 1980–1986

# 19  Arrested but Still Defiant

On January 22, 1980, the day he expected the government to arrest him, Sakharov was determined to follow his usual routine.[1] In the early afternoon, in a limousine the academy provided him, he set off for the Lebedev Institute to attend its weekly seminar on theoretical physics. Although he had had no formal duties at the institute since 1969, he retained an office there and enjoyed the intellectual stimulation the seminars provided. As his limousine traversed the Krasnokholmskii Bridge, the police, who had closed the bridge to other vehicles, stopped Sakharov's car and surrounded it. Two KGB agents quickly got into the car and ordered the driver to take Sakharov to the procurator's office. On their arrival, the agents hustled him to the office of the deputy procurator, Alexander Rekunkov, who read to him the January 8 decree of the Presidium of the Supreme Soviet rescinding the awards and medals he had won, as well as the title of Hero of Socialist Labor, as punishment for various actions of his—none of them specified—that had supposedly harmed the Soviet Union. Rekunkov then informed Sakharov that to prevent him from talking to foreigners, the government was exiling him to Gorky, a city five hundred miles east of Moscow that was closed to foreigners. When Rekunkov asked Sakharov to indicate receipt of the decree by signing a separate sheet of paper on which were written the last few sentences of the decree, Sakharov noted that neither Brezhnev (who in 1977 had become chairman of the Supreme Soviet) nor the Presidium secretary had signed the decree; instead, their names were typed onto it. This seemed to Sakharov symbolic of the decree's illegality and of the illegality of the punishment the government had prescribed, and he defiantly refused the deputy procurator's request. To substantiate his objections, he pointedly reminded Rekunkov that the awards he had received were for services he once performed for his country and thus could not be conjured out of existence simply because the government was now angry with him.[2] Undeterred by this, Rekunkov told Sakharov that he had to leave for Gorky immediately and could not even return home to collect any belongings he might want to take with him. But the deputy procurator did allow him to call Bonner, who was still unaware of what was happening. In their conversation, Sakharov transmitted the information that she could, if she wished, accompany him to Gorky but that she had only two hours

---

1. In describing the events of the day, I have relied mainly on the narrative in Sakharov's memoirs, pp. 510–13, and in "The Exile of Sakharov," *Chronicle of Current Events*, no. 56 (April 30, 1980): 74–75.
2. Ioirysh, *Uroki A. D. Sakharova*, 11. The idea of stripping Sakharov of his awards and title was not a new one. Andropov had suggested it, as well as expulsion from the Academy of Sciences, in September 1973. "Zapiska komiteta gosudarstvennoi bezopasnosti pri Sovete Ministrov SSR (September 1973)," Korotkov, Melchin, and Stepanov, *Kremlevskii samosud*, 334.

to pack and do whatever else she had to do before a car would come to take her to the airport.

There was never any doubt that Bonner would join her husband in exile. By 1980 the couple had gone through too much together to endure separately this new test of their mettle. Nor did she hesitate, while she was frantically packing, to ask Ruf and Liza (who by this time was living in Sakharov and Bonner's apartment) to ask everyone they knew, especially foreign correspondents, to publicize the events that were unfolding and to characterize what the government was doing to Sakharov as a violation of human rights and Soviet law. Given their experience with the Soviet press, Sakharov and Bonner both considered foreign reporters useful conduits for information that would place their activities in a favorable light, rather than as neutral observers of the events they reported, and on this occasion the couple were especially intent on using the foreign press to their advantage. Given their situation, their intentions are entirely understandable. Because the telephone in their apartment mysteriously went dead immediately after Bonner's conversation with Sakharov ended, as did the pay phones in the immediate vicinity of the apartment, Liza had to walk a considerable distance to find one that worked. Finally she did, and before that phone went dead as well, she was able to contact Grigorii Podiapolskii's daughter, Natalia, who transmitted the news of Sakharov's arrest and impending exile to another dissident, who in turn called a foreign correspondent. Only in this circuitous way did news of Sakharov's arrest and exile reach the outside world.

While Liza was carrying out her critical mission, KGB agents transported Sakharov to Domodedovo Airport south of Moscow, where, after a two-hour hiatus, Bonner finally arrived, accompanied by Liza and Ruf. Sakharov and Bonner of course were greatly relieved to see each other and to know that, regardless of what might happen to them in Gorky, they could still live together. Bonner, in particular, had feared for some time that Sakharov, like Solzhenitsyn, would be exiled abroad and that, unlike Natalia Solzhenitsyna, she would not be allowed to join her husband. In the phrase Bonner later used to summarize the nearly seven years they would spend in Gorky, she and Sakharov were now "alone together" and for that reason felt a strange sense of elation on the plane ride to Gorky; even the presence of twelve KGB agents on the aircraft could not dampen their spirits. They had no inkling at the time that after Bonner left their apartment in Moscow, KGB agents had searched it and confiscated papers and documents that were of great personal value, such as Sakharov's Nobel Diploma, as well as items of no political significance at all, such as copies of scientific articles Sakharov had already submitted for publication. It was a measure of how significant and sensitive the government considered Sakharov's arrest and exile that Andropov ordered his principal deputy, Semën Tsvigun, to fly to Gorky simultaneously in a separate airplane so that nothing untoward might happen to ruin the operation after the plane carrying Sakharov and Bonner landed.[3]

---

3. Sakharov, *Memoirs*, 513–14; "The Exile of Sakharov," 75. That Tsvigun was also Brezhnev's brother-in-law suggests that the general secretary himself had directed, or at least organized, the whole operation. Rubenstein and Gribanov, *KGB File*, 241.

In exiling Sakharov, the Soviet leadership hoped to silence him without rupturing its relations with the West, which were already strained severely by the Soviet invasion of Afghanistan. For this reason, killing Sakharov was not a real option. Nor, despite the collapse of détente, was putting him on trial on charges sufficiently plausible for gullible Western elites to believe. However precarious his physical health, Sakharov was still strong enough psychologically not to incriminate himself or other dissidents, as Piotr Iakir had done in 1973, in exchange for lenient treatment. From the government's perspective, it was far better to exile Sakharov internally to a city like Gorky, where the KGB could keep him under surveillance—which it could not do if, like Solzhenitsyn, he were exiled abroad. When Andropov first proposed exiling Sakharov to Gorky, no one in the Politburo objected in principle to the punishment, and only Chernenko and Viktor Grishin expressed a preference for a city farther from Moscow. In his memoirs Anatolii Dobrynin, the longtime Soviet ambassador to the United States, claims unpersuasively that the Kremlin hierarchs considered Sakharov relatively unimportant and not really dangerous to the regime in his own right. But Dobrynin also writes that, as "the constant focus of anti-Soviet campaigning abroad," Sakharov had to be dealt with, and sending him someplace where foreigners could not get to him made perfect sense.[4] In Andrei Gromyko's assessment, "The question of Sakharov has ceased to be a purely domestic matter. He finds an enormous number of responses abroad. All the anti-Soviet scum, all this rabble revolves around Sakharov. It is impossible to ignore this situation any longer."[5]

To minimize the Western protests Gromyko feared, the Soviet leadership tried to rid themselves of Sakharov as quickly as possible. In fact, it was precisely to avoid, or at least to minimize, such protests that the Politburo accepted Andropov's recommendation that Sakharov not be tried in court despite his being indictable, under Articles 64 and 70 of the Criminal Code of the RSFSR, respectively, for treason and anti-Soviet agitation.[6] Significantly, Sakharov states in his memoirs, as he did in an interview in 1987, that he was never shown, and was skeptical of the existence of, any document originating in the Politburo, the Council of Ministers, or the Supreme Soviet formally ordering the KGB to take action; the document Rekunkov read that revoked Sakharov's medals and awards contained nothing about banishing him to Gorky, despite Rekunkov's efforts to leave Sakharov with the impression that it did.[7]

4. Dobrynin, *In Confidence*, 512–13. The urgency with which the government removed Sakharov from Moscow was partly a reflection of the fact that the Olympics were to begin there shortly. With Sakharov incommunicado, foreign reporters covering the games would not be able to interview him.

5. "Politburo Meeting (January 3, 1980)," in Rubenstein and Gribanov, *KGB File*, 247.

6. "Andropov and Rudenko to the Central Committee (December 26, 1979)," in Rubenstein and Gribanov, *KGB File*, 245, 247.

7. Sakharov, *Memoirs*, 511. In his memoirs, Sakharov states that when the government rescinded his exile, it still would not confirm the existence of a decree formally exiling him in 1980. He goes on to write that the only decree he saw that pertained to his exile was "the one stripping me of my awards." Ibid., 616. Of course, a document formally exiling Sakharov may someday be found. But the circumstances surrounding both the beginning of Sakharov's exile and the end of

Sakharov's exile, of course, was illegal and unconstitutional. Only a court could order a Soviet citizen into exile; indeed, from Sakharov's initial arrest to the end of his exile in December 1986, he was never accused of a crime, not even informally.[8] In addition, as Sofia Kalistratova, who was herself an attorney, pointed out, the terms of Sakharov's exile (not just the simple fact of it) were lawless: the maximum term for internal exile, in Soviet law, was five years; Sakharov's exile was indefinite. In addition, most of the restrictions that were placed on his activities once he was settled in Gorky had no explicit sanction in Soviet law.[9] Finally, Article 9 of the Universal Declaration of Human Rights, which the Soviet Union had agreed to uphold by signing the Helsinki Accords, explicitly forbade "arbitrary exile."[10]

But legalisms such as these were irrelevant to the delicate assignment the KGB was ordered to carry out. Sakharov was no ordinary dissident. By the mid 1970s, long before the Afghan invasion, he had become the foremost symbol in the West of opposition to the Soviet regime—far more so, it must be said, than Solzhenitsyn, whose strident attacks on capitalism and Western materialism after establishing residence in the West severely diminished his credibility.[11] Moreover, Sakharov, unlike Solzhenitsyn, spoke the language of Western liberalism. His reiteration and defense of human rights resonated deeply with intellectual elites in the West who, whatever their moral myopia about the Soviet Union and communism, took for granted the values Sakharov was championing, such as freedom of speech, the right of unfettered access to information, and the right of people to choose their place of residence. This was all the more reason for the Soviet leadership to try to silence Sakharov without at the same time turning him into a martyr.

### Settling In, Reluctantly, in Gorky

On their arrival in Gorky, Sakharov and Bonner were taken directly to what would be their home for almost the next seven years—a four-room apartment in an eleven-story building at 214 Gagarin Street.[12] Inside they found waiting for them the deputy procurator for the Gorky District, an apparatchik named Perelygin, who informed Sakharov of the restrictions he would henceforth have to abide by: under no circumstances could he travel beyond the city limits, meet with foreigners, or communicate by telephone or through the mails; in addition, he would have to report periodically to the police and would be kept

---

it nearly seven years later suggest that the government did not want to leave a paper trail making its culpability explicit.

8. Andrei Sakharov, "Statement on Manuscript Theft (November 10, 1982)," ibid., 683.

9. Sofia Kalistratova, "Lawlessness: A Lawyer's Notes," in Babyonyshev, *On Sakharov*, 24–27.

10. Paul Sieghart, "The Sakharov Case and International Law," *Fifth International Sakharov Hearing: Proceedings, April 1985*, ed. Allan Wynn (London, 1986), 16.

11. See, in this regard, Aleksandr I. Solzhenitsyn, *A World Split Apart: Commencement Address Delivered at Harvard University, June 8, 1978* (New York, 1978).

12. Bonner, *Alone Together*, 24. The apartment was on the first floor, above which neither Sakharov nor Bonner was allowed to go. Tatiana Yankelevich, conversation with author, January 13, 2004.

under nearly constant surveillance.[13] The only benefit Sakharov derived from the highly irregular manner in which the Soviet government chose to dispose of him was that because no formal directive was ever issued for his arrest and exile and then distributed to the various institutions with which he was associated professionally, the functionary at the Academy of Sciences charged with dispensing the monthly stipends to academicians refused the order of his superior to stop sending stipends to Sakharov. As a result, he continued to be paid by the academy as if nothing untoward had happened to him.[14] In this particular instance, as was often the case in the Brezhnev era, the government's cruelty was tempered by its incompetence.

The Soviet leaders of course were aware that Sakharov's exile, no matter how smoothly it was executed, could not be kept secret. The fact that it was announced in *Izvestiia* in its evening edition of January 22 and followed shortly by attacks on Sakharov in various Soviet newspapers suggests that the government wanted to get out its version of what had happened and why before Western governments and organizations could condemn it.[15] On January 23, an article in *Izvestiia* entitled, in English translation, "A Just Decision," that was written by (or for) the journalist K. Batmanov, derided Sakharov as a tool of Western imperialism who had betrayed the Soviet people. Claiming that Sakharov had already passed state secrets to American and West European journalists and diplomats, Batmanov derided him as a renegade and an apostate who, while serving "a foreign master," engaged in politics because he was burned out as a scientist.[16] On January 28, TASS lent its voice to the chorus of calumny, calling Sakharov a warmonger acting at the instigation of the most aggressive imperialist circles in the West. On January 30, the gazette of the Supreme Soviet appeared with the decree depriving Sakharov of his awards and title appended to it.[17] The same day, *Literaturnaia gazeta* described Sakharov's life as an object lesson in how a person of weak character (Sakharov) could be manipulated ideologically by "a vain egomaniac" (Bonner).[18] Over the next two weeks the polemics diminished in both number and intensity, but on February 15, perhaps in anticipation of retribution by Western scientists and governments, they resumed, most vehemently in an article in *Komsomolskaia pravda* arguing that the egomania Sakharov had developed in the 1950s as a result of his contributions to thermonuclear weaponry was the reason the "humanism" he espoused

13. Sakharov, *Memoirs*, 514–15.

14. Janouch, "My 'Meetings' and Encounters with Andrei Dmitrievich Sakharov," 378–79.

15. Sakharov, *Memoirs*, 516.

16. K. Batmanov, "A Just Decision," in *Chronicle of Human Rights* 37 (January–March 1980): 12. According to an Israeli physicist, Gary Lipkin, the Soviet government circulated not only Batmanov's charge that Sakharov, by the time he was exiled to Gorky, was past his prime as a physicist; it also claimed that it had sent him to Gorky to spare him further embarrassment from this. Gary Lipkin, "Andrei Sakharov i Institut Veitsmana," in Altshuler et al., *On mezhdu nami zhil*, 392.

17. "In the Presidium of the USSR Academy of Sciences," *TASS*, January 28, 1980, reprinted in *Chronicle of Human Rights*, no. 37 (January–March 1980): 15; Sakharov, *Memoirs*, 516.

18. B. L. Altshuler, "Nou-khau," in Altshuler et al., *On mezhdu nami zhil*, 57.

later in his life was not merely "false" but "pathologically inhuman."[19] Also on February 15, an article in *Novoe vremia* (*New Times*) accused Sakharov of attempting to establish an organization joining dissidents and foreigners in a common effort to undermine the Soviet state.[20]

In his memoirs Sakharov claims that in the hours after his arrest he responded passively, too passively, to the measures being taken against him.[21] His responses to Rekunkov during their meeting suggest the opposite, however, and by the time he arrived in Gorky he was determined to raise his voice yet again against his own government, summoning all the eloquence he could muster in an effort to show the world it could not silence him. Sakharov's message, in essence, was that the Soviet government was obliged by its own laws and by the simple fact of his own humanity to treat him well, which in practical terms meant abrogating his exile immediately.

Sakharov's campaign, now that he was in Gorky, required Bonner's participation and that of her family as well. As in the past, they responded magnificently to the challenge. On the evening of January 22, Liza and Ruf held an informal press conference at the Chkalov Street apartment, where they told the reporters assembled there the truth about what had happened that day.[22] Over the next few days, the apartment came to resemble a "madhouse," as reporters, friends, acquaintances, and even people entirely unknown to the family milled about, awaiting word of further developments.[23] On January 27, Sakharov, from Gorky, issued a statement notable for its open defiance: virtually everything that had been done to him since the afternoon of January 22, he insisted, was illegal as well as a violation of the Universal Declaration of Human Rights; for that reason he was prepared "to stand public and open trial" to demonstrate his innocence of the accusations against him.[24] Sakharov pointedly cited in his appeal not only dissidents and political prisoners other than himself but also members of ethnic and religious minorities whose dissent had caused them to be arrested and sent to prison or to labor camps. The implication—conspicuously absent in the appeals he had issued in 1973—was that his arrest, coupled as it was with punitive actions against other opponents of the regime, could hardly be considered the result of purely personal failings, which was precisely how the government, by stressing Sakharov's malleability and Bonner's duplicity, was depicting it.

To reinforce the impression that he could not be intimidated, on January 30, two days after Bonner had read his statement to foreign correspondents, Sakharov told Perelygin, who had summoned him to the procurator's office in Gorky, that because his exile was illegal, the restrictions imposed on him were illegal as well, particularly the injunction against meeting with foreign reporters. Calmly but with his customary directness and precision, Sakharov told

19. Quoted ibid.
20. "The Exile of Sakharov," 76–77.
21. Sakharov, *Memoirs*, 512.
22. Ibid., 517.
23. Ibid.
24. Andrei Sakharov, "Statement of January 27, 1980," ibid., 675.

Perelygin that he would not comply with these restrictions and would not even register officially as a permanent resident of Gorky, as Perelygin demanded.[25] His only concession—which he retracted in a letter he wrote to Perelygin the same evening—was to acknowledge having heard the deputy procurator's warnings of punitive measures in the event he violated the terms of his exile. But beyond that Sakharov was unwilling to go, and he left Perelygin's office as defiant as when he had entered it. In his confrontations with Soviet bureaucrats like Perelygin, Sakharov, like the Russian revolutionaries of the late nineteenth century, tried at times to reverse the roles of accuser and defendant, in this case holding Perelygin responsible for the decisions of his superiors by exposing these decisions to a foreign audience he fervently hoped would condemn them. For Sakharov's stratagem to work, Bonner's assistance and the assistance of foreign reporters were absolutely essential, and Sakharov's defense was as much an exercise in public persuasion as it was a reiteration of legal principles.

In their efforts to gain public support, Sakharov and Bonner were successful. Although the protests they generated were not sufficient to cause the government to rescind Sakharov's exile or even to make the terms of it less onerous, they probably prevented the government from treating him more harshly. Although the dissidents in the Soviet Union raised their voices on his behalf, the support Sakharov received from abroad was more significant politically. The United States Congress passed a concurrent resolution condemning Sakharov's exile, as did the European Parliament, the Dutch government, and the Italian and Spanish Communist parties, whose advocacy of a communism more humane than the Soviet model included supporting Soviet dissidents like Sakharov.[26] In addition, Jacques Chaban-Delmas, the president of the French National Assembly, cut short his visit to Moscow in protest after Sakharov was arrested.[27] Western intellectuals, despite the penchant of many of them for claiming a moral equivalence between Western democracy and Soviet Communism, spoke out on Sakharov's behalf with surprising vehemence. Either in public statements or in private telegrams to Brezhnev, French physicists, American college presidents, and two hundred physicists at the European Center for Nuclear Research made clear their displeasure with what the Soviets had done, while twenty-five American Nobel laureates warned the Soviet leader that American scientists would not stand idly by if the Soviet Union's treatment of their fellow prize winner did not improve. In England, four Oxford professors wrote a pointed letter to the *Times* of London rejecting the Soviet government's insinuation that Sakharov had taken up politics because he had deteriorated as a physicist. Of all the protests that occurred, clearly the most ominous from the perspective of the Soviet government was the decision on February 24 by the council of the National Academy of Sciences in the United States to suspend for six months all bilateral

25. Ibid., 521–22. In the six months following Sakharov's exile, the KGB demanded more than fifty times that Sakharov do this, and each time he refused. Ibid., 526.
26. "Western Responses," *Chronicle of Human Rights*, no. 37 (January–March 1980): 21–24.
27. Rubenstein, *Soviet Dissidents*, 274.

contacts with the Soviet Academy of Sciences. This meant that American scientists with membership in the National Academy who wished to receive Soviet scientists in the United States or to visit them in the Soviet Union or even just to contact them for the purpose of exchanging ideas and information would now have to make their own arrangements.[28]

Because Bonner had brought to Gorky the transistor radio she and Sakharov used in Moscow to receive broadcasts from Radio Liberty, Voice of America, and other stations that included information about the dissidents and the support they received in the West, she and Sakharov were fairly well informed of Western protests on Sakharov's behalf. When in March the police installed a jamming device near their apartment building, the couple simply went outside, walked far enough away from the device to avoid its effects, and listened to the stations they preferred with little difficulty.[29] Undoubtedly Sakharov and Bonner were gratified by the protests, especially those from dissidents and others in the Soviet Union who lacked the immunity Western critics enjoyed, though they were equally concerned when the individuals responsible for these protests were punished. In one case, a protester in Makhachkala in the Caucasus got seven years in prison and two years in exile for standing in the town center for an hour with a sign calling for Sakharov's release and the government's adherence to human rights.[30] But they were disappointed, even enraged, by the virtual silence of Sakharov's colleagues in the Academy of Sciences.[31] To be sure, Sakharov was not expelled from the academy, and his nameplate on the door to the office he maintained at the institute (which was an arm of the academy and directly responsible to it) was not removed in all the years he was at Gorky.[32] No motion to dismiss him was ever introduced in the academy, and the issue of his exile never came up in the course of official business.[33] Only the few academicians who personally loathed Sakharov ever discussed the matter, and they apparently did so only privately.[34] But members of the academy who were sympathetic to Sakharov were silent as well.[35] In keeping with the government's wish that Sakharov be silenced but without causing contacts and exchanges with American scientists to cease, the consensus in the academy, in short, was that its members should simply ignore him.[36] This was the principal reason for the lack of pressure from the Soviet government to expel him.[37]

28. "Western Responses," 22–26.

29. Sakharov, *Memoirs*, 515, 527.

30. Sharansky, *Fear No Evil*, 313.

31. Sakharov, *Memoirs*, 515–16.

32. V. A. Zuckerman, "Academician Andrei Dmitrievich Sakharov," in Altshuler et al., *Facets of a Life*, 684.

33. Joel Lebowitz, "Ogromnaia dukhovnaia sila," in Altshuler et al., *On mezhdu nami zhil*, 376–87.

34. A. B. Migdal, "K portretu Andreia Sakharova," in Altshuler et al., *On mezhdu nami zhil*, 437; editor's note, *Chronicle of Human Rights*, no. 37 (January–March 1980): 16.

35. Sakharov, *Memoirs*, 515–16.

36. Altshuler, "Misunderstanding Sakharov," 232.

37. Sakharov, *Memoirs*, 517.

In this case, unlike the Nuzhdin affair in 1964, the interests of the academy and the government coincided. Both thought Sakharov's expulsion from the academy a bad idea because its likely consequences would be harmful to their particular interests. As Geoffrey Hosking and others have argued, the academicians were concerned, above all, to defend their privileges, such as traveling abroad to scientific conferences and having access to Western scientific journals. Both of these, of course, would be threatened if Western scientists curtailed all contacts with them in retaliation for their expelling Sakharov.[38] Moral principle, or even the impulse to close ranks around a member of their own profession who was treated badly, was a factor only to scientists such as Feinberg and Vitalii Ginzburg. Apart from their political views, they were friends of Sakharov as well as colleagues, and they lobbied their colleagues not to expel him from the academy (an endeavor that was actually unnecessary) at least partly out of a sense of personal loyalty.[39]

In the Lebedev Institute itself, roughly the same dynamic prevailed. To be sure, members of the theoretical department opposed Sakharov's exile as a matter of principle, and while they apparently did nothing to protest it, the head of the department, Vitalii Ginzburg, and other members lobbied privately to prevent Sakharov's expulsion from the institute. In addition, they deputized Ginzburg to plead on their behalf with Communist Party officials that they be allowed to contact and visit Sakharov. In this they were mostly successful, and seventeen members of the institute visited Sakharov in Gorky from 1980 to 1986, some more than once.[40] But if Evgenii Feinberg's recollections of the whole matter are accurate, the majority of the scientists who expressed interest in seeing Sakharov "had scientific interests closest to his own"—which suggests they went to Gorky at least partly for the benefits of talking physics with Sakharov rather than as a gesture of solidarity.[41]

The response of the Soviet scientific establishment to Sakharov's arrest and exile, in sum, was almost exclusively one of calculated indifference; only a few scientists, among them Kapitsa, responded favorably to requests from Bonner for assistance.[42] Soviet scientists did not persecute Sakharov more than the government wished them to (principally by expelling him from the scientific

38. Geoffrey Hosking, *The Awakening of the Soviet Union* (Cambridge, Mass., 1991), 49.

39. Unlike Ginzburg, who was a full member of the academy, Feinberg, at the time of Sakharov's exile, was only a corresponding member. D. S. Chernavskii, "Vizit v Gorkii," in Altshuler et al., *On mezhdu nami zhil*, 758.

40. Ibid.; E. Feinberg, "Pamiati velikogo grazhdanina," *Literaturnaia gazeta*, December 20, 1989, 10; Vladimir Ya. Fainberg, "Precursor of Perestroika," *Physics Today*, August 1990, 44.

41. Feinberg, "Biographical Sketch," 8.

42. In Kapitsa's case, he and Khariton appealed to Andropov in November 1980 to treat Sakharov more humanely—after refusing a request from Ruf Bonner the previous January to condemn the original decision to exile him. But when Andropov refused their request, they protested no further. Sakharov, *Memoirs*, 303, 517; Altshuler, "Nou-khau," 60. Limiting himself to halfway measures was typical of Kapitsa's remonstrations on Sakharov's behalf. In 1973, when Soviet scientists circulated a letter denouncing Sakharov, Kapitsa, to his credit, refused to sign it. But he did not defend Sakharov publicly either. Iurii Rost, "Akademik," *Literaturnaia gazeta*, November 16, 1988, 12.

institutions to which he belonged), but they did little or nothing to help him. In both cases, self-interest was the dominant motive—fear of the adverse effects expulsion might have on their contacts with Western scientists, along with a desire to benefit professionally from any conversations they would have with Sakharov about physics. As it happened, the National Academy of Sciences in the United States, despite the efforts of Soviet scientists to prevent it, instituted a boycott on scientific contacts on February 24, which continued until 1984.[43] But the public silence Soviet scientists observed continued for many years, in some cases beyond the rescission of Sakharov's exile in December 1986. If they expressed any opposition, they did so privately, and for this reason the bitterness Sakharov and Bonner felt for the Soviet scientific establishment never disappeared. In October 1980 Sakharov sent a letter to Anatolii Alexandrov, the president of the Academy of Sciences, angrily reproaching him and his colleagues for not opposing his exile at a time when their intervention might have succeeded in reversing it. Nineteen years later Bonner was still criticizing Sakharov's colleagues publicly for what she considered their unconscionable cowardice.[44] In fact, it was in response to criticism such as hers that Alexandrov in 1990 claimed that he and Keldysh had been responsible for preventing Sakharov's expulsion from the Academy of Sciences—which was manifestly untrue—and that once Sakharov was in exile, there was nothing they or anyone else in the academy could have done for him. Life in Gorky, Alexandrov added gratuitously and self-servingly, was not as terrible as Sakharov's supporters imagined it was, and the isolation it entailed was no worse than what Sakharov had experienced at Arzamas.[45]

Surprisingly, Sakharov's living conditions in Gorky were not as onerous as they might have been. The apartment he and Bonner were assigned in the building on Gagarin Street had six rooms (which included a kitchen and a bathroom). Large by Soviet standards, the apartment was even more commodious for the couple because the relatives who had lived with them in Moscow were now either abroad or forbidden to join them in Gorky. As a result, Sakharov and Bonner had a fair amount of space, as well as time, to themselves.[46] Moreover, as a disabled war veteran, Bonner had access, even in Gorky, to the special stores from which ordinary Soviet citizens were barred. Although she was not allowed to enter these stores, the items she needed were delivered to her.[47] When asked in 1988 what life had been like in Gorky, Sakharov described it as "tranquil,"

43. "Western Responses," 25; Bailey, *Making of Andrei Sakharov*, 355.

44. Andrei Sakharov, "Open Letter to Anatoly Aleksandrov, President of the USSR Academy of Sciences (October 20, 1980)," in Babyonyshev, *On Sakharov*, 220–21; Moroz, "Vozvrashchenie iz ssylki," 272–73; Elena Bonner, "Komu nuzhny mify," *Ogonëk* 11 (March 1990): 25.

45. "Akademik Aleksandrov otvechaet," 61–62. To make the academy's inaction appear more honorable than Bonner described it, Alexandrov also compared it favorably to Pasternak's expulsion from the Writers' Union in 1958, after he won the Nobel Prize for Literature. Because it had occurred more recently, when the current Soviet leadership was in power, Alexandrov did *not* mention Solzhenitsyn's expulsion in 1967 from the same Writers Union that expelled Pasternak.

46. Sakharov, *Memoirs*, 515. In May 1980 Ruf Bonner emigrated to the United States.

47. Bonner, *Alone Together*, 200.

and in his memoirs he freely acknowledges that exile in Gorky was preferable to prison or confinement in a labor camp.[48]

The life Sakharov and Bonner led had a comforting rhythm to it. Every six weeks or so, Bonner would depart for Moscow, where she would stay in the apartment the couple retained there for anywhere from ten to fifteen days—during which she would buy foods and other items not available in Gorky and gather up books Sakharov requested—and then return to Gorky. In the nearly seven years that Sakharov was in Gorky, Bonner made approximately 150 such trips.[49] In addition, the couple were allowed to have a car. Sakharov used it only rarely, and Bonner, though she drove it in Gorky, took the train to Moscow. On the way passengers occasionally accosted her and denounced her husband, of whose treason they were certain.[50] When Bonner was in Gorky, the couple followed a normal routine, in which they went food shopping, watched television, went to the movies, and when the weather was good, indulged in the age-old Russian recreation of picking mushrooms.[51] The police had no objection to Sakharov's ordering books from the bookstore of the Academy of Science in Moscow, and while the couple could not invite acquaintances who lived in Gorky to visit them, they were permitted to visit one couple, the Khainovskiis, who were not only old friends of theirs but distant relatives of Bonner.[52]

Along with the material comforts Sakharov and Bonner enjoyed, what made life in Gorky tolerable were the visits the authorities permitted from Soviet scientists. In all likelihood the government calculated that by allowing these visits, it would lessen the adverse effects Sakharov's exile had on the country's image abroad. Presumably, when Sakharov's colleagues returned from Gorky, they would report that he was reasonably well and fully able to pursue his scientific work even without access to scientific institutes in Moscow. On reaching the West, this information would then persuade Western scientists who were boycotting the Soviet Union to reverse their decision and resume the scientific contacts the Soviet government considered essential.[53] Once the scientists who wished to visit Sakharov in Gorky had been vetted by the KGB, the only real restriction on their visits was that politics not be discussed.[54] From 1980 to 1986, Linde, Fradkin, Kalashnikov, Fainberg, and Feinberg all visited Sakharov after

48. Sakharov, *Memoirs*, 551; Sakharov and Adamovich, "Zhit' na zemle i zhit' dolgo," 173.

49. Sakharov, *Memoirs*, 548; Altshuler, "On nebyl naiven," 234.

50. Sakharov, *Memoirs*, 595; Edward Kline, conversation with author, June 10, 2008; Nikolai Grachev, "U dveri," in Ivanova, *Andrei Dmitrievich*, 184. Grachev was one of the militiamen who stood watch at Sakharov's apartment in Gorky.

51. Sakharov, *Memoirs*, 599–600.

52. Ibid., 549.

53. Ibid., 550; Liebowitz, "Ogromnaia dukhovnaia sila," 381. To convince public opinion in the West that Sakharov was being well treated, the Soviets also importuned politically pliant members of the Academy of Sciences to misinform foreign scientists about Sakharov's exile. Among the lies the latter were told was that Sakharov had a personal secretary in Gorky to tend to his needs. Sakharov, *Memoirs*, 550.

54. There were three visits in 1980, two in 1982, seven in 1983, three in 1984, two in 1985, and three in 1986. Chernavskii, "Osnova vselennoi mozhet raspadat'sia," 69; I. M. Drĕminym, "Gor'kovskaia papka," in Altshuler et al., *On mezhdu nami zhil*, 883.

accepting this condition.[55] The only physicist who came without official permission was Misha Levin, who arranged through a mutual friend to meet Bonner at a specified location in Gorky while attending a scientific conference there from which Sakharov was barred.[56] Given that the government, for its own reasons, approved of these visits, traveling to Gorky to talk physics with Sakharov hardly qualified as an act of courage, much less an expression of dissidence. But the visits helped to relieve Sakharov's isolation and raised his spirits considerably.

Still, neither Sakharov nor Bonner could forget the fact that they were personae non gratae. Nor could they ignore the toll that living in exile exacted as it continued year after year. The arrangements they had to abide by seemed designed to rob them of their autonomy and independence and thus of their dignity as human beings. Particularly galling was the constant surveillance by the KGB and the uniformed police, which made it easy for the couple to believe that their exile would never end. The authorities kept tabs on the couple mostly by tailing them wherever they went. But they also enlisted the services of "civilians," including for some time an older woman who euphemistically introduced herself to Sakharov as his "landlady" but whose late husband had once been a KGB agent. The woman showed up every day at Sakharov's apartment—occasionally, to perpetuate her cover, she came with sheets and towels—and simply sat for several hours in a room in the apartment that was reserved for her, after which she departed for the local KGB headquarters, where she informed the officials there of Sakharov's and Bonner's activities.[57] Not coincidentally, the apartment building where the couple lived also served as a safe house for KGB agents between sensitive assignments, and several KGB officials lived in the building as well.[58] Because the landlady deliberately left the window in her room unlocked, KGB agents on several occasions entered the apartment without any difficulty when Sakharov and Bonner were out and then rummaged through the couple's belongings for documents and other items they thought their superiors would find useful. These robberies continued until July 1980, when Sakharov realized how the landlady was facilitating them and thereafter refused to let her in. To limit the unfavorable publicity a confrontation over the issue would have caused, the police raised no objections when Sakharov complained, and no other "landladies" ever appeared at his door.[59]

Given their concerns about foreign protests, the authorities carefully calibrated, and occasionally recalibrated, the severity of Sakharov's restrictions. In the first week he and Bonner were in Gorky, he was allowed to receive visitors. But the KGB then began screening them, detaining those it deemed politically unacceptable and even, in three cases, sending them to psychiatric hospitals. With the exception of scientists, the KGB eventually allowed Sakharov no visitors

55. Drēminym, "Gor'kovskaia papka," 883.
56. M. L. Levin, "Eti gor'kie vstrechi v Gor'kom," *Kuranty*, May 21, 1991, 5.
57. Sakharov, *Memoirs*, 515, 528.
58. Klose, *Russia and the Russians*, 223.
59. Sakharov, *Memoirs*, 527–28.

at all, and when he and Bonner, in attempting to relieve their isolation, tried to make long-distance or international telephone calls, the telephones in the nearby post office they had to use went dead.[60] Sakharov was also tailed by policemen everywhere he went, even when he took out the garbage, and there were times during his exile when as many as thirty-five KGB agents (in addition to ordinary policemen) were assigned to him.[61] In the spring of 1983, at about the same time the police set up command posts—one outside the apartment building, another outside the apartment itself—to turn away would-be visitors, Sakharov and Bonner realized that the telephones in neighbors' apartments they had previously used for local calls were now malfunctioning as well—even though they worked perfectly after the couple returned home. What this meant in terms of their everyday lives, quite apart from reducing their ability to communicate with supporters and to generate protests, was that Sakharov and Bonner now had no way of summoning medical assistance in the event of an emergency.[62] Of course their apartment itself was bugged by the KGB, and whenever Sakharov and Bonner wanted to communicate something they thought should remain private, they wrote it on slates.[63] To foster the false impression that there was nothing amiss in their lives, the KGB sent American and West European media film it had shot earlier of Sakharov and Bonner talking nonchalantly on the telephone.[64]

The Soviet government harassed Sakharov in Gorky for the same reason it had sent him there, namely, to prevent him from continuing his dissidence, which required that he communicate with supporters both in the Soviet Union and in the West. In this respect the isolation he experienced in Gorky was different from what he had experienced earlier at Arzamas: whereas at Arzamas it was the privileges Sakharov enjoyed, as much as the military projects he was working on, that had to be kept secret from the Soviet people, in Gorky it was the ideas he espoused and the moral authority he gave to these ideas that required his continued separation from the outside world. But the actions the government took after January 1980 to silence him had the additional purpose of weakening the dissident movement to the point where it would disappear entirely. By the time the government sent Sakharov into exile, the movement had been so debilitated by the arrest and subsequent punishment of its leading members that, without Sakharov to publicize the travails of dissidents less well known than he, without his bearing witness at trials and demonstrations, and without his signature proudly affixed to petitions calling on the Soviet Union to abide by its own laws and legal principles, it might simply cease to exist. The celebrity and moral authority Sakharov brought to the dissident movement were essential to its survival, and so the stakes in his struggle to retain a modicum of personal

60. Ibid., 518, 526.
61. Ibid., 526–27, 549.
62. Ibid., 581–82.
63. Bonner, *Alone Together,* 113.
64. Ibid., 196–97.

freedom once he was in Gorky transcended the limits of his own personal predicament. What was at stake was the fate of the dissident movement itself. Thus there was no reason, out of a sense of modesty, for Sakharov to remain silent.[65]

The government's ultimate objective in harassing Sakharov was to break him—to wear him down sufficiently that he would, on his own volition, relinquish his views or at least recognize that trying to advance them from Gorky was not worth the toll it took on his physical and emotional health. Sometimes the tactics the government used to achieve its objective were utterly juvenile. During their periodic burglaries of his apartment, KGB agents occasionally deposited cockroaches among papers of his they deemed too trivial to steal.[66] More sinister, and far more threatening to Sakharov, were the multiple thefts of his memoirs. In March 1981, while he was at a dentist's office receiving treatment, agents trailing him took his only copy of the memoirs after Sakharov unwisely left the bag that contained them in the reception area.[67] In October 1982, after finishing another version, Sakharov had a large portion of it snatched from him by KGB agents while he was sitting in his car, possibly after being drugged.[68] Finally, in December 1982, agents claiming to be detectives accosted Bonner on the train she was taking from Gorky to Moscow and took the section of the memoirs she had with her, along with a movie camera and movies she and Sakharov had taken of themselves to counter the misleading footage the KGB had pawned off in the West as authentic. Roi Medvedev, who had previously disparaged Sakharov during the press campaign in 1973, fell even lower in Sakharov's estimation when he told a foreign reporter a few days after this happened that because Sakharov knew state secrets, he had no right to write memoirs at all. The KGB's theft of them, Medvedev sniffed, was something he and Bonner should have expected.[69]

To some extent, the thefts were trial balloons to test what the foreign reaction might be to more extreme measures the government might take in the future.[70] In addition, they may simply have been a way of preventing publication in the West of a book that credibly depicted the Soviet system in an unflattering light.[71]

---

65. Sakharov, *Memoirs*, 551.

66. Bonner, *Alone Together*, 111–12.

67. Ibid., 7; Sakharov, *Memoirs*, 529–31. After the KGB robbed his apartment several times, Sakharov began taking with him all important documents, including his memoirs, wherever he went. But on this particular occasion he agreed to the suggestion of the receptionist in the dentist's office—who may have worked for the KGB—that he leave with her his bag containing not only the memoirs but also his personal diary and drafts of essays on Pushkin and Faulkner. Possibly by prearrangement, she later gave the bag to KGB agents when they arrived. In his memoirs Sakharov berates himself for not having made a second copy—which, in the absence of a copy machine, would not have been easy. Bonner, "Chetyre daty," 177; Sakharov, *Memoirs*, 530.

68. Sakharov, *Memoirs*, 532–33; Andrei Sakharov, "Letter to Vitaly Fedorchuk (October 23, 1982)," ibid., 681.

69. Ibid., 535–37.

70. Ibid.

71. In his memoirs, Sakharov refers elliptically to Bonner's transmitting the memoirs to the Yankelevichs in America but does not describe how she did this. Sakharov, ibid., 531. Nor did Efrem Yankelevich when I asked him in February 2004.

But the principal reason for stealing Sakharov's memoirs, one suspects, was to rob their author of his ability to function as a rational being, which Sakharov always considered the sine qua non of his own and everyone else's humanity. If he could not do this, if he could not create and sustain an intellectual life for himself, he would be just as dead as if he had been physically killed. Sakharov, it seems, was aware of this, and understood how much, both for himself and for the regime, was riding on the survival and eventual publication of his memoirs. In the statement he sent to Western reporters decrying the theft of his memoirs in March 1981, Sakharov noted pointedly that the KGB, by stealing these and other documents critically important to him, was trying "to deprive me of my memories, the record of my ideas, and the possibility of any intellectual life, even in solitude."[72] Like the censors in Stalin's time who obliterated from history books not just any mention of Trotsky's supposed malfeasance but all evidence of his very existence, the KGB in the early 1980s tried to rob Sakharov, and everyone who might be interested in who he was and what he stood for, of the record he had compiled of his life up to that time. By stealing Sakharov's memoirs, the regime was encroaching on the prerogative especially dear to him of reconstructing his own life as he saw it, of telling his story truthfully so that the values and principles it illuminated would be understandable. Telling the truth about himself was for Sakharov a human right no less sacred and universal than the other human rights he championed. In fact, his difficulties in preserving his memoirs and getting them to people in the West who might be favorably influenced by them seemed emblematic of all the other difficulties he was experiencing.

No matter how well they lived in purely material terms, exile for Sakharov and Bonner was a very difficult burden for both of them to bear; in Sakharov's words, it "strained our strength and our nerves to the limit."[73] Because of the role Bonner played as her husband's only real conduit to the outside world, his exile in some ways placed more of a burden on her than on him. In poor health when Sakharov began his exile in 1980, she suffered at least one serious heart attack and several "cardiac seizures" in the course of it.[74] But Sakharov suffered as well. He often despaired that his exile might never end, and he shared Bonner's conviction in 1983 that the KGB was quite literally killing them.[75] At one point in their exile, the couple selected cemetery plots for themselves.[76]

## Doing Physics Again

Under the circumstances, the scientific work Sakharov did in Gorky was a welcome diversion and in lifting his spirits truly therapeutic. Exile gave Sakharov more time to devote to physics than he had in the 1970s, when fighting for human rights on a global scale took priority. But in the early 1980s this was

72. Andrei Sakharov, "Statement of March 17, 1981," ibid., 680.
73. Ibid., 551.
74. Ibid., 581–82.
75. Ibid., 583; Elena Bonner, "Otvet na voprosy frantsuzskogo Komiteta 15-i (November 1983)," *Materialy samizdata*, no. 6/84 (February 27, 1984), AS 5159: 1–3.
76. Altshuler, "On nebyl naiven," 235.

no longer possible, and without the continuous flow of dissidents, reporters, and ordinary citizens seeking his opinions or assistance, he could concentrate on the cosmological issues with which he had first grappled in the 1960s and 1970s. These issues concerned the origins, development, and eventual fate of the universe—a topic sufficiently large that it minimized, perhaps even trivialized, the oppression Sakharov was experiencing. Compared with the universe, the Soviet Union was a transient phenomenon, of little or no consequence in the larger scheme of things. For Sakharov raising cosmological questions was just as gratifying psychologically as it was stimulating intellectually, and because the answers he proposed to these questions were purely theoretical and speculative, he had no need of the scientific institutes, with their laboratories and other equipment, from which he was now excluded.[77] Whatever articles he needed for his work, even those by non-Russian scientists, the authorities allowed him to receive. Some of these were forwarded by the institute; others he received directly from colleagues and scientific institutes abroad.[78] There were so many of them, in fact, that, by his own admission, he had trouble reading them all.[79]

In defining the limits of Sakharov's autonomy as a scientist, the Soviet government displayed the same bewildering mixture of leniency and repression it showed in establishing the other terms of his exile. For example, the government allowed him to submit the articles he wrote in Gorky to Soviet scientific journals, even the most prestigious ones, such as the *Journal of Experimental and Theoretical Physics,* which published them. At the same time, however, the censors excised the dedications Sakharov included in these articles because they considered them politically provocative. In fairness to the government, several of these were clearly calculated to antagonize: one was to Bonner, and another was to Philip Handler, former president of the American Academy of Sciences, recently deceased, who in the fall of 1973 had strongly protested the press campaign against Sakharov.[80] Still, Sakharov had been so thoroughly marginalized politically by his confinement in Gorky that the government would have gained more than it lost in terms of public relations had it simply allowed the dedications to remain.

In Gorky Sakharov worked on a variety of topics in what he called "fundamental science."[81] One of these was string theory, which hypothesized the existence of additional dimensions beyond the three spatial ones and the single temporal one that are perceptible. String theory was one of the most promising and controversial topics in theoretical physics, its proponents claiming that once it was understood completely and corroborated empirically, it might yield the Unified Theory explaining the four principal forces in the universe—gravity, electromagnetism, the strong nuclear force, and the weak nuclear force—that physicists

77. Moroz, "Vozvrashchenie iz ssylki," 303.
78. Vasiliev, "Tri poezdki v Gor'kii," 189; Tatiana Yankelevich, conversation with author, January 13, 2004. Scientific articles were the only material Sakharov received freely in the mail.
79. I. M. Dremin, "Otlychennyi ot 'Iashchika,'" in Altshuler et al., *On mezhdu nami zhil,* 286.
80. Pimenov, "Kakim on byl," 212; Altshuler, "Nou-khau," 75, 91.
81. Moroz, "Vozvrashchenie iz ssylki," 303.

from Einstein onward had been trying to discover.[82] Another topic Sakharov worked on was "quantum chromodynamics," in which he tried to estimate the "coupling constant" between quarks and the gluon field, which Sakharov described as analogous to an electromagnetic field.[83] Yet another concerned "multisheet" models of the universe, on which he wrote an article that appeared in 1982.[84] In the article, Sakharov tried to reconcile the so-called multisheet model, in which the universe is presumed to expand and contract, with the second law of thermodynamics, which holds that the entropy (or the disorder and chaos) of a closed system (the universe) inexorably increases. The second law implies (when it is applied to the universe as a whole) that the conditions that exist in the universe must change with every cycle of expansion and contraction and that these changes are irreversible.[85] But the laws of mechanics, as Sakharov noted, are, in fact, reversible in terms of time. In both his 1979 article on the reversibility of time and the article that appeared in 1982, he tried to resolve this contradiction by speculating that there was a point, not in the "infinitely distant past" but also not long after the creation of the universe, at which time could move either forward or backward.[86] Extrapolating from this scenario to that of a universe that is expanding and contracting sequentially, Sakharov thought that at the point at which the universe stops expanding and starts contracting (and also when it stops contracting and starts expanding again), time will also reverse itself. Since "physical and informational processes" run backward whenever time does, entropy increases regardless of the direction in which "time's arrow" is pointing; therefore there is no violation of the second law of thermodynamics.[87]

A related issue in cosmology that Sakharov grappled with at Gorky concerned the possibility of multiple universes.[88] In 1984, in a paper entitled, in English translation, "Cosmological Transitions with a Change in Metric Signature," he speculated that because of "quantum tunneling," different regions of the universe (such as the center of a black hole) have different combinations of temporal and spatial dimensions—or, in the terminology cosmologists used, different "metric signatures."[89] Sakharov inferred from this the astonishing and mind-numbing

82. B. L. Altshuler, "Scientific Method of A. D. Sakharov," in *Sakharov Memorial Lectures in Physics*, ed. L. V. Keldysh and V. Ya. Fainberg (New York, 1992), 1:2; Brian Greene, *The Elegant Universe: Superstrings, Hidden Dimensions, and the Quest for the Ultimate Theory* (New York, 2000).

83. Sakharov, *Memoirs*, 541; Andrei Sakharov, "An Estimate of the Coupling Constant between Quarks and the Gluon Field," *Soviet Physics JETP* 52 (1980): 175–76, reprinted in Sakharov, *Collected Scientific Works*, 233–37.

84. Sakharov, "Cosmological Models"; Andrei Sakharov, "The Baryonic Asymmetry of the Universe," *Soviet Physics JETP* 49 (1979): 594–99, reprinted in Sakharov, *Collected Scientific Works*, 115–30.

85. Andrei Sakharov, "Many-Sheeted Cosmological Models of the Universe," *Journal of Experimental and Theoretical Physics* 56, no. 4 (October 1982): 705–9.

86. Sakharov, *Memoirs*, 544. In explicating Sakharov's hypothesis, I have relied largely on the summary in his memoirs, pp. 542–44.

87. Ibid., 544.

88. Ibid., 545.

89. A. D. Sakharov, "Cosmological Transitions with a Change in Metric Signature (1984)," *SLAC Translation 0211* (Stanford, 1984). See also Altshuler et al., "Personalia," 12.

suggestion that the number of universes that are similar to ours, in that they all contain the possibility of intelligent life, is actually infinite.[90] Several cosmologists prior to Sakharov had advanced the hypothesis of multiple universes existing simultaneously, all of them arising out of "primordial space" but each of them entirely separate and "ignorant" of one another; taken together, these universes comprised a Mega Universe. Sakharov, however, speculated that these multiple universes are sequential rather than simultaneous, distinct temporally rather than spatially (and thus very similar to, perhaps even identical to, the universe or universes he posited in his multisheet theory). Out of each contraction of the universe, Sakharov suggested, a truly new universe is created, one that is "oblivious" to all the universes that came before it. Sakharov argued, furthermore, that because black holes "violate symmetry at the stage of collapse," they might, by their very existence, preclude or make highly unlikely the emergence of "highly organized structures," such as living organisms, in the universe that follows the universe that contained them.[91] But Sakharov also speculated that the gradual evaporation of black holes, along with baryon decay, will "smooth out" the "inhomogeneities" black holes create, so that smooth and turbulent universes will follow one another sequentially, with the possibility of intelligent life in at least some of them.[92] In short, the turbulent universe we inhabit (that is, a universe with black holes and baryon asymmetry) was preceded by, and will be succeeded by, a smooth universe, one lacking black holes and baryon asymmetry.

About the correctness of Sakharov's speculations only a theoretical physicist or cosmologist can render a serious judgment. But to the historian or biographer concerned with the relationship between Sakharov's physics and the events that were transpiring in his personal life, these speculations, by their very remoteness from everyday reality, were in all likelihood important for the therapeutic effect they had in making that reality more endurable while also contradicting the erroneous conclusion he had come to that, notwithstanding the effects of his exile, he was beginning to lose his analytical and intuitive powers as a physicist.[93] At a time in his life when politics was largely off-limits to him, it was especially gratifying for Sakharov to know that he was still capable of first-rate work in his chosen profession.

## Hunger Strike

Ironically, as Sakharov's scientific work expanded in scope to encompass the entire universe, his political concerns narrowed. His attention, increasingly, was on Bonner and her prospective daughter-in-law, Liza Alexeeva, who by the time of Sakharov's exile was still waiting for the exit visa she needed to leave the country and join Bonner's son, Alexei, in America, where the couple were to

90. Sakharov, "Cosmological Transitions," 21.
91. Sakharov, *Memoirs*, 546.
92. Ibid.
93. Ibid., 540.

marry. Given Sakharov's isolation and political powerlessness, Liza and Alexei were virtually the only persons in the Soviet Union whose mistreatment or harassment he had any real hope of alleviating.

The preeminence Bonner's family enjoyed in Sakharov's use of time and energy became apparent in the spring of 1981, when Liza's application for a visa was finally denied—despite earlier assurances from the authorities that she would receive it. The year before, for assisting Sakharov at the time of his exile, Liza had been threatened with arrest and physical violence and as punishment was refused permission to visit him in Gorky.[94] As a result, she had little reason to think these assurances were credible. Nevertheless, when the rejection came, she was shaken and distraught. Sakharov and Bonner, who were obviously concerned about her, decided that the methods they were using had failed and that more extreme measures were required.

The tactic they adopted, in November 1981, was one that Sakharov had first used in 1974, namely, a hunger strike. In assessing it, one must remember that it followed months of protests that were entirely futile. Liza had been harassed and persecuted by the government since the spring of 1978, when she moved into Sakharov's apartment in Moscow, and a few weeks later applied for an exit visa. In response, the government forbade her from taking her final examinations at the teachers' institute where she and Alexei had been enrolled; shortly afterward she lost her job as a computer operator. In September 1979, Liza attempted suicide when several of the Leningrad hijackers convicted in 1970 were released from prison and given permission to emigrate to Israel but refused Bonner's request that one of them claim Liza as his fiancée so that she might leave the country when they did.[95]

Making matters worse for Liza was the opposition of her parents to her relationship with Alexei, her living with Sakharov and Bonner, and her efforts to join Alexei in America, all of which seemed to imply approval of Sakharov's dissidence. This enraged Liza's father, a retired army officer, who refused, as was his legal right, to provide the statement visa applicants needed from their parents absolving the applicants of any debts owed their parents. Adding insult to injury, the government in February 1980 allowed Alexei's wife and daughter to leave the Soviet Union for the United States. Immediately following their departure, there appeared in the Sunday supplement to *Izvestiia* an article claiming that Alexei had repented his adultery and requested his wife's forgiveness, which she magnanimously granted him, and that the couple, now happily reconciled, would be reunited in America. All this, of course, was nonsense, and Alexei's divorce became final in July 1980.[96]

Throughout 1980 and early 1981, Sakharov did what he could to resolve the matter. In June 1980, in protest of Liza's inability to leave the country, he stopped

94. Ibid., 556.
95. Ibid., 552–54.
96. Ibid., 555.

corresponding with Soviet scientists who were still in contact with him, and in September he told Vitalii Ginzburg that unless Liza received a visa, he would no longer receive scientists in Gorky.[97] In that same year he sent a telegram to Brezhnev and a letter to the vice president of the Academy of Sciences, stressing in each of them that Liza was an innocent victim of the regime, rather than an opponent of it, who was being punished unfairly for the dissidence of others, specifically his own and Bonner's. In late 1980 and early 1981, he addressed comparable letters to Alexandrov, Zeldovich, and Khariton, while Bonner issued appeals to the West on Liza's behalf. But none of this had any effect, and the KGB's harassment of Liza continued. In response, in order to strengthen the legal case for her receiving a visa—which was often granted to facilitate the reunification of families—Sakharov and Bonner arranged through Edward Kline, an American friend and supporter, for Alexei and Liza to be married by proxy in the United States. With Alexei present and Kline standing in for his bride, the marriage was performed on June 9, 1981, in Montana, one of only two states in the country that recognized proxy marriages. Unexpectedly, the marriage had the salubrious effect of reconciling Liza's parents to her daughter's situation, and they dropped their opposition to her leaving the Soviet Union. Liza's father, as a result of the proxy marriage, even wrote to Brezhnev requesting his intervention. But the government remained as unyielding as ever, and Sakharov and Bonner decided that only a hunger strike, which they believed would capture the attention of Western public opinion, would bring the desired result. Coincidentally, Brezhnev was scheduled to visit West Germany in November, and the couple decided that the hunger strike should begin then, believing that the Western media would likely cover the two events simultaneously. In October Sakharov sent telegrams to Brezhnev and Alexandrov announcing his intentions, and on November 22, one day before Brezhnev arrived in Bonn, he and Bonner began fasting, permitting themselves only mineral water, which maintained their internal electrolyte balance.[98]

Despite the danger it posed to their health and perhaps even to their lives, Sakharov and Bonner continued their hunger strike for the next twelve days, during which time news of their protest prompted twenty American Nobel laureates, French and Norwegian scientists, the Communist mayor of Florence, Italy, and the United States Senate to express support for the couple and to call upon the Soviet government to grant Liza the visa she needed.[99] In the Soviet Union, Roald Sagdeev added his voice to the chorus of disapproval by asking Alexandrov to intervene with Andropov on Liza's behalf so that Sakharov and Bonner could end their hunger strike.[100]

97. Andrei Sakharov, "From Exile in Gorky (June 1, 1981)," *Chronicle of Human Rights*, no. 43 (July–September 1981): 18; A. Sakharov, "To the Head of the Theoretical Department of FIAN, V. L. Ginzburg (September 14, 1980)," *Chronicle of Current Events*, no. 60 (December 31, 1980): 102.

98. Sakharov, *Memoirs*, 556–59.

99. Ibid., 563–64.

100. Sagdeev, *Making of a Soviet Scientist*, 252–53.

The response was not uniformly favorable, however. For the first time in Sakharov's career as a dissident, an action of his was criticized sharply by other dissidents, including several who on other occasions had been supportive. Lidiia Chukovskaia, whose fondness for Sakharov was immense, thought his hunger strike an act of self-indulgence especially inappropriate at a time when dissidents such as Sharansky, who was still in prison, needed support, certainly more than Bonner's daughter-in-law.[101] Grigorenko wrote to Sakharov stating that by fasting he was endangering his life for a relatively trivial objective, and he implored him to end his protest immediately. Revolt Pimenov, who also wrote to Sakharov, argued strenuously that the happiness Alexei and Liza would experience if Liza received a visa was not worth the suffering Sakharov and Bonner were experiencing.[102] In the United States, the scientists Jeremy Stone and Joel Lebowitz, who were both supporters of his, implored them to stop what they were doing, while in the Soviet Union Vitalii Ginzburg and Evgenii Feinberg voiced the same objections Grigorenko and Pimenov had expressed—namely, that the tactic Sakharov had adopted in this particular instance, because it was so physically dangerous, was not commensurate with its objective.[103] Sidney Drell, another American physicist who admired Sakharov, regretfully concluded that the hunger strike damaged Sakharov's "political authority" among the many scientists in the West who agreed with his ideas and usually endorsed the means he adopted to achieve them.[104]

Far from being chastened by such criticism, Sakharov was emboldened by it. The implication that he was acting more out of loyalty to a family member than on the basis of moral principle clearly annoyed him and only strengthened his resolve not to give in—either to the Soviet government or to his critics. Sakharov, like Bonner, was quite stubborn, especially when he believed his principles were involved, and in this instance he thought his commitment to his principles, if not the principles themselves, was being maligned unfairly. Even though his affection for Liza, which he readily acknowledged, was entirely genuine, he also believed that the hunger strike was motivated primarily by moral principle, and only secondarily by the practical consideration that only a tactic as radical as a hunger strike had any chance of success. Of these two justifications, the moral argument, not surprisingly, was the one he stressed. He explained his decision in a letter he sent to foreign scientists just a week before he began the fast: "The KGB, by making Liza a hostage for my public activity, has not only caused her and Alexei many years of suffering, but has changed this from a personal matter into a public, even a political, affair. The fight for Liza and Alexei has become a necessary, logical component of my long-term defense of human rights, of an open society, of law, of humaneness, of international security and confidence.

101. Migdal, "K portretu Andreia Sakharova," 437.
102. Sakharov, *Memoirs*, 560.
103. Ibid., 565; Ginzburg, "O fenomene Sakharova," 239.
104. Ginzburg, "O fenomene Sakharova," 238; Sidney Drell, "Neobkhodim novyi podkhod," in Altshuler et al., *On mezhdu nami zhil*, 283.

It is important for me that those friends who are speaking out in my defense around the world understand my feelings on this subject."[105]

Of course Sakharov felt personally responsible for Liza, and never denied that, in the punishment she suffered, she was effectively his surrogate.[106] But he was also able to divorce his personal feelings from the moral principles he believed he was championing by supporting her. On December 1, in response to criticism that in fasting he had allowed his compassion for an individual he deeply cared about to cloud his judgment and obscure his sense of moral propriety, he proclaimed that the hunger strike he and Bonner had begun nine days earlier was nothing less than "a battle for freedom to leave the country and to return, a battle for freedom in general."[107] In fact, Liza's inability to receive the exit visa was the equivalent on a smaller scale of his own inability over the years to persuade the Soviet government to provide for the Soviet people the entire panoply of human rights they deserved. In his memoirs, Sakharov summarized his reasoning as follows: "The authorities' refusal to let [Liza] rejoin Alexei may have been the immediate cause of our hunger strike, but in a broader sense, it was the consequence of all that had happened to us, including exile in Gorky, and a continuation of my struggle for human rights and the freedom to choose one's country of residence—not in the abstract, but in a situation in which Lusia and I had from the beginning felt a direct responsibility."[108] Far from disqualifying Sakharov from acting on Liza's behalf, his closeness to her actually heightened his responsibility to defend and protect her, an obligation he undertook freely not only because he cared deeply for her but also because, as a consequence of his own isolation, she was one of the few people he had a real chance of helping.

That Sakharov was in exile when he began his hunger strike had no bearing on the guiding principle to which he tried to adhere throughout his career as a dissident that there could be no distinction between the abstract moral principles he espoused and the individual human beings in whom these moral principles inhered: unless he championed the cause of particular individuals, these moral principles would remain mere abstractions. Whatever the practical considerations a hunger strike—when to begin it, how to publicize it, how long to continue it if the government was not forthcoming in responding to it, what he and Bonner should do in case the government tried to force them to eat, and so on—the moral calculus that required him to fast, once he decided that that would be his method of protest, was consistent with the integral connection in Sakharov's philosophy of human rights between the individuals who were

105. Andrei Sakharov, "Three Letters Concerning the Hunger Strike (November 15, 1981)," in Babyonyshev, *On Sakharov*, 271.

106. Andrei Sakharov, "Obrashchenie v zashchitu A. Bolonkina (April 3, 1981)," *Materialy samizdata*, no. 13/81 (June 1, 1981), AS 4319: 1.

107. Sakharov, *Memoirs*, 567.

108. Ibid., 561.

entitled to human rights and these rights themselves, in all their universality and moral clarity.

Despite their worsening physical condition, Sakharov and Bonner continued their hunger strike into December. Not even their hospitalization on December 4 (which of course was involuntary) could change their minds. On that day KGB agents broke into their apartment and transported them to separate hospitals. Following his admission and confinement to a hospital bed, Sakharov (who thought Bonner was in the same hospital) refused all medical procedures until they were reunited. Four days later, after physicians threatened to begin feeding both of them forcibly, an official from the KGB visited each of them and told them that if they ended their hunger strike immediately, Liza would receive the exit visa she desired. Sakharov replied that before he could consider the offer, he would have to discuss it with his wife. The next day, December 9, Bonner was taken to his room, whereupon she and Sakharov agreed to end their hunger strike, seventeen days after starting it.[109] Perhaps the principal factor in the government's decision to capitulate was the fear expressed by Alexandrov and others in the Academy of Sciences that if Sakharov died as a result of his hunger strike, the contacts with Western scientists that still existed after his exile would be curtailed. In fact, in the interest of avoiding a potential public relations disaster for the Soviet Union, Alexandrov appealed directly to Brezhnev to grant Liza a visa.[110]

Overjoyed by their sudden and unexpected success, Sakharov issued a statement on December 12, shortly before leaving the hospital, in which he described the hunger strike and all the protests it engendered as "a struggle not only for our children's life and happiness, not only for my own honor and dignity, but also for every human being's right to freedom and happiness, for the right to live in accordance with one's ideals and beliefs, and in the final analysis—it was a struggle for all prisoners of conscience."[111] On December 14, visa in hand, Liza left the Soviet Union for the United States, where in Boston she and Alexei were finally reunited, this time as husband and wife. On December 22, Sakharov suffered a "heart spasm" and on December 26 an actual heart attack.[112] But not even these medical crises, as serious as they were, could diminish the satisfaction he and Bonner experienced. For Sakharov, his triumph over the Soviet system, quite apart from its political dimensions, was meaningful for what it revealed about the depth of his relationship with Bonner. As he put it, the hunger strike was perhaps "our finest hour, a proof of our mutual love and commitment."[113]

109. Ibid., 562–72.
110. Feinberg, "Dlia budushchego istorika," 687–88.
111. Sakharov, *Memoirs*, 573.
112. Ibid., 574–75.
113. Ibid., 575.

# 20 Finding Hope in Quantum Physics

The exhilaration Sakharov felt when Liza finally received an exit visa did not last long. However gratifying it was in personal terms, his success in forcing the Soviet government to capitulate momentarily could not obscure the harsh reality that the dissident movement, by 1981, was in extremis. In the late 1970s the government decided to destroy the dissident movement in its entirety, and sending Sakharov to Gorky was just one of many steps it took to achieve its objective.[1] Indeed, in the months that followed Sakharov's victory in December 1981, the government's persecution accelerated. By the summer of 1982, Helsinki Groups in Lithuania and Ukraine had been crushed, and in the fall of that year the Moscow Helsinki Group, which had always been preeminent in its relation to the other groups, disbanded.[2] In the early 1980s, Sakharov, when he was not preoccupied with Liza, did what little he could to reverse these developments, mostly by protesting the persecution of individual dissidents, many of whom were members of these various groups, even before they or their families asked him to. On behalf of Tatiana Osipova and her husband, Ivan Kovalev, he petitioned Andropov to permit the couple conjugal visits after they were sent, on separate occasions, to the same labor camp for their activities on behalf of the Moscow Group—but his petition was simply ignored.[3] Orlov,[4] Velikanova,[5] Viktor Brailovskii,[6] Gleb Iakunin,[7] Ivan Kovalev's father, Sergei,[8] the Georgian dissident Merab Kostava,[9] the Ukrainian dissident and poet Vasilii Stus,[10] and Anatolii Marchenko[11] were just a few of the other individuals on whose

1. Richard Sakwa, *Gorbachev and His Reforms, 1985–1990* (New York, 1991), 202.
2. "The Political and Social Thinking of Andrei Sakharov," *Samizdat Bulletin*, no. 157 (May 1986): 6.
3. Sakharov, *Memoirs*, 539; A. D. Sakharov, "To Dr. Linus Pauling, Winner of the Lenin Peace Prize and the Nobel Prize for Chemistry (May 4, 1981)," *Chronicle of Current Events*, no. 62 (July 14, 1981): 131.
4. Andrei Sakharov and Naum Meiman, "Open Letter to the Madrid Conference," *Samizdat Bulletin*, no. 108 (April 1982).
5. A. Sakharov et al., "Kto osuzhden (August 29, 1980)?" *Materialy samizdata*, no. 17/81 (May 4, 1981), AS 4076: 1.
6. Andrei Sakharov, "On Behalf of Viktor Brailovsky (December 5, 1980)," *Chronicle of Human Rights*, no. 40 (October–December 1980): 12–13.
7. Sakharov et al., "Kto osuzhden?" 1.
8. Sakharov, "To Dr. Linus Pauling," 131.
9. Sakharov, *Memoirs*, 540.
10. A. Sakharov, "In Defense of the Poet Vasily Stus (October 19, 1980)," *Chronicle of Current Events*, no. 58 (November 1980): 80–81.
11. Sakharov, *Memoirs*, 539. Marchenko had been arrested, for the sixth time, in March 1981, partly for writing a letter to Kapitsa on Sakharov's behalf. When he learned of this, Sakharov felt an obligation to reciprocate, and perhaps for this reason directed his appeal for Marchenko to Kapitsa, who ignored it. The disdain he felt for Kapitsa as a result of this increased after

behalf Sakharov intervened either publicly or privately, but to no avail, while he himself was in exile.

Sakharov mourned the demise of the dissidents very deeply. He, of course, was one of them, and the emotional ties he had developed over the years with the dissidents he defended made the incarceration of each of them a personal tragedy. This in turn darkened Sakharov's political views, in particular his estimation of the chances of the Soviet system reforming itself. In 1982 he acknowledged that he had "no hope" that the Soviet Union, under current circumstances, could be forced to democratize (the reader will recall that for Sakharov democratization was not democracy but rather a form of glasnost), and in 1983 he and Bonner began to wonder "when, if ever, better times would arrive."[12] Also in 1982, Sakharov began reflecting on some of the choices he had made in earlier phases of his career as a dissident, in particular his decision in 1970 to join the Human Rights Committee. He did not go so far as to conclude that his decision was a mistake. Instead, he tried to redefine its objectives retroactively to place his joining it in a more favorable light. In contrast to what he had believed when he joined the committee, Sakharov now claimed that he had never thought it could actually persuade the government to provide human rights to the Soviet people or educate the people about why they were legally and morally entitled to them; the most he ever believed the committee could do (or so he said in 1982) was to assist selected individuals who had been unlawfully arrested. Had the committee tried to do more than that, he now said, it would have frightened away the authorities, who "did not want *any* expression of independence, any independent source of information either inside the country or reaching the West."[13] Despite his misgivings about the committee, Sakharov had higher hopes for it when it was established than his subsequent assessment seems to suggest. What is notable about his attempt in 1982 to minimize retroactively the committee's ambitious agenda is his stressing the futility of any strategy more ambitious than the minimalist approach he was forced to adopt in 1980. In short, Sakharov was backdating his pessimism in the early 1980s to the early 1970s, when he and the other members of the committee were actually quite hopeful about the future. This in itself is a measure of how profoundly his pessimism had overtaken him.

Sakharov's belief that the dissidents now had little chance of changing the Soviet Union reinforced the low opinion he already had of socialism and the Soviet Union and of the Western elites who either ignored the evils of Soviet Communism or found ways of excusing them. In Gorky, Sakharov persisted in calling the Soviet Union totalitarian, writing in his "Letter from Exile," which appeared in the *New York Times* and several West European newspapers, that

---

Marchenko's death in December 1986 from the effects of a hunger strike he was conducting in Chistopol Prison. In February 1987 Sakharov publicly criticized Kapitsa for what he considered his cowardice six years earlier. Ibid., 613–14; "The Exile of Sakharov," 91–92; Andrei Sakharov, "Interview mit dem Sowjetischen und Dissidenten Roy Medwedew," *Der Spiegel*, February 2, 1987, 10.

12. Sakharov, *Memoirs*, 582; "Andrei Sakharov o pravozashchitom dvizhenii: Otchety na voprosy V. Chalidze (April 26, 1982)," *SSSR: Vnutrennie protivorechiia* 5 (1982): 9.

13. "Andrei Sakharov o pravozashchitom dvizhenii," 6. Emphasis in original.

totalitarianism took the form in the Soviet Union of a closed, almost hermetically sealed state with a largely militarized economy that was strictly controlled by a highly centralized bureaucracy.[14] What was worse, the Soviet system was relentlessly and implacably expansionist, possessed of a messianism born of an ideology that served to justify the repression it inflicted domestically.[15] But because the Soviet system, despite its moral bankruptcy, had "substantial accomplishments to its credit," and because the Soviet people had nothing to compare it with, except the same system in earlier times when conditions were worse, they tolerated and endured, rather than protested and condemned, its numerous deficiencies, such as inadequate medical care, an inferior educational system, and a sluggish economy that at times could not even produce enough food to keep people alive. For this reason the kind of consciousness raising the dissidents had been attempting since the early 1970s was bound to fail.[16]

Sakharov's opinion of the Soviet people, already low in the late 1970s, diminished even further in the early 1980s. On several occasions during this period he expressed his disappointment with and even anger at them. In his "Letter from Exile," written in the spring of 1980, he implied that the vices of which the Soviet people were plainly guilty predated the Soviet Union and were as much a reflection of certain deficiencies in the Russian national character as they were the result of the debilitating effects of living under communism for nearly seventy years. The Soviet people, he charged, were egoistic, hypocritical, naïve, nationalistic, and anti-Semitic.[17] The fact that they were ignorant of other societies, specifically those in the West, that might provide a positive model for them to emulate was no excuse for "the ideology of the Soviet philistine" that pervaded the masses and the elite and enabled the people to rationalize, explain away, or simply ignore the numerous injustices they either heard about or observed directly in their daily lives.[18] The following passage from Sakharov's letter captures the bitterness he felt toward his fellow citizens for their cynical acquiescence in the malfeasance of which the Soviet government was clearly guilty:

> The people of our country submit uncomplainingly to all the shortages of meat, butter, and many other products—though they do grumble at home. They put up with the gross social inequality between the elite and the ordinary citizens. They endure the arbitrary behavior and cruelty of local authorities. They know about the beatings and deaths of people in police stations but as a rule keep quiet. They do not speak out—sometimes they even gloat—about the unjust treatment of dissidents. They are silent about any and all foreign policy actions.[19]

Although Sakharov was too diplomatic to say so explicitly, the clear implication is that in Soviet Communism the Soviet people got what they deserved.

14. Andrei Sakharov, "A Letter from Exile (May 4, 1980)," in Babyonyshev, *On Sakharov*, 224.
15. Ibid., 225, 233.
16. Ibid.; Sakharov, *Memoirs*, 579.
17. Sakharov, "Letter from Exile," 232.
18. Ibid.
19. Ibid., 233.

In the letter Sakharov underscored his contempt for the Soviet people by comparing them adversely to people in the West, whose collective mentality he described admiringly as "practical" and "efficient."[20] Unlike the *homo sovieticus* he condemned, Western man (as he called him) was not so blinded by the need for immediate gratification that he would refrain from aspiring to "great goals," by which Sakharov meant seeking for oneself and one's progeny a world more humane and more advanced technologically than the one that now existed.[21] At the same time he reserved perhaps his most withering criticism in the early 1980s for Western intellectuals, whom he repeatedly chastised for their apathy, cowardice, disengagement, and intellectual masochism. These defects, he claimed, had the effect of rendering Western political elites and opinion makers, who relied on Western intellectuals for guidance, largely oblivious to Soviet failures and moral transgressions, which in Sakharov's opinion were demonstrably worse than anything for which Western governments could be criticized. This lack of moral discernment on the part of Western intellectuals had the calamitous effect, he said, of inuring the West to the mortal threat Soviet totalitarianism posed to it; for this reason everyone in the West not yet afflicted with this moral myopia had an obligation to combat it as forcefully and as persistently as he could.[22] Sakharov was hardly subtle in condemning the defects of Western intellectuals, and in his implication that these defects were primarily ethical and intellectual, his criticisms (as distinct from his solutions) were surprisingly similar to Solzhenitsyn's.

As the victories he scored against the regime diminished radically and the price he paid for them increased, Sakharov retreated to a purely ethical politics, a politics of existential protest that was not really a form of politics at all. For the first time since he had become a dissident in 1968, Sakharov was reduced to advocating human rights for their own sake. For all intents and purposes, no one in the government and very few among the Soviet people were still listening to him, and those that were were in no position to help. By the time that Sakharov was in Gorky, whatever chance there was of convincing the Soviet government to reform itself had long passed. But whereas this ethical politics would be an admission of weakness for someone less convinced of his moral rectitude, for Sakharov it was a source of strength, a means of preserving the ideals he and the other dissidents stood for until circumstances changed and the prospects of influencing Soviet society improved, as he was certain they would. In 1982, Sakharov explained why protesting "for its own sake" was a moral imperative for him and why, for the immediate future, it was the tactic he had an obligation to adopt: "The strength of the struggle for human rights does not lie in its organization or the number of its participants. It is a moral strength, a strength of unconditional rightness. This movement cannot disappear without a trace.

20. Ibid., 229.
21. Ibid.
22. Andrei Sakharov, "How to Preserve World Peace (August 16, 1981)," in Babyonyshev, *On Sakharov*, 264–65.

A word already spoken lives on, and new people with their unique destinies and souls continually make new contributions."[23]

In the 1980s Sakharov spoke the language of pure moral exhortation not because he thought it would change things but because he knew it would not. Under the circumstances, the most he and the remaining dissidents could do was to help individuals unlawfully arrested or imprisoned; changing the political system ultimately responsible for these particular injustices was beyond the realm of possibility.[24] He expressed this perception in a declaration he issued in June 1980 on behalf of the imprisoned dissident Viktor Nekipelov: "[I]n today's world, there is much that is terrible and unjust. But the fate of one man, who does so much for others, is something worth fighting for."[25] No matter how inauspicious were the prospects of his protests changing the political system that made his protests necessary, Sakharov felt obliged to speak out whenever human rights were violated, and the reason he did so was clear and unambiguous: "When people are confronted with a visible, concrete situation," he wrote in 1982, "they are objectively responsible not only for their actions, but for their inaction."[26]

The idleness Sakharov experienced in exile enabled him to reiterate at greater length the dissident agenda he had formulated earlier in his life. But the substance of his dissidence remained the same. Among the demands he made of the Soviet government were that it adhere to the Helsinki Accords,[27] issue a general amnesty for political prisoners,[28] and end its barbaric practice of incarcerating in psychiatric hospitals dissidents and others who were mentally sound.[29] He also proclaimed yet again the indivisibility of domestic and foreign policy, reminding everyone who could still hear him that countries that provide human rights domestically act peacefully abroad, and those that fail to do so should be condemned not only by their own people but by people everywhere.[30] He continued to advocate—albeit equivocally and unenthusiastically—a multiparty system over the monopoly of power the Communist Party still enjoyed.[31] He also reiterated his unshakable faith in the virtues, if not the inevitability, of

23. Andrei Sakharov, UPI interview, January 19, 1982, reprinted in *Chronicle of Current Events*, no. 64 (June 30, 1982): 111.

24. A. Sakharov, "Political Prisoners' Day (October 28, 1981)," *Chronicle of Current Events*, no. 63 (December 31, 1981): 169.

25. Andrei Sakharov, "Zaiavlenie 'v zashchitu Viktora Nekipelova' (June 14, 1980)," in *Materialy samizdata*, no. 29/80 (August 23, 1980), AS 4039: 2.

26. "Andrei Sakharov o pravozashchitom dvizhenii," 8.

27. Andrei Sakharov, "World Security, Human Rights Linked—Sakharov," *Los Angeles Times*, September 9, 1980, 5.

28. "Political Prisoners' Day (October 30, 1980), *Chronicle of Human Rights*, no. 40 (October–December 1980): 14.

29. Sakharov, "Political Prisoners' Day (October 28, 1981)," 169.

30. Andrei Sakharov, "Zaiavlenie uchastnikam predstoiashchego v noiabre 1980 Madridskogo soveshchaniia—35—i stranam, podpisavshim Zakliuchitel'nyi Akt Khel'sinkskogo soveshchaniia (August 8, 1980)," in *Materialy samizdata*, no. 29/80 (August 22, 1980), AS 4045: 1–3.

31. In his "Letter from Exile," the most Sakharov could say on behalf of a multiparty system in the Soviet Union was that there "probably" should be one. Sakharov, "Letter from Exile," 234.

convergence, which he later said was what sustained him intellectually through-out his years in exile.[32] After the Polish trade union movement Solidarity or-ganized massive strikes that directly challenged the legitimacy of the Polish Communist Party, Sakharov, just as he had in 1977 in the case of Charter 77 in Czechoslovakia, expressed strong support for his fellow dissidents outside the Soviet Union, calling the members of Solidarity his "brothers" and commend-ing them for their nonviolent tactics.[33]

On the less programmatic, more philosophical issues that had concerned him in earlier phrases of his career, Sakharov spoke out from Gorky as well. Most prominently, he repeated his long-standing vision of science and scientists as agents of the moral improvement of humanity. But he also was aware that this moral improvement required first of all that the moral degeneration of human-ity, which in a nuclear age could lead to the obliteration of everyone and every-thing, be brought to a halt. This meant that scientists' primary responsibility was to prevent mankind from misusing the achievements of science for pernicious, and possibly even catastrophic, purposes. Far from assisting humanity in its in-exorable advancement to a state of moral perfection, scientists would have their hands full, at least for the immediate future, simply trying to prevent mankind from destroying itself. In a letter he sent in 1981 to an international confer-ence in New York that was organized for the explicit purpose of honoring him, he warned again, just as he had in the late 1970s, of the danger human beings posed to themselves, and he emphasized as well the responsibility this placed on scientists to protect them.[34] After restating unapologetically his view that experts should perform the essential role in a just society of subjecting social problems "to unbiased and searching examination," Sakharov elaborated on what he thought the role of scientists in society should be:

> With some important exceptions (primarily affecting totalitarian countries), sci-entists are not only better informed than the average person, but also strive for and enjoy more independence and freedom. Freedom, however, always entails responsibility. Scientists and other experts already influence or have the capacity to influence public opinion and their governments. (That influence should not be exaggerated but it is substantial.) My view of the situation of scientists in the contemporary world has convinced me that they have special professional and social responsibilities.[35]

In an appeal he sent to Soviet scientists in 1982, Sakharov reiterated the obligation he believed scientists had to defend other scientists when they were

---

32. Sakharov and Adamovich, "Zhit' na zemle i zhit' dolgo," 170; Andrei Sakharov, "Pis'mo uchastnikam vstrechi v Sorbonne (September 24, 1983)," in *Materialy samizdata*, no. 41/83 (Octo-ber 31, 1983), AS 5063: 2.

33. Andrei Sakharov et al., "Message to the Polish Interfactory Strike Committee (n. d.)," *Chronicle of Human Rights*, no. 40 (October–December 1980): 13.

34. Andrei Sakharov, "The Responsibility of Scientists (March 24, 1981)," in Babyonyshev, *On Sakharov*, 205–11.

35. Ibid., 206.

persecuted, whether for their political views or simply because they performed their jobs in ways that antagonized their superiors.[36] In 1983, in his message on accepting the Szilard Award, given by the American Physical Society, Sakharov cited Einstein, Bohr, and Leo Szilard as scientists whose commitment to peace and human rights should be emulated by other members of their profession.[37] Of course Sakharov was too modest to include himself in this litany of titans, but the society's decision to honor him in this fashion leaves no doubt that scientists abroad respected him for more than his scientific accomplishments and considered him a model of the socially conscious scientist.

## The Indeterminacy of Nature and Human Affairs

Sakharov's views changed little or not at all while he was in exile. But with time on his hands, he reassessed aspects of his dissidence and clarified the philosophical assumptions that had given rise to it. In the latter case, Sakharov finally made explicit his conviction that the course of human history was unpredictable and that any theory of human behavior and history that claimed predictive value was not only erroneous but positively dangerous. Although the enormous differences between physics and politics in their subject matter and methodology should make one wary of drawing parallels between them in explaining Sakharov's intellectual development, in this case there was a direct connection. In 1982, when Sakharov was still refining his multisheet model of the universe—which the reader will recall sharply contradicted the models other cosmologists had proposed of a steady-state universe, and of a purely and inexorably inflationary one—he wrote a letter to Boris Altshuler in which he expressed his doubts about the correctness not just of his own model but of all the models cosmologists had proposed.[38] The only thing he could do in response to these doubts, he acknowledged to Altshuler, was to posit his theories and then await their empirical corroboration, if indeed such corroboration even existed. In Sakharov's words, "we shall wait [because] the future will show who is right."[39] In this there is nothing extraordinary or unusual. He was simply expressing the caution and healthy respect for empirical evidence any good physicist, even a theoretical one, should have. But he then went on in his letter to posit a fundamental unpredictability in the universe, an unpredictability he considered beneficial because it restored to the individual the possibility of changing the world in ways that were socially useful. In explaining his position, Sakharov made clear that the physical world and the world of human affairs were ultimately governed by the same principles and that the reason one could say very little about the future on the basis of what existed in the present was

36. A. Sakharov, "Letter to Soviet Scientists (March 30, 1982)," *Chronicle of Current Events*, no. 64 (June 30, 1982), 105–6.

37. Andrei Sakharov, "Acceptance Speech for the Szilard Award (April 1983)," in *Memoirs*, 663.

38. The letter is included in B. L. Altshuler, "On nebyl naiven," in Ivanova, *Andrei Dmitrievich*, 230–31.

39. Ibid., 230.

that there was really not one future but an infinite number of them. Because the actions and behavior of human beings determined which of these futures would come about, no one could know a priori, on the basis of some abstract theory of history, what the future would be.

In his letter to Altshuler, the skepticism Sakharov expressed about theories purporting to explain nature and the universe he simply transferred to theories that purported to explain human behavior. According to Sakharov, there was a fundamental indeterminacy in both the physical world and human affairs. The famous thought experiment of Schrödinger's cat—which the German scientist conjured as a way of demonstrating the indeterminacy that existed in the subatomic world of quantum physics—could just as easily be considered descriptive of how human history evolved—namely, as the result of human beings' interacting with their environment in unpredictable ways.[40] What Sakharov wrote to Altshuler on this particular point deserves to be quoted at length. It is one of his most significant philosophical statements and the only one in which he explicitly linked the assumptions that were at the core of his dissidence with the views he held about nature and the universe:

> Fortunately, the future is unpredictable, and it is also, because of quantum effects, indeterminable. The laws of quantum theory, with their notions of probability, refer not only to science. In history as well, and also in the fate of the individual, the future is not only unpredictable, but in any given moment, it simply doesn't exist. Various scenarios are possible, some of which directly contradict one another. Whether humanity survives or not, whether a particular political prisoner perishes, and so on—the results can depend on the efforts of individuals, on their actions (or lack of action) at the present time. This is like the situation of "Schrödinger's cat" in quantum mechanics where the outcome of an experiment (the fate of the"cat") is determined not by the trajectories of "mindless" electrons, but by the free will of the observer, by the decisions he makes.[41]

The implication of this for theories like Marxism-Leninism that claimed predictive value was that they were unequivocally wrong. Such theories, as

40. In Schrödinger's experiment, there is a box containing a cat, a vial of poison, and a hammer, along with radioactive matter and a detector that can record its decay. These things are arranged so that when an atom of the radioactive matter decays, the hammer smashes the vial of poison, the poison is released, and the cat dies. In the experiment, the detector is turned on just long enough for there to be the same chance that an atom in the radioactive material decays as there is that none of them does. Ordinary experience suggests that after the detector is turned on, the cat is either dead or alive depending on whether or not an atom has been released. But Schrödinger believed that the principles of quantum physics dictated that only when someone opened the box and observed its contents would the cat be either dead or alive. Prior to that moment, there were only probabilities, in this case an equal probability, that the cat was dead or alive; in fact, before the box was opened, there were two "worlds" that existed simultaneously, in one of which the cat was dead, in the other of which the cat was alive. For a description and comprehensible explanation of the experiment, see John Gribben, *In Search of Schrödinger's Cat: Quantum Physics and Reality* (New York, Bantam Books, 1984), 203, and Paul Davies, *God and the New Physics* (New York, 1983), 114.

41. Altshuler, "On nebyl naiven," 230–31.

Sakharov stated in an interview he gave in 1980, "pretend to know ultimate truths," but in fact they know nothing of the sort, and for that reason those who accept them almost always lack "flexibility and tolerance."[42] For Sakharov that was reason enough to be concerned. In claiming to know with complete certainty what the future would bring, there was not only intellectual arrogance but an implicit sanction of whatever methods the advocates of such theories believed were necessary to achieve their objectives, which were held to be desirable precisely because they were deemed to be inevitable. The result, in the Soviet Union, was Stalinism, which Sakharov considered not the betrayal or repudiation of Bolshevism and Marxism-Leninism but their logical (though hardly inevitable) extension.

One might think that this "uncertainty principle" would produce a pervasive pessimism, a belief that since the future was unknowable, striving for a better one would be pointless.[43] But this is not what Sakharov concluded. Instead, he argued that the uncertainty inherent in the nature of things was actually a cause for guarded optimism. True, the unpredictability of the future meant that there were no objective laws determining it. But precisely for that reason human beings were free to influence the future. Indeed, if they chose their actions carefully and were scrupulous both in their objectives and in the means they chose to achieve these objectives, they could create new social and political realities, such as convergence, that were superior to those that existed. Progress, while hardly inevitable, was nonetheless possible.

Sakharov expressed this view most clearly and succinctly a few years later, in 1988, in an interview he gave to *Molodezh Estonii.*[44] In response to a question about whether he believed in the existence of fate, he replied that he did not "except in the general sense of an internal logic to the unfolding of events."[45] After noting that this logic pertained to the entire universe as well as in the affairs of human beings, Sakharov said that "the future is unpredictable and indeterminable, that it is created by all of us, step by step in our unending and intricate interactions."[46] In response to the next question—whether he thought "everything is in the hands of God or in the hands of Man"—Sakharov replied that "the freedom to choose belongs to man" and that that is why "the role of the individual [in history] is great."[47] Even though fate, in the limited role Sakharov ascribed to it, "places individuals at some key point in history," Sakharov added, what individuals do in their lives is contingent upon their own choices and decisions, not on some impersonal mechanism, such as the dialectic, that presumably is embedded in nature and thus the ultimate cause of all

---

42. Andrei Sakharov, "Otvety na voprosy Korrespondenta Lakkua/ital'ianskoe agentsvo ANSA (1980)," in *Materialy samizdata,* no. 18/80 (May 19, 1980) AS3963: 6.
43. "Uncertainty principle" is the phrase Werner Heisenberg coined for a fundamental tenet of quantum physics.
44. Sakharov and Bonner, "I Tried to Be on the Level of My Destiny," 328–41.
45. Quoted in Altshuler, "On nebyl naiven," 235.
46. Ibid.
47. Ibid.

history.[48] Paradoxically, the very indeterminacy in nature that for others was conducive to despondency was for Sakharov a potentially liberating phenomenon, making possible the moral improvement of humanity as a whole, by forcing every individual to rely on his own devices in improving himself and his environment. It was for precisely this reason that Sakharov often said that the future is unpredictable and that it is a very good thing for humanity that it is.[49]

## Revisiting Nuclear Weapons and Arms Control

The one significant change in Sakharov's views that occurred while he was in Gorky concerned nuclear weapons and deterrence. Previously he had considered deterrence effective in preventing nuclear war. To be sure, in the late 1970s he came to believe its effectiveness was only temporary and that the only permanent guarantee of peace was disarmament, which would be a concomitant of convergence. In the early 1980s, however, Sakharov questioned whether deterrence was effective even as a temporary expedient. The problem with deterrence was that it required a certain symmetry: while nuclear weapons might be effective in deterring a nuclear attack, they were no longer effective in deterring a conventional attack. The assumption on which the United States had based its policy of containment since the Cold War began was that its nuclear capability would deter the Soviet Union from launching a conventional invasion of Western Europe: the casualties American servicemen in Western Europe would suffer as a result of an invasion would justify an American nuclear strike on the Soviet Union. Sakharov, however, now rejected that assumption, arguing that nuclear war had become so unimaginable to American policymakers that not even the deaths of American soldiers in Western Europe would prompt the United States to launch a nuclear attack. Nuclear weapons had lost their power to deter because the threat to use them, at least on the part of the Americans, was no longer credible. For that reason, Sakharov argued that a Soviet conventional attack on Western Europe (or anywhere else) could be repelled only by conventional forces and that the West should therefore increase those forces to the point where their deterrent value would be credible.[50] In short, American conventional forces would replace American nuclear weapons in deterring the Soviets from using their conventional forces aggressively. The only circumstance under which Sakharov could now envision the United States launching a nuclear strike on the Soviet Union was in response to a Soviet nuclear strike on the United States. And the Soviets might actually launch such a strike because they

48. Ibid.

49. Altshuler, "Nou-khau," 68.

50. The scenario Sakharov discounted of a Soviet conventional invasion triggering an American nuclear response was explicated clearly by Charles Krauthammer in articles he wrote in the 1980s. See, for example, "Some Allies: Whose Side Are They on?" *Washington Post*, April 25, 1986, A19. In these articles, Krauthammer noted that American officials, for good reason, never acknowledged publicly what this scenario implied about American military personnel in Europe—namely, that they were there, for all intents and purposes, to die. To repel a Soviet invasion, there would have to have been many more of them.

no longer considered credible the Americans' threat to retaliate with nuclear weapons—and also because there were elements in the Soviet military who believed that the Soviet Union could fight and win a nuclear war.

Sakharov presented his argument in a letter he sent to the Pugwash Conference on nuclear weaponry and arms control in September 1982,[51] in his acceptance speech on receiving the Szilard Award,[52] and in his open letter to Sidney Drell on the danger of thermonuclear war. Sakharov wrote the letter in response to articles Drell had written on the subject that he gave to Bonner while in Moscow in December 1982; Sakharov's response, which the KGB confiscated when Bonner tried to mail it from Moscow, he finally mailed successfully from Gorky, and it appeared as an article in the American journal *Foreign Affairs* in July 1983.[53] In his letter to Drell, Sakharov explained at length why he believed the West, and the United States in particular, should increase its conventional forces to the point where there would exist, for the first time in the Cold War, strategic parity in conventional forces as well as nuclear ones:

> For a long time, beginning as far back as the end of the 1940s, the West has not been relying on its "conventional" armed forces as a means sufficient for repelling a potential aggressor and for restraining expansion. There are many reasons for this—the West's lack of political, military, and economic unity; the striving to avoid a peacetime militarization of the economy, society, technology, and science; the low numerical levels of the Western nations' armies. All that at a time when the U.S.S.R. and the other countries of the socialist camp have armies with great numerical strength and are rearming them intensively, sparing no resources. It is possible that for a limited period of time the mutual nuclear terror had a certain restraining effect on the course of world events. But, at the present time, the balance of nuclear terror is a dangerous remnant of the past! In order to avoid aggression with conventional weapons one cannot threaten to use nuclear weapons if their use is inadmissible. One of the conclusions that follows here—and a conclusion you draw—is that it is necessary to restore strategic parity in the field of conventional weapons.[54]

In his letter to Drell, Sakharov's call for parity in conventional weapons was clear. But when he elaborated in the same letter on the reason he thought such parity was necessary—because nuclear weapons were no longer a credible deterrent to conventional warfare—what he was really saying was that nuclear weapons were no longer a credible deterrent to *any* kind of warfare and therefore had no moral justification at all. Because the circumstances that originally justified them had changed, nuclear weapons had lost their raison d'être and should be abolished. In his letter to Drell, Sakharov made this point obliquely.

51. "Text of Sakharov's Letter to Pugwash Parley on Soviet Policy," *New York Times*, September 10, 1982, 6.

52. Sakharov, "Acceptance Speech for the Szilard Award," 660–63.

53. Andrei Sakharov, "The Danger of Thermonuclear War: An Open Letter to Dr. Sidney Drell," *Foreign Affairs* 61, no. 5 (Summer 1983): 1001–16.

54. Ibid., 1006–7.

But in his Szilard Award acceptance speech (which someone delivered on his behalf), he made it explicitly. After answering in the affirmative the question he posed to himself whether "nuclear terror" had served over the past forty years "as a deterrent against war," he continued as follows:

> Nuclear deterrence is gradually turning into its own antithesis and becoming a dangerous remnant of the past. The equilibrium provided by nuclear deterrence is becoming increasingly unsteady; increasingly real is the danger that mankind will perish if an accident or insanity or uncontrolled escalation draws it into a total thermonuclear war. In light of this it is necessary, gradually and carefully, to shift the functions of deterrence onto conventional armed forces, with all the economic, political and social consequences this entails. It is necessary to strive for nuclear disarmament.[55]

But Sakharov did not favor the immediate abolition of nuclear weapons. For the foreseeable future, arms control, rather than disarmament, was what the two nuclear superpowers needed to negotiate. Disarmament remained an objective only for the long run. In the short term, nuclear weapons would be useful in negotiations as bargaining chips, essential in ensuring that arms reductions were symmetrical, which was the only way nuclear peace could be maintained before total disarmament occurred. In Sakharov's scheme of things, each of the two nuclear superpowers would reduce, and eventually abolish, its nuclear arsenals (including the missiles, such as the SS-20s, that delivered them) if, and only if, the other superpower did so as well. But before either power would do this, it would have to be convinced (at least in the case of the Soviet Union) that it could not achieve a first-strike capability by building up its nuclear forces. And it would be convinced of this only if the other power demonstrated its willingness to match that buildup with one of its own. Once again Sakharov accepted the correctness of the cliché common among American critics of arms control that to build down, there are times, as in the early 1980s, when one has to build up.

Sakharov stated his position in a several ways. In the letter he sent to Alexandrov in October 1980, in which he condemned his colleagues in the academy for their collective indifference to his exile and confinement, he argued that "genuine disarmament" was possible only if it proceeded from "a strategic balance of power."[56] In his letter to Drell, Sakharov noted that while "it is impossible to win a nuclear war…as long as there are nuclear weapons in the world, there must be a strategic parity of nuclear forces so that neither side will venture to embark on a limited or regional nuclear war."[57] Arms control for the purpose of achieving disarmament, in other words, was a lengthy process, involving difficult and protracted negotiations into which the United States should enter only

55. Sakharov, "Acceptance Speech for the Szilard Award," 661–62.
56. Sakharov, "Open Letter to Anatoly Aleksandrov," 213.
57. Sakharov, "Danger of Thermonuclear War," 1016.

from a position of strength. It should have delivery systems like Cruise missiles, the MX, and Pershing IIs already operational so that the Soviet Union would have some incentive for reducing, and eventually eliminating, not only its intermediate range missiles like the SS-20s but its arsenal of ICBMs as well.[58] For this reason Sakharov emphatically rejected Drell's call for a nuclear freeze, and the fact that such a freeze was wildly popular among the elites in both Western Europe and America when Drell recommended it probably reduced even further Sakharov's already low opinion of them.[59]

The blind devotion of these elites to a nuclear freeze was for Sakharov another manifestation of their intellectual and moral obtuseness. In his view, a nuclear freeze was a terrible idea. If put into place, it would produce a situation precisely the opposite of what its advocates wanted and predicted. To Sakharov it hardly mattered whether a nuclear freeze was unilateral or multilateral; in either case it would increase, rather than diminish, the chances of nuclear war. If the United States, for example, froze its production of nuclear weapons unilaterally, the Soviet Union would not only continue to produce nuclear weapons but probably accelerate the production of them, and the result would be a growing asymmetry in the two arsenals that might cause the Soviet Union to consider or even carry out a nuclear strike. The fact that Soviet ICBMs were currently in silos vulnerable to a nuclear attack—which would ordinarily deter the Soviets from launching a strike of their own—was essentially negated because they were MIRVed sufficiently so that firing them in a first strike was a viable option. This is particularly true since the Soviets (according to Sakharov) were aware that American missiles, in the absence of the MX, were just as vulnerable to Soviet missiles as Soviet missiles were to American ones.[60] But a bilateral freeze was hardly better than a unilateral one. Although Sakharov did not say so explicitly, he knew that the United States' delivery systems, principally its ICBMs, were older than Soviet systems and thus more prone to malfunction. For this reason, a bilateral freeze without any allowance for replacing missiles that became obsolete or simply stopped working would be destabilizing, leading to the asymmetry Sakharov rightly considered dangerous to peace.

Sakharov's animadversions on a nuclear freeze hardly endeared him to those in the West who saw it as an alternative to the arms race and a deus ex machina that would end the Cold War. Closer to home, his implication that Soviet leaders might carry out a nuclear first strike infuriated them. For one thing, it called into question Brezhnev's repeated statements that the Soviet Union would never use nuclear weapons first.[61] For another, it showed Sakharov to be profoundly

58. Sakharov, *Memoirs*, 539; Sakharov, "Acceptance Speech for the Szilard Award," 662.
59. Sakharov, "Danger of Thermonuclear War," 1009–10.
60. Ibid., 1013.
61. Holloway, *Soviet Union and the Arms Race*, xv. Whether Brezhnev was telling the truth was a matter of heated debate in the West. Richard Pipes argued in 1977 that the Soviets truly believed they could fight and win a nuclear war—which made a first strike a conceivable option, perhaps even an attractive one. Many others, among them Robert Arnett, disagreed. David Holloway

suspicious of the Soviet Union, ready to ascribe to it nefarious intentions, including a willingness to risk the lives of millions of people. Not surprisingly, the reaction from the Soviet government to Sakharov's statements on nuclear weapons and deterrence, in particular his letter to Drell, was swift, menacing, and in some ways even more personally defamatory than the press campaign in 1973. On the very day the letter to Drell appeared in *Foreign Affairs*, *Izvestiia* attacked it.[62] In an article signed (but not necessarily written) by four academicians and entitled, in English, "When Honor and Conscience are Lost," the authors (or author) cited Sakharov's letter to Drell as evidence of treason—a kind of betrayal of the Soviet Union in which Sakharov publicly displayed not only his hatred of the Soviet system and the Soviet people but his willingness to assist in the destruction of the Soviet Union itself.[63] For all his pretensions to the moral high ground, Sakharov in reality was a warmonger who hypocritically tried to disguise his calls for "a war against his own country" with bogus claims to be serving the cause of international peace.[64] The fact that Sakharov was a scientist and thus knew all too well the consequences of the nuclear war he was inciting only heightened his infamy.[65]

The various statements Sakharov made that contradicted Soviet policy on nuclear weaponry and deterrence gave the authorities the excuse they needed to charge him with betraying national security—which effectively foreclosed what little chance there still was of his being allowed to emigrate or of the government's exiling him abroad.[66] With Sakharov now confined to the Soviet Union, seemingly for the rest of his life, he remained, as it were, a stationary target, and the rhetorical attacks on him escalated. Just before the letter to Drell appeared, the government revived the suspicion it had first raised in 1973 that Sakharov was mentally ill. In an interview he gave to *Newsweek* in June, Alexandrov said he detected "a psychic shift" in Sakharov.[67] One month later, perhaps as a way of gauging the Western reaction should the Soviet government incarcerate

maintained in 1983 that while the Soviet civilian leadership did not think nuclear war was winnable, the Soviet military prepared for one as if it were. Pipes, "Why the Soviet Union Thinks It Could Fight and Win a Nuclear War," 21–34; Robert L. Arnett, "Soviet Attitudes Towards Nuclear War: Do They Really Think They Can Win?" *Journal of Strategic Studies* 2, no. 9 (September 1979): 172–91; Holloway, *Soviet Union and the Arms Race*, 52–54. None of these views obviates the thesis that the Soviets sought nuclear parity, or even superiority, because they realized it would bring significant *political* benefits even if nuclear weapons were never used.

62. Presumably the Soviets possessed a copy of the letter before it was published in America, probably one of those Bonner mailed from Moscow that never reached its recipient.

63. A. A. Dorodnitsyn et al., "Kogda teriaiut chest' i sovest'," *Izvestiia*, July 3, 1983, 4. Ironically, just as Sakharov believed (with good reason) that the article was actually written by a propagandist such as Iurii Zhukov or Iurii Kornilov, the author or authors of the article claimed (without offering any evidence) that Sakharov's letter to Drell had been ghostwritten. Sakharov, *Memoirs*, 584.

64. Dorodnitsyn et al., "Kogda teriaiut chest' i sovest'," 4.

65. Ibid.

66. Sagdeev, *Making of a Soviet Scientist*, 253–54.

67. Quoted in Sakharov, *Memoirs*, 597.

Sakharov in a psychiatric hospital, Andropov intimated to a delegation of visiting American senators that the Soviet physicist was simply crazy.[68]

The rhetorical onslaught continued, with increasing intensity and vituperation, for the rest of the summer and into the fall. In July the most salacious and condemnatory parts of Nikolai Iakovlev's book *CIA Target—The USSR*, which had been published earlier in the year, appeared in the magazine *Smena (Change)*, which had over one million readers.[69] In the excerpts *Smena* published, Iakovlev excoriated Sakharov as a Kadet, a weak and unpatriotic fool, and an unwitting tool of his overbearing, scheming, and deceitful wife, who herself was an agent of "the Zionists."[70] For good measure, Iakovlev attacked Bonner's children as "loafers" and pointedly distinguished them from Sakharov's own children, who he noted were wise enough to distance themselves from their befuddled father and his duplicitous spouse.[71] Incredibly, Iakovlev had the temerity, after his diatribes appeared in *Smena*, to visit Sakharov in Gorky, ostensibly so he could interview him for another journal but actually for the purpose of unnerving him. Sakharov, after refuting Iakovlev's calumnies as calmly and as logically as he could, uncharacteristically lost his composure when Iakovlev continued to impugn Bonner's character and behavior and slapped him. A few days later Bonner lodged a formal complaint against her husband's tormentor, but to no one's surprise the authorities ignored it.[72] In October the journal *Chelovek i zakon (Man and the Law)*, whose readership was almost nine million, published yet another of Iakovlev's assaults, this one directed mainly at Bonner, whom it described as a sexual predator with an almost satanic proclivity for seducing older men and then absconding with their life savings. In the lurid portrait of Bonner the article painted, which obviously bore no relation to reality, Sakharov came across as a hapless victim of his wife's machinations on behalf of the CIA and evil Zionists, "to be pitied more than hated for the ease with which people stronger than he cynically used him for their own nefarious purposes."[73] By the time the campaign came to an end, approximately four months after it began, Sakharov had received almost three thousand letters denouncing him.[74]

## Health Problems and Hunger Strikes

In September 1982, well before this new press campaign began, Bonner applied for a visa to go abroad for another operation on her eye. Through the

68. Ibid.

69. Nikolai Iakovlev, "Put' vniz," *Smena* 14 (July 1983): 26–27. See also Andrei Sakharov, "A Letter to My Colleagues (November 1983)," *Samizdat Bulletin*, no. 130 (February 1984): 2. In 2003 a new edition of Yakovlev's book was published in Moscow. Rubenstein and Gribanov, *KGB File*, 281.

70. Iakovlev, "Put' vniz," 27.

71. Ibid.

72. Sakharov, *Memoirs*, 589–92.

73. Ibid., 586–87. This was how the KGB, in less lurid tones, regularly described their relationship. Rubenstein and Gribanov, *KGB File*, 270, 303, 305, 307–8, 318, 325. See also an internal TASS memorandum from 1984 claiming that Bonner "regularly goads [Sakharov] into actions hostile to the Soviet state and society." Ibid., 288.

74. Bonner, *Alone Together*, 91.

winter and spring of 1982–1983, her application languished. When she suffered a heart attack in April 1983, her request became urgent; only from doctors outside the Soviet Union could she receive the expert care her cardiac problems now desperately required. But the government was not about to acquiesce, and the press campaign convinced Sakharov that in the absence of drastic and dramatic action on his part, it might never do so. Finally, in September, Sakharov decided to conduct another hunger strike.[75] But Bonner, who remembered the toll the previous one had taken on his frail constitution, argued against it. In D. S. Chernavskii's formulation of their dilemma, if Sakharov did nothing for Bonner, he endangered her life, but going on a hunger strike for Bonner might endanger his own.[76] Reluctantly, Sakharov complied with Bonner's wishes.[77]

However, in October 1983 and January 1984, Bonner suffered additional heart problems. These convinced Sakharov he had no choice but to start fasting, a tactic that had worked once before and might work again.[78] He was well aware how barbaric many in the West considered the force-feedings the government used on other dissidents who fasted. For this reason, he could be reasonably sure that any hunger strike he began, even if he was not forced to eat, would generate publicity and considerable sympathy in the West. But again Sakharov hesitated. He and Bonner feared that the government would use a hunger strike as a pretext for arresting her, and for that reason asked the American ambassador to grant Bonner temporary asylum in the American embassy if, in the event Sakharov began fasting, her arrest appeared imminent. But Bonner remained uneasy about this course of action, and Sakharov deferred a final decision to the spring. On May 2 the government essentially resolved the issue for him: on that day KGB agents detained Bonner at the Gorky airport just before she boarded a flight to Moscow and detained her briefly.[79] At that point Sakharov concluded he had little to lose and much to gain by a hunger strike. He began fasting the same day, and the fact that Bonner was released pending a trial did not cause him to stop. On May 7 Sakharov was taken to Semashko Hospital, and on May 11 he was, for the first time, force-fed intravenously—which did not prevent TASS from alleging that Sakharov's hunger strike was actually faked.[80] Although he suffered what might have been a minor stroke when the injections began, the hospital continued them until May 15, when the medical personnel attending him began feeding him by shoving food down his mouth. This proved so painful

75. Andrei Sakharov, "The Hunger Strike Appeal (May 8, 1984)," ibid., 241; Sakharov, *Memoirs*, 581–83.

76. Chernavskii, "Vizit v Gorkii," 762. Sakharov surely knew that, if done violently enough, force-feeding could be fatal. One dissident, Iurii Kuk, had died in 1981 as a result of it. "Torture by Clamp and Spoon," *U.S. News and World Report*, February 24, 1986, 31.

77. A. Sakharov, "Letter to Anatoly Alexandrov (October 15, 1984)," in *Memoirs*, 700.

78. Sakharov, "The Hunger Strike Appeal," 240. According to Altshuler, his anger at his scientific colleagues for refusing to support Bonner's visa application was another factor in Sakharov's decision. Altshuler, "Nou-khau," 68.

79. Bonner, *Alone Together*, 241; Andrei Sakharov, "A Letter to the Family (November 24, 1985)," in *Memoirs*, 689.

80. Bonner, *Alone Together*, 234–36; Sakharov, *Memoirs*, 689–90.

that occasionally, when his "feeding team" (as he called the orderlies and nurses who attended him) was "at full strength"—that is, when one person tied him down and held him while others held his nose, opened his mouth, and forced food down it—Sakharov would relent and swallow voluntarily. But most of the time he valiantly but vainly resisted.[81]

Over the next two weeks, as the doctors administered psychotropic drugs (and even tried hypnosis) in a fruitless effort to cause Sakharov to end his hunger strike, his physical condition worsened to the point where he was near death.[82] Finally, on May 27 he relented and agreed to eat voluntarily. The hunger strike, his third in ten years, was over. But the authorities refused to release him from the hospital, where he remained for the rest of the spring and almost all of the summer. On September 7, Sakharov began another fast but abandoned it the next day when he was told that if he stopped, he would be released from the hospital and thus could see Bonner again after a hiatus of four months.[83] In what was for Sakharov a rare moment of self-pity, he told Misha Levin after his release that while he was fasting, he understood how the slaves in Rome must have suffered while being crucified.[84]

Sakharov's hunger strike prompted the same vituperation his earlier fasts had evoked from the Soviet government. TASS, on May 4, inveighed against what it called his "blatant calumnies and malicious lies defaming our country, our system and the Soviet people," which, through Bonner, supposedly had reached the West and emboldened the "anti-Soviet centers" there to try to undermine the Soviet system.[85] Similar assaults appeared in the Soviet press in the weeks that followed, and in August, in response to accusations in the West that Sakharov was being detained against his will in a Soviet hospital, the KGB sent to a West German newspaper a videotape of Sakharov and Bonner taken prior to the hunger strike that the KGB had doctored to make it seem current. Foolishly, the newspaper swallowed the hoax and sold the tape to ABC News in the United States, which just as foolishly broadcast it.[86]

As was the case when Sakharov fasted on behalf of Liza Alexeeva, his hunger strike in 1984 prompted criticism, some of it intense, from people ordinarily sympathetic to him. His critics included Jeremy Stone, who, in the *International Herald Tribune,* repeated the objections he had made against Sakharov's hunger strike in 1981—namely, that it was self-serving and a distraction from far more pressing matters.[87] Another was Vitalii Ginzburg, who believed that by

81. Sakharov, *Memoirs,* 691.

82. B. L. Altshuler, quoted in Ivanova, *Andrei Dmitrievich,* 30; "The Sakharov Tragedy Continues," *Samizdat Bulletin* 136 (August 1984): 1.

83. Sakharov, "Letter to Anatoly Alexandrov," 705.

84. Altshuler, "Nou-khau," 90.

85. Quoted in Bonner, *Alone Together,* 232.

86. "Operation Sakharov: The KGB Weaves a Tangled Web," *U.S. News and World Report,* March 3, 1986, 7.

87. Jeremy J. Stone, "Sakharov: A Scientist's Rebellion," *International Herald Tribune,* May 29, 1984, 6; Bonner, *Alone Together,* 73–74.

fasting Sakharov was doing for Bonner something he would not do for other dissidents—a charge that was true but hardly damning, since Bonner, after all, was his wife.[88] As if on cue, Roi Medvedev also weighed in, claiming that Sakharov was fasting not for Bonner but to secure an end to his own exile.[89] Most hurtful of all was the reaction of Sakharov's children. On May 15 they sent Bonner a telegram urging her to convince their father to end his hunger strike: if he did not relent, they would have no choice but to request that the procurator's office bring criminal charges against her for inciting their father to commit suicide.[90] Despite the fact that the KGB had knowledge of the letter before his children sent it and may even have written it for them and then forced them to sign it, Sakharov was so angry and distressed by the distrust and animosity the letter revealed that he refused to have any contact with his children for the next eighteen months, until November 1985.[91] Now, more than ever, Bonner's children were also Sakharov's.

What worried him the most throughout his hunger strike and hospitalization was Bonner's precarious legal status in the wake of her arrest. Although she was released immediately, in the ensuing investigation she was threatened with treason, a crime for which she could have been executed.[92] In the end, the government charged her with "anti-Soviet slander" under Article 190-1 of the RSFSR Criminal Code. On August 10 she was tried, convicted, and sentenced to five years of internal exile in Gorky. The implications of this were enormous: not only could Bonner no longer carry out in Moscow the essential errands she had run for Sakharov since his exile began; more ominously, the regime now had sound legal grounds for denying Bonner the exit visa she needed to go abroad.[93] In reacting to all of this, Sakharov probably shared Altshuler's surmise that the Soviets had charged and convicted Bonner to punish Sakharov for his letter to Drell, which by the time of Bonner's arrest had circulated widely in the West.[94] On a purely emotional level, Sakharov was infuriated by Bonner's travails: someone close to him was being treated unfairly. But intellectually he viewed her case the way he did that of any other Soviet dissident or citizen whose rights had been violated, and he tried to defend her with the same arguments he used on behalf of people he hardly knew. On August 1, even before Bonner was tried, he charged in a public declaration that when the government had arrested, detained, tried, convicted, and sentenced her, it was acting in violation of Soviet law. Since he, not Bonner, was the real object of the government's animus, he should be the defendant or at least a codefendant in the case; the fact

88. Bonner remained very bitter about Ginzburg's charge, and in 1990 criticized him publicly for it. Bonner, "Komu nuzhny mify," 25.
89. Sakharov, "Interview mit Roy Medwedew," 10.
90. Sakharov, "Letter to the Family (November 24, 1985)," 690.
91. Ibid.; Bonner, *Alone Together*, 73–74.
92. Bonner, *Alone Together*, 69.
93. Sakharov, *Memoirs*, 599.
94. Altshuler, "Nou-khau," 89.

that he was not involved legally in her case only underscored its fundamental fraudulence.[95]

Four months later, on November 29, Sakharov filed an administrative complaint, in which he pointed out the various irregularities, inconsistencies, and outright violations of the law in the government's treatment of Bonner. That Soviet law was mobilized to silence him—which is what he believed was the government's real objective—was an example of precisely the kind of oppression that had caused him to become a dissident in the first place. In his complaint Sakharov enumerated the shortcomings of the legal case against his wife with the same relentless logic and attention to evidence he had shown in previous years in defending countless individuals whose human rights had been violated. Procedurally, because Bonner's trial took place in Gorky rather than in Moscow, where the alleged crimes had supposedly been committed, the verdict it produced was illegal. Also, Article 190-1, by any fair reading, required the person making statements slanderous of the Soviet Union to know they were false. But since Bonner thought the statements she was disseminating were true, she could not be charged legitimately with violating that particular article. Moreover, since the statements were actually Sakharov's, he should be the defendant in the case. Finally, because Bonner had a heart ailment and was also a disabled veteran, her sentence, under Soviet law, should have been reduced.[96]

Confined to Gorky, distraught by the government's seemingly relentless persecution of his family and other dissidents, Sakharov found solace in the ideas and principles he championed. Ideas created for Sakharov an "alternate universe," a mental sphere in which abstractions like human rights were just as real as the human beings—principally Liza, Bonner, and Sakharov himself—who were denied them. Understandably, Sakharov's struggle on behalf of himself and his family caused him to minimize the significance of other events that occurred at the time, even those that bore directly on his own situation. Conspicuously missing from Sakharov's memoirs—which were written not long after the events they describe—is any mention of the deaths of Suslov and Brezhnev in 1982; the interregnum from 1982 to 1985 in which one gerontological invalid, Andropov, was succeeded by another, Konstantin Chernenko; and the ascension to power of a much younger man, Mikhail Gorbachev, in 1985. If Sakharov's memoirs were the only source one had for the nearly six years he spent in Gorky, one could easily draw the conclusion that the Soviet Union, like Oceania in Orwell's *1984*, was a faceless, totalitarian monolith in which nothing changed and very little happened. This, of course, was not the case. The decline of the Soviet economy that began imperceptibly in the early 1960s accelerated in the late 1970s and early 1980s. Unbeknownst to Sakharov, several Soviet sociologists and economists, among them Tatiana Zaslavskaia and Abel Aganbegian, recognized the threat this posed to the Soviet system and

95. A. Sakharov, "Zaiavlenie (August 1, 1984)," in *Vospominaniia*, 2, 523.
96. A. Sakharov, "Administrative Complaint (November 29, 1984)," in *Memoirs*, 693–97.

briefed Gorbachev on what might be done to reverse it. In the 1970s Sakharov had been fairly sensitive to changes that occurred in the country in addition to those involving the dissidents. But in the early 1980s he knew less about events outside his immediate circle in Gorky, some of which would eventually affect his own life profoundly.

When Sakharov ended his hunger strike in September 1984 without Bonner's receiving the exit visa she requested, it was only a matter of time before he began another one. In a letter to Alexandrov in February 1985, he threatened to start fasting again and to resign from the academy as well if a visa was not forthcoming from the authorities. The only reason he postponed his fast was that he thought Chernenko's dire medical condition would detract attention from it.[97] But by April, the situation had been clarified: Chernenko was dead, and Gorbachev, with the timely assistance of Gromyko, was now firmly in control.[98] On April 16 Sakharov began another hunger strike. On April 21 he was again taken to Semashko Hospital, where he was force-fed and in all likelihood given psychotropic drugs to reduce his resistance.[99] He had hoped this fast would force the authorities to pardon Bonner as the first step to granting her a visa, possibly on May 9, the fortieth anniversary of the end of World War II in Europe.[100] But neither a pardon nor a visa was forthcoming. Having started his hunger strike, Sakharov felt he had no choice now but to continue it, and the force-feedings continued into the summer.

On July 11, having heard nothing from or about Bonner for almost three months, Sakharov reconsidered his strategy and ended his fast. In response, the KGB quickly released him from the hospital—which it had not done when Sakharov ended his hunger strike the year before—probably because it feared Sakharov's continued hospitalization might generate protests at a conference to monitor compliance with the Helsinki Accords that was scheduled to convene in Ottawa, Canada on August 1. Thinking that Gorbachev would be more receptive to his request if he was no longer fasting, Sakharov had composed a letter to Gorbachev at the end of June (which he did not send) again requesting the exit visa Bonner needed.[101] But when the KGB publicly described Sakharov's decision as a capitulation, he decided, on July 27, to start again. Hospitalization followed immediately, and force-feedings resumed. Before becoming incommunicado, however, Sakharov had managed to mail his letter to Gorbachev, with a copy to Gromyko.[102] In the letter he coupled his request for a visa with what he thought

97. A. Sakharov, "Prezidentu AN SSSR A. P. Aleksandrovu (February 12, 1985)," in *Vospominaniia*, 2, 540–41. In the end, he never resigned from the academy.

98. On the specifics of the succession, see Dusko Doder and Louise Branson, *Gorbachev: Heretic in the Kremlin* (New York, 1990), 60–65.

99. Sakharov, "Letter to the Family," 690; Bonner, *Alone Together*, 153.

100. Bonner, *Alone Together*, 139.

101. Ibid., 152; Sakharov, *Memoirs*, 599–600.

102. Sakharov, *Memoirs*, 600. In his memoirs Sakharov states that he sent the letters "on or about July 29." Ibid. It seems almost certain, however, that if he (as opposed to Bonner) sent the

was an inducement for the Soviet leader to respond favorably. Sakharov noted that he was tired of politics and wanted to devote his attention entirely, or almost entirely, to physics. As he put it, he wanted "to discontinue [his] public activities [i.e., his dissidence] apart from exceptional circumstances."[103] Anticipating the criticism this would prompt from other dissidents if the letter became public that he was betraying his most cherished principles, Sakharov wrote that, given Bonner's condition, getting her the visa and the medical treatment she needed took precedence over everything else and that in any case his ability to influence events politically from Gorky was minimal. What Sakharov wrote in his letter to Gorbachev was true, and in regard to his lack of political influence it is worth nothing that in the summer of 1985, while he was incommunicado in Semashko Hospital, the United Nations, after reporting him "missing," conducted only the most cursory search "to find him."[104] Indeed, public criticism from the West was less than what it had been during Sakharov's earlier hunger strikes and hospitalizations—while criticism from dissidents and others in the Soviet Union was just as great. This time it was Evgenii Feinberg who leveled the charge, albeit in letters he chose not to publicize, that Sakharov was acting selfishly—that he was seeking for his wife something that was inaccessible to the other 270 million Soviet citizens.[105] Sakharov replied that Bonner was his wife, and he would do whatever was necessary to save her life. In addition, if he did not make good on the threat he had issued to go on a hunger strike, he would lose what little leverage with Alexandrov and the academy he still possessed.[106]

For these reasons Sakharov persevered in his campaign, even as his physical condition worsened. By the middle of August, his normal weight of 175 pounds had plummeted to 138 pounds, in response to which his doctors prescribed intravenous and subcutaneous infusions of nutrients. But the infusions were exceedingly painful and caused his legs to swell terribly, preventing him from walking for several days.[107] On August 30 Sakharov's stepson, Alexei, began his own hunger strike outside the Soviet embassy in Washington. This heightened awareness of Sakharov's plight: on September 10 the United States Congress passed a nonbinding, concurrent resolution expressing "solidarity" with him and Bonner and objecting to the Soviets' treatment of them. When the State Department, shortly afterward, promised to remonstrate with the Soviet government, Sakharov concluded that his hunger strike had generated all the publicity it was likely to produce, and for that reason he could now end it.[108]

---

letters, in the sense of physically mailing them, he had to have done so before he was hospitalized on July 27.

103. Ibid. As early as the fall of 1982, in a note he appended to a copy he sent to Anatolii Alexandrov of a letter written for the chairman of the KGB, Sakharov had expressed a desire to devote most of his time to physics. Sakharov, "Letter to Vitaly Fedorchuk," 682.

104. Altshuler, "Nou-khau," 100.

105. Feinberg, "Dlia budushchego istorika," 691–92.

106. Ibid., 693.

107. Sakharov, *Memoirs*, 601.

108. Ibid., 602; Bonner, *Alone Together*, 160; Altshuler, "Nou-khau," 101.

## 21 The Soviet Leadership Softens

In the late summer of 1985, when Bonner's prospects of going abroad and Sakharov's of leaving Gorky never seemed worse, the new Soviet leadership, unbeknownst to both of them, was reconsidering its refusal to grant Bonner a visa. On August 29 the Politburo discussed her application formally. Gorbachev, who, as general secretary, chaired the meeting, ascribed Bonner's behavior to her "Zionism," and Chebrikov, the head of the KGB, expressed the commonly held view among the Soviet leadership that Sakharov was little more than Bonner's puppet. Nevertheless they decided to approve her application. But they also agreed on several conditions Bonner would have to accept before she could leave the country: while abroad, she could not discuss political matters, hold press conferences, or under any circumstances talk to Western reporters.[1] On September 5 Sergei Sokolov, the same KGB official who in May had tried unsuccessfully in a personal meeting to get Sakharov to renounce convergence and his views on nuclear weaponry, visited him on behalf of the Politburo to secure his agreement to these conditions, which now required that Sakharov enumerate in a written statement all the secret scientific information he possessed.[2] Chebrikov, in particular, was afraid that if Sakharov had not already divulged this information to Bonner, he might divulge it to her in the future, probably just before she went abroad, and then she would share it with interested Westerners, including representatives of Western intelligence agencies. Chebrikov's expectation, or at least his hope, was that such a statement from Sakharov might somehow prevent her from revealing what she knew while she was in the West. Sokolov also sought from Sakharov assurances that Bonner would not defect once she left the country and that he himself, because of what he was privy to, would never try to emigrate. When Sokolov presented these conditions, Sakharov was noncommittal on those that applied to Bonner, promising merely to inform her of them. As for himself, he told Sokolov he would be happy to produce a statement promising never to leave the Soviet Union but that, in reality, the whole issue was moot: if he applied for an exit visa, he would never be granted one—which meant that if Bonner went abroad, given the strength of their marriage, she would never defect.[3] On October 6 Bonner, who independently of Sakharov had concluded that his hunger strike should end, communicated her wishes to him by including in a letter a line from Pushkin the couple had previously agreed would be a signal for him to cease. On October 23 Sakharov did so. The next day Bonner received an exit visa—but with the demand that she leave

1. Dobrynin, *In Confidence*, 553; Altshuler, "Nou-khau," 101.
2. Sakharov, "Letter to the Family," 692.
3. Sakharov, *Memoirs*, 602.

the country immediately. She insisted, however, that before she could leave she needed time to help her husband recover from the effects of the hunger strike, and the authorities, albeit reluctantly, acquiesced. In late November Bonner flew to Italy, where Alexei and Efrem met her. From there, in early December, she traveled on to the United States, where, in January 1986 in Boston, she underwent heart bypass surgery. On June 2 she returned to Moscow and two days later finally arrived back in Gorky, to which, despite her visa, she was still legally confined. As it happened, Bonner never approved of the conditions Sokolov had asked Sakharov to present to her, and in the United States she discussed political issues publicly once her health permitted it.[4]

While Bonner was away, Sakharov pursued the same causes he had advocated when she was with him—thereby refuting the claim that he was her puppet. On February 19, 1986, he issued yet another appeal, in the form of a letter to Gorbachev, for a general amnesty for prisoners of conscience, claiming that most of them had been wrongly charged under Article 190-1, which required that the person charged with defaming the Soviet Union knew that the statements he made were false. Because Sakharov recognized in Gorbachev a native intelligence that might make it possible to deal with him pragmatically, he included in his appeal an acknowledgment that if a general amnesty was not possible, he would be satisfied with one for the political prisoners he cited specifically in his letter.[5] Sakharov also tried to appeal to Gorbachev's political interests as well as his patriotism, arguing that amnesty would benefit both the Soviet Union and (although he did not use the term) Gorbachev's own policy of perestroika. He knew when he wrote the letter that the chances of Gorbachev's responding favorably to it were small. Fifteen days before Sakharov issued his appeal, the general secretary, in an interview with a correspondent from *L'Humanité*, had denied that there were political prisoners in the Soviet Union and, responding to a question about Sakharov, specifically replied that his living conditions were "normal" and his exile perfectly legal.[6] But Sakharov hoped that Gorbachev would eventually order the release of all political prisoners and that despite what he had said in the interview, he would allow Sakharov at some point to return to Moscow.

Not even Gorbachev's handling of the Chernobyl disaster in April 1986—in which 31 people died instantly or shortly afterward, 134 others came down with radiation sickness, and some 1,000,000 more were exposed to radioactive fallout after one of the four reactors at the nuclear power plant near the town of that name melted down—caused Sakharov to relinquish the hopes he had placed in

---

4. Ibid., 603–5.

5. Coppen, "Public Life of Andrei Sakharov," 254; Andrei Sakharov's Appeal for Prisoners of Conscience on February 19, 1986, 99th Cong., 2d sess., *Congressional Record* 132, pt. 21:29945–47. When Gorbachev became general secretary in March 1985, Sakharov commented: "It looks as if our country's lucky. We've got an intelligent leader." Quoted in Andrew and Mitrokhin, *Sword and the Shield*, 332.

6. Mikhail Gorbachev, "Answers to *l'Humanité*," in *Selected Speeches and Articles* (Moscow, 1987), 329.

the general secretary.[7] Eventually Sakharov would conclude from the accident that "an essentially new reality" had arisen that required "international legislation" mandating the placement of nuclear reactors deep enough under the earth's surface so that, in case of similar meltdowns, no radiation would escape into the atmosphere.[8] He was chagrined by how quickly Gorbachev had reverted to the political habits he had developed as a loyal party apparatchik when he forbade the Soviet press from reporting the accident for several weeks. But because the press reports of the accident, when they finally appeared, drastically minimized its effects, he did not comprehend the magnitude of the disaster until Vladimir Fainberg and Arkadii Tseitlin visited him in Gorki at the end of May and passed on secret information that underscored the magnitude of the accident.[9] For that reason, Sakharov's anger at Gorbachev was not as great as it might have been had he learned of the accident immediately.

The first hint Sakharov had that the government was softening its opposition to him came in December 1985, when physicists from the Lebedev Institute, who had been barred from seeing him for well over a year, were allowed again to come to Gorky. A month later, one of these visitors, Andrei Linde, asked him on behalf of the KGB if he would be willing to work in Moscow on magnetically confined fusion reactors. Linde's offer was issued privately, and Sakharov, who was understandably skeptical of the KGB's intentions, rejected it by telling Linde that his scientific interests at present were in cosmology and field theory, not controlled fusion.[10] The following May, however, Viktor Louis, who was known for launching trial balloons for the Soviet leadership, claimed in an article he wrote for a Western newspaper that Sakharov was "respected by the overwhelming majority of the Russian people" and that, whatever his transgressions, "he is on our side of the barricades."[11]

Once Sakharov stopped his hunger strike and Bonner received the exit visa she requested, the Soviet leadership could consider the more fundamental issue of Sakharov's confinement in Gorky. Although hardliners in the KGB and the Communist Party, such as Egor Ligachev, favored continuing it, both Gorbachev and Alexander Yakovlev, the chief architect of perestroika, recognized that any improvement in Soviet-American relations required his release. Moreover, by 1986 Gorbachev and Sakharov agreed sufficiently on how the Soviet Union should be reformed (though not on the reasons for its reform) that releasing Sakharov would be a way of demonstrating that perestroika was real and that its objectives included the liberalization of significant aspects of the Soviet

7. Bailey, *Making of Andrei Sakharov*, 374; Roger Bate, "Chernobyl's Real Victims," January 24, 2002, http://www.techcentralstation.com/1051/envirowrapper.jsp?PID=1051–450&CID=1051–012402A.

8. Sakharov, *Memoirs*, 612–13; Altshuler, "Scientific Method of A. D. Sakharov," 2. In the late 1980s, Sakharov repeatedly called for such legislation. See, for example, Sakharov and Adamovich, "Zhit' na zemle i zhit' dolgo," 167, and "Akademik A. D. Sakharov," *Vestnik Akademii nauk SSSR* 5 (1989): 118.

9. Sakharov, *Memoirs*, 608.

10. Ibid., 606–7.

11. Quoted in Bonner, *Alone Together*, 263.

system.[12] Also, releasing Sakharov would deprive the remaining dissidents of a martyr who aggravated anti-Soviet sentiments in the West.[13]

Gorbachev, however, could not order Sakharov's release unilaterally, and given the opposition to it from the likes of Ligachev and Viktor Chebrikov, he could not do so immediately. He needed the support of the Politburo and the acquiescence, if not the support, of the KGB. To secure these, Yakovlev had Andrei Grachev and Nikolai Shishkin, both in the International Information Department of the Central Committee (in which capacity they had access to Sakharov's works, including *Reflections*, which Grachev had read), generate arguments that Ligachev and other opponents in the Politburo would find congenial. The point the two men stressed in making the case for Sakharov's release was the practical one that keeping him in Gorky was simply not worth the adverse publicity it still generated.[14] Because he deemed the KGB's opposition implacable, Yakovlev, with Gorbachev's approval, imposed strict secrecy on Shishkin's and Grachev's activities, and through the summer and early fall of 1986 Chebrikov remained ignorant of what was afoot. During this period, in fact, the government maintained publicly its long-standing position, going back to the first days of Sakharov's exile, that the government had always treated him humanely and in a way that was consistent with Soviet law. In October, the deputy procurator in Gorky made this point directly to Sakharov in the course of refusing his request to pass along to Gorbachev another letter requesting the release of political prisoners—the first one in which Sakharov explicitly requested his own release.[15] Undaunted by the refusal, Sakharov simply mailed the letter—which he describes in his memoirs as "the imperceptible tremor that touched off the avalanche"—directly to Gorbachev three weeks later.[16]

By the end of November, Yakovlev's initiative had achieved the desired effect, and on December 1 the Politburo agreed in principle to Sakharov's release.[17] One week later, Anatolii Marchenko, at the age of forty-eight, died in a labor camp from the effects of a hunger strike he had been conducting since the beginning of August. Sakharov was disconsolate when he learned of this.[18]

12. Grachev, *Kremlevskaia khronika*, 96–97; Doder and Branson, *Gorbachev*, 172–74; Brown, *Gorbachev Factor*, 165.

13. Brown argues that Gorbachev's ultimate objectives were more radical than those of the dissidents, and for that reason he considered further persecution nonsensical. Brown, *Gorbachev Factor*, 157. But the general secretary did not anticipate that his reforms would cause the dissidents who remained active politically, such as Sakharov, to radicalize *their* objectives, eventually to a degree that Gorbachev would not and could not accept.

14. Ibid., 164–65, 324; Grachev, *Kremlevskaia khronika*, 96. In an interview in the late 1980s, Len Karpinskii, who was on the periphery of the dissident movement, also justified Sakharov's release on grounds of Soviet national interest. Len Karpinsky, "The Autobiography of a Half-Dissident," in *Voices of Glasnost: Interviews with Gorbachev's Reformers*, ed. Stephen F. Cohen and Katrina vanden Heuvel (New York, 1989), 300.

15. Brown, *Gorbachev Factor*, 164–65; Sakharov, *Memoirs*, 611–12.

16. Sakharov, *Memoirs*, 612.

17. Brown, *Gorbachev Factor*, 165; D. S. Cherniaev, *Shest' let s Gorbachevym: Po dnevnikovym zapisiam* (Moscow, 1993), 125–26. Significantly, Ligachev was absent when the Politburo met to resolve the matter. S. A. Kovalev, "Etot patsient," in Ivanova, *Andrei Dmitrievich*, 172.

18. Sakharov, *Memoirs*, 613–14.

Because of his multiple arrests, Marchenko had suffered more than most of the dissidents, and the duration and intensity of his suffering evoked in Sakharov a visceral, almost paternalistic concern for his welfare. But Marchenko's death, ironically, was the catalyst that triggered Sakharov's release. The adverse publicity the death precipitated caused the government to look for something to overshadow it, and releasing Sakharov, who was far better known in the West than Marchenko, served that purpose very well.[19] On the evening of December 15, an electrician appeared suddenly at Sakharov's apartment in Gorky and installed a telephone; the KGB agent who accompanied him told Sakharov to expect a call—he did not say from whom—the next day. The following afternoon, when the telephone rang and Sakharov answered, he heard one of Gorbachev's assistants telling him that the next voice he would hear would be Gorbachev's. In the brief conversation that followed, the general secretary informed the Soviet physicist that the decree rescinding Sakharov's title and awards would itself be rescinded, that he could return to Moscow immediately, and that Bonner would be free to do so as well.[20] After Gorbachev related that the new president of the Academy of Sciences, Guri Marchuk, would be coming to Gorky shortly to work out the details of his return, Sakharov brought up Marchenko, admonishing Gorbachev for his death and requesting that the general secretary "look one more time at the question of releasing persons convicted for their beliefs."[21] When Gorbachev was noncommittal, Sakharov, in violation of the protocol that applied when talking to a head of state (or, in Gorbachev's case, the equivalent of a head of state), simply thanked him and said goodbye.[22]

Three days later, on December 19, Marchuk arrived at Sakharov's apartment, where he read Sakharov and Bonner what he said was the decree of the Presidium of the Supreme Soviet pardoning Bonner and revoking the 1980 decree authorizing Sakharov's exile, which Sakharov had assumed did not exist[23] Moreover, Marchuk (unlike Gorbachev) said nothing about the honors the government had stripped from Sakharov at the time he was exiled. Instead, he insisted that Sakharov's release was conditional upon his promising "to refrain from further anti-social behavior"—a condition Sakharov branded illegal and unfair: even if he wanted to refrain from such behavior, the government had no business requiring him to do so.[24] But the academy president also made a point of telling Sakharov that many of the political prisoners he was concerned about had been released and that the cases of several others were under review. Also on December 19, in

19. Pimenov, "Kakim on byl," 216–17; Philip Taubman, "Sakharov in New Era," *New York Times,* December 25, 1986, 3.

20. Sakharov, *Memoirs,* 614–15.

21. Ibid., 616.

22. Ibid.

23. Sakharov never saw the decree from which Marchuk read, and in the interview in which he mentioned this, he left open the possibility it never existed. Sakharov and Adamovich, "Zhit' na zemle i zhit' dolgo," 174.

24. Sakharov, *Memoirs,* 616–17.

the middle of a press conference devoted to nuclear testing in the atmosphere, the deputy minister of foreign affairs, Vladimir Petrovskii, in response to a pre-arranged question, announced that the Academy of Sciences and other organizations had received and approved a request from Sakharov "to move to Moscow."[25] He also noted that the Supreme Soviet had decided—presumably, on its own—to pardon Bonner. The only reason Petrovskii gave for these decisions was Sakharov's "long absence" from the Soviet capital.[26] The unmitigated mendacity of this explanation understandably angered Sakharov and Bonner, who were still mourning Marchenko. But they were not about to miss their chance to return home to the city where prior to 1980 they had spent almost all their lives.

On December 22, Sakharov and Bonner left Gorky for Moscow, arriving at the Iaroslavl Station the next day to a throng of reporters waiting for them. For forty minutes Sakharov patiently answered their questions. Modestly, he stated that he had not really explored political issues while in exile, but now that he was free he would do so. But most of his time he would spend on physics, specifically on cosmological questions and issues involving elementary particles.[27] He described his conversation with Gorbachev and the installation of the telephone that preceded it, and in response to a question about Afghanistan remarked vaguely that "more resolute measures" to end the war there must be taken.[28] He expressed his personal sorrow, and Bonner's, over Marchenko's death and referred to his earlier letters to Gorbachev imploring him to release "prisoners of conscience" still denied the freedom to which they were entitled.[29]

Anyone viewing the assemblage of reporters and listening to the questions they asked on that bitterly cold day in December would have recognized immediately how difficult it was going to be for Sakharov to give up politics as the Soviet government demanded and focus his attention on science. Now that Gorbachev had made it a matter of legitimate public concern, politics, no matter how much Sakharov wished to avoid it, could not help but remain an integral and essential aspect of his life. Indeed, one suspects that he was not altogether displeased by this. From 1980 to 1986 Sakharov had remained committed to the political issues that concerned him at a time in his life when the easiest, and in purely medical terms the most prudent, thing for him to do would have been to eschew any involvement in politics and devote his time and energy to science and the well-being of his family. Instead, he had found himself drawn inexorably into a series of confrontations with the government that required him to jeopardize his health and even his life.

Sakharov returned to Moscow in December 1986 just as much the political figure he had been when he left the city nearly seven years earlier. He would remain one for the three years that were left to him. But the kind of politics he would engage

25. Ibid., 617.
26. Ibid.
27. Moroz, "Vozvrashchenie iz ssylki," 282.
28. Ibid., 283.
29. Ibid., 284.

in now that perestroika made possible an ever-increasing degree of public involvement in governance was very different. For the twenty years of his dissidence, Sakharov had practiced, by choice as well as necessity, a politics of rhetorical moral exhortation in which organizational skills and a willingness to make compromises and build alliances were rarely necessary.[30] The moral politics Sakharov engaged in was one of ideas and principles that could not be tested empirically because the government refused to allow the Soviet people to share in governance. As a result, the principles Sakharov espoused retained the pristine clarity they had when he conceived them, undiluted by the dynamics of a political system that exposed ideas and principles to individuals and interest groups that would accept them only if they were modified to meet their particular and often parochial needs. Earlier, pragmatism and practicality rarely mattered. To be sure, Sakharov was capable of couching his objectives pragmatically when the occasion required it, as he did in the early 1970s when he still believed he could win the government's approval by appealing to the self-interest of its leaders. But in all his years as a dissident he was never a participant in a political process in which the players freely sacrificed some of their principles in order to secure the acceptance of others.

Thus the challenge Sakharov faced when he emerged at the Iaroslavl Station was not whether he could stay away from politics and do physics instead, but rather whether he could adjust to the new political realities in the Soviet Union and function effectively in a political environment for which, by temperament, vocational training, and personal experience, he seemed to be singularly ill suited. This period of Sakharov's life would be like no other in requiring him, if he wished to be politically effective, to compromise on principles and ideas he believed in—without at the same time dissipating the immense moral authority he possessed. For the first time in his life, Sakharov would have to assume the role of politician, and it was within the context of the new kind of politics toward which Gorbachev was slowly leading a reluctant party and a skeptical public that he would have to make several serious and significant decisions. Would he assist the general secretary of the Communist Party in the titanic effort he had begun to reform the Soviet Union in order to save it? Or would he try to thwart that effort on the grounds that the Soviet Union was no longer worth saving? Would he support and oppose the government as the occasion demanded, in an effort of his own to redirect perestroika in a direction he thought was consistent with the vision of convergence and human rights to which he still adhered? Or would he consider this strategy a form of politics incompatible with the ethical principles it was intended to advance? These were the questions Sakharov had to answer as he began what would turn out to be the final chapter of his life, and in many ways the most extraordinary one. Given Sakharov's stature and reputation for moral probity, how he answered these questions would profoundly affect not only the fortunes of Gorbachev and the reforms he was trying to implement but the survival of the Soviet Union itself.

30. Dmitrii Simes makes roughly the same point in *After the Collapse: Russia Seeks Its Place as a Great Power* (New York, 1999), 29.

# PART VII

# The Conscience of Perestroika: 1986–1989

# 22 Return to Moscow

On his first full day back in Moscow, Sakharov returned to the Lebedev Institute to attend its weekly seminar on theoretical physics. If he did so in the expectation that he could resume his activities as if nothing had changed since he was last there in January 1980, he was wrong. As he entered the seminar, the scientists who were present applauded him, and during the course of it an adoring crowd waited anxiously outside for him to emerge—proof that not everyone in Moscow believed the falsehoods the Soviet press had spread about Sakharov in the years he was in Gorky.[1]

After a lifetime of tumultuous experiences, of soaring triumphs matched by gnawing disappointments, a part of the man wanted to avoid politics entirely and in the phrase he used in his memoirs to describe his real intentions, "to dream of science" instead.[2] But his celebrity and newfound accessibility made this impossible. The lifting of restrictions on whom Sakharov could speak to prompted a steady stream of visitors to the Chkalov Street apartment he happily reoccupied. Among these was a delegation from the Council on Foreign Relations in New York that included two former secretaries of state, Henry Kissinger and Cyrus Vance; former American ambassador to the United Nations, Jeane Kirkpatrick; former secretary of defense Harold Brown; and various other luminaries in the American foreign-policy establishment.[3] However much Sakharov may have wanted to do physics, he quickly found he lacked the time for it. Although he faithfully attended the weekly seminars and periodic conferences the institute sponsored, original research was largely precluded: in the three years until his death in December 1989, he produced only one scientific paper, a postscript to an article by Zeldovich on whether it was possible to create the universe from nothing.[4] In addition, in the fall of 1987 he agreed to chair the Commission on Cosmomicrophysics the Academy of Sciences had established several years earlier to coordinate research on the subject, which couples the physics of elementary particles with the cosmology of the early universe.[5] But that, to Sakharov's genuine regret, was the extent of his involvement in physics.

1. Tsukerman and Azarkh, "Liudi i vzryvy," 124; Janouch, "My 'Meetings' and Encounters with Andrei Dmitrievich Sakharov," 382–83.
2. Andrei Sakharov, *Moscow and Beyond: 1986 to 1989*, trans. Antonina Bouis (New York, 1992), 35.
3. Ibid., 12–14.
4. Feinberg, "A Biographical Sketch," 9; Andrei Sakharov, "Postscript to Zeldovich's article, 'Is it Possible to Create the Universe 'From Nothing'?" *Priroda* 4 (April 1988), cited in Sakharov, *Memoirs*, 723.
5. Sakharov had refused an identical offer in the spring of 1987 after the incumbent in the position, Zeldovich, passed away. M. Yu. Khlopov, "They Expect a Good Program from Us," in Drell and Kapitza, *Sakharov Remembered*, 227–28.

In May 1988 he told an interviewer, only partly tongue in cheek, that to do physics properly, without distractions, he would have to return to Gorky, where he had the solitude to concentrate on the scientific issues that interested him.[6]

But Sakharov was not sorry he had chosen politics over physics, and he used his newfound freedom to advance the causes he had championed as a dissident.[7] For all that had transpired in his life, he was, in essence, the same man he had always been, his personal quirks and idiosyncrasies still as expressive of his intellectual independence as his political convictions were. Visitors to Sakharov's apartment after 1986 often encountered him wearing slippers, faded jeans, and the cowboy shirts for which he had a distinctly un-Russian weakness. With stacks of letters on the bookcase and errant kitchen tiles reattached with tape to the wall from which they had fallen, the apartment exuded the same sense of amiable chaos visitors had commented on in the late 1960s and 1970s.[8] The times, however, were very different. Certainly Sakharov's living conditions were markedly better. Upon his return from exile, the government offered him what by Soviet standards was a luxurious apartment in the building where Khariton lived, which was reserved exclusively for academicians. But Sakharov and Bonner preferred the more modest accommodations with which they were familiar, and they remained on Chkalov Street. Sakharov's only concession to the demands he knew would now be made on him by admirers, reporters, and petitioners was to use the apartment one floor below, which the government offered him on the recommendation of the Academy of Sciences, both as a study and as a sanctuary to which he could retreat when the flood of visitors became unbearable.[9]

As the solicitude of the academy suggested, the last three years of Sakharov's life were marked by his personal rehabilitation and, to an extent, by his political vindication as well, as the Soviet government transformed into policy several of the recommendations he had made as a dissident. By what it permitted him to do and what it permitted the Soviet press to say about him, the Soviet government, without a formal edict or explanation, made clear that whatever Sakharov's transgressions might have been in the past, much, if not all, was now forgiven, at least implicitly. In February 1987 Sakharov made his first public appearance in Moscow in seven years—at the "Moscow Forum for a Nuclear-Free World and the Survival of Mankind," where he spoke three times on nuclear weapons and democratization in the Soviet Union. At the conclusion of the forum he was even allowed to hold a press conference at the Ministry of Foreign

6. Gennady Zhavoronkov, "Alone with Everyone: Andrei Sakharov at Home," *Moscow News*, May 15, 1988, 16.

7. Ibid.

8. Ibid.; Gennady Zhavoronkov, "What Was He Like, What Will We Be Like?" *Moscow News*, December 31, 1989, 10.

9. Tatiana Yankelevich, conversation with author, January 13, 2004. The couple originally preferred an apartment on the same floor, but the other residents on the floor were "fearful" of them. Zhavoronkov, "What Was He Like?" 10.

Affairs to answer questions about his role in it.[10] In March he had lunch with Margaret Thatcher at the British embassy in Moscow—which would have been unthinkable just four months earlier—and in May he conferred with the French prime minister, Jacques Chirac, at the Academy of Sciences. A month later, in a ceremony at the French embassy, he received an honorary diploma from both the French Academy of Sciences and the Academy of Moral and Political Sciences, along with the medal of the Institute of France.[11] By the summer of 1987, the government permitted the publication, in the magazine *Teatr,* of a review Sakharov had written of a new production of Mikhail Bulgakov's play *The Heart of a Dog.* Not since the mid-1960s had an article of his—except those that dealt with physics—appeared in an official Soviet publication, and the fact that the review included his argument that technological progress should not be achieved at the expense of man's spirituality underscored how radically not only Sakharov's life but conditions in the country as well had changed under Gorbachev's new brand of leadership.[12]

*Teatr* had a limited readership, and even after Sakharov's review appeared in it, very few in the Soviet Union were aware of how far his rehabilitation had proceeded. In November 1987, however, there appeared in *Moscow News*—which did have a mass circulation—an interview with Sakharov that touched on some of the most sensitive issues in Soviet politics, including Stalinism and its relevance to contemporary conditions; in the answers he gave he stressed "the absolute necessity" of telling the truth about it.[13] In the summer of 1988, while on a visit to Leningrad, Sakharov appeared for the first time on Soviet television, on the program *The Fifth Wheel,* where he discussed perestroika, glasnost, and the need for even greater ideological and economic pluralism in Soviet society.[14] That fall, the Supreme Soviet, in a formal declaration, ordered that the awards and honors it had rescinded in 1980 be restored to him, and on October 20, 1988, following his nomination by Sagdeev, the Academy of Sciences voted Sakharov onto its presidium, a signal honor not even his most optimistic supporters during the years he was in exile could have imagined he would ever receive.[15] On that same day, the government lifted the ban on foreign travel it had imposed on Sakharov since his days at Arzamas; in doing so it was probably influenced by the testimony of Khariton, who at a meeting of the Politburo a few days earlier emphasized that the scientific information Sakharov possessed was by now obsolete and that even if it was not, he could be trusted not to divulge it.[16] Two weeks later, Sakharov, accompanied by Sagdeev and Evgenii Velikhov, the vice

10. Sakharov, *Moscow and Beyond,* 15–25.

11. Ibid., 27–28, 30.

12. Ibid., 40–41; A. D. Sakharov, "Veriu v razum," *Teatr* 8 (1987): 114.

13. Andrei Sakharov, "It's an Absolute Necessity to Speak the Truth: Impressions of the Film 'Risk,'" *Moscow News,* November 8, 1987, 14.

14. Sakharov, *Moscow and Beyond,* 53. A. D. Sakharov, Pervoe na sovetskom televidenii interv'iu programme 'Piatoe koleso,' Leningrad, in "Chetyre interv'iu," *Zvezda* 5 (May 1991): 126–27.

15. Sakharov, *Moscow and Beyond,* 65–66; David Remnick, "Sakharov Will Visit U.S. on His First Trip to West," *Washington Post,* October 22, 1988, A1.

16. Sakharov, *Moscow and Beyond,* 67.

president of the Academy of Sciences, traveled to the United States. There the three men attended conferences in Washington, New York, and Boston of the International Foundation for the Survival and Development of Humanity, on whose board of directors Sakharov, Sagdeev, and Velikhov served. In Washington, Sakharov was also received warmly at the White House, where he spoke at some length with President Reagan and Vice President Bush, and at the State Department, where he met with Secretary of State Shultz. (This was in sharp contrast to Solzhenitsyn's situation in 1975, when President Ford and Secretary of State Kissinger refused to meet with him because they feared that doing so would harm détente.) In New York and Washington, Sakharov was feted and presented with a variety of awards, among them the prestigious Albert Einstein Peace Prize, by organizations representing the elite of American science. On the return trip to the Soviet Union, he stopped off in Paris, where Bonner joined him, to participate in celebrations marking the fortieth anniversary of the Universal Declaration of Human Rights. While in the French capital, he was also granted a private meeting with the French president, François Mitterand.[17]

In February 1989, Sakharov went abroad again, first to Italy, where he had an audience with the pope and received honorary degrees from the universities of Bologna and Siena, and then to Canada, where he conferred with Prime Minister Mulroney. From Ottawa he and Bonner went to the United States, where between meetings and formal events they were able to relax with Tania and Alexei and their families in the Boston area. On Sakharov's last trip to the United States, in the summer of 1989, he devoted himself largely to finishing his memoirs, which had become so long that he decided to publish the sections dealing with events after his return to Moscow as a separate book.[18] By this time Sakharov's health, from both fatigue and his omnipresent heart condition, had deteriorated considerably: he gasped for breath after taking no more than seven or eight steps, and some thought his speech was slurred.[19] For this reason, the opportunity to enjoy yet again the emotional support he received from Bonner's children (as opposed to his own children, who continued to shun him) was irresistible.[20] Without respites such as these, he might literally have worked himself to death.

Sakharov's political rehabilitation was not uncontested, and the time it took—just short of two years—was proof that there were some in the government and the scientific elite who opposed it. The rehabilitation was carefully calibrated, so much so that the extent of it at any particular time could be considered a fairly good barometer, from 1987 to 1989, of the progress of perestroika. Resistance to it took many forms. The KGB, which had wanted Sakharov's internal exile to

17. Ibid., 67–73; Remnick, "Sakharov Will Visit U.S," A15.

18. Sakharov, *Moscow and Beyond*, xix, 100–105; Lourie, *Sakharov*, 389.

19. Remnick, *Lenin's Tomb*, 279.

20. Still estranged from his daughters, Sakharov was chagrined especially by the depths to which his son, Dmitrii, had sunk: by the mid 1980s, Dmitrii had dropped out of MGU and medical school successively, had married and divorced, and was drinking heavily. He was also unable to hold a job for very long. Sakharov, *Moscow and Beyond*, 35; Lourie, *Sakharov*, 364.

continue indefinitely, much preferred that he reoccupy the apartment on Chkalov Street—on this the KGB and Sakharov were in rare agreement—because it was already bugged. In fact, it was the KGB that had the apartment one floor below it vacated and reserved for him; with the additional space, there would be more reason for Sakharov to want to return to it.[21] At many stages in the process of Sakharov's rehabilitation, the Soviet government, whether deliberately or as a result of bureaucratic incompetence, took back with one hand what it gave with the other. For example, just when Sakharov was freely visiting the French embassy to receive the honors that were bestowed upon him, the government, as a way of reminding the former dissident that he was still not entirely free from its clutches, disallowed a seminar French and Soviet physicists were hoping to hold with him. With the same purpose in mind, the KGB vandalized his car.[22] Throughout the late 1980s Sakharov was also criticized in the Soviet press, though without the personal animus that had marked earlier attacks, and in December 1987 the government refused to permit the publication of an interview he had given to *Argumenty i fakty* advocating reductions in nuclear weapons.[23] Similarly, the interview Sakharov gave on Soviet television in Leningrad in June 1988 was broadcast without the segment of it in which he criticized the government's handling of the ethnic conflict in Nagorno-Karabakh in the Caucasus between Azeris and Armenians.[24]

Not all of the criticism that followed Sakharov's return to Moscow came from government officials and apparatchiki who had loathed him from his days as a dissident. There were some in the movement for greater reform in the Soviet Union—including several former dissidents, such as Marchenko's widow, Larissa Bogoraz—who criticized Sakharov for what they considered his excessive willingness to compromise his principles in an effort to reach a modus vivendi with the government. Implicit in their criticism was that Sakharov was far too accepting of Gorbachev's bona fides as a reformer.[25] But the vast majority of the criticism came from elements in the Soviet elite that considered ending Sakharov's exile a mistake. Fully 82 of the 234 academicians present opposed Sakharov's elevation to the presidium of the Academy of Sciences, and undoubtedly a goodly number of those who voted for the nomination did so merely because they considered it the politic thing to do.[26] One such individual, surely, was the academician S. V. Vonsovskii, who in the winter of 1989 praised Sakharov publicly as "our honor, our conscience, and our pride" after having denounced him viciously in *Pravda* sixteen years earlier, when the press campaign against

21. Coleman, *Decline and Fall of the Soviet Empire,* 434.
22. Sakharov, *Moscow and Beyond,* 31–32.
23. Ibid., 41.
24. Ibid., 53. The interview Sakharov gave to *Argumenty i fakty* finally appeared in December 1989, shortly after his death, as "Novoe politicheskoe myshlenie neobkhodimo," *Argumenty i fakty,* December 19–25, 1989, 4–5. When the text of the interview was published in *Zvezda* in 1991, the deleted material had been restored to it. See Sakharov, Pervoe na sovetskom televidenii interv'iu, 126–27.
25. Sakharov, *Moscow and Beyond,* 7.
26. Remnick, "Sakharov Will Visit U.S.," A1.

Sakharov and Solzhenitsyn began, as a mouthpiece of "highly reactionary circles" and "an instrument of propaganda hostile to the Soviet Union and other socialist nations."[27]

## Continuing the Struggle for Human Rights

Under the circumstances, it was only natural for Sakharov, for a long time after returning to Moscow, to be wary of the government's attempts at reconciliation. The survival instincts he had developed as a dissident could not be suppressed easily or immediately, and the fact that his rehabilitation proceeded slowly and fitfully was all the more reason to think that the agenda he had developed earlier as a dissident was still relevant and that the protracted course of his own rehabilitation was proof that perestroika itself was incomplete. Foremost among his concerns were the political prisoners still languishing in prisons or labor camps: how well or badly they were treated, how many of them there were, how close they were to being released, and whether those who were released had been amnestied or merely pardoned became the principal criteria by which he would determine the moral health of Soviet society.[28] For Sakharov, the fact that he himself was now free only underscored how essential it was, as a matter of principle, that everyone should be free. In an interview he gave to Soviet reporters barely days after his exile ended, Sakharov professed his "moral duty" to facilitate the release of political prisoners and claimed that glasnost would have no meaning if the government continued to hold them illegally.[29] In January 1987, Sakharov wrote directly to Gorbachev that "without an amnesty [of political prisoners], it will be impossible to bring about a decisive moral change in our country, to overcome the inertia of fear, indifference, and hypocrisy."[30] One year later, on the occasion of their first face-to-face encounter, Sakharov asked the general secretary point-blank to release the roughly two hundred "prisoners of conscience" who were still incarcerated in various prisons, psychiatric hospitals, and labor camps around the country, and in October 1988, seeing that not all of them had been released, he refused to accept the decorations the government was considering restoring to him.[31]

Among the other issues Sakharov raised even more forcefully now that he was no longer a dissident involved the relationship between human rights and foreign policy. Once again he stressed that governments that treated their own people humanely were inclined to act pacifically in their foreign policy; the corollary Sakharov now drew from this axiom was that if the Soviet Union were to release all of its political prisoners, the likelihood of an atmosphere of trust in

27. Ioirysh, *Uroki A. D. Sakharova*, 42. The diatribe of which Vonsovskii was a cosigner is in Sakharov, *Memoirs*, 632.

28. A. Sakharov, "Neizbezhnost' perestroiki (March 25, 1988)," in *Inogo ne dano*, ed. Iu. N. Afanasiev (Moscow, 1988), 129.

29. Walker, "Sakharov Casts Doubt on Feasibility of SDI," *Times*, December 29, 1989, 8.

30. Sakharov, *Moscow and Beyond*, 5.

31. B. L. Altshuler et al., "Academik Andrei Dmitrievch Sakharov," in Altshuler et al., *On mezhdu nami zhil*, 20; Frank von Hippel, "Nashe sotrudnichestvo," ibid., 743–44.

international relations would be considerably greater.[32] Moreover, since human rights, by definition, were universal, persons living outside the Soviet Union had the same obligation to protest their violation inside the Soviet Union that Soviet citizens had to protest their violation in other countries. Sakharov, throughout his life, was nothing if not consistent in this regard. From 1987 to 1989 he condemned—to cite just a few examples—the detention of the Chinese dissident Fang Lizhi,[33] the death sentences meted out in China to those convicted of organizing the demonstrations for democracy in Tiananmen Square,[34] and the refusal of Saddam Hussein in Iraq to grant its Kurdish minority the right to secede from Iraq and form their own nation.[35] In his conversation with Mitterand, Sakharov made a point of bringing up Saddam's barbaric persecution of the Kurds.[36]

In addition, Sakharov continued to champion the ethnic minorities in the Soviet Union that were still oppressed, most notably the Crimean Tatars, whose inalienable right, as he saw it, to return to and settle in their ancestral homeland in the Crimea he reiterated after 1986 with the same eloquence and moral passion he had shown earlier in his life. The one minority Sakharov was less concerned about in the late 1980s was the Jews, both because most Soviet Jews who wished to emigrate in the Gorbachev era were allowed to do so and because the discrimination against those who remained in the Soviet Union had eased considerably. But the Tatars were still denied the right to choose their place of residence—which for Sakharov was emblematic of the moral depravity of the Soviet system as a whole. Thus he tried to advance this objective for the Tatars with the same fervor he had previously shown on behalf of Soviet Jews. In a conversation with Alexander Yakovlev in March 1988, Sakharov requested that all the Tatars who wished to return to the Crimea—not just those whom the Soviet government deemed deserving of it—be allowed to do so. To Sakharov, the government's largesse seemed more like the granting of a privilege than the acknowledgment of a universal right.[37]

More broadly, Sakharov remained committed to helping anyone whose human rights had been violated, regardless of the class or category of the population to which they belonged. Although in the late 1980s he was especially sensitive to the persecution of both the Tatars and the Meskhi Turks, whose massacre by Uzbeks in Uzbekistan in June 1989 he immediately and forthrightly protested, one did not have to be a Tatar or a Meskhi Turk for Sakharov to be

32. Andrei Sakharov, "The Breakthrough Must Be Continued and Widened," *Moscow News*, December 6, 1987, 2; Andrei Sakharov, "Of Arms and Reforms," *Time*, March 16, 1987, 40–41.

33. Daniel Sutherland, "Sakharov Appeals to Beijing," *Washington Post*, December 16, 1988, A37, 47.

34. Steve Connor, "Stop the Death Sentences in China, Pleads Sakharov," *Daily Telegraph*, June 20, 1989, 2; A. Sakharov, "Obrashchenie Mezhregional'noi gruppy narodnykh deputatov SSSR (June 1989)," in *Vospominaniia* 2:574.

35. Andrei Sakharov, "Obrashchenie k parizhskoi mezhdunarodnoi konferentsii po probleme kurdov (October 13, 1989)," *Russkaia mysl'*, October 20, 1989, 3.

36. Sakharov, *Moscow and Beyond*, 74.

37. Ibid., 50.

moved to react.[38] In theory, everyone who was denied human rights was deserving of Sakharov's solicitude, and the only limits he was willing to accept on his own interventions were practical ones, such as his calculation of whether his intervention would be effective. Sometimes, however, he acted without thinking through the implications of his involvement—which is not to say that his intervention was unproductive. In August 1988, while vacationing at a resort on the Black Sea, Sakharov took up the cause of a waitress whose fiancé, because he had a criminal record, was not allowed to marry her. Sakharov's humane and commonsensical view was that criminals should be allowed to marry once they served their sentence, and he sent a telegram to the bureaucrat who had denied the couple a marriage license protesting the injustice that had been done. To the surprise and delight of the waitress, the chairman relented and granted her and her fiancé the license.[39]

Sakharov's interventions were reflective of his identity as an *intelligent,* and he espoused the intelligentsia's concern for the emancipation of the individual in the years that remained to him. In April 1989, in an interview that appeared in *Knizhnoe obozrenie* (*Book Review*), Sakharov agreed emphatically with the interviewer's statement that Soviet society must assist in the full development of the individual personality. He also made the point that the reform of the Soviet Union must be based primarily on moral principle.[40] In a similar vein, the platform upon which Sakharov ran as a candidate to the Congress of People's Deputies in the spring of 1989 included "the defense of the rights of the individual personality."[41] It may indeed have been his commitment to the intelligentsia's ethos of moral protest that Sakharov had in mind when, in April 1987, in response to the charge that by supporting perestroika he was betraying the principles he had held as a dissident, he stated that politically as well as personally he was exactly the same person he was ten years earlier.[42]

Still, Sakharov was different from the intelligentsia in his willingness, on many occasions between 1987 and 1989, to accept a partial victory when seeking a total victory would result in gaining nothing at all. In these years Sakharov engaged willingly in practical politics, with all the compromises and accommodations that that required. For that reason he had to calculate exactly how much of his agenda he could hope to achieve in any particular situation. In the case of the Meskhi Turks, for example, Sakharov pragmatically advised them, in the interest of preventing further massacres, to accept the offer Nikolai Ryzhkov tendered on behalf of the government that they be resettled not in their homeland in Georgia, where they wanted to go, but rather in various regions of the RSFSR. (To Sakharov's chagrin, his advice was rejected.) In the case of the Crimean Tatars, Sakharov carefully refrained from calling for the Crimea to

38. Ibid., 137–40.
39. Ibid., 52–53.
40. Sakharov, "V narode vsegda sokhraniaiutsia nravstvennye sily," 6–7.
41. "Programma A. D. Sakharova," *Knizhnoe obozrenie,* April 7, 1989, 6–7.
42. Bill Keller, "Sakharov's Pro-Gorbachev's Stand: Attacked, He Stands His Ground," *New York Times,* April 3, 1987, A1.

be an autonomous Tatar republic, as some Tatars were demanding, because he considered it impractical. In his view, there were not enough Crimean Tatars, even with the inclusion of all those living elsewhere in the Soviet Union, to warrant such a republic; as an alternative, he suggested that those who moved to the Crimea simply settle near one another.[43] Finally, despite his belief that political prisoners in the Soviet Union on their release should be amnestied rather than pardoned because a pardon implied an acknowledgment of guilt, he recommended that they should accept the pardons the government offered them as a condition of their release. Indeed, he even counseled them to sign the statement the government demanded that they promise not to engage in illegal actions in the future.[44] For this, he was criticized strongly by Bogoraz and Boris Altshuler.[45] But in contrast to his critics, Sakharov did not believe he was dissipating the moral capital he and other dissidents had accumulated by seeking satisfaction of their objectives within the Soviet system, especially now that Gorbachev was genuinely trying to reform it.

## Space-Based Missile Defenses and Arms Control

Another issue on which Sakharov spoke out passionately was the Strategic Defense Initiative, or SDI, as it came to be abbreviated, after President Reagan first announced it in a speech to the American people in 1983. Sakharov was opposed to SDI, and he made his opposition known on numerous occasions from December 1986 to December 1989. He believed the initiative was nothing less than a threat to world peace and an inducement to nuclear war.

SDI entailed the construction of a missile defense shield in space in which missiles launched from satellites previously placed in orbit around the earth would intercept and destroy offensive missiles the Soviet Union (or any other hostile power with the same capability) might launch against the United States. Sakharov believed that SDI was destabilizing and ineffective simultaneously: because it would not do what it was intended to do—namely, shoot down enemy missiles before they landed—any benefits from scientific spin-offs hardly warranted the expense, time, and energy required to build the system.[46] SDI, in sum, would not work. While Sakharov did not believe that the cost of a Soviet SDI would actually bankrupt the Soviet economy and cause the Soviet system to collapse, he was convinced that if the Soviets followed the Americans and decided to build one, money and precious resources better used for perestroika would be wasted. Also, SDI would divert attention from the imperative of reducing Soviet conventional forces, which since the early 1980s Sakharov had considered more critical than nuclear deterrence to the maintenance of peace.[47] But

43. Sakharov, *Moscow and Beyond*, 50, 139.
44. Ibid., 6; "Conversation with Andrei Sakharov and Elena Bonner," 5.
45. Sakharov, *Moscow and Beyond*, 7.
46. Sakharov, "Novoe politicheskoe myshlenie neobkhodimo," 4; Sakharov, "Of Arms and Reforms," 43.
47. Sakharov, *Moscow and Beyond*, 22; Arno Penzias, "Sakharov i SOI," in Altshuler et al., *On mezhdu nami zhil*, 485; Sakharov, "Of Arms and Reforms," 40–41.

despite these cogent reasons for not building a missile defense shield, Sakharov feared that Gorbachev would feel compelled to respond to the American initiative with a Soviet one. For this reason, there was a genuine urgency in his criticisms of SDI, and he often phrased them in the form of a plaintive plea to the general secretary that he think carefully about the whole project before endorsing it. Even if a Soviet SDI would not cause the Soviet Union to collapse, it could very easily cause perestroika to collapse, and with it the very real chance of a sharp reduction in international tensions. In Sakharov's view, because missile defenses, conventional forces, domestic reform, and world peace were all intimately connected, a change in any one of them would automatically affect all the others.

Sakharov's objections to space-based missile defenses were both practical and conceptual: these defenses would not work given the current state of technology, and if they did, their effect would be precisely the opposite of what their advocates believed. In Sakharov's view, a missile defense shield that was capable of repelling or deterring a missile attack would actually increase the chances of an attack, though paradoxically the attacker could be the country that possessed such a shield, rather than the country that lacked it. In Sakharov's scenario, the country that possessed a space-based defense might be emboldened to carry out a nuclear first strike of its own because it believed this defense made it invulnerable, or far less vulnerable, to retaliation by the country it attacked.[48] But there was another contingency, just as dangerous and far more likely to occur: that the country against which SDI was directed would either construct its own missile defense shield or simply build and deploy more offensive missiles than the defense shield of its adversary could intercept. Thus the original advantage SDI conferred would be neutralized. In the alternative, the country without SDI could try to shorten the "boost phase" of its offensive missiles, making it much harder for missiles launched from satellites to intercept them.[49] But regardless of how the country that lacked its own defense shield reacted, its response would have the effect of re-creating the original stalemate that had caused its adversary to construct a missile defense shield in the first place. Indeed, this new stalemate would be more dangerous than the original one because, with space-based defenses shown to confer no permanent advantage, the temptation on both sides to deploy more offensive missiles or to develop more destructive ones would be greater.[50]

For Sakharov, however, the principal problem with space-based missile defenses was a practical one. The current state of technology in defensive weaponry was inadequate to develop missiles launched from space-based satellites that were not themselves extremely vulnerable to interception or deception.

48. Moroz, "Vozvrashchenie iz ssylki," 317–18.
49. "Conversation with Andrei Sakharov and Elena Bonner," 8. Another possibility Sakharov considered was that the country lacking a space-based missile would develop missiles with a sub-ballistic trajectory (which Cruise missiles had) but with intercontinental range (which Cruise missiles lacked). Sakharov, "Of Arms and Reforms," 43.
50. Interview with Zora Safir, 9; Sakharov, "Novoe politicheskoe myshlenie neobkhodimo," 4.

Space mines, decoys, jamming devices, and other antisatellite weapons could be developed fairly quickly that would neutralize a space-based missile-defense shield in much the same way that comparable instrumentalities were developed to cripple a land-based ABM system.[51] As Sakharov pointed out, "[I]t is much easier and cheaper to overcome space defenses than to create them."[52] Given that SDI, for the foreseeable future, would not work, the best thing the Soviet Union should do in response to the American initiative was absolutely nothing. Sakharov viewed space-based missile defenses as little more than a cul-de-sac in the perpetual search for strategic advantage in the Cold War. In the formulation he often used in interviews to encapsulate his objections, space-based defenses would be like "a Maginot Line in space—expensive and ineffective."[53]

From this Sakharov drew the logical conclusion that in the interest of reducing the chances of nuclear war, the best thing the superpowers could do was to reduce their arsenals of offensive weaponry, especially intercontinental ballistic missiles. Practically speaking, this meant that reductions in these weapons should not be held hostage to reductions in other weapons, especially ones like SDI that were useless. Allowing the failure of negotiations on weapons that would not work to preclude an agreement on weapons that would, such as ICBMs, would be counterproductive and irrational. But this was precisely the impasse at which the United States and the Soviet Union found themselves when Sakharov, in February 1987, made a suggestion he thought might break it: that negotiations on SDI be decoupled from those on offensive weapons systems so that a failure to achieve an agreement on the former would not preclude agreements on the latter. Barely three months after terminating a punishment it had imposed for what it considered his near-treasonous activities, the Soviet government adopted Sakharov's suggestion.

To appreciate how constructive this suggestion was, one must bear in mind the negotiating position of the Soviet government before adopting it. In July 1986 President Reagan had proposed to Gorbachev that the superpowers eliminate entirely their arsenals of offensive missiles (in which the Soviets had an advantage) in exchange for the United States' postponing the deployment of SDI. Because he wanted SDI not merely postponed but eliminated, Gorbachev rejected the proposal. Three months later, at the Reykjavik summit, Gorbachev surprised Reagan by offering a deal of his own in which the Soviet Union would

---

51. Sakharov, *Moscow and Beyond*, 22; Sakharov, "Of Arms and Reforms," 42.

52. Andrei Sakharov, "Things Are Better, but...," *U.S. News and World Report*, January 12, 1987, 31.

53. Sakharov, *Moscow and Beyond*, 22. Frank Gaffney, among others, has pointed out that the decoys and other antisatellite weapons that critics like Sakharov believed made SDI ineffective are themselves vulnerable to interdiction. Frank J. Gaffney, Jr., "Bush, Missile Defense, and the Critics," *Commentary* 111, no. 2 (February 2001): 33–34. But Gaffney's contention, while valid, suggests an unending cycle of technological innovations, of measures and countermeasures, in which any advantage is only temporary. In light of this, countries considering space-based defenses should weigh the temporary security such defenses provide against the expenditure of resources required not only to construct such a defense but to modernize it every time an adversary develops technologies neutralizing its effectiveness.

reduce its conventional forces and agree to both the elimination of IRBMs in Europe and a 50 percent reduction in overall nuclear arsenals if the United States would abandon SDI. Reagan—who for all his anticommunist rhetoric yearned for a nuclear-free world—was sorely tempted, on receiving Gorbachev's proposal, to accept it. But in the end, his faith in SDI as a means of ensuring America's security prevailed, and the two leaders left the summit without an agreement. The Soviets then reverted to the position they had taken prior to the summit that reductions in offensive weapons were strictly conditional upon limitations on the deployment of SDI.[54] With the two superpowers thus once again at loggerheads, Sakharov made his very opportune suggestion in February 1987, in a speech at a forum in Moscow on a "Nuclear Free World and the Survival of Mankind."[55]

At the forum he urged the government to "untie the package"—that is, to negotiate SDI and reductions in offensive weaponry separately.[56] Because the United States would not abandon SDI despite sound reasons for doing so and because the missile shield would not work if it were built, its abandonment should not be a precondition for reductions in offensive weapons, which Sakharov believed were in the best interests of the Soviet Union. If these arms reductions were deep enough, there would no longer be any need for SDI, and the United States, however belatedly, would stop work on it. But even if the United States persisted in SDI, the Soviet Union could deploy cheaper countermeasures, such as decoys and cruise missiles (which fly at altitudes too low for space-based weapons to reach them) in the unlikely event SDI proved effective against ballistic missiles. This, at any rate, was the reasoning behind Sakharov's proposal.[57]

By this time Gorbachev's thinking had evolved to the point where he viewed reductions in offensive weapons not just as a bargaining chip in negotiations on SDI. Evidently he realized they were politically useful as well, namely, as a way of demonstrating his commitment to improving Soviet-American relations, which in turn would facilitate perestroika. Reductions in offensive weapons, in other words, should be negotiated for their own sake. For this reason, it was hardly an accident that Anatolii Dobrynin, the longtime Soviet ambassador to the United States and now the head of the International Department of the Communist Party Secretariat, was in the audience at the forum when Sakharov spoke. Dobrynin left immediately after Sakharov finished and transmitted to his superiors the gist of Sakharov's suggestion and the reasons he had given for the Soviet government to adopt it.[58] Two weeks later, Gorbachev offered to

---

54. For an exposition and analysis of the negotiations, see Glynn, *Pandora's Box,* 347–53, and Doder and Branson, *Gorbachev,* 208.

55. Prior to the speech, his first in public since the 1960s, Sakharov had made his proposal in newspaper interviews. One of these, to *Literaturnaia gazeta* in January 1987, was not published because it included a statement of his opposition to a Soviet SDI. Sakharov, *Moscow and Beyond,* 18; Walker, "Sakharov Casts Doubt on Feasibility of SDI," 8; Litinskii, "Ob A. D. Sakharove i vokrug," 401.

56. Strobe Talbott, *The Master of the Game: Paul Nitze and the Nuclear Peace* (New York, 1988), 360.

57. Sakharov, "Of Arms and Reforms," 43. See also Moroz, "Vozvrashchenie iz ssylki," 317–18.

58. Von Hippel, "Nashe sotrudnichestvo," 742.

negotiate reductions in offensive missiles—albeit only on IRBMs—irrespective of the impasse on SDI. In the months that followed, the United States and the Soviet Union hammered out an agreement, the Intermediate Range Nuclear Forces (INF) treaty, in which the United States and the Soviet Union agreed to eliminate all of their missiles with a range between 310 and 3,200 miles; specifically, the Soviets would scrap their SS-4s, -12s, -20s, and -23s, while the Americans would do the same with their Pershing IIs and Cruise missiles in Europe.[59] This marked the first time in the history of arms control negotiations that the superpowers had agreed to the elimination of an entire class or category of weapons—and Sakharov could rightly consider himself partly responsible for it. As it was, he wholeheartedly applauded the INF agreement when Gorbachev and Reagan signed it in December 1987.[60] One can only imagine how pleased he would have been had he lived to see the signing of the Strategic Arms Reduction Treaty (START) in May 1992, in which the United States and four successor states of the Soviet Union—Russia, Ukraine, Kazakhstan, and Belarus—agreed to "deep reductions" in strategic offensive weapons, specifically ICBMs and submarine-launched ballistic missiles (SLBMs).[61] This treaty, too, was partly the result of Sakharov's suggestion, and it was fortunate for him that he lived long enough to hear the Soviet foreign minister, Eduard Shevardnadze, announce (in September 1989) his government's willingness to negotiate reductions in ICBMs regardless of the status of SDI—an offer the Soviet Union presented formally at the Malta summit between Gorbachev and President Bush three months later.[62]

The INF agreement the Soviet Union signed in 1987 was not just a vindication of Sakharov's view that negotiations on offensive weapons should be decoupled from those on SDI. More broadly, the agreement seemed to confirm his longstanding conviction that the liberalization of the Soviet Union was a prerequisite of arms control, and to the extent that reductions in nuclear weapons freed up resources for perestroika, that arms control was conversely a prerequisite of liberalization. Characteristically, Sakharov never mentioned this in anything he wrote, nor did he ever congratulate himself publicly for his prescience. But in the solitude of his own deliberations, he surely was aware of it. The INF and START treaties were both achievements to which Sakharov contributed significantly, and they both could be cited in support of his conviction that countries that observed human rights at home were less likely to act aggressively abroad.

Sakharov, however, did not consider Gorbachev's decoupling of negotiations sufficient incentive for the United States to take the Soviet Union seriously as a partner in reducing international tensions and lessening the chances of nuclear

59. Adèle Lamoureux, "The INF Agreement: 'The Beginning of the Beginning,' " http://perc. ca/PEN/1987–11/lamoureux.html.

60. Sakharov, "Neizbezhnost' perestroiki," 133.

61. Treaty between the United States of America and the Union of Soviet Socialist Republics on the Reduction and Limitation of Strategic Offensive Arms (START Treaty), http://www.ceip. org/files/projects/npp/resources/start1text.html.

62. Sakharov, *Moscow and Beyond,* 23.

war. Instead, he tried to impress upon the Soviet government the need for additional concessions. Specifically, he called for the reduction by 50 percent of the Soviet Union's entire arsenal of strategic weapons. In addition, he advised that the preponderance of the missiles that remained once this reduction was completed be either based on submarines (SLBMs) or placed on land on mobile launchers (like the American MX). The reason for this was that the more vulnerable an offensive missile was to its own destruction, the more incentive there was to fire it preemptively; and since Soviet missiles in fixed silos were exceedingly vulnerable, the chances of a preemptive nuclear strike (and thus the chances of a full-blown nuclear war) would diminish if they were replaced by missiles that were less vulnerable, namely, those that were mobile. Moreover, by reducing its nuclear arsenal so drastically, the Soviet government could devote to perestroika and other pressing domestic obligations the resources, attention, and energy that would otherwise be expended on the increasingly costly task of maintaining this arsenal.[63]

But for all the benefits, intangible as well as material, that reducing nuclear weaponry would bring, the cause of domestic reform in the Soviet Union could not succeed, according to Sakharov, unless there were also significant reductions in the size of Soviet conventional forces. In interviews, public speeches, and private conversations with members of the Soviet leadership, including Gorbachev, he tried to convince the Soviet leadership of this.[64] Nuclear weapons, he pointed out, were comparatively cheap: unlike soldiers, missiles and warheads did not have to be fed, housed, or paid. Nor did they require large numbers of people to operate them. The most effective way of increasing funding for civilian projects, if one chose to do so by reducing funds that would otherwise be earmarked for the military, was by reducing expenditures not on nuclear weapons but on conventional forces. Specifically, Sakharov called for a 50 percent reduction of Soviet conventional forces and argued that the best way to do this was by reducing the term of service for draftees by half, from two years to one. Because most recruits were now literate and many already knew how to drive cars and operate machinery, the basic training they needed was considerably less than what had been needed earlier in the country's history. As a result, reducing the term of service would not reduce overall military effectiveness.[65] Finally, Sakharov stressed that the heads of their various branches of the Soviet military should always be civilians. This would reduce the chance of "Bonapartism" (i.e., the military's seeking political power), and was probably the reason he believed the officer corps need not be significantly reduced.[66]

Quite apart from the beneficial effects that reductions in Soviet conventional forces would have on perestroika, these reductions were necessary for the ripple effect they would have on negotiations to reduce nuclear weapons. In the late

63. Ibid., 19–20; Sakharov, "Novoe politicheskoe myshlenie neobkhodimo," 4; Andrei Sakharov, "Fifty Percent Is More Than Just Half," *New Times* 38 (1988): 21; Interview with Zora Safir, 7.

64. Sakharov, *Moscow and Beyond*, 41, 153–54.

65. Sakharov and Adamovich, "Zhit' na zemle i zhit' dolgo," 175.

66. See, for example, Sakharov, *Moscow and Beyond*, 36; and "Stepen' svobody: Aktual'noe interv'iu," 28.

1980s Sakharov resurrected the argument he had first articulated in Gorky earlier in the decade: because the principal threat to nuclear peace was the threat Soviet conventional forces posed to Western Europe (rather than the threat Soviet nuclear forces posed to the United States), the United States would be more amenable to reducing its nuclear arsenal—which in turn would make the Soviet Union more amenable to reducing its own nuclear arsenal—if the Soviets were to reduce their conventional forces unilaterally.[67] Sakharov made this point in a variety of venues, most forcefully in an interview with Leonid Ryzhkov in Moscow after a Pugwash Conference in October 1988. Two months later, in a speech before the United Nations General Assembly, Gorbachev announced in effect, that he was taking Sakharov's advice. The Soviet Union, he said, would reduce its conventional forces unilaterally. But it would do so by only 10 percent (that is to say, from 5 million to 4.5 million).[68] Sakharov, in response, called for this 10 percent reduction to be followed by additional ones. If the government should balk at these, or if the reduction it ordered should for some reason fail to spur reductions in the superpowers' nuclear arsenals, he offered a fallback position: that NATO and the Warsaw Pact agree to a demilitarized zone between their forces of some 150–200 kilometers. In that way, a surprise attack would be less likely to succeed, and the fear of one would be less likely to prompt preemptive action. As a result, the chances of a conventional war in Europe—which would surely escalate into a nuclear war between the United States and the Soviet Union—would be greatly diminished.[69]

## A Relationship of Guarded and Conditional Respect

Issues of defense, while obviously important to Sakharov in the last years of his life, did not rivet his attention the way perestroika did. This enormous undertaking, on which Gorbachev embarked for the purpose of strengthening the Soviet Union, had the paradoxical effect of accelerating its collapse.[70] Since Gorbachev's ascension to power in 1985 was hardly preordained, one can reasonably argue that with a different, more conservative general secretary in the late 1980s, the Soviet Union would not have collapsed in 1991—though it probably would have done so at a later date.[71] Although Sakharov did not live to see the collapse, his views on perestroika contain genuine insights into the reasons for it.

67. Sakharov, "Neizbezhnost' perestroiki," 134; Sakharov and Adamovich, "Zhit' na zemle i zhit' dolgo," 175; Michael Gordon, "Sakharov Urges Moscow to Cut Size of its Military," *New York Times,* November 16, 1988, A13.

68. After Gorbachev announced the reduction, the defense minister, Sergei Akhromeev, who strongly opposed it, resigned his position in protest. McCauley, *Gorbachev,* 139.

69. Andrei Sakharov, "A Trustworthy Policy," *New Times* 24 (1988): 13; Sakharov, "Neizbezhnost' perestroika," 134; Sakharov, "Novoe politicheskoe myshlenie neobkhodimo," 5.

70. This view is not uncommon among Sovietologists who have written about the Soviet Union's collapse. See, for example, Terry McNeill, "In Defense of Realism," in *Rethinking the Soviet Collapse: Sovietology, the Death of Communism and the New Russia,* ed. Michael Cox (London, 1998), 52.

71. This is more or less the argument of Myron Rush in his article "Fortune and Fate," *National Interest* 31 (Spring 1993): 19–25. The entire issue is devoted to the collapse of the Soviet Union.

Sakharov and Gorbachev, while very different in their temperament and life experiences, both favored the Soviet Union's reform. Both men—Sakharov more easily than Gorbachev, who retained an allegiance to the Leninism Sakharov had jettisoned in the early 1970s—rejected the worst excrescences of Stalinism and hoped to substitute for what remained of it in the Soviet Union a more humane and efficient political and economic system that would satisfy the material and spiritual needs of the Soviet people. But they sharply disagreed on what this system should entail and thus on the extent to which perestroika should be pursued. For Gorbachev perestroika was a means to an end—namely, a Soviet Union whose better treatment of its people would have the effect of making it more competitive with the United States, a country with the wherewithal to flourish in an age when science and technology were advancing more rapidly than at any other time in human history. For Sakharov perestroika was an end in itself.[72] A "restructured" Soviet Union—quite apart from the fact that it would mark the imminence of convergence—was preferable because it would provide the Soviet people with human rights and foster respect for the individual personality. What is more, perestroika for Sakharov was not something the Soviet leadership should grant the Soviet people out of a sense of paternalistic magnanimity. While as a dissident he had seemed to approve of the Soviet government's improving the lives of its people in this fashion, viewing them essentially as the beneficiaries rather than the instruments of reform, by the late 1980s he believed that reform should be an undertaking in which the Soviet people were equal participants with the Soviet government. For Sakharov, perestroika was not a reward for good behavior. Nor should the Soviet people be grateful upon receiving it. Rather, they were entitled to it by virtue of their common humanity.

But Gorbachev, unlike Sakharov, could not shed the elitism and paternalism both men possessed when, at different times, they came originally to the problem of social reform—Gorbachev in the early 1980s when briefings from economists and others caused him to recognize that the status quo could not long survive, Sakharov in the late 1960s when he wrote *Reflections*. As Sakharov himself astutely observed, while Gorbachev spoke favorably of popular participation in governance, its reality made him acutely uncomfortable. Subsequent events would bear out the accuracy of Sakharov's observation. The general secretary never quite rid himself of the debilitating illusion ultimately fatal to his political career that the government (or more precisely, the Communist Party) was the only legitimate instrument of reform and the sole arbiter of which reforms should be enacted.[73] In the end, perestroika was doomed not just by Gorbachev's fidelity to Leninism and Bolshevism, however attenuated it was by 1990 and 1991. It was doomed equally by his fidelity to the paternalism so deeply embedded in Russian history and culture.[74]

---

72. Sakwa, *Gorbachev and His Reforms*, 176.

73. Andrei Sakharov, "Taking a Tough New Line," *U. S. News and World Report*, January 30, 1989, 50.

74. Sakharov recognized Gorbachev's inability and unwillingness to renounce Leninism and Bolshevism and criticized him for it. "Sakharov, Bonner on Gorbachev, Restructuring," interview

The personal relationship Sakharov and Gorbachev established in 1988 reflected their political and philosophical differences. Although Gorbachev attended the banquet hosted by the forum on nuclear weapons in February 1987 at which Sakharov floated his decoupling proposal, the two men did not actually meet or speak to each other.[75] Not until January 1988 did they do so. At that time Sakharov, in his role as director of the International Foundation for the Survival and Development of Humanity, joined other members of the organization for a meeting with Gorbachev in the Kremlin, at which he passed to the general secretary a list of remaining political prisoners.[76] Sakharov's initial impression was that Gorbachev was "intelligent, self-possessed, and quick-witted in discussion" and that "the policies he was pursuing at the time [were] consistently liberal, fostering a gradual growth of democracy by means of fundamental reforms."[77] Thereafter, their relationship was marked by mutual respect, though never affection, along with the realization that the policies they each pursued made the maintenance of civility essential. One of Gorbachev's reform-minded advisers, Georgii Shakhnazarov, advised the general secretary that Sakharov was someone with whom one could "do business," and when Gorbachev paid his last respects at the Academy of Sciences immediately preceding Sakharov's funeral, he told Bonner that with Sakharov's passing he had lost "my one honest opponent."[78] But Gorbachev was also irked when Sakharov disagreed with him publicly, as he did repeatedly at the two Congresses of People's Deputies the Soviet physicist attended as a delegate. Indeed, when *Argumenty i fakty* conducted a poll in October 1989 that showed Sakharov to be a more popular political figure than Gorbachev, the general secretary threatened to fire the editor who published the results.[79] Gorbachev, in the final analysis, could not control Sakharov, and that fact alone, irrespective of the latter's substantive criticisms of perestroika, was a source of genuine irritation for the general secretary, who had absorbed from the political system he grew up in its operative assumption that the Soviet people should behave politically like docile children. This seems to explain the condescension with which Gorbachev wrote about Sakharov in his memoirs, in

by Jean-Pierre Barou, *Sueddeutsche Zeitung,* January 26, 1989, reprinted in Eisen, *Glasnost Reader,* 346. But he did not discern the paternalism in the latter's entire approach to governance and social change. Nowhere in Sakharov's voluminous writings, at any rate, is there any criticism of Gorbachev's paternalism or even any mention of it.

75. Sakharov, *Moscow and Beyond,* 26.

76. Ibid., 45. Sakharov remarked to the American scientist Frank von Hippel, who was with him when he met Gorbachev, that the circumstances under which he had last been in the Kremlin were very different: on that occasion he was going to see Beria. Von Hippel, "Nashe sotrudnichestvo," 743.

77. Sakharov, ibid.

78. Georgii Kh. Shakhnazarov, *Tsena svobody: Reformatsiia Gorbacheva glazami ego pomoshchika* (Moscow, 1993), 393; Bonner, "Komu nuzhny mify?" 25. Gorbachev received rather different advice from the chameleon-like Kapitsa, who told the general secretary that Sakharov was vain, naïve, and ambitious. Mikhail Gorbachev, *Memoirs* (New York, 1995), 296.

79. "Obshchestvennoe mnenie o narodnykh deputatakh," *Argumenty i fakty,* October 7–13, 1989, 1; Jack Matlock, *Autopsy of an Empire: The American Ambassador's Account of the Collapse of the Soviet Union* (New York, 1995), 264.

which he opined at one point patronizingly on how sad he felt at the Second Congress of People's Deputies when he watched the Nobel Prize–winning physicist "indiscriminately squander the respect he commanded" by focusing his attention on "idle issues."[80]

For his part, Sakharov, while always respectful of Gorbachev, was never awed by him. In fact, he seemed to play the role of Gorbachev's conscience, exhorting him on the basis of moral principle not to waver in his commitment to reform as he explored the outer limits of perestroika. Sakharov seemed to calibrate his public support of Gorbachev, rationing it very carefully on the basis of the general secretary's willingness to expand his program of reform to coincide with Sakharov's more radical one. When Gorbachev agreed to do so, Sakharov applauded him, but when he refused, Sakharov criticized him and warned darkly of the harmful consequences that would follow. Indeed, from 1987 to 1989, Sakharov seemed to radicalize his own positions precisely when Gorbachev had finally accepted them; thus there was always some political distance between the two men. Sakharov's objective, of course, was to lure Gorbachev to follow him. But he was always careful not to allow too much or too little distance between his positions and Gorbachev's: if his were too far ahead of Gorbachev's, he would lose whatever influence he had on him, while if they were too close to the general secretary's, Sakharov would lose credibility among the more radical reformers, such as Iurii Afanasiev and Galina Starovoitova, whose good opinion he considered quite important.[81] As it was, several former dissidents, such as Malva Landa, criticized Sakharov for supposedly being too supportive of and too chummy with the Soviet leader.[82] In January 1988, in a talk he gave at a Moscow restaurant to former members of the Helsinki Groups that existed in the late 1970s, Sakharov summarized his strategy toward Gorbachev and perestroika as follows: "It seems to me essential that we preserve our fundamental positions on all the basic questions we face in this new situation, but at the same time explore all possibilities in this new situation to direct the movement [for reform] in the proper direction. We should also show flexibility in discovering new paths. Flexibility and fidelity to one's principles are hardly compatible, but we have to find some way to combine them."[83] This task Sakharov imposed on

80. Gorbachev, *Memoirs*, 298.

81. By training a historian, Afanasiev, like Sakharov, decried the falsification of Soviet history, claiming on one occasion that as a result of it "we do not recognize ourselves in the mirror." In the late 1980s Afanasiev openly admitted that his advocacy of reform was a form of repentance for his inaction earlier, when Sakharov was in Gorky. Perhaps as compensation for this, unlike Sakharov, he spoke frequently of perestroika as "a revolution" and implied that that was the reason he supported it. Iu. N. Afanasiev, "Perestroika i istoricheskoe znanie," in Afanasiev, *Inogo ne dano*, 505; Yuri Afanasyev, "The Agony of the Stalinist System," in Cohen and vanden Heuvel, *Voices of Glasnost*, 100; Iurii Afanasiev, "Govorim o proshlom, no reshaetsia budushchee sotzializma," *Moskovskie novosti*, May 10, 1987, 11. In 1990 Afanasiev helped found Democratic Russia, an organization that tried to bring all reform-minded organizations in the Soviet Union under its umbrella. Tragically, Starovoitova, who continued to fight for democracy and human rights after the Soviet Union collapsed, was murdered under mysterious circumstances in November 1998.

82. Sakharov, *Moscow and Beyond*, 12.

83. Quoted in Frantishek Ianoukh, "Nas sblizila prazhskaia vesna," in Altshuler et al., *On mezhdu nami zhil*, 851.

himself was a difficult one, but he performed it skillfully and without sacrificing his own principles.

Sakharov never doubted that perestroika, or some facsimile of it, was necessary. Given that Soviet society was "profoundly ill," the Soviet people "morally degraded," and the Soviet government "an administrative-command structure of control" that sustained itself parasitically by adopting technological advances developed in the West, the Soviet leadership had no choice but to reform the Soviet Union if it wanted the country to remain competitive with the West (here Sakharov's justification of reform coincided with Gorbachev's).[84] But because Soviet youth were even more demoralized, in the literal sense of the word, than their parents were, unless reform were consummated quickly, it was likely to be either whittled away incrementally or stopped abruptly with Gorbachev's removal from power, which was always a distinct possibility. While Gorbachev himself would never abuse the power he had to the extent of reinstating mass repression (or so Sakharov predicted in January 1989), the person who succeeded him as general secretary might very well do so.[85]

Eventually, Sakharov soured on perestroika when it became clear to him, in late 1988 and early 1989, that Gorbachev's version of it left the basic attributes and institutions of the Soviet state intact—the police, the *nomenklatura*, a planned economy, and the concentration of political power in the Communist Party.[86] Because the Communist Party was both the principal instrument and the principal object of reform, he was not at all surprised that perestroika was increasingly being executed by people who had good reason to oppose it. Indeed, it was precisely to circumvent the party that Gorbachev created in the spring of 1989 a new institution, the Congress of People's Deputies, through which he could continue perestroika at precisely the pace he desired. But this in turn created a contradiction that neither Gorbachev nor anyone else in the Soviet leadership was able to acknowledge, much less resolve. While perestroika necessarily entailed a diminution of the power of the state, Gorbachev, who was in charge of the state, found that the only way he could overcome opposition to perestroika was by increasing the state's power. In short, the means Gorbachev adopted to achieve his ends contradicted his ends and could easily subvert them.

By the end of 1988, Sakharov had come to the conclusion that the power Gorbachev had accumulated, no matter how wisely or benevolently he exercised it, was not only dangerous to perestroika but incompatible with it.[87] By the summer of 1989, his concerns had deepened to the point where he believed that Gorbachev was capable—like Napoleon in 1799—of a coup d'état that would subvert the very goals he had originally supported.[88] What drove Sakharov to contemplate such a profoundly disturbing contingency was Gorbachev's election

---

84. Sakharov, "Neizbezhnost' perestroiki," 122–23.
85. Interview with Zora Safir, 2.
86. "Z" [Martin Malia], "To the Stalin Mausoleum," *Daedalus* (Winter 1990): 301.
87. A. Sakharov, "Perestroika: Kto protiv?" *Ogonëk* 50 (December 1988): 13.
88. Sakharov, *Moscow and Beyond*, 133.

in late May to the chairmanship of the Supreme Soviet of the Congress of People's Deputies after the other two candidates for the position withdrew before the balloting even began.[89] It seemed to Sakharov that Gorbachev was grasping for "unlimited personal power" and that the only way to protect himself against charges of corruption—the general secretary had already been accused of taking bribes in Stavropol before coming to Moscow in 1978—was through direct and popular election.[90]

At the same time, Sakharov seemed to recognize that Gorbachev's new power was really empty power and that the more he accumulated, the more he seemed beholden to those in the party who opposed perestroika, such as Vadim Medvedev, who in 1988 had succeeded Yakovlev as Central Committee secretary for ideology.[91] As Sakharov described the situation in the summer of 1989, the enemies of perestroika were now the executors of it. Because he was trying to please everyone simultaneously, Gorbachev would soon have to choose definitively between placating those outside the party who wanted reforms more radical than those he considered safe and sufficient and appeasing those within the party who recognized the threat these more radical reforms would pose to their own power and privileges. In November 1989, in an interview with a reporter from a Polish newspaper published in Warsaw, Sakharov suggested that the general secretary had opted for the latter, confessing somberly that the recent attacks on glasnost in the Soviet press were "very disturbing."[92]

Still, he always acknowledged that there was no acceptable alternative to Gorbachev, and he supported him consistently, though by no means uncritically, after returning to Moscow in December 1986. Sakharov's support was not unconditional: should Gorbachev abandon perestroika entirely, he would withdraw it. But as long as this did not happen, Sakharov would play the role of the loyal opposition, appealing to Gorbachev's better nature and his political interests, to ensure that the general secretary would not renege on his commitments. For example, in an interview in April 1987 with the publisher of *U.S. News and World Report,* Sakharov urged Gorbachev to continue glasnost—which Gorbachev had instituted to facilitate perestroika—not just because it was intrinsically meritorious, but also because it benefited Gorbachev more than it did his conservative critics.[93] Sakharov did not wish Gorbachev ill. Whatever his faults and inadequacies as a leader, he was the only hope the reformers had, the only person in the Soviet Union in a position to translate their demands into policy.[94] Even when Sakharov became disenchanted with Gorbachev, as he did in the last two months

89. Ibid., 122; Anatolii Sobchak, *Khozhdenie vo vlast': Rasskaz o rozhdenii parlamenta* (Moscow, 1991), 129–30.

90. Sakharov, *Moscow and Beyond,* 132–33.

91. Ibid., 61, 130–31.

92. Interview with Andrei Sacharov, *Polityka* (Warsaw), November 25, 1989, 7.

93. Andrei Sakharov, "Glasnost: There's No Turning Back," *U. S. News and World Report,* April 20, 1987, 31.

94. Sakharov, "Trustworthy Policy," 14.

of his life, he recognized and stated publicly, as in the interview he gave to the Warsaw newspaper in late November 1989, that if Gorbachev were toppled from power, whoever succeeded him would almost surely be worse.[95]

Gorbachev, in Sakharov's estimation, could either propel the Soviet Union toward greater reform or restore the complacency and stagnation that had existed before he came to power (though not as quickly or thoroughly as his successor would). Accordingly, Sakharov counseled Western governments to adopt toward the general secretary the position he had recommended they take toward détente a decade earlier. Western governments should support Gorbachev but nonetheless keep their eyes open so that if he should slacken in his commitment to reform, they could take concrete steps, such as halting all forms of cooperation, to ensure that reform would resume. Ideally, the mere threat of withholding cooperation would be sufficient to ensure that such a step would never actually be necessary.[96]

Not surprisingly, this was a theme Sakharov stressed on his trips to the West. In a speech in November 1988 to the New York Academy of Sciences he told his audience that Gorbachev "should be helped," but because "not all of the problems [in the Soviet Union] have been solved," that help should be offered critically.[97] Given the opposition to perestroika Gorbachev faced within the party, some backsliding on his part was to be expected. But this was precisely why the West should do all it could to prevent it.[98] In Sakharov's view, Western support—both rhetorical and substantive—for perestroika would help to counterbalance opposition from the Communist Party, the police, and the armed forces.[99] And if for some reason this support should be insufficient to prevent Gorbachev from capitulating to his opponents, or if for reasons of his own he should decide to abandon perestroika, the West's withdrawal of its support would cause him to change his mind and order perestroika's resumption. On reflection, Sakharov's argument is not entirely convincing or consistent: why should the threat to withdraw Western support be enough to restore perestroika if that support was not enough to prevent opponents of perestroika, or Gorbachev himself, from stopping it in the first place? But whatever it lacked in cogency, Sakharov's argument shows how integral he considered the West to the fate of perestroika and ultimately of the Soviet Union itself.

95. "Interview with Andrei Sacharov," 7. Five days before his death, Sakharov amended his scenario: a coup by hardliners would embolden others even more reactionary to overthrow them. But the result would be the same—the end of perestroika and reform. Andrei Dmitrievich Sakharov, "Istina odnogo cheloveka (December 9, 1989)," *Komsomol'skaia Pravda*, December 16, 1989, 2.

96. Sakharov, *Moscow and Beyond*, 73; Carla Hall, "Dinner with Andrei," *Washington Post*, November 14, 1988, B11.

97. Gary Lee, "Sakharov Says Soviet Union Continues to Violate Human Rights," *Washington Post*, November 12, 1988, A16.

98. Interview with Zora Safir, 14; "A. Sakharov, "Ia aktivno podderzhivaiu perestroiku," *Izvestiia*, February 6, 1989, 6.

99. Sakharov, "There's No Turning Back on Glasnost," 31.

# 23  A Different Kind of Perestroika

What, then, did Sakharov think the reform of the Soviet Union required? How, if at all, did his proposals and prescriptions evolve from 1987 to 1989, and how much did they correspond to what Gorbachev was enacting concurrently under the aegis of perestroika?

On the Soviet economy, Sakharov's views became more radical. In 1987 and through most of 1988, as Gorbachev proposed reforms that modified economic relations without changing the economic institutions themselves—such as allowing individual enterprises limited freedom in how they functioned but with the state continuing to own them—Sakharov was largely silent, focusing his attention on other matters.[1] But in December 1988 he spoke out forcefully. In an interview with Zora Safir, a reporter for the Voice of America, he proclaimed that "without a market economy and without competition...economic restructuring is doomed to difficult times ahead and to a lack of effectiveness."[2] Two months later, in an interview he gave to *Moscow News*, Sakharov stated that the substantive purpose of his candidacy for election to the Congress of People's Deputies was "to deepen and further perestroika" and that in furtherance of that objective he favored "a free market for labor, the means of production, raw materials, and intermediate products."[3] In addition, collective and state farms that were inefficient should be dissolved immediately, and industries shown to be nonprofitable "should be either leased out or sold to shareholders"; of those that were left, the largest should be broken up into smaller ones "to encourage capitalism and to eliminate monopoly pricing."[4]

Sakharov's endorsement of capitalism, which he reiterated in the platform he formulated on behalf of his candidacy, was obviously something Gorbachev could never accept.[5] For the general secretary, economic reform—indeed, reform of any kind—should not exceed the limits imposed by the socialism he espoused. Certainly the laws on industrial and state enterprise Gorbachev announced in late 1986 and the reforms the Central Committee plenum considered in June 1987 fell far short of what Sakharov would advocate eighteen months later.[6] The question remains, however, what Sakharov actually meant by "capitalism." Significantly, he did not call for a free market per se, only for a free market for labor. Similarly, he did not call for the complete dismantling of the collective farms, only for the dismantling of those that were unprofitable.

1. Sakwa, *Gorbachev and His Reforms*, 279.
2. Interview with Zora Safir, 6.
3. Andrei Sakharov, "For Peace and Progress," *Moscow News*, February 5, 1989, 8.
4. Ibid.
5. "Programma A. D. Sakharova," 6.
6. Sakwa, *Gorbachev and His Reforms*, 279; Sakharov, *Moscow and Beyond*, 10.

Nor did he call for the denationalization of state property.[7] Rather, what Sakharov seems to have envisioned, at least for the immediate future, was a mixed economy in which state-owned and privately owned enterprises competed vigorously with each other, in much the same way they were meant to do in the 1920s under Lenin's New Economic Policy (NEP). As Sakharov stated explicitly in June 1989, there should be "a pluralization of the economy so that all forms of property will finally become legally and economically equal."[8] But the neo-NEP Sakharov advocated was really the NEP in reverse. Instead of evolving toward socialism, as the Bolsheviks thought the original NEP would do, this new mixed economy would evolve toward capitalism—a nonrapacious and regulated form of capitalism—in which there would be no monopolies to curtail competition, and much of the cradle-to-grave security to which the Soviet people had grown accustomed would be preserved.[9] In this respect it is significant that in his memoirs, in the context of describing convergence—which for Sakharov remained the point at which all ongoing historical processes come to an end—he stated that economically it entailed "a market and competition."[10]

Sakharov's belief that this humane capitalism could be achieved in the Soviet Union through a process of evolution, without a formal mandate from the government or any other institution in society, was notable for what it suggested about socialist systems that sought to transform themselves into capitalist ones. The kind of transformation Sakharov advocated was the opposite of what the Soviet Union initiated in the 1920s and 1930s and of what other countries experienced at other times in the twentieth century. He proposed the demolition, rather than the construction, of an enormous apparatus of state control and ownership, which the political elite understandably had a vested interest in preserving. For this reason, proceeding from socialism to capitalism was more difficult, at least politically, than proceeding from capitalism to socialism. As a consequence, it would have to be done gradually. This was Sakharov's principal insight when he considered the economic reform of the Soviet Union, and his insistence on a gradualist approach, in which the capitalist sector of the economy was given time to demonstrate its superiority over the socialist one, was predicated on the belief that the Soviet people and their leaders, whatever their current deficiencies, would eventually be rational enough to set aside any preference they still had for socialism.

Ironically, Sakharov's scenario of socialism evolving into capitalism is reminiscent of how Marx and Engels, in the *Communist Manifesto,* imagined capitalism evolving into socialism. It is often ignored or forgotten that the violent revolution Marx and Engels believed would install the proletariat in power would be a purely political one; nowhere in the *Manifesto* is there any indication that the

7. Sakharov reiterated his point about the collective farms in his interview with Grigory Tsitriniak (June 1989), reprinted in *Perils of Perestroika: Viewpoints from the Soviet Press, 1989–1991,* ed. Isaac J. Tarasulo (Wilmington, Del., 1992), 338.

8. Ibid., 343.

9. Sakharov, *Moscow and Beyond,* 145; "Programma A. D. Sakharova," 3.

10. Sakharov, *Moscow and Beyond,* 160.

proletariat, once in power, would eliminate private property immediately. Conspicuously absent among the steps Marx and Engels predicted the proletariat would take in preparation for the emergence of communism and a classless society was the nationalization, by government fiat, of the means of production. The only economic asset the bourgeoisie would lose immediately was land; all other private property would disappear gradually, as the result of the elimination of things like unearned income and private inheritance.[11] In Marx and Engels' scenario, as well as in Sakharov's, the government would not decree the existence of a new economic system but instead initiate a process by which this new system would emerge. As a result, one could say legitimately that, in Marx and Engels' scenario, capitalism (as an economic system) would evolve into socialism just as gradually as socialism would evolve into communism—and that both of these transformations would be just as gradual as the evolution of a socialist into a capitalist economic system under Sakharov's scenario.

In the last weeks of his life Sakharov became impatient with the slow pace of economic reform under Gorbachev and rejected the gradualism he had previously advocated. On December 1, 1989, he joined Afanasiev, Gavriil Popov, Vladimir Tukhonov, and Arkady Murashev—all of them, like Sakharov, duly elected delegates to the Second Congress of People's Deputies—in calling for a two-hour general strike if the party did not relinquish its monopoly of power and if the government did not pass a law ending the collective ownership of land.[12] But Sakharov died two weeks later without clarifying when he thought the transition to private ownership should begin, how quickly it should proceed, or even how strongly he favored it.

However essential economic reform was to the survival of the Soviet Union, Sakharov always recognized, from 1987 to 1989, the primacy of politics in ensuring that the government behaved humanely. While cognizant of the Chinese model, in which the economy was liberalized while political institutions were left largely intact, Sakharov much preferred that these institutions be altered first and that the Communist Party relinquish its monopoly of power.[13] As he mentioned in an interview in June 1989, economic relationships derived ultimately from political ones (in contrast to the Marxist-Leninist view), and a political elite like the Soviet one that sought to save itself by changing the former before changing the latter was bound to weaken or even destroy itself. The Chinese, he said, were destined to fail in reforming their own system, and the Soviets would surely fail if they made the mistake of imitating them.[14] Sakharov

11. Karl Marx and Friedrich Engels, *The Communist Manifesto* (London, 1967), 104–5.

12. Sakharov et al., "Appeal of a Group of People's Deputies of the USSR (December 1, 1989)," 717–18. This was one of many instances in which Sakharov joined forces with moderate reformers, some of them originally supportive of Gorbachev, who believed the corrective to the current stagnation was not democracy but rather a smaller and less bureaucratic government. It was Popov, not surprisingly, who coined the term "administrative command system," which Sakharov used as well, to describe the Soviet Union. Peter Reddaway and Dmitri Glinski, *The Tragedy of Russia's Reforms: Market Bolshevism against Democracy* (Washington, 2001), 105.

13. Sakharov et al., "Appeal of a Group of People's Deputies of the USSR" (December 1, 1989), 721–22.

14. A. D. Sakharov, "S"ezd ne mozhet sdelat' vse srazu…," *Literaturnaia gazeta,* June 21, 1989, 11.

defined politics broadly. Among other requirements, it encompassed the rule of law, which in his mind required the abolition of Article 6 of the Soviet Constitution, which ratified the Communist Party's monopoly of power. Sakharov did not call publicly for the abolition of the article until the summer of 1989. But before then he sought to limit the party's power by calling attention to its abuses. For Sakharov, these abuses were evidence that perestroika was not automatic or irreversible and that Gorbachev had to be watched constantly so that any backsliding could be pointed out and condemned. In late 1988, for example, he joined Sergei Zalygin, the editor of *Novyi mir,* in protesting—by means of a letter to Gorbachev himself—the recent rescission of permission for *Novyi mir* to serialize *The Gulag Archipelago.* Possibly as a result of this letter, the government reversed itself.[15] In a similar vein, Sakharov took the opportunity, while meeting with Yakovlev in late 1988, to register his strong objection to the illegal detention of Armenians who had formed a committee to publicize the mistreatment of Armenians in Azerbaijan. A few months earlier, he had expressed his concern about new restrictions the government imposed on public demonstrations.[16]

Sakharov appreciated and publicly applauded the steps the government had taken to ensure the rule of law and thus prevent its own exercise of arbitrary power. For example, the resolution passed at the Nineteenth Party Conference in the summer of 1988 committing the party to the creation of a "socialist legal state" in the Soviet Union seemed to be precisely the evidence Sakharov was seeking that the Soviet government shared his commitment to the rule of law; indeed, the elimination in 1989 of Articles 70 and 190-1 of the RSFSR Criminal Code, under which so many dissidents had been unjustly punished, was undoubtedly a personal vindication.[17] Had Sakharov lived to see it, he would have strongly approved of the abolition of censorship in August 1990, which, as John Miller has pointed out, effectively made possible private enterprise in the dissemination of information in the Soviet Union.[18] He no doubt would have been pleased as well with the emergence in the spring of 1991 of a Soviet press virtually indistinguishable from a Western one in its reporting the news rather than disseminating the party line, which had been the principal purpose of the Soviet press since the early 1920s.

But had he lived longer, Sakharov would also have been disturbed by the slowness with which the government acted in seeking to achieve the rule of law. In particular he would have regretted the fact that in 1991 half of the media and most of the printing presses in the Soviet Union still remained in the hands of the Communist Party.[19] Similarly, he would have been chagrined by the extraordinary powers, such as the right to impose martial law and to issue decrees

15. Sakharov, *Moscow and Beyond,* 65.
16. Ibid., 56, 79.
17. John Miller, *Mikhail Gorbachev and the End of Soviet Power* (New York, 1993), 111. These articles, which the reader will recall were omnibus clauses effectively criminalizing any public statement of which the government disapproved, were replaced by an article declaring unlawful only incitements to violence that had as their purpose either the overthrow of the government or "the change of the Soviet state and social order." Quoted ibid., 99.
18. Ibid., 99.
19. Ibid., 99–100.

unilaterally, that Gorbachev possessed as Soviet president, a position he assumed in 1990.[20] Sakharov was greatly concerned by Gorbachev's steady accretion of power in the summer and fall of 1989 and thought that unless his power was accompanied by legal limits on how it would be exercised, whoever succeeded Gorbachev, or perhaps even Gorbachev himself, might use it to undo the progress perestroika had achieved and restore the repressive status quo that existed under Brezhnev.

To the end of his life, Sakharov remained cognizant of how fragile the rule of law was in a country such as Russia, with its long history of rulers exercising power arbitrarily. As a dissident, he believed that moral exhortation, coupled with appeals to rational self-interest, was all that anyone could do to strengthen it. In the late 1980s, however, Sakharov recognized that the new realities perestroika had created meant that there were other tactics he and others who shared his belief in the rule of law could utilize to secure its acceptance. One of these was expanding glasnost—Gorbachev's policy of publicizing some, but not all, of the shortcomings of Soviet society for the purpose of facilitating perestroika. To raise public awareness of the actual process by which laws were made, people should know who was drafting the laws, the content of the drafts, and how they were changed, if at all, in the course of being debated by those in government who were responsible for making them. After the First Congress of People's Deputies convened in May 1989, Sakharov concluded that laws should be legislated, rather than issued by fiat, and that the congress should be the institution empowered to do this. This, in turn, made it imperative that the Soviet people, to whom the congress was ultimately accountable, should know how the legislative process worked.[21]

But a working knowledge of how laws were made was not enough to ensure that these laws would be just or that the government, after making them, would obey them. It was also necessary, according to Sakharov, that people have the right to influence the process of lawmaking itself, in particular by demonstrating their preferences in public gatherings and if necessary public protests. In January 1989 he stated flatly that freedom of assembly was now the human right most critical to the establishment of a just and humane society in the Soviet Union and that the "collective rights" of which freedom of assembly was one example had become more important to the average Soviet citizen than the "individual rights" (for example, the right to petition the government for redress of particular grievances) to which Soviet citizens were equally entitled.[22] By collective rights, Sakharov did not mean rights that only a collective entity, like a nation, possessed. Rather, he meant individual rights that were exercised collectively. Persons who assembled peacefully to express their opinions were therefore exercising a right—the right to free expression—that inhered in individuals. But because under Gorbachev a mass politics was now possible, Sakharov

20. Stephen Kotkin, *Armageddon Averted: The Soviet Collapse, 1970–2000* (New York, 2001), 148.
21. Sakharov, *Moscow and Beyond*, 127–28.
22. "Sakharov, Bonner on Gorbachev, Restructuring," 345.

thought it especially important that the right to express individual opinions collectively in public arenas be guaranteed.

But even glasnost and the exercise of individual rights collectively were insufficient to ensure the rule of law in the Soviet Union. These would have to be accompanied by genuine pluralism, which meant true democracy and a multiparty system. Sakharov did not favor pluralism and democracy merely in the abstract. He won election to the Congress of People's Deputies in the spring of 1989, and once elected, showed his commitment to democracy by doing everything he could to ensure that others would come to share it. When Gorbachev was elected chairman of the Supreme Soviet by the congress in the absence of any opposition or alternative candidacies, Sakharov walked out of the congress in protest and later told the Soviet leader bluntly that the Soviet Union had held bogus elections for seventy years and did not need any more of them.[23]

By the end of 1988, Sakharov had come to the conclusion that a multiparty system was desirable, and in the months that followed he made clear how essential it was that such a system emerge in the Soviet Union.[24] In April 1989 he stated flatly that perestroika could not succeed if those who were directing it were oblivious to the demands for reform the Soviet people were making simultaneously and without direction or encouragement from the government. In Sakharov's opinion, the only way the Soviet leadership could adequately respond to these demands was by allowing the advocates of reform to establish their own political parties and to participate in the political process democratically.[25] Even before the Congress of People's Deputies convened in May 1989, he condemned the procedures under which it would operate as "undemocratic."[26]

To his lasting credit, Sakharov was among the small number of former dissidents who understood after 1985 how essential pluralism and democracy were to the success of perestroika, and he frequently upbraided Gorbachev personally for failing to offer himself as a candidate in an election in which the Soviet people as a whole, as opposed to the members of an elected assembly like the congress, participated. On several occasions, Sakharov shrewdly advised the general secretary that being elected popularly would enhance his legitimacy and strengthen his ability to withstand the forces in the country, particularly the police and the military, that wanted perestroika to fail.[27] Indeed, by 1989 democracy had become for Sakharov the only bulwark against a resurgence of repression, and he thought Gorbachev could reform the Soviet Union more thoroughly, more quickly, and without as much risk to his own political security if he had a direct electoral mandate to do so. To be sure, Sakharov made a sharp distinction between democracy and mob rule. Like many Russians, he feared and disliked the latter. But he never equated or conflated the two phenomena,

23. Elena Bonner, "On Gorbachev," *New York Review of Books,* May 17, 1990, 17.
24. Interview with Zora Safir, 15.
25. Sakharov, "V narode vsegda sokhraniaiutsia nravstvennye sily," 6.
26. Interview with Zora Safir, 1.
27. Sakharov, "S"ezd ne mozhet sdelat' vse srazu...," 11.

as many Russians did, and he saw the rule of law as the best bulwark against democracy's degeneration into anarchy. This was how Sakharov described the relationship between political pluralism and the rule of law in January 1989: "The establishment of the rule of law is justified by our history in which man has been the victim of dictatorship by the state. However, the law has to protect man from the excesses of the state, the crowd, the masses, and the mass media and give preference to a pluralist society. And if a society is pluralist...it will watch over moral principles."[28]

To a Western reader, Sakharov's concerns about the excesses of the masses might seem strange given the long-standing pattern in Russian and Soviet history of the state's exercising enormous power. But the fear of anarchy and mob rule has been a prominent feature of Russian political culture, as many commentators on the subject have pointed out, and the fact that Sakharov shared this fear is not surprising. The elitism implicit in the advisory boards he first advocated in *Reflections* was certainly consistent with this. But what is remarkable about Sakharov's concerns is that in the last years of his life he came to see democracy not just as something different from mob rule but as an antidote to it. When asked in an interview in 1988 if he still hoped political leaders would "heed the opinions of scientists more than they do today," Sakharov replied that he hoped these leaders would pay attention not only to scientists' conclusions but to "public opinion."[29] Whenever Sakharov, from 1987 to 1989, advocated the establishment of these advisory boards of experts (as he did in his platform for election to the First Congress of People's Deputies), he made clear that the influence they exercised should be tempered by the larger democracy in which they existed, in which the political leaders would not only be accountable to the people but also receive input on the various public issues that concerned them.[30] In the democracy Sakharov now preferred, the people would not permit the experts to divine their best interests, and the views of experts would not be the only ones the government considered in making policy. Equal consideration, perhaps even greater consideration, would be given to the views of ordinary people.

## Nagorno-Karabakh and Sakharov's Vision of a New Union

In supporting democracy, Sakharov's operative assumption was that the Soviet people were rational enough to practice it wisely. Of course this contradicted his statements that the Soviet people were hypocritical, materialistic, and selfish. But given his priorities, this did not matter very much. By the time of his death, democracy had become a moral imperative legitimizing the reforms he envisioned for the Soviet Union and an essential prerequisite of them. On only one issue—the clash between Armenians and Azeris over Nagorno-Karabakh—did

28. "Sakharov, Bonner on Gorbachev, Restructuring," 345–46.
29. Sakharov, "Fifty Percent Is More Than Just Half," 22.
30. Sakharov, "Programma A. D. Sakharova," 6.

he argue after returning to Moscow that democracy should be deferred to some future date because the people involved were not ready for it.

Nagorno-Karabakh was an autonomous region inside Azerbaijan in the Caucasus. Seventy percent of its population was Armenian and Christian, while the majority of the population in Azerbaijan was Muslim. For years, antagonism between the two peoples had been building, and by the 1980s the consensus among the Armenians in Nagorno-Karabakh was that the region should become an integral part of Armenia, despite the absence of a common border. With the weakening of Moscow's authority in the late 1980s, the resentments that had been held in check in the Brezhnev era finally exploded, and the unwillingness of the central government in Moscow to suppress them only weakened the Soviet system further.

Beginning in the winter of 1988, large numbers of Armenians in Nagorno-Karabakh and in Armenia itself began to agitate openly for the transfer of Nagorno-Karabakh to Armenia, and an Azeri pogrom against Armenians in Sumgait, the third largest city in Azerbaijan, lent special urgency to their demand. Correspondingly, many Azeris were concerned that compatriots of theirs who were living in Nagorno-Karabakh would be discriminated against or even persecuted if the transfer the Armenians demanded were to occur. Both sides invoked the principal of self-determination, and in purely ethical terms they both had legitimate grounds for doing so. The Armenian majority in Nagorno-Karabakh wanted to live within a larger (though geographically divided) Armenia, while the Azeri minority in Nagorno-Karabakh feared that, in this larger Armenia, they would lose their rights and possibly even their ethnic identity. Because their respective interests, under the circumstances, were irreconcilable, hostilities continued between the two groups until the collapse of the Soviet Union in 1991.

When he first devoted attention to the conflict, Sakharov's sympathies lay primarily with the Armenians. In the dichotomous lens through which he viewed the dispute, and indeed all the other conflicts involving national and ethnic minorities that racked the Soviet Union in its final years, his inclination was to favor the underdog, whom he saw in this case as the Armenian minority in Azerbaijan rather than the Azeri minority in Nagorno-Karabakh. That Bonner's father was Armenian may also have contributed to Sakharov's position. In the context of a different ethnic conflict, involving Abkhazians in Georgia who wanted their homeland incorporated into the RSFSR, Sakharov stated on one occasion that "the freedom and rights of larger nations should not be bought at the expense of smaller ones, which are entitled to special consideration." Applied to Nagorno-Karabakh, this suggested that the Armenians there should have their aspirations satisfied.[31] In addition, Sakharov thought the transfer of Nagorno-Karabakh justified on the grounds of self-determination, a principle he considered expressive not only of democracy but also of the right every

31. Sakharov, *Moscow and Beyond*, 108.

individual possessed to determine his place of residence. In this sense, the Armenians in Nagorno-Karabakh were like the Jewish refuseniks of the 1970s.

Accordingly, Sakharov did what he could, beginning in the winter of 1988, to facilitate the transfer. In March he wrote a letter to Gorbachev recommending it and sent a copy of the letter to *Moscow News*.[32] In response, Yakovlev and another of Gorbachev's advisers, Valentin Falin (who was also in charge of *Novosti*, the Soviet news agency), met separately with Sakharov to discuss the matter.[33] Sakharov, in his meeting with Yakovlev, termed the Armenians' demand for the transfer "reasonable" and claimed that if the Soviet government had originally agreed to it, the massacre of Armenians in Sumgait would never have occurred.[34] Soviet policy on the whole issue of Nagorno-Karabakh he denounced vehemently in his memoirs as "inexcusably vacillating and unprincipled," as well as "unjust, one-sided, and provocative."[35]

In response to the criticisms Sakharov leveled at the government, Yakovlev took the party line: that by altering the "national structure of the [Soviet] state"—which is what Yakovlev said the transfer would precipitate—the government would usher in a veritable civil war between nationalities not only in the Caucasus but all over the Soviet Union; left unsaid but clearly implicit in his reply was that the Soviet Union might even collapse as a result of it.[36] Yakovlev's argument did not satisfy Sakharov. As he explained in his original letter to Gorbachev, the government's willingness to redress the Armenians' grievance was nothing less than a "touchstone" of perestroika and a test of Gorbachev's commitment to it.[37]

In the months that followed his exchange with Yakovlev, Sakharov's views underwent a subtle but significant transformation. Whereas in March he had thought that Nagorno-Karabakh, in keeping with the principle of self-determination, should become an integral (though geographically discrete) part of Armenia, by July he had come to the conclusion that while the disputed territory should not be subordinated in any way to Azerbaijan, "an administration responsible only to Moscow" should be established there to govern it.[38] Such an arrangement, if adopted, might ease tensions and allow cooler heads on both sides to prevail. But the government rejected Sakharov's proposal shortly after he offered it, and by the time it accepted the idea, in January 1989, the conflict had

---

32. Andrei Sakharov, "Otkrytoe pis'mo," *Materialy samizdata* 26/88 (June 17, 1988) AS6222: 3. Although *Moscow News* printed only an abridged version of the letter, it appeared in full in Leningrad in the newspaper *Rubikon*. Two critical responses to Sakharov's letter appeared in *Moscow News* in subsequent issues: Gadzhi Gadzhiev, "Pis'mo akademiku Andreiu Sakharovu s kritikoi ego pis'ma o Nagornom Karabakhe," *Moskovskie novosti*, April 3, 1988; and M. S. Khalatov et al., "Glavnomu redaktoru gazety 'Moskovskie novosti,'" *Moskovskie novosti*, reprinted in *Materialy samizdata*, no. 39/88 (August 19, 1988), as AS6276: 1–2, and AS6277: 1–4, respectively.
33. Sakharov, *Moscow and Beyond*, 47–48.
34. Ibid., 49.
35. Ibid., 46.
36. Ibid., 49.
37. Andrei Sakharov, "Otkrytoe pis'mo," 5.
38. Sakharov, *Moscow and Beyond*, 53.

reached a point of no return.[39] A visit to the region Sakharov made in December 1988 at Yakovlev's request and with Gorbachev's explicit approval enabled him to see firsthand the degree to which passions there had made compromise impossible. On his visit, Sakharov was accompanied by Bonner, Starovoitova, Leonid Batkin, and Andrei Zubov, the last of whom, before leaving Moscow, proposed that a referendum be held to resolve the dispute. When he learned of Zubov's proposal, Sakharov considered it "worth discussing."[40] But once he was in the Caucasus, he revised his position. The vehement opposition both Armenians and Azeris expressed to a referendum when Sakharov broached the idea convinced him that Zubov's proposal, in the parlance of conflict resolution, was a nonstarter.[41] The only practical course of action was for the Soviet government to administer Nagorno-Karabakh from Moscow until "events run their course"—by which Sakharov meant a cooling of passions sufficient to allow serious negotiations between the parties to begin.[42]

Reduced to its essentials, the position Sakharov had reached at the time of his death a year later was that the problem of Nagorno-Karabakh was unsolvable and that neither side had a monopoly of moral virtue in the matter. The claims of the Azeri minority in Nagorno-Karabakh were just as compelling, in terms of self-determination and individual rights, as those of the Armenian minority in Azerbaijan. Evaluating the problem merely as an ethical matter would not facilitate a practical solution. The most anyone could hope for in the immediate future was that Armenians and Azeris would exercise restraint and avoid force and violence until a new union could be created in which the territories they inhabited would be separate union republics. Whether these republics would be ethnically homogenized by large-scale but presumably voluntary population transfers, Sakharov did not say. Over the long run there was only one solution: a genuine federalism in which the legitimate aspirations of both minorities to self-determination were satisfied.[43] To his credit, Sakharov was able, in the case of Nagorno-Karabakh, to perceive the moral ambiguities in a conflict that admitted no mutually acceptable solution. To this extent, he showed how far his thinking had evolved since his days as a dissident, when his very powerlessness afforded him the luxury of evaluating social problems without any obligation to contemplate solutions to them that recognized their practical complexities.

What, then, would Sakharov's new union look like? How different would it be from the existing union, and what virtues would it possess that would make disputes like that over Nagorno-Karabakh impossible, or at least highly unlikely? Although Sakharov stated in February 1989 that he preferred Lenin's original concept of a "union of equal states," the union he envisioned bore little

39. Ibid., 54.
40. Ibid., 77.
41. Ibid., 77–91.
42. Interview with Zora Safir, 4.
43. Sakharov, "Istina odnogo cheloveka," 2; "Sakharov o Karabakh (1989)," *Golos Armenii*, December 19, 1990, 4.

relation to what Lenin intended.[44] Indeed, it was very different from anything Gorbachev, before 1991, was willing to consider.

To ensure that the minorities in the Soviet Union were treated fairly, Sakharov advocated what he called a "horizontal" federalism.[45] All the "national subdivisions" of this union, which would take the form of republics, would have equal rights, as would the people who lived in them.[46] Political sovereignty would reside in these republics, in much the same way it resided, in Rousseau's conception, in people who were living in a state of nature before government became a practical necessity. But just as the people in Rousseau's imagined past relinquished their sovereignty to a government because they needed an external entity to protect them, these republics would voluntarily relinquish a measure of their sovereignty to this larger union once they recognized that they could not survive without it. Significantly, the union Sakharov envisioned would have jurisdiction over foreign policy and defense.[47] But apart from those two areas, the center in his union would have far less power than the Soviet government possessed. The republics would retain considerable autonomy—enough of it, in fact, to make secession, while legally an option, in practice unnecessary.[48] Sakharov's union would be a voluntary union, with only those powers that its constituent republics decided to delegate to it on the basis of enlightened self-interest.

Sakharov described this voluntary union comprehensively for the first time in the summer of 1989, in his speech to the Congress of People's Deputies on June 9. In the fall of that year, he enumerated its powers and described its structure in greater detail. The center (as the central government would be called) would be in Moscow and would be responsible not only for defense and foreign policy but also for transportation and communication between the republics. There would be a common currency and an all-union military, though the republics could devise their own currency for internal use and create their own armed forces that could be merged, if this became necessary, with those of the center. At their discretion, the republics could devolve additional powers to the center. But each republic would have complete economic independence, with the right to enter into direct economic contacts with other countries. They would also have their own legal and judicial systems, though cases could be appealed to a supreme court of the union; the president of the union, who would be elected by the constituent republics, would have the power to grant pardons and annul sentences considered excessive or unjust. Each republic could have its own language, but Russian would be the language in which interrepublic and center-republic relations would be conducted.[49]

44. Sakharov, "For Peace and Progress," 8.

45. A. Sakharov, "Perestroika: Kto protiv," 14.

46. Andrei Sakharov, "Speech to the Congress of People's Deputies (June 9, 1989)," in *Moscow and Beyond*, 154.

47. Ibid., 154–55; Sakharov, "Stepen' svobody: Aktual'noe interv'iu," 26.

48. Interview with Zora Safir, 3.

49. A. Sakharov and G. Starovoitova, "Proekt platformy mezhregional'noi gruppy narodnykh deputatov SSSR (November–December 1989)," in *Materialy samizdata*, no. 6/90 (November–December 1989), AS 6440: 5–7.

About this edifice of relationships Sakharov envisioned, several observations are appropriate. First, he occasionally described what he was calling for as a confederation.[50] But if by a confederation one means an arrangement of sovereign states that lacks a central authority or government to oversee the tasks these states have decided to share, then he was proposing not a confederation but a federation, albeit one that was very loose, certainly less restrictive than what the Founding Fathers prescribed for the United States. Second, Sakharov's federalism was very different from the version Gorbachev was advocating. While Sakharov's vision involved a devolution of power to smaller political entities, where ultimate political authority resided and whose material and spiritual welfare was the reason the center existed, Gorbachev's aim in granting autonomy to the constituent elements of the Soviet Union was actually to strengthen the center by increasing the Soviet people's allegiance to it. Indeed, Gorbachev hoped that the federalism he finally accepted, in the union treaty of July 1991, would save the Soviet Union, not weaken it.[51] Third, while Gorbachev finally accepted in 1991 a good deal of what Sakharov had advocated in 1989, his acceptance came too late to achieve this objective.[52] By 1991, the kind of federalism Gorbachev was proposing, or more precisely acquiescing in, was no longer sufficient to satisfy many of the national and ethnic minorities, especially those in the Baltics and the Caucasus. The most they were willing to accept—and the Baltics not even that—was a confederation like the Confederation of Independent States that functioned, mostly on paper, after the Soviet Union collapsed on January 1, 1992. Finally, one can argue that if the Soviet Union had to collapse, it would have been better if it had done so as a result of the government's adopting Sakharov's kind of federalism rather than in the way it actually did, in response to a failed coup that only aggravated the social and political antagonisms that had prompted the coup attempt. Sakharov's new union, by contrast, would come about when the institutions and constituencies of the old union consented, as a matter of rational self-interest, to the substitution of the new union for the old.

Sakharov never called explicitly for the destruction of the Soviet Union. But the kind of union he envisioned would have been very different from the one that existed when he died. With its federalism, market economy, democracy, and observance of human rights, it would have been more like the United States than the Soviet Union. This in turn suggests a subtle change in Sakharov's vision of convergence, the closest thing to an idée fixe in his political thought. Convergence for him had always meant the merging of capitalism and socialism—as late as 1987, at the Forum for a Nuclear Free World, Sakharov called it "a rapprochement of the socialist and capitalist systems"—into an amalgam that

---

50. Ibid., 7; Sakharov, "Draft Constitution," 26–27.

51. Sakharov, "Stepen' svobody: Aktual'noe interv'iu," 26; Andrei Sakharov, "The Real Russia," *Observer*, June 25, 1989, 15. The treaty—which, to the detriment of the Communist Party, would have drastically decentralized political power in the Soviet Union—was what prompted party hardliners to stage a coup on August 19, the day before the treaty was to go into effect.

52. Miller, *Mikhail Gorbachev*, 175.

retained, serendipitously, the best qualities of each of them.[53] But in the last years of his life he seemed to alter the ingredients that went into this amalgam, so that when it was finally formed, it would contain more elements drawn from the Western way of organizing society—principally its free market, federalism, and democracy—than from the Soviet way of doing so, the only virtue of which was the cradle-to-grave security it provided. None of this, however, reduced the role perestroika would play in convergence. To Sakharov, the former was a prerequisite of the latter, and thus when Gorbachev seemed to lose his enthusiasm for perestroika, Sakharov feared that convergence had stalled as well.[54] In his opinion, a great deal, perhaps even the survival of the planet, was riding on the fortunes of perestroika. The convergence of which it was a precondition was the only permanent solution to the threat nuclear weapons posed to international peace, especially when they were in the hands of dictators whose very lack of legitimacy caused them to act aggressively in foreign policy. In this respect Sakharov recognized that weapons were the result, not the cause, of international tensions.[55] On several occasions in the late 1980s Sakharov even stated that convergence was necessary to prevent the destruction of civilization.[56] And since perestroika was a prerequisite of convergence, it, too, was necessary to prevent the destruction of civilization. In Sakharov's mind, perestroika and convergence were inextricably linked, and each of them was not only inherently good but an alternative (in the case of convergence the only alternative) to things like nuclear war that were inherently bad. For this reason Sakharov often spoke in the late 1980s of the virtues of perestroika and convergence simultaneously, and in his 1989 election platform, he extolled convergence as "the sole route to the elimination of the threat of the destruction of humanity."[57]

The importance Sakharov ascribed to convergence lay partly in the fact that it was, in his opinion, just one of several possible outcomes of the predicament in which humanity presently found itself. Unfortunately, convergence was not inevitable. In the absence of any metahistorical mechanism like the dialectic to preordain its emergence, its realization depended on individuals' making the right choices. To be sure, Sakharov shared with the communists the confidence that history at some point comes to an end. But in contrast to the communists, he believed that history could easily end in catastrophe, either in the annihilation of all humanity in a nuclear war or in its extinction as a result of the gradual exhaustion of the earth's resources. Equally conceivable was that humanity would continue simply to muddle through, avoiding a nuclear holocaust but also failing, for whatever reason, to achieve convergence. According to Sakharov, there was no single way in which history would end, as there was in

53. Sakharov, *Moscow and Beyond*, 21.
54. Sakharov and Adamovich, "Zhit' na zemle i zhit' dolgo," 176.
55. Sakharov, "Neizbezhnost' perestroiki," 134.
56. Sakharov, *Moscow and Beyond*, 64; Sakharov, "Of Arms and Reforms," 40; Sakharov, "The Breakthrough Must Be Continued and Widened," 2; Sakharov, "For Peace and Progress," 8.
57. "Programma A. D. Sakharova," 7.

Marxism and communism.[58] Nor, despite his concerns about nuclear war and ecological disaster, were there only two ways in which history could end. Instead, the future was indeterminable, with many possible outcomes, perhaps even an infinite number of them, and the one that would actually emerge would reflect the choices people made in their everyday lives, largely ignorant of the larger consequences that followed. Sakharov's obligation was thus to educate people, particularly people like Gorbachev whose actions were especially consequential, about the larger implications of what they were doing. Indeed, this role was entirely consistent with his vision of the humane and socially responsible scientist.

In the last years of his life, Sakharov included ecological catastrophes with nuclear war among the horrors only convergence could prevent. This is how he paired these two threats and the role that convergence would play in eliminating them in an article he wrote in 1989:

> Humanity finds itself in the twentieth century in the unprecedented situation in which there is a real danger of humanity's destroying itself. The result of a major thermonuclear war can only be the ruin of civilization, the suffering of millions, and the social and biological degradation of the lives of those who survive, as well as of the lives of their descendants.... No less threatening is the multifaceted ecological danger: the progressive poisoning of those who live near plants for the intensification of agriculture that emit chemical, electrical, and metallurgical waste products; the destruction of forests; the exhaustion of natural reservoirs; the irreversible violation of the equilibrium in nature between organic and inorganic structures; and worst of all, the disturbance of the human gene pool and that of other species. We may already be on the road to ecological ruin.
>
> But I am convinced that the only conclusive way of avoiding the thermonuclear and ecological ruin of humanity, and of resolving other problems of a global dimension, is through a fundamental and mutual coming together, in which economic, political, and ideological relationships are enveloped, of the global systems of capitalism and socialism. This is, in my conception of things, convergence.[59]

Among the most salient and consequential virtues of convergence was the protection of the environment. In reaching this conclusion, Sakharov was completely consistent with his earlier position in which a Promethean faith in science and technology was tempered by the conviction that considerable care had to be taken in applying them so that nature and the environment were not harmed or destroyed in the process. While science and technology were absolutely essential to the creation of a good society, they were not themselves

58. There is evidence that the Soviet leadership in the late 1980s had adopted a vision of the future closer to Sakharov's than either Sakharov or the Soviet leadership was prepared to admit. The party's ideologist, Vadim Medvedev, stated in September 1988 that while socialism and capitalism would not merge because both systems were part of "the same human civilization," their paths would "cross." Quoted in Sakwa, *Gorbachev and His Reforms*, 323.

59. Andrei Sakharov, "Konvergentsiiu, mirnoe sosushchestvovanie," in *50/50: Opyt slovaria novogo myshleniia* (Moscow, 1989), 14–15.

inherently good. Rather, they were instruments of human will and thus morally neutral—capable of benefiting humanity but also of destroying it.

In keeping with this, Sakharov protested strongly any encroachments on the environment he considered exceptionally harmful. In December 1988, he and three other academicians sent a telegram to Gorbachev and Ryzhkov in which they strongly condemned the construction of the Volga-Chograi Canal. They objected specifically to the increased salinization the canal produced in the Kalmyk region, which would kill off most of the four million osetra sturgeon there. In addition, the canal was an economic boondoggle, its costs far exceeding its benefits.[60] Also in 1988, in the interview he gave at the conclusion of the Pugwash Conference, Sakharov expressed his concern that forests in the Soviet Union were being destroyed for no good reason, and he also bemoaned what he called "the chemicalization" of people's lives.[61] In June 1989 he decried the exposure of cotton growers in Uzbekistan to pesticides that were harmful to humans.[62] Throughout the late 1980s he called on the Soviet leadership to be truthful about ecological disasters like Chernobyl. Thus he was genuinely pleased when, in the spring of 1989, immediately following the rupture of a gas pipeline, the Soviet press reported the incident and Gorbachev acknowledged publicly that the government bore responsibility for it.[63] This was another instance in which the general secretary, in effect, adopted a position for which Sakharov had previously argued, namely, that the calamities technology caused should be reported no less faithfully than its triumphs.

But while Sakharov was obviously concerned about the depredations science and technology could inflict on the environment, the preponderance of his time and energy, in terms of ecology, was spent on disabusing the Soviet people of the delusion that nuclear technology was inherently harmful. He endeavored to demonstrate that nuclear energy, generated peacefully in reactors made safe by placing protective domes over them and by using water rather than graphite as a coolant and a moderator, could be a boon to humanity.[64] The human race, he stated in 1988, needed nuclear energy because chemical fuels were being depleted rapidly, and the cost of using solar, tidal, wind, or geothermal energy was still prohibitive.[65] Indeed, Sakharov included the right to live in an ecologically safe and secure environment among the human rights he cited in the draft constitution he produced in the last months of his life.[66]

At the same time, he characterized the more extreme environmentalism to which many in the 1980s were prone as irrational, even as a form of collective

60. Sakharov, *Moscow and Beyond*, 93–94; "Akademik A. D. Sakharov," 117.

61. Sakharov, "Fifty Percent Is More Than Just Half," 22.

62. Andrei Sakharov, "The Real Russia," 15.

63. Andrei Sakharov, "Vstupitel'noe slovo"; Grigorii Medvedev, "Chernobyl'skaia tetrad'," *Novyi mir* 6 (June 1989): 4; Miller, *Mikhail Gorbachev*, 68.

64. Andrei Sakharov, "We Cannot Do Without Nuclear Power Plants, But…," *World Marxist Review*, February 1, 1990, 22.

65. Ibid., 21.

66. Sakharov, "Draft Constitution," 26.

hysteria.[67] Sakharov considered the principal obstacle to nuclear energy a psychological one. But he also believed that if the case for nuclear energy in general and for underground nuclear reactors in particular (that they were less expensive and less vulnerable to terrorism than surface reactors), were presented cogently, people would see their virtues and support their use.[68] No system, he readily acknowledged, was foolproof. But most of the risks involved in nuclear energy could be minimized by several simple precautions and correctives. In addition to using water as a coolant and moderator, underground reactors could be built with "shades" to contain the release of radioactive material; in the event these precautions failed, the reactors themselves could be shut down, closed up, and, unlike surface reactors, burned.[69] All in all, Sakharov considered the advantages of nuclear energy well worth the risks, and by the late 1980s he was sufficiently convinced that the Soviet people—whatever their failings in other respects—were mature enough and rational enough to recognize this. "People aren't fools" is how he summarized his position in an interview he gave in October 1988.[70]

Sakharov's commitment to democracy followed logically from comments such as this. He expressed this commitment in actions as well as words, participating in what was perhaps the most powerful impetus to democracy in the Gorbachev era—the emergence in the Soviet Union of a civil society. By a civil society one means a society in which there are independent organizations that protect the individual from the state. Obviously the number of organizations that must exist in a society for it to be truly a civil one is arbitrary. But by any reasonable criterion, Soviet society in the late 1980s had become, or was in the process of becoming, a civil society. By 1988, there were some thirty thousand informal political organizations in the Soviet Union, and by early 1989 that number had doubled.[71]

By participating in this process, Sakharov advanced it, and his mere presence in the organizations he joined gave them additional legitimacy. The first organization he participated in was the International Foundation for the Survival and Development of Humanity, which was established by Evgenii Velikhov and the American physicist Jerome Wiesner in 1987. At the suggestion of Wiesner, who was in Moscow for the aforementioned Forum for a Nuclear-Free World, Sakharov agreed not only to join the organization but to serve on its board of directors—this in spite of his long-standing reluctance to risk a repetition of his experience with the Human Rights Committee in the early 1970s. The fact that he assumed administrative responsibilities as a member of the foundation was perhaps a measure of Wiesner's powers of persuasion. But Sakharov's

67. Sakharov and Adamovich, "Zhit' na zemle i zhit' dolgo," 167.

68. Sakharov, "Fifty Percent Is More Than Just Half," 22.

69. Sakharov and Adamovich, "Zhit' na zemle i zhit' dolgo," 164; Andrei Sakharov, "My ne vprave derzhat' narod v strakhe," *Leninskaia smena,* October 30, 1988, 192. Not all scientists agreed with Sakharov on the relative safety of underground nuclear reactors. See von Hippel, "Nashe sotrudnichestvo," 744.

70. Sakharov, "My ne vprave derzhat' narod v strakhe," 192.

71. Petro, *Rebirth of Russian Democracy,* 147.

enthusiasm waned when he realized that the foundation was not as effective in implementing its objectives as he had hoped. While he did not resign from the organization, he gradually scaled back his involvement to the point where, by his own testimony, he was fulfilling his responsibilities only cursorily.[72] In his memoirs he justified his conduct by claiming that he had "neither the strength nor the desire to do more."[73]

Sakharov's experiences in other organizations in the late 1980s were more satisfying. In the summer of 1988, Afanasiev, Len Karpinskii, Iurii Kariakin, and Leonid Batkin approached Sakharov while he and Bonner were on vacation in Protvino to secure his assistance in forming Moscow Tribune, which they envisioned as an "embryonic legal opposition" to counter what they saw as the government's recent backsliding on perestroika and glasnost.[74] What bothered them were recent curbs on public demonstrations and on freedom of the press, the undemocratic procedures under which the recently concluded Nineteenth Party Conference had been conducted, and the increased powers recently accorded to the Ministry of the Interior. Sakharov agreed to join the organization, and although he left most of the day-to-day work to others, he served ably and conscientiously on its organizing committee.[75] Perhaps because its numbers and influence were so small—barely one hundred people belonged to it when it was established formally in October 1988—Sakharov hardly mentions Moscow Tribune in his memoirs other than to say it was "an interesting and important undertaking."[76]

Far more consequential was the group Memorial, which Sakharov joined in the spring of 1988, not long after it had been founded by Lev Ponomarev and several others who believed the pace at which perestroika was proceeding was too slow. How Sakharov became a member of Memorial is revealing. Shortly before the Nineteenth Party Conference in the early summer of 1988, the founders of Memorial conducted an informal poll in Moscow to determine whom they should ask to serve on the organization's governing body. Sakharov was among the top votegetters, and when the founders informed him of this and of what they hoped their organization would accomplish, he readily agreed to become an active member.[77]

The purpose of Memorial, as its name suggests, was to preserve the memory, individually and collectively, of the victims of Stalinism. It would achieve this by establishing archives, a museum, and a library, all of which, by providing a repository for the victims' recollections, would give them a credibility they might otherwise not possess. In addition, a physical monument to the victims, probably in Moscow, would serve to symbolize their horrible fate. But the organization

72. Sakharov, *Moscow and Beyond*, 42–44. Edward Kline, conversation with author, June 10, 2008.
73. Ibid., 44.
74. Ibid., 56.
75. Ibid. 56–57.
76. Ibid., 57; Sakwa, *Gorbachev and His Reforms*, 201.
77. Sakharov, *Moscow and Beyond*, 57–58.

would do more than merely memorialize. For those who were too young to have any recollection of Stalin's crimes, it would inform and instruct and in that way serve as an informal school in which the Soviet people would learn their government's history. Also, Memorial would assist the victims of Stalinism who were still alive, mostly through the distribution of funds its leaders would raise and then deposit in a bank account—a prerogative unavailable to ordinary Soviet citizens before the advent of perestroika.[78]

In response the government tried to co-opt the organization by establishing a commission of its own to foster remembrance, which it believed would be sufficient to prevent a recurrence of Stalinism. It also refused to register Memorial as a legal organization, which would allow it to have its own bank account. In rejecting the group's demand for one, the government argued that since the Ministry of Culture had been entrusted at the Nineteenth Party Conference with the task of setting up a commission to perform the functions Memorial wanted to perform, whatever money Memorial raised rightfully belonged to the Ministry of Culture. Sakharov found this reasoning absurd, and when he met with Alexander Degtiarev, one of Vadim Medvedev's subordinates, to protest the government's obduracy and animus toward Memorial, he told him that the very essence of a public organization like Memorial was its independence; indeed, if the government refused to allow it to register as a public organization, he and the other members would meet anyway in apartments around Moscow.[79] As it happened, Memorial was duly registered only after Sakharov's death, in response to a request Bonner made of Gorbachev personally on the day of Sakharov's funeral.[80] But Sakharov's remonstrances were significant nonetheless. Through his objections, he was not only defending an organization to which he had committed himself but literally instructing the Soviet leadership on the characteristics of a civil society and what a civil society required from the government to function properly.

Memorial was not without its critics. One was Alexander Solzhenitsyn, who from his home in the United States, objected to Memorial's decision, which Sakharov supported, to focus on Stalin's crimes rather than on those of Lenin and Soviet Communism generally. Sakharov shared Solzhenitsyn's abhorrence of the latter. But taking into account the practical reality that not everyone in Memorial agreed with him and that therefore attacking Lenin might cause the government to disband the organization entirely, Sakharov insisted pragmatically that Memorial should limit its attention, at least for a time, to Stalin and Stalinism.[81]

What made Memorial something more than simply a means of instilling remembrance was that it looked forward as well as backward. Its purpose was not just to memorialize crimes already committed but also to prevent crimes that

78. Ibid.; Sakwa, *Gorbachev and His Reforms,* 98.
79. Sakharov, *Moscow and Beyond,* 60–61.
80. Tatiana Yankelevich, conversation with author, January 13, 2004.
81. Sakharov, *Moscow and Beyond,* 58–59.

might otherwise be committed in the future. Indeed, its operative assumption was that only by remembering past crimes could the commission of future ones be prevented. In this respect Memorial was trying to be proactive, and its emphasis on the rule of law and the autonomy of the individual made it the one organization Sakharov joined about which he had no serious qualms either while he was a member or retrospectively.[82] Nowhere in his writings can one find any criticism of it.

In Memorial Sakharov was still acting as a dissident, seeking to influence policy without participating in the process by which policy was made. This would soon change. With his election in the spring of 1989 to the First Congress of People's Deputies, he became a politician. He offered himself as a candidate, formulated a program he would follow if elected, and for two weeks in late May and early June played a prominent role in the inaugural congress of the first institution in Russia since the Constituent Assembly in 1918 that represented, however imperfectly, the wishes and interests of the people as a whole rather than those of the Communist Party. Prior to the congress, Sakharov was a figure familiar to and respected by a small proportion of the educated elite. To the rest of the population he was either unknown or a dim memory from an earlier era. When the congress was over, he was a national figure with mass popularity.[83] The outpouring of grief and adulation that followed Sakharov's death in December 1989 would not have been possible without his nomination, election, and participation in the congress in the winter and spring of that year.

# 24 The Congress of People's Deputies

There were moments of high drama at the First Congress of People's Deputies after it convened in late May 1989. Sakharov was involved in several of them. But the one that captured most poignantly his ambivalent attitude toward both Gorbachev and the program of reform the latter believed would save the Soviet Union occurred on June 9, the last day the congress was in session. The assembled delegates were contemplating a resolution supportive of perestroika. Sakharov thought the resolution did not go far enough. By this time in his political evolution, the perestroika he favored was more radical and should be carried out more rapidly than the version Gorbachev preferred. Never one to remain silent when a matter dear to him was under discussion, Sakharov asked Gorbachev, who was presiding over the proceedings, to give him fifteen minutes

---

82. Anatolii Rybakov, "Memorial," *Literaturnaia gazeta*, August 31, 1988, 2.

83. Archie Brown, who considered the influence the dissidents had on perestroika to be minimal, states nevertheless that at the time of his death, Sakharov was "the most respected upholder of democratic and liberal values in the country." Brown, *Gorbachev Factor*, 8, 10.

to explain why he was voting against the concluding resolution. Gorbachev, however, allowed him only five, and when Sakharov simply kept speaking after his allotted time expired, Gorbachev promptly turned off his microphone so that none of the deputies save those in the first few rows could hear him. But the microphones that the television and radio stations had installed in the chamber were still functioning, and Sakharov's oration in its entirety reached the much larger audience outside the chamber that was watching or listening to the proceedings.[1]

What this incident illustrates is how reformers more radical than Gorbachev caused him to lose control of the congress, so that by the time it concluded, his political authority was arguably less than what it had been when the session began. To the degree to which the conflicts and divisions among the delegates increased as the proceedings unfolded, the congress not only mimicked the collapse of the Soviet Union but contributed to its collapse as well. The question this raises, of course, is why Gorbachev created the congress—for which there was no precedent in the entire history of the Soviet Union—in the first place.

The answer is that Gorbachev realized not long after perestroika began that the Communist Party was an imperfect instrument for reforming the Soviet system. For perestroika to succeed, the party had to relinquish its monopoly of power. But if it did so, Gorbachev would lose whatever chance he had of controlling perestroika, which in the wrong hands could become a mass movement for the abolition of the entire regime. To the end of his tenure as general secretary, Gorbachev considered perestroika a policy implemented by the elite and imposed on the populace from the top down. There was, in sum, a glaring contradiction between how the policy would be implemented and the result it was intended to produce.

In the first three years of perestroika, Gorbachev was oblivious to this contradiction or chose to ignore it. But by the summer of 1988, the reforms he had carried out earlier in the year and in 1987 had so alienated large segments of the Party and the *nomenklatura* that the delegates to the Nineteenth Party Conference in 1988 refused to agree to any additional reforms. This in turn convinced the general secretary to change his strategy: since he could not abolish the Communist Party or force the rescission of its monopoly of power, he would create another institution, one more amenable to reform than the party, that could serve as the vehicle through which perestroika would continue. Instead of confronting the party, he would go around it. In this endeavor Gorbachev had the unwitting assistance of party hard-liners, who, while shrewd in recognizing that perestroika meant a sharp diminution of their power and privileges, seemed clueless about Gorbachev's plan to implement it. Foolishly, the delegates to the party conference, after voting down Gorbachev's proposal to elect party secretaries (including the general secretary) by secret ballot, agreed to Gorbachev's proposal to create a Congress of People's Deputies. A half year later, a special

1. Sakharov, *Moscow and Beyond*, 149–50.

session of the Supreme Soviet amended the constitution to permit the creation of this institution, which would become, upon its convocation, the chief legislative body of the Soviet Union.[2] In Richard Sakwa's formulation, the creation of the Congress of People's Deputies allowed perestroika to progress from a means of liberalizing the Soviet Union, in which the authorities could grant or withdraw reforms as circumstances warranted, to a means of democratizing the country, in which the people, acting through their elected delegates to the congress, could demand reforms as an inalienable right and play a role in the formulation, discussion, and legislation of these reforms.[3] In creating the congress, Gorbachev thought that he could have it both ways: while the Congress might be difficult to control, if he could carefully calibrate the amount of reform it would legislate, he could circumvent the party, which disliked reform, while co-opting the radicals outside the party, who wanted too much reform.

What actually happened once the congress convened showed that Gorbachev had outsmarted himself and that even the most carefully crafted plans in politics have unintended consequences. The forces in Soviet society expressed through the congress seriously undermined the legitimacy of the Soviet system and two years later caused the entire union to collapse.[4] Some 200 million people watched the proceedings of the congress on Soviet television, and it was obviously with this in mind that Bonner once described the congress as the school where the Soviet people learned what was wrong with their country.[5] To the extent that Gorbachev set in motion the train of events that resulted in this, he contributed, albeit unwittingly and unintentionally, to his own downfall.

To ensure that the Communist Party would dominate the congress, the government prescribed procedures for the nomination and election of deputies that were blatantly undemocratic, though not sufficiently so as to preclude popular participation entirely. According to the government commission that devised it, the congress would be comprised of 2,250 deputies—as would the congresses that would follow it on a biannual basis—and it would meet (or so it was anticipated) for roughly two weeks. These deputies would review and, if necessary, amend legislation passed by the Supreme Soviet, a smaller body the congresses would elect that would meet when they were not in session. This Supreme Soviet (which would replace the Supreme Soviet in the Soviet government that already existed) would have a chairman, who would be elected by the congress, and a vice chairman, who would be selected by the chairman; the soviet itself would consist of 542 delegates serving staggered five-year terms.[6] Because the

2. Sakharov, *Moscow and Beyond*, 79, 96; Leon Aron, *Yeltsin: A Revolutionary Life* (New York, 2000), 230.

3. Sakwa, *Gorbachev and His Reforms*, 196.

4. In one deputy's opinion, the congress led to "the demystification" of the Soviet government's power. Quoted in "Z" [Malia], "To the Stalin Mausoleum," 327.

5. Aron, *Yeltsin*, 299; Bonner cited in David Holloway, "The Expanding Agenda: Democracy and Human Rights" (conference on "A. D. Sakharov: His Legacy Ten Years Later," Stanford University, Stanford, Calif., December 10, 1999), 7.

6. Sakwa, *Gorbachev and His Reforms*, 134, 144; David Lane, *Soviet Society under Perestroika* (London, 1992), 63.

soviet was smaller and would meet more frequently than the congresses—by law it would be in session for forty weeks annually—it would legislate on behalf of the congresses and, by extension, on behalf of the Soviet people.[7]

Competitive elections would be held for only two-thirds of the seats in the congress. The 750 deputies for which there were no competitive elections would be selected by organizations such as the Komsomol, the Academy of Sciences, various artistic and literary institutions, and the Communist Party. These organizations, if they wished, could stage their own competitive elections, with candidates limited to their membership. But they also had the option of simply selecting a slate of deputies equal to the number that was prescribed for them. Gorbachev, who feared that in competitive elections party members who favored perestroika would lose to those opposed to it, made sure that only one hundred candidates (almost all of them supporters of perestroika) were nominated for the hundred seats the Communist Party was guaranteed.[8] Of the remaining fifteen hundred delegates, half of these would be elected from territorial districts roughly equal in population and the other half by the various union republics, autonomous republics, autonomous regions, and autonomous districts.[9]

The process by which individuals were chosen to run in districts that were determined territorially had two stages to it. A candidate first had to be nominated at a public meeting of no fewer than 500 people, half of whom had to approve the nomination before it could proceed to the next stage in the process, a second public meeting, at which the identical requirements applied. But registration committees packed with party activists vetted the candidates that were nominated and had considerable influence in some instances over who was admitted to the public meetings at which the nominations were entered and considered.[10] When the actual elections to the congress were held on March 26, 1989, 2,901 candidates competed for the 1,500 seats to be filled by popular election. Three hundred eighty-five of these seats had only one candidate nominated to fill them; 953 had two candidates, and 162 had three or more. In those districts in which a candidate failed to win the 50 percent of the vote needed for election, a runoff was to be held a short time later between the two candidates who received the most votes in the initial balloting. If a candidate failed to win 50 percent of the vote even with no opposition (because a majority of voters had crossed out his name or left the ballot unmarked), the candidate was considered defeated and a new election was held to fill the seat. Although over 80 percent of the deputies who were elected were Communists and party members, most of these favored perestroika. But 20 percent of the Communist Party candidates lost, including thirty-four who, with no opposition, failed to receive the requisite 50 percent of the vote. Voter turnout was high—in Moscow 83.5 percent of the eligible voters cast ballots—and the Communist Party did

7. McCauley, *Gorbachev*, 109.
8. Ibid., 105.
9. Sakharov, *Moscow and Beyond*, 96.
10. Sakwa, *Gorbachev and His Reforms*, 135; Aron, *Yeltsin*, 255.

worst in precisely those parts of the country, namely, the cities, where turnout was highest.[11]

Sakharov himself declared his candidacy in January 1989 after refusing several pleas in the summer and fall of 1988 that he serve on the Supreme Soviet of the government.[12] The reason he changed his mind was that he realized that the congress, unlike the Supreme Soviet, might function independently of the Communist Party; even if it did not, it would still provide a forum from which he could publicize his own objectives. But there remained the practical matter of his nomination and election. In this he had several options. Perhaps the easiest one was to be elected (or selected) by the Academy of Sciences, which was allotted thirty seats in the congress. Absent in the regulations allotting seats to organizations like the academy was any directive prescribing how exactly these organizations were to choose their deputies. Another possibility was to run in one of the territorial districts. This option conformed more closely to Sakharov's democratic inclinations, and it also had the advantage of conferring on him, in the event he won, greater legitimacy as a spokesman for the Soviet people than if he were elected or selected solely by the academy.

Sakharov, perhaps unwisely, allowed his name to be put in nomination for one of the seats allotted to the academy. Because the academy had determined that five of these seats would be filled by scientific societies affiliated with it, only twenty-five of the original thirty seats reserved for the academy would be contested. At the meeting on January 18 at which the twenty-five nominees were to be selected, Sakharov, who had been nominated by over fifty scientific institutes, failed to receive the required majority of votes from those comprising the so-called plenum—which consisted of the members of the presidium of the academy and the governing boards of its eighteen separate departments—that the academy had created to vote on the nominations it received.[13] Because the number of nominations (twenty-three) was less than the number of seats (twenty-five) it could fill, the academy allotted five more seats to the scientific societies affiliated with it, leaving twenty seats to be contested by the twenty-three candidates, one of whom was Sakharov.

Many of Sakharov's supporters in the academy, as well as other scientists not committed to his candidacy, disliked the way the academy had reduced the number of seats that could be contested. Sakharov, too, thought its actions unseemly, and he considered running instead in a territorial district in Moscow. In fact, he was nominated in five separate districts in the city and in Arzamas, Kamchatka, the Kola peninsula east of Finland, and one district in Leningrad. In one of the Moscow districts where he was nominated, twenty-five thousand Muscovites crammed into the Dom Kino, the headquarters of the Cinematographers'

---

11. McCauley, *Gorbachev*, 106–7; Sakwa, *Gorbachev and His Reforms*, 136–38, 140–41.

12. Sakharov, *Moscow and Beyond*, 96.

13. Ibid., 96–98; Brown *Gorbachev Factor*, 189; Robert G. Kaiser, *Why Gorbachev Happened: His Triumphs and His Failure* (New York, 1991), 270–71; "Chei Kandidat Sakharov?" *Komsomol'skaia Pravda*, January 27, 1989, 2.

Union, to see his nomination approved by a vote of 947–0.[14] At this point, Boris Yeltsin, who had been nominated in the same Moscow district in which Sakharov's nomination was approved unanimously, offered his support if Sakharov agreed to run somewhere else. To this quid pro quo Sakharov, perhaps surprisingly, agreed. But a short time later, when Bonner objected that what Yeltsin had proposed, while not morally wrong, would have the effect of harming the human rights movement in the Soviet Union, Sakharov changed his mind.[15] He decided not to run in any territorial district at all. Instead, he would refocus his attention on the academy, hoping that if he could win the nomination again, this time its plenum would approve it. His stated reason was his desire to reinvigorate the academy and his belief that he could do this most credibly and effectively if he represented the organization at the congress.[16] On February 4 Sakharov issued a statement making public his intentions, and in the weeks that followed he did what he could to win support in the academy, which scheduled a meeting to select its remaining nominees on March 18.

On that day, only eight of the twenty-three candidates who had survived the first round of balloting in January received the requisite majority approval, leaving twelve of the twenty seats at issue still unfilled. New elections, open to anyone, were therefore scheduled for April 13. Once again—for the third time—Sakharov was nominated. This time, however, his nomination was supported by nearly all of the more than two hundred organizations affiliated with the academy. This support had the effect of neutralizing the opposition to Sakharov's candidacy among many of those on the plenum, including the academy president, Guri Marchuk (who had gone to Gorky in December 1986 to negotiate the terms of Sakharov's return to Moscow). Coupled with a public demonstration on Sakharov's behalf by several thousand scientific workers outside the academy's headquarters on the Leninskii Prospekt, this support convinced the plenum to approve Sakharov's nomination.[17] On April 14 the actual balloting took place, and since approval of his nomination was tantamount to election, he was effectively elected to the congress on that day.[18]

In the nearly six weeks between his election to the congress on April 14 and its convocation on May 25, Sakharov campaigned on behalf of his platform with a facility quite remarkable when one remembers that very little in his previous roles as physicist and dissident had prepared him for it. In May he spoke at enormous

14. "Chei Kandidat Sakharov?" 2; Arkadii Murashev, "Mezhregional'naia deputskaia," *Ogonëk*, August 4–11, 1990, 6.

15. Sakharov, *Moscow and Beyond*, 99; Bonner, "Chetyre daty," 178.

16. Pimenov, "Kakim on byl," 219. Sakharov's arrangement with Yeltsin had no practical implications in light of his subsequent decision to run only for a seat reserved for the academy. Still, he regretted it. Sakharov, *Moscow and Beyond*, 99.

17. Sakharov, *Moscow and Beyond*, 105; Kaiser, *Why Gorbachev Happened*, 271; Graham, *Science in Russia and the Soviet Union*, 189.

18. Sakharov, *Moscow and Beyond*, 107. Among the candidates of the Academy of Sciences whose nominations were approved when Sakharov's was were his fellow physicist Roald Sagdeev and the economist Nikolai Shmelev. Both were politically close to Sakharov and the other delegates to the congress professing liberal and semiradical views. Brown, *Gorbachev Factor*, 189.

rallies in Luzhniki, the stadium and sports complex in Moscow, organized by Moscow Tribune. At one of these rallies, he rehearsed, before two hundred thousand spectators, the themes he planned to stress at the congress itself.[19] In May he also traveled to Syktyvar, the capital of the Komi Autonomous Republic, to campaign for Revolt Pimenov, who was in a runoff election for a seat in the congress. After endorsing Pimenov's candidacy, Sakharov taped a statement on his behalf that was broadcast on Soviet television and also advocated his election at several public meetings. Before the congress convened, Sakharov was also elected by his fellow deputies-to-be to a smaller caucus that would prepare a proposed agenda for the congress to follow. As it turned out, the Soviet government preempted the caucus, which never met, and imposed its own agenda on the congress. Significantly, its first order of business, after the Supreme Soviet of the congress had been elected, was the election of the soviet's chairman.[20]

Sakharov's platform was an intriguing mixture of idealism and pragmatism. Substantively, he pledged himself to the transformation of the Soviet Union into what was essentially a Western state.[21] The Soviet Union, he said, should be "a just state," based on the rule of law and a firm commitment to peace and progress, providing the goods and services, such as comprehensive medical care, that in the West were characteristic of the welfare state.[22] To achieve "social and national justice," perestroika should be "widened and deepened" through the instrument of glasnost, which he said should be extended to include the opening of state and party archives, the establishment of a permanent commission to oversee the KGB, and a thoroughgoing reform of Soviet prisons.[23] But Sakharov recognized the futility of calling for reforms to which the Soviet government could not agree: he called merely for multicandidate rather than multiparty elections and underscored his willingness to work with the government by describing as "Leninist" the union of equal states he wanted the Soviet Union to become.[24] Even if the last was only a rhetorical device to win support from those who might otherwise reject the reforms he was proposing, his invocation of Lenin was a clever gambit. By disguising the transformation of the Soviet Union as a restoration of arrangements that its founder had sanctioned, Sakharov was signaling the Soviet people that he was not a wild-eyed radical and that the Soviet leadership could negotiate with him seriously and on the basis of a convergence of interests. It is extremely unlikely that Sakharov, in 1989, truly believed there was anything in Leninism worth preserving or resurrecting. Rather, his reference to Lenin reveals his political acumen, specifically his willingness and ability to soften the sharp edges of his proposals in a way that served his own interests effectively.

This did not mean, however, that when the congress convened on May 25, Sakharov allowed his ultimate objectives to be vitiated by the imperfections of the institution in which he was now a participant. Several of his supporters were

19. Ibid., 116.
20. Ibid., 114.
21. Aron, *Yeltsin*, 264.
22. "Programma A. D. Sakharova," 6.
23. Ibid.
24. Ibid.

fearful, before he ran for election, that that would happen.[25] Their fears turned out to be groundless. Sakharov, far from repudiating his ideals and objectives, reiterated them at the congress with an eloquence and consistency that seemed to embolden him to view the congress itself as a potential vehicle for the radical transformation of Soviet society. In this respect Sakharov, in the spring of 1989, was like Mirabeau and others in the Estates-General in France exactly two hundred years earlier who had tried to change that institution into a genuine national assembly representing the entire French nation and responsive to the wishes of the French people as a whole. What caused Sakharov to want the Congress to undergo a similar transformation was his suspicion that Gorbachev intended the congress as an instrument for enhancing his personal power, principally through his election pro forma as the chairman of the Supreme Soviet.[26] But Sakharov shrewdly recognized that he could use the congress for his own purposes, as a platform from which to speak to and for the Soviet people as a whole. This in fact is what he did. Televising the proceedings of the congress afforded prominent and outspoken deputies the opportunity to engage in political consciousness raising on a scale unimaginable just a few years earlier.[27] In his memoirs Sakharov writes approvingly of how the congress performed the pedagogical function he envisioned for it:

> The twelve days of the Congress completely demolished the illusions that had lulled everyone in our country and the rest of the world to sleep. Speeches by people from the four corners of the country, from both left and right, painted a merciless picture of what life is really like in our society—the impression in the minds of millions of people transcended anyone's personal experience, however tragic it might be, as well as the cumulative efforts of newspapers, television, literature, movies, and the other mass media in all the years of glasnost.... The Congress burned all bridges behind us. It became clear to everyone that we must go forward or we will be destroyed.[28]

Given Sakharov's objectives, Boris Yeltsin's criticism that the congress could not transform the moral authority it had into political power and Jack Matlock's that it was too large and unwieldy to legislate effectively seem largely irrelevant.[29] Despite his shyness and reserve, Sakharov welcomed the coverage the congress received and benefited from it politically.[30]

He spoke to the congress on the day it convened. In his speech, he stated clearly and unambiguously that it should act primarily as a legislature. He said

25. A. E. Shabad, "Sakharova—V deputaty," in Ivanova, *Andrei Dmitrievich*, 111–12.

26. Interview with Zora Safir, 1–2.

27. In addition to the television coverage the congress received, newspapers across the country reported on its proceedings, and *Pravda* and *Izvestiia* provided transcripts of them. To be sure, *Izvestiia* edited the transcripts it printed, with the result that some of what Sakharov said at the congress, including the last portion of his oration on the last day of the proceedings, was omitted. Sakharov, *Moscow and Beyond*, 150.

28. Ibid., 120.

29. Miller, *Mikhail Gorbachev*, 118–19; Aron, *Yeltsin*, 303; Jack Matlock, *Autopsy of an Empire: The American Ambassador's Account of the Collapse of the Soviet Union* (New York, 1995) 205–6.

30. "Obshchestvennoe mnenie o narodnykh deputatakh," 1.

that he favored the adoption of a resolution stating that the congress had "the exclusive right to adopt laws for the USSR, and to appoint people to the highest posts of the USSR, including the Chairman of the Council of Ministers, the Chairman of the Committee of People's Control, the Chairman of the Supreme Court, the Procurator General, and the Chief Arbiter of the USSR"; toward this end, the Soviet Constitution should be amended accordingly.[31] He stressed that the congress should not be a "rubber stamp" for the Communist Party, the Supreme Soviet, or the chairman of the Supreme Soviet, whoever that might be.[32] If it were, then whatever democracy existed in the Soviet Union was a bogus democracy, a sham and smoke screen for the small elite still running the country. For this reason it was essential that the election of the chairman be deliberative rather than hasty, and he implored the deputies to delay so that Gorbachev and any others who might seek the position could present themselves and their credentials for the deputies' consideration. To Sakharov, the election of the chairman had profound symbolic as well as substantive importance: it was nothing less than a test of the government's commitment to perestroika and of its willingness to allow the Soviet people, through the agency of the congress, a role in implementing it.

Gorbachev, however, would have none of this. As if to demonstrate that the authoritarianism Sakharov rejected still prevailed, he interrupted Sakharov and told him to hurry and finish his remarks. Both in this particular instance and in many others in which the two men crossed swords publicly, one senses that Gorbachev was as irritated by Sakharov's impudence in challenging him as he was flustered by the substantive arguments Sakharov presented. In this case, Sakharov was concerned that by electing the chairman too quickly, without proper consideration, the congress would effectively be yielding power to the person who held the position, with the result that it would be reduced to "a congress of voters" and nothing more.[33] But Gorbachev had the support he needed and was elected to the position immediately (though not unanimously, because eighty-seven deputies left their ballots blank or crossed out his name). To show his disdain for the entire procedure, Sakharov got up from his seat after the balloting began and with everyone in the congress watching him, walked out of the chamber.[34] The next day, when Gorbachev asked him why he had left, Sakharov replied that the Soviet Union had had "seventy years of elections without alternative candidates" and did not need any more of them.[35]

Sakharov spoke to his fellow deputies twelve times while the congress was in session and gave interviews to newspapers and journals. In that way he contributed mightily to the educational task the congress performed of illuminating

31. Sakharov, *Moscow and Beyond*, 118; "S"ezd narodnykh deputatov SSSR," *Izvestiia*, May 26, 1989, 4.

32. Sakharov used the term in his interview with Iurii Rost a few weeks later to describe what he feared the congress would become in relation to the Supreme Soviet. Sakharov, "S"ezd ne mozhet sdelat' vse srazu...," 11.

33. Sakharov, *Moscow and Beyond*, 118.

34. Ibid., 122.

35. Bonner, "On Gorbachev," 17.

many of the problems, deficiencies, and inadequacies of the Soviet system that for decades the government had largely succeeded in concealing. Of course not everyone at the congress considered this socially useful, and when Sakharov was the one who was exposing the country's problems, the reaction was especially fierce. What particularly enraged his critics was an interview he had given while in Canada three months earlier in which he condemned the war in Afghanistan very harshly and accused Soviet helicopter pilots of shooting Soviet soldiers on the ground to prevent them from being taken prisoner.[36] On June 2, Sergei Chervonopiskii, a Komsomol secretary who had lost both legs in combat in Afghanistan, read out at the congress a petition signed by Soviet paratroopers denouncing Sakharov and denying his charges. At the end of his diatribe Chervonopiskii extolled the virtues of "state power, our motherland, and Communism"; the clear implication was that Sakharov, by impugning the Soviet armed forces, was a traitor.[37] When Chervonopiskii was finished, other delegates followed his example and denounced Sakharov in what the latter believed was an organized and prearranged campaign to discredit him, different only in intensity and duration from previous campaigns in 1973 and 1980. One of his attackers, a high school teacher from Gazalkent in Uzbekistan, condemned him for insulting "the whole army, the whole people, [and] all those who died."[38] To Anatolii Sobchak, the future mayor of St. Petersburg, who was present in the hall when Sakharov was attacked, the assaults on his character were reminiscent of "the spirit of 1937"—a clear reference to Stalin's Terror—and proved that "the instincts of Stalinism" were still powerful in Soviet politics.[39]

Sakharov was not intimidated by these attacks on his integrity and patriotism. If anything, they emboldened him to escalate his criticisms of the war. He immediately denied the charge that he had impugned the Soviet military and two days later, on June 4, called the invasion and occupation of Afghanistan "a criminal adventure" and "a crime of the Fatherland" for the perpetration of which the Soviet government must be held accountable.[40] Still, the attacks showed Sakharov how powerful were the forces in Soviet society opposing perestroika and how easily Gorbachev could become the captive of them. Accordingly, on the last day of the congress, June 9, he sought to persuade not only the assembled deputies but also Gorbachev himself of the absolute necessity of continuing perestroika. In their concluding resolution, "The Basic Directions of Domestic and Foreign Policy of the USSR," the delegates expressed support for perestroika. The resolution called for improvements in social entitlements, such as raising the level of pensions to that of the minimum wage; guaranteeing civil liberties and due process in the administration of justice; harmonious

36. Sobchak, *Khozhdenie vo vlast'*, 42–43.
37. Quoted in Sakharov, *Moscow and Beyond*, 134.
38. Quoted ibid., 135.
39. Sobchak, *Khozhdenie vo vlast'*, 48.
40. "S"ezd narodnykh deputatov SSSR," *Pravda*, June 5, 1989, 3.

relations between the various republics within a larger framework that was consistent with "Leninist principles of federation"; and the assignment of political power to the Soviet people, who would exercise it through subsequent sessions of the congress.[41] But to Sakharov, these commitments, while welcome, were not sufficient. He asked Gorbachev, who was presiding, to give him fifteen minutes to explain why he was voting against the concluding resolution. What followed was the incident described in the beginning of this chapter.

Sakharov began his remarks by warning ominously of the dangers of concentrating so much power in the presidency of the Supreme Soviet. Indeed, the very manner in which Gorbachev had assumed the position, in a bogus election in which he faced no competition, was evidence enough of how easily this power could be abused in the future. As the ultimate cause of this, Sakharov pointed directly to Article 6 of the Soviet Constitution, which sanctified the Communist Party as "the leading and guiding force of Soviet society."[42] Thus, to avoid similar abuses in the future, Article 6 should be abolished.[43] In addition, Sakharov proposed limiting the KGB's jurisdiction to "international security" (so that, like the American CIA, it would be barred by law from involvement in purely domestic affairs). He then reiterated his earlier recommendation that the congress retain "the exclusive right to elect and recall the top officials of the USSR."[44] After a *tour d'horizon* touching on foreign policy, the nationalities, the military, and the need for a resolution committing the country and the government to the rule of law, Sakharov concluded with a plea for genuinely autonomous soviets to replace the Communist Party as the principal political institution in the country.[45] In a final rhetorical flourish, he ironically repeated the Leninist slogan from 1917, "All Power to the Soviets," as a way of indicating that the soviets he advocated, unlike Lenin's, would be an instrument of democracy and humane values.[46] The irony in Sakharov's invocation of this slogan was not lost on Gorbachev and the other deputies to whom it was directed. Nor could they have been oblivious to what Sakharov had just done—namely, advanced the goal posts beyond where they had been before he began speaking and beyond where Gorbachev, absent any pressure from Sakharov, was willing to go. By taunting the general secretary the way he did—and invoking Lenin's slogan was surely a taunt—Sakharov was trying to force him to exceed the limits of reform he had previously established and accept Sakharov's agenda instead. Finally, to underscore his dissatisfaction with what the congress had done (or more precisely, had failed to do), Sakharov remained seated when the other deputies stood at attention for the playing of the "Hymn to the Soviet Union," which formally ended the congress.[47]

41. Sakharov, *Moscow and Beyond*, 145–46.
42. *Constitution (Fundamental Law) of the Union of Soviet Socialist Republics* (Moscow, 1977), 21.
43. Sakharov, *Moscow and Beyond*, 152.
44. Ibid., 152–53.
45. Ibid., 153–56.
46. Ibid., 156.
47. Ginzburg, "O fenomene Sakharova," 248. On the basis of what Sakharov supposedly told him, Ginzburg also claims that he refused to stand because he did not like the hymn as a piece of music. Given Sakharov's character and his behavior at the congress prior to this incident, this is unlikely. Sakharov did not do things so dramatic and fraught with symbolism for a trivial reason.

## The Interregional Group and the Draft Constitution

Whatever its deficiencies, the congress greatly accelerated the emergence of a civil society in the Soviet Union. One of the organizations it inspired was the Interregional Group of People's Deputies (IRG). This organization, which was formed in the last days of the congress, initially consisted of 388 deputies. They met in the evenings at the Moskva Hotel.[48] At the meeting on July 29–30, 1989, at which the IRG was formally established, Sakharov, who had attended earlier meetings when the congress was still in session, was elected one of five cochairs; the others were Yeltsin, Afanasiev, Popov, and Viktor Palm, who, as an Estonian, represented the three Baltic republics in the organization.[49] Sakharov remained an active member of the group until his death.[50] In that capacity, he contributed to the creation of a civil society in the same way he did as a member of Moscow Tribune and Memorial—not merely by advocating a civil society but by participating in an organization whose very existence was proof that such a society was in the process of emerging.

The IRG took positions on issues it considered essential to the reform of the country. It favored a multiparty system, a free market, civil and legal rights, and private property, and it sponsored discussions and generated position papers on these and other issues. As its agenda suggests, the organization existed both to inform and to advocate.[51] But its principal purpose was to serve as a political pressure group, forcing Gorbachev and the political leadership of the country to the left so that perestroika would be enlarged to the point at which the Soviet Union would become, for all intents and purposes, a social democracy. Although its members did not consider it a political party, in practice the IRG did almost everything a political party in a democracy does.[52] The only reason its leaders refrained from calling it a political party was that parties other than the Communist Party were in practice, if not formally, prohibited in the Soviet Union; for that reason the government refused to allow the group to publish a newspaper or to set up its own bank account.[53] Under the circumstances, the decision not to call the IRG a party or to endow it with the accoutrements of a party was wise.

By the time the second congress convened, the objective of the IRG was not to pressure it the way it did the first congress, cajoling its deputies to contemplate changes they might not otherwise consider, but to undermine it. In the view of the IRG, neither the congress nor the general secretary was any longer a viable instrument of reform; rather, both intended, or were powerless to prevent,

48. Aron, *Yeltsin*, 311; Sakharov, *Moscow and Beyond*, 147.

49. Michael Urban, *The Rebirth of Politics in Russia* (New York, 1997), 162. Although Sakharov was in the United States when the meeting was held, he was elected a cochairman anyway, finishing fifth among the thirteen persons nominated for the five cochairmanships. Yeltsin received the most votes. Aron, *Yeltsin*, 312; Interv'iu A. D. Sakharova parizhskoi gazetoi "Mond," September 1989, reprinted in Skonechnaia and Tsypkina, *Sakharov: Takim on byl*, 72.

50. Sakharov, *Moscow and Beyond*, 147.

51. Ibid., xii; McCauley, *Gorbachev*, 153.

52. Urban, *Rebirth of Politics*, 162.

53. McCauley, *Gorbachev*, 111; Interviu A. D. Saharova parizhskoi gazette "Mond," 72–73.

counterreform and repression—a perception that prompted Gorbachev to charge that the organization was nothing more than a "gangster group" bent on undermining his leadership.[54] Despite such rhetoric—or possibly because of it—Sakharov wanted the members of the IRG who served in the congress to proclaim themselves the parliamentary opposition even though the group commanded the allegiance of only 229 of the 2,250 deputies.[55]

For Sakharov the IRG was exactly the right instrument for pressuring Gorbachev: a loose organization without bylaws, a single chairman, or a binding program, with power exercised by individuals elected democratically. Indeed, in its lack of centralized leadership, the IRG was a microcosm of the loose federalism Sakharov thought should characterize the Soviet Union of the future. But as the fate of perestroika and reform became even more precarious in the fall of 1989, Sakharov pragmatically revised his position. Despite its diminished numbers—or perhaps because with fewer members it could act cohesively and purposefully on behalf of specific objectives—he called upon the IRG to act as a genuine faction, deliberately pressing for the adoption of the program to which he and Galina Starovoitova had contributed.[56] Sakharov held a long-standing aversion to organizations even remotely resembling in their structure the "democratic centralism" Lenin had prescribed for the Communist Party. The fact that Sakharov, in the last weeks of his life, thought a structured organization necessary to achieve his objectives and those of the IRG shows how little confidence he had in Gorbachev to continue perestroika.

Ironically, much of Sakharov's time in November and early December 1989 was taken up by a task he had agreed to undertake at the request of Gorbachev himself. This was the drafting of a new constitution to replace the so-called Brezhnev Constitution of 1977, which Gorbachev rightly thought did not reflect the new realities of perestroika and glasnost. In the spring of 1989 the Soviet government created a commission to draft this new constitution. The list of proposed members shows that the commission was stacked: Gorbachev would serve as its chairman, and every member was also a member of the Communist Party. Not surprisingly, some in the congress thought the whole project a hoax, but when Sagdeev nominated Sakharov from the floor because he thought that at least one of the commission's members should not be from the party, Sakharov, rather than reject the nomination, agreed to serve on the condition (as he told Gorbachev from the speaker's rostrum) that he "have the right to propose alternative formulations and principles, and to take issue with recommendations that I oppose."[57] Gorbachev, probably calculating that with Sakharov on the commission he could effectively co-opt him and thereby neutralize his political

54. Urban, *Rebirth of Politics,* 163; Hedrick Smith, *The New Russians* (New York, 1990), 503.

55. "O narodnom deputate A. D. Sakharove rasskazyvaet narodnyi deputat Galina Starovoitova," 66. It bears mention that more than twice as many deputies (561) belonged to Soiuz, a nationalist organization opposed to perestroika. Kaiser, *Why Gorbachev Happened,* 381.

56. A. Sakharov and G. Starovoitova, "Proekt platformy mezhdregional'noi gruppy," 5–7. Their contribution concerned the relationship between the nationalities and the center.

57. Sakharov, *Moscow and Beyond,* 129–30.

opposition, agreed immediately to his demand and declared him a member of the commission before the deputies could vote on his nomination. In the end, Sakharov, Yeltsin, and seventeen first secretaries of regional party organizations comprised the commission.[58] Almost certainly Sakharov knew when he accepted Sagdeev's nomination that he would find little support for any changes he might recommend to the draft constitution. But the concessions he won from Gorbachev ensured that he could offer his own draft if he wished, which he could use pedagogically to point out the deficiencies in the one the commission had written.

At the time of his death, Sakharov was still revising his draft. But even in its unfinished form it stands as a summa of everything he believed after the end of his exile. Lofty in its rhetoric, far-reaching in its objectives, and enamored of universal principles, Sakharov's constitution was also quite detailed in the institutional arrangements it prescribed. For example, it called for a bicameral legislature and a president elected directly for a five-year term. In addition, it recommended a mixed economy in which privately owned enterprises would compete with state-owned ones—somewhat like the NEP but with the former eventually outproducing the latter. In keeping with the federalism Sakharov preferred, the Soviet Union would have a different name—the Union of Soviet Republics of Europe and Asia—and the administration in Moscow that would oversee the union would be responsible only for foreign policy, defense, and interrepublic communications. The union would also be strictly voluntary, and the existing republics and autonomous regions of the Soviet Union would be free not to join it. The only limitation on the autonomy of the republics and regions choosing to join the new union was a purely practical one: in the interest of ensuring an orderly transition to the new arrangements, the current borders would be inviolable for a ten-year period.[59]

To the inhabitants of the new union, the constitution guaranteed that no one would live in poverty and that medical care and education would be both adequate and universal. In foreign policy, the union would strive to achieve convergence, and in the interest of peace it would promise "no first use" of nuclear weapons. All international covenants the Soviet Union signed, as well as those the new union signed, would have the force of law within the new union regardless of who was elected to its various offices. In addition, Sakharov described in his draft the scenario he hoped would follow the establishment of the union: the capitalist and socialist sectors of the world would gradually merge by adopting similar and ultimately identical policies, and a single world government would eventually appear that would exercise its authority benignly, humanely, and democratically.[60] In its claim to contain a set of principles under which all humanity would live peacefully and happily, Sakharov's constitution

---

58. Ibid., 130; Sakwa, *Gorbachev and his Reforms*, 130.
59. Sakharov, *Moscow and Beyond*, xiii–xiv; Sakharov, "Draft Constitution," 26–27.
60. Sakharov, "Draft Constitution," 26.

was distinctive and in the history of constitutions, both proposed and adopted, quite possibly unique.

Anatolii Sobchak remarked that it was the only constitution he knew of that listed the spiritual contentment of the people among its objectives.[61] The second and third articles explicitly provide that "the aim of the people of the Union of Soviet Republics of Europe and Asia and its government bodies is to ensure a happy and meaningful life, material and spiritual freedom, welfare, peace and security for all citizens of the country and for all inhabitants of the planet irrespective of their race or nationality, sex, age or social status.... The development of the European-Asian Union is grounded in the moral and cultural traditions of Europe and Asia and of the whole of mankind, all races and nations."[62]

To achieve these objectives, the government that oversaw this new union would pursue a liberal agenda: everyone in each of the republics and autonomous regions that comprised the union had "the right to life, freedom, and happiness," and was obliged in return to respect "the social, economic, and civil rights of the individual."[63] Everyone possessed freedom of movement (no small thing to Sakharov), and no one could be confined in a psychiatric hospital without a good reason. The death penalty was forbidden everywhere in the union, there were no secret police forces ostensibly protecting what Sakharov called "public and state order," and both pluralism and tolerance had the status of constitutional principles.[64] What is most remarkable about Sakharov's constitution, particularly when one considers it from the perspective of his many years as a dissident, is the apparent ease with which he was able to give concrete expression to the lofty moral principles in which he believed. By translating abstract ideals into specific and detailed institutional arrangements that would preserve and protect these ideals, Sakharov was doing something no other dissident had ever done. The emphasis in his constitution, despite a few lapses (such as the rote applicability of international law regardless of its content), was on practicality. Although there were several aspects of these arrangements, mostly having to do with procedure (such as the precise order in which elections to the various government offices would be held, and how disputes between the two chambers of the legislature would be resolved), about which Sakharov was silent, the document he produced, even in its unfinished form, stands as a monument to his successful transition from a lonely dissident issuing moral anathemas against the Soviet government into an active participant in the more prosaic, but also more consequential, task of devising new institutions for this same government that were as practical and effective as they were ethical and humane.[65] By the very act of drafting a constitution, Sakharov seemed to be suggesting that moral exhortations alone were not enough to create a just society.

61. Sobchak, *Khozhdenie vo vlast'*, 139.
62. Sakharov, "Draft Constitution," 26.
63. Ibid.
64. Ibid.
65. Ioirysh, *Uroki A. D. Sakharova*, 61.

## Last Days

In addition to writing and revising his constitution, Sakharov devoted his attention in the last weeks of his life to the abolition of Article 6, which still had the force of law under the old constitution. The first time Sakharov called for its abolition publicly was in his concluding oration to the first congress in June.[66] By the fall it seemed clear to him that the Communist Party's primary concern was to perpetuate itself and its leaders, who had lost interest in serving the people they claimed to represent. Thus, instead of trying to reform the party or to circumvent it (which is what Gorbachev had tried to do), critics should foster alternatives to it. While Sakharov did not live long enough to participate in the creation of a new political party (apart from advocating, in the last speech he delivered, that the IRG become the practical equivalent of a party), he did consider the Communist Party and Article 6 the principal obstacles to the continuation of perestroika. Conversely, he saw the abolition of this particular article as precisely that to which Gorbachev would have to agree if his stated commitment to perestroika were to be taken seriously.[67] In Sakharov's words, "the Party should not have any particular constitutional privileges that would put it in a preferential position in regard to other social groups."[68] A few days after the interview in which he made this observation, Sakharov joined Popov, Afanasiev, Tikhonov, and Murashev in proclaiming publicly that "the abrogation of Article 6 would deliver a blow to the partocracy, a blow of immense strength. It would have tremendous political significance: for perestroika in the first place, for us to believe that perestroika is irreversible."[69] At the same time, Sakharov was careful not to call for the abolition of the Communist Party, much less the dismantling or destruction of the Soviet Union.

While none of Sakharov's allies was enamored of Article 6, a few of them considered his campaign to eliminate it tactically unwise. Sobchak thought Sakharov was "too far out in front" on the issue, advocating something that the Second Congress, scheduled to convene on December 12, would be disinclined even to consider. Indeed, when Sakharov (who was a deputy in the congress by virtue of his having served in the previous one) immediately introduced a motion to discuss the issue, it got the support of only 839 of the 2,033 deputies who were present.[70] Given that a minimum of 60 percent of the deputies opposed abolition, Sobchak preferred that the reformers run their own candidates against Communist Party candidates whenever possible.[71] Within the government itself, Gorbachev, Yakovlev, and Shevardnadze shared Sakharov's view that

66. Andrei Sakharov, "A Speech to the People's Congress," *New York Review of Books,* August 17, 1989, 25. I am unaware of anyone in the Soviet Union calling for the abolition of Article 6 before Sakharov.
67. "Istina odnogo cheloveka," 2; "O narodnom deputate A. D. Sakharove rasskazyvaet narodnyi deputat Galina Starovoitova," 65.
68. "An Interview with Andrei Sakharov," 3.
69. Sakharov et al., "Appeal of a Group of People's Deputies of the USSR," 721.
70. Sobchak, *Khozhdenie vo vlast',* 128–29; Sakwa, *Gorbachev and His Reforms,* 185.
71. Sobchak, *Khozhdenie vo vlast',* 129–31.

Article 6 should be abolished, albeit for very different reasons. But like Sobchak they did not want this to happen immediately, and they were adamant that it not be done legislatively by the Congress of People's Deputies; their preference was that the new constitution simply lack a comparable provision.[72] Gorbachev also advanced the argument, which could fairly be considered disingenuous, that since the party's monopoly of power had been established prior to the first Soviet constitution (and thus to all subsequent ones), it could not be abolished by revising the existing constitution. Only a new constitution could achieve what Sakharov wanted.[73]

In the end, Article 6 was abolished—at the third congress in March 1990, one month after the Central Committee of the Communist Party recommended doing so. The party consented to its loss of political primacy because even party officials opposed to perestroika had come to recognize that, however much they benefited from the article, not abolishing it would bring down the system completely.[74] By this time Sakharov was dead and his victory a posthumous one. When he had tried to speak to the congress on December 12 in support of his motion to discuss the matter, Gorbachev, from the chair, made clear his extreme irritation and with the television cameras rolling, forced the Nobel Prize winner from the podium. As a result, the motion was soundly defeated.[75] In the encounters between Gorbachev and Sakharov, in the very different ways they behaved toward one another, one sees in microcosm two very different visions of how the Soviet Union should be reformed. Gorbachev restricted reform to that which he or his surrogates dispensed incrementally and unilaterally, without regard for the demand for it in the society at large, while Sakharov saw reform as an expression of popular sentiment to which the leaders of a nation, regardless of whether they were elected or not, should be responsive.

This radicalization of Sakharov's views in the month before he died included the tactics he advocated to achieve them. In the same statement he signed with Afanasiev and the others calling for the abolition of Article 6, he also proposed a two-hour work stoppage in Moscow for December 11; its purpose was to pressure the second congress not only to abolish Article 6 but to enact laws on land and property. On December 11, in a speech at the Lebedev Institute, Sakharov justified the work stoppage on the even more radical grounds that it would help destroy "the administrative-command system that is leading us to the edge of ruin."[76] This was the closest he would come to advocating the dismantling of the Soviet system by nonparliamentary means. Although Soviet miners in Vorkuta had struck for the abolition of Article 6 earlier that fall, Sakharov's adoption of nearly the same tactic was exceedingly risky. The laws legalizing strikes that had been promulgated only four months earlier included the requirement that

---

72. Brown, *Gorbachev Factor*, 194; McCauley, *Gorbachev*, 161.
73. Matlock, *Autopsy of an Empire*, 275.
74. Sobchak, *Khozhdenie vo vlast'*, 134, 136; Brown, *Gorbachev Factor*, 193–94.
75. McCauley, *Gorbachev*, 154; Matlock, *Autopsy of an Empire*, 275.
76. Quoted in Altshuler, "A kogda upadesh—Eto nevazhno," 122.

they follow a cooling-off period and the failure of arbitration, neither of which Sakharov and his allies envisioned or provided for when they called for a work stoppage—which for all intents and purposes was a strike, albeit a self-limiting one.[77] To many reformers who agreed with Sakharov on the objectives of the work stoppage, the risks it entailed exceeded its possible benefits, and several supporters of Sakharov in the academy who were also deputies to the congress, such as Ginzburg and Vitalii Goldanskii, were critical as well.[78]

In the end, Sakharov's call was largely ignored.[79] But this only caused him to redouble his efforts, and on December 14 he reiterated before a caucus of IRG deputies the themes he had stressed in the previous months. Heatedly he defended his call for a work stoppage, citing the places (Lvov, Vorkuta, and the Donets coal fields) where workers had conducted them. He also pointed out that the numerous discussions his request prompted had the salubrious effect of attracting people to the political process.[80] Just as emphatically, he repeated his demand for the abolition of Article 6, describing it as "the most important political act which the country needs today."[81] Finally, Sakharov exhorted the deputies to declare themselves a formal opposition and to invite all the other deputies who did not belong to the IRG but who agreed with its objectives to join it in seeking to end the Communist Party's monopoly of power; unless this happened, reform could not continue. Without referring to Gorbachev by name, Sakharov made clear that the general secretary, surrounded as he was by new, more conservative advisers, could no longer be trusted to advance his original policies:

> The leaders bring the country to a catastrophe by delaying the process of pere-
> stroika for years. They are leaving the country during these years in a state where
> everything will be crumbling, crumbling intensively. All the plans to go over to an
> intensive market economy will prove unrealizable, and disenchantment within
> the country is already growing. This disenchantment makes it impossible for this
> country to follow an evolutionary road in its development. The only road, the
> chance of an evolutionary road, is to make perestroika radical.[82]

Implicit in Sakharov's analysis of the situation was that if perestroika were not radicalized in the ways he suggested, then elements in the country demanding changes even more radical than what he and other reformers advanced would radicalize their tactics as well, possibly even resorting to violence.

When the meeting adjourned, Sakharov sat for an interview with journalists from Kazakhstan at a nearby hotel.[83] The interview was a long one, perhaps

77. Sakwa, *Gorbachev and His Reforms*, 158, 213.
78. Elena Bonner, "U nego byl kharakter pobitelia," 4.
79. Hosking, *Awakening of the Soviet Union*, 183.
80. Andrei Sakharov, "The Last Address," *Moscow News*, December 31, 1989, 10.
81. Ibid.
82. Ibid.
83. Remnick, *Lenin's Tomb*, 282.

longer than he anticipated, and one can imagine how tired he was by the time he returned home. The eighteen-hour days he had been working since the end of the summer had taxed his already-weakened constitution to the limit. Perhaps the prudent thing for Sakharov to have done that evening would have been to relax.[84] But he planned to deliver a speech the next day at the congress and needed time to reread the draft he had written and make whatever changes he considered necessary. The debate the next day would surely be tumultuous, and Sakharov, always a stickler for clarity, wanted his words to be precise. One of the items he planned to discuss was of special importance: the congress was considering an amendment to the Criminal Code fixing at nine months the maximum time a person could be detained before trial. Sakharov considered the time period excessive for both practical and ethical reasons, and while the specific issue before the congress was strictly procedural—namely, by what means the Criminal Code could be changed to reflect the existence and prerogatives of the congress—what really animated Sakharov was the issue of pretrial detention itself.[85] This kind of incarceration had profoundly troubled him in all the years he was a dissident, and there is a certain poignancy in the fact that in this, the last speech he would write, he resumed the role he had played so courageously for so many years in the face of almost universal opprobrium.

Sakharov never delivered the speech. After eating dinner with Bonner, he retreated to the study downstairs to take a nap. He left instructions with his wife to wake him two hours later so he could resume work on the speech. But when she came to wake him, he was dead, his heart having stopped beating after a major attack of arrhythmia, from which he had suffered for many years.[86]

84. Lebowitz, "Ogromnaia dukhovnaia sila," 387. According to Tatiana Yankelevich (in a conversation on January 13, 2004), Sakharov's health was by this time so precarious that he believed he had little time to live—which explains the urgency that attended his activities in the last weeks of his life. She does not believe that that caused the simultaneous radicalization of his views.

85. A. D. Sakharov, "O chem on ne uspel skazat' (December 14, 1989)," *Literaturnaia gazeta,* December 27, 1989, 2.

86. Lourie, *Sakharov,* 398; Tatiana Yankelevich, conversation with author, January 13, 2004; A. E. Shabad, "Narodnoe dostoianie (kak ne khoronili Sakharova)," in Altshuler et al., *On mezhdu nami zhil,* 768. There is disagreement on the circumstances of Sakharov's death. Coleman claims that Sakharov left Bonner at nine o'clock in the evening and that she found him dead two hours later, lying on the floor next to the door to the study with the key he used to enter it still in the door—which leaves open the possibility that Sakharov died before he even entered the study. Pimenov states that Bonner found Sakharov dead at 10:30 p.m.—in contrast to Tatiana Yankelevich, who pinpoints the time as 11:00 p.m.—while Boris Altshuler contends that Sakharov died from heart failure, which caused him to fall while coming out of a pantry (presumably in the upstairs apartment), and that Bonner did not attend to him immediately because his falling made no noise. Coleman, *Decline and Fall of the Soviet Empire,* 116; Tatiana Yankelevich, conversation with author, January 13, 2004; Pimenov, "Kakim on byl," 220–21; Altshuler, "A kogda upadesh," 140. Lourie's brief account, based on an interview with Bonner (who according to Lourie was told by Sakharov to wake him at nine o'clock, not eleven o'clock, in the evening), seems the most accurate. Yankelevich confirms it, and I have followed it here.

# 25 Apotheosis Postmortem

In the four days between Sakharov's death, on December 14, and his funeral, on December 18, Gorbachev negotiated the terms of the funeral with the same ambivalence he had demonstrated when Sakharov was alive. Even in death, Sakharov was someone whose support he wanted, whose reputation he envied, and whose political opposition he resented. Moreover, how Gorbachev reacted to Sakharov's passing could have repercussions for the general secretary's standing both at home and abroad. The official obituary in *Pravda,* signed by Gorbachev and fifty-five other government and party officials, perfectly reflected this ambivalence and uncertainty. It described Sakharov simply as "a well-known public figure" to whom "a gross injustice was done" when he was exiled to Gorky.[1] But it failed to indicate what Sakharov had done to warrant such treatment, nor did it cite any of the ideas he expressed or the causes he advanced. One sees the same reluctance to speak frankly about Sakharov in Gorbachev's actions at the second congress on the day after Sakharov died. On the one hand, he ascended the podium to proclaim melodramatically that with Sakharov's passing, "a part of our heart is gone," and a short time later he spoke warmly to *Moscow News* about his erstwhile interlocutor and critic. On the other hand, he refused to declare an official day of mourning and rejected pleas that the congress adjourn on the day of Sakharov's funeral. The most the general secretary was willing to permit was the observance at the congress of a minute of silence.[2]

Shortly after Sakharov died, Gorbachev sent his future foreign minister, Evgenii Primakov, to Sakharov's apartment to offer Bonner the option of a public funeral, suitable for a member of the Politburo, in the Hall of Columns across from the Kremlin, where Lenin and Stalin had lain in state.[3] In addition, a government commission the congress established to organize the funeral and the disposition of Sakharov's remains proposed that he be buried in the Novodevichii Cemetery, where Khrushchev, among other notables, was buried.[4] But Bonner rejected both of these recommendations, and given Sakharov's undeniable prominence, the Soviet leadership had no choice but to accede to her desire that he be laid to rest in the Vostriakhovskoe Cemetery, where Ruf Bonner was also buried and where Elena wanted to be buried as well. An additional factor in Bonner's insistence on Vostriakhovskoe was the fact that it was not patrolled

---

1. "Andrei Dmitrievich Sakharov," *Pravda,* December 16, 1989, 4.
2. Kaiser, *Why Gorbachev Happened,* 311; Remnick, *Lenin's Tomb,* 283; "Vchera v Kremle," *Komsomol'skaia Pravda,* December 16, 1989, 1.
3. Remnick, *Lenin's Tomb,* 286.
4. Pimenov, "Kakim on byl," 222; "Vchera v Kremle," 1.

by militia, as Novodevichii was, and was thus more accessible to ordinary Soviet citizens who wished to pay their respects.[5]

Bonner recognized that Sakharov's passing was a political event of considerable magnitude. The Soviet people, not to mention foreign dignitaries who wished to come, should have access to the various events, particularly the funeral itself, that would commemorate it. Accordingly, she agreed to a public viewing of Sakharov's body in the Palace of Youth on December 16 and 17 and also to the commission's recommendation that the funeral the following day be outdoors at the Luzhniki sports complex, which could accommodate the large of number of people expected to attend it. Sakharov's funeral, in other words, should be a "civil funeral," consistent with his commitment to glasnost and the creation in the Soviet Union of a civil society.[6] In contrast to the funerals of Soviet leaders, which were invariably indoors, Sakharov's would be outdoors and thus, at least symbolically, open to everyone.

On December 16 and 17, more than ten thousand people passed by Sakharov's open coffin, which was adorned in red and black crepe. Some had waited outside in the cold for six hours for the opportunity, however brief, to pay their respects, and it took five hours for everyone to do so. The diversity of those who were there—miners, Armenian nationalists, Congress deputies, members of the Ukrainian nationalist organization Rukh—showed the breadth, as well as the depth, of Sakharov's popularity.[7] The next morning, his body was taken to the Academy of Sciences building on Leninskii Prospekt, where Gorbachev and six other Politburo members expressed their condolences; Gorbachev himself signed the guest book and later told a reporter that Sakharov deserved the Nobel Prize he had won. While talking briefly to Bonner, he agreed to her request that Memorial be allowed to register as a lawful and legitimate public organization.[8] From the academy, the coffin was transported to the Lebedev Institute, where for two hours several of its members and representatives of other scientific institutes eulogized their late colleague.[9]

The funeral itself was a massive demonstration of the respect and affection, even adoration, that had developed for Sakharov in the three years since he returned to Moscow from Gorky. The cortege that followed his coffin increased in size as it made its way from the institute to Luzhniki, and the crowd that finally assembled for the funeral in an enormous parking lot outside the stadium ranged, according to various estimates, from fifty thousand[10] to one hundred

5. Pimenov, "Kakim on byl," 222; Ioirysh, *Uroki A. D. Sakharova,* 87; Tatiana Yankelevich, conversation with author, January 13, 2004.

6. Pimenov, "Kakim on byl," 222; Shabad, "Narodnoe dostoianie," 766–67.

7. Pimenov, "Kakim on byl," 222; "Moskva proshchaetsia s A. D. Sakharovym," *Spetsial'noe prilozhenie—Russkaia mysl',* December 22, 1989, 7.

8. Remnick, *Lenin's Tomb,* 287.

9. Pimenov, "Kakim on byl," 223; Shabad, "Narodnoe dostoianie," 770.

10. Remnick, *Lenin's Tomb,* 287.

thousand[11] or even two hundred thousand.[12] Again, the diversity of the crowd was as impressive as its size: miners, intellectuals from Moscow and the other major cities of the Soviet Union, Ukrainians, Latvians, Estonians, Lithuanians, and undoubtedly people of other nationalities were among the mourners, many of whom carried placards with the number 6 crossed out on them—a reference to Sakharov's campaign to eliminate Article 6 from the Soviet Constitution.[13]

Given Sakharov's belief in the universality of human rights, the absence of foreign leaders at his funeral was regrettable, though perhaps, given the requirements of realpolitik, understandable. President Bush rejected Ambassador Matlock's suggestion that he send an emissary from the United States to Sakharov's funeral, as President Reagan had sent Bush himself, when Bush was vice president, to the funerals of Brezhnev, Andropov, and Chernenko. Instead, Bush ordered Matlock to represent the United States.[14] Lech Walesa, who wanted to attend the funeral, was unable to because his flight from Warsaw was diverted to Leningrad.[15] But the king of Norway sent a formal message of condolence, and Solzhenitsyn, from Vermont, stated that he grieved "our irretrievable loss" and sent a basket of white roses that Bonner placed near Sakharov's coffin in the Palace of Youth.[16] Even Roi Medvedev spoke highly of him on Soviet television.[17]

At the funeral itself, some twenty-five speakers, including Afanasiev, Sobchak, Yeltsin, Popov, and Vytautus Landisbergis, the Lithuanian reformer who would be elected president of Lithuania three months later, eulogized Sakharov effusively. So did Sergei Kovalev, who made a point of refuting the charge that Sakharov had not really suffered in his lifetime because he never spent time in prison. According to Kovalev, Sakharov, by publicly protesting violations of human rights, actually "sat in prison a thousand times with each of us, with friends, with people he never met."[18] Another eulogist, the prominent reformer and expert on Russian literature Dmitrii Likhachev, recalled Sakharov as "a prophet in the original sense of the word who called his contemporaries to a moral reawakening in the future."[19] Other speakers compared him to Gandhi, Tolstoy, and Martin Luther King.[20] Bonner, who in silent tribute wore the fur hat her husband had often worn himself, chose not to speak formally, confining her public comments to a plea that the funeral service be peaceful and orderly—a

11. "14 dekabria 1989 goda v Moskve skonchalsia Andrei Dmitrievch Sakharov," *Russkaia mysl'*, December 22, 1989, 1; "Miting v Luzhnikiah," *Spetsial'noe prilozhenie*, 7.

12. Matlock, *Autopsy of an Empire*, 280.

13. Remnick, *Lenin's Tomb*, 287–88; Alexander Nekrich, "Sakharov: narod i vlast'," *Spetsial'noe prilozhenie*, 6.

14. Matlock, *Autopsy of an Empire*, 277–78.

15. Walesa finally arrived in Moscow that evening, in time to attend the *pominka*, the traditional funeral feast, organized by Bonner at which Yeltsin, who had joined the funeral procession on the way to Luzhniki, was present as well. Edward Kline, conversation with author, June 10, 2008.

16. Quoted in Skonechnaia and Tsypkina, *Sakharov: Takim on byl*, 87.

17. Ioirysh, *Uroki A. D. Sakharova*, 82.

18. Remnick, *Lenin's Tomb*, 288; Pimenov, "Kakim on byl," 223; Kovalev quoted in *Spetsial'noe prilozhenie*, 7.

19. Quoted in *Spetsial'noe prilozhenie*, 7.

20. Remnick, *Lenin's Tomb*, 288.

reference few Russians of her generation would miss to the tumult at Stalin's funeral that caused some of the spectators to be trampled to death.[21] As it was, the sadness people felt was very real—it was said that even the militia on duty when Sakharov was buried were red-eyed from grief.[22]

The tributes to Sakharov continued for days, even weeks, after he died. His apartment on Chkalov Street quickly became a shrine to his memory: people left carnations at the door and lit candles around the photograph of him that stood next to it. On a motion of the deputies, the seat Sakharov had occupied at the second congress was left empty for the remainder of the term, and when the third congress convened the following March, its deputies, as a way of honoring the contributions Sakharov had made to the institution, literally created a seat for him, which remained empty for the duration of its proceedings.[23] Immediately after Sakharov died, the national flags of the three Baltic republics—Estonia, Latvia, and Lithuania—were flown at half-staff, and in Vilnius, the capital of Lithuania, where several thousand people had gathered to honor Sakharov's memory, the radio station observed a moment of silence.[24] The Baltics had always been of special concern to Sakharov, and the outpouring of grief there reflected it. But the adulation Sakharov's passing engendered elsewhere was no less genuine. From December 16–18 there were ceremonies honoring him in Kiev, where thirty thousand residents of the city, many with lit candles, gathered in a city stadium to pay tribute to him. In Vinnitsa, a crowd of one thousand observed a moment of silence; in Erevan, fifty thousand attended a memorial meeting; and in Vorkuta, a memorial tribute organized by the local strike committee observed a moment of silence in Sakharov's memory. There were similar tributes in Novosibirsk and Cheliabinsk.[25] In Leningrad, in the city's principal sports complex, forty thousand people, many holding the red, white, and blue flag of Russia with black bows attached to it, bore witness to Sakharov's commitment to human rights. In addition, sixty thousand gathered on Palace Square in Leningrad to pay their respects. When the formal proceedings had finished, some of the mourners, as a way of indicating that they considered Sakharov the successor of the noble army officers who on Palace Square had tried to overthrow the monarchy in 1825, carried Sakharov's portrait to the Trubetskoi Bastion, where several of the officers (called Decembrists because the revolt occurred in December) had been incarcerated.[26]

In the months that followed this initial paroxysm of grief, the tributes continued, though understandably they were less emotional and fewer in number. At the same time, they were planned with an eye to permanence: streets, town squares, schools, libraries, and even several mountains in the Soviet Union

21. Ibid., 288.

22. Alexander Ginzburg, "Na sleduiushchi den': Nachalo puti k sakharovskoi Konstitutsii," *Russkaia mysl'*, December 22, 1989, 1.

23. Remnick, *Lenin's Tomb*, 284; Ginzburg, "O fenomene Sakharova," 247.

24. Aron, *Yeltsin*, 315; "Strana proshchaetsia Sakharovym," *Russkaia mysl'*, December 22, 1989, 16.

25. "Strana proshchaetsia Sakharovym."

26. Ibid.

were named for Sakharov. In 1992, on what would have been his seventy-first birthday, his bust was unveiled in a ceremony in the main corridor of the Lebedev Institute, where he had spent a good deal of his career as a physicist. It is fair to presume that those who were honoring Sakharov in this fashion were impressed more by his commitment to moral principle and his struggle for human rights than by anything he accomplished as a physicist, however impressive his scientific accomplishments were. But the physicists who admired Sakharov also seemed to recognize that the ethical principles he had championed were of a piece with the qualities that made him an estimable physicist, and it was entirely fitting that his bust was placed directly opposite that of his mentor, Igor Tamm, who was not only Sakharov's teacher but also a model of how a scientist should act in the larger society.[27]

Foremost among the virtues Sakharov's mourners memorialized were the sense of moral purpose and the belief in the civilizing properties of reason that Tamm and other scientists, at both FIAN and Arzamas, had recognized in him long before he involved himself in politics. Of all the personal qualities Sakharov embodied, his commitment to living ethically on the basis of rational principles was the attribute his admirers, whether they were politically minded or not, most fervently wanted to cultivate in themselves, not only as a way of ensuring Sakharov a kind of immortality but also as a means of their own moral improvement. Ironically, Sakharov may have been in death more than he ever was in life a model of the moral rectitude he believed his countrymen should possess. To Sagdeev and Iurii Kariakin, an expert on Dostoevskii who had collaborated with Sakharov on Moscow Tribune, Sakharov was not merely an admirable human being who had lived his life ethically; he was, respectively, "our moral compass" and "the perfect moral compass" of the Soviet Union.[28] To Ales Adamovich, he should be emulated because he believed that "moral law, rationally arrived at, was such an absolute principle as to be a law of nature."[29] In Ilia Zaslavskii's succinct description of the man, Sakharov was nothing less than "the conscience of our country,"[30] which was more or less how Iurii Liubimov,[31] Gennadii Aigi,[32] the editors of *Posev* and *Grani* in a joint declaration they issued from Western

27. B. L. Altshuler et al., "Ot redkollegii," in Altshuler et al., *On mezhdu nami zhil*, 8. Sakharov was also honored by the government of Sweden, which in 1991 issued a postage stamp commemorating his commitment to "uphold the fundamental principles for peace between men," and by the European parliament in Strasburg, which established a prize in Sakharov's name after his death for people or institutions that fostered the principles he had espoused. Of the many honors Sakharov received during his lifetime, the most imaginative was the International Astronomical Union's naming an asteroid after him in 1979. Given Sakharov's political activities at the time, it is unlikely that the union was honoring him solely for his accomplishments as a physicist. Drell, "Andrei Sakharov and the Nuclear Danger," 38; Ales Adamovich, "V etom dome, nakhodias' v ssyle...," in Ivanova, *Andrei Dmitrievich*, 15; "Asteroid 'Sakharov,'" in Altshuler et al., *On mezhdu nami zhil*, 909.

28. Sakharov, *Moscow and Beyond*, xvi; Remnick, *Lenin's Tomb*, 283.

29. Quoted in "Proshchanie s Andreem Dmitrievichem Sakharovym," *Literaturnaia gazeta*, December 20, 1989, 1.

30. Remnick, *Lenin's Tomb*, 284.

31. Quoted in "Moment of Grief," *Moscow News*, December 31, 1989, 8.

32. Gennadii Aigi, "Sovest' i sviatost'," *Spetsial'noe prilozhenie*, 2.

Europe,[33] and Liudmila Alexeeva[34] all described him. Along these lines, one of the banners that was held up by the spectators at Sakharov's funeral bore the inscription "Andrei Dmitrievch: the Mind, the Honor, and the Conscience of our Era."[35] Five months later, at the annual May Day celebrations in Moscow, some of the marchers in Red Square carried posters of Sakharov that called him simply "The Conscience of the Nation."[36] What all of these tributes had in common was the assumption, or the hope, that Sakharov's virtues were transferable and that by internalizing them people could perpetuate the values he stood for, and perhaps even make Sakharov himself immortal. Sonia Sorokina, in the special edition of *Russkaia mysl* that was published after Sakharov died, made this intimation of immortality explicit:

> I am glad I had the good fortune to live in 'the era of Sakharov'....Andrei Sakharov is dead....No, he is NOT DEAD, since he cannot be purged from our memories; one cannot forget him. It is impossible to forget not only his good ideas, but also the warm glow of his eyes, his soft smile, his views that were those of the intelligentsia, his inexhaustible virtue. No, Andrei Dmitrievich is not dead.[37]

But it was not only as a repository of the nation's conscience and the avatar of a new morality that would be collectively ennobling that Sakharov was eulogized. It was also Sakharov as truth teller—someone who spoke the hard truths about the Soviet Union—that captivated the public's imagination, or at least the imagination of the educated elite, in the period immediately following his death. Irina Ilovaiskaia, writing in *Russkaia mysl*, extolled Sakharov's "indefatigable search for truth" and stated that "in his own person and in his own life he reflected an evangelical impulse to repudiate all the lies" the Soviet leadership repeated endlessly.[38] Several deputies to the second congress included in a tribute that appeared in an Estonian newspaper the statement that from Sakharov they learned "how not to live a lie."[39]

What these tributes clearly suggested was that Sakharov was an *intelligent* in the original, pre-Soviet sense of the word. Occasionally this characterization was explicit: Anatolii Levitin-Krasnov, in his contribution to the same memorial edition of *Russkaia mysl* to which Sorokina contributed, called Sakharov "the pride of the Russian intelligentsia," while on some of the notes and placards left near Sakharov's coffin at the Palace of Youth were written the words "The Finest Flower of the Russian Intelligentsia."[40] To tell the truth regardless of the consequences was the attribute of the intelligentsia Sakharov most visibly personified, and

33. "Redaktsii zhurnalov 'Posev' i 'Grani,'" *Spetsial'noe prilozhenie*.
34. Quoted ibid.
35. "Miting v Luzhnikakh," 7.
36. Remnick, *Lenin's Tomb*, 327.
37. Quoted in *Spetsial'noe prilozhenie*, 6.
38. Irina Ilovaiskaia, "Pamiati A. D. Sakharova," *Russkaia mysl'*, December 22, 1989, 1.
39. "Uchastniki Tret'ego s"ezda, nezavisimykh zhurnalistov (December 16, 1989)," *Spetsial'noe prilozhenie*, 3.
40. Levitin-Krasnov quoted in *Spetsial'noe prilozhenie*, 6; Matlock, *Autopsy of an Empire*, 278.

many of those who mourned his passing considered it essential that his membership in this social category so redolent of an unquenchable moral fervor be acknowledged. In a similar vein, Roald Sagdeev evoked the intelligentsia's original commitment to individual liberation when he noted, in a tribute that appeared in print on December 20 in a special edition of *Literaturnaia gazeta,* that Sakharov "struggled not just for freedom in the abstract, for all, but for every individual in particular."[41] Irina Ilovaiskova was no less perceptive when she wrote about Sakharov that "he loved not the abstraction of humanity, but concrete individuals."[42]

While Sakharov would probably have been pleased and gratified by these tributes, which captured essential elements of his personality and political philosophy, one can say with some assurance that by the rest of what transpired after his passing he would have been genuinely embarrassed: the placards, the burning candles, the intimations of immortality, the fulsome praise that made him seem more like a deity than a man. Praise was something he instinctively disliked. But as a scientist, Sakharov would also have objected to some of the tributes because they were factually inaccurate, and he almost certainly would have repudiated those that were suffused with Christian images of martyrdom and repentance.[43] Despite Bonner's wishes, which she expressed on Soviet television of December 17, that her husband not be turned in death into a religious icon, that is precisely what many of those who mourned his passing tried to do.[44] At Sakharov's funeral, there were many signs that said simply "forgive us."[45] The same thing was written on one of the wreaths that were laid next to his coffin in the Palace of Youth.[46] The writer and human rights activist Iu. A. Karabchievskii, in a tribute to Sakharov that appeared in 1990, confessed on behalf of the Soviet people that "we are all guilty before Andrei Dmitrievich."[47] When a memorial plaque was affixed in that same year to the house where Sakharov had lived in Gorky, Boris Nemtsov, who was both a scientist and a resident of the city, commented publicly that the unveiling of the plaque was "the first step to repentance."[48] And in a notebook someone left outside Sakharov's Moscow apartment shortly after he died in which mourners could express their condolences, one person wrote the following: "Forgive us for all the misfortune that

41. Quoted in "Proshchanie s Andreem Dmitrievichem Sakharovym," 1.

42. Ilovaiskaia, "Pamiati A. D. Sakharova," 1.

43. Tatiana Yankelevich, conversation with author, August 21, 2001.

44. Ioirysh, *Uroki A. D. Sakharova,* 84. In April 2003 Bonner objected strenuously to a plan to build a monument to Sakharov. Her reason was not that a monument would cause his admirers to deify him. Rather, she felt that Sakharov's principles were now unpopular and that a monument would do nothing to rehabilitate them. Michael Wines, "Sakharov's Widow Opposes Moscow Plan to Build Monument," *New York Times,* April 17, 2003, A5.

45. V. F. Turchin, "Scientist and Prophet," in Altshuler et al., *Facets of a Life,* 638; Matlock, *Autopsy of an Empire,* 278; Stanislav Kondrashov, "The Life of Andrey Sakharov," *New Times* 52 (1989): 25.

46. Adam Hochschild, *The Unquiet Ghost: Russians Remember Stalin* (New York, 1995), 122; Oleg Moroz, "Prilozhenie" to Khariton, "Radi iadernogo pariteta," 737.

47. Quoted in "V etom dome, nakhodias' v ssylke...," in Ivanova, *Andrei Dmitrievch,* 17.

48. Quoted ibid., 13.

we caused you. Forgive us for the fact that now only good things will be said of you by those who did not do so while you were alive. Words will not help, and we did not safeguard your life. But I believe we will safeguard your memory. Forgive us."[49]

In this national morality play Sakharov's mourners constructed, Sakharov, in Oleg Moroz's apt description, played the role of "a saint spurned," of someone whose message of moral redemption was rejected the entire time he was alive by a populace too concerned with material things to care for the spiritual and ethical dimensions of earthly life.[50] All one could do, now that this paragon of moral virtue was dead, was "to bow one's head" before him and try to inculcate in oneself the "holiness" he embodied.[51] Sakharov, like Jesus, was a martyr who, in the words of V. Iadvorzhetskii, a member of the union of theater arts in Gorky, "went up on the cross for us."[52] "Every revolution has its saint," Vitalii Korotich observed, "and Andrei Dmitrievich is the saint and martyr of perestroika. If God sent Jesus to pay for the sins of humankind, then a Marxist God somewhere sent Andrei Sakharov to pay for the sins of our system."[53]

Of course the critical question one should ask about these tributes is not whether they were accurate or whether Sakharov would have approved of them but whether the Soviet people drew from them the conclusion that they should adopt Sakharov's substantive positions on political issues in addition to emulating the moral righteousness he exuded. Did those who admired Sakharov in life and mourned him in death try merely to perpetuate in their own lives the personal qualities in Sakharov they found admirable purely as a means of moral and spiritual self-improvement? Or did Sakharov's death prompt in the mourners a sober examination and acceptance of the political and philosophical objectives he tried so persistently and energetically to advance—human rights, the rule of law, international peace, ecological awareness, and convergence? Was Sakharov's legacy a substantive one, and if so, did it have any effect on the course of events in the two years the Soviet Union existed after Sakharov's death and in the various successor states that emerged when it collapsed? To answer these questions requires an examination of his influence postmortem.

49. Quoted in Remnick, *Lenin's Tomb*, 285.

50. Moroz, "Prilozhenie," to Khariton, "Radi iadernogo pariteta," 737. According to I. D. Novikov, writing in 1991, the majority of the Soviet people considered Sakharov their "saintly conscience." I.D. Novikov, "Ob Andree Dmitrieviche," in Altshuler et al., *On mezhdu nami zhil*, 446.

51. "Uchastniki Tret'ego s"ezda, nezavisimykh zhurnalistov," 3; Aigi, "Sovest' i sviatost'," 2.

52. Quoted in "V etom dome, nakhodias' v ssylke...," in Ivanova, *Andrei Dmitrievich*, 15. Two years after Sakharov's death, A. B. Migdal described the Soviet physicist as a prophet whose "way to Golgotha was difficult." Migdal, "K portretu Andreia Sakharova," 441.

53. Kaiser, *Why Gorbachev Happened*, 313. Misha Levin, who was Jewish, analogized Sakharov's suffering as a dissident to the Old Testament figure Job. Ioirysh, *Uroki A. D. Sakharova*, 86.

# Conclusion  Sakharov's Legacy

In assessing Sakharov's influence after his death, the first thing to determine is the effect he had on the collapse of the Soviet Union, arguably the most significant event of the late twentieth century. Though he made a substantial contribution to this event, he never advocated the overthrow of the Soviet system or did anything with the conscious intention of causing it.

He contributed mostly by pressuring Gorbachev to continue and to widen perestroika, which instead of preventing or retarding the collapse of the Soviet system, had the paradoxical and wholly unintended effect of accelerating it. About Sakharov's relationship to perestroika one must be precise. The relevant point is not that Gorbachev advocated some of the things Sakharov advocated or that their views on the need for reform and on the kinds of reform needed largely coincided until Sakharov radicalized his agenda in 1989 to the point where Gorbachev could no longer accept it. It could easily have been sheer coincidence that Sakharov and Gorbachev supported the same things. Rather, the point is that Gorbachev proposed certain reforms at least partly because he found Sakharov's arguments for them convincing. Between their views on reform there was not just a correlation but a causal relationship.

In this respect, it does not matter whether Gorbachev was merely a reformer who never shed his belief in Marxism-Leninism[1] or a transformer who by the time the union collapsed had repudiated the substance, if not the legitimizing rhetoric, of Soviet Communism.[2] What is important is that a good deal of what Gorbachev prescribed for the Soviet Union was Sakharovian in content: efficient and honest government; the rule of law; truth telling about the present and past; freedom of assembly, the press, and information; popular participation in government; decentralization of the Soviet economy; and a measure of federalism in interrepublic relations.[3] Obviously the two men disagreed on the extent to which and the rate at which these principles could be given practical expression. And they disagreed on why they should be adopted. But they agreed on their inherent correctness and that the Soviet Union required them.

The same was true of foreign policy, where Gorbachev eventually accepted Sakharov's view that human rights were of international concern and thus properly a subject of negotiations with the United States.[4] On Afghanistan, Gorbachev finally adopted Sakharov's position that Soviet intervention there had

---

1. This is the view of Dmitrii Simes and Alexander Yakovlev. It was shared by Gorbachev's late wife Raisa. Simes, *After the Collapse,* 32–33.
2. See, for example, Brown, *Gorbachev Factor,* especially 306–18.
3. Sakwa, *Gorbachev and His Reforms,* 21–22.
4. McCauley, *Gorbachev,* 81.

been a colossal blunder (if not exactly a crime) and that the best thing the Soviets could do was withdraw.[5] More broadly, Shevardnadze, in July 1988, repeated Sakharov's earlier admonition that Soviet foreign policy should be based on universal moral principle. Five months later, speaking at the UN General Assembly, Gorbachev himself articulated Sakharov's view that the world economy was rapidly becoming a monolith. "A single organism outside of which not a single state can develop normally" is how the general secretary described it.[6] From this he drew the conclusion, which also came from Sakharov, that international relations should be "democratized"—that the problems countries faced in their bilateral relations should be solved internationally and that their foreign policies should be guided by the moral interests of their peoples. For this reason, he said, the Soviet Union would henceforth be bound by international covenants such as the Universal Declaration of Human Rights.[7] All countries, Gorbachev insisted, had to respond rationally to ecological threats, and he named the unrestricted proliferation of nuclear weapons as the most dangerous of these. On purely military matters, Gorbachev promised to reduce the size of Soviet armed forces unilaterally, and he even called for the establishment by the United Nations of assemblies of experts, including scientists, with whom the member nations would consult on matters of mutual concern.[8]

Of course Sakharov and the dissidents were not the only ones who had advocated the principles and policies Gorbachev now espoused. Some of the others who did—like Alexander Yakovlev, whose support for perestroika was more the result of his experiences as ambassador to Canada in the 1970s than of any affinity he had for the dissidents—were closer personally to Gorbachev than Sakharov was.[9] For this reason, analysts of perestroika such as Archie Brown and Alexander Shtromas have minimized the dissidents' influence on Gorbachev, arguing that the impetus to reform in the late 1980s came mostly from "within-system reformers" like Georgii Shakhnazarov, who by eschewing open dissidence retained a credibility with the Soviet leadership that the dissidents lacked.[10] The implication of this argument is that the dissidents, in opposing the Soviet system openly, behaved foolishly.

5. Ibid., 138.
6. Ibid., 139; Mikhail Gorbachev, "Speech to the UN General Assembly (December 7, 1988)," in Foreign Broadcast Information Service-SOV-88-236, December 8, 1988, 11.
7. Gorbachev, "Speech to the UN General Assembly," 16.
8. Ibid., 17, 19.
9. Brown, *Gorbachev Factor*, 75, 81, 105; David Pryce-Jones, *The War That Never Was: The Fall of the Soviet Empire, 1985–1991* (London, 1995), 420.
10. Brown, *Gorbachev Factor*, 8; Alexander Shtromas, *Political Change and Social Development: The Case of the Soviet Union* (Frankfurt, 1981), 67–82. An American historian of Russia, writing in 1977, minimized the dissidents as "largely a Western media creation" whose importance was exaggerated by a Soviet leadership that was "paranoid" and "hysterical." Richard Hellie, "The Structure of Russian History," *Russian History* 4, no. 1 (1977): 18. For the opposite argument, with which I agree, that the dissidents influenced perestroika and thus contributed indirectly to the Soviet Union's collapse, see Robert Horvath, *The Legacy of Soviet Dissent: Dissidents, Democratisation and Radical Nationalism in Russia* (London, 2005), 1–8, 50–149, 236–38.

But several of these reformers have testified to the influence of the dissidents in general, and of Sakharov in particular, in the genesis and evolution of their ideas. Fëdor Burlatskii, an adviser to Khrushchev and Andropov who was close enough to Gorbachev to accompany him to the Geneva and Reykjavik summits, states that when he first met Sakharov in 1970, the latter seemed to him akin to "a prophet" and "a seer" whose views, as expressed in *Reflections,* contained "an entirely new and original perspective on the contemporary world."[11] In his memoir, *Kremlevskaia khronika,* Andrei Grachev states explicitly that in the works of Sakharov to which he had access "were first formulated the postulates of the New Thinking [i.e., perestroika and glasnost]." Among the works he read was *Reflections,* his copy of which he carefully guarded.[12] Another adviser to Gorbachev who was influenced by the dissidents was Anatolii Cherniaev, who before serving Gorbachev directly had been a chief deputy to Boris Ponomarev, the head of the international department of the Central Committee.[13] Even Leonid Shebarshin, who headed the first main directorate of the KGB from 1989 to 1991, expressed in an interview in the early 1990s his respect for both Sakharov and Solzhenitsyn.[14]

As for Gorbachev himself, Sakharov's influence on his thinking was profound, so much so that the general secretary, who was not known for his modesty and always prided himself on his intellectual self-sufficiency, felt compelled eventually to acknowledge it. In his memoirs, which were published in the mid-1990s, he listed Sakharov and the dissidents along with Khrushchev and Kosygin among those who "left their mark—if not on our political structures, then on our minds."[15] Gorbachev perused the file the KGB had accumulated on Sakharov before permitting him to return to Moscow in December 1986, and the insights he gained from reading it strengthened his commitment to perestroika and glasnost and colored his judgment of what these policies should entail.[16] Of course the extent to which Gorbachev was willing to reform the Soviet Union

11. Fëdor Burlatskii, *Vozhdi i sovetniki: O Khrushchev, Andropove i ne tol'ko o nikh...* (Moscow, 1990), 346. Robert English, in *Russia and the Idea of the West: Gorbachev, Intellectuals and the End of the Cold War* (New York, 2000), 287, notes that almost all of the Gorbachev-era reformers he interviewed for his book testified to the influence of *Reflections* on the development of their own ideas.

12. Grachev, *Kremlevskaia khronika,* 97. In fact, the KGB, by saving the dissidents' works, inadvertently became a conduit for the transmission of their ideas to the Soviet leadership. Urban, *Rebirth of Politics in Russia,* 46.

13. Brown, *Gorbachev Factor,* 20.

14. Pryce-Jones, *War That Never Was,* 363.

15. Gorbachev, *Memoirs,* 349.

16. Peter Reddaway, "The Role of Popular Discontent," *National Interest* 31 (Spring 1993): 60. Speaking at the Library of Congress in Washington in May 1992, Gorbachev admitted that he had read the works of Soviet dissidents much earlier than that, when he was first party secretary in Stavropol in the mid-1970s. Although Gorbachev did not mention Sakharov in his lecture, it is likely that what he read of the dissidents' works included something, or several things, by Sakharov. At the very least, the general secretary in January 1987 read the summary of Sakharov's views that Shevardnadze had prepared for him in the form of a lengthy memorandum in which he noted that Sakharov's opinions on political issues should be considered seriously. Aron, *Yeltsin,* 763; Gorelik, *World of Andrei Sakharov,* 351.

never quite matched Sakharov's evolving expectations, and by the time of his death Sakharov believed that Gorbachev had become an impediment to the further advancement of perestroika. But the degree to which the two men agreed on what reform required at a minimum was remarkable. At the very least, the congruence in their views was greater than it would have been had Gorbachev been guided solely by the opinions of in-house reformers such as Yakovlev and Shevardnadze.

Sakharov's influence on perestroika was very real and had the practical effect, albeit only temporarily, of legitimizing these policies among the reformers outside the Soviet leadership who were urging it to reform more rapidly and more systematically than it intended. Not surprisingly, Sakharov's death in 1989 served to galvanize these efforts. In January 1990 Iurii Afanasiev acknowledged Sakharov's impact on the evolution of his own ideas and credited him with playing a critical role in the creation of a genuine political opposition.[17] In addition, the organization calling itself Democratic Russia that was formed in 1990 to advance the principle that the state exists to protect the individual stated explicitly in its platform that its values and objectives were based partly "on the humanistic ideas of our great contemporary, Andrei Dmitrievich Sakharov."[18] For Len Karpinskii, another reformer who found the pace of perestroika insufficient, Sakharov was "a moral-intellectual force—an example of honesty and bravery" who contributed significantly to "the ideology of democratization and perestroika."[19]

For this reason one might say that Sakharov's ghost hovered unmistakably in August 1991 over the crowds that gathered outside the White House (where the Russian parliament was located) to show their opposition to the farcical coup that party leaders opposed to perestroika were attempting. Boris Nemtsov, who stood with Yeltsin outside the White House in open defiance of the plotters, said later that much of his motivation for doing so was traceable to Sakharov, and Evgenii Evtushenko, the perennial weather vane of Soviet politics, read a poem to the crowd that evoked the image of Sakharov "coming to the aid of our parliament" after "shyly wiping his cracked spectacles"—the latter perhaps an allusion to Sakharov's ability to emerge from the intelligentsia to participate openly and effectively in politics.[20]

Through 1990 and 1991, Sakharov's popularity (which his death had the effect of increasing) remained great, and it was probably bolstered by the publication of works of his that had previously been forbidden: *Reflections* appeared in *Voprosy filosofii* in 1990, and his memoirs were serialized in *Znamia* in 1990 and 1991.[21] In 1994, the Sakharov Archives in Moscow were officially opened, and

17. John Dunlop, *The Rise and Fall of the Soviet Empire* (Princeton, 1993), 112–13.

18. "Sozdan izbiratel'nyi blok 'Demokraticheskaia Rossiia,'" *Ogonëk* 6 (February 1990): 17.

19. Karpinsky, "Autobiography of a Half-Dissident," 300.

20. Coleman, *Decline and Fall of the Soviet Empire*, 369; Evtushenko quoted in Iain Elliot, "Three Days in August: On-the-Spot Impressions," in *Russia at the Barricades: Eyewitness Accounts of the August 1991 Coup*, ed. Victoria E. Bonnell, Ann Cooper, and Gregory Freidin (Armonk, N.Y., 1994), 294.

21. Stephen White, *After Gorbachev* (New York, 1993), 91.

in the same year an American branch was established at Brandeis University in the United States.[22] Also in the 1990s Sakharov's apartment in Gorky was made into a museum; a Sakharov Museum and Public Center was opened in Moscow; and the street in Arzamas where Sakharov lived in the early 1950s was named for him.[23] The respect Sakharov commanded did not derive merely from the personal qualities he displayed as a dissident. It was also the result of the substantive positions he had taken. When in 1990 a group of reformers in Uzbekistan set out to write a constitution for a transformed Uzbek Republic, they consulted the constitution Sakharov had drafted in the fall of 1989. The same was true in 1990 of the advisers around Yeltsin who drafted a Declaration of Sovereignty for the RSFSR.[24] In 1991, a poll of 1,953 people by the All-Union Center for the Study of Public Opinion showed that 54 percent of them considered Sakharov to have been a man of "high moral caliber," while only 3 percent believed he had acted "in the interests of the enemies of the Soviet Union." Fully 55 percent said that Sakharov's views on social and political issues were close to theirs. In addition, 50 percent agreed with the proposition that throughout his years as a public figure Sakharov had sought to elevate the moral caliber of the Soviet people, and 45 percent agreed that he had had much success, or some success, in achieving his objectives. On substantive issues, 71 percent shared Sakharov's view that the invasion of Afghanistan was "a crime," and 63 percent thought the Soviet Union in its policies should follow "a Western path of development."[25]

Although opinion polls can vary greatly in their results depending on how their questions are worded, the results on Sakharov, in their totality, show unmistakably that the Soviet people in 1990–1991 not only remembered him but regretted his absence. When asked in one poll in December 1990 to name the individuals the Soviet people needed most to extricate them from the crisis they faced, 48 percent of the respondents named Sakharov, a figure exceeded only by the 58 percent who named Jesus. Lenin, by contrast, was named by 36 percent and Gorbachev by only 26 percent.[26] Among the dissidents in Eastern Europe, Sakharov's popularity, though not as pervasive as it was in the Soviet Union, was no less intense among the dissidents there. The Polish writer and poet Czeslaw

22. Altshuler et al., "Ot redkollegii," 8; http://library.brandeis.edu/50th/phase3.html#1994. The archives were transferred to Harvard University in 2004.

23. Altshuler et al., "Ot redkollegii,"; M. D. Frank-Kamenetskii, "Pari. O chem sporiat fiziki," in Altshuler et al., *On mezhdu nami zhil,* 721.

24. Matlock, *Autopsy of an Empire,* 395; Reddaway and Glinski, *Tragedy of Russia's Reforms,* 161, 661.

25. Iurii Levada, *Chelovek i legenda: Obraz A. D. Sakharova v obshchestvennom mnenii* (Moscow, 1991), 3, 7, 18, 24, 26, 30. Not everyone shared these sentiments. To diminish them, Vladimir Kriuchkov, Chebrikov's successor as KGB chief, in 1990 sponsored the creation of the Andrei Sakharov Union of Democratic Forces, the activities of which consisted mostly of publishing a newspaper, *Tsentr,* that polemicized against Bonner as well as Sakharov. Also, advocates of National Bolshevism such as Vladimir Zaburin and V. Samoilov denounced as unprincipled and unpatriotic not only Sakharov but also those responsible for the cult that emerged around him after his death. Horvath, *Legacy of Soviet Dissent,* 116–17; Vladimir Zaburin, "Razgovor s mukhami, ili monolog na kukne," *Molodaia gvardiia* 8 (1990): 212, 216–17; V. Samoilov, "Razgul Sakharovshchiny," *Molodaia gvardiia* 9 (1990): 260–63.

26. "Social Barometer," *Moscow News,* December 16–23, 1990, 9.

Milosz was surely exaggerating in 1990 when he said about Sakharov that "the whole part of Europe from which I come is indebted to [him], for its newly rein-vented freedom is to a large degree the result of his courage."[27] Eastern Europe abandoned communism for many reasons, most of them having little to do with Sakharov. But the fact that someone like Milosz, who contributed greatly to the collapse of communism in Poland, believed that Sakharov had played a role in this collapse is evidence that his influence on this phenomenon was far from negligible.

Sakharov's influence after his death even extended to America. In January 2005 President George W. Bush credited Natan Sharansky's book *The Case for Democracy*, which he had read in galleys the previous fall and winter, with provid-ing "a glimpse of how I think on foreign policy."[28] What Bush had in mind in particular was Sharansky's view that democracy and the protection of human rights domestically were a prerequisite of international peace—an idea the pres-ident emphasized in his second inaugural address. This idea, of course, was also central to Sakharov's views on foreign affairs, and there is reason to believe that Sharansky's advocacy of it (and thus Bush's as well) is traceable to Sakharov. Sharansky, in addition to calling the Soviet scientist "my teacher" and dedicat-ing the book to him, credited the Soviet Union's defeat in the Cold War partly to "the courage of dissidents like Sakharov and Orlov."[29]

In post-Soviet Russia, however, Sakharov's popularity waned considerably, de-spite the similarities between his views and many of the public pronouncements Boris Yeltsin made as Russia's president. Rhetorically, Yeltsin often sounded like Sakharov. His election platform in 1990 was one that Sakharov could have en-dorsed enthusiastically, and in May 1990, at the Russian Congress of People's Deputies, Yeltsin proclaimed that "the most important, primary sovereignty in Russia [ought to be] the sovereignty of the individual."[30] Outside the White House in August 1991, Yeltsin told the crowd assembled there that its foremost weapon against the treacherous plotters who were bent on restoring the old order was "the enormous will [the Soviet people possessed] to defend the ideals of freedom, democracy, and human worth."[31] Not long after the coup collapsed, he even proclaimed that decommunization entailed the assertion of universal moral values and that "the free coming and going of Russia's citizens abroad" was

27. Czeslaw Milosz, introduction to Bonner, "On Gorbachev," 14.

28. Quoted in Amy Doolittle, "Bush Committed to Winning War on Terror," *Washington Times*, January 12, 2005, A8.

29. Natan Sharansky, *The Case for Democracy: The Power of Freedom to Overcome Tyranny and Terror* (New York, 2004), xix, 12, 113, 137, 145. Sharansky (who changed his first name from "Anatolii" to "Natan" when he moved to Israel in 1986) kept a bust of Sakharov on his desk while serving in the Sharon government in 2003–2005. After leaving office Sharansky stated explicitly that the assertion of the Bush Doctrine that democracy and peace are causally related was traceable intel-lectually to Sakharov. Natan Sharansky, "Defending and Advancing Freedom," *Commentary* 120, no. 4 (November 2005): 60–61.

30. "S"ezd narodnykh deputatov RSFSR. Stenograficheskii otchet," *Sovetskaia Rossiia*, May 25, 1990, quoted in Aron, *Yeltsin*, 377.

31. Quoted ibid., 464.

among the most prominent of them.[32] At the seventh Congress of People's Deputies in December 1992, Yeltsin stated that the state should serve the individual
and not the reverse, and as late as March 1997 he reiterated that what he sought
for Russia was "an order based on law."[33] In the same oration he proclaimed
that "an order that suppresses the individual, his freedom, his initiative, and his
dignity cannot become the basis of a modern society."[34] Two years later, in nomi-
nating Sakharov for *Time* magazine's "Person of the Century," Yeltsin claimed to
have been influenced by Sakharov and for that reason professed himself "intensively aware" of how much he missed "his wisdom, firmness, and honesty."[35]

But Yeltsin was more a populist than a liberal, and Sakharov, who never
entirely trusted Yeltsin and was dubious of his intellect, had good reason to
question the sincerity of his convictions.[36] Although the two men seemed to
share the same objectives, Sakharov always suspected that Yeltsin's conversion
to democracy and human rights was the consequence of political calculation.[37]
In any case, the two men were never close either personally or politically, and
when Yeltsin's policies in the late 1990s seemed to repudiate his liberal rhetoric,
people who had been close to Sakharov, most notably Bonner, were chagrined
but hardly surprised.[38]

Of all the things Yeltsin did that antagonized Sakharov's supporters in the
1990s, the most infuriating—even more than the corruption he tolerated and
the cronyism he embraced—was the war the Russian government waged on
Chechnya. What the war came to symbolize for these people was not only the
lawlessness and lack of respect for civilized behavior that increasingly pervaded
life in post-Soviet Russia but the waning of Sakharov's influence, of which the
war seemed irrefutable proof. In much the same way the Afghan invasion sym-
bolized for Sakharov all that was wrong in the Soviet Union in the late 1980s, the
war on Chechnya came to encapsulate for Bonner and the others who wished
to perpetuate Sakharov's legacy all that was wrong in Russia in the late 1990s.
Not only the cruelty of the tactics that were employed in the war but its lack of a
coherent rationale above and beyond the reassertion of Russian hegemony over
a non-Russian minority made comparisons with Afghanistan inescapable. Had
Sakharov been alive, he undoubtedly would have opposed the war in Chechnya
and for the same reasons he opposed the war in Afghanistan.[39] For this reason,
Bonner could have been speaking for Sakharov as well as for herself when in
January 2000 she condemned the tactics Russian forces were using in Chechnya
as "genocidal" and claimed they were proof that Russia was degenerating into

32. Quoted ibid., 466.
33. Ibid., 500; quoted ibid., 652.
34. Quoted ibid., 652.
35. Boris Yeltsin, "Who Should Be the Person of the Century?" *Time*, December 20, 1999, 29.
36. Pryce-Jones, *War That Never Was*, 421–22.
37. Simes, *After the Collapse*, 69–70; Matlock, *Autopsy of an Empire*, 246.
38. John Morrison, *Boris Yeltsin: From Bolshevik to Democrat* (New York, 1991), 110.
39. Gail Lapidus expressed the same idea at the Stanford conference on Sakharov's legacy
in 1999.

a police state.[40] A month later she signed a petition several former dissidents were circulating that called the new Putin regime "the introduction of modernized Stalinism."[41] Obviously Bonner was not mollified by Putin's gesture in February 2000 of laying flowers on Sakharov's grave.[42]

Sakharov might not have accepted Bonner's description of Russia as a police state, but he surely would have been appalled by the violations of human rights it committed, the pervasive cronyism and corruption it tolerated, and the ecological calamities it tried to conceal. Moreover, the pervasive pursuit of private wealth, the gangster style of politics, and the emergence of Mafia-like enterprises engaged in gun running, drugs, and other illicit activities suggested that by the mid-1990s Sakharov's vision of a society based on the rule of law was increasingly unlikely to be realized in Russia.[43] Contributing to this was the "ecocide" that was occurring simultaneously. By keeping secret from the Russian people scientific, economic, and technological matters it deemed essential to national security, including incidents in which governmental negligence caused great harm to the environment, the government essentially exempted itself from the requirement of accountability that Sakharov considered a prerequisite of genuine and lasting reform.[44] Just as in the Soviet Union before Gorbachev, the government of Russia was now doing pretty much what it wanted for the simple reason that very few people knew what it was doing. Coupled with the diminution in the political strength of the democratic movement that began not long after the Soviet Union collapsed, this lack of accountability created the sense among many Russians that the law was something to be evaded, at best an instrument for advancing personal interests in defiance of the general welfare. The result was a society in which, in Anne Applebaum's apt phrase, it no longer paid to be decent—a state of affairs with which Andrei Sakharov would have been thoroughly disgusted.[45]

The results of an opinion survey of Russians in 2000 and 2001 show how widespread were the pessimism and cynicism such attitudes reflected. When asked what they disliked about the Soviet Union, a majority of respondents pointed to

40. Quoted in Stephen F. Cohen, *Failed Crusade: America and the Tragedy of Post-Communist Russia* (New York, 2001), 184.

41. Quoted in John Lloyd, "The Logic of Vladimir Putin," *New York Times Magazine*, March 19, 2000, 65.

42. Charlemagne [pseud.], "Vladimir Putin, Russia's Post-Cold-Warrior," *Economist*, January 8, 2000, 51. A year later, Bonner condemned as "a profanation of history" Putin's resurrection of the old Soviet anthem, retitled "Gimn Rossiiskoi Federatsii" and with new lyrics by the lifelong Stalinist Sergei Mikhalkov, who had supplied the words for the Soviet original. Ion Mihai Pecapa, "Putin's Duality (August 5, 2005)," http://www.frontpagemag.com/Articles/ReadArticle.asp?ID=19003.

43. Stephen Handelman, *Comrade Criminal: Russia's New Mafiya* (New Haven, 1995). David Satter, in *Darkness at Dawn: The Rise of the Russian Criminal State* (New Haven, 2003), shows convincingly that the lawlessness in the mid-1990s continued into the new century and if anything, became more blatant and pervasive.

44. The Russian government took this action in 1997. Aleksei Iablokov, "O sobliudenii ekologicheskikh prav cheloveka v Rossii," in *Razmyshleniia o progresse, mirnom, sosushchestvovanii i intellektual'noi svobode*, 183, 184–87.

45. Anne Applebaum, "A Dearth of Feeling," *New Criterion* 15, no. 2 (October 1996): 15.

its inefficiency and corruption rather than its violations of human rights. Conversely, those who praised the Soviet system claimed that prior to perestroika its superiority consisted not only in the job security and economic stability it provided but also in the political stability its denial of personal freedom guaranteed. For the economic decline that occurred in the late 1980s a majority of respondents blamed Gorbachev and perestroika rather than the communist system itself. And when asked what they thought of the civil liberties Sakharov favored, while a majority still approved of them in principle, they did not think that exercising them would improve their lives. Indeed, only 30 percent of respondents thought they were now living in a "law-governed state," while fully 69 percent believed either that the communist system should be restored or that the existing system should be replaced by a dictatorship.[46]

All of this suggests that barely a decade after the collapse of the Soviet Union the yearning for a strong government, willing and able to violate individual rights if that was deemed necessary to provide stability and order, was so pervasive that not even Sakharov could have neutralized it. The problem was not just that public opinion is fickle and that people have short memories. It was much larger and, in historical terms, much deeper. When Sakharov questioned the moral legitimacy of the Soviet Union and tried to pressure the regime to base its legitimacy on values that were more to his liking, he was going against the grain not just of Soviet political culture but of Russian national culture—with its paternalism, its implicit equation of democracy with anarchy, and its insufficient reverence for the inherent worth of the individual. In the end, the humane and ethical liberalism Sakharov espoused simply did not have deep roots in Russian culture, and for this reason it was really Sakharov, rather than the Soviet Union, that was out of step with Russian history. This attaches to Sakharov's struggles against the Soviet government a certain nobility that might have been missing had these struggles succeeded. But it also lends to his life a poignancy reflective of the fact that, in nearly everything he attempted, he was trying to change radically and in a matter of a few decades the culture of a country that, by the time he was born, had existed for centuries. As a result, this culture could change, if it changed at all, only slowly and incrementally. Given what we know now about what happened in Russia in the late 1990s, it is hard to imagine a scenario for Russia in the twenty-first century in which the values and principles Sakharov championed are triumphant. Russia is not ready for Sakharov. Perhaps one day it will be.

This does not mean that Sakharov was unimportant or that there are no lessons to be learned or insights to be gained from his life. Despite the disjunction between his values and the present incapacity of Russian culture to absorb

---

46. Stephen White, "Russia's Disempowered Electorate," in *Russian Politics under Putin,* ed. Cameron Ross (Manchester, Eng., 2004), 82–84, 87–88. The difficulty the Sakharov Museum in Moscow has had in raising funds since its opening in 1996 is perhaps in keeping with these polling results. The museum's fortunes were hardly enhanced in 2003 when an exhibit critical of the Orthodox Church caused its director and curator to be convicted of "inciting religious hatred." Sophia Kishkovsky, "Sakharov Museum Falls on Hard Times," October 2, 2007, http://www.iht.com/articles/2007/10/02/africa/moscow.php#end_main.

them, there nevertheless are sound reasons for persons both in Russia and in the West to be concerned with him, to revisit the choices he made, the actions he took, and the ideas he espoused.

Perhaps the first thing that is important to note about Sakharov is that his appearance as a dissident in the late 1960s was to be expected. The contradiction in the Soviet Union between the vocational autonomy it granted its educated elite and the political freedom it denied this same elite made the emergence of people like Sakharov virtually inevitable. Because the Soviets were committed to modernizing Russia's society and economy while perpetuating their monopoly of political power, they necessarily withheld with one hand what they granted with the other. In the language of familial relations, they treated Sakharov the physicist as an adult but Sakharov the human being and Soviet citizen as a child. From this dichotomy, to which not everyone in the Soviet elite was oblivious, the Soviets generated the dissidence of which Sakharov's was perhaps the most eloquent and outstanding example.

But the appearance of dissidents like Sakharov did not guarantee they would be successful in convincing either the Soviet leadership or the Russian people to accept their agenda. What is so disheartening about Bonner's animadversions about Putin, her concern that Russia under his leadership is degenerating into a form of neo-Stalinism, is how few Russians share it. While Sakharov's appearance on the stage of Russian history in the late twentieth century was not surprising in light of the modernizing agenda the Soviet leadership followed practically since the October Revolution in 1917, the failure of his ideals to retain support much beyond his own death was perhaps to be expected. The gap between what Sakharov wanted and the culture that limits what the Russian people now want is presently too great and is likely to remain so for the foreseeable future.

But Sakharov's story is also instructive as a study of personal character. For anyone who shares the humane values Sakharov championed and who admires the courage and fortitude he showed in trying to convince others of their correctness over the implacable opposition of a powerful government, his life provides a moral example few others can match. Of course Sakharov was not a saint, as both he and Bonner readily acknowledged. His not volunteering for military service in World War II was hardly heroic, and his rationale for not doing so was self-serving. He neglected Klava at times during their marriage, and it is hard to believe that his estrangement from his children was entirely their fault or a product exclusively of factors beyond his control. There were times when his concern for Bonner's family seemed to skew his priorities—for example, in the early 1980s when his campaign to secure an exit visa for Liza precluded his helping others whose predicament was more serious. One can also lament the toll Sakharov's dissidence took on other people close to him, principally Bonner's children, without concluding that he should have forsaken his dissidence because of it.[47]

---

47. Easily the most jaundiced view of Sakharov is David Shipler's. In *Russia: Broken Idols, Solemn Dreams* (New York, 1984), 207–8, 370–72, he describes Sakharov and Bonner as supercilious snobs unconcerned with ordinary people and their problems. What is worse, he claims they have no

Nor was Sakharov's political judgment unerring. He made mistakes. There were people he misjudged, issues he analyzed incorrectly, and expectations that were never met. In the first category one might include Chalidze; in the second, the moral equivalence claimed in *Reflections* between the United States and the Soviet Union; and in the third, the whole concept of convergence, which, as a vision of the future, has been rendered largely moot by the collapse of communism everywhere in the world except in backwaters such as Cuba and North Korea. (China remains an exception but only a partial one given the changes in the economy that occurred there in the late twentieth century.) Given the way Sakharov described convergence, it is perhaps appropriate that this is the case. Convergence, for Sakharov, was really an ahistorical or posthistorical concept useful more for the hope it provided than as an analytical tool in understanding the political realities that confronted him. What is more, it seemed to entail the suppression of human nature: it implied that there was one good way to live and that the values that informed how people would live after convergence occurred were timeless, absolute, and universal. Of course, in the last years of his life Sakharov came to question the inevitability of convergence, and in all the years he advocated it he never argued that people should be coerced into accepting it. But there is something unsettling about a vision so monolithic that it fails to take into account the diversity of human experience, the multiplicity of ways in which a just society may be organized, and the possibility that the uniformity in the social arrangements people devise for themselves once convergence exists might stifle human creativity rather than foster it. The implication in Sakharov's advocacy of convergence was that those who rejected it suffered from an absence or deficiency of rationality. But surely one could question convergence on both moral and practical grounds based on arguments that were entirely reasonable.

But Sakharov was right about much more than he was wrong. He was right about détente—that for the Soviets it was a means of expanding political influence and achieving nuclear parity. He was right, more generally, about arms control—that it was not an end in itself and that it could be successful only if the tensions that made it necessary were defused. He was right about the mechanics of nuclear deterrence and the role conventional forces played in keeping the nuclear peace in Europe. And his original decision in the early 1950s to design thermonuclear weapons for the Soviet Union was morally defensible because the logic of deterrence he invoked to justify it was sound. In addition, Sakharov called attention to the despoliation of nature in the Soviet Union earlier than practically anyone else, and his role in the Nuzhdin affair, in which he thwarted the expansion of Lysenko's nefarious influence on Soviet science, was

_____

understanding of freedom of the press, viewing reporters simply as conduits for the propagation of their own "party line." Bonner, in particular, is shrill and intolerant of criticism, and both of them are like the Soviet leaders they criticized—which makes them hypocrites as well as implicitly authoritarian. There may be some small truth in what Shipler writes regarding the press. But the fact that nearly every other description of Sakharov—of which there are over one hundred—either contradicts Shipler completely or presents a more temperate and nuanced evaluation suggests that his description is, at best, one-sided and incomplete and, at worst, mostly wrong.

exemplary. Finally, without Sakharov to prod him, Gorbachev in 1987 and 1988 might not have reformed the Soviet Union as much as he did.

However gently he expressed it, Sakharov's liberalism was a tough-minded liberalism, and it harbored no illusions about the malevolence of the Soviet Union. But it was not merely its tough-mindedness that made Sakharov's liberalism attractive. There is something truly uplifting about the ethical vision he first conjured as a dissident, and then practiced as a reformer in the Gorbachev era, of a society based on the rule of law and the protection of human rights. The most precious of these rights, as far as Sakharov was concerned, were the right to choose one's place of residence, the right of critics of the government to a presumption of sanity, and the right of everyone to due process in the administration of justice. For Sakharov, legality and the adherence to legal norms were a way of ensuring that every individual received not only the protection from the state needed to fulfill his potential as a human being but also the material comforts and security without which the kind of liberation Sakharov professed would be impossible. Sakharov's insistence on ecological consciousness and his belief that scientists had a critical role to play in instilling it are especially impressive. Unless the earth is protected and its natural resources preserved, he seemed to be saying, everything humanity has achieved culturally and intellectually will be seriously jeopardized. Indeed, Sakharov's vision of the humane and socially responsible scientist, shorn of the elitism that was initially a part of it, is one that offers a reasonable compromise between the extremes of unbridled Prometheanism on the one hand and a reflexive environmentalism that sees technology as inherently evil on the other. Finally, one should include among Sakharov's accomplishments his formulation of self-determination as an instrument of individual advancement rather than as a rhetorical device to justify revolutionary movements like the Bolsheviks that once in power subordinated the individual's rights to the collective interests of the party and the state.

But Sakharov was not so wedded to his own ideas that he was unable to reevaluate and revise them as circumstances warranted. He changed his mind and evolved intellectually. Clearly he was able in the 1980s to shed the elitism evident earlier in his life in *Reflections* and other writings.[48] This made possible his transition from dissident to political leader after returning to Moscow in 1986. If, unlike Vaclav Havel in Czechoslovakia and Lech Walesa in Poland, Sakharov never wielded power in an executive capacity, he understood the practical politics of perestroika better than any of the other dissidents who sought to reform the Soviet Union in the late 1980s.[49] At the same time, he remained true to his

---

48. Somewhat like Sakharov in his earlier years, Vaclav Havel believed that democratically elected leaders should use their power paternalistically to elevate the masses to a higher state of human consciousness. But while Sakharov eventually jettisoned his elitism, Havel retained his even after his election as president of Czechoslovakia in the Velvet Revolution. Chandler Rosenberg, "The Dissident Mind: Vaclav Havel as Revolutionary Intellectual," *Journal of the Historical Society* 6, no. 3 (September 2006): 465–80.

49. Michael Scammell includes Havel and Walesa with Sakharov among the dissidents in Russia and Eastern Europe who in his opinion successfully managed the transition to political

most cherished ideals and ethical principles, most notably "the absolute necessity," as he called it, "to speak the truth."[50]

But Sakharov's greatest achievement was in transcending the political culture that produced him. As a Russian who lived almost his entire life under a
regime that denied people human rights, he was able nevertheless to comprehend the concept of human rights, to grasp their centrality in a just society, and
to champion them tirelessly and eloquently under circumstances that cowed
lesser men into silence. At the same time he universalized them into principles
no less timeless and absolute than those the intelligentsia had advocated a century earlier. In doing so, he was acting like the *intelligent* he always was. But
Sakharov avoided the fanaticism into which this moral absolutism could easily
have degenerated—as it did in the case of the intelligentsia with the advent of
the revolutionary movement in the late nineteenth century—because he never
subordinated his respect for the individual personality to his desire to serve
all of humanity. In assessing the claims of the individual when they conflicted
with those of collectivities such as the nation or the working class or the state,
Sakharov never wavered in choosing the former over the latter. In his commitment to individual rights and in the constancy of purpose with which he sustained this commitment over a lifetime, Sakharov was one of the rare figures in
history from whom one can draw inspiration as well as enlightenment.

---

leadership. Of all the others who have written about Sakharov, the dissidents, and perestroika, to
the best of my knowledge only Peter Reddaway and Dmitri Glinski have noted this transformation
in Sakharov. They also seem to share Scammell's conviction, and mine, that Sakharov did not
betray his principles in the process. Michael Scammell, "The Prophet and the Wilderness," 36;
Reddaway and Glinski, *Tragedy of Russia's Reforms,* 229, 668.

50. Sakharov, "It's an Absolute Necessity to Speak the Truth," 14.

# Bibliography

**Part I. Writings, Public Statements, Letters, and Interviews of Sakharov**

*1947*

"Generation of the Hard Component of Cosmic Rays." In *Collected Scientific Works*, edited by
   D. ter Haar, D. V. Chudnovsky, and G. V. Chudnovsky, 239–54. New York: Marcel Dekker,
   1982: 239–54.
"Theory of Nuclear Transitions of the Type O-O." Candidate of Science thesis, FIAN.

*1948*

"Excitation Temperature in a Gas-Discharge Plasma." In *Collected Scientific Works*, 43–47.
"Interaction of the Electron and the Positron in Pair Production." In *Collected Scientific Works*,
   255–80.
"Miuonnyi kataliz." *Otchet FIAN SSSR*, 1948, 41–43.

*1951*

"Theory of a Magnetic Thermonuclear Reactor, Part II." In *Collected Scientific Works*, 11–22.

*1957*

"Radioactive Carbon in Nuclear Explosions and Nonthreshold Biological Effects." In *Soviet
   Scientists on the Danger of Nuclear Tests*, edited by A. V. Lebedinsky, 39–49. Moscow: Foreign
   Languages Publishing House, 1960.
"Reactions Produced by Mu-Mesons in Hydrogen." In *Collected Scientific Works*, 7–10. With
   Ia. B. Zeldovich.

*1958*

"Nuzhny estestvenno-matematicheskie shkoly." *Pravda*, November 19, 1958, 3. With
   Ia. Zeldovich.

*1965*

"Igor' Evgen'evich Tamm (k sedesiateliiu so dnia rozhdeniia)." *Uspekhi fizicheskikh nauk* 86, no. 2 (June 1965): 353. With V. L. Ginzburg and E. L. Feinberg.

"The Initial Stage of an Expanding Universe and the Appearance of a Nonuniform Distribution of Matter." In *Collected Scientific Works,* 65–83.

"Magnetic Cumulation." In *Collected Scientific Works,* 23–27. With others.

"The Symmetry of the Universe." In *Sakharov Remembered: A Tribute by Friends and Colleagues,* edited by Sidney D. Drell and Sergei P. Kapitza, 217–23. New York: American Institute of Physics, 1991.

"U chenyi i grazhdanin—akademiku I. Ye. Tammu—70 let." *Izvestiia,* July 8, 1965, 6.

*1966*

"Establishment Intellectuals Protest to Brezhnev." In *An End to Silence: Uncensored Opinion in the Soviet Union: From Roy Medvedev's Underground Magazine "Political Diary,"* edited by Stephen F. Cohen, 177–79. New York: W. W. Norton, 1982. With others.

"Magnetoimplosive Generators." In *Collected Scientific Works,* 29–41.

"Maximum Temperature of Thermal Radiation." In *Collected Scientific Works,* 137–39.

"The Quark Structure and Masses of Strongly Interacting Particles." In *Collected Scientific Works,* 205–21. With Ya. B. Zeldovich.

"To the Supreme Soviet of the RSFSR." In *The Demonstration in Pushkin Square,* edited by Pavel Litvinov, 14–15. Boston: Gambit, 1969. With others.

"Vacuum Quantum Fluctuations in Curved Space and the Theory of Gravitation." In *Collected Scientific Works,* 167–69, 171–77.

*1967*

"Quark-Muonic Currents and Violation of CP Invariance." In *Collected Scientific Works,* 89–92.

"Scientists and the Danger of Nuclear War." In Cohen, *An End to Silence,* 228–34. With Ernst Henry.

"Vacuum Quantum Fluctuations in Curved Space and the Theory of Gravitation." In *Collected Scientific Works,* 167–69, 171–77.

"Violation of CP Invariance, C Asymmetry, and Baryon Asymmetry of the Universe." In *Collected Scientific Works,* 85–88.

*1968*

*Progress, Coexistence and Intellectual Freedom.* Edited with an introduction, afterword, and notes by Harrison E. Salisbury. New York: W. W. Norton, 1968.

"Sushchestvuet li elementarnaia dlina." *Fizika v shkole* 2 (1968): 6–15.

*1969*

"Antiquarks in the Universe." In *Collected Scientific Works,* 93–104.

*1970*

"A Multisheet Cosmological Model." In *Collected Scientific Works,* 105–14.

"Otkrytoe obrashchenie k Prezidentu SShA R. Niksonu i Predsedateliu Prezidiuma Verkhovnogo Soveta SSSR N. V. Podgornomu, 28 dekabria 1970." In *Sobranie dokumentov samizdata* 7 (Munich: RFE/RL, 1972), no. AS512, 1–2.

"Otkrytoe pis'mo L. I. Brezhnevu v sviazi s nasil'stvennym pomeshcheniem Zh. A. Medvedeva v psikhiatricheskuiu bol'nitsu (June 6, 1970)." In *Sobranie dokumentov* samizdata 7 (RFE/RL: 1972), no. AS471, 1–2.

"Pis'mo Presidium Verkhovnogo Soveta SSSR." In *Sobranie dokumentov samizdata* 6 (RFE/RL: 1972), no. AS435, 1–2. With V. I. Chalidze, A. S. Volpin, and P. I Iakir.

"Pis'mo v zashchitu R. Pimenova I B. Vaila: Predsedateliu Verkhovnogo Suda RSFSR." In *A. Sakharov v bor'be za mir,* edited by Ia. Trushnovich, 191–92. Frankfurt/Main: Possev-Verlag, 1973. With others.

"Prezidiumu Verkhovnogo Soveta SSSR." *Posev* 11 (1970): 62. With V. N. Chalidze, A. S. Volpin, and P. I. Iakir.

"Printsipy Komiteta prav cheloveka." *Posev* 12 (1970): 23. With others.

"A Reformist Program for Democratization." In Cohen, *An End to Silence,* 317–27. With Roy Medvedev and Valentin Turchin.

## 1971

"Delo Abel'sona i dr. (December 23, 1971)." In *Sobranie dokumentov samizdata* 16 (RFE/RL: 1972), no. AS660-v, 33–34. With V. I. Chalidze and A. N. Tverdokhlebov.

"Dokumenty iuridicheskoi praktiki delo Bukovskogo (November 29, 1971)." In *Sobranie dokumentov samizdata* 16 (RFE/RL: 1972), no. AS660-v, 5–6. With V. Chalidze, A. Tverdokhlebov, and A. S. Volpin.

"Let Soviet Citizens Emigrate (October 7, 1971)." In *Sakharov Speaks,* edited by Harrison E. Salisbury. New York: Vintage Books, 1974: 160–63.

"Memorandum (March 5, 1971)." In *Memoirs,* 641–49. New York: Alfred A. Knopf, 1990.

"Mnenie Komiteta prav Cheloveka po probleme lits, priznannykh psykhicheski bol'nymi (July 3, 1971)." In *Sobranie dokumentov samizdata* 24 (RFE/RL: 1977), no. AS1268, 2–4. With A. N. Tverdokhlebov, V. N. Chalidze, and I. P. Shafarevich.

"Obrashchenie k General'nomu prokuroru i ministru iustitsii SSSR s pros'boi garantirovat' glastnosti sudoroizvodstva i sobliudeniia vsekh predusmotrennykh zakonom prav obviniaemogo na predstoiashchem protsesse V. Bukovskogo (December 1971)." In *Sobranie dokumentov samizdata* 24 (RFE/RL: 1977), no. AS1283, 1. With M. A. Leontovich, I. P. Shafarevich, and A. A. Galich.

"Obrashchenie Komiteta prav cheloveka k Vsemirnomu kongressu psikhiatrov." *Posev* 11 (1971): 4–5.

"O strannom protsesse v Sverdlovske (July 16, 1971)." *Khronika tekushchikh sobytii* 21 (September 11, 1971). In *Sobranie dokumentov samizdata* 10b (RFE/RL: 1972), no. AS1000, 8. With V. Chalidze.

"Otkrytoe pis'mo Ministru vnutrennikh del N. A. Shchelokovu v podderzhku V. Fainberga i V. Borisova, a takzhe drugikh lits, podvergshikhsia repressiiam v marte 1971 g. (March 30, 1971)." In *Sobranie dokumentov samizdata* 8 (RFE/RL: 1972), no. AS609, 1–2.

"Pamiati Igoria Evgen'evicha Tamma." *Uspekhi fizicheskikh nauk* 105, no. 1 (September 1971): 163. With V. L. Ginzburg, M. A. Markov, and E. L. Feinberg.

"Pis'mo N. V. Podgornomu v zashchitu A. Ye. Levitina-Krasnova (May 23, 1971)." In *Sobranie dokumentov samizdata* 9 (RFE/RL: 1972), no. AS685, 1.

"Prezidiumu Verkhovnogo soveta SSR: O presledovanii evreev-repatriatov v Sovetskom Soiuze (May 20, 1971)." *Posev* 6 (1971): 12.

"Privetstvie g-nu U Tantu pos slutsaiu obeda, organizuemogo Mezhdunarodnoi Ligoi prav cheloveka v ego chest' (December 2, 1971)." In *Sobranie dokumentov samizdata* 24 (RFE/RL: 1977), no. AS1272, 1.

"To the Members of the USSR Supreme Soviet: Request for a Pardon." *Chronicle of Current Events,* no. 21 (September 11, 1971): 278. With others.

## 1972

"Appeal to the General Secretary of the Central Committee and the USSR Prosecutor General (January 18, 1972)." In *Sakharov Speaks,* 236.

"51 in Soviet Ask Amnesty for Political Prisoners." *New York Times,* November 19, 1972, 2.

"Komitet prav Cheloveka, Obrashchenie v Presidium VS/SSSR o vosstanovlenii prav nasil'stvenno pereselennykh narodov (April 21, 1972)." In *Sobranie dokumentov samizdata* 24 (RFE/RL: 1977), no. AS1254, 1. With others.

Letter to Brezhnev, Kosygin, and Podgorny, January 1, 1972. Sakharov Archives. Brandeis University, Waltham, Mass.

"Mnenie Komiteta po povodu doklada A. N. Tverdokhlebova o bor'be sovetskogo zakonodatel'stva s paraziticheskim obrazom zhizni (June 29, 1972)." In *Sobranie dokumentov samizdata* 24 (RFE/RL: 1977), no. AS1256, 1–3. With A. N. Tverdokhlebov, V. N. Chalidze, and I. P Shafarevich.

"On the Problem of Restoring the Rights of Persons and Peoples Violated in the Course of Forcible Resettlement (March 16, 1972)." In *Sakharov Speaks*, 237–38.

"Otkrytoe obrashchenie k psikhiatram vsego mira s prizyvom vystupit' v zashchitu Semena Gluzmana (November 15, 1972)." In *Sobranie dokumentov samizdata* 24 (RFE/RL: 1977), no. AS1221, 1.

"Postscript to Memorandum (June 1972)." In *Memoirs*, 649–52.

"Telegram to Rudenko on Admission to Trial of Lubarsky (October 27, 1972)." Cited in the *Chronicle of Current Events*, no. 28 (December 31, 1972): 21. With others.

"Telegram to the RSFSR Supreme Soviet (June 7, 1972)." *Chronicle of Current Events*, no. 26 (July 5, 1972): 263–64.

"The Topological Structure of Elementary Charges and CPT Symmetry." In *Collected Scientific Works*, 199–204.

"To the Presidium of the Supreme Soviet USSR (April 21, 1972)." In *Sakharov Speaks*, 238–39. With V. N. Chalidze, A. N. Tverdokhlebov, and I. P. Shafarevich.

"To the USSR Supreme Soviet: An Appeal for Amnesty (May 1972)." In *Sakharov Speaks*, 239–40. With others.

"To the USSR Supreme Soviet: On the Abolition of the Death Penalty (September 1972)." In *Sakharov Speaks*, 240. With others.

"A Voice Out of Russia." Interview by Jay Axelbank. *Observer,* December 3, 1972, 29.

*1973*

"Andrei Sakharov Demands International Investigation: An Open Appeal." *Samizdat Bulletin*, no. 3 (July 1973).

"Announcement of the Committee for Human Rights (July 9, 1973)." *Samizdat Bulletin*, no. 5 (September 1973). With Grigory Podyapolsky and Igor Shafarevich.

"Appeal to the Chilean Government about Pablo Neruda." In *Sakharov Speaks*, 243–44.

*A. Sakharov v bor'be za mir.* Edited by Ia. Trushnovich. Frankfurt/Main: Possev-Verlag, 1973.

"A Clarification (September 12, 1973)." In *Sakharov Speaks*, 1974: 208–10.

"I Assume Full Responsibility (November 28, 1973)." *Samizdat Bulletin*, no. 10 (February 1974).

"In Support of the Appeal of the International Committee for the Defense of Human Rights (December 29, 1973)." In *Sakharov Speaks*, 244–45.

Interview with a Lebanese Correspondent, October 11, 1973. In *Sakharov Speaks*, 223–26.

Interview with Olle Stenholm. In *Memoirs*, 623–30.

Interview with Mikhail P. Malyarov, First Deputy Soviet Prosecutor. In *Sakharov Speaks*, 179–92.

Interview with Western Correspondents, August 21, 1973. In *Sakharov Speaks*, 194–207.

Interv'iu dannoe im po telefonu iz Moskvy Korrespondentu zapadnogermanskogo zhurnala "Shpigel," September 17, 1973. In *Sobranie dokumentov samizdata* 25 (RFE/RL: 1977), no. AS1474, 1–8.

Introduction to *Sakharov Speaks*, 29–54.

"A Letter to the Congress of the United States (September 14, 1973)." In *Sakharov Speaks*, 211–15.

"Letter to Smirnov (October 3, 1973)." *Chronicle of Human Rights*, no. 4 (September–October 1973): 35–36.

"Letter to Yury Andropov (January 23, 1973)." *Chronicle of Human Rights*, no. 1 (November 1972–March 1973): 48–49.

"Let the Red Cross In." *Observer*, September 9, 1973, 2.

"My Place Is in My Homeland (November 30, 1973)." *Samizdat Bulletin*, no. 10 (February 1974).

"Obrashchen k Predsedateliu GA OON s prizyvom zapretit' pytki (November 11, 1973)." *Materialy samizdata* 1/76 (January 16, 1976) AS2451-a: 3.

"O moei pozitsii (October 9, 1973)." In *Andrei Dmitrievich: Vospominaniia o Sakharove*, edited by Tatiana I. Ivanova, 160–62. Moscow: Terra, 1990.

"An Open Letter to the United Nations Educational, Scientific and Cultural Organization (UNESCO) (March 22, 1973)." *Samizdat Bulletin*, no. 2 (June 1973). With others.

"Otkrytoe obrashchenie v sviazi s priznaniem Iu. Shikhanovicha dushevnobol'nym (July 5, 1973)." In *Sobranie dokumentov samizdata* 25 (RFE/RL: 1977), no. AS1445, 1–2. With E. Bonner and G. Podiapolskii.

"Otkrytoe pis'mo Genrichu Belliu ob A. Amal'rike i L. Ubozhko (May 27, 1973)." In *Sobranie dokumentov samizdata* 28 (RFE/RL: 1978), no. AS1521, 1–2.

"Otkrytoe pis'mo rektoru tel'avivskogo universiteta prof. Iuvalu Neemanu v zashchitu engeniia levicha (May 30, 1973)." In *Za i protiv: 1973 god, dokumenty, fakty, sobytiia*, 46. Moscow: PIK, 1991.

"Otkrytoe pis'mo v zhurnal 'Shpigel,' s zamechaniiami ob opublikovannom variante ego interv'iu shvedskomu televideniiu (July 29, 1973)." In *Sobranie dokumentov samizdata* 25 (RFE/RL: 1977), no. AS1456, 1–2.

"Otvety na voprosy, kasaiushcheesia Komiteta prav Cheloveka (January 1973)." In *Sobranie dokumentov samizdata* 24 (RFE/RL: 1977), no. AS1246, 1–3. With I. Shafarevich and G. Podiapolskii.

"O zaiavlenii Evgeniia Barabanova (September 19, 1973)." In *Sobranie dokumentov samizdata* 25 (RFE/RL: 1977), no. AS1476, 1. With G. Podiapolskii.

"Pis'mo Iu. V. Andropovu s pros'boi otpustit' na poruki Viktora Khaustova (October 28, 1973)." In *Sobranie dokumentov samizdata* 25 (RFE/RL: 1977), no. AS1476, 1. With E. Bonner.

"Pragmatism versus Morality (November 20, 1973)." *Samizdat Bulletin*, no. 10 (February 1974).

"Sakharov Favors House Trade Curbs." *New York Times*, October 8, 1973, 5.

"Sakharov on Receiving the Award of the International League for the Rights of Man (December 5, 1973)." In *Sakharov Speaks*, 227–29.

"Soviet Physicist Pleads for Dissenters." *New York Times*, August 3, 1972, 3.

"Statement of the Human Rights Committee (October 1, 1973)." In *Sakharov Speaks*, 217–21.

"A Talk with Soviet Dissident Andrei Sakharov." *New York Post*, August 23, 1973.

"Text of the Sakharov Reply to Lawyer." *New York Times*, October 8, 1973, 4.

"To L. I. Brezhnev, General Secretary of the CC CPSU (May 18, 1973)." In *Sakharov Speaks*, 1974.

"To the Secretary-General of the UN, Mr. Kurt Waldheim (June 25, 1973)." In *Sakharov Speaks*, 241–43. With Grigory Podyapolsky.

"Zaiavlenie A. Sakharova po povodu napadok na nego v sovetskoi pechati." In *A. Sakharov v bor'be za mir*, 172–74.

*1974*

"Address of Academician Andrei D. Sakharov at Meeting Organized by the International Committee for the Defense of Human Rights (June 5, 1974)." *Samizdat Bulletin*, no. 17 (September 1974).

"Andrei Sakharov's Appeals to Leonid Brezhnev and Richard Nixon (June 24, 1974)." *Samizdat Bulletin*, no. 17 (September 1974).

"An Appeal by S. Kovalev and A. Sakharov (December 27, 1974)." *Samizdat Bulletin*, no. 23 (March 1975).

"Appeal from Moscow Regarding Solzhenitsyn (February 13, 1974)." *Samizdat Bulletin*, no. 12 (April 1974).

"Appeal to General Suharto (April 4, 1974)." *Chronicle of Current Events*, no. 32 (July 17, 1974): 101.

"Appeal to the World's Scientists (July 9, 1974)." *Chronicle of Current Events*, no. 34 (December 31, 1974): 73–74.

"Blagodarstvennoe pis'mo Sakharova pri prisuzhdenii premiia 'Chino del' Duko' (September 24, 1974)." *Khronika tekushchikh sobytii* 33 (December 10, 1974): 61–62.

"The Case of the German Residents of Estonia (August 8, 1974)." *Chronicle of Human Rights*, no. 10 (July–August 1974): 11–12.

"Declaration (December 28, 1974)." *Samizdat Bulletin*, no. 23 (March 1975).

"Declaration of a Hunger Strike (June 28, 1974)." *Chronicle of Current Events*, no. 32 (July 17, 1974): 96.

"Declaration on Solzhenitsyn (January 5, 1974)." In *Sakharov Speaks*, 232–33. With Alexander Galich, Vladimir Maximov, Vladimir Voinovich, and Igor Shafarevich.

"Documents on Behalf of Dzhemilev (July 16, 1974)." *Chronicle of Current Events*, no. 32 (July 17, 1974): 31–33.

"General'nomu Sekretariu TsK KPSS K. U. Chernenko (February 21, 1984)," (letter). Sakharov Archives. Brandeis University, Waltham, Mass.

"I Appeal to You with Respect and Hope." *New York Times*, February 10, 1974, sec. 4: 16.

"In Answer to Solzhenitsyn." *New York Review of Books*, June 13, 1974, 3–4.

"In Defense of Khaustov (March 6, 1974)." *Samizdat Bulletin*, no. 19 (November 1974).

"In Defense of Ostapov (March 28, 1974)." *Chronicle of Human Rights*, no. 8 (March–April 1974): 32–33.

"In Defense of Plyushch and Shikhanovich (February 12, 1974)." *Chronicle of Human Rights*, no. 7 (January–February 1974): 29–30. With others.

"In Defense of Scientists (July 17, 1974)." *Chronicle of Human Rights*, no. 10 (July–August 1974): 15–16. With Igor Shafarevich.

"In Support of Siniavskii (October 1974)." Cited in *Chronicle of Current Events*, no. 35 (March 31, 1975): 149.

Interview with the BBC, August 22, 1974. *Chronicle of Current Events*, no. 34 (December 31, 1974): 74–75.

Interv'iu, dannoe korrespondentu ezhenedel'nika "Sandi Taims," o vysylke A. Solzhenitsyna iz SSSR i o "Moskovskom obrashchenii," February 20, 1974. In *Sobranie dokumentov samizdata* 28 (RFE/RL: 1978), AS1593, 1–3.

Interv'iu, dannoe korrespondentu gazety "Tribiun de Zhenev" o knige "Arkhipelag GULag" i o svobode slova i material'nom polozhenii v SSSR, January 20, 1974. In *Sobranie dokumentov samizdata* 28 (RFE/RL: 1978), no. AS1579, 1–4.

"It Is Immoral to Treat Human Suffering as 'Internal Affairs' (September 5, 1974)." *Samizdat Bulletin*, no. 19 (November 1974).

"Letter to Brezhnev (June 25, 1974)." *Chronicle of Current Events* (July 17, 1974), 104.

"Letter to Senator Henry Jackson, Secretary of State Henry Kissinger, and the US Congress (October 21, 1974)." *Chronicle of Human Rights*, nos. 11–12 (September–December 1974): 8–10.

"Mikhail Kheifits Is Convicted (September 15, 1974)." *Chronicle of Human Rights*, nos. 11–12 (September–December 1974): 36.

"Obrashchenie k General'nomu Sekretariu OON K. Val'dkhaimu s pros'boi posodeistvovat' vozvrashcheniiu krymskikh tatar na rodinu (January 1974)." In *Sobranie dokumentov samizdata* 12 (RFE/RL: 1974), AS1725, 1–2. With others.

"Obrashchenie v Mezhdunarodnyi PEN-klub i Evropeiskoe soobshchestvo pisatelei v sviazi s otkazom v razreshenii na vyezd v SShA Aleksandru Galichu (January 16, 1974)." In

*Sobranie dokumentov samizdata* 28 (RFE/RL: 1978), no. AS1546, 1–2. With E. Bonner and V. Maksimov.

"Obrashchenie v zashchitu Mustafy Dzhemileva (November 20, 1974)." In *Sobranie dokumentov samizdata* 12 (RFE/RL: 1974), no. AS1946-a, 4.

"On Aleksandr Solzhenitsyn's *Letter to the Soviet Leaders.*" In *The Political, Social and Religious Thought of Russian "Samizdat": An Anthology,* edited by Michael Meerson-Aksenov and Boris Shragin, 291–301. Belmont, Mass.: Nordland Publishing Co., 1977.

"An Open Letter (November 7, 1974)." *Samizdat Bulletin,* no. 22 (February 1975).

"An Open Letter to Leonid Brezhnev and Gerald Ford (November 20, 1974)." *Samizdat Bulletin,* no. 25 (May 1975).

"An Open Letter to Leonid Brezhnev from Andrei Sakharov (October 24, 1974)." *Samizdat Bulletin,* no. 25 (May 1975).

"Otkrytoe pis'mo akademiku V. A. Engel'gardtu (May 29, 1974)." In *Sobranie dokumentov samizdata* 29 (RFE/RL: 1978) no. AS1651, 1–2.

"Otvety na voprosy frantsuzskogo korrespondenta po povodu A. I. Solzhenitsyna (January 8, 1974)." In *Sobranie dokumentov samizdata* 28 (RFE/RL: 1978), no. AS1545, 1–2.

"Restrictions on the Freedom to Choose One's Domicile (September 11, 1974)." *Chronicle of Human Rights,* nos. 11–12 (September–December) 1974: 32.

"Sakharov: Hardliners Gaining Power in Kremlin." *Washington Post,* January 21, 1974, A14.

"Sakharov's Hunger Strike." *Chronicle of Human Rights,* no. 10 (July–August 1974): 21–22.

*Sakharov Speaks.* Edited by Harrison E. Salisbury. New York: Vintage Books, 1974.

"Sakharov Speaks Out for Dr. Shtern (December 13, 1974)." *Samizdat Bulletin,* no. 27 (July 1975).

"Scaler-Tensor Theory of Gravitation." In *Collected Scientific Works,* 195–97.

"Slushanie A. Sakharova v Danii (November 22, 1974)." *Posev* 6 (June 1975): 13–14.

"Statement by Academician Sakharov (August 2, 1974)." *Survey* 20, no. 4 (Autumn 1974): 111–12.

"Statement in Defense of Pirogov and Nekipelov to International League for the Rights of Man, International Committee for the Defense of Human Rights, and Amnesty International (May 28, 1974)." *Chronicle of Human Rights,* nos. 13–14 (May–June 1974): 13–14.

"To Amnesty International." *Chronicle of Current Events,* no. 32 (July 17, 1974), 102. With A. Tverdokhlebov.

"To the International League for the Rights of Man (February 27, 1974)." *Samizdat Bulletin,* no. 13 (May 1974). With others.

"Tomorrow: The View from Red Square." *Saturday Review,* August 24, 1974, 12–14, 108, 110.

"The 26th Anniversary of the Declaration of Human Rights (December 10, 1974)." *Samizdat Bulletin,* no. 24 (April 1975).

"Zaiavlenie 'K probleme finansovykh operatsii Vneshtorgbanka i Vneshposyltorga SSSR' (December 15, 1974)." *Materialy samizdata* 7/75 (February 14, 1975), AS2012: 1.

"Zaiavlenie o Vsesoiuznom agentstve po avtorskim pravam kak ob orudii tsenzury v sviazi s interv'iu B. Pankina ot 12.23.73 (January 5, 1974)." In *Sobranie dokumentov samizdata* 28 (RFE/RL: 1978), no. AS1542, 1–2. With A. Galich, V. Maksimov, V. Voinovich, and I. Shafarevich.

"Zaiavlenie v zashchitu Lidii Chukovskoi po povodu ee iskliucheniia iz Soiuza pisatelei SSSR (January 9, 1974)." In *Sobranie dokumentov samizdata* 28 (RFE/RL: 1978), no. AS1544, 1.

*1975*

"Andrei Sakharov on Emigration (April 22, 1975)." *Chronicle of Human Rights,* no. 15 (May–June 1975): 9–11.

"Andrei Sakharov's Appeal to the Congress of the United States of America (January 28, 1976)." *Samizdat Bulletin,* no. 23 (March 1975).

"Appeal for Amnesty (August 16, 1975)." *Chronicle of Current Events,* no. 37 (1978): 56–57. With others.

"Appeal for Dzhemilev (December 3, 1975)." *Chronicle of Current Events*, no. 38 (1978): 125.

"Appeal for Osipov (September 27, 1975)." *Chronicle of Current Events*, no. 37 (1978): 7.

"The Case of Sergei Kovalev (December 1975)." In *Alarm and Hope*, 20–24. New York: Vintage Books, 1978.

"Declaration on Florescul (October 30, 1975)." *Chronicle of Current Events*, no. 38 (1978): 110.

"Declaration on Former Political Prisoners (October 30, 1975)." *Chronicle of Current Events*, no. 38 (1978): 110.

"Druzh'ia i vragi Sakharova." *Khronika tekushchikh sobytii,* December 31, 1975, 3.

"In Defense of Leonid Plyushch (October 23, 1975)." *Chronicle of Human Rights*, nos. 17–18 (October–December 1975): 18.

"In Defense of Mustafa Dzhemilev ( June 27, 1975)." *Chronicle of Human Rights*, no. 16 ( July–September 1975): 10.

"Mass Formula for Mesons and Baryons with Allowance for Charm." In *Collected Scientific Works*, 223–26.

*My Country and the World.* New York: Vintage Books, 1975.

"The Need for an Open World ( July 10, 1975)." *Bulletin of the Atomic Scientists* 31, no. 9 (November 1975): 8–9.

"Nobel Acceptance Speech (December 11, 1975)." In *Alarm and Hope*, 3–18.

"Obrashchenie v 'Mezhdunarodnuiu Amnestiiu, Gen. sekr. Martinu Ennalsu i mezhdunarodnoi obshchestvennosti v zashchitu Andreia Tverdokhlebova i Mikoly Rudenko' (April 18, 1975)." *Materialy samizdata* 18/75 (May 2, 1975) AS2129: 1.

"On Behalf of the Political Prisoners of Moldavia (November 1975)." *Samizdat Bulletin*, no. 33 ( January 1976).

"An 'Open Letter' to Amnesty International and the World Federation of Democratic Jurists, Asking Them to Help Sergei Kovalev and Andrei Tverdokhlebov, Both Members of the AI Soviet Section Whose Trials Are Expected to Take Place Soon (October 20, 1975)." In *Sobranie dokumentov samizdata* 30 (RFE/RL: 1978), no. AS2371, 145–46.

"Otkrytoe pis'mo predsedateliu KGB Iu. V. Andropovu s trebovaniem prekratit' presledovanie chelov ego sem'i ( January 6, 1975)." *Materialy samizdata* 5/75 ( January 31, 1975) AS1996: 1–2.

Pis'mo Prezidentu AN SSSR akademiku Keldysh M. V., March 25, 1975. Sakharov Archives. Brandeis University. Waltham, Massachusetts.

"Political Prisoner's Day." *Chronicle of Human Rights*, nos. 17–18 (October–December 1975): 24–25. With others.

"Sakharov Calls for UN to Save Kurds." *Sunday Times*, March 30, 1975, 1.

"Spectral Density of Eigenvalues of the Wave Equation and Vacuum Polarization." In *Collected Scientific Works*, 179–94.

"Thousands Held in Russia—Sakharov." *Los Angeles Times*, December 9, 1975, 1, 7.

"To Non-Soviet Readers of My Book 'My Country and the World' (October 1, 1975)." *Samizdat Bulletin*, no. 34 (February 1976).

"What the Nobel Prize Means, by Sakharov." *Sunday Times*, October 12, 1975, 10.

"Why I Speak Out Alone." *Observer Review,* June 8, 1975, 19.


*1976*

"Address of September 25, 1976 Sent to International League for Human Rights." In *Alarm and Hope*, 33–34.

"Appeal for Bukovsky (October 29, 1976)." In *Alarm and Hope*, 36–37.

"Appeal for Davidovich (March 7, 1976)." Quoted in *Chronicle of Current Events*, no. 39 (March 12, 1976): 198. With others.

"Appeal for Kovalev ( January 9, 1976)." *Chronicle of Current Events*, no. 39 (March 12, 1976): 212–13. With others.

"Declaration of Support for a Symposium on Jewish Culture in the USSR (November 29, 1976)." In *Alarm and Hope*, 147.

"General'nomu sekretariu OON, Glavam gosudarstv-chlenov Soveta Bezopasnosti, Prezidentu Livana (October 1976)." In *Vospominaniia*. Vol. 2, 482. Moscow: Prava cheloveka, 1996.

"Glavam pravitel'stv stran-uchastnits Khel'sinksogo Soveshchaniia (November 29, 1976)." *Khronika tekushchykh sobytii* 43 (December 31, 1976): 87–88.

"In Defense of Yefrem Yankelevich (June 11, 1976)." *Samizdat Bulletin*, no. 47 (March 1977).

Interview with AP Correspondent George Krimsky, December 6, 1976. In *Alarm and Hope*, 84–87, 90–93.

Interv'iu ital'ianskoi gazette "Korr'era della Sera," February 25, 1976. In *Khronika tekushchykh sobytii* 39 (March 12, 1976): 70–71.

Interv'iu norvezhskomu korrespondentu, October 30, 1976. In *Khronika tekushchykh sobytii* 44 (March 16, 1977): 105–8.

"Message to Ford and Carter (October 11, 1976)." In *Alarm and Hope*, 43–44.

"Obrashchenie k Predsedateliu GA OON s prizyvom zapretit' pytki." *Materialy samizdata* 1/76 (January 16, 1976) AS2451-a: 1–4. With others.

"Osvobozhdenie Vladimira Bukovskogo (October 1976)." *Khronika tekushchykh sobytii* 43 (December 31, 1976): 6. With Lev Kopelev.

"Otkrytoe obrashchenie (February 23, 1976)." *Khronika tekushchykh sobytii* 39 (March 12, 1976): 69. With others.

"Pamiati Efima Davidovicha (April 1976)." *Khronika tekushchykh sobytii* 40 (May 20, 1976): 76–77. With others.

"Plea to Amnesty International (October 29, 1976)," In *Alarm and Hope*, 36. With others.

"Pobeda sil razuma i gumannosti (December 18, 1976)." *Khronika tekushchykh sobytii* 43 (December 31, 1976): 9. With P. Grigorenko and Iu. Orlov.

"Postscript to 'Open Letter from Mothers and Wives of Political Prisoners' (March 19, 1976)." *Chronicle of Human Rights*, nos. 20–21 (April–June 1976): 27. With Yury Orlov.

"Prezidiumu XXV s"ezda KPSS (February 19, 1976)." *Khronika tekushchykh sobytii* 39 (March 12, 1976): 50–51. With Petr Grigorenko.

"Protest Over Detention of Alexander Ginzburg (June 7, 1976)." In *Alarm and Hope*, 149–50.

"Sakharov Seeks Open World." *Guardian*, April 1, 1976, 6.

"Soveshchaniiu evropeiskikh kommunisticheskikh partii (July 23, 1976)." *Khronika tekushchykh sobytii* 42 (October 8, 1976): 86–87. With Iu. Orlov and V. Turchin.

"A Statement (April 17, 1976)." *Chronicle of Human Rights*, nos. 20–21 (April–June 1976): 15–16.

"Telegram to President-Elect Carter (November 3, 1976)." In *Alarm and Hope*, 44–45.

"To the Workers' Defense Committee (November 20, 1976)." In *Memoirs*, 684–85.

"The Trial of Andrei Tverdokhlebov (April 4, 1976)." *Chronicle of Current Events*, no. 40 (May 20, 1976): 4–5.

"Vsem uchenym mira s prizyvom vystupat' v zashchitu Sergeia Kovaleva (November 1976)." *Materialy Samizdata* 4/76 (December 27, 1976) AS2756: 1–5. With others.

"V zashchitu Andreia Tverdokhlebova (April 1976)." In *Delo Tverdokhlebova*, 97. New York: Izdatelstvo khronika, 1976. With others.

"V zashchitu Zosimova (October 26, 1976)." *Khronika tekushchykh sobytii* 43 (December 31, 1976): 86–87. With others.

"A Welcome to *Kontinent*." In *Kontinent*, xvi–xvii. London: Andrei Deutsch, 1976.

"Zaiavlenie, adresovannoe v Mezhdunarodnuiu Amnestiiu, v OON, rukovoditeliam gosudarstv i politicheskikh partii (September 30, 1976)." Sakharov Archives. Brandeis University, Waltham, Mass.

"Zaiavlenie (April 1976)." In *Delo Tverdokhlebova*, 81. New York: Izdatelstvo khronika, 1976. With others.

"'Zaiavlenie o dele Tverdokhlebova' nakanune passmotreniia Verkhovnym sudom RSFSR kassatsionnoi zhaloby (May 3, 1976)." *Materialy samizdata* 15/76 (May 7, 1976), AS2525: 1–3.

*1977*

ABC Interview, March 25, 1977. In *Alarm and Hope,* 53–54, 116–17.

"Address to the Second Sakharov Hearing (October 30, 1977)." In *Alarm and Hope,* 129–32.

"Alarm and Hope (1977)." In *Alarm and Hope,* 99–111.

"Appeal on Behalf of Naum Meiman and Iurii Goldfarb (September 9, 1977)." In *Alarm and Hope,* 156.

"Appeal on Behalf of Orlov ( July 11, 1977)." In *Alarm and Hope,* 153. With others.

"Appeal on Behalf of Pyotr Ruban ( January 3, 1977)." In *Alarm and Hope,* 42.

"Appeal to the Belgrade Conference Participants (October 4, 1977)." *Chronicle of Current Events,* no. 47 (November 30, 1977), 103.

"Appeal to the Parliaments of All Helsinki-Signatory States (October 3, 1977)." In *Alarm and Hope,* 157–59.

CBS Interview, February 10, 1977. In *Alarm and Hope,* 48–49, 115–16.

"Cut Off by KGB." *Observer,* January 9, 1977, 9.

"Defense of the Khailo Family." Cited in *Chronicle of Current Events,* no. 48 (March 14, 1978): 127.

"Diskriminatsiia krymskikh tatar prodozhaetsia (November 14, 1977)." *Khronika tekushchikh sobytii* 47 (November 30, 1977): 69–70.

"In Defense of Alexander Ginzburg (February 4, 1977)." *Chronicle of Human Rights,* no. 25 ( January–March 1977): 10–11. With Igor Shafarevich.

"In Support of Charter 77 (February 12, 1977)." *Chronicle of Human Rights,* no. 25 ( January–March 1977): 67. With others.

Interview in *France-Soir,* February 23, 1977. In *Alarm and Hope,* 52–53, 94–95.

Interview in *Newsweek,* February 24, 1977. In *Alarm and Hope,* 25–26, 134–38.

Interview on Swedish/Norwegian Radio and Television, April 4, 1977. In *Alarm and Hope,* 117–19.

Interview with *Corriere della Sera,* January 26, 1977. In *Alarm and Hope,* 139–44.

"Letter to Carter ( January 21, 1977)." In *Alarm and Hope,* 46–48.

"Letter to the Amnesty International Symposium on the Abolition of the Death Penalty (September 19, 1977)." In *Memoirs,* 653–56.

"Letter to the *New York Times* (October 10, 1977)." In *Alarm and Hope,* 159–62.

"A Look at the Past Year (December 14, 1977)." *Chronicle of Current Events,* no. 48 (March 14, 1978): 173–74.

"Message to the Venice Biennale (November 4, 1977)." In *Alarm and Hope,* 113.

"Obrashchenie v zashchitu Mal'vy Landy (May 12, 1977)." In *Trevoga i nadezhda: Odin god obshchestvennoi deiatel'nosti Andreia Dmitrievicha Sakharova,* 115. New York: Khronika, 1978.

"Obrashchenie v zashchitu sem'i Chudnovskikh ( July 23, 1977)." In *Trevoga i nadezhda,* 117.

"100-dnevnaia golodovka politzakliuchennykh Mordovskikh lagerei—Trebovanie statusa politzakliuchennogo (April 21, 1977)." *Khronika tekushchikh sobytii* (May 25, 1977): 47. With M. Landa, E. Bonner, and T. Khodorovich.

"On Receiving the Joseph Prize (November 4, 1977)." In *Alarm and Hope,* 162.

"Pentecostals (December 12, 1977)." *Chronicle of Current Events,* no. 48 (March 14, 1978): 138.

"Reply to Carter (February 17, 1977)." In *Alarm and Hope,* 50–52.

"Reply to Gusev (March 5, 1977)." In *Alarm and Hope,* 81–84.

"Repressii protiv grupp 'Khel'sinki,' Arest Ginzburga, Orlova, Rudenko, Tikhogo, Shcharanskogo ( January 5, 1977)." *Khronika tekushchikh sobytii* 44 (March 16, 1977): 10.

"Sharansky Appeal (March 19, 1977)." In *Alarm and Hope,* 151–52.

"Speech to the AFL-CIO Convention in Los Angeles (November 28, 1977)." In *Alarm and Hope,* 163–67.

"Statement on Moscow Bomb ( January 12, 1977)." In *Alarm and Hope,* 59–63.

"Statement on Vladimir Rubtsov ( January 18, 1977)." In *Alarm and Hope,* 64–65.

"Telegram to President-Elect Carter (January 3, 1977)." In *Alarm and Hope,* 42.

"Telegram to USSR Prosecutor General Rudenko and MVD Minister Shchelokov Asking Them to Prevent a New Falsified Trial of Mustafa Dzhemilev (November 15, 1977)." *Sobranie dokumentov samizdata* 30 (RFE/RL: 1978), AS3210, 644. With Petr Grigorenko and Reshat Dzhemilev.

"Telegramma. Predsedateliu Prezidiuma Verkhovnogo Soveta L. Brezhnevu (December 30, 1977)." *Materialy samizdata* 4/78 (January 20, 1978) AS3122: 1. With Elena Bonner.

"To Academician B. N. Ponomaryov and Academician A. P. Alexandrov (November 15, 1977)." *Chronicle of Current Events,* no. 47 (November 30, 1977): 165–66.

"To the President of Yugoslavia, Josip Broz Tito (November 25, 1977)." *Chronicle of Current Events,* no. 48 (March 14, 1978): 172.

"To the Psychiatrists of the World (October 17, 1977)." *Chronicle of Current Events,* no. 47 (November 30, 1977): 164. With N. Meiman, P. Grigorenko, and S. Kallistratova.

"V drugikh lageriakh i tiur'makh (November 30, 1977)." *Khronika tekushchikh sobytii* 47 (November 30, 1977): 108. With P. G. Grigorenko.

"Zaiavlenie (April 21, 1977)." *Khronika tekushchikh sobytii* 45 (May 25, 1977): 47. With M. Landa, E. Bonner, and T. Khodorovich.

"Zaiavlenie A. D. Sakharova n press-konferentsii 10 Noiabria g." In *Trevoga i nadezhda,* 135–36.

"Zaiavlenie Genprokuroru SSSR R. Rudenko po povodu proizvola i narushenli zakonnosti rabotnikami KGB vo vermin obyskov i na vyemke v dome 3 Gamsakhurdia (April 14, 1977)." *Materialy samizdata* 21/77 (July 25, 1977) AS2949: 1–3. With P. Grigorenko and S. Kallistratova.

*1978*

"About the Belgrade Conference (March 9, 1978)." *Chronicle of Current Events,* no. 48 (March 14, 1978): 174–75.

Afterword to *Alarm and Hope,* 168–81.

"An Appeal (December 10, 1978)." *Chronicle of Human Rights,* no. 32 (October–December 1978): 5–7. With others.

"Appeal on Behalf of Yakov Vagner (May 6, 1978)." *Chronicle of Current Events,* no. 51 (December 1, 1978): 155–56.

"The Human Rights Movement in the USSR and Eastern Europe: Its Goals, Significance, and Difficulties (November 8, 1978)." In *On Sakharov,* edited by Alexander Babyonyshev, 257–58. New York: Alfred A. Knopf, 1982.

"Human Rights Struggle Will Continue." *Guardian Weekly,* August 27, 1978.

"In Defense of Ginzburg (February 2, 1978)." *Chronicle of Current Events,* no. 48 (March 14, 1978): 12. With others.

"In Defense of Sharansky (March 8, 1978)." *Chronicle of Current Events,* no. 48 (March 14, 1978): 14.

"In Defense of Vins (February 18, 1978)." *Chronicle of Current Events,* no. 48 (March 14, 1978): 22.

Interview with a French journalist, September 14, 1978. *Chronicle of Current Events,* no. 51 (December 1, 1978): 195.

Interview with Andrei Sakharov. BBC, July 3, 1978, 12–16.

Interview with *L'Express,* December 25, 1978. *Chronicle of Current Events,* no. 52 (March 1, 1979): 134.

Interview with the Italian journal *Grazie,* January 31, 1978. *Chronicle of Current Events,* no. 48 (March 14, 1978): 174.

"Letter to Handler and Stone on Scientific Contacts (May 1978)." *Chronicle of Current Events,* no. 51 (December 1, 1978): 176.

"Letter to L. I. Brezhnev and N. A. Shchelokov (July 4, 1978)." *Chronicle of Current Events,* no. 51 (December 1, 1978): 122.

"Mirovoi obshchestvennosti, vsem veruiushchim, vsem vystupaiushchim za sobliudenie prav cheloveka (April 16, 1978)," *Materialy samizdata* 30/78 (August 11, 1978) AS3311: 1.

"Mirovoi obshchestvennosti v zashcitu Balisa Gaiauskasa (April 16, 1978)," *Khronika tekushchikh sobytii* 49 (May 14, 1978): 16–17.

"Nuclear Energy and the Freedom of the West." *Bulletin of the Atomic Scientists* 34, no. 6 (June 1978): 12–14.

"Obrashchenie k mirovoi obshchestvennosti s prizyvom podderzhat' trebovanie Eduarda Kuznetsova o predostavlenii emu svidaniia (January 16, 1978)." *Materialy samizdata* 7/78 (February 3, 1978) AS3148: 1–2. With Elena Bonner.

"Obrashchenie k sootechestvennikam i mirovoi obshchestvennosti s prizyvom borot'sia za osobozhdenie A. Podrabineka (May 22, 1978)," *Materialy samizdata* 21/78 (June 2, 1978) AS3248: 1. With others.

"Otkrytoe pis'mo v zashchitu Gregoriia Gol'shteina (March 8, 1978)." *Materialy samizdata* 37/78 (November 3, 1978) AS3369: 1–2.

"Pis'mo A. D. Sakharovu (October 1978)." *Khronika tekushchykh sobytii* 51 (December 1, 1978): 84.

"Predislovie." In *Vykhod iz labirinta*, by Evgenii Gnedin, 5–9. New York: Chalidze Publications, 1982: 5–9.

"Predislovie k 'O vremeni i o sebe.'" *Posev* 8 (1978): 59–60.

"Request on Behalf of Pyotr Vins' Family (January 3, 1978)." *Chronicle of Current Events*, no. 48 (March 14, 1978): 22.

"Statement (July 20, 1978)." *Chronicle of Human Rights*, no. 31 (July–September 1978): 30.

"Statement Concerning the Moscow Olympiad in 1980 (September 14, 1978)." *Chronicle of Current Events*, no. 51 (December 1, 1978): 194–95.

"To the International Olympic Committee; To the President of the IOC, Lord M. Killanin (June 26, 1978)." *Chronicle of Current Events*, no. 51 (December 1, 1978): 194. With others.

*Trevoga i nadezhda: Odin god obshchestvennoi deiatel'nosti Andreia Dmitrievicha Sakharova.* New York: Khronika, 1978.

"12 maia 1978-goda—Den' Gluzmana (May 11, 1978)." *Materialy samizdata* 30/78 (August 11, 1978) AS3318: 1.

"Zaiavlenie (December 2, 1978)." In *Vospominaniia*, 2:490–91.

"Zaiavlenie v Verkhovnyi sovet sssr ob amnestii politicheskikh zakliuchennykh (October 30, 1978)." *Materialy samizdata* 36/78 (October 27, 1978) AS3360: 1–2. With others.


## 1979

"Andrei Sakharov on Science and Society (December 6, 1979)." *Chronicle of Human Rights*, no. 36 (October–December 1979): 25–26.

"Answers to Questions from the Italian Journalist Laccua (December 21, 1979)." *Chronicle of Current Events*, no. 55 (December 31, 1979): 65–67.

"Baltic Dissidents in Soviet Urge Freeing of 3 Republics." *New York Times*, August 25, 1979, 3.

"The Baryonic Asymmetry of the Universe." In *Collected Scientific Works*, 115–30.

"Czechoslovak Trials and Moscow Support." *Chronicle of Human Rights*, no. 36 (October–December 1979): 19. With others.

Interview with the *Washington Post*, January 1, 1979. *Chronicle of Current Events*, no. 52 (March 1, 1979): 134–35.

"Letter to Giscard d'Estaing (March 1979)." Cited in *Chronicle of Current Events*, no. 53 (August 1, 1979): 123.

"Letter to Scientific Colleagues (March 10, 1979)." *Chronicle of Human Rights*, no. 33 (January–March 1979), 29.

"Message to the 1979 Sakharov Hearings (September 5, 1979)." *Samizdat Bulletin*, no. 78 (October 1979).

"On an Article in the Newspaper *Le Figaro* (November 30, 1979)." Cited in *Chronicle of Current Events*, no. 55 (November 30, 1979): 65.

"On the Persecution of the Journal 'Searches' (January 1979)." *Chronicle of Current Events,* no. 52 (March 1, 1979): 25. With others.

"Open Appeal (November 5, 1979)." *Chronicle of Current Events,* no. 54 (November 15, 1979): 13. With Elena Bonner.

"Otkrytoe obrashchenie (October 24, 1979)." *Khronika tekushchikh sobytii* 54 (November 15, 1979): 137.

"O zadachakh, predlagavshikhsia na mekhmate MGU abiturientam-evreiam (June 12, 1979)." *Khronika tekushchikh sobytii* 54 (November 15, 1979): 138.

"Perepiska s Genrikhom Bëllem." In *Vospominaniia* 2:476–79.

"Predsedateliu PVS SSSR L. I. Brezhnevu." *Khronika tekushchikh sobytii* 54 (November 15, 1979): 137–38.

Review of *Disturbing the Universe,* by Freeman Dyson. *Washington Post Book World,* September 23, 1979, 1, 8.

"Sakharov—For General Amnesty April 28, 1979)." *Samizdat Bulletin,* no. 78 (October 1979).

"Sakharov in Defense of the Crimean Tatars (January 31, 1979)." *Chronicle of Human Rights,* no. 33 (January–March 1979): 11.

"Statement on Charter-77 (July 31, 1979)." *Chronicle of Human Rights,* no. 35 (April–June 1979): 15.

"Tolstovskii fond. N'iu-Iork, SShA (September 27, 1979)." *Khronika tekushchikh sobytii* 54 (November 15, 1979): 138.

*1980*

"Amerikanskomu fizicheskomu obshchestvu federatsii amerikanskikh uchenykh (December 1980)." *Materialy samizdata* 14/81 (April 10, 1981) AS4271: 1.

"Appeal to the Madrid Conference on Behalf of Orlov (December 1, 1980)." *Chronicle of Current Events,* no. 60 (December 31, 1980): 88.

"Cosmological Models of the Universe with Reversal of Time's Arrow." In *Collected Scientific Works,* 131–36.

"An Estimate of the Coupling Constant between Quarks and the Gluon Field," In *Collected Scientific Works,* 233–37.

"In Defense of the Poet Vasily Stus (October 19, 1980)." *Chronicle of Current Events,* no. 58 (November 1980): 80–81.

"Kto osuzhden (August 29, 1980)?" *Materialy samizdata* 17/81 (May 4, 1981) AS4076: 1. With others.

"A Letter from Exile (May 4, 1980)." In Babyonyshev, *On Sakharov,* 223–40.

"Lev Kopelev Is under Fire (February 3, 1980)." *Chronicle of Current Events,* no. 56 (April 30, 1980), 82.

"Mass Formula for Mesons and Baryons." In *Collected Scientific Works,* 227–32.

"Message to the Polish Interfactory Strike Committee." *Chronicle of Human Rights,* no. 40 (October–December 1980): 13.

"Nachal'niku Teoreticheskogo otdela FIAN akademiku V. L. Ginzburgu (September 14, 1980)." *Materialy samizdata* 41/80 (November 28, 1980) AS4136: 2.

"Ob"edinennomu mezhzavodskomu stachechnomu komitetu (August 30, 1980)." *Materialy samizdata* 35/80 (October 13, 1980) AS4092: 1. With others.

"On Behalf of Viktor Brailovsky (December 5, 1980)." *Chronicle of Human Rights,* no. 40 (October–December 1980): 12–13.

"Open Letter on Afghanistan (July 27, 1980)." In *Memoirs,* 657–59.

"Open Letter to Anatoly Aleksandrov, President of the USSR Academy of Sciences (October 20, 1980)." In Babyonyshev, *On Sakharov,* 212–22.

"Otkrytoe pis'mo (January 18, 1980)." *Materialy samizdata* 6/80 (February 18, 1980) AS3859: 1–2.

"Otvety na voprosy korrespondenta Bi-Bi-Si Ch. E. Birbaura 17/I-1980 g." Sakharov Archives. Brandeis University, Waltham, Mass.

"Otvety na voprosy korrespondenta Lakkua/ital'ianskoe agentsvo ANSA (1980)." *Materialy samizdata* 18/80 (May 19, 1980) AS3963: 6.

"Our Mail (February 12, 1980)." *Chronicle of Current Events,* no. 56 (April 30, 1980): 84.

"Political Prisoners Day (October 30, 1980)." *Chronicle of Human Rights,* no. 40 (October–December 1980): 14. With others.

"Sakharov Demands Hearing on Open Court." *Times* (London) (February 27, 1980, 9.

"Sakharov Proposes Soviet Withdrawal." *New York Times,* January 3, 1980, A13.

"Sakharov's Statement of January 27, 1980." In *Memoirs,* 673–75.

"Some Thoughts on the Threshold of the Eighties (February 18, 1980)." In Babyonyshev, *On Sakharov,* 241–43.

"Statement of January 27, 1980." In *Memoirs,* 673–75.

"Statement on Moscow Olympics (April 26, 1980)." *Chronicle of Current Events,* no. 56 (April 30, 1980): 87–88.

"Statement on Telegram to Alexandrov (March 3, 1980)." *Chronicle of Current Events,* no. 56 (March 3, 1980): 85.

"Statement on the Two Summonses (February 3, 1980)." *Chronicle of Current Events,* no. 56 (April 30, 1980): 81–82.

"Statement to Rekunkov (February 23, 1980)." *Chronicle of Current Events,* no. (April 30, 1980): 83–84.

"Telegram to Alexandrov (March 3, 1980)." *Chronicle of Current Events,* no. 56 (April 30, 1980): 85.

"To the Editor of 'Nature' Magazine (October 6, 1980)." *Samizdat Bulletin,* no. 92 (December 1980).

"To the Head of the Theoretical Department of FIAN, V. L. Ginzburg (September 14, 1980)." *Chronicle of Current Events,* no. 60 (December 31, 1980): 102.

"Vitse-prezidentu AN SSSR akademiku Velikhovu E. P. (August 12, 1980)." *Materialy samizdata* 41/80 (November 28, 1980) AS4135: 1–5.

"World Security, Human Rights Linked—Sakharov." *Los Angeles Times,* September 9, 1980, 5.

"Zaiavlene dlia pressy (May 21, 1980)." *Materialy samizdata* 33/80 (September 29, 1980), AS4082: 2.

"Zaiavlenie uchastnikam predstoiashchego v noiabre 1980 Madridskogo soveshchaniia-35—i stranam, podpisavshim Zakliuchitel'nyi Akt Khel'sinkskogo soveshchaniia (August 8, 1980)." *Materialy samizdata* 29/80 (August 22, 1980), AS4045: 1–3.

"Zaiavlenie 'v zashchitu Viktora Nekipelova' (June 14, 1980)." *Materialy samizdata* 29/80 (August 23, 1980), AS4039: 2.

*1981*

"Andrei Sakharov: An Autobiographical Note (March 24, 1981)." In Babyonyshev, *On Sakharov,* xi–xiv.

"Announcement of Intention to Begin a Hunger Strike (November 15, 1981)." In Babyonyshev, *On Sakharov,* 270–71.

"Appeal to Shevardnadze on Behalf of Kostava (December 30, 1981)." *Chronicle of Current Events,* no. 63 (December 31, 1981): 174.

"From Exile in Gorky (June 1, 1981)." *Chronicle of Human Rights,* no. 43 (July–September 1981): 18

"Glave delegatsii SShA na konferentsii b Madride g-nu Maksu Kempelmenu (January 29, 1981)." Sakharov Archives. Brandeis University, Waltham, Mass.

"How to Preserve World Peace (August 16, 1981)." In Babyonyshev, *On Sakharov,* 262–69.

Interview with Kevin Klose, June 1, 1981. *Chronicle of Human Rights,* no. 43 (July–September 1981): 17–21.

"Letter to an American Colleague [Sidney Drell] (January 30, 1981)." *Samizdat Bulletin,* no. 97 (May 1981).

"Letter to Brezhnev on Behalf of Elizaveta Alekseyeva (May 26, 1981)." *Chronicle of Current Events,* no. 63 (December 31, 1981): 128–29.

"Letter to Foreign Colleagues (October 1981)." *Chronicle of Current Events,* no. 63 (December 31, 1981): 131–32.

"Obrashchenie v zashchitu A. Bolonkina (April 3, 1981)." *Materialy samizdata* 13/81 (June 1, 1981), AS4319: 1.

"Open Letter (February 8, 1981)." *Chronicle of Current Events*, no. 61 (March 16, 1981): 202. With others.

"Political Prisoners' Day (October 28, 1981)." *Chronicle of Current Events*, no. 63 (December 31, 1981): 169.

"Reply to Lebowitz and Stone (November 27, 1981)." In Babyonyshe, *On Sakharov*, 272.

"Reply to Sidney Drell's Telegram (December 2, 1981)." Cited in *Chronicle of Current Events*, no. 63 (December 31, 1981): 134.

"The Responsibility of Scientists (March 24, 1981)." In Babyonyshev, *On Sakharov*, 205–11.

"Save Anatoly Marchenko (October 7, 1981)." *Chronicle of Current Events*, no. 63 (December 31, 1981): 30–31.

"Statement of March 17, 1981." In *Memoirs*, 680.

"Telegrams to Alexandrov and Velikhov (October 21, 1981)." *Chronicle of Current Events*, no. 63 (December 31, 1981): 129.

Telegram to Brezhnev (October 21, 1981)." *Chronicle of Current Events*, no. 63 (December 31, 1981): 129.

"To Dr. Linus Pauling, Winner of the Lenin Peace Prize and the Nobel Prize for Chemistry (May 4, 1981)." *Chronicle of Current Events*, no. 62 (July 14, 1981): 131.

"Two Appeals (March 22, 1981, and April 3, 1981)." In Babyonyshev, *On Sakharov*, 260.


## 1982

"Andrei Sakharov o pravozashchitnom dvizhenii (April 26, 1982)." *SSSR: Vnutrennie protivorechiia* 5 (1982): 5–9.

*Collected Scientific Works.* New York: Marcel Dekker, 1982.

"In Defense of Boris Altshuler (May 31, 1982)." *Chronicle of Current Events*, no. 64 (June 30, 1982): 114.

"In Defense of Ivan Kovalev (April 3, 1982)." *Chronicle of Current Events*, no. 64 (June 30, 1982): 4–5.

"Letter to Soviet Scientists (March 30, 1982)." *Chronicle of Current Events*, no. 64 (June 30, 1982): 104–6.

"Letter to Vitaly Fedorchuk (October 23, 1982)." In *Memoirs*, 681–82.

"Many-Sheeted Cosmological Models of the Universe." *Journal of Experimental and Theoretical Physics* 56, no. 4 (October 1982): 705–9.

"Open Letter to the Madrid Conference." *Samizdat Bulletin*, no. 108 (April 1982). With Naum Meiman.

"Pis'mo Al'tshuleru." In Altshuler, B. "On nebyl naiven." In Ivanova, *Andrei Dmitrievich*, 230–31.

"Pis'mo sovetskim uchenym (March 30, 1982)." *Materialy samizdata* 17/82 (May 30, 1982) AS4631: 1–3.

"A Reply to Slander (October 1982)." *New York Review of Books*, July 21, 1983, 8–11.

"Statement on Manuscript Theft (November 10, 1982)." In *Memoirs*, 682–83.

"Telegram to the American Astronomer Gehrels (February 21, 1982)." *Chronicle of Current Events*, no. 64 (June 30, 1982): 113.

"Telegramma v Presidium VS SSSR s prizyvom amnestirovat' uznikov sovesti v sviazi s 60-letiem SSSR (December 7, 1982)." *Materialy samizdata* 10/83 (March 7, 1983) AS4868: 2.

"Text of Sakharov's Letter to Pugwash Parley on Soviet Policy." *New York Times*, September 10, 1982, 6.

"To the President of France, Citizen Mitterand (January 20, 1982)." *Chronicle of Current Events*, no. 64 (June 30, 1982): 103–4.

"Two Years in Gorky (January 24, 1982)." *Samizdat Bulletin*, no. 108 (April 1982).

UPI interview, January 19, 1982. *Chronicle of Current Events*, no. 64 (June 30, 1982): 109–11.

"Vstrecha so Zbignevom Romashevskim (October 1982)." *Materialy samizdata* 20/83 (May 9, 1983) AS4929: 2.

"V zashchitu Georgiia Vladimova (February 19, 1982)." *Materialy samizdata* 15/82 (April 15, 1982) AS4623: 1.

"V zashchitu Sof'i Kalistratovoi (February 24, 1982)." *Materialy samizdata* 15/82 (April 15, 1982) AS4624: 1–2.

*1983*

"Acceptance Speech for the Szilard Award (April 1983)." In *Memoirs,* 660–63.

"The Danger of Thermonuclear War: An Open Letter to Dr. Sidney Drell." *Foreign Affairs* 61, no. 5 (Summer 1983): 1001–16.

"Deposition (November 19, 1983)." In *Alone Together,* by Elena Bonner, 43–47. New York: Alfred A. Knopf, 1986.

Foreword to *Russia's Underground Press: The Chronicle of Current Events,* by Mark Hopkins, vii. New York: Praeger Publishers, 1983.

Foreword to *The Vavilov Affair,* by Mark Popovsky, vii–viii. Hamden, Conn.: Archon Books.

"A Letter to My Colleagues (November 1983)." *Samizdat Bulletin,* no. 130 (February 1984): 2.

"Message to the Norwegian Government (February 24, 1983)." In Bonner, *Alone Together,* 201–2.

"Obrashchenie v zashchitu Iurii Shikhanovicha (November 24, 1983)." *Materialy samizdata* 47/83 (December 19, 1983) AS5111: 1.

"Pis'mo uchastnikam vstrechi v Sorbonne (September 24, 1983)." *Materialy samizdata* 41/83 (October 31, 1983), AS5063: 2.

"Prezidentu akademiku A. P. Aleksandrovu (May 19, 1983)." Sakharov Archives. Brandeis University, Waltham, Mass.

*1984*

"Administrative Complaint (November 29, 1984)." In *Memoirs,* 693–97.

"Appeal to Academician Lazarevich (November 10, 1984)." In "The Sakharov Phenomenon," by V. L. Ginzburg. In *Andrei Sakharov: Facets of a Life,* edited by Boris Altshuler et al., 285–86. Gif-Sur-Yvette, France: Éditions Frontières, 1991.

"Cosmological Transitions with a Change in Metric Signature (May 1984)." SLAC Translation 0211. Stanford: AD-EX Translations, 1984, 2–24.

"General'nomu Sekretariu Tsk KPSS K. U. Chernenko (February 21, 1984)," (letter). Sakharov Archives. Brandeis University Waltham, Mass.

"The Hunger Strike Appeal (May 8, 1984)." In Bonner, *Alone Together,* 241.

"Letter to Anatoly Alexandrov (October 15, 1984)." In *Memoirs,* 698–706.

"Sakharov's Letter Called on U.S. to Shelter Wife." *New York Times,* May 19, 1984, 4.

"Uchastnikam konferentsii v Stokgol'me (January 12, 1984)." In *Vospominaniia* 2: 515–16.

"Zaiavlenie (August 1, 1984)." In *Vospominaniia* 2:523.

*1985*

"A Letter to the Family (November 24, 1985)." In *Memoirs,* 689–93.

"Pis'mo Lazarevichu (January 16, 1985)." In "O fenomene Sakharova," by B. L. Ginzburg. In *On mezhdu nami zhil...,* edited by B. L. Altshuler et al. Moscow: Praktika, 1996: 225–26.

"Prezidentu AN SSSR A. P. Aleksandrovu (February 12, 1985)." In *Vospominaniia* 2: 540–41.

*1986*

Andrei Sakharov's Appeal for Prisoners of Conscience on February 19, 1986. *Congressional Record.* 99th Cong., 2d sess. Vol. 132, pt. 21:29945–47.

"General'nomu sekretariu TsK KPSS M. S. Gorbachevu (October 22, 1986)." In Ginzburg, "O fenomene Sakharova," 227–29.

"Letter to Academician Marchuk." Cited in "Misunderstanding Sakharov," by B. L. Altshuler. In Drell and Kapitza, *Sakharov Remembered: A Tribute by Friends and Colleagues,* 247.
"The Political and Social Thinking of Andrei Sakharov." *Samizdat Bulletin,* no. 157 (May 1986): 1–12.
"Sakharov Says He Plans to Renew Civil Rights Advocacy in Moscow," *New York Times,* December 21, 1986, 1, 14.
Transcript of interview given by the Sakharovs in Moscow. *New York Times,* December 25, 1986, 3. With Elena Bonner.

*1987*

"Akademik Iakov Borisovich Zel'dovich." *Pravda,* December 5, 1987, 3. With others.
"The Breakthrough Must Be Continued and Widened." *Moscow News,* December 6, 1987, 2.
"A Conversation with Andrei Sakharov and Elena Bonner." *SIPIscope* 15, no. 2 (June–July 1987): 3–11.
"Glasnost: There's No Turning Back." *U. S. News and World Report,* April 20, 1987, 31.
"Gorbachev's Courageous Reform Plan." *U.S. News and World Report,* February 16, 1989, 13.
Interview mit dem Sowjetischen Historiker und Dissidenten Roy Medwedew. *Der Spiegel,* February 2, 1987, 10.
Interview with Voice of America, January 1987. Cited in Andrei Sakharov, *Moscow and Beyond: 1986 to 1989,* 11. New York: Alfred A. Knopf, 1990.
Interviu, 1987. In "Vozrashchenie iz ssylki (Istoriia odnogo interviu)," by Oleg Moroz. In Ivanova, *Andrei Dmitrievich,* 271–366.
"It's an Absolute Necessity to Speak the Truth: Impressions of the Film 'Risk,'" *Moscow News,* November 8, 1987, 14.
"Of Arms and Reforms." *Time,* March 16, 1987, 40–43.
"On Accepting a Prize." *New York Review of Books,* August 13, 1987, 49.
"Sakharov on Human Rights Goals." *Physics Today* 40, no. 4 (April 1987): 4.
"Statement of Andrei Sakharov to the Helsinki Review Conference in Vienna." *Samizdat Bulletin,* no. 167 (March 1987).
"There's No Turning Back on Glasnost." *U.S. News and World Report,* April 20, 1987, 31.
"Things Are Better, but…" *U.S. News and World Report,* January 12, 1987, 31.
"Veriu v razum." *Teatr* 8 (1987): 113–15.

*1988*

"Appeal for Armenian Earthquake Victims (December 1988)." Cited in *Moscow and Beyond,* 72.
"Armenians Facing Genocide in Dispute, Sakharov Says." *Washington Post,* November 26, 1988, A16.
"Calm and Wisdom." *Moscow News,* April 3, 1988, 4.
"Fifty Percent Is More than Just Half." *New Times* 38 (1988): 21–22.
"In Support of Charter-77 (January 26, 1988)." In Frantisek Janouch, "My 'Meetings' and Encounters with Andrei Dmitrievich Sakharov," by František Janouch. In Altshuler et al., *Andrei Sakharov,* 387–88.
Interview with Zora Safir, December 4, 1988. Sakharov Archives. Brandeis University. Waltham, Mass.
Interv'iu Bolgarskoi zhurnalistke zhanne avisai. Moskva, July 1988" *Zvezda* 5 (1991): 127–39.
"I Tried to Be on the Level of My Destiny." *Molodezh Estonii,* October 11, 1988. In *The Glasnost Reader,* edited by Jonathan Eisen. New York, 1990: 328–41. With Elena Bonner.
"Kommentarii akademika A. D. Sakharova po povodu etoi stenogrammy, sdelannye im 8 iiulia 1988 g." In Altshuler et al., *On mezhdu nami zhil,* 866.
"A Man of Unusual Interests." *Nature,* February 25, 1988, 671–72.
"My ne vprave derzhat' narod v strakhe." *Leninskaia smena,* October 30, 1988, 187–93.

"Neizbezhnost' perestroiki (March 25, 1988)." In *Inogo ne dano,* edited by Iu. N. Afanasiev, 122–34. Moscow: Progress, 1988.

"On Gorbachev: A Talk with Andrei Sakharov (November 14, 1988)." *New York Review of Books,* December 22, 1988, 28–29.

"An Open Letter to Mikhail Gorbachev (March 21, 1988)." *Samizdat Bulletin,* no. 181 (Spring 1989).

"Otkrytoe pis'mo." *Materialy samizdata* 26/88 (June 17, 1988) AS6222: 3.

"Perestroika: Kto protiv?" *Ogonëk,* December 1988, 13–14.

Pervoe na sovetskom televidenii interv'iu programme "Piatoe koleso," Leningrad, July 14, 1988. In "Chetyre interv'iu." *Zvezda* 5 (1991): 126–27.

"Postscript to Zeldovich's article 'Is It Possible to Create the Universe from Nothing?'" *Priroda* 4 (April 1988). Cited in *Memoirs,* 723.

"Remarks Honoring Edward Teller (November 16, 1988)." In "Physics, the Bomb, and Human Rights," by Sidney D. Drell and Lev B. Okun. In Drell and Kapitza, *Sakharov Remembered,* 119–20.

"A Trustworthy Policy." *New Times* 24 (1988): 13–14.


*1989*

"Akademik A. D. Sakharov." *Vestnik Akademii nauk SSSR* 5 (1989): 116–18.

"The Appeal of a Group of Peoples' Deputies of the USSR (December 1, 1989)." In Altshuler et al., *Andrei Sakharov,* 717–18. With V. A. Tikhonov, G. Kh. Popov, A. N. Murashev, and Yu. N. Afanasyev.

"At the Academy or Nowhere." *Moscow News,* February 19, 1989, 9.

"Blokada Armenii." *Russkaia mysl',* October 20, 1989, 15.

"Draft Constitution." *New Times* 52 (1989): 26–27.

"The Fate of Raul Wallenberg." *Moscow News,* September 10, 1989, 6.

Foreword to *No, I Do Not Complain,* by František Janouch. In "My Meetings and Encounters with Andrei Dmitrievich Sakharov," by František Janouch. In Altshuler et al., *Andrei Sakharov,* 397.

Foreword to *Armenian Tragedy,* by Yuri Rost, ix. New York: St. Martin's Press, 1990.

"For Peace and Progress." *Moscow News,* February 5, 1989, 8.

"Glasnost and Democratization: An Afterword." In *Small Fires: Letters from the Soviet People to Ogonyok Magazine, 1987–1990,* edited by Christopher Cerf and Marina Albee, 111–13. New York: Summit Books, 1990.

"Ia aktivno podderzhivaiu perestroiku." *Izvestiia,* February 6, 1989, 6.

Interview in *Ottawa Citizen,* February 1989. Cited in Altshuler, "Misunderstanding Sakharov," 247.

An Interview with Andrei Sacharov, Warsaw, *Polityka,* November 25, 1989, 1–7.

Interv'iu A. D. Sakharova parizhskoi gazette "Mond," September 1989. In *Sakharov: Takim on byl,* 69–70. Zhitomir: Golos grazhdanina, 1991.

"Istina odnogo cheloveka (December 9, 1989)." *Komsomol'skaia pravda,* December 16, 1989, 2.

"Istiny ne stareiut (September 27, 1989)." *Kuranty,* May 21, 1991, 4–5.

"Konvergentsiiu, mirnoe sosushchestvovanie." In *50/50: Opyt slovaria novogo myshleniia,* 13–17. Moscow: Progress, 1989, 13–17.

"The Last Address." *Moscow News,* December 31, 1989, 10.

"The Last Speech at FIAN (December 11, 1989)." In Altshuler et al., *Andrei Sakharov,* 720–24.

"Lionskaia lektsiia (September 27, 1989)." In *Vospominaniia* 2: 705–12.

"Neproiznesennaia rech' (December 14, 1989)." In *Vospominaniia* 2: 601–3.

"Novoe politicheskoe myshlenie neobkhodimo." *Argumenty i fakty,* December 19–25, 1989, 4–5.

"Obrashchenie k parizhskoi mezhdunarodnoi konferentsii po probleme kurdov (October 13, 1989)." *Russkaia mysl',* October 20, 1989, 3.

"Obrashchenie Mezhregional'noi gruppy narodnykh deputatov SSSR (June 1989)." In *Vospominaniia* 2:574.

"O chem on ne uspel skazat' (December 14, 1989)." *Literaturnaia gazeta,* December 27, 1989, 2.

"Pis'mo: Slovo chitatelia." *Ogonёk,* January 7–14, 1989, 5. With others.

"Proekt platformy mezhregional'noi gruppy narodnykh deputatov SSSR (November–December 1989)." *Materialy samizdata* 6/90, AS6440: 5–7. With G. Starovoitova.

"Programma A. D. Sakharova." *Knizhnoe obozrenie,* April 7, 1989, 6–7.

"The Real Russia." *Observer,* June 25, 1989, 15.

"Reply to Chervonopisky (June 2, 1989)." In *Moscow and Beyond,* 133–35.

"Sakharov, Bonner on Gorbachev, Restructuring." Interview by Jean-Pierre Barou. *Sueddeutsche Zeitung,* January 26, 1989. In Eisen, *The Glasnost Reader,* 341–46.

"Sakharov Defends Armenian Dissidents." *Chicago Tribune,* February 9, 1989, 1, 16.

"Sakharov o Karabakh (1989)." *Golos Armenii,* December 19, 1990, 4.

"S"ezd ne mozhet sdelat' vse srazu…" *Literaturnaia gazeta,* June 21, 1989, 11.

"Speech to the Congress of People's Deputies (June 9, 1989)." In *Moscow and Beyond,* 150–56.

"A Speech to the People's Congress." *New York Review of Books,* August 17, 1989, 25–26.

"Stepen' svobody: Aktual'noe interv'iu." *Ogonёk,* July 1989, 26–29.

"Svoimi vospominaniami o Dmitrii Ivanoviche Sakharove delitsia ego syn, A. D. Sakharova (January 17, 1989)." In Ivanova, *Andrei Dmitrievich,* 267–69.

"Taking a Tough New Line." *U. S. News and World Report,* January 30, 1989, 50.

"To the Madrid Conference on East-West Trade and Economic Relations (January 16, 1989)." Sakharov Archives. Brandeis University, Waltham, Mass. With Elena Bonner.

"V narode vsegda sokhraniaiutsia nravstvennye sily." *Knizhnoe obozrenie,* April 7, 1989, 6–7.

"Vstupitel'noe slovo." In "Chernobyl'skaia tetrad'," by Grigorii Medvedev, *Novyi mir* 6 (June 1989): 3–4.

"Vystuplenie na grazhdanskoi panikhide po Sof'e Vasil'evne Kalistratovoi (December 8, 1989)." *Russkaia mysl',* December 22, 1989, 4.

"Vystuplenie na vstreche s kollektivom Uralmashzavoda (September 15, 1989)." In *Vospominaniia* 2: 575–88.

"We Cannot Do without Nuclear Power Plants, But…" *World Marxist Review,* February 1, 1990, 21–22.

"Zhit' na zemle i zhit' dolgo." *Iskusstvo kino* 8 (1989): 162–76. With Ales Adamovich.

*1990*

*Memoirs.* New York: Alfred A. Knopf, 1990.

*Moscow and Beyond: 1986 to 1989.* New York: Alfred A. Knopf, 1990.

*1991*

"Vospominaniia." *Znamia* 1–5 (1991).

*1996*

*Vospominaniia.* 2 vols. Moscow: Prava cheloveka, 1996.

## Part II. Works about Sakharov and Other Relevant Materials

Adamsky, Victor, and Yurii Smirnov. "Moscow's Biggest Bomb: The 50-Megaton Test of October 1961." *Cold War International History Project* 4 (Fall 1994): 3, 19–21.

Adler, Stephen L. "Induced Gravitation." In Sakharov, A. D. *Collected Scientific Works,* edited by D. ter Haar, D. V. Chudnovsky, and G. V. Chudnovsky, 263–69. New York: Marcel Dekker, 1982.

Afanasiev Iurii. "Govorim o proshlom, no reshaetsia budushchee sotzializma." *Moskovskie novosti*, May 10, 1987, 11, 13.

——. "Perestroika i istoricheskoe znanie." In *Inogo ne dano*, edited by Iu. N. Afanasiev, 491–506. Moscow: Progress, 1988.

Agurskii, Mikhail, ed. "Chto zhdet Sovetskii Soiuz? Sbornik statei po povodu 'Pis'mo vozhdiam' A. Solzhenitsyna." Self-published, 1974.

"Aid to Underdeveloped Nations." Interview of Professor Max Millikan. *Tech Engineering News*, April 1969, 25.

Albright, Joseph. "The Pact of Two Henrys." *New York Times Magazine*, January 5, 1975, 16–34.

Alexandrov, A. P. "Kak delali bombu." *Izvestiia*, July 23, 1988, 3.

Alexandrov G. et al. "Pozitsii, chuzhdaia narodu." *Pravda*, September 5, 1973, 3.

Alexeyeva, Ludmilla. *Soviet Dissent: Contemporary Movements for National, Religious, and Human Rights.* Middletown, Conn.: Wesleyan University Press, 1985.

Alexeyeva, Ludmilla, and Paul Goldberg. *The Thaw Generation: Coming of Age in the Post-Stalin Era.* Pittsburgh: University of Pittsburgh Press, 1993.

Almond, Mark. "1989 without Gorbachev." In *Virtual History: Alternatives and Counterfactuals*, edited by Niall Ferguson, 392–415. New York: Basic Books, 1999.

Altshuler, Boris, et al., eds. *Andrei Sakharov: Facets of a Life.* Gif-Sur-Yvette, France: Editions Frontières, 1991.

Altshuler, Boris, et al., eds. *On mezhdu nami zhil: Vospominaniia o Sakharove.* Moscow: Praktika, 1996.

Altshuler, L. V. "Tak my delali bombu." *Literaturnaia gazeta*, June 6, 1990, 13.

Amalrik, Andrei. *Will the Soviet Union Survive Until 1984?* New York: Harper & Row, 1981.

Amalrik, Andrei et al. "Goriacho pozdravliaem Andreia Dmitrievicha Sakharova." *Posev* 11 (November 1975): 5.

Andrew, Christopher, and Oleg Gordievsky. *KGB: The Inside Story of Its Foreign Operations from Lenin to Gorbachev.* New York: Harper Collins, 1990.

Andrew, Christopher, and Vasilio Mitrokhin. *The Sword and the Shield: The Mitrokhin Archive and the Secret History of the KGB.* New York: Basic Books, 1999.

Applebaum, Anne. "A Dearth of Feeling." *New Criterion* 15, no. 2 (October 1996): 5–17.

Arbatov, Georgi. *The System: An Insider's Life in Soviet Politics.* New York: Times Books, 1992.

Arnett, Robert L. "Soviet Attitudes Towards Nuclear War: Do They Really Think They Can Win?" *Journal of Strategic Studies* 2, no. 9 (September 1979): 172–91.

Aron, Leon. *Boris Yeltsin: A Revolutionary Life.* New York: St. Martin's Press, 2000.

Astashenkov, P. T. *Kurchatov.* Moscow: Molodaya gvardia, 1968.

Babyonyshev, Alexander, ed. *On Sakharov.* New York: Alfred A. Knopf, 1982.

Babyonyshev, Alexander, R. Lert, and E. Pechuro, eds. *Sakharovskii sbornik-1981.* Moscow: Kniga, 1991.

Bailes, Kendall E. "The Politics of Technology: Stalin and Technocratic Thinking among Soviet Engineers." *American Historical Review* 79, no. 2 (April 1974): 445–69.

——. *Technology and Society under Lenin and Stalin: Origins of the Soviet Technical Intelligentsia, 1917–1941.* Princeton: Princeton University Press, 1978.

Bailey, George. *Galileo's Children: Science, Sakharov, and the Power of the State.* New York: Arcade Publishing, 1990.

——. *The Making of Andrei Sakharov.* New York: Allen Lane, 1989.

Barabashev, Alexei. "In the Human Chain at the White House." *Woodrow Wilson Center Report* 3, no. 3 (November 1991): 2.

Bate, Roger. "Chernobyl's Real Victims (January 24, 2002)." http://www.techcentralstation.com/1051/envirowrapper.jsp?PID=1051–450&CID=1051–012402A.

Bergman, Jay. "The Idea of Individual Liberation in Bolshevik Visions of the New Soviet Man." *European History Quarterly* 27, no. 1 (January 1997): 57–92.

——. "Valerii Chkalov: Soviet Pilot as New Soviet Man." *Journal of Contemporary History* 33, no. 1 (January 1998): 135–52.

Berlin, Isaiah. *Russian Thinkers,* edited by Henry Hardy and Aileen Kelly. New York: Pelican Books, 1979.

Berlinski, David. "Where Physics and Politics Meet: The Extraordinary Life of Edward Teller." *Weekly Standard*, November 26, 2001, 33–36.

Beschloss, Michael R., and Strobe Talbott. *At the Highest Levels: The Inside Story of the End of the Cold War.* Boston: Little, Brown, 1993.

Bethe, Hans. "Sakharov's H-bomb." *Bulletin of the Atomic Scientists* 46, no. 8 (October 1990): 8–9.

Bhagwatti, Jagdish. "The Underdeveloped World." *Tech Engineering News*, April 1969, 30.

Billington, James H. *Fire in the Minds of Men: Origins of the Revolutionary Faith.* New York: Basic Books, 1980.

Bjorken, J. "Elementary Particle Physics." In Sakharov, *Collected Scientific Works*, 141–45.

Blau, Eleanor. "Humanist Manifesto II Offers a 'Survival' Philosophy." *New York Times*, August 26, 1973, 1, 51.

Bobkov, Filipp. *KBG i vlast'.* Moscow: Veteran MP, 1995.

Bohlen, Celestine. "Sakharov Describes Loneliness of Life in Gorki." *Washington Post*, January 11, 1987, A26, A28.

Bonnell, Victoria E., Ann Cooper and Gregory Freidin, eds. *Russia at the Barricades: Eyewitness Accounts of the August 1991 Coup.* Armonk, N.Y.: M. E. Sharpe, 1994.

Bonner, Elena. *Alone Together.* New York: Alfred A. Knopf, 1986.

——. "Do dnevnik: k izdaniiu Sobraniia sochinenii A. D. Sakharova." *Znamia* 11 (2005): 62–128. Unpublished copy received from Tatiana Yankelevich.

——. "Komu nuzhny mify?" *Ogonëk*, March 1990, 25.

——. "Letter to the Editor." *New York Times*, October 27, 1999, A26.

——. *Mothers and Daughters.* New York: Vintage Books, 1993.

——. "On Gorbachev." *New York Review of Books*, May 17, 1990, 14–17.

——. "U nego byl kharakter pobeditelia." *Kuranty*, May 21, 1991, 5.

——. "Vladimir Potemkin." *Wall Street Journal*, June 17, 2003, A16.

——. *Vol'nye zametki k rodoslovnoi Andreia Sakharova.* Moscow: Prava cheloveka, 1996.

——. "What Happened Is That Nothing Happened." *Moscow News*, August 5–12, 1990, 5.

Boobbyer, Philip. *Conscience, Dissent and Reform in Soviet Russia.* London: Routledge, 2005.

Borzenkov, E. "Nedostoinye deistviia." *Pravda*, September 5, 1973, 3.

Breslauer, George W., and Philip E. Tetlock, eds. *Learning in U.S. and Soviet Foreign Policy.* Boulder: Westview Press, 1991.

Brinton, William M., and Alan Rinzler. *Without Force or Lies: Voices from the Revolution of Central Europe in 1989–90: Essays, Speeches, and Eyewitness Accounts.* San Francisco: Mercury House, 1990.

Brown, Archie. *The Gorbachev Factor.* New York: Oxford University Press, 1996.

Brumberg, Abraham, ed. *In Quest of Justice: Protest and Dissent in the Soviet Union Today.* New York: Praeger Publishers, 1970.

Brzezinski, Zbigniew. *Power and Principle: Memoirs of the National Security Advisor, 1977–1981.* New York: Farrar, Straus, Giroux, 1983.

Bukovsky, Vladimir. *To Build a Castle: My Life as a Dissenter.* New York: Viking Press, 1978.

——. "Who Resists Gorbachev?" *Washington Quarterly* (Winter 1989), 5–22.

Bulanov, A. L., and I. A. Krylova. "Sootnoshenie politiki i iadernoi voiny: Analiticheskii obzor literatury: 1955–1987." *Voprosy filosofii* 5 (1988): 110–24.

Burlatskii, Fëdor. *Vozhd i sovetniki: O Khrushchev, Andropov i ne tol'ko nikh…* Moscow: Izdatel'stvo politicheskoi literatury, 1990.

Burnham, James. *The Managerial Revolution: What Is Happening in the World.* New York: John Day Co., 1941.

Buwalda, Petrus. *They Did Not Dwell Alone: Jewish Emigration from the Soviet Union 1967–1990.* Baltimore: Johns Hopkins University Press, 1997.

Campbell, Louise. "Sakharov: Soviet Physicist Appeals for Bold Initiatives." *Science*, August 8, 1969, 556–58.

Carter, Jimmy. *Keeping Faith: Memoirs of a President.* New York: Bantam Books, 1982.

"The Case of the German Residents in Estonia." *Chronicle of Human Rights*, no. 10 (July–August 1974): 11–12.

Chakovskii, A. "Chto dal'she: razmyshleniia po prochtenii novoi knigi Garrisona Salsberi." *Literaturnaia gazeta,* February 14, 1973, 14.

Chalidze, Valery. *To Defend These Rights: Human Rights and the Soviet Union.* New York: Random House, 1974.

Charlemagne [pseud.]. "Vladimir Putin, Russia's Post-Cold-Warrior." *Economist,* January 8, 2000, 51.

"Chei kandidat Sakharov." *Komsomol'skaia Pravda,* January 27, 1989, 2.

Cherniaev, A. S. *Shest' let s Gorbachevym: Po dnevnikovym zapisiam.* Moscow: Progress, 1993.

*A Chronicle of Human Rights.* New York: Khronika Press, 1972–83.

Clark, Bruce. *An Empire's New Clothes: The End of Russia's Liberal Dream.* New York: Vintage Books, 1995.

Clemens, Walter C. "Sakharov: A Man for Our Times." *Bulletin of the Atomic Scientists* 27, no. 10 (December 1971): 4–6.

Cohen, Stephen F., ed. *An End to Silence: Uncensored Opinion in the Soviet Union from Roy Medvedev's Underground Magazine "Political Diary."* New York: W. W. Norton, 1982.

———. *Failed Crusade: America and the Tragedy of Post-Communist Russia.* New York: W. W. Norton, 2001.

Cohen, Stephen F., and Katrina Vanden Heuvel, eds. *Voices of Glasnost: Interviews with Gorbachev's Reformers.* New York: W. W. Norton, 1989.

Coleman, Fred. *The Decline and Fall of the Soviet Empire: Forty Years That Shook the World from Stalin to Yeltsin.* New York: St. Martin's Press, 1996.

Connor, Steve. "Stop the Death Sentences in China, Pleads Sakharov." *Daily Telegraph,* June 20, 1989, 2.

Conquest, Robert. *The Great Terror: A Reassessment.* New York: Oxford University Press, 1990.

———. *Tyrants and Typewriters: Communiqués from the Struggle for Truth.* Lexington, Mass.: D. C. Heath, 1989.

*Constitution (Fundamental Law) of the Union of Soviet Socialist Republics.* Moscow: Novosti, 1985.

Coppen, David Peter. "The Public Life of Andrei Sakharov, 1966–1989: A Bibliographical Chronicle." Master's thesis, University of Illinois at Urbana-Champaign, 1998.

Cox, Michael, ed. *Rethinking the Soviet Collapse: Sovietology, the Death of Communism, and the New Russia.* London: Pinter, 1998.

Dallin, Alexander. "New Thinking in Soviet Foreign Policy." In *New Thinking in Soviet Politics,* edited by Archie Brown. New York: St. Martin's Press, 1992.

Davies, Paul. *God and the New Physics.* New York: Simon & Schuster, 1983.

De Boer, S. P., E. J. Driessen, and H. L. Verhaar, eds. *Biographical Dictionary of Dissidents in the Soviet Union, 1956–1975.* The Hague: Martinus Nijhoff, 1982.

"Delo Beriia." *Izvestiia TsKPSS* 2 (February 1991): 141–208.

*Delo Tverdokhlebova,* edited by Valery Chalidze. New York: Izdatelstvo khronika, 1976.

"Deputaty ot Akademii nauk SSSR." *Izvestiia,* April 21, 1989, 3.

Djilas, Milovan. *The New Class: An Analysis of the Communist System.* New York: Praeger Publishers, 1957.

Dobbs, Michael. "Soviet Reforms Lagging, Sakharov Warns." *Washington Post,* September 10, 1988, A14.

Dobrynin, Anatoly. *In Confidence: Moscow's Ambassador to America's Six Cold War Presidents (1962–1986).* New York: Random House, 1995.

*Documents and Materials, 19th All-Union Conference of the CPSU, Report and Speeches by Mikhail Gorbachev, General Secretary of the CPSU CC.* Moscow: Novosti, 1988.

Doder, Dusko, and Louise Branson. *Gorbachev: Heretic in the Kremlin.* New York: Penguin Books, 1990.

Doolittle, Amy. "Bush Committed to Winning War on Terror." *Washington Times,* January 12, 2005, A8.

Dornan, Peter. "Andrei Sakharov: The Conscience of a Liberal Scientist." In *Dissent in the USSR: Politics, Ideology, and People,* edited by Rudolph L. Tökés. Baltimore: Johns Hopkins University Press, 1975.

Dorodnitsyn, A. A. et al. "Kogda teriaiut chest' i sovest'." *Izvestiia,* July 3, 1983, 4.

Dorozynski, Alexandre. *The Man They Wouldn't Let Die.* New York: Macmillan Co., 1965.

Draper, Theodore. "Appeasement and Détente." *Commentary* 61, no. 2 (February 1976): 27–38.

Drell, Sidney D. "Andrei Sakharov and the Nuclear Danger." *Physics Today* 53, no. 5 (May 2000): 37–41.

Drell, Sidney D., and Sergei P. Kapitza, eds. *Sakharov Remembered: A Tribute by Friends and Colleagues.* New York: American Institute of Physics, 1991.

Drell, Sidney D., and Lev Okun. "Andrei Dmitrievch Sakharov." *Physics Today* 43, no. 8 (August 1990): 26–36.

Dunlop. John. *The Rise of Russia and the Fall of the Soviet Empire.* Princeton: Princeton University Press, 1993.

Durch, William J. *The ABM Treaty and Western Security.* Cambridge, Mass.: Ballinger Publishing Co., 1988.

Easterhas, Erno. "The Tragic State of Soviet Workers." *Los Angeles Times,* March 19, 1975, 7.

Eisenhower, Susan, and Roald Z. Sagdeev. "Sakharov in His Own Words." *Physics Today* 43, no. 8 (August 1990): 51–54.

Ellman, Michael, and Vladimir Kontorich. "The Collapse of the Soviet System and the Memoir Literature." *Europe-Asia Studies* 49, no. 2 (1997): 259–79.

Eltsin, Boris. "Pochemu ia golosoval protiv." *Russkaia mysl',* February 16, 1990, 6.

Emelianov, V. S. "Kurchatov, kakim Ia ego znal." *Iunost'* 4 (1968): 83–93, and 5 (1968): 88–95.

English, Robert. *Russia and the Idea of the West: Gorbachev, Intellectuals, and the End of the Cold War.* New York: Columbia University Press, 2000.

Erugin, N. "Otpoved' klevetniku." *Pravda,* August 31, 1973, 3.

Fainberg, Vladimir. "Precursor of Perestroika." *Physics Today* 43, no. 8 (August 1990): 40–45.

Fairbank, Charles. "The Suicide of Soviet Communism." *Journal of Democracy* 1, no. 2 (Spring 1990): 18–26.

Feinberg, E. L. *Epokha i lichnost'. Fiziki. Ocherki i vospominaniia.* Moscow: Nauka, 1999.

———. "Pamiati velikogo grazhdanina." *Literaturnaia gazeta,* December 20, 1989, 10.

Feld, Bernard T. "Sakharov Chooses Survival." *Tech Engineering News,* April 1969, 5.

"The Final Act of the Conference on Security and Cooperation in Europe, Aug. 1, 1975, 14 I.L.M. 1292 (Helsinki Declaration)." http://www1.umn.edu/humanrts/osce/basics/finact75.html.

Fish, M. Steven. *Democracy from Scratch: Opposition and Regime in the New Russian Revolution.* Princeton: Princeton University Press, 1995).

Fortescue, Stephen. *The Academy Reorganized: The R&D Role of the Soviet Academy of Sciences since 1961.* Canberra: Australian National University Press, 1983.

———. *The Communist Party and Soviet Science.* London: Macmillan, 1987.

"14 dekabria 1989 goda v Moskve skonchalsia Andrei Dmitrievch Sakharov." *Russkaia mysl',* December 22, 1989, 1.

Frish, S. E. *Skvoz' prizmu vremeni.* Moscow: Politizdat, 1992.

Furth, Harold P. "Controlled Fusion Research." In Sakharov, *Collected Scientific Works,* 49–54.

Gaddis, John Lewis. *We Now Know: Rethinking Cold War History.* New York: Oxford University Press, 1998.

Gaffney, Frank, Jr. "Bush, Missile Defense, and the Critics." *Commentary* 111, no. 2 (February 2001): 29–36.

———. "Poor Pact." *New Republic,* October 25, 1999, 17–18.

Gaidar, E. T. *Dni porazhenii i pobed.* Moscow: Vagnus: 1996.

Galbraith, John Kenneth. *The New Industrial State.* Boston: Houghton Mifflin, 1967.

Gathman, Roger. "The Moral Complexity of Sakharov." *Christian Science Monitor,* April 4, 2002, 21.

Gellner, Ernest. *Encounters with Nationalism.* Oxford: Blackwell, 1994.

Gilligan, Emma. *Defending Human Rights in Russia: Sergei Kovalyov: Dissident and Human Rights Commissioner 1969–2003.* New York: Routledge, 2004.

Ginzburg, Alexander. "Na sleduiushchii den': Nachalo puti k sakharovskoi konstitutsii." *Russkaia mysl',* December 22, 1989, 1–2.

Glebov, Oleg, and John Crowfoot, eds. *The Soviet Empire: Its Nations Speak Out: The First Congress of People's Deputies, Moscow, 25 May to 10 June 1989.* New York: Harwood Academic Publishers, 1989.

Glendon, Mary Ann. *A World Made New: Eleanor Roosevelt and the Universal Declaration of Human Rights.* New York: Random House, 2001.

Glynn, Patrick. *Closing Pandora's Box: Arms Races, Arms Control, and the History of the Cold War.* New York: Basic Books, 1992.

Goldanskii, Vitalii I. "Scientist, Thinker, Humanist." *Physics Today* 43, no. 8 (August 1990): 47–49.

Golovin, I. N. *I. V. Kurchatov: A Socialist-Realist Biography of the Soviet Nuclear Scientist.* Bloomington, Ind.: Selbstvarlag Press, 1968.

Goncharov, German. "The American Effort," *Physics Today* 49, no. 11 (November 1996): 45–48.

———. "Beginnings of the Soviet H-Bomb Program." *Physics Today* 49, no. 11 (November 1996): 50–54.

———. "The Race Accelerates." *Physics Today* 49, no. 11 (November 1996): 56–61.

Gorbachev, Mikhail. *Memoirs.* New York: Doubleday, 1996.

———. *On My Country and the World.* New York: Columbia University Press, 2000.

———. "O proekte novoi programmy KPSS." *Pravda,* July 26, 1991, 1–2.

———. *Perestroika: New Thinking for Our Country and the World.* London: Collins, 1987.

———. *Selected Speeches and Articles.* Moscow: Progress, 1987.

———. "Speech to the UN General Assembly (December 7, 1988)." Foreign Broadcast Information Service-SOV-88–236, December 8, 1988, 11–19.

———. "Zakliuchitel'noe slovo M. S. Gorbacheva na 28 s"ezde KPSS." *Pravda,* July 14, 1990, 1.

Gorbanevskaya, Natalia. *Red Square at Noon.* London: Deutsch, 1972.

Gordon, Michael. "Sakharov Urges Moscow to Cut Size of Its Military." *New York Times,* November 16, 1988, 14.

Gorelik, Gennady. "The Metamorphosis of Andrei Sakharov." *Scientific American* 280, no. 3 (March 1999): 98–101.

Gorelik, Gennady, with Antonina W. Bouis. *The World of Andrei Sakharov: A Russian Physicist's Path to Freedom.* New York: Oxford University Press, 2005.

Grachev, A. S. *Kremlevskaia khronika.* Moscow: Eksmo, 1994.

Graham, Loren R. *The Ghost of the Executed Engineer: Technology and the Fall of the Soviet Union.* Cambridge, Mass.: Harvard University Press, 1993.

———. "Knowledge and Power." *Sciences* 20, no. 8 (October 1980): 14–32.

———, ed. *Science and the Soviet Social Order.* Cambridge, Mass.: Harvard University Press, 1990.

———. *Science in Russia and the Soviet Union: A Short History.* New York: Cambridge University Press, 1993.

———. *What Have We Learned about Science and Technology from the Russian Experience?* Stanford: Stanford University Press, 1998.

Greene, Brian. *The Elegant Universe: Superstrings, Hidden Dimensions, and the Quest for the Ultimate Theory.* New York: Vintage Books, 2000.

Gribben, John. *In Search of Schrödinger's Cat: Quantum Physics and Reality.* New York: Bantam Books, 1984.

Griffith, William. "An Analysis of the Sakharov Paper." *Tech Engineering News,* April 1969, 27.

Grigorenko, Petro G. *Memoirs.* New York: W. W. Norton, 1982.

Gumbel, Peter. "Soviet Leaders Receive Appeals by Intellectuals." *Wall Street Journal,* May 16, 1988, 12.

Gustavson, Thane. "Why Doesn't Soviet Science Do Better Than It Does?" In *The Social Context of Soviet Science,* edited by Linda L. Lubrano and Susan Gross Solomon. Boulder: Westview Press, 1980: 31–68.

Gwertzman, Bernard. "3 in Russia Move to Defend Rights." *New York Times*, November 16, 1970, 1, 8.

Hahn, Gordon M. *Russia's Revolution from Above: Reform, Transition, and Revolution in the Fall of the Soviet Communist Regime*. New Brunswick: Transaction Publishers, 2002.

Hall, Carla. "Dinner with Andrei." *Washington Post*, November 14, 1988, B1, B11.

Handelman, Stephen. *Comrade Criminal: Russia's New Mafiya*. New Haven: Yale University Press, 1995.

Haslam, Jonathan. "Stalin's War or Peace: What If the Cold War Had Been Avoided." In Ferguson, *Virtual History*.

Hayward, Max, ed. *On Trial*. New York: Harper & Row, 1967.

Hellie, Richard. "The Structure of Russian History." *Russian History* 4, no. 1 (1977): 1–22.

Hirsch, Daniel, and William G. Mathews. "The H-Bomb: Who Really Gave Away the Secret?" *Bulletin of the Atomic Scientists* 45, no. 1 (January–February 1990): 22–30.

Hochschild, Adam. *The Unquiet Ghost: Russians Remember Stalin*. New York: Penguin Books, 1995.

Hoge, James. "Sakharov Urges West: Keep Pushing Détente." *Los Angeles Times*, December 2, 1975, 2, 7.

Hollander, Paul. *Political Will and Personal Belief: The Decline and Fall of Soviet Communism*. New Haven: Yale University Press, 1999.

Holloway, David. "The Expanding Agenda: Democracy and Human Rights." Paper delivered at conference "A. D. Sakharov: His Legacy Ten Years Later." Stanford University, Stanford, Calif., December 10, 1999.

——."New Light on Early Soviet Bomb Secrets." *Physics Today* 49, no. 11 (November 1996): 26–27.

——. "Soviet Scientists Speak Out." *Bulletin of the Atomic Scientists* 49, no. 4 (May 1993): 18–19.

——. "Soviet Thermonuclear Development." *International Security* 4, no. 3 (1979–1980): 192–97.

——. *The Soviet Union and the Arms Race*. New Haven: Yale University Press, 1983.

——. *Stalin and the Bomb: The Soviet Union and Atomic Energy 1939–1956*. New Haven: Yale University Press, 1994.

Hopkins, Mark. *Russia's Underground Press: The Chronicle of Current Events*. New York: Praeger Publishers, 1983.

Horvath, Robert. *The Legacy of Soviet Dissent: Dissidents, Democratisation and Radical Nationalism in Russia*. London: Routledge, 2005.

Hosking, Geoffrey. *The Awakening of the Soviet Union*. Cambridge, Mass.: Harvard University Press, 1991.

"How to Speak Out on Sakharov et al." *Nature*, November 13, 1980, 105–6.

Iatzkov, Anatoli. "Atom i razvelka." *Voprosy istorii estestvoznaniia i tekhniki* 3 (1992): 103–7.

Iliopoulos, J. "The Baryon Number of the Universe." In Sakharov, *Collected Scientific Works*, 147–50.

Ilovaiskaia, Irina. "Pamiati A. D. Sakharova." *Russkaia mysl'*, December 22, 1989, 1.

Ioirysh, A. I. *Uroki A. D. Sakharova: Gosudarstvenno-politicheskie vzgliady*. Moscow: URSS, 1996.

Isaacson, Walter. *Kissinger: A Biography*. New York: Simon & Schuster, 1992.

Ivanova, Tatiana I., ed. *Andrei Dmitrievich: Vospominaniia o Sakharove*. Moscow: Terra, 1990.

Jackson, Henry M. "First, Human Détente." *New York Times*, September 9, 1973, 4, 17.

Jackson, James. O. "Russian Dissident Wins Nobel Peace Prize." *Chicago Tribune*, October 10, 1975, 1, 15.

"Jews Tell of KGB Threat." *Times*, December 28, 1973, 5.

Joravsky, David. *The Lysenko Affair*. Chicago: University of Chicago Press, 1970.

Josephson, Paul R. *Physics and Politics in Revolutionary Russia*. Berkeley: University of California Press, 1991.

——. *Red Atom: Russia's Nuclear Program from Stalin to Today*. New York: W. H. Freeman, 2000.

Kagarlitsky, Boris. *Farewell to Perestroika: A Soviet Chronicle*. London: Verso, 1990.

Kaiser, Robert G. *Russia: The People and the Power*. New York: Pocket Books, 1976.

——. *Why Gorbachev Happened: His Triumphs and His Failure.* New York: Simon & Schuster, 1991.

Kaku, Michio. *Visions: How Science Will Revolutionize the 21st Century.* New York: Anchor Books, 1998.

Kalugin, Oleg. *The First Directorate: My 32 Years in Intelligence and Espionage against the West.* New York: St. Martin's Press, 1994.

Kapitsa, P. L. *Nauka i sovremennoe obshchestvo.* Moscow: Nauka, 1998.

——. "The Scientist Who Talked Back to Stalin." *Bulletin of the Atomic Scientists* 46, no. 3 (April 1990): 26–33.

Kaufman, Burton I. *The Presidency of James Earl Carter, Jr.* Lawrence: University Press of Kansas, 1993.

Keldysh, M. V., and V. Ya. Fainberg, eds. *Sakharov Memorial Lectures in Physics.* New York: Nova Science Publishers, 1992.

Keller, Bill. "Sakharov's Pro-Gorbachev's Stand: Attacked, He Stands His Ground." *New York Times,* April 3, 1987, A1.

Kelley, Donald R. *The Solzhenitsyn-Sakharov Dialogue: Politics, Society, and the Future.* Westport, Conn.: Greenwood Press, 1982.

Khariton, Yuli, and Yuri Smirnov. "The Khariton Version." *Bulletin of the Atomic Scientists* 49, no. 4 (May 1993): 20–31.

*Khronika tekushchikh sobytii.* New York: Khronika Press, 1968–1984.

Khrushchev, Nikita Sergeevich. *Khrushchev Remembers: The Last Testament.* Boston: Little, Brown, 1974.

Khrushchev, Sergei. *Khrushchev on Khrushchev: An Inside Account of the Man and His Era.* Boston: Little, Brown 1990.

——. *Nikita Khrushchev and the Creation of a Superpower.* University Park: Pennsylvania State University Press, 2000.

Kishkovsky, Sophia. "Sakharov Museum Falls on Hard Times (October 2, 2007)." http://www.iht.com/articles/2007/10/02/africa/moscow.php#end_main.

Kissinger, Henry. *Years of Upheaval.* Boston: Little, Brown, 1982.

Kline, Edward. *Moskovskii Komitet prav cheloveka.* Moscow: Prava cheloveka, 2004.

Klose, Kevin. *Russia and the Russians: Inside the Closed Society.* New York: W. W. Norton, 1984.

——. "Sakharov Tired; Movement Battered." *Washington Post,* November 28, 1977, A12.

Knight, Amy. *Beria, Stalin's First Lieutenant.* Princeton: Princeton University Press, 1993.

Kon, Igor. "Sotsiologiia." In *Filosofskaia entsiklopediia.* Vol. 5. Moscow: Sovetskaia entsiklopediia, 1970, 92.

Kondrashov, Stanislav. "The Life of Andrey Sakharov." *New Times* 52 (1989): 24–25.

Kornilov, Iurii. "Postavshchik klevety." *Literaturnaia gazeta,* July 18, 1973, 9.

Korotkov, A. V., S. A. Melchin, and A. S. Stepanov, eds. *Kremlevskii samosud.* Moscow: Rodina, 1994.

Kotkin, Stephen. *Armageddon Averted: The Soviet Collapse, 1970–2000.* New York: Oxford University Press, 2001.

Kraminova, Natalia. "Galina Starovoitova in Season." *Moscow News,* July 15–22, 1990, 16.

Kramish, Arnold. *Atomic Energy in the Soviet Union.* Stanford: Stanford University Press, 1959.

Krauthammer, Charles. "Arms Control: The End of an Illusion." *Weekly Standard,* November 1, 1999, 21–27.

——. "Some Allies: Whose Side Are They on?" *Washington Post,* April 25, 1986, A19.

Krivonosov, Iu. I. "Landau i Sakharov v 'razrabotkakh' KGB." *Voprosy istorii estestvoznaniia i tekhniki* 3 (1993): 123–31.

Lamoureux, Adèle. "The INF Agreement: 'The Beginning of the Beginning.'" http://perc.ca/PEN/1987-11/lamoureux.html.

Lane, David. *Soviet Society under Perestroika.* London: Routledge, 1992.

Laqueur, Walter. *The Dream That Failed: Reflections on the Soviet Union.* New York: Oxford University Press, 1994.

———. *Fin de Siècle and Other Essays on America and Europe.* New Brunswick: Transaction Publishers, 1997.

Lee, Gary. "Sakharov Arrives in U.S., Ending 30-Year Travel Ban." *Washington Post*, November 7, 1988, A25–A26.

———. "Sakharov Praises Gorbachev's Vow to Cut Troops." *Washington Post*, December 9, 1988, A20.

———. "Sakharov Says Soviet Union Continues to Violate Human Rights." *Washington Post*, November 12, 1988, A16.

Leonhard, Wolfgang. "The Domestic Politics of the New Soviet Foreign Policy." *Foreign Affairs* 52, no. 1 (October 1973): 59–74.

Levada, Iurii. *Chelovek i legenda: Obraz A. D. Sakharova v obshchestvennom mnenii.* Moscow: Informatsionnoe agentstvo data, 1991.

———. "Social Barometer." *Moscow News*, December 16–23, 1990, 9.

Le Vert, Suzanne. *The Sakharov File: A Study in Courage.* New York: Silver Burdett Press, 1986.

Levin, M. L. "Eti gor'kie vsrechi v Gor'kom." *Kuranty*, May 21, 1991, 5.

Lewin, Moshe. *The Gorbachev Phenomenon: Expanded Edition.* Berkeley: University of California Press, 1991.

Lipkin, Harry J. "Elementary Particles." In Sakharov, *Collected Scientific Works,* 271–80.

Lipman, Masha. "Putin's KGB Way." *Washington Post*, April 17, 2001, A17.

Litvinov, Pavel, ed. *The Demonstration in Pushkin Square.* Boston: Gambit, 1969.

———. *The Trial of the Four: A Collection of Materials on the Case of Galanskov, Ginzburg, Dobrovolsky and Lashkova, 1967–68.* New York: Viking Press, 1972.

Lloyd, John. "The Logic of Vladimir Putin." *New York Times Magazine*, March 19, 2000, 65.

Lourie, Richard. *Sakharov: A Biography.* Hanover, NH: Brandeis University Press, 2002.

———. "The Smuggled Manuscript: Translating Sakharov's Memoirs." *New York Times Book Review*, June 3, 1990, 3, 30–31.

Lozansky, Edward, ed. *Andrei Sakharov and Peace.* New York: Avon Books, 1985.

Malia, Martin. *The Soviet Tragedy: A History of Socialism in Russia, 1917–1991.* New York: Free Press, 1994.

Marchenko, Anatoly. *To Live Like Everyone.* New York: Henry Holt, 1989.

Marx, Karl, and Friedrich Engels. *The Communist Manifesto.* London: Penguin Books, 1967.

*Materialy samizdata.* Munich: RFE/RL, 1975–1991.

Matich, Olga. "Vasilii Aksenov and the Literature of Convergence: *Ostrov Krym* as Self-Criticism." *Slavic Review* 47, no. 4 (Winter 1988): 642–51.

Matlock, Jack E. *Autopsy of an Empire: The American Ambassador's Account of the Collapse of the Soviet Union.* New York: Random House, 1995.

McCauley, Martin. *Gorbachev.* New York: Longman, 1998.

McFaul, Michael. *Russia's Unfinished Revolution: Political Change from Gorbachev to Putin.* Ithaca: Cornell University Press, 2001.

McLean, Hugh, and Walter N. Vickery, eds. *The Year of Protest, 1956: An Anthology of Soviet Literary Materials.* New York: Vintage Books, 1961.

McMillan, Priscilla Johnson. "Dr. Strangelove." *Los Angeles Times Book Review*, October 28, 2001, 3–4.

Medvedev, Roy A. *Let History Judge: The Origins and Consequences of Stalinism.* New York: Columbia University Press, 1989.

Medvedev, Zhores. *The Medvedev Papers.* New York: St. Martin's Press, 1971.

———. "New President of the Soviet Academy." *Nature*, December 18, 1975, 566.

———. *On Socialist Democracy.* New York: W. W. Norton, 1977.

———. *On Soviet Dissent.* New York: Columbia University Press, 1980.

———. *The Rise and Fall of T. D. Lysenko.* New York: Columbia University Press, 1969.

———. "The Sakharov I Knew." *Observer*, July 7, 1974, 9.

———. *Soviet Science.* New York: W. W. Norton, 1978.

Meerson-Aksenov, Michael, and Boris Shragin, eds. *The Political, Social and Religious Thought of Russian "Samizdat": An Anthology.* Belmont, Mass.: Nordland Publishing Co., 1977.

*Memorandum akademika Sakharova. Tekst, otliki, diskussiia.* Frankfurt/Main: Posev, 1970.

"Mezhdunarodnye otnosheniia i ideologicheskaia bor'ba." *Kommunist* 14 (September 1973): 221–22.

Miller, John. *Mikhail Gorbachev and the End of Soviet Power.* New York: St. Martin's Press, 1993.

Millikan, Max. "Aid to Underdeveloped Nations." *Tech Engineering News,* April 1969, 25–27.

Milosz, Czeslaw. Introduction to "On Gorbachev," By Elena Bonner, *New York Review of Books,* May 17, 1990, 14.

"Moment of Grief." *Moscow News,* December 31, 1989, 8–9.

Morozov, A. "Razrushiteli." *Smena* 9–10 (1946): 11–12.

Morrison, John. *Boris Yeltsin: From Bolshevik to Democrat.* New York: Dutton, 1991.

Morrison, Philip. "On the Relevance of the Sakharov Paper." *Tech Engineering News,* April 1969, 7–9.

Murarka, Dev. "Sakharov Hits Back." *Observer,* September 9, 1973, 2.

Murashev, Arkadii. "Mezhregional'naia deputskaia." *Ogonëk,* August 4–11, 1990, 6–8.

Murphy, Kenneth. *Retreat from the Finland Station: Moral Odysseys in the Breakdown of Communism.* New York: Free Press, 1992.

*Nauchno-prakticheskaia konferentsiia, posviashchennaia 73-i godovshchine so dnia rozhdeniia A. D. Sakharova.* Moscow: Iuridicheskaia literatura, 1994.

Newhouse, John. *Cold Dawn: The Story of SALT.* Washington, D.C.: Pergamon-Brassey's, 1989.

"Notes on People." *New York Times,* July 22, 1972, 17.

Nove, Alec. *Glasnost' in Action: Cultural Renaissance in Russia.* Boston: Unwin Hyman, 1989.

"Obshchestvennoe mnenie o narodnykh deputatakh." *Argumenty i fakty,* October 7–13, 1989, 1.

"O budushchem Rossii: Press-konferentsiia A. I. Solzhenitsyna (November 16, 1974)." *Posev* 12 (December 1974): 6.

"O lichenii Sakharova A. D. gosudarstvennykh nagrad SSSR." *Vedomosti Verkhovnogo Soveta Soiuza Sovetskikh Sotsialisticheskikh Respublik* 5 (May 1980): 99.

"Operation Sakharov: The KGB Weaves a Tangled Web." *U.S. News and World Report,* March 3, 1986, 37.

Oppenheimer, Robert. "Physics in the Contemporary World." *Bulletin of the Atomic Scientists* 4, no. 3 (March 1948): 65–68, 85–86.

Orlov, Yuri. *Dangerous Thoughts: Memoirs of a Russian Life.* New York: William Morrow, 1991.

Osipov, Vladimir. "Piat' vozrazhenii Sakharovu." In *Tri otnosheniia k rodine,* 73–80. Frankfurt/Main: Posev, 1978.

Osnos, Peter. "Too Many Protests." *Washington Post,* January 13, 1975, A9.

Pasternak, Boris. *Doctor Zhivago.* New York: Pantheon Books, 1991.

Pecapa, Ion Mihai. "Putin's Duality (August 5, 2005)." http://www.frontpagemag.com/Articles/ReadArticle.asp?ID=19003.

Petro, Nicolai N. "Perestroika from Below: Voluntary Socio-Political Associations in the RSFSR." In *Perestroika at the Crossroads,* edited by Alfred J. Reiber and Alvin Z. Rubenstein, 102–35. Armonk, N.Y.: M. E. Sharpe, 1991.

———. *The Rebirth of Russian Democracy: An Interpretation of Political Culture.* Cambridge, Mass.: Harvard University Press, 1995.

Pipes, Richard, ed. *The Russian Intelligentsia.* New York: Columbia University Press, 1961.

———. "Why the Soviet Union Thinks It Could Fight and Win a Nuclear War." *Commentary* 64, no. 1 (July 1977): 21–34.

Pisar, Samuel. *Of Blood and Hope.* Boston: Little, Brown, 1980.

"Pis'mo chlenov Akademii nauk SSSR." *Pravda,* August 29, 3.

Plyushch, Leonid. *History's Carnival: A Dissident's Autobiography.* New York: Harcourt Brace Jovanovich, 1979.

Pomerantsev, V. "Ob iskrennost' v literature." *Novyi mir* 12 (December 1953): 218–45.

Pond, Elizabeth. "Sakharov Glum about Future of Rights in U.S.S.R." *Christian Science Monitor,* August 10, 1976, 22.

"Professor Weisskopf Discusses Scientific Implications of Sakharov's Proposal." *Tech Engineering News,* April 1969, 29.

"Programma Kommunisticheskogo partii sovetskogo soiuza." *Pravda,* August 8, 1991, 4.

"Proshchanie s Andrei Dmitrievichim Sakharovym." *Literaturnaia gazeta,* December 20, 1989, 1, 10.

Pryce-Jones, David. *The War That Never Was: The Fall of the Soviet Empire, 1985–1991.* London: Phoenix Press, 1995.

Rabkin, Jeremy. "The Legacy of Eleanor Roosevelt: The Promise and Problems of a Universal Declaration of Human Rights." *Weekly Standard,* May 28, 2001, 29–33.

*Razmyshleniia o progresse, mirnom sosushchestvovanii i intellektual'noi svobode: Materialy konferentsii k 30-letiiu raboty A. D. Sakharova.* Moscow: Prava cheloveka, 1998.

Reddaway, Peter. "Dissent in the Soviet Union." *Problems of Communism* 32, no. 6 (November–December 1983): 1–15.

———. "Russian Appeal to World Council of Churches." *Times* (London), October 26, 1974, 6.

———, ed. *Uncensored Russia: Protest and Dissent in the Soviet Union.* New York: American Heritage Press, 1972.

Reddaway, Peter, and Dmitri Glinski. *The Tragedy of Russia's Reforms: Market Bolshevism against Democracy.* Washington, D.C.: United States Institute of Peace Press, 2001.

Reed, Thomas, and Arnold Kramish. "Trinity at Dubna." *Physics Today* 49, no. 11 (November 1996): 30–35.

Rees, Martin. *Before the Beginning: Our Universe and Others.* Reading, Mass.: Helix Books, 1998.

Remnick, David. "Deep in the Woods." *New Yorker,* August 6, 2001, 32–40.

———. "The First and the Last." *New Yorker,* November 18, 1996, 118–22.

———. *Lenin's Tomb: The Last Days of the Soviet Empire.* New York: Vintage Books, 1994.

———. "The Missing Man." *New Yorker,* May 21, 2001, 37–38.

———. *Resurrection: The Struggle for a New Russia.* New York: Vintage Books, 1998.

———. "Sakharov Will Visit U.S. on His First Trip to West." *Washington Post,* October 22, 1988, A1.

Resis, Albert, ed. *Molotov Remembers: Inside Kremlin Politics: Conversations with Felix Chuev.* Chicago: Ivan R. Dee, 1993.

Rhodes, Richard. *Dark Sun: The Making of the Hydrogen Bomb.* New York: Simon & Schuster, 1995.

———. *The Making of the Atomic Bomb.* New York: Simon & Schuster, 1986.

Richter, James G. *Khrushchev's Double Bind: International Pressures and Domestic Coalition Politics.* Baltimore: Johns Hopkins University Press, 1994.

Rosenberger, Chandler. "The Dissident Mind: Vaclav Havel as Revolutionary Intellectual." *Journal of the Historical Society* 6, no. 3 (September 2006): 465–80.

Ross, Cameron. *Russian Politics under Putin.* Manchester, Eng.: Manchester University, 2004.

Rost, Yuri. "Akademik." *Literaturnaia gazeta,* November 16, 1988, 12.

———. "Ushel chelovek." *Literaturnaia gazeta,* December 20, 1989, 10.

Rothberg, Abraham. *The Heirs of Stalin: Dissidence and the Soviet Regime, 1953–1970.* Ithaca: Cornell University Press, 1972.

Rubenstein, Joshua. *Soviet Dissidents: Their Struggle for Human Rights.* Boston: Beacon Press, 1980.

Rubenstein, Joshua, and Alexander Gribanov, eds. *The KGB File of Andrei Sakharov.* New Haven: Yale University Press, 2005.

Rumiantsev, A., M. Mutin, and V. Mshveniaradze. "Akatual'nye voprosy bor'by protiv antikommunizma." *Pravda,* October 13, 1969, 4–5.

Rybakov, Anatolii. "Memorial." *Literaturnaia gazeta,* August 31, 1988, 2.

Sagdeev, Roald. *The Making of a Soviet Scientist.* New York: Wiley, 1994.

———. "Russian Scientists Save American Secrets." *Bulletin of the Atomic Scientists* 49, no. 4 (May 1993): 32–36.

———. "Science and Perestroika: A Long Way to Go." *Issues in Science and Technology* 4, no. 4 (1988): 48–52.

"Sakharov Applies for Visit to Oslo." *New York Times,* October 21, 1975, 10.

"Sakharov Plea Rejected by Dr. Kissinger." *Times* (London), October 17, 1975, 5.

Sakwa, Richard. *Gorbachev and His Reforms, 1985–1990.* New York: Prentice-Hall, 1991.

*Samizdat Bulletin.* San Mateo: Samizdat Publications, 1973–1990.

Samoilov, V. "Razgul Sakharovshchini." *Molodaia gvardiia* 9 (1990): 260–63.

Satter, David. *Darkness at Dawn: The Rise of the Russian Criminal State.* New Haven: Yale University Press, 2003.

Saunders, George, ed. *Samizdat: Voices of the Soviet Opposition.* New York: Monad Press, 1974.

Scammell, Michael. "The Prophet and the Wilderness." *New Republic,* February 25, 1991, 29–36.

——. *Solzhenitsyn: A Biography.* London: Hutchinson, 1985.

Schroeter, Leonard. *The Last Exodus.* Seattle: University of Washington Press, 1979.

Seaborg, Glenn T. *Kennedy, Khrushchev, and the Test Ban.* Berkeley: University of California Press, 1981.

Sestanovich, Stephen. "The Hour of the Demagogue." *National Interest* 25 (Fall 1991): 1–15.

"S"ezd narodnykh deputatov SSSR." *Izvestiia,* May 26, 1989, 4–5.

"S"ezd narodnykh deputatov SSSR." *Izvestiia,* May 27, 1989, 2–5.

"S"ezd narodnykh deputatov SSSR." *Izvestiia,* June 11, 1989, 3–8.

"S"ezd narodnykh deputatov SSSR." *Pravda,* June 5, 1989, 3.

Shabad, Theodore. "Life Is Too Closely Imitating Art." *New York Times,* September 9, 1973, sec. 4, 4.

——. "Pressure Only Spurs Soviet Dissidents." *New York Times,* September 21, 1973, 3.

——. "Soviet Portrays Sakharov as Backer of Chile's Junta." *New York Times,* September 26, 1973, 3.

Shakhnazarov, Georgii. *Tsena svobody: Reformatsiia Gorbacheva glazami ego pomoshchnika.* Moscow: Rossika, Zeys, 1993.

Sharansky, Natan. *The Case for Democracy: The Power of Freedom to Overcome Tyranny and Terror.* New York: Public Affairs, 2004.

——. "Defending and Advancing Freedom." *Commentary* 4 (November 2005): 60–61.

——. *Fear No Evil.* New York: Random House, 1988.

Shatz, Marshall S. *Soviet Dissent in Historical Perspective.* New York, 1980.

Shatz, Marshall S., and Judith E. Zimmerman, eds. *Vekhi: Landmarks.* Armonk, N.Y.: M. E. Sharpe, 1994.

Shevardnadze, Eduard. *The Future Belongs to Freedom.* New York: Free Press, 1991.

Shipler, David. *Russia: Broken Idols, Solemn Dreams.* New York: Penguin Books, 1984.

Shragin, Boris. "Oppozitsionnye nastroeniia v nauchnykh gorodkakh." *SSSR: Vnutrennie protivorechiia* 1 (1991): 100–119.

Shtromas, Alexander. *Political Change and Social Development: The Case of the Soviet Union.* Frankfurt/Main: Verlag Peter Lang, 1981.

Shtromas, Alexander, and Morton A. Kaplan, eds. *The Soviet Union and the Challenge of the Future.* New York: Paragon House, 1988.

Simes, Dmitrii. *After the Collapse: Russia Seeks Its Place as a Great Power.* New York: Simon & Schuster, 1999.

Skidmore, David. *Reversing Course: Carter's Foreign Policy, Domestic Politics, and the Failure of Reform.* Nashville: Vanderbilt University Press, 1996.

Skonechnaia, A. D., and F. L. Tsypkina, eds. *Sakharov: Takim on byl.* Zhitomir: Golos grazhdanina, 1991.

Smith, Gaddis. *Morality, Reason, and Power: American Diplomacy in the Carter Years.* New York: Hill and Wang, 1986.

Smith, Hedrick. "The Intolerable Andrei Sakharov." *New York Times Magazine,* November 4, 1973, 42–46, 50–61, 64–71.

——. *The New Russians.* New York: Random House, 1990.

——. *The Russians.* New York: Ballantine Books, 1976.

Smolin, Lee. *The Life of the Cosmos.* New York: Oxford University Press, 1997.

Snow, C. P. *The Physicists.* Boston: Little, Brown, 1981.

Sobchak, Anatolii. *For a New Russia: The Mayor of St. Petersburg's Own Story of the Struggle for Justice and Democracy.* New York: HarperCollins, 1992.

——. *Khozhdenie vo vlast': Rasskaz o rozhdenii parlamenta.* Moscow: Novosti, 1991.
*Sobranie dokumentov samizdata.* 30 vols. Munich: RFE/RL, 1972–1978.
Solzhenitsyn, Aleksandr I. *Letter to the Soviet Leaders.* New York: Harper & Row, 1974.
——. *The Oak and the Calf: Sketches of Literary Life in the Soviet* Union. New York: Harper & Row, 1980.
——. "Peace and Violence." *Index* 2, no. 4 (Winter 1973): 49–51.
——. "Sakharov and the Criticisms of 'A Letter to the Soviet Leaders.'" In *Kontinent,* 14–23. Garden City: Anchor Press, 1976.
——. *A World Split Apart: Commencement Address Delivered at Harvard University, June 8, 1978.* New York: Harper & Row, 1978.
Solzhenitsyn, Alexander I. et al. *From under the Rubble.* Boston: Bantam Books, 1976.
Sonin, Anatoly. "How the A-bomb Saved Soviet Physicists' Lives." *Moscow News,* April 1, 1990, 16.
Sorokin, Pitirim. *Russia and the United States.* New York: E. P. Dutton, 1944.
"Soviet Physicist Pleads for Dissenters." *New York Times,* August 3, 1972, 3.
"Soviet Physicists Rebuked by Party." *New York Times,* October 26, 1970, 10.
"Sozdan izbiratel'nyi blok 'Demokraticheskaia Rossia'." *Ogonëk,* February 1990, 17.
Special Issue of *Moscow News,* December 31, 1989.
*Spetsial'noe prilozhenie—Russkaia mysl',* December 22, 1989.
Starovoitova, Galina. "Ia uzhe obespechila sebia memuarami." *Nezavisimaia gazeta,* July 30, 1991, 5.
Sternberg, Hilary. "Sakharov and Solzhenitsyn: Champions of Freedom." *Index* 2, no. 4 (1973): 5–12.
Stites, Richard. *Revolutionary Dreams: Utopian Vision and Experimental Life in the Russian Revolution.* New York: Oxford University Press, 1989.
Stix, Thomas H. "Plasma Physics. "In Sakharov, *Collected Scientific Works,* 55–57.
Stone, Jeremy. "Sakharov: A Scientist's Rebellion." *International Herald Tribune,* May 29, 1984, 6.
"Strana proshchaetsia Sakharovym." *Russkaia mysl',* December 22, 1989, 16.
*The Strange Death of Soviet Communism.* Special issue of *National Interest* 31 (Spring 1993).
Sudoplatov, Pavel, and Anatoli Sudoplatov. *Special Tasks: The Memoirs of an Unwanted Witness, a Soviet Spymaster.* Boston: Little, Brown, 1994.
Susskind, L. "Matter-Antimatter Asymmetry." In Sakharov, *Collected Scientific Works,* 151–55.
Sutherland, Daniel. "Sakharov Appeals to Beijing." *Washington Post,* December 16, 1988, A37, A47.
Szilard, Leo. *Voice of the Dolphins, and Other Stories.* New York: Simon & Schuster, 1961.
Talbott, Strobe. *Endgame: The Inside Story of SALT II.* New York: Harper & Row, 1979.
——. *The Master of the Game: Paul Nitze and the Nuclear Peace.* New York: Alfred E. Knopf, 1988.
Tarasulo, Isaac J., ed. *Perils of Perestroika: Viewpoints from the Soviet Press, 1989–1991.* Wilmington: SR Books, 1992.
Taubman, Philip. "Sakharov in New Era." *New York Times,* December 25, 1986, 3.
Thomas, Daniel C. *The Helsinki Effect: International Norms, Human Rights, and the Demise of Communism.* Princeton: Princeton University Press, 2001.
Thomas, D. M. *Alexander Solzhenitsyn: A Century in his Life.* New York: St. Martin's Press, 1998.
Thorne, Kip S. *Black Holes and Time Warps: Einstein's Outrageous Legacy.* New York: W. W. Norton, 1995.
"Torture by Clamp and Spoon." *U.S. News and World Report,* February 24, 1986, 31.
"Treaty between the United States of America and the Union of Soviet Socialist Republics on the Reduction and Limitation of Strategic Offensive Arms (START Treaty)." http://www.ceip.org/files/projects/npp/resources/start1text.html.
Tretiakov, V. "Strategiia i taktika." *Posev* 3 (March 1971): 2.
Trimble, Jeff. "Sakharov's Bold Challenge." *U.S. News and World Report,* January 30, 1989, 49–50.
Trotsky, Leon. *Literature and Revolution.* Ann Arbor: University of Michigan Press, 1960.
Tsukerman, V. A., and Z. M. Azarkh. "Liudi i vzryvy." *Zvezda* 11 (1990): 93–129.

Tucker, Robert C. *The Soviet Political Mind: Stalinism and Post-Stalin Change.* New York: W. W. Norton, 1971.

Tucker, William. "The Permanent Energy Crisis." *Weekly Standard,* March 17, 2003, 16–17.

*XXVIII s"ezd Kommunisticheskoi partii sovetskogo soiuza: 2-13 iulia, 1990 goda.* Moscow: Steno-grafischeskii otchet, 1990.

Urban, Michael. *The Rebirth of Politics in Russia.* New York: Cambridge University Press, 1997.

Vance, Cyrus R. *Hard Choices: Critical Years in America's Foreign Policy.* New York: Simon & Schuster, 1983.

"Vchera v Kremle." *Komsomol'skaia pravda,* December 16, 1989, 1.

Von Hippel, Frank. "Declaration to the American Physics Society on the Study of Water-Cooled Nuclear Reactors." *Review of Modern Physics* 47 (1975): S110–S111.

——. "Revisiting Sakharov's Assumptions." *Science and Global Security* 1, nos. 3–4 (1990): 185–86.

Voshchanov, P. "On operedil vremia." *Komsomol'skaia Pravda,* December 16, 1989, 1.

Vucinich, Alexander. *Empire of Knowledge: The Academy of Sciences of the USSR (1917–1970).* Berkeley: University of California Press, 1984.

Walker, Christopher. "Sakharov Casts Doubt on Feasibility of SDI." *Times,* December 29, 1986, 8.

——. "Scientist's Joy of Freedom Marred by Fate of Marchenko." *Times,* December 24, 1986, 10.

Weiner, Norbert. "How U.S. Cities Can Prepare for Atomic War" *Life,* December 18, 1950, 77–86.

Weissberg-Cybulski, Alexander. *The Accused.* New York: Simon & Schuster, 1951.

Wells, H. G. *The Shape of Things to Come.* New York: Macmillan, 1933.

White, Stephen. *After Gorbachev.* New York: Cambridge University Press, 1993.

——. *Gorbachev in Power.* New York: Cambridge University Press, 1990.

Williams, Robert. *Klaus Fuchs, Atom Spy.* Cambridge, Mass.: Harvard University Press, 1987.

Wines, Michael. "Sakharov's Widow Opposes Moscow Plan to Build Monument." *New York Times,* April 17, 2003, A5.

Wynn, Allan, ed. *Fifth International Sakharov Hearing: Proceedings, April 1985.* London: Andre Deutsch, 1986.

Yakovlev, Alexander. *A Century of Violence in Soviet Russia.* New Haven: Yale University Press, 2002.

Yakovlev, Egor. "In Search of an Accord." *Moscow News,* January 14, 1990, 3–4.

Yakovlev, Nikolai. *CIA Target—the USSR.* Moscow: Progress, 1982.

——. "Put' vniz." *Smena,* July 1983, 26–27.

Yankelevich, Efrem. "Vspominaia podrobnosti." Unpublished manuscript.

Yeltsin, Boris. "Who Should Be the Person of the Century?" *Time,* December 20, 1999, 29.

——. *Zapiski prezidenta.* Moscow: Ogonëk, 1994.

York, Herbert F. *The Advisors: Oppenheimer, Teller, and the Superbomb.* San Francisco: W. H. Free-man, 1976.

"Z" [Malia, Martin]. "To the Stalin Mausoleum." *Daedalus,* Winter 1990, 295–343.

Zaburin, Vladimir. "Razgovor s mukhami, ili monolog na kukne." *Molodaia gvardiia* 8 (1990): 206–30.

Zacharias, Jerrold. "To Solve World Problems." *Tech Engineering News,* April 1969, 28.

*Za i protiv: 1973 god, dokumenty, fakty, sobytiia.* Moscow: PIK, 1991.

Zaloga, Stephen. *Target America: The Soviet Union and the Strategic Arms Race, 1945–1964.* No-vato, Calif.: Presidio, 1993.

Zhavoronkov, Gennady. "Alone with Everyone: Andrei Sakharov at Home." *Moscow News,* May 15, 1988, 16.

Zubok, Vladislav, and Constantine Pleshakov. *Inside the Kremlin's Cold War: From Stalin to Khrushchev.* Cambridge, Mass.: Harvard University Press, 1996.

# Index